TURKEY
ISTANBUL
Xanthi
Sapai
Peplos
Kavala
Alexandroupolis
THASOS
Samothrace Town
SAMOTHRACE
LIMNOS
Aegean Sea
SPORADES
LESVOS
Mitilini
Skyros
SKYROS
CHIOS
Hios
TURKEY
Kato Aetos
ANDROS
SAMOS
Raches
Agios Kirykos
KEA
TINOS
MYKONOS
IKARIA
KITHNOS
SIROS
Hora
THE CYCLADES
PATMOS
SERIFOS
PAROS
NAXOS
Naxos
LEROS
SIFNOS
KALYMNOS
Kalimnos
Kos
KOS
AMORGOS
Pollonia
Adamas
SIKINOS
IOS
Folegandros
MILOS
DODECANESE
ASTIPALEA
NISSIROS
SIMI
FOLEGANDROS
Oia
Fira
ANAFI
TILOS
Rodos
SANTORINI
HALKI
RHODES
KASTELLORIZO
Sea of Crete
Karpathos
KARPATHOS
Rethymnon
Heraklio
Agios Nikolaos
KASOS
CRETE
© MOON.COM
TIRANA
MACEDONIA
BULGARIA
Seres
Xanthi
ALBANIA
Thessaloniki
Katerini
Kerkira
GREECE
Aegean Sea
NORTH AEGEAN
IONIAN ISLANDS
SPORADES
Mitilini
TURKEY
Agrinio
Chalkida
Izmir
Adriatic Sea
ATHENS
CYCLADES
DODECANESE
Rodos
Mediterranean Sea
Heraklio
CRETE
0 50 mi
0 50 km
© MOON.COM
D0018305

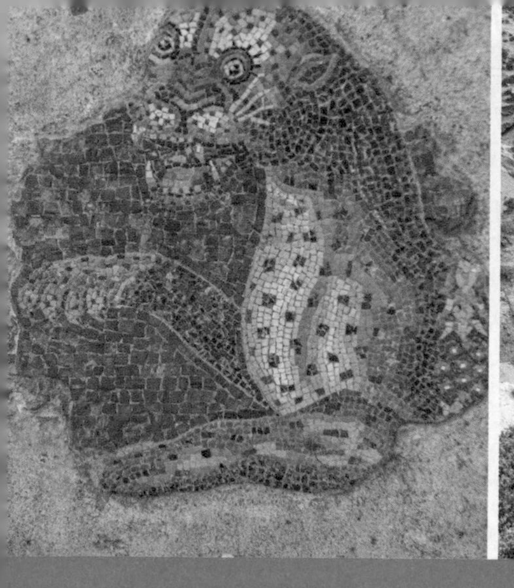

DISCOVER

Greek Islands & Athens

"Happy is the man, I thought, who, before dying, has the good fortune to sail the Aegean Sea."

—*Nikos Kazantzakis*

There's a winding mountain road in Karpathos that leads down to a sliver of liquid turquoise paradise, cut between two jagged rocks like a bite of an ice cream sandwich. The view itself is stunning: With each turn of the road, the browns and greens of the mountainside give way to the dazzling blues of the Aegean. The light, a hazy glow that has inspired countless artists and writers, reflects off silvery olive trees and catches the ripples of the sea. The air is satisfyingly thick and salty, and as you inhale the scent of wild sage and oregano, it feels like you are sitting, in the best way possible, inside a giant mug of tea.

Karpathos is just one of more than 6,000 Greek islands, flung haphazardly across the Mediterranean like dozens of coins dropped from a great height. Each is a holistically sensual and unique experience, from the lunar dunes of Milos to the lush forests of Samothrace. You'll find dazzling displays of earnest humanness: villages precariously carved into cliff sides where old men finger *komboloi* (prayer beads) and drink syrupy coffee, domed churches painted ochre,

Clockwise from top to left: a beautiful tiger mosaic in Delos; Milos island beach; the Greek flag; House of Cleopatra on Delos; souvenirs in a Mykonos shop; sun-dried octopus in Crete.

octopuses drying in the sun, and bodies of every shape and size baking under the hot sun like loaves of bread. Each of the 202 inhabited islands has its own vibe, character, landscape, and specialties, and you can find one to soothe any ailment, tickle any fancy, or live any adventure.

It's increasingly easy to travel across the Aegean and Ionian seas. Each year, the Greek government adds new, or bolsters existing, ferry lines. Budget airlines fly regularly from European cities to Ikaria, Lesvos, and Corfu, and new eco-lodges and hotels are built every season. Islands are offering more amenities to travelers, including windsurfing, yoga, and well-preserved hiking trails. The Greek islands continue to inspire and delight with their beauty, and there's never been a better time to visit.

Clockwise from top to left: a boat on a Mykonos beach; fresco of leaping bulls in Knossos, Crete; bright green olives commonly grown throughout the region; ancient ruins on the island of Delos.

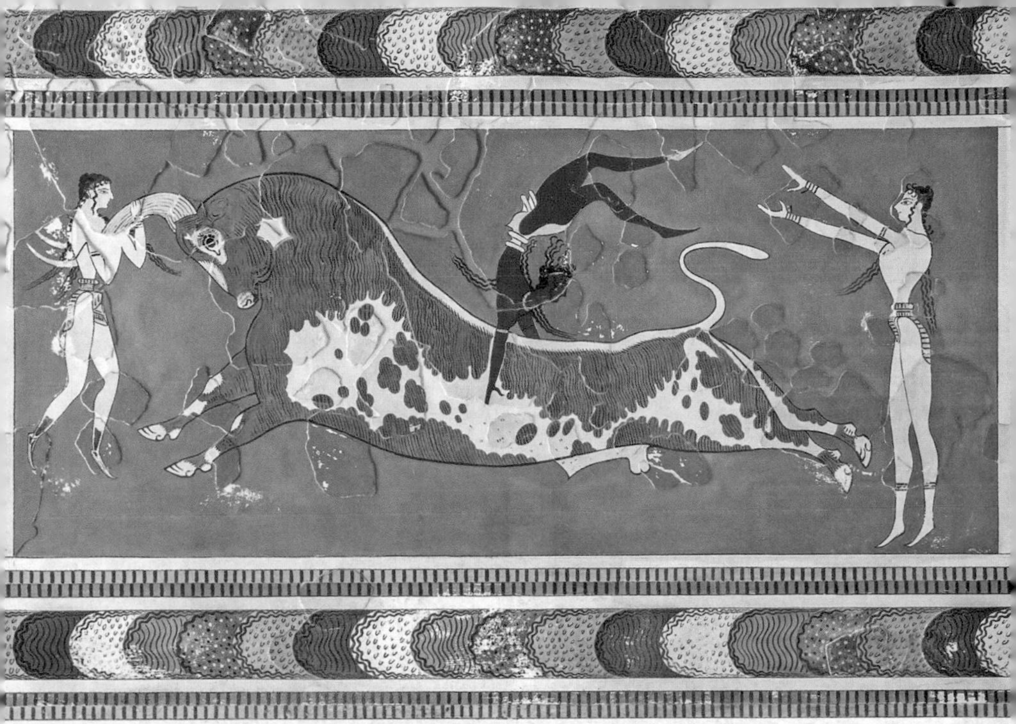

10 TOP EXPERIENCES

1 Finding your favorite **beach.** From party spots (Mykonos) to hippie hangouts (Anafi) to unbelievable lunar landscapes (Milos), the Greek Islands have you covered (page 27).

2 Visiting the birthplace of Apollo and Artemis at **Delos Archaeological Site,** just a short boat ride from Mykonos (page 134).

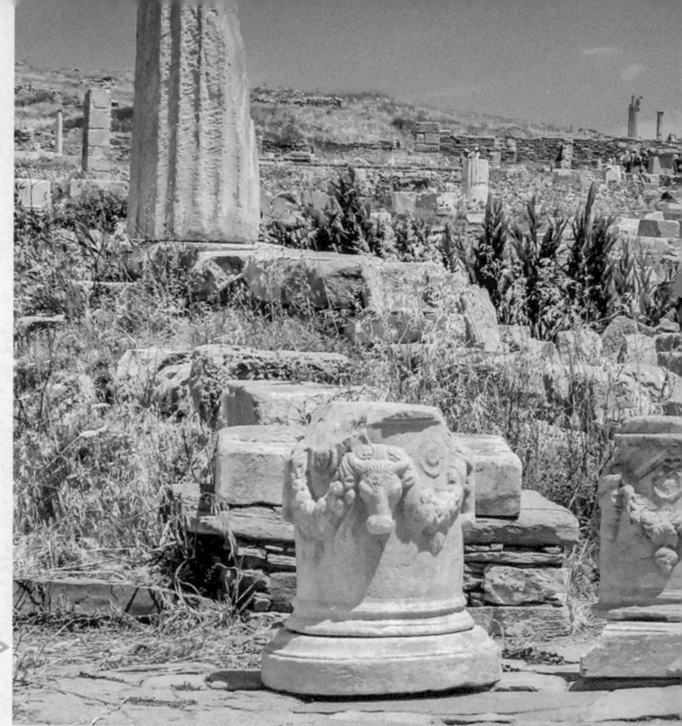

3 Taking a **boat trip from Milos** (called a *gyro tis Milos*) to access the island's wildest beaches and most secluded swimming spots (page 156).

^
^
^

4 Catching a glimpse of the **Acropolis** from rooftops, streets, and other corners of the Athens—especially at sunset (page 49).

5 Visiting **Olympos Village,** aka the city of living folklore, on Karpathos. Isolated from the rest of the island (and world), this traditional village has been allowed to preserve its past (page 218).

6 Sampling chilled ouzo accompanied by seafood meze at an ***ouzeri*** on Lesvos, known as home of the famed Greek drink (page 303).

>>>

7 Exploring **The Sanctuary of the Great Gods** on Samothrace, one of the most important (and mysterious) archaeological sites in all of Greece (page 267).

<<<

8 Losing track of time on **Ikaria,** one of the world's famed Blue Zones, and a place where time itself seems to be a philosophical concept (page 287).

>>>

9 Exploring **Chania Town.** The Venetian harbor town is not only the most beautiful city on Crete—it's a stunning portal to some of the island's most amazing scenery, beaches, and food (page 449).

10 Walking through **Skyros' Hora,** an endless maze of cobblestone streets and whitewashed houses with flat roofs that you can climb onto (page 345).

Planning Your Time

Where to Go

Athens

Why go: Fantastic ruins, street art, top-notch restaurants, excellent people watching

There's never been a better time to visit the birthplace of Western civilization. Despite the economic crisis, the Greek spirit has persevered, and there's an explosion of creativity, with new **shops, museums,** and **restaurants** opening at a rapid clip. Come for the old, too; no visit to Greece is complete without at least a glimpse of the marvelous **Parthenon.** Piraeus port is a gateway to most of the islands, and you'll likely pass through here at some point.

Cycladic Islands

Why go: Endless turquoise seas, whitewashed villages

SANTORINI

Thousands of years ago, a cataclysmic volcano made Santorini what it is today: an architectural marvel of cave dwellings precariously perched on the lip of the red caldera. For **romance, luxury,** and truly out-of-this-world **views,** come to Santorini. This is an island best visited in the late fall or early spring, when the tourists have gone and you can drink in the caldera view alone. It's one of the most crowded islands in Greece, so come in the off-season to appreciate its sensual vibe.

MYKONOS

Greece's most notorious **party island** is the place to come for excellent **gourmet meals,** endless **nightlife,** and **fantastic music.** But there's a

the Acropolis of Athens

tranquil, authentic side to this island as well, and it has the most harmonic **architecture** of all the Cycladic islands. True clubbers should come in July or August; the rest of you will enjoy Mykonos in September or June. Just a boat ride away is the **Delos Archaeological Site,** located on an uninhabited island.

FOLEGANDROS

Once totally off the grid, Folegandros is becoming more touristic, but that doesn't detract from this beautiful island's subdued charm. Come for the **beaches,** the **hiking,** and the bougainvillea-laced towns. Its hora is one of the most beautiful in the Cyclades. It still attracts a **bohemian,** if well-heeled, crowd.

MILOS

With more than 70 fantastic **beaches,** ranging from black sand to strange white rock formations that look like a lunar landscape, Milos is a **geologist's dream island.** Most of the beaches are accessible only by boat, and it's a true pleasure to spend the day cruising around, lazily jumping into the sea.

NAXOS

As soon as you arrive at the port, you'll see the heart-stoppingly beautiful **Temple of Apollo.** The biggest island of the Cyclades is home to fantastic ruins, expansive sand **beaches, traditional mountain villages,** and some truly excellent **restaurants.**

ANAFI

Seemingly lost in time and last on the Santorini line, tiny Anafi is the island that everyone else forgot about. All the better for you, since you can enjoy this hippie island's **pristine beaches** and **glorious sunsets** without the crowds. There's not much to do besides lounge and swim, usually naked, and that's exactly the point.

Dodecanese Islands

Why go: Roman, Byzantine, and Ottoman history; adventure travel

Fyriplaka beach, Milos island

Greek Islands for Families

When choosing an island for family travel, look for places that offer something for everyone. Your sullen teenaged son might perk up at the thought of vacation in Mykonos, but his eight-year-old sister won't have a very fun time. In general, Greeks love children and will do their all to accommodate your pickiest eaters and most rambunctious kids.

boat with tourists on a Porto Katsiki beach, Lefkada

BEST ISLANDS FOR FAMILIES

Based on my experience, **Naxos** is a perfect family place: There's hiking, nightlife, beaches, museums, and plenty of tour operators providing water sport activities. **Kalymnos, Lesvos,** and **Lefkada** also have a variety of activities for every age level and interest, from 3 to 83. Boat rides are always a good option, as are walking tours and hanging out on an organized beach where you'll find activities to suit everyone. Another option is to choose really chill islands, like **Anafi, Samothrace,** or **Alonnisos,** where you can relax, let the stress of real life melt away, and enjoy some cell phone-free quality time with your family.

TRY TO AVOID

Stay away from places that are overly crowded, like **Zakynthos** or **Santorini,** as you'll spend a lot of time standing in lines or on crowded beaches.

KARPATHOS

Faraway Karpathos has some of the Mediterranean's best **windsurfing,** and some of the Greek islands' best-kept **secret beaches.** The island also has a curiously large portion of Greek-Americans, who return home every summer and have lent a decidedly American flair to the island.

RHODES

Rhodes has something of a **party** reputation, but it's so much more than a hedonistic island. With some of the best-preserved **Ottoman** and **medieval era ruins** around and some stunning **nature,** Rhodes has something for everyone.

KALYMNOS

Once the epicenter of sponge diving in the Aegean, Kalymnos is now better known for its **extreme sports:** between its dramatic mountainscape and craggy boulders, it's the perfect place for **rock climbers** and **divers.**

Northeast Aegean Islands

Why go: Authentic experiences without the crowds; excellent seafood

SAMOTHRACE

Difficult to get to, Samothrace rewards those who make the journey with endless **hiking trails** full of waterfalls and natural swimming pools. The island is full of wild goats and attracts a decidedly **hippie crowd,** who camp in the forest and swim naked. This is an island for letting your spirit loose.

IKARIA

The delightfully endearing wacky aunt of the Greek islands, Ikaria is a magical little place. The laid-back and philosophical character of the locals is truly inspiring, and the social cohesion, **excellent food,** and **therapeutic hot springs** all contribute to one of the biggest centenarian populations in the world. Ikaria literally runs on a different time: everything opens at night!

LESVOS

Greece's third-largest island warrants a visit: It's the home of both **ouzo** and **Sappho,** and boasts some stunning **natural landscapes,** from petrified forests to kilometer-long beaches. And let's not forget the **food,** which is some of the best in Greece. Lesvos has borne the brunt of the refugee crisis, which is all the more reason to visit and support the island.

Sporades Islands

Why go: Tranquility, hiking, horses

ALONNISOS

Lovely Alonnisos feels like a world away: Covered in vegetation, the island is a **nature lover's paradise,** with fantastic **beaches** and plenty of **hiking** trails. It has one of the most beautiful horas in the Aegean, and a relaxed, happy vibe.

SKYROS

You'll probably fall madly in love with the tiny **Skyrian horses,** plus the **fantastic food,** strangely abandoned landscape in the south of the island, the lovely locals, the beautiful hora, and the generally **off-the-beaten-path vibe** of Skyros.

Ionian Islands

Why go: Stunning beaches, Italian influence, and picturesque coves

CORFU

Walking around Corfu Town, you'll be forgiven for thinking you're in Italy. From the architecture to the food, Corfu has a strong **European flair.** There's excellent cuisine, beautiful **beaches,** and enough **museums** to spend your whole vacation just looking at art.

ZAKYNTHOS

Home to **Shipwreck Bay,** one of Greece's most famous beaches, Zakynthos has some of the most unbelievably blue waters you've ever seen. Now an **adrenaline junkie's paradise,** the island becomes overrun with families in the summer, but the colors alone are worth the crowds.

LEFKADA

One of only two islands you can drive to, Lefkada is all pine trees and winding roads, and water that might be even more beautiful than Zakynthos', but with half the crowds. Popular with Italians, Israelis, and Greek families, Lefkada has a laid-back vibe that makes it a **family-friendly** destination.

Crete

Why go: Tradition, mountains, beaches, food

The largest of the Greek islands, Crete is a universe unto itself. It would take a lifetime to experience everything this island has to offer. Come for the fantastic **history, museums,** beautifully preserved port towns, local character, and of course, the **food.** (Don't tell anyone, but it's the best in Greece.)

Choosing Your Island

If You Want...	Island	Why Go?	Plane Access?	Mainland Access Port/ Length of Ferry Ride
Solitude and Bohemian Vibes	Skyros (page 341)	Easy to access, Skyros still retains an off-the-beaten-path feeling.	yes*	Kymi in Evia (1.5 hours)
	Anafi (page 193)	Watch sunsets that rival Santorini's, without the crowds.	no	Piraeus (passing through Santorini, 9-11 hours), or direct from Santorini (1.5 hours)
	Folegandros (page 136)	Hike, watch the sunset, or kick back and do nearly nothing.	no	Piraeus (6-10 hours)
Hiking	Alonnisos (page 322)	Trek across a wild island teeming with wildflowers and endemic herbs.	no	Volos and Agios Konstantinos (3 hours), or Kymi in Evia (2.5 hours)
	Samothrace (page 261)	A mountainous interior attracts hikers, and secluded beaches are crowd-free.	no	Alexandroupoli (2 hours)
Adventure Sports	Zakynthos (page 382)	Take in Shipwreck Bay and the Blue Caves, followed by the adventure sport of your choice.	yes	Kyllini (1 hour) or Patras (3.5 hours)
	Kalymnos (page 244)	Craggy Kalymnos is a dream come true for divers and rock climbers.	yes*	Piraeus (up to 11 hours)
	Karpathos (page 204)	Windsurf this windy island and visit Olympos, one of Greece's oldest villages.	yes*	Piraeus (17 hours)
Nightlife	Mykonos (page 113)	Go clubbing, enjoy excellent cuisine, and take a trip to Delos Archaeological Site.	yes	Piraeus (2.5-4.5 hours)

Museums	Corfu (page 358)	Visit excellent museums, preserved forts, and a harbor town that feels a little like Venice.	yes	Igoumenitsa (1 hour 45 minutes)
Ancient Ruins	Rhodes (page 222)	Rhodes has preserved ruins and monuments, from the medieval old town to a cliffside Acropolis.	yes	Piraeus (14-24 hours)
	Naxos (page 170)	Visit the Temple of Apollo and meander through traditional villages.	yes*	Piraeus (4-5 hours)
Traditional Villages	Ikaria (page 276)	Ikaria offers a slice of authentic Greece. The island is also semi-nocturnal, thanks to a history of dodging pirate invasions.	yes*	Piraeus (6-8 hours)
Romance	Santorini (page 85)	Indulge in romance, luxury, and incredible views.	yes	Piraeus (4-9 hours)
Arresting Landscapes	Milos (page 150)	Visit more than 70 beaches and marvel at the volcanic landscape.	yes*	Piraeus (3-6 hours)
Cuisine	Lesvos (page 297)	Lesvos is the home of ouzo, Sappho, and some of the best bites in Greece.	yes	Piraeus (9 hours)
	Crete (page 423)	Greece's largest island boasts a varied landscape, the Palace of Knossos, and the best food in Greece.	yes	Piraeus (up to 18 hours)
A Family Vacation	Lefkada (page 403)	Lefkada is laid-back, easy to access, and has something for everyone.	yes	None (most travelers fly or drive)

* domestic flights only

When to Go

High Season (June-August)

Summer, when temperatures (and prices!) soar, is the high season in Greece. Business is in full swing, and you'll find everything open, usually for longer hours. Though the weather is great (28-40°C/82-104°F), the crowds can be relentless, especially in August (and particularly the middle two weeks of the month). If you're going to travel during this time, be prepared to make plenty of reservations and wait in lots of lines, especially if you're going to blockbuster islands like Mykonos, Santorini, or Crete.

Shoulder Season (April-May and September-October)

The months bookending the summer season (particularly May and September) are great times to visit the islands. The crowds aren't so intense, the weather is mild but warm enough to enjoy the beaches (12-25°C/54-77°F in fall, 9-25°C/48-77°F in spring), and you'll be able to snag reservations that would be impossible in mid-August. By October the weather has usually cooled down, but you can still swim.

Low Season (November-March)

Aside from a few islands with a substantial population and other forms of economy, you'll find nearly everything on the islands closed. Only islands with larger populations, like Crete, Lesvos, and Corfu, have plenty of restaurants, stores, museums, etc. that stay open all year. The weather is cold and rainy (6-16°C/43-61°F), and boat services are greatly reduced, especially to the smaller islands. Some islands might be worth visiting for specific holidays. Skyros, for example, has a great festival during pre-Lent Carnival (usually in February), but try going to Anafi in November and you'll be sorely disappointed.

Before You Go

Passports and Visas

You'll need a valid passport to enter Greece (or an I.D. card if you're coming from another EU country). Greece is part of the Schengen zone, so Americans, Australians, Canadians, and Brits are granted three months to travel around without applying for a visa. If you wish to stay longer, you'll need to get a six-month tourist visa from your country's Greek embassy.

Vaccinations

You don't need to take any specific vaccines to come to Greece, but when traveling, it's a good idea to be up to date on all your shots. Greece does have free healthcare, so if you run into any medical issue and you don't have insurance, rest assured that you'll be treated properly and humanely in the hospitals.

Transportation

AIR

Depending on which island you're visiting, it can be convenient to fly directly to that island's airport (Crete, Mykonos, Corfu) or to the Eleftherios Venizelos Airport in Athens (35 km/22 mi from the city center). From Athens you can connect to islands through the domestic airlines. Depending on which island you're visiting, your flight from Athens will take around 45 minutes to an hour.

BOAT

A comprehensive ferry system travels between the islands and the mainland ports.

To get to **Crete,** the Cycladic islands **(Santorini, Mykonos, Folegandros, Milos, Naxos, Anafi),** and the Dodecanese islands **(Karpathos, Rhodes, Kalymnos)** you'll go from Piraeus port near Athens. There are also two other ports, Rafina and Lavrio, with service to Cycladic islands.

For the Ionian island of **Corfu,** you will leave from Igoumenitsa port (7 hours from Athens). For **Zakynthos,** you will leave from Kyllini (3 hours from Athens) or Patras (2 hours from Athens). **Lefkada** is not accessible via mainland port; most travelers drive or fly to reach this destination.

To get to the Sporades island of **Alonnisos,** you'll need to leave from Volos (4 hours from Athens). It's also possible to reach Alonnisos from Agios Konstantinos (2 hours from Athens) and Kymi in Evia (2 hours from Athens). **Skyros,** another Sporades island, is only reachable from Kymi.

In terms of the Northeast Aegean Islands covered in this book, boats for **Lesvos** and **Ikaria** leave from Piraeus; to get to **Samothrace** you must fly first to Alexandroupoli in the northeast of the country.

What to Take

Greeks are a pretty chic bunch, and you'll look out of place with rumpled shirts and cut-off jeans. Pack a few **nicer summer outfits,** especially if you're spending time on Mykonos, Santorini, or Crete. Choose breathable fabrics like linen and cotton, and pack at least one pair of **sandals** and one pair of **sturdy shoes** for walking. Women should bring a **modest outfit** that covers the knees, shoulders, and chest for visiting churches.

If you're going to do a lot of walking or hiking, bring **hiking shoes,** a **hat,** and a couple of pairs of **socks.** You can buy granola bars and water bottles in Greece. Most of the islands don't have drinkable tap water, so it won't help to bring a reusable water bottle unless it has a water filter. If you want to cut down on plastic waste, bring a **reusable water bottle** that can filter water.

You can buy snorkel gear, like masks and flippers, on the spot (a snorkel mask costs about €10), but it's useful to bring your own **beach towel.** Most accommodations have towels, but they don't always have towels specifically for the beach, and you might be charged if you forget to bring it back to the hotel. You'll want to bring a **phone charger, power adapter, credit** and **debit cards,** and your **driving license** if you're planning on renting a vehicle. Outlets take either Type C 220V/50Hz or Type F 230V/50Hz standard European plugs (two round prongs). Get an **electronic converter** that adapts to both for any devices that are not dual voltage.

If you're prone to seasickness, it's a good idea to bring some **medicine,** as well as **mosquito repellent** and plenty of **sunscreen.** Add a **hat** and some **sunglasses** and you're good to go.

Best of the Cycladics: Naxos, Mykonos, and Anafi

It's tempting to cram as much as you possibly can into a trip to a foreign country, but I really urge you not to when it comes to the islands. You could spend one day on each island, but you will be exhausted and burned out (and possibly sunburned) by the end of it. Instead, choose one island per three to five days, depending on its size, and depending on how relaxed you want to be.

Ten days is enough time to get a mix of both high-end and more tranquil islands. Head first to Naxos, the largest of the Cycladic islands, before heading to Mykonos for a hedonistic whirlwind. Recover and relax on the island of Anafi, which boasts the same spectacular sunsets as Santorini, with none of the crowds.

In Naxos, I recommend renting a car. You can get around on foot on Anafi, and in Mykonos parking is a nightmare.

Day 1: Athens

If you've arrived in Athens the night before, take a day to soak up some of the city's most important sites, including the **Acropolis** and **Parthenon,** a quick walk through **Anafiotika,** and a glass of wine from one of the city's many delicious **wine bars.**

Day 2: Naxos

Take the earliest possible ferry from Piraeus port (10 km/6 mi southwest of central Athens; easily accessed via metro from Athens, but arrive early to avoid missing your boat!). You'll arrive a few hours later in fertile Naxos, the largest of the Cycladic islands. Visit the **Temple of Apollo** and go have lunch at **Yema Agapis.** Spend an hour or two walking around **Hora** and up in the **Kastro.** Eat dinner at **Axiotissa Taverna,** the best restaurant on an island full of amazing food.

Day 3: Naxos

Get the blood pumping with an early morning **hike** through Mt. Zas' 6-km (3.75-mi) loop from Arai Spring. The first half is well-marked; beyond the cave you'll just follow the beaten foot path. Then, drive over to the cozy seaside village of **Moutsouna** for a grilled fish lunch, before heading down to **Psili Ammos** for a relaxing afternoon by the sea.

Day 4: Naxos

Devote a day to exploring the mountainous interior of the island, where **charming traditional villages** dot the landscape and the view. As you drive up increasingly winding road, the scenery becomes more and more breathtaking. A good trip is to go from Sangri to Halki (you must try the custard pie from **To Spitiko Galaktobouriko**) to Apiranthos, before stopping in Koronos for a very late lunch at **Matina & Stavros' Taverna.** Consult the map beforehand; the most circuitous route is often the safest and best paved road to travel.

Day 5: Naxos to Mykonos

Spend the morning relaxing on **Alyko Beach** and exploring the many coves and abandoned hotel covered in artistic graffiti. In the late afternoon, take the fast boat to Mykonos (35 minutes), where you can catch the sunset at the aptly named **180 Degrees Sunset Bar** in Hora. Hunker down in your hotel; Mykonos is going to get you good tomorrow.

Day 6: Day Trip to Delos Archaeological Site

Take the 9am boat to **Delos** and spend your allotted four hours wandering around this amazing piece of living history. On your return, head directly for **Super Paradise Beach** and spend the afternoon sipping champagne and dancing with beautiful people. Cap off the evening with some debauchery at **Jackie O.**

Greece's Best Beaches

You're here for the sand and waves, aren't you? Here's a roundup of Greece's most picturesque coastlines, from the Ionian to the Aegean:

BEST PARTY BEACH

Super Paradise, Mykonos: Don't come here to relax. This is a beach to see and be seen, and to party *a lot* thanks to the mega clubs and bars that line it (page 128).

BEST HIPPIE PARADISE

Megalos Roukounas, Anafi: This long stretch of sand turns into a bohemian paradise each summer, with plenty of free campers and nudists running about (page 200).

BEST WINDSURFING BEACH

Devil's Bay, Karpathos: All the professional windsurfers head to this windy cove to skim along the waves. If you can't join 'em, admire 'em. It looks like they're flying (page 213).

BEST SECRET COVES

Alyko Beach, Naxos: This beautiful long sandy beach in Naxos has plenty of secret spots thanks to the dozens of coves that cut through the beach, plus an abandoned hotel that's now covered in artwork (page 182).

BLUEST WATER

Porto Katsiki, Lefkada: For an impossibly blue waters—seriously, it's like Mother Nature just made up a brand-new color—make a beeline to Porto Katsiki (page 414).

Egremni, Lefkada: Accessible only by boat, this is the only other beach that gives Porto Katsiki a run for its money in terms of blue hues. Stretch out along 2.5 km (1.5 mi) of white sand and just drink in the scenery (page 414).

relax and bathe in crystal clear water of Balos beach

MOST UNIQUE

Balos Bay, Crete: There are too many beautiful beaches in Crete, but the geographical wonder of Balos Bay—pink sand, impossibly turquoise water—might just be the most spectacular. Come early in the morning to beat the crowds (page 457).

Sarakiniko Beach, Milos: Comprising salt-eroded volcanic rock, this beach makes you feel like you're walking on the moon (page 164).

Day 7: Mykonos

You've probably felt better, huh? Take a leisurely car drive through the island's interior roads, and head to one of the more secluded beaches, such as Agios Sostis on the northern coast, where you can enjoy a delicious meal at the seaside taverna. Before sunset, head to **Scorpios** for a cocktail, and then let the night take you…

Days 8-9: Anafi

Head out of Mykonos to Anafi (the easiest way is to take a boat through Santorini; the whole journey takes 5 hours). It would defeat the whole purpose of Anafi if I were to give you an itinerary. Instead, spend your days lounging around the **beach,** occasionally walking the **trails.** If you see only one beach, make it **Megalos Roukounas.** If you do nothing else, you've done it correctly.

Day 10: Anafi to Athens

Take the ferry back to Athens (8 hours) feeling relaxed and completely rejuvenated.

Best of the Dodecanese: Rhodes and Karpathos

In the far-flung Dodecanese islands, your cell phone picks up Turkish coverage and the radio statically plays Turkish pop songs. History is rife here, and though these islands are increasingly popular with the package tourist crowd, there's still a way around that. Fly first to Rhodes before heading to Karpathos. You'll want to book a car in Rhodes, and for at least part of the time in Karpathos. From Karpathos, you can fly back to Athens.

Day 1-2: Athens to Rhodes

There's no need to spend a full day on the ferry—fly directly from Athens to Rhodes (2 hours).

You'll want at least two days to explore the Old Town of Rhodes at your own pace. Don't miss the **Jewish Quarter** or the **Street of the Knights of Rhodes,** which ends at the **Palace of the Grand Master.** When you're done exploring, there are plenty of great restaurants in Rhodes Town to satisfy your appetite.

Day 3: Rhodes

To beat the crowds, head out early to the **Valley of the Butterflies,** a 45-minute drive from Rhodes Town. Today's other can't-miss sight is the city's **Acropolis,** with stunning coastal views.

Day 4: Rhodes

After so much sightseeing, take advantage of Rhodes' quieter beaches in the south. Spend the day at the **Isle of Prasonisi,** which is popular with windsurfers.

Day 5: Rhodes to Karpathos

You can take the ferry (6 hours) or fly (40 minutes) to craggy Karpathos, which is the best place in Greece to try your hand at **windsurfing**—even beginners should sign up for lessons at Chicken Bay. Drive to the seaside village of **Finiki** to have freshly grilled fish and stuffed calamari with the fishermen.

Day 6: Karpathos

Grab a coffee and a freshly baked doughnut for breakfast and stroll along the backstreets of **Pigadia** before hopping a **boat tour** (departing at 8:30am) to the three best beaches on the island: **Achata, Kyria Panagia,** and **Apella.**

Day 7: Karpathos

Early in the morning (no later than 8:30am to beat the crowds) head to **Olympos Village,** which has survived intact since the 7th century. After lunch in Olympos, drive down to **Diafani** for an afternoon at the beach, followed by a seaside dinner at one of the fish tavernas lining the harbor.

Day 8: Karpathos

Apella is one of my favorite beaches in Greece. I know you saw it by boat, but head back here to spend a full, proper Greek vacation day floating in the sea and satiating yourself in the small taverna at the top of the beach.

Day 9: Karpathos to Athens

Board a flight back to Athens.

Hiking Through the Islands

Local islands are cleaning up their hiking trails, and there's never been a better time to walk through the islands. Depending on what island and trail you choose, you'll stumble upon ruins, coastal views, and endemic plants.

SAMARIA GORGE, CRETE

16 km (10 mi) one-way

Walk through a wildflower-covered gorge that ends with a dip in the sea (page 459).

CORFU TRAIL, CORFU

220-km (137-mi) loop; can be hiked in sections

Hike through well-marked paths on this intense route that circles all of Corfu, passing through villages, across streams, and through forests (page 378).

MOUNT ZAS, NAXOS

8-km (5-mi) loop

Scale the mountain where it's said Zeus was born. The views will make you feel as though you're floating above Naxos (page 187).

FONIAS RIVER, SAMOTHRACE

5 km (3 mi) one-way

Trek along a river to a large pool (perfect for a dip) and waterfall (page 271).

FOLEGANDROS' NORTHWEST COAST

Three separate trails (2-5.5 km/1.25-3.5 mi each) lead across the northwest coast of Folegandros, which is populated by only a few homes and farms. Depending on which trail you choose, you can access churches, a lighthouse, or hidden beaches and coves (page 147).

waterfall cascading through the cliffs on Fonias River

ALONNISOS

This herb-scented island is basically a walker's paradise. Start off with the small walk between the port and Palio Alonnisos; at the end of your hike you can reward yourself with a slice of cake from Hayati (page 325).

Best of the Northeast Aegean: Ikaria and Lesvos

For a taste of a less touristy side of Greece, head to Ikaria and Lesvos, where it's all about the food, the vibes, and the traditional nightlife. Note that there's only one weekly direct ferry (the day of the week varies throughout the year; best to book this directly with a tour operator) between the two islands, so plan your trip accordingly.

I recommend renting a car in both islands, especially in Ikaria, where time is a philosophy and buses run sporadically.

Day 1: Athens to Lesvos

Catch an early morning flight to Lesvos, arriving in Mytilini. Go directly for a swim in **Tarti Beach** before heading back to Mytilini when the sun gets too hot. Spend the afternoon wandering around the port town, ducking into the fantastic **Therirade Museum.** Cap off the evening with a visit to an ***ouzeri*** for ouzo and meze.

Day 2-3: Lesvos

Spend the next two days on the island's west coast, basing yourself in **Skala Eressou.** A full day should be spent relaxing on the beach, while the second day should be devoted to exploring the nature in the area, like the wetlands and the **petrified forest.** Bird watchers can book a half-day excursion with Eleni Galinou.

Day 4: Lesvos to Ikaria

It's a long ferry ride (10 hours) to Ikaria, the island that operates mostly at night, but I promise it's worth it. If you arrive at night, head directly to the **Christos Raches village,** where things only start opening around 10pm. Extra points if there's a ***panigiri*** going on, but even if there's not, walk around the village, stopping for drinks and food at any of the cafés and tavernas dotting the village square.

Day 5: Ikaria

Since you're already on the west coast, stay in the area for the day, heading to the seaside village of **Armenistis** for lunch at **MaryMary.** Spend the afternoon at **Nas,** a hippie paradise well-known for the ruins of an ancient temple dedicated to the goddess Artemis. Finish the day with dinner at **Anna.**

Day 6: Ikaria

Explore the southeast coast of the island. Spend the morning at the fantastic **Seychelles** beach, before driving up the southern coast to **Therma,** which has some of the best hot springs in Europe. In between make a stop at the **Rock of Icarus.**

Day 7: Ikaria to Athens

Take a ferry back to Athens (6.5 hours) the next morning.

Therma village on Ikaria island

Know Your History

History and archaeology buffs will have a field day in Greece (pun intended). Although nearly all the islands have some sort of ruins and museums, Samothrace, Crete, and Delos (accessible from both Mykonos or Naxos) have particularly fabulous places to visit. Download **Topos Text** to your phone, which has geolocated more than 5,000 ancient ruins across Greece, and complements them with excerpts of ancient texts.

PALACE OF KNOSSOS, CRETE

The best preserved of the Minoan palaces, the Palace of Knossos is a testament to the ferocious strength and power of the mysterious Minoan civilization (page 434).

DELOS ARCHAEOLOGICAL SITE, DELOS

This uninhabited island (accessible by way of Mykonos) was a sacred place for ancient Greeks, and is one of the most important Panhellenic sanctuaries. Walk around temples, theaters, former houses, and truly magnificent mosaics (page 134).

TEMPLE OF APOLLO, NAXOS

The huge marble gate—actually an unfinished temple dedicated to Apollo—is one of the most arresting sights in Greece, and the first thing you'll see as your ferry boat docks in Naxos (page 176).

SANCTUARY OF THE GREAT GODS, SAMOTHRACE

Feel the energy at this mysterious temple complex dating back to the 7th century BC. The site was used to worship the "Great Gods," but the true meaning behind the place still has archaeologists scratching their heads (page 267).

the stunning Temple of Apollo in the early morning light

PARTHENON, ATHENS

One of the most awe-inspiring places in Western civilization, the Parthenon, still stands in all its glory above the Acropolis (page 43).

Best of the Sporades: Skyros and Alonnisos

I love the Sporades islands for their laid-back vibe and lush nature, but it's a bit difficult to navigate between them. Either choose one of the two, or count an extra day (as detailed below) to go between Alonnisos and Skyros. In Alonnisos, you won't need a car, but I suggest hiring one in Skyros for at least part of the time you're there.

Day 1: Athens to Skyros

You'll need to catch the bus from Athens to Kymi

to take the ferry (1.5 hours) to Skyros (there are no boats from Piraeus). You'll arrive in the evening; head to **O Pappous Kai Ego** for dinner.

Day 2: Skyros

Explore **Hora** in the morning, taking time to walk up to the **Monastery of St. George** for incredible views of the beaches below. Then, head to **Molos Beach** (which you viewed from above) for seaside relaxation.

Day 3: Skyros

Drive down to the wild, deserted southern part of Skyros, where you can visit **Rupert Brooke's grave** and hike out to **Cape Lithari lighthouse.** On your drive back north, say hello to the local ponies at **Mouries Farm,** and have dinner at the adjacent taverna.

Day 4: Skryos to Alonnisos

You'll need to catch the ferry back to Volos before grabbing another one from the same port to Alonnisos. The whole thing, unfortunately, will take you around 8 hours, but at least the boat ride is beautiful! Be sure to pack snacks.

Day 5: Alonnisos

Stock up on provisions like homemade spanakopita (spinach pie) at **Ikos Traditional Products** before heading out for **Chrisi Milia Beach.** In the afternoon, explore the traditional village of **Palio Alonnisos,** then enjoy a meal on the grapevine-strewn terrace of **Astrofegia.**

Day 6: Alonnisos

Tour the **National Marine Park of Alonnisos** by boat, keeping an eye out for dolphins and monk seals, which you might spot if you're lucky. Lunch will be included on your tour. In the evening, watch the sunset from the cliffside Byzantine church of **Agioi Anargyroi.**

Day 7: Alonnisos to Athens

The easiest way to return to Athens is to take the ferry from Alonnisos to Kymi ([AU] hours). From there, you can take the bus back to central Athens.

National Marine Park of Alonnisos

Best of the Ionian Coast: Corfu and Lefkada

Fly into Corfu, and spend three days exploring the island's stunning architecture and sampling the Venetian-inspired food. There's no easy way to get around the Ionian islands, but you can take the boat and the bus from Corfu to arrive a few hours later in Lefkada, where you can spend a few days soaking up the impossibly blue beaches and beautiful mountains.

You don't need a car for the first day in Corfu; the rest of the time I recommend renting one.

Day 1: Arrive in Corfu

Fly directly into Corfu. I hope you've taken a morning flight so you can fortify yourself with an excellent pudding from **Alexis Dairy Store** for breakfast. Spend the morning walking around the winding old roads of Corfu Town, before visiting the **Palaio Frourio (Old Fort)**. For comparison's sake, walk over to the **Neo Frourio (New Port)** as well. If you only have time to visit one museum, make it the **Corfu Museum of Asian Art.** Indulge in dinner at the wine bar **Salto.**

Day 2: Corfu

Drive across the island to the western side, working your way down by alternating between the villages and the little coves. Visit Durrell's favorite beach, **Myrtiotissa,** and eat at one of the excellent **mountain tavernas.**

Day 3: Corfu

Head up the island's northern coast, making sure to stop in the fabulously preserved village of **Palia Perithia.** Leave the car behind and start off on a three-hour hike around **Mt. Pantokrator,** the highest point in Corfu; you'll be able to see all the way to Italy. Head to **Longas beach** for the sunset.

Day 4: Corfu to Lefkada

It's a bit difficult to navigate between the Ionian islands. To get to Lefkada, you'll need to take the ferry from Corfu to the mainland (1.5 hours), and then a bus to Lefkada (2 hours). You'll arrive by early afternoon, which is enough time to explore the Caribbean-inspired **Lefkada Town** and have an Italian-inspired dinner at **Nissi Mediterranean Kuzina.**

Day 5: Lefkada

Rent a car and drive down the island's fabulous west coast, stopping in **Egremni** and **Porto Katsiki beach**. Pack a picnic before you set out for the day, and buy some honey and bee pollen from the many handmade shacks along the side of the road. Drive to **Rachi restaurant** for the sunset and a delicious gourmet dinner at bargain prices.

Before you head back to your hotel, book a paragliding expedition for tomorrow from the guys at **Parapente Paramotor** outside of Rachi.

Day 6: Lefkada

Spend the morning flying like a bird on your **paragliding** excursion. If you're still on an adrenaline high, head to **Vasilikis Beach** on the south side of the island to try your hand at **windsurfing,** or head to the calmer **Ammoussa beach** for some **snorkeling.**

Day 7: Day Trip to Meganisi

There are several satellite islands dotting Lefkada. Take the morning to visit the small, colorful island of Meganisi by hopping on a boat from Nidri. A €20 boat tour includes **swimming** stops and a **taverna** stop. You'll be back in Lefkada around 5pm, which is enough time to catch an evening flight to Athens.

Bohemian Greece

The truth is, there's no island left that's completely off the grid—we are no longer in the 1970s. That being said, there are a few islands that attract a more artistically minded traveler, or someone looking for something a bit more alternative.

SAMOTHRACE

Samothrace is definitely a bohemian island, popular with hippies and reggae fans who camp among the trees. The fact that it's so hard to get to acts as a sort of filter, protecting it from mass-packaged tourists (page 261).

ANAFI

Anafi has all the spectacular landscapes and sunsets of Santorini without the crowds. It draws a very eclectic mix of Greek and foreign tourists, and by July it turns into a haven for nudists and bonvivants, with free camping and contemporary art festivals (page 193).

IKARIA

Ikaria already has the coolest people of any island, and attracts a similar sort of tourist—though be warned that in August it's wall-to-wall people. You'll find plenty of yoga and meditation workshops here to help get you in the mood (page 276).

ALONNISOS

Lovely Alonnisos is a favorite with Greeks, who come for the relaxed beaches. It attracts a lot of walkers, hitchhikers, and travelers in cutoff shorts just having a good time (page 322).

FOLEGANDROS

Folegandros is increasingly becoming a "cool" island, so visit while it's still somewhat under the radar. You'll find sparsely populated beaches, a beautiful hora, and a free-spirit vibe (page 136).

MYKONOS

Mykonos was once a fantastic bohemian spot thanks largely to gay culture, and although it's been commercialized, there's a carefree hedonistic vibe that's impossible to escape (page 113).

Athens (Αθήνα)

Athens (pop. 5 million) has long been defined by its ancient past. Here, after all, is the birthplace of democracy, a seaside capital where sun-bleached relics like the Parthenon, Hadrian's Arch, and the ancient agora continue to stand. After the ancient Greek empire fell, Athens was reduced to a pastoral village, which it remained until its establishment as modern Greece's capital in the 1800s.

Today's Athens would be completely foreign to Aristotle and Plato, though they would still recognize the Parthenon, which, particularly when lit up at night, is an incredible sight to see. The city is a modern mash of contradictions, with neoclassical buildings next to 1960s high rises, and contemporary art galleries buttressed by stone ruins. Recent economic problems have had a destabilizing effect on Athens,

Highlights

Look for ★ to find recommended sights, activities, dining, and lodging.

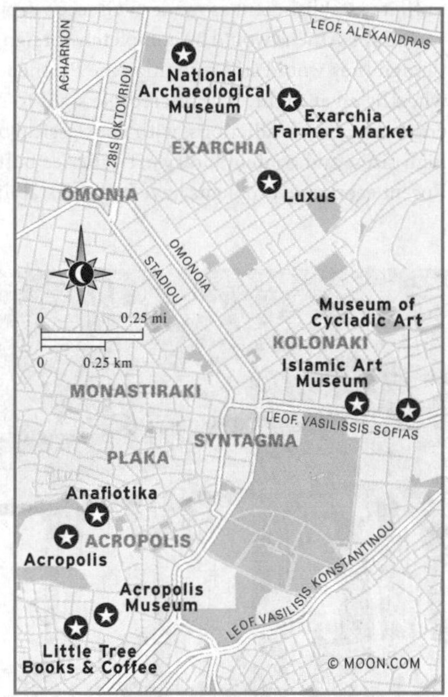

★ **Acropolis:** The most iconic archaeological site in Western civilization is even more impressive in person (page 43).

★ **Acropolis Museum:** Adjacent to the ruins, the newly refurbished Acropolis Museum houses archaeological findings from the Acropolis in a sleek, modern building (page 49).

★ **Anafiotika:** Beat the crowds in Plaka by heading to this neighborhood right above it, which feels like a Greek island town in the middle of the city (page 50).

★ **Islamic Art Museum:** After checking out the fabulous collection of Islamic art, head to the rooftop café. It's the most beautiful in Athens (page 52).

★ **National Archaeological Museum:** Peruse the world's most impressive collection of Greek antiquities (page 54).

★ **Exarchia Farmers Market:** Buy fresh fruits and vegetables at Athens' best farmers market, held every Saturday. Produce is seasonal, and if you come in August, you'll taste the best figs of your life (page 54).

★ **Museum of Cycladic Art:** Picasso himself was so inspired by the minimal Cycladic statues that most of his modern oeuvre is based on these simple lines. Check out the fantastic collection for yourself (page 56).

★ **People-Watching in Koukaki:** The charming residential neighborhood of Koukaki, in the shadow of Acropolis, is a must for people-watching—and the shaded tree-lined garden at **Little Tree Books & Coffee** is the best spot to do so (page 71).

★ **Exarchia:** Café by day, bar by night, **Luxus** is a good anchor for exploring Exharchia, Athens' most alternative neighborhood, which is known for its literary and political scene (page 74).

and thousands of people have left in search of other opportunities. But Athens can never be fully beaten down, and it is now indeed on the rise: New museums and cultural centers, including the wonderful Stavros Niarchos Foundation Cultural Center, have been built; the bohemian set has returned to set up community projects, fusion restaurants, and art spaces; and immigrants from across Africa, the Middle East, and Asia have breathed new life into forgotten neighborhoods.

Orientation and Planning

NEIGHBORHOODS

Syntagma

Syntagma is the beating heart of Athens—or perhaps more accurately, its brain. The main square of Syntagma is home to the Parliament, where ministers pour in and out during weekdays and crowds gather to protest during particularly fiery moments of social upheaval. The joke in Athens is that all roads lead to Syntagma, which is sort of true. You'll most likely pass here at some point, either taking the shopping pedestrian road of Ermou down to Monastiraki and Plaka, or to eat at one of the restaurants in the area. Some of Athens' best hotels are located here, but like the center of any metropolis, it doesn't have much of a neighborhood vibe.

Monastiraki, Plaka, and Koukaki

The neighborhood of **Plaka** is considered the first neighborhood in modern Athens. Built under the shadow of Acropolis (the rock on which the Parthenon sits), it is the most touristic part of Athens and is unmissable for any visitor to the city. Plaka has that quintessential Greek look so many tourists are after (bougainvillea, narrow roads), and although there are gems to be found, it's really jam-packed with tourists in the summer. **Monastiraki,** to the north, is a bit more edgy, with plenty of bars and restaurants and a nice flea market. **Koukaki,** located south of Acropolis, is a mostly residential neighborhood that in recent years has become increasingly hip; there are great restaurants, cafés, and shops, all within spitting distance of Acropolis but with a lot fewer tourists.

Gazi and West Athens

To the west of the city center you'll find the industrial area of **Gazi:** the name comes from the gaswork companies that were here. These days, it's a trendy neighborhood with great cafés, bars, and a lively arts and music scene. **Kermaikos, Metaxourigia,** and **Thisio** all buttress Gazi and have also been undergoing their own gentrified renaissance.

Psyrri, Omonia, and Exarchia

In the north part of Athens you'll find the central roundabout of Omonia Square, which acts as a de facto walking bridge between the neighborhoods of Psyrri and Exarchia. All three spots have their own character, with a certain kind of grittiness that has caused the US State Department to put out a travel alert on the neighborhood of Exarchia. That's total hogwash; **Exarchia** is a fantastic alternative neighborhood that's staunchly anti-fascist, and it remains a beacon for artists, poets, leftists (and anarchists). It's full of bookstores, cafés, record shops, and vintage stores, and an excellent farmers market on Saturdays. Demonstrations between protestors and police happen with semi-regularity, but the only big days to watch out for are November 17 (anniversary of Athens Polytechnic Uprising)

Previous: Inside the Parthenon atop the Acropolis; the changing of the guards outside Parliament; this Golden Funeral Mask of Agamemnon from the Trojan War is on display at the National Archaeological Museum.

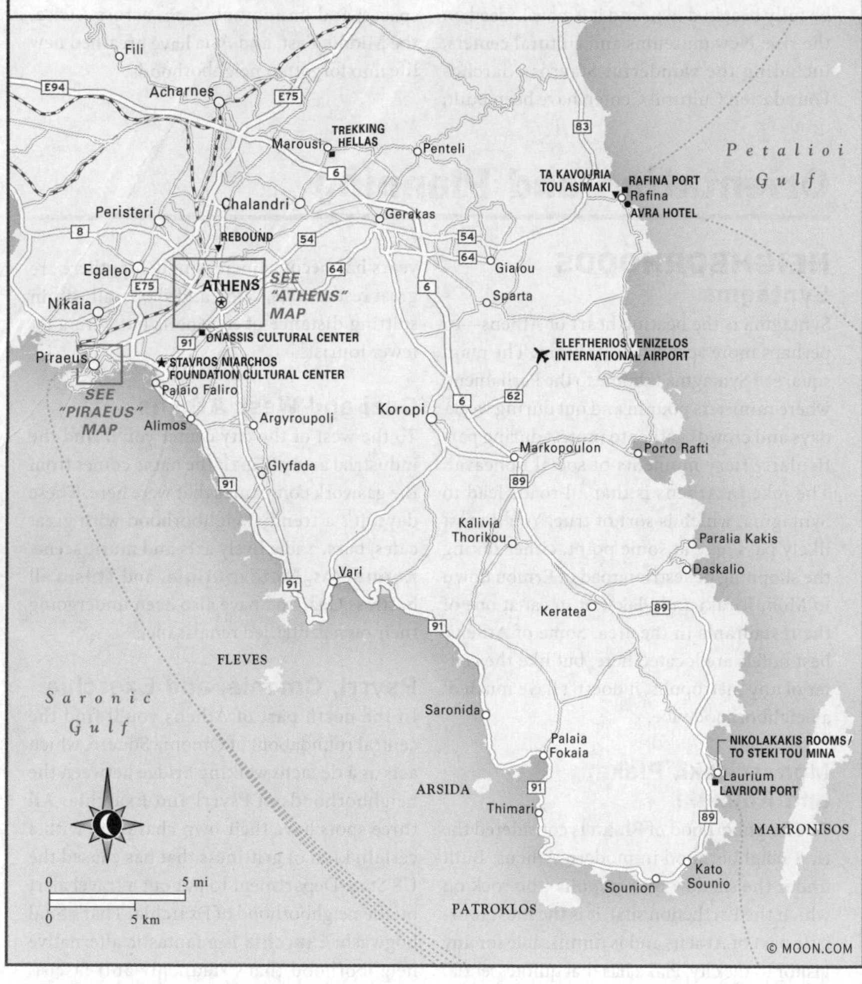

and December 6 (anniversary of the murder of 15-year-old Alexandros Grigoropoulos by police).

Psyrri centers on Iroon Square and is another vibrant and colorful neighborhood, though with less of a political slant. There's a lot of really good street art around Psyrri, especially along Louka Nika Street, and there are some cool bars, restaurants, shops, and cafés. **Omonia** can get a bit dodgy by night, and there's a decent amount of pickpocketing in the area; watch out.

Kolonaki

Considered the most aristocratic of Athens' downtown neighborhoods, Kolonaki ("little column" in Greek) is located on the slopes of Mount Lycabettus, east of Syntagma, and attracts a who's who of Athenians. There's a mix of neoclassical and modern buildings, the cute

Kolonaki Square, and a number of important museums.

Pangrati and Mets

Located behind the National Gardens, Pangrati and Mets are two residential neighborhoods that are rapidly becoming known for their slightly Brooklyn-ish, slightly Parisian vibe, while remaining quintessentially Athenian. These two spots are among my favorites in Athens: tranquil, full of locals, with plenty of quirky architectural details. There are lots of good restaurants and bars around here as well, plus a growing number of design shops and clothing stores.

PLANNING YOUR TIME

Most visitors heading to the Greek islands tack on Athens as a one-day bookend to their ferry trips. How wrong they are. Athens is a truly fantastic city, but if you want to get to know it outside of its major tourist sites, you'll want to spend at least three or four days here. You'll need a full day to visit Acropolis and see some museums, but the real joy of Athens comes from walking around its neighborhoods, sitting in cafés and people watching, soaking up the art that's around every corner, and scratching just a little bit below the Parthenon surface.

INFORMATION AND SERVICES

There are plenty of **bank branches and ATMs** around central Athens. Note that ATM fees start at around €2.50. The **National Bank of Greece** (Karageorgi Servias at Stadiou, Syntagma; tel. 210/334 0500) has a 24-hour automated exchange machine. Capital controls imposed during the financial crisis have since been lifted, and lines are usually pretty short.

The **central post office** is near Omonia (Eolou 100; Mon.-Fri. 7:30am-8:30pm, Sat. to 2:30pm), and there's another one in Syntagma, though it's always crowded and understaffed, and the underpaid postal workers are usually grumpy (Plateia Syntagma, Mon.-Fri. 7:30am-8:30pm, Sat. to 2:30pm, Sun. 9am-1:30pm).

Pharmacies are a dime a dozen; there seems to be one on each corner. Public hospitals in Greece will treat you with or without insurance, and the **central clinic** is open 24/7 (Asklipiou 31; tel. 210/367 4000).

The main tourist office, the **EOT** (Dionysiou Areopagitou 18-20; tel. 210/331 0347; www.visitgreece.gr), has knowledgeable staff, free brochures, and maps of the city.

SAFETY

The emergency number for police is **100.** There are two main **police** buildings in Ambelokipi (Leof. Alexandras 173; tel. 210/770 5711; www.astynomia.gr) and Syntagma (210/725 7000). Tourist police are located in Koukai (Veikou 43-45; tel. 210/920 0724 for office, 171 for 24/7 service; daily 8am-10pm). However, police in Athens are a mixed bag. Though they can sometimes be helpful, they've been accused of colluding with the Nazi-party Golden Dawn, and are not always helpful, even in extreme circumstances. I met one man outside the American Embassy who had been attacked in plain sight of five police officers; despite his screams for help, they didn't lift a finger. Tourist police are better equipped to deal with issues immediately pertaining to foreign tourists (lost passports, for example).

That said, Athens is a generally safe city, though some areas are definitely worth avoiding, especially at night, like the backstreets of Omonia. As in any big capital city, visitors should exercise caution. The sexual harassment is on par with the rest of Europe: existent, annoying, but generally not physically harmful. LGBTQ+ travelers are mostly safe in central Athens, especially in LGBTQ+-friendly neighborhoods like Exarchia and Gazi. Hate crimes against immigrants have unfortunately been increasing, and though tourists haven't been attacked, be cautious, especially if you find yourself suddenly near a far-right protest.

Itinerary Ideas

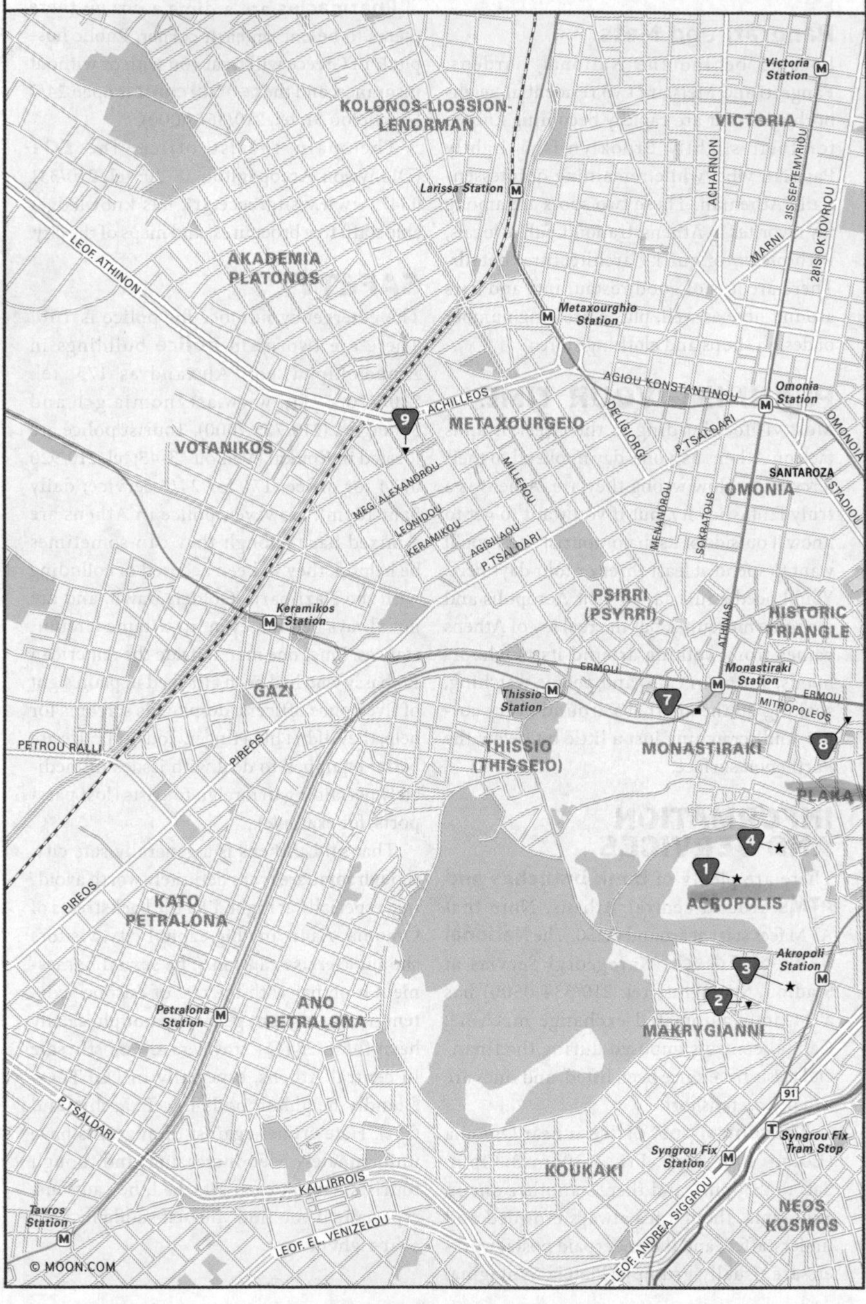

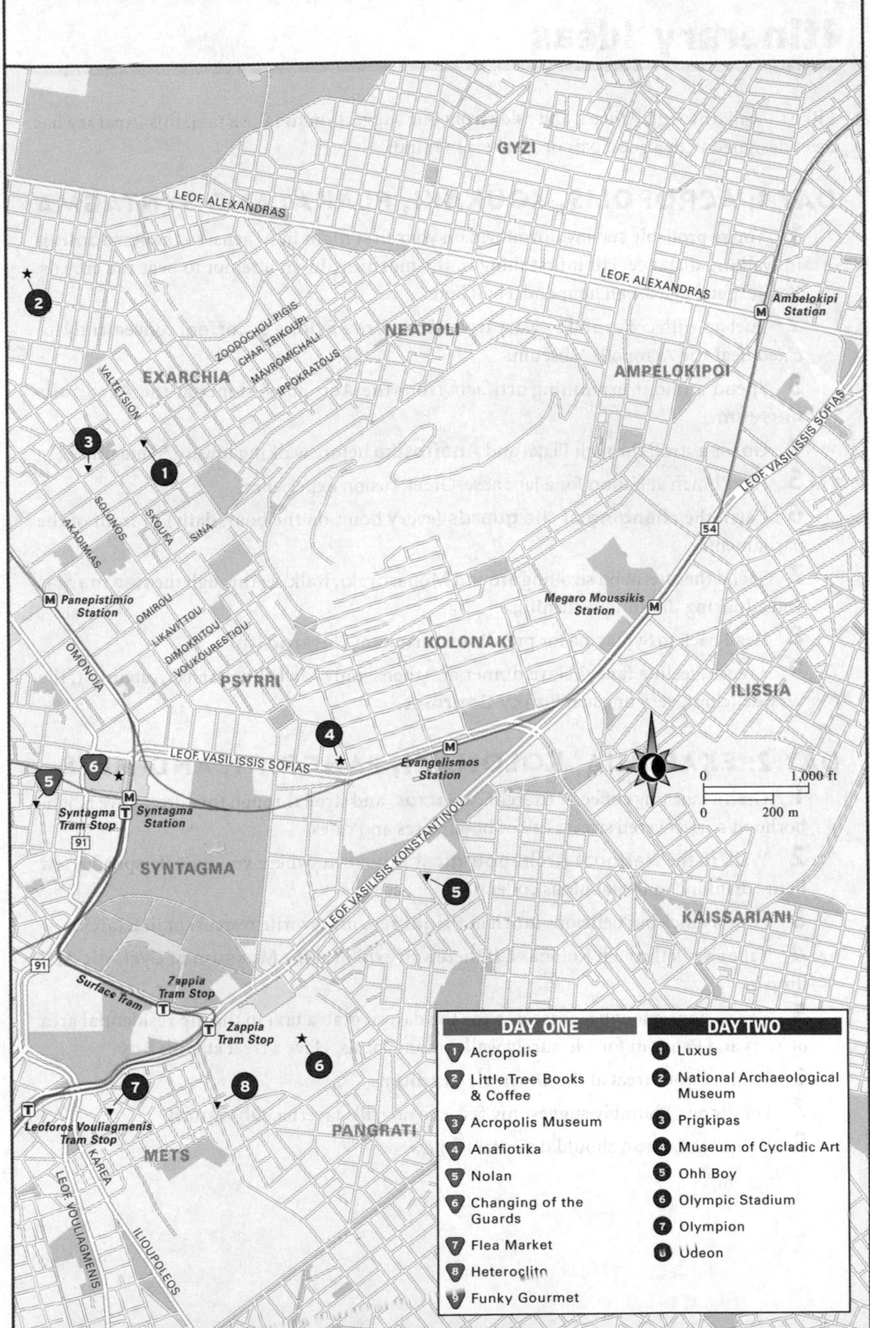
GYZI
LEOF. ALEXANDRAS
LEOF. ALEXANDRAS
Ambelokipi Station
NEAPOLI
ZOODOCHOU PIGIS
CHAR. TRIKOUPI
MAVROMICHALI
IPPOKRATOUS
EXARCHIA
VALTETSION
AMPELOKIPOI
LEOF. VASILISSIS SOFIAS
SOLONOS
SKOUFA
SINA
AKADIMIAS
54
Panepistimio Station
OMIROU
LIKAVITTOU
DIMOKRITOU
VOUKOURESTIOU
Megaro Moussikis Station
KOLONAKI
OMONOIA
PSYRRI
ILISSIA
LEOF. VASILISSIS SOFIAS
Evangelismos Station
0 1,000 ft
0 200 m
Syntagma Tram Stop
Syntagma Station
91
SYNTAGMA
LEOF. VASILISIS KONSTANTINOU
KAISSARIANI
91
Surface Tram
Zappia Tram Stop
Zappia Tram Stop
Leoforos Vouliagmenis Tram Stop
PANGRATI
METS
KAREA
LEOF. VOULIAGMENIS
ILIOUPOLEOS
DAY ONE
1 Acropolis
2 Little Tree Books & Coffee
3 Acropolis Museum
4 Anafiotika
5 Nolan
6 Changing of the Guards
7 Flea Market
8 Heteroclito
9 Funky Gourmet
DAY TWO
1 Luxus
2 National Archaeological Museum
3 Prigkipas
4 Museum of Cycladic Art
5 Ohh Boy
6 Olympic Stadium
7 Olympion
8 Udeon

Itinerary Ideas

I like to walk through Athens, and aside from one suggestion to take a taxi, this itinerary has been designed with a good pair of sneakers in mind.

DAY 1: ACROPOLIS, KOUKAKI, PLAKA, AND SYNTAGMA

1 You're probably staying downtown on your first night in Athens, so the **Acropolis** is in walking distance. Hit it first thing in the morning, in an attempt to beat the crowds. You'll spend at least an hour and a half here.

2 Fuel up with coffee and a pastry from **Little Tree Books & Coffee,** conveniently located near the Acropolis Museum.

3 Spend an hour examining artifacts from the Acropolis' slopes at the **Acropolis Museum.**

4 Go for a stroll through Plaka and **Anafiotika** before walking toward Syntagma.

5 Have lunch at **Nolan** for a Japanese-Greek fusion experience.

6 Catch the **changing of the guards** (every hour, on the hour, daily) in front of the parliament.

7 Spend the afternoon strolling around Monastiraki, walking through the **flea market** and admiring the antique furniture.

8 Head back to Syntagma for pre-dinner drinks at **Heteroclito.**

9 Are you feeling fancy? Have dinner at Athens' only Michelin-starred restaurant, the very delicious, very unusual **Funky Gourmet.**

DAY 2: EXARCHIA, KOLONAKI, PANGRATI, AND METS

1 Grab a morning coffee in Exarchia at **Luxus,** and stroll through this alternative neighborhood's art-covered streets full of bookstores and cafés.

2 Walk to the **National Archaeological Museum,** where you'll likely spend a few hours drinking in the fabulous collection.

3 Have a quick but delicious lunch at **Prigkipas,** my favorite restaurant in Exarchia.

4 Take a walk through Kolonaki. If there's an exhibit at the **Museum of Cycladic Art,** drop in.

5 You've done enough sightseeing for the day, so grab a taxi to the hip residential area of Mets and Pangrati for a leisurely walk among locals. Have a treat at **Ohh Boy.**

6 Walk off your treat at the **Olympic Stadium.**

7 For dinner, I humbly suggest my favorite no frills taverna, **Olympion.**

8 Drinks at **Odeon** should definitely follow.

Sights

If you're going to be in Athens for several days and want to do a lot of sightseeing, consider buying the €30 ticket that provides entry to the Acropolis, the Ancient Agora, Hadrian's Library, the Temple of Olympian Zeus, Aristotle's Lyceum, and the Roman Agora. It's valid for five days and can be bought at any of these sights.

Art lovers will be happy to hear that a €15 ticket, valid for three days, provides entry to the National Archaeological Museum, the Byzantine & Christina Museum, the Numismatic Museum, and the Epigraphic Museum.

SYNTAGMA

Syntagma Square

Plateia Syntagma; free

This is the main square of Athens. Here you'll find the Parliament, where the constitution was granted in 1843 (Syntagma means "constitution" in Greek.) There are a couple of cafés lining the square and a fountain in the center. Politics are still present today; this is often a main point for protests and demonstrations. In fact, the best way to experience the square would be during one of the protests (democracy in action!), which happen with semi-regularity. Otherwise, I suggest walking the perimeter of the square, stopping at the **Changing of the Guards** in front of Parliament.

Changing of the Guards

Plateia Syntagmatos; free

Every hour, on the hour, of every day—even at 3am on Tuesday—the fantastically costumed evzones (guards) perform an elaborate changing-of-guards ritual in front of the Tomb of the Unknown Soldier, which honors any Greek soldier that was ever killed in any Greek war. On Sundays at 11am, the affair is elevated to a whole marching platoon, accompanied by a band.

There's always a crush of tourists (and pigeons) photographing the changing of the guards. For a more intimate experience head down toward the Presidential Palace behind the National Gardens. Located on a quiet residential street, the "palace" (it's really more of a townhouse) is guarded by evzones who still perform the hourly exchange. Note that these are the most respected soldiers in Greece, and you can't get too close to them; if you do, they'll bang their Ottoman-era rifles against the ground as a warning.

National Gardens

Leoforos Vasilissis Sofias and Leoforos Vsilissis Amalias; 7am-dusk; free

Greece used to be a monarchy, and in 1938, Queen Amalia designed these lovely royal gardens as a leafy repose. Apparently, Amalia was so enthralled with her slice of greenery she spent up to three hours a day tending to the plants. No need to be royalty to visit now; it's a pleasure to stroll through the gardens. There's a café and playground as well as a zoo. In addition to the Presidential Palace entrance, there's another one next to the Parliament, so after the Changing of the Guards, you can easily enter the garden. The gardens are built around **Zappeio Palace,** built in 1870 and now open to the public with occasional concerts and performances.

PLAKA AND ACROPOLIS

★ Acropolis

Acropolis; tel. 210/321 4172; http://odysseus.culture.gr/index_en.html; Apr.-Oct. 8am-8pm, Nov.-Mar. 8am-5pm, last entry 30 minutes before closing; €20

The heartbeat of Athens—and, some would argue, all of Western civilization—is even more stunning in person than in photos. What personally touches me about Acropolis is the indelible energy of the place: Despite the hordes of tourists, it's a truly spiritual

Athens

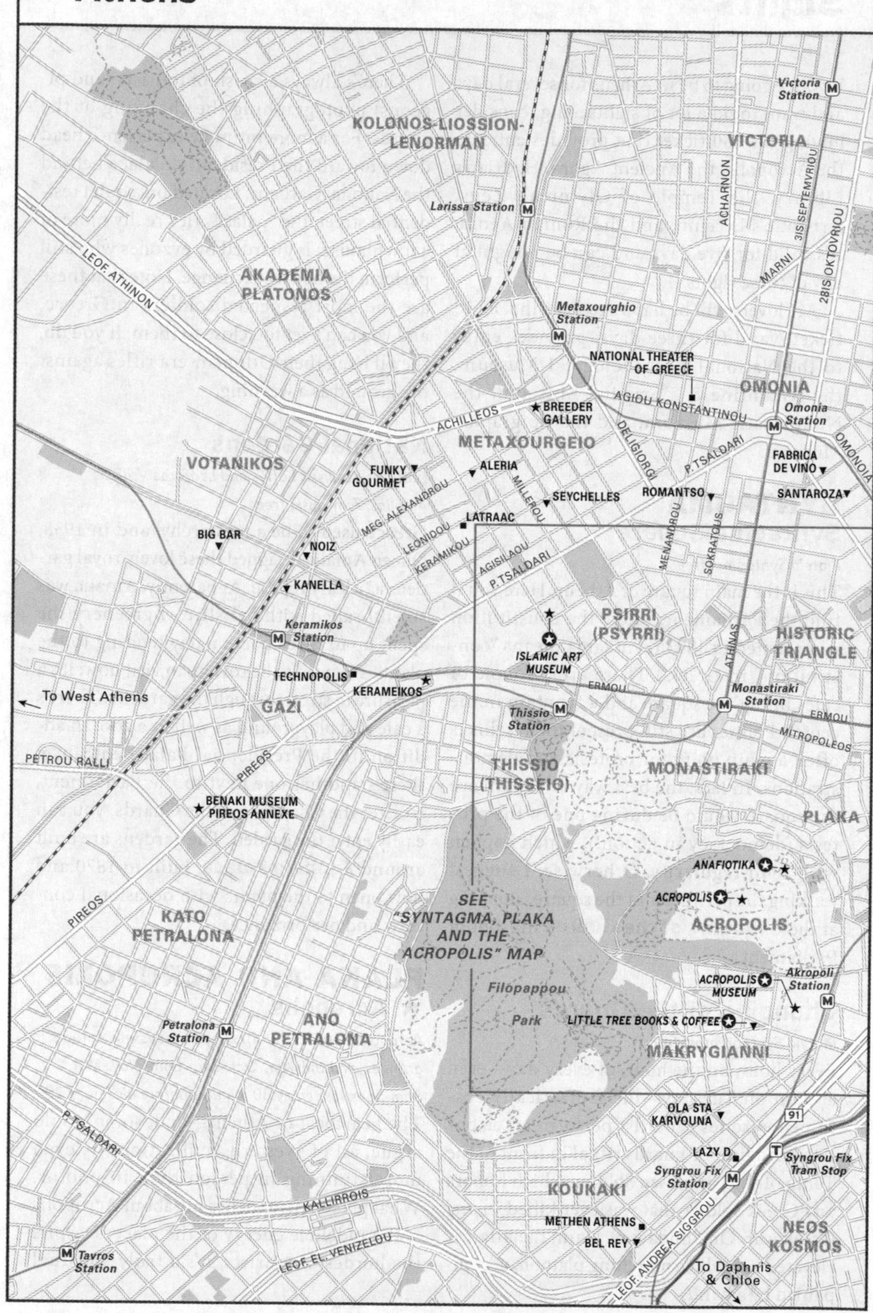
KOLONOS-LIOSSION-LENORMAN
Victoria Station
VICTORIA
Larissa Station
ACHARNON
3IS SEPTEMVRIOU
28IS OKTOVRIOU
MARNI
LEOF. ATHINON
AKADEMIA PLATONOS
Metaxourghio Station
NATIONAL THEATER OF GREECE
OMONIA
Omonia Station
AGIOU KONSTANTINOU
BREEDER GALLERY
ACHILLEOS
METAXOURGEIO
DELIGIORGI
OMONOIA
P. TSALDARI
VOTANIKOS
FUNKY GOURMET
ALERIA
MILLEROU
FABRICA DE VINO
SANTAROZA
ROMANTSO
SEYCHELLES
MEG. ALEXANDROU
LATRAAC
LEONIDOU
KERAMIKOU
AGISILAOU
MENANDROU
SOKRATOUS
BIG BAR
NOIZ
KANELLA
PSIRRI (PSYRRI)
HISTORIC TRIANGLE
ATHINAS
Keramikos Station
ISLAMIC ART MUSEUM
TECHNOPOLIS
KERAMEIKOS
ERMOU
Monastiraki Station
To West Athens
GAZI
Thissio Station
MITROPOLEOS
PETROU RALLI
PIREOS
THISSIO (THISSEIO)
MONASTIRAKI
BENAKI MUSEUM PIREOS ANNEXE
PLAKA
ANAFIOTIKA
ACROPOLIS
SEE "SYNTAGMA, PLAKA AND THE ACROPOLIS" MAP
KATO PETRALONA
ACROPOLIS MUSEUM
Akropoli Station
Filopappou Park
LITTLE TREE BOOKS & COFFEE
Petralona Station
ANO PETRALONA
MAKRYGIANNI
OLA STA KARVOUNA
91
P. TSALDARI
LAZY D
Syngrou Fix Tram Stop
Syngrou Fix Station
KOUKAKI
KALLIRROIS
METHEN ATHENS
BEL REY
NEOS KOSMOS
LEOF. ANDREA SIGGROU
Tavros Station
LEOF. EL. VENIZELOU
To Daphnis & Chloe

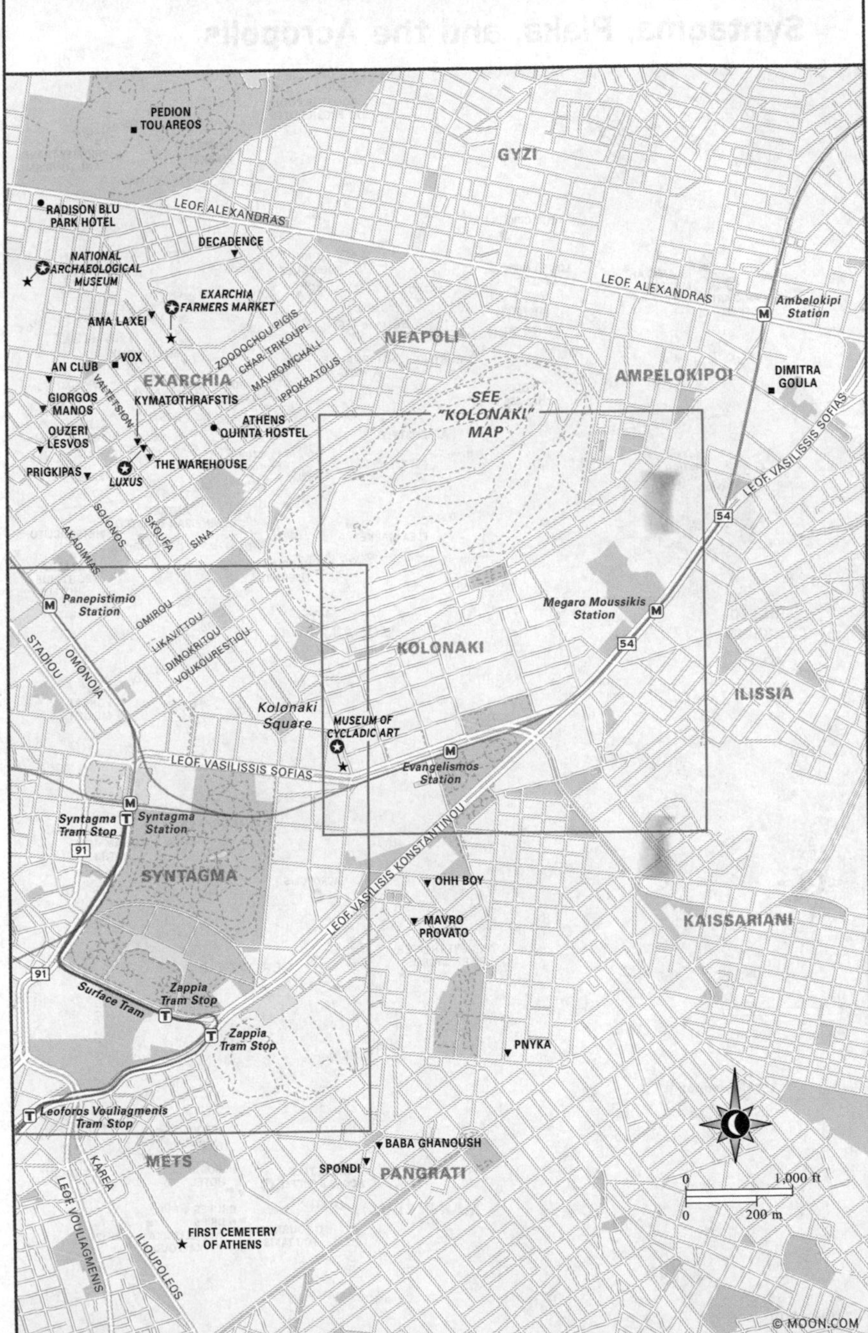
PEDION TOU AREOS
GYZI
RADISON BLU PARK HOTEL
LEOF. ALEXANDRAS
DECADENCE
NATIONAL ARCHAEOLOGICAL MUSEUM
EXARCHIA FARMERS MARKET
AMA LAXEI
Ambelokipi Station
NEAPOLI
ZOODOCHOU PIGIS
CHAR. TRIKOUPI
MAVROMICHALI
IPPOKRATOUS
VOX
AN CLUB
EXARCHIA
VALTETSIOU
AMPELOKIPOI
DIMITRA GOULA
GIORGOS MANOS
KYMATOTHRAFSTIS
SEE "KOLONAKI" MAP
ATHENS QUINTA HOSTEL
OUZERI LESVOS
THE WAREHOUSE
PRIGKIPAS
LUXUS
LEOF. VASILISSIS SOFIAS
54
SOLONOS
SKOUFA
SINA
AKADIMIAS
Megaro Moussikis Station
Panepistimio Station
OMIROU
LIKAVITTOU
DIMOKRITOU
VOUKOURESTIOU
STADIOU
OMONOIA
KOLONAKI
ILISSIA
Kolonaki Square
MUSEUM OF CYCLADIC ART
Evangelismos Station
Syntagma Tram Stop
Syntagma Station
91
SYNTAGMA
LEOF. VASILISIS KONSTANTINOU
OHH BOY
MAVRO PROVATO
KAISSARIANI
Surface Tram
Zappia Tram Stop
PNYKA
Leoforos Vouliagmenis Tram Stop
BABA GHANOUSH
METS
SPONDI
PANGRATI
KAREA
0
1,000 ft
200 m
LEOF. VOULIAGMENIS
FIRST CEMETERY OF ATHENS
ILIOUPOLEOS
© MOON.COM

Syntagma, Plaka, and the Acropolis

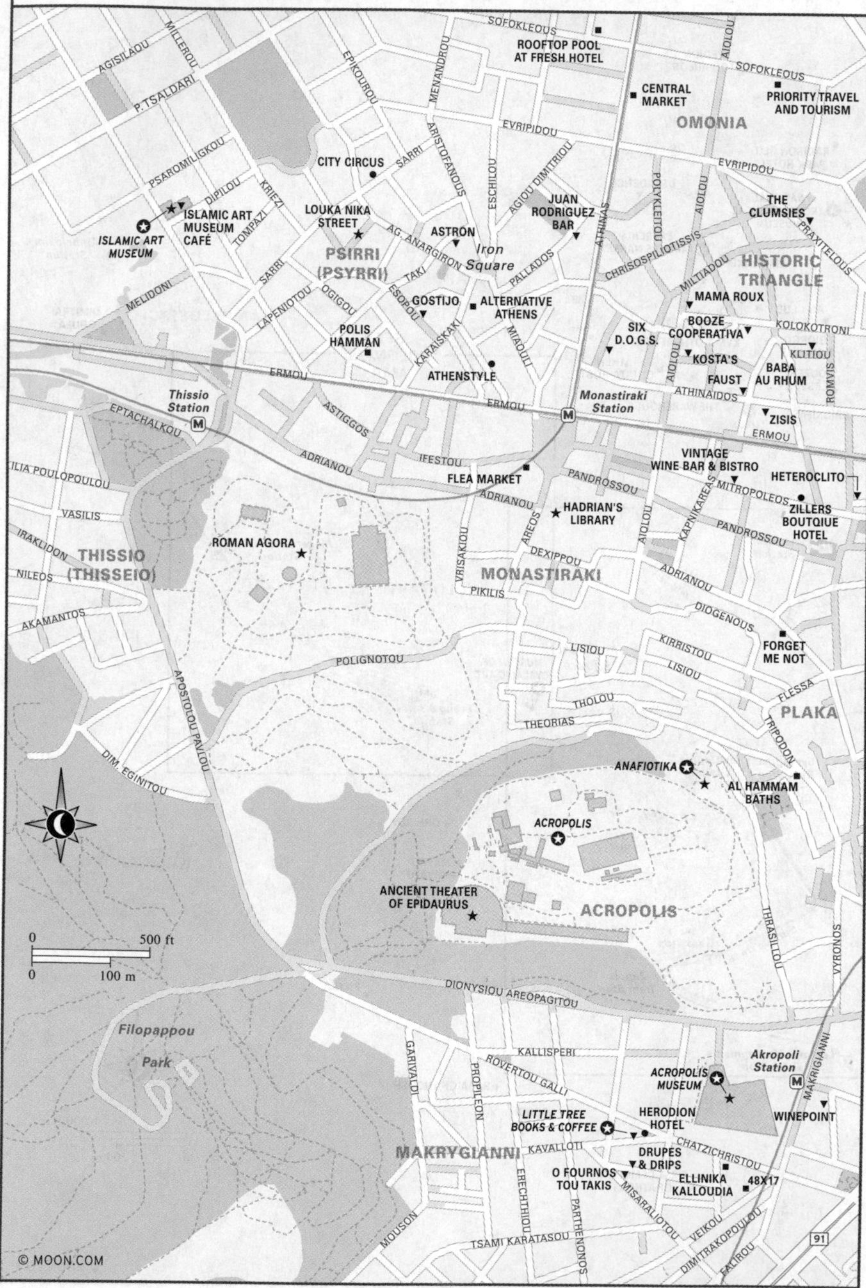
SOFOKLEOUS
ROOFTOP POOL AT FRESH HOTEL
CENTRAL MARKET
PRIORITY TRAVEL AND TOURISM
OMONIA
EVRIPIDOU
CITY CIRCUS
ISLAMIC ART MUSEUM
ISLAMIC ART MUSEUM CAFÉ
LOUKA NIKA STREET
ASTRON
JUAN RODRIGUEZ BAR
THE CLUMSIES
PSIRRI (PSYRRI)
Iron Square
HISTORIC TRIANGLE
GOSTIJO
ALTERNATIVE ATHENS
MAMA ROUX
BOOZE COOPERATIVA
SIX D.O.G.S.
KOSTA'S
FAUST
BABA AU RHUM
POLIS HAMMAN
ATHENSTYLE
Thissio Station
Monastiraki Station
ZISIS
VINTAGE WINE BAR & BISTRO
HETEROCLITO
FLEA MARKET
HADRIAN'S LIBRARY
ZILLERS BOUTQIUE HOTEL
ROMAN AGORA
THISSIO (THISSEIO)
MONASTIRAKI
FORGET ME NOT
PLAKA
ANAFIOTIKA
AL HAMMAM BATHS
ACROPOLIS
ANCIENT THEATER OF EPIDAURUS
ACROPOLIS
Filopappou Park
Akropoli Station
ACROPOLIS MUSEUM
WINEPOINT
LITTLE TREE BOOKS & COFFEE
HERODION HOTEL
MAKRYGIANNI
DRUPES & DRIPS
O FOURNOS TOU TAKIS
ELLINIKA KALLOUDIA
48X17
0 500 ft
0 100 m
© MOON.COM

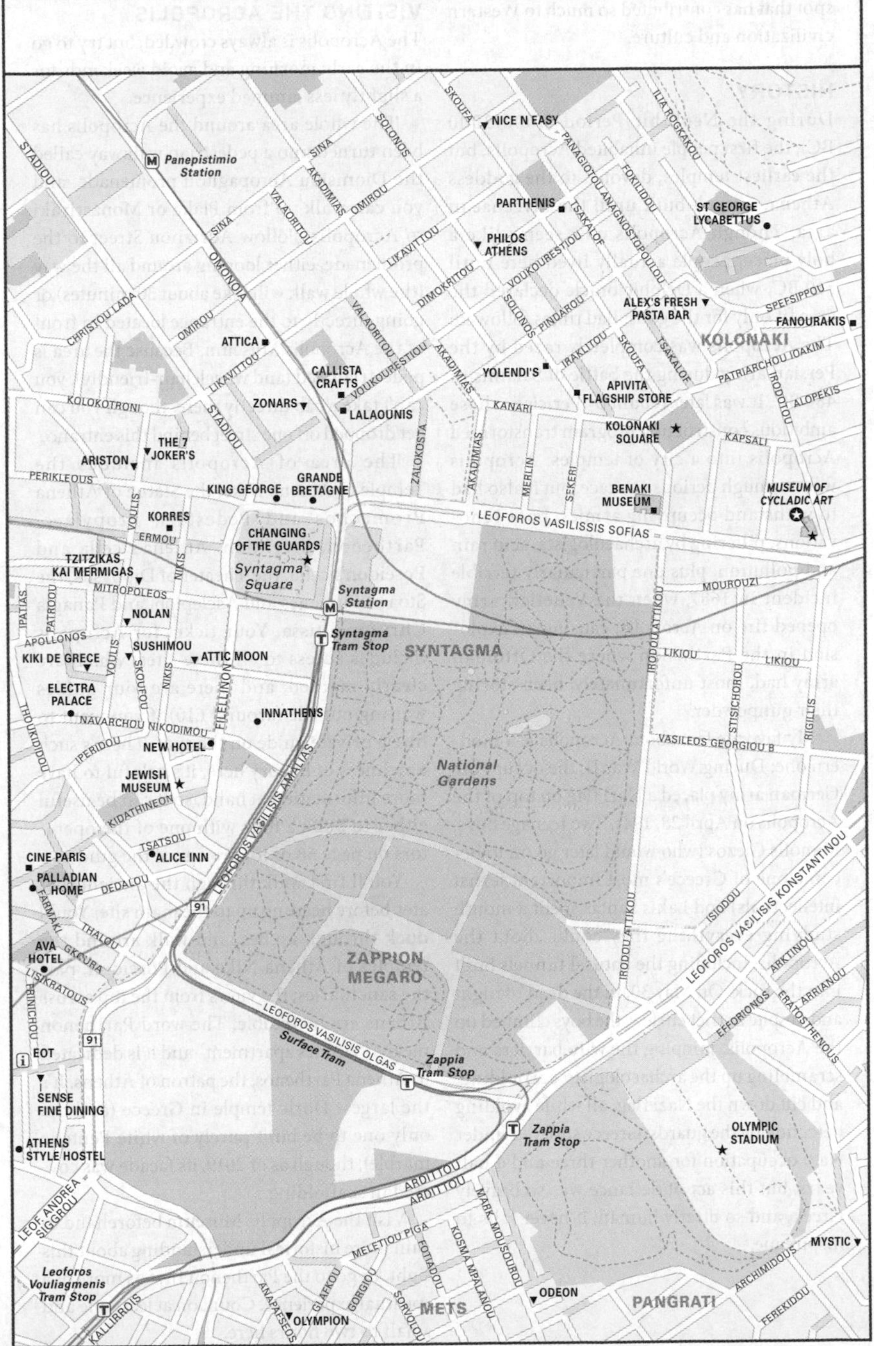
Panepistimio Station
NICE N EASY
PARTHENIS
ST GEORGE LYCABETTUS
PHILOS ATHENS
ALEX'S FRESH PASTA BAR
FANOURAKIS
KOLONAKI
ATTICA
CALLISTA CRAFTS
YOLENDI'S
APIVITA FLAGSHIP STORE
ZONARS
LALAOUNIS
KOLONAKI SQUARE
THE 7 JOKER'S
ARISTON
GRANDE BRETAGNE
KING GEORGE
BENAKI MUSEUM
MUSEUM OF CYCLADIC ART
KORRES
CHANGING OF THE GUARDS
Syntagma Square
TZITZIKAS KAI MERMIGAS
Syntagma Station
NOLAN
Syntagma Tram Stop
SYNTAGMA
SUSHIMOU
ATTIC MOON
KIKI DE GRECE
ELECTRA PALACE
INNATHENS
NEW HOTEL
National Gardens
JEWISH MUSEUM
CINE PARIS
ALICE INN
PALLADIAN HOME
AVA HOTEL
ZAPPION MEGARO
EOT
Surface Tram
Zappia Tram Stop
SENSE FINE DINING
Zappia Tram Stop
OLYMPIC STADIUM
ATHENS STYLE HOSTEL
MYSTIC
Leoforos Vouliagmenis Tram Stop
ODEON
PANGRATI
METS
OLYMPION
STADIOU
SINA
SOLONOS
AKADIMIAS
OMIROU
VALAORITOU
SKOUFA
ILIA ROGKAKOU
PANAGIOTOU ANAGNOSTOPOULOU
FOKILIDOU
TSAKALOF
VOUKOURESTIOU
LIKAVITTOU
DIMOKRITOU
PINDAROU
SPEFSIPPOU
OMONOIA
CHRISTOU LADA
PATRIARCHOU IOAKIM
IRAKLITOU
IRODOTOU
ALOPEKIS
KANARI
KOLOKOTRONI
ZALOKOSTA
MERLIN
SEKERI
KAPSALI
PERIKLEOUS
LEOFOROS VASILISSIS SOFIAS
ERMOU
VOULIS
NIKIS
MOUROUZI
MITROPOLEOS
IPATIAS
PATROOU
APOLLONOS
IRODOU ATTIKOU
LIKIOU
FILELLINON
THOUKIDIDOU
NAVARCHOU NIKODIMOU
STISICHOROU
RIGILIS
IPERIDOU
VASILEOS GEORGIOU B
LEOFOROS VASILISIS AMALIAS
KIDATHINEON
TSATSOU
DEDALOU
FARMAKI
THALOU
GKEURA
LISIKRATOUS
FRINICHOU
LEOFOROS VASILISSIS KONSTANTINOU
ISIDOU
ARKTINOU
ARRIANOU
EFFORIONOS
ERATOSTHENOUS
LEOFOROS VASILISIS OLGAS
ARDITTOU
MARK. MOUSOUROU
LEOF ANDREA SIGGROU
MELETIOU PIGA
FOTIADOU
KOSMA MPALANOU
ARCHIMIDOUS
FEREKIDOU
GLAFKOU
GORGIOU
SORVOLOU
ANAPAFSEOS
KALLIRROIS
91

spot that has contributed so much to Western civilization and culture.

HISTORY

During the Neolithic Period (4000-3000 BC), the first people inhabited Acropolis, but the earliest temples, devoted to the goddess Athena, weren't built until the Mycenaean area. Though Acropolis now seems like a holy place, people actually lived here until 510 BC, when a Delphic oracle declared the area fit only for the gods. Bad times followed: The Acropolis was completely razed by the Persian army during the battle of Salamis in 480 BC. It was later rebuilt by Pericles, whose ambitious construction program transformed Acropolis into a city of temples. Acropolis went through periods of peace, but it also had to withstand occupying armies, poor renovations, pilfering by archaeologists, acid rain and pollution, plus one particularly terrible incident in 1687, when the Venetian army opened fire on Acropolis, causing an explosion in the Parthenon where the Ottoman army had, most unfortunately, been storing their gunpowder.

My favorite fact about Acropolis is a modern one: During World War II, the occupying German army placed a Nazi flag on top of the Acropolis on April 28, 1941. Two teenage boys, Manolis Glezos (who would later go on to become one of Greece's most important leftist intellectuals) and Lakis Santas spent a month studying everything they could about the Acropolis, including the natural tunnels built into the rock. On May 30, in the dead of night and despite a strict curfew, the boys climbed up the Acropolis, jumping the wire barriers and scrambling up the archaeologists' scaffolding, and cut down the Nazi flag, all while avoiding detection by the guards. Greece suffered under Nazi occupation for another three and a half years, but this act of defiance was so bravely Greek, and so utterly human, it never fails to inspire me.

VISITING THE ACROPOLIS

The Acropolis is always crowded, but try to go in the early morning and avoid weekends for a slightly less jammed experience.

The whole area around the Acropolis has been turned into a pedestrian walkway called the Dionisiou Aeropagitou promenade, and you can walk up from Plaka or Monastiraki to Acropolis. Follow Adrianou Street to the promenade, either looping around all the way (the whole walk will take about 30 minutes) or going directly to the entrance located in front of the Acropolis Museum. Because the area is pedestrianized (and wheelchair-friendly), you can't take a cab directly there, though you can get dropped off one street behind this entrance.

The area of Acropolis includes the Temple of Athena Nike, the Statue of Athena Promachos and Pedestals, Propylaea, Parthenon, Erechtion, Athena's cella and Poseidon's cella, the Theater of Dionysus, the Stoa of Eumenes and Asclepion, and Panagia Chrysopolitissa. Your ticket for Acropolis includes access to all these sites, which are clearly marked, and there are tour guides waiting outside (around €10) if you want to hire a private guide on the spot. There's such a richness of history here, it's helpful to have more information at hand, so it can be useful either to book a tour with one of the operators on page 58 or to hire one of the guides.

You'll first walk through the ancient theater before heading up to the main site. You'll duck through arches, and walk around the temples of Athena Nike and Poseidon, past the sanctuaries; the views from the top across Athens are incredible. The word Parthenon means "virgin's apartment" and it is dedicated to Athena Parthenos, the patron of Athens. It's the largest Doric temple in Greece (and the only one to be built purely of white Pentelic marble), though as of 2019, its facade was covered in scaffolding.

Visit the Acropolis Museum beforehand to gain more historical understanding about this sight, or go to the Parthenon first as more of a spiritual experience. Count on at least one and a half to two hours here.

TOP EXPERIENCE

Acropolis Views

the view of Acropolis and Parthenon from the Grande Bretagne Hotel

As beautiful as it is up close, the Acropolis is just as arresting from far away, and one of my favorite things to do in Athens is to catch a glimpse of it from rooftops, streets, and other corners of the city. It never fails to fill my soul. The creamy white Parthenon atop Acropolis changes colors throughout the day (my favorite time is sunset) and is lit up at night, like an orange jewel atop all of Athens.

Here are some of the more interesting vantage points in the city:

- **Filopappou Park:** This elevated area provides breathtaking views of the city, including the Acropolis.
- **Rooftop Pool at the Hilton Hotel:** The largest and deepest pool in the city also boasts views of Athens' most famous monument. Grab a lounge chair and spend the whole day, if you like.
- **Al Hammam Baths:** At this Turkish-style bathhouse, you can take in a view of the Acropolis along with your cup of tea.
- **SENSE Fine Dining:** Chow down on French-inspired gourmet plates while peeping at the Acropolis.
- **Hotels:** A number of our recommended hotels boast Acropolis views, from the budget-friendly **Athens Style Hostel** to the luxe **Electra Palace.**

★ Acropolis Museum

Dionysiou Areopagitou 15; tel. 210/900 0900; www.theacropolismuseum.gr/en; Nov.- Mar. Mon.-Thu. 9am- 5pm, Fri. 9am-10pm, Sat.-Sun. 9am-8pm, Apr.-Oct. Mon. 8am-4pm, Tues.-Sun. 8am-8pm, Fri. 8am-10pm, last admission 30 minutes before closing; €5 Nov.-Mar., €10 Apr.-Oct.

Built at the foot of the southern slope of Acropolis, this newish museum opened in 2009. All modernist glass and filled with light, it houses many of the archaeological findings from Acropolis.

The museum is built over an archaeological site, and the architects cleverly constructed a glass walkway so you can see the excavation as you walk into the museum. The collection is housed across three levels. The foyer gallery displays more recent findings (mostly clay objects and vases) from Acropolis' slopes. The Archaic Gallery on the first floor is my personal favorite; it's full of statues (some real, some replicas), including the five Caryatids, the columns of women who held up the Erechtheion (temples that housed the cult of Athena and Poseidon, who, according to myth, duked it out for the patronage of Athens). On the top floor is the Parthenon Gallery, a glass atrium that showcases the temple's 160-meter (525-foot) long (!) frieze. The British Museum has a good portion of the frieze, as well as the Parthenon Marbles; in the Acropolis Museum the gaps are filled in with plaster facsimiles (you'll be able to tell the difference from the color gradient).

★ Anafiotika

Built in the shadow of the Acropolis, Plaka is like a village within Athens, and every tourist loves to come here. It is beautiful, but it's also disappointingly touristic. For a respite from the crowds, walk up into Anafiotika, the village within a village within a city. When Plaka was first being constructed in the 1800s, builders were brought over from the island of Anafi, as Anafiots were thought to be the best builders in the Cycladics. During the day, the builders worked on neoclassical-style mansions for the wealthy; by night they constructed rough-and-tumble island-style homes for themselves. These homes are still inhabited today, and it truly feels like you're wandering through a Greek island. There are no cafés, restaurants, or shops; instead, just get lost in the tiny streets, stopping occasionally to pet a stray cat and soaking up the fantastic architecture.

Anafiotika is located at the northeast corner of Acropolis. To get here from Adrianou street in Plaka, follow any of the small streets up, in the direction of the Acropolis.

Roman Agora

Adrianou 24; tel. 210/321 0185; http://odysseus.culture.gr/index_en.html; May-Oct. 8am-8pm, Nov.-Apr. 8am-3pm; €8

If Acropolis was the soul of Ancient Athens, then the Agora was its brain: This was where business, politics, administrative duties, and social activity took place. Immeasurable contributions to Western civilization were made here. Socrates proposed his philosophical ideas here, for a start.

It's worth taking an hour to walk along the well-maintained grounds, and to supplement your visit by popping into the museum (your ticket counts for both). Parts of the Agora are still quite well maintained, especially the Gate of Athena Archegetis, financed by Julius Caesar. Also worth an up-close visit is the Tower of the Winds, an eight-sided Pentelic marble clocktower that still stands in all its timeless glory.

Hadrian's Library

North of the Roman Agora; tel. 210/324 9350; daily 8:30am-3pm; http://odysseus.culture.gr/h/3/eh355.jsp?obj_id=2370; €4

Hadrian's Library was constructed in AD 132 by Emperor Hadrian. There were music and lecture rooms as well, and an impressive collection of papyrus scrolls. None of that, of course, can be seen today; all that remains is one restored wall and an 11th-century church. The site is worthwhile only if you've gotten the Acropolis Pass. Otherwise, you can get a good idea of the sight by walking along the fenced perimeter and peeking through.

Temple of Olympian Zeus

tel. 210/922 6330; http://odysseus.culture.gr/index_en.html; 8am-8pm; €8

Partly built in the 6th century BC by Peisistratos, the Olympian Zeus was once one of the largest temples in Greece. Decorated with 104 Corinthian columns, construction

1: a detail of the Caryatids inside Parthenon **2:** the labyrnith streets of Anafiotika, above Plaka and below Acropolis **3:** the Acropolis Museum

1

2

3

was touch-and-go for seven centuries (turns out it's expensive to build huge temples to gods). Construction was eventually completed by Emperor Hadrian in AD 131. Only 15 columns remain now, but it's an arresting site, all the more so for being in the center of Athens. Your multi-site Acropolis ticket (€30) includes access here.

Jewish Museum

Nikis 39; tel. 210/32 25 582; www.jewishmuseum.gr; Mon.-Fri. 9am-3pm, Sun. 10am-2pm; from €6

Greece historically had a sizeable Jewish population, especially in the north of the country. During World War II and the subsequent Nazi occupation of Greece, a considerable number of Jews were shipped off to death camps. In some rare cases—like on the island of Zakynthos, where a heroic mayor hid all the Jews—people were saved. These stories, along with the tremendous cultural contribution of Judaism to Greece (since the 3rd century BC) are on display at the small but important Jewish Museum. You'll find recouped objects Nazis took from Greek Jews, as well as original religious manuscripts, traditional costumes, and religious and folk artworks.

GAZI AND WEST ATHENS

Benaki Museum Pireos Annexe

Pireos 138; tel. 210/345 3111; www.benaki.gr; Thurs.-Sun. 10am-6pm, Fri.-Sat. 10am-10pm, closed Aug.; €6

You can't miss this giant, salmon-pink building on the otherwise industrial avenue of Pireos; it's the contemporary answer to the main Benaki museum. They have great exhibits featuring Greek and international artists (check website, exhibits change every few months), as well as events in the airy courtyard. There's a nice café and gift shop, too.

Kerameikos

Ermou 148; tel. 210/346 3552; http://odysseus.culture.gr/index_en.html; Apr.-Oct. daily 8am-8pm, reduced hours Nov.-Mar.; €8 including museum, or free with Acropolis ticket

This fantastic archaeological site is located northeast of Acropolis. The name comes from the potters (*kerameis*) who inhabited this area around 3000 BC. In the 6th century, it was used as a cemetery; it wasn't until 1861, when another construction project was going on nearby, that Kerameikos was rediscovered.

The area has two monumental gates: the Dipylon (the city's main entrance) and the Sacred Gate (the gate used by pilgrims during the annual Eleusian pilgrimage). There's a helpful map of the site at the main entrance on the right; you'll walk through the ancient streets and see the remains of buildings. The most impressive part of the site is the **Street of the Tombs,** where Athens' most important residents were buried. Replicas of the monuments from the funerals are on display here; all of the actual finds from the site are located in the on-site **Kerameikos Archaeological Museum,** which has the same hours as the main site.

Breeder Gallery

Iasonos 45; tel. 210/331 7527; http://thebreedersystem.com/gallery; Tues.-Fri. noon-8pm, Sun. noon-6pm; free

Probably the most important contemporary art gallery in Athens, Breeder is the place to see the work of contemporary Greek designers, and occasionally international artists as well. Check their website to see what shows are up. The chic white space hosts video, installation, sculpture, and painting exhibits, and attracts an in-the-know art crowd.

PSYRRI

★ Islamic Art Museum

Koumpari 1, Keramikos; tel. 210/367 1000; www.benaki.org; Wed. and Fri.-Sat. 10am-6pm, Thurs. 10am-11:30pm, Sun. 10am-4pm; €9

I wouldn't say that I'm suggesting this

1: a couple walk through Psyrri in downtown Athens **2:** the view of Lycabettus from Anafiotika **3:** grafitti in downtown Athens

1
2
3
DOG·DAYS·ARE·HERE
2018

museum solely because of its fantastic rooftop café that features an incredible watercolor fresco and is my personal favorite spot to grab a coffee in all of Athens (maybe in all of Europe?!)... but the café is definitely a great excuse to look at some of the world's most important Islamic art. There are more than 8,000 objects from the 12th to 19th century, mostly from the private holdings of collector Antonis Benakis, amassed while he was living in Alexandria. There are some truly fantastic ceramics, a perfectly intact ivory chess board from the 14th century, and the reconstructed interior of a 17th-century Egyptian mansion. You'll want to spend at least an hour and a half here.

Iroon Square

In Greek, *iroon* means heroes: All the streets around this square are named after the heroes of the Greek War of Independence. Today, it's a lively neighborhood meeting spot, lined with cafés and restaurants, where live music often bleeds out of the buildings in the summer months.

Louka Nika Street

This small alley in Psyrri is like a living, outdoor art gallery: The walls are painted by local and foreign artists, and the endless colorful murals will vie for your attention. The murals are constantly changing, so if you visit one year, don't expect to find the same thing on your next trip! It's located off Syrri street, across the large Hbh (IVI) Theater.

EXARCHIA

★ National Archaeological Museum

28is Oktovriou 44; tel. 213/214 4800; www.namuseum.gr/en; Nov.-mid-Apr. Tues. 1pm-8pm, Wed.-Mon. 8:30am-4pm, mid-Apr.-Oct. Tues. 12:30pm-8pm, Wed.-Mon. 8am-8pm; €10 Apr. 1-Oct. 31, €5 Nov. 1-Mar. 31

This is considered one of the world's most important museums, thanks to its stunning collection of Greek antiquities. There are more than 11,000 items spread across the 8,000-square-meter (86,111-square-foot) neoclassical building. The exhibits are presented thematically and include a fantastic prehistoric collection (the gold masks are next-level), an Egyptian room, a sculptures wing, and some impressive frescoes from Santorini. You could easily spend a whole day here.

★ Exarchia Farmers Market

Kallidromiou Street; Sat. 9am-5pm

Each neighborhood has its own *laiki* (market), but Exarchia's is considered the best, and it attracts shoppers from across the city. Every Saturday, orange tents go up and crates upon crates of fruits and vegetables are placed on plastic tables. The produce changes with the season; for your sake, I hope you're here when it's apricot season (which only lasts 20 days in May) or better yet, fig season (August). You'll also find oils, beeswax candles, flowers and plants, spices, and jams. This is an excellent place to stock up on food if you're staying in an Airbnb or want to pack a picnic.

KOLONAKI

Byzantine and Christian Museum

22 Vassilissis Sofias Ave.; tel. 213/213 9572; Tues.-Sun. 8am-3pm; €4, under 18 free

For a truly immersive overview of Greece's Byzantine history, be sure to visit this gem of a museum, housed on the grounds of the former Villa Ilissia, home to the eccentric Sophie de Marbois-Lebrun, Duchess of Plaisance. There are 25,000 different artifacts spanning 17 centuries, including costumes, icons, engravings, jewelry, frescoes, sculptures, and more. Everything is extremely well-arranged and lit, blessedly placed in chronological order and with clear English translations. It's one of the most important Byzantine history museums in the world.

Benaki Museum

Koumpari 1; 210/367 1000; www.benaki.gr; Wed. and Fri. 9am-5pm, Thurs. and Sat. 9am-noon, Sun. 9am-3pm; €9, free Thurs.

Think of the Benakis as the Rockefellers of

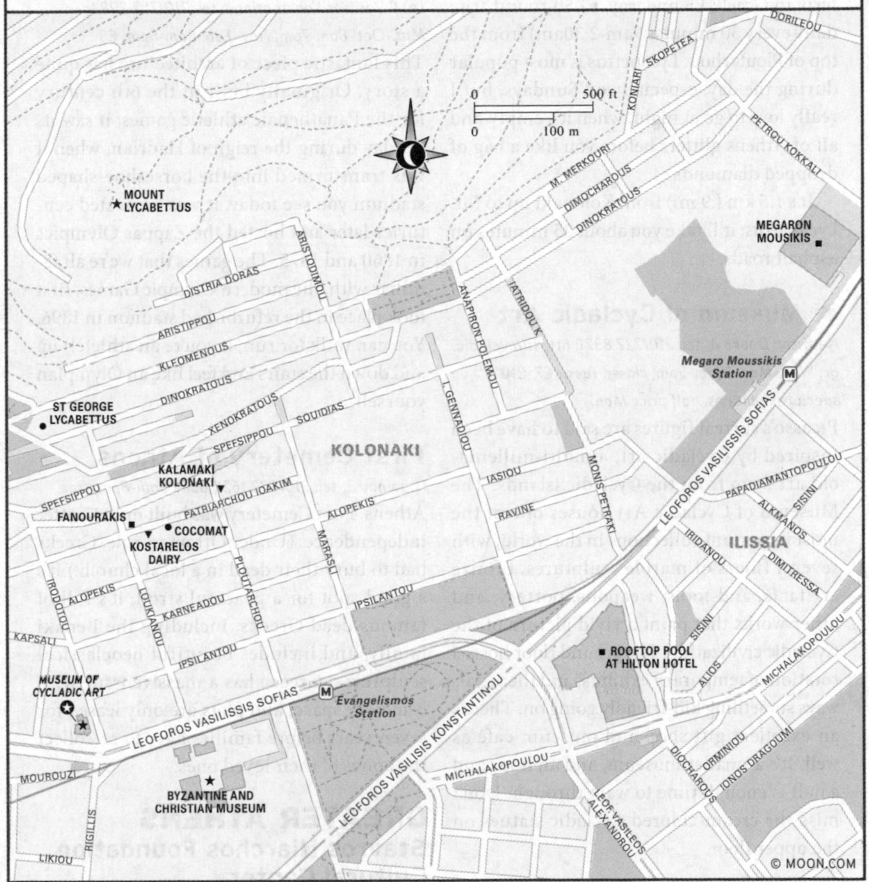

Greece (via Egypt, where they partly lived): wealthy aristocrats who, whatever you may think of class structure and money, at least contributed to the preservation of their country's cultural heritage. In 1931 the family donated their Athenian residence, along with more than 37,000 Islamic and Byzantine objects. Nearly 70,000 more pieces spanning centuries from the Bronze Age to World War II have since been added, and the museum underwent extensive renovations and reopened in 2000. The paintings by El Greco and Theodoros Poulakis are worth seeking out. You'll want to spend at least two to three hours here, depending on how much of an art lover you are.

There are two other Benaki museum branches: the Islamic Art Museum in Keramikos and the Pireos Annexe for contemporary art. A pass for all three costs €20 and is valid for three months.

Mount Lycabettus

Lycabettus, the hill that looms over Kolonaki and Exarchia, has some of the best panoramas of Athens. You can either climb to the top (on a clear day, you can easily see to Piraeus port) or take the 10-minute funicular railway (*teleferik* in Greek; €5 one way, €7.50 round trip; daily every 30 minutes 9am-2:30am) from the top of Ploutarhou. Lycabettus is most popular during the day, especially on Sundays, but I really love to go at night, when it's empty and all of Athens glitters before you like a bag of dropped diamonds.

It's 1.5 km (.9 mi) from Kolonaki up to Mt. Lycabettus; it'll take you about 25 minutes on asphalt roads.

★ Museum of Cycladic Art

Neofitou Douka 4; tel. 210/722 8321; https://cycladic.gr; Wed.-Mon. 10am-5pm, closed Tues.; €7, €10 special exhibitions, half price Mon.

Picasso's surreal figures are said to have been inspired by Cycladic art, a multi-millenia-old art form from the Cycladic islands. The Museum of Cycladic Art houses one of the most important collections in the world, with several floors of marble sculptures, bronze artifacts, and tools, weapons, pottery, and other works that paint a vivid picture of the Cycladic civilization. The ground floor hosts a rotation of temporary exhibits, and there's always something kid-friendly going on. There's an excellent gift shop and museum café as well. It's a smaller museum, and an hour and a half is enough time to walk through. Don't miss the cream-colored Cycladic statues on the upper floor.

Kolonaki Square

The heart of Kolonaki is this tree-lined square. In the middle of the square you'll find a small, ancient column, after which the whole area is named. This square features plenty of shops and cafés, usually filled with upscale clientele (in the winter time, it's not uncommon to see little old ladies with their fur coats and pearls). Coffee here is overpriced, but the people watching is worth it.

PANGRATI AND METS

Olympic Stadium

Leof. Vasileos Konstantinou; tel. 210/752 2984; Mar.-Oct. 8am-7pm, Nov.-Feb. 8am-5pm; €5

This fantastic piece of architecture has quite a story. Originally built in the 6th century for the Panathenaic athletic games, it saw its heyday during the reign of Hadrian, when it was transformed into the horseshoe-shaped stadium you see today. It was excavated centuries later and hosted the Zappas Olympics in 1860 and 1875. The games that we're all familiar with, the modern Olympic Games, first took place in the refurbished stadium in 1896. You can walk (or run, if you're an athlete!) up and down the stairs and feel like an Olympian yourself.

First Cemetery of Athens

Logginou 3; tel. 210/922 1621; daily 8am-8pm; free

Athens' First Cemetery was built in 1837, after independence. (Under Ottoman rule, Greeks had to bury their dead in a local church.) It's a good spot for a peaceful stroll; it's full of famous dead Greeks, including the Benaki family, and includes beautiful neoclassical sculptures. Greece has a massive issue with cemetery space, and plots are only leased for seven years before families have to re-collect the bones of their loved ones.

GREATER ATHENS

Stavros Niarchos Foundation Cultural Center

Leof. Andrea Siggrou 364, Kallithea; tel. 216/809 1000; www.snfcc.org; Apr.-Oct. 6am-noon, Nov.-Mar. 6am-8pm, certain areas open later for events; free

Shipping giant Stavros Niarchos has given a great deal to the cultural scene in Athens. The most impressive contribution so far is the Stavros Niarchos Foundation Cultural Center, a gleaming chrome and glass building designed by Renzo Piano that opened in 2017. There's a fantastic 21-hectare (52-acre) park complete with a pool, playgrounds, and a grassy lawn. This is also the new home of the National Ballet, National Opera, and National Library. Check their website; in addition to fantastic performances, they often have free concerts and events, especially in the summer.

There are free shuttle buses leaving every hour from Syntagma Square (check website); you can also take a taxi (approx. €10 euros). It's worth coming out here for a concert or performance, or if you have kids who desperately need some space to run around.

Recreation

PARKS

Athens is not the greenest city in Europe, by a long stretch—some neighborhoods are bitterly devoid of any greenery. In the past few years, with the economic crisis and the influx of refugees arriving in the city, parks were used as makeshift camps, and some of them became epicenters of drug dealing and use, and prostitution. As of 2019, police had begun aggressively cleaning up the parks in the center of Athens, and they've become more hospitable places for families and children.

FILOPAPPOU

Also known as the Hill of Muses, Filopappou is an elevated area that's beloved for its breathtaking views of the city, including Acropolis. It's a weekend haunt for Athenians who come to picnic in the shade, or to wander through the rambling paths that crisscross the park. The walk to the top is pretty easy, and takes about 30 minutes from the bottom to the summit. It's located just west of Acropolis, and is next to Koukaki.

PEDION TOU AREOS

One of the largest public parks in Athens, Pedion Tou Aereos has undergone a pretty dramatic face-lift in the past few months. On the west side of the park there's still a bit of dealing going on, but the park is full of wide avenues, benches, and blooming trees. It sits between Kypseli and Exarchia, and is reminiscent of big parks in New York: you'll find a diverse group of people, from old Greek ladies knitting to young Eritrean mothers, to spandex-clad joggers. The park occasionally hosts markets and cultural events.

LATRAAC

Leonidou 63-65; 213/045 3377; daily noon-3pm and 5:30pm-10:30pm, café till 1am; free

This very cool—albeit very small—skate park attracts long-haired long-boarders who perform tricks in the wooden bowl while their admirers watch them from the adjacent café. The park occasionally hosts music events, and the café offers a decent selection of drinks and food.

HIKING

Aside from Filopappou and Lycabettus, there's not a lot of hiking to do in Athens, but there are some great spots outside of the city, including Cape Sounio and Ymittos. Consider booking a hike with **Trekking Hellas** (Gounari 96; 210/331 0323; www.trekking.gr; 4-hour guided treks from €40), which offers a variety of outdoor activities around Attica and Peloponnesus.

ROOFTOP POOLS

Athens is a city of rooftops, and on many of those you will find pools. Lounging poolside is a preferred Athenian activity in summertime when it's just too hot to wait for the beach. Most hotels sell day passes to non-guests.

FRESH HOTEL

Sofokleous 26; tel. 210/524 8511; daily 10am-7pm; €20

One of the best pool deals in Athens is at Fresh Hotel, which has a small pool on the building's 9th floor. All guests receive a complimentary coffee or soft drink upon arrival. Located just behind Omonia Square.

HILTON HOTEL

46 Vasilissis Sofias Ave.; tel. 210/728 1000; daily 8am-9pm; €25 Mon.-Fri., €40 Sat.-Sun.

Should you find yourself in Athens with no prospect of going to the beach, positively drenched in sweat and without hope, remember: the Hilton Athens (located in Kolonaki) swimming pool is here for you. The largest and deepest outdoor pool in the city is on the hotel's rooftop and offers stunning vistas of Acropolis and Lycabettus. Come at 8am, grab a lounge chair, and spend the whole day. You can order drinks and food from the bar and café.

HAMMAM AND BATHHOUSES

POLIS HAMMAM

Avliton 6; tel. 210/321 2020; www.polis-hammam.gr; Mon.-Fri. noon-11pm, Sat.-Sun. 11am-11pm; bath with scrub from €27

Located in a tiny alley in Psyrri, and a bit difficult to find, Polis Hammam has the cheapest bath-scrub offer in the city. They have plenty of other treatments, too, including massages, facials, and cupping in an Ottoman-style hammam. Check their website; they often have offers and deals.

AL HAMMAM BATHS

Tripodon 16 and Ragava 10, Plaka; tel. 211/012 9099; www.alhammam.gr; daily 11am-9pm; bath with scrub from €35

Four hundred years of Ottoman rule had a lasting effect in some respects, and one is that Athenians embraced the Turkish-style bathhouses. One of the most beautiful is Al Hammam Baths, a small bathhouse outfitted with marble, tiles, and glittering chandeliers. In addition to enjoying a steam and scrub, you can lounge like a pasha in the small terrace café, admiring the view of the Acropolis and drinking a cup of tea.

TOURS

I do not recommend going on the double-decker or air-conditioned city bus tours. Much of Athens happens at a street level, and to be honest, unlike Barcelona or Paris, there aren't enough landmark attractions that are worth seeing from the inside of a car. Also, tickets are expensive, and you can cover much of Athens by foot, with or without a tour guide.

If you'd prefer to travel without a guide but still want the down low on Athenian history and culture, consider downloading to your phone **Topos Text** (https://topostext.org; free), a "reference tool for Greek civilization." Each archaeological site is geo-tagged and links to ancient texts and literature from that location.

ALTERNATIVE ATHENS

Karaiskaki 28; tel. 211/012 6544; www.alternativeathens.com; daily 9am-8pm; from €40

Offering tours led by local Greeks, both in and outside of Athens, this is a reputable and fun tour group. You can customize tours based on your interests—say, street art in Exarchia—and according to your budget and how much time you have. There are good mythology tours, as well as food and museum tours. The company skews to the alternative. Tours are also LGBTQ-friendly.

CULINARY BACKSTREETS ATHENS

4 Platia Omonias; https://culinarybackstreets.com/category/cities-category/athens; from €120

Greek food—with all its layered complexities, political nuances, and delicious tastes—is really worth getting to know. Book a tour with the folks of Culinary Backstreets to learn more about this country's incredible gastronomy. You'll find out how different Greek foods are made, take a trip to the Central Market, taste products from local vendors, and try a few restaurants, depending on which tour you book. It'll be a journey for your mind and your stomach. Tours are around five and a half hours, and the price includes the food sampled.

Nightlife and Entertainment

Athenians love to have a good time, and you'll find plenty of bars, cafés, clubs, discos, and more around the city. Bars can fill up from 6pm, for a pre-dinner drink, and the more popular places will be packed by 11pm. Clubs don't get going till at least 1 or 2am, and parties can last until 6am.

Around the city you'll notice plenty of posters advertising shows, events, festivals, concerts, and more. These are both neighborhood-specific (in Exarchia you'll find flyers for squat parties, for example), and Athens-wide events. These posters are a great way to find out about events that happen outside of your usual Google-search.

A word of warning: Though cigarette smoking is illegal in Greece, that rule is regularly flouted by everyone, including the country's health minister, who famously went on a televised conference a few years ago with a cigarette in hand. In fact, Greeks are the 14th heaviest smokers in the world. There are a few places that strictly enforce the no-smoking rule (all the wine bars, for example), but most of the time you will be inhaling a lot of secondhand smoke.

NIGHTLIFE DISTRICTS

The areas around **Monastiraki** and **Gazi** are the two best known areas for nightlife, albeit a bit mainstream. Both are filled to the brim with raucous parties all weekend long (in the summer, the weekend stretches through the whole week).

I prefer to go out in **Exarchia, Kerameikos** (in West Athens), or **Mets;** these are more laid-back areas, with dingy basement clubs where everyone dresses in black and bops around to punk, or relaxes in café-bars discussing everything from art to leftist politics to broken hearts. They are more "hipster" areas, but they're also blessedly inter-generational. (I've gone out on weekends in **Exarchia,** for example, and ended up deep in conversation with septuagenarians.)

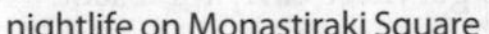

nightlife on Monastiraki Square

BARS

Syntagma

THE CLUMSIES

Praxitelous 30; tel. 210/323 2682; Sun.-Thurs. 10am-2am, Fri.-Sat. 10am-4am

Day-drinkers, rejoice: The Clumsies, which bills itself as an all-day bar, is here for you. Two champion bartenders opened this excellent cocktail bar, and from 10am they sling innovative and delicious cocktails in a space filled with natural light. There's a "secret" private room in the back, complete with fireplace, billiard table, and a bookcase filled with leather-bound books (reservation only).

BABA AU RHUM

Klitiou 6, Plaka; tel. 211/710 9140, Mon.-Fri. 7pm-3am, Sat. 7pm-4am

Regularly ranked amongst the world's best cocktail bars, Baba au Rhum is the sophisticated granddaddy of Athens' new wave bar scene. The focus is on the drinks, which the bartenders expertly execute at top speed on busy weekend nights. As the name suggests, rum makes a big appearance on the menu, but the bartenders are also happy to whip you up something special based on another spirit.

BOOZE COOPERATIVA

Kolokotroni 57; tel. 211/405 3733; www.boozecooperativa.com; Mon.-Sat. 11am-3am, Sun. 11am-midnight

Technically, it's illegal to smoke indoors, but one enterprising smoker realized that if he created his own political party and, thus, a party meeting space, smokers in his café could continue to puff away unmolested. Enter Booze Cooperativa, a café-bar that hosts art exhibits and concerts for the hip and beautiful, under a cloud of smoke. It bills itself as a "brain hub"; check their website for upcoming events.

THE 7 JOKER'S

Voulis 7; tel. 210/321 9225; Mon.-Thurs. 10am-4:30am, Fri.-Sat. 10am-6am, Sun. 2pm-4:30am

Locals refer to it as just "Joker's," and this cozy café-bar, filled to the brim with all sorts of circus-y objects like giant chandeliers and kitschy lamps, is a great place for a cocktail. It gets quite packed, but the atmosphere is great.

Monastiraki

JUAN RODRIGUEZ BAR

Pallados 3; tel. 210/322 4496; Sun.-Thurs. 9am-3am, Fri.-Sat. 9am-4:30am

This see-and-be-seen bar gets incredibly packed on weekends (with people and cigarette smoke), but the bartenders make excellent drinks, the atmosphere is fun and funky, and there's always a DJ in the pack spinning some groovy tunes. There's nice bar food as well.

Exarchia

SANTAROZA

Asklipiou 69; tel. 215/510 1784; Sun.-Thurs. 6pm-3:30am, Fri.-Sat. 6pm-4:30am, closed July-Aug.

A new addition to the bar scene (they opened in 2018) in Exarchia, this one reminds me of my favorite bars in Brooklyn, with excellent, vibe-y decor, great drinks, enough snacks to keep me satisfied, and super music. There are cool bartenders and an even cooler crowd, aged up to mid-30s. "We were voted the sexiest bar in Athens," one of the bartenders archly told me, so get there early for a seat.

THE WAREHOUSE

Valtetsiou 21; tel. 215/540 8002; warehouseproject.gr; daily 9am-2:30am

A local favorite drawing a beautiful crowd throughout the day, this café shifts from expertly pulled espressos to an impressive wine list after sunset. There's a very good selection of food as well, from breakfast to dinner.

Mets

ODEON

Mark. Mousourou 19; tel. 210/922 3414; daily 9am-2am

This is a neighborhood favorite, thanks to its cute and cozy atmosphere, nice bartenders, and groovy music. Nice in the evening and in the morning, too, it's a bit reminiscent of an old-school *kafeneion* (traditional Greek coffeehouse), and there's a small area with outdoor seating.

WINE BARS

Syntagma

★ HETEROCLITO

2 Fokionos and Petraki; tel. 210/323 9406; Mon.-Thurs. 12:30pm-midnight, Fri.-Sat. 12:30pm-1:30am, Sun. 6pm-11pm; glasses from €5

Greece has some of the oldest vineyards in the world, but its reputation is mainly for having overly sweet, Mediterranean Manischewitz-style wine. Forget all that and head to Heteroclito, a cozy wine bar with a Parisian vibe that serves some of Greece's most interesting wines, originating from Crete to Macedonia. Trust the advice of the knowledgeable bartenders, and be sure to order a meat and cheese plate to justify drinking a whole bottle.

Plaka and Acropolis

KIKI DE GRECE

Ipitou 4; tel. 210/321 1279; daily noon-1am; glasses from €3.50

Inspired by 1920s French actress Kiki de Montparnasse's bold statement that all she needs to survive is bread, an onion, and a bottle of wine, Kiki de Grece offers all three, albeit in the form of wine by the glass and delectable appetizers. It's a cozy bar on a pedestrian street, though it gets crowded quickly so come early to snag a seat.

VINTAGE WINE BAR & BISTRO

Mitropoleos 66-68; 213/029 6570; daily from 4pm; glasses from €5

With over 500 wines to choose from, the spacious Vintage Wine Bar & Bistro lets customers order half glasses of Greek and international labels. The owners used to run a restaurant, and that's reflected in the excellent and extensive menu of shared plates and snacks, all made with local ingredients. If you're feeling flush, they have several magnums you can purchase. This spot is popular with a more mature crowd.

WINEPOINT

2 Porinou Athens; tel. 210/922 7050; daily 1pm-2am; glasses from €5, tasting €25

Walking around ruins all day, no matter how beautiful, can be exhausting. Head to Winepoint, located blessedly close to the Acropolis, for a boozy pick-me-up. This bright and colorful space has more than 270 Greek labels (30 of which are available by the glass). Winepoint also offers 90-minute wine tastings

coffee shops and bars in a street of Plaka

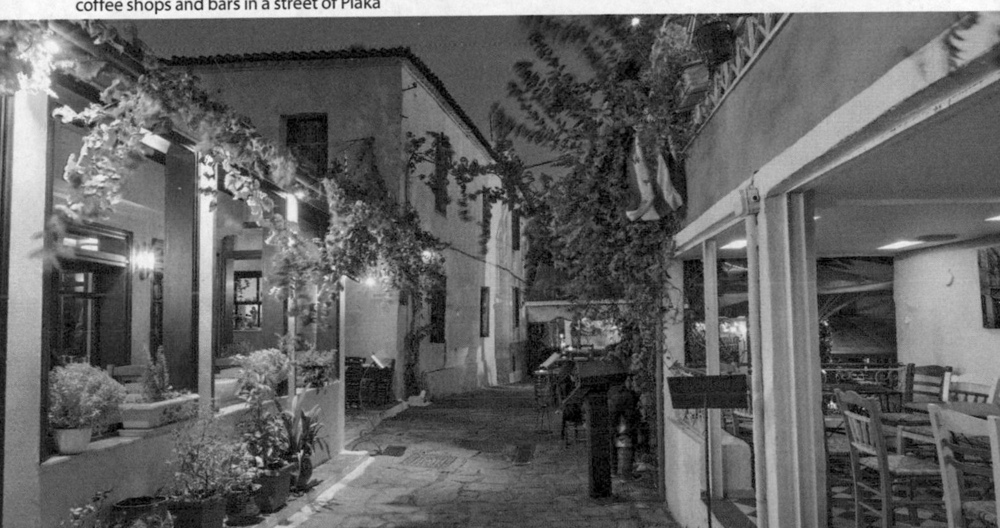

every day, from 1pm to 8pm, accompanied by a meat and cheese plate.

Omonia

FABRICA DE VINO

Emanouil Benaki 3; tel. 210/321 4148; daily 1pm-1am; glasses from €7

Located a stone's throw away from seedy Omonia Square, Fabrica de Vino makes up for its lack of curb appeal with a fun and dynamic atmosphere, and a great selection of Greek wines. There are snacks, too, either traditional meze or Spanish-style pinchos and tapas.

MUSIC VENUES AND CLUBS

Most of the below places either have cover charges of around €5 or ticket charges from €5-30 for concerts. Often the cover charge will include one beverage (beer or soft drink).

Monastiraki

FAUST

Kalamiotou 11; tel. 210/323 4095; www.faust.gr; Mon. 8:30pm-midnight, Tues.-Wed. noon-3pm and 8:30pm-midnight, Thurs.-Sun. 12:30am-4am

Faust is a small club on a Monastiraki side street with a frenetic energy and good beats, especially on Saturday. Check the website for events.

SIX D.O.G.S.

Avramiotou 6-8; tel. 210/321 0510; https://sixdogs.gr; Sun.-Thurs. 10am-3am, Fri.-Sat. 10am-7am

Bringing the biggest names in Greek and international electronic music, this is a great place to see some live acts and DJs, and dance your butt off. They also occasionally have art exhibitions. There's no dress code, but everyone looks Boiler Room cool.

Psyrri

ROMANTSO

Anaxagora 3; tel. 216/700 3325; www.romantso.gr/?Lang=En; daily, depends on events

Housed in the former printing plant of the infamous magazine *ROMANTSO*, this fantastic creative hub serves as both an "incubator" for artists and start-ups, and a cultural center. This place is a must visit, as they have all sorts of events going on, from live music acts to hoop dancing. Check the website for upcoming events.

ASTRON

Taki 3; tel. 698/388 5327; Thurs.-Sat. 10pm-7am

There's not a huge techno scene in Athens, so techno-lovers congregate at Astron, a tiny, hard-to-find club with no signage. Check their Facebook page, or Resident Advisor (www.residentadvisor.net), the electronic music scene's main media site for upcoming acts. Admission is free but the party doesn't get started till 3am.

Exarchia

DECADENCE

Poulcherias 2; tel. 697/441 4214; 9pm-late; €5 entrance

In the '80s, Decadence was the coolest address in Greece. It shuttered and people forgot about it, but in 2017 it reopened to local fanfare. Located in a dilapidated townhouse in Exarchia with a basement dance floor, it's a fun place to dance away an evening.

AN CLUB

Solomou 13-15; tel. 210/330 5056; www.anclub.gr; €5 entrance

For punk and grunge, head to AN Club, a small underground club that showcases local bands and some lesser-known international acts. The floor is sticky, the dress code is black, and there's only a suggestive distinction between dance floor and stage, but it's got a fun(ky) vibe. Also, punks are always the nicest people—and hardcore anti-fascists to boot. Check the website for upcoming shows, and go make some cool friends.

REBOUND

Mithimnis 43; Sun. midnight-6am; €6 entrance

This is the most cult-y dance place in Athens: a basement that only opens on Saturdays after midnight. Everyone is dressed in black, the

coffeehouse), and there's a small area with outdoor seating.

WINE BARS

Syntagma

★ HETEROCLITO

2 Fokionos and Petraki; tel. 210/323 9406; Mon.-Thurs. 12:30pm-midnight, Fri.-Sat. 12:30pm-1:30am, Sun. 6pm–11pm; glasses from €5

Greece has some of the oldest vineyards in the world, but its reputation is mainly for having overly sweet, Mediterranean Manischewitz-style wine. Forget all that and head to Heteroclito, a cozy wine bar with a Parisian vibe that serves some of Greece's most interesting wines, originating from Crete to Macedonia. Trust the advice of the knowledgeable bartenders, and be sure to order a meat and cheese plate to justify drinking a whole bottle.

Plaka and Acropolis

KIKI DE GRECE

Ipitou 4; tel. 210/321 1279; daily noon-1am; glasses from €3.50

Inspired by 1920s French actress Kiki de Montparnasse's bold statement that all she needs to survive is bread, an onion, and a bottle of wine, Kiki de Grece offers all three, albeit in the form of wine by the glass and delectable appetizers. It's a cozy bar on a pedestrian street, though it gets crowded quickly so come early to snag a seat.

VINTAGE WINE BAR & BISTRO

Mitropoleos 66-68; 213/029 6570; daily from 4pm; glasses from €5

With over 500 wines to choose from, the spacious Vintage Wine Bar & Bistro lets customers order half glasses of Greek and international labels. The owners used to run a restaurant, and that's reflected in the excellent and extensive menu of shared plates and snacks, all made with local ingredients. If you're feeling flush, they have several magnums you can purchase. This spot is popular with a more mature crowd.

WINEPOINT

2 Porinou Athens; tel. 210/922 7050; daily 1pm-2am; glasses from €5, tasting €25

Walking around ruins all day, no matter how beautiful, can be exhausting. Head to Winepoint, located blessedly close to the Acropolis, for a boozy pick-me-up. This bright and colorful space has more than 270 Greek labels (30 of which are available by the glass). Winepoint also offers 90-minute wine tastings

coffee shops and bars in a street of Plaka

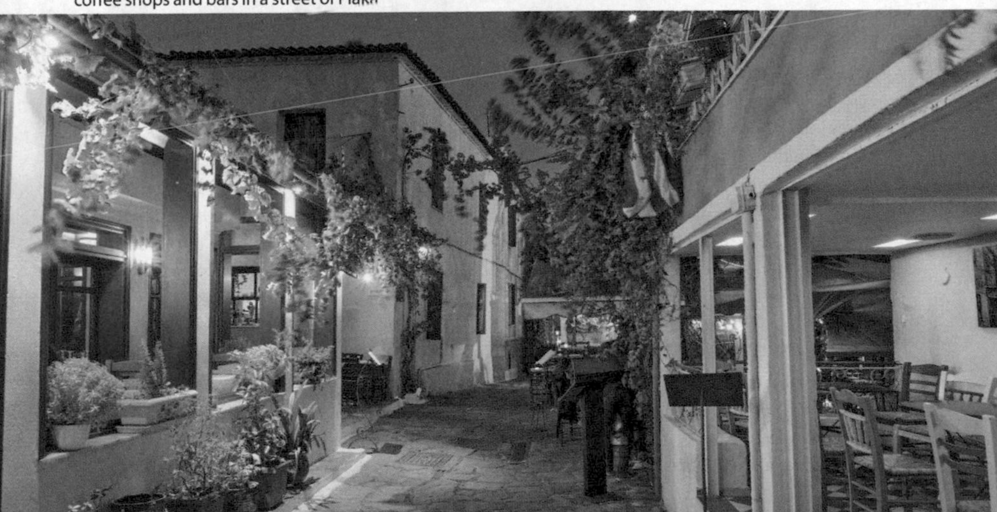

every day, from 1pm to 8pm, accompanied by a meat and cheese plate.

Omonia

FABRICA DE VINO

Emanouil Benaki 3; tel. 210/321 4148; daily 1pm-1am; glasses from €7

Located a stone's throw away from seedy Omonia Square, Fabrica de Vino makes up for its lack of curb appeal with a fun and dynamic atmosphere, and a great selection of Greek wines. There are snacks, too, either traditional meze or Spanish-style pinchos and tapas.

MUSIC VENUES AND CLUBS

Most of the below places either have cover charges of around €5 or ticket charges from €5-30 for concerts. Often the cover charge will include one beverage (beer or soft drink).

Monastiraki

FAUST

Kalamiotou 11; tel. 210/323 4095; www.faust.gr; Mon. 8:30pm-midnight, Tues.-Wed. noon-3pm and 8:30pm-midnight, Thurs.-Sun. 12:30am-4am

Faust is a small club on a Monastiraki side street with a frenetic energy and good beats, especially on Saturday. Check the website for events.

SIX D.O.G.S.

Avramiotou 6-8; tel. 210/321 0510; https://sixdogs.gr; Sun.-Thurs. 10am-3am, Fri.-Sat. 10am-7am

Bringing the biggest names in Greek and international electronic music, this is a great place to see some live acts and DJs, and dance your butt off. They also occasionally have art exhibitions. There's no dress code, but everyone looks Boiler Room cool.

Psyrri

ROMANTSO

Anaxagora 3; tel. 216/700 3325; www.romantso.gr/?Lang=En; daily, depends on events

Housed in the former printing plant of the infamous magazine *ROMANTSO*, this fantastic creative hub serves as both an "incubator" for artists and start-ups, and a cultural center. This place is a must visit, as they have all sorts of events going on, from live music acts to hoop dancing. Check the website for upcoming events.

ASTRON

Taki 3; tel. 698/388 5327; Thurs.-Sat. 10pm-7am

There's not a huge techno scene in Athens, so techno-lovers congregate at Astron, a tiny, hard-to-find club with no signage. Check their Facebook page, or Resident Advisor (www.residentadvisor.net), the electronic music scene's main media site for upcoming acts. Admission is free but the party doesn't get started till 3am.

Exarchia

DECADENCE

Poulcherias 2; tel. 697/441 4214; 9pm-late; €5 entrance

In the '80s, Decadence was the coolest address in Greece. It shuttered and people forgot about it, but in 2017 it reopened to local fanfare. Located in a dilapidated townhouse in Exarchia with a basement dance floor, it's a fun place to dance away an evening.

AN CLUB

Solomou 13-15; tel. 210/330 5056; www.anclub.gr; €5 entrance

For punk and grunge, head to AN Club, a small underground club that showcases local bands and some lesser-known international acts. The floor is sticky, the dress code is black, and there's only a suggestive distinction between dance floor and stage, but it's got a fun(ky) vibe. Also, punks are always the nicest people—and hardcore anti-fascists to boot. Check the website for upcoming shows, and go make some cool friends.

REBOUND

Mithimnis 43; Sun. midnight-6am; €6 entrance

This is the most cult-y dance place in Athens: a basement that only opens on Saturdays after midnight. Everyone is dressed in black, the music is exclusively dark wave, and you probably won't make any friends (this is a locals only joint to the max, and has been since the 1970s). That being said, every Athenian you meet will have spent at least part of their life dancing away here, and you should, too. Located in Kypseli (the neighborhood above Exarchia).

LGBTQ+

Generally speaking, Athens is safe for the LGBTQ+ community, though trans people are still more marginalized than others in the community. Outside of some Golden Dawn hangouts deep in Piraeus, you will be fine. Each June, there's a gay pride parade through Athens, and it remains one of the more popular times of the year for LGBTQ+ tourists to visit. Though there are LGBT-specific bars, nearly all places in downtown Athens are LGBT-friendly.

That being said, homophobia and transphobia are frustrating realities anywhere in the world. In 2018 the gay HIV activist Zak Kostopoulos was beaten to death in Omonia. Police presented the case as a botched robbery, but gay activists and friends of Zak insist that he was murdered in an act of hate.

Gazi and West Athens

BIG BAR

Falesias 12; tel. 694/628 2845; www.barbig.gr; Tues., Thurs., Sun. 10pm-3am, Fri.-Sat. 10pm-5am

One of the longest-running gay clubs in Athens, BIG offers fun parties that are advertised for bears and chasers; but in reality, all kinds of men and women party here. The smoking—illegal only in theory—is intense for non-Greeks. Best parties are on Saturday.

NOIZ

Leof. Konstantinoupoleos 78; tel. 210/346 7850; Sun., Mon., Wed., Thurs. 11:45pm-4am; Fri-Sat 11:45pm-6am

Noiz is the stalwart of the Athens LGBT club scene. It's marketed as a lesbian club, but in recent years, it's become more popular with gay men (and straight people). There are theme nights and international DJs.

CINEMA

Plaka

CINE PARIS

Kidathineon 22; tel. 210/322 2071; www.cineparis.gr

Athens' first outdoor cinema, Cine Paris was built in the 1920s by a Greek hairdresser who used to live in Athens. The rooftop theater has fantastic views of Acropolis, which can be a bit distracting from the movie! New films are shown weekly.

Exarchia

VOX

Themistokleous 82; tel. 210/330 1020

On the ground level of a pedestrian street in Exarchia, Vox features a lovely open-air courtyard where you can buy beer and snacks. They also have the most interesting movie selection; check their Facebook page for titles.

THEATER AND DANCE

NATIONAL THEATER OF GREECE

Agiou Konstantinou 22; tel. 528/817 0171; www.n-t.gr

Built in 1880 by Ernst Ziller (architecture buffs can stay at Ziller's Hotel), the National Theater (located in Omonia) is both a fantastic building and a great place to catch a show at one of the four stages. This is one of the best places to enjoy a theater performance in Athens, thanks to a well-curated list of international and local shows, some of which are quite experimental. Check the website for a schedule.

ONASSIS CULTURAL CENTER

107-109 Syngrou Avenue; www.onassis.org/initiatives/onassis-stegi

Onassis is the other big Greek shipping name to know. More easily accessible than the Niarchos Center, the Onassis Cultural Center stages a fantastic, diverse selection of music, theater, and dance performances. Greece has a particularly strong dance theater scene; if choreography from Papaioannou (an internationally renowned local choreographer) is playing, go see it! There's also a great fine dining restaurant on the top floor. The cultural center is located in Neos Kosmos (closest to Koukaki).

TECHNOPOLIS

Technopolis; tel. 210/346 1589; www.technopolis-athens.com

This industrial space, located in Gazi, is now a museum, but I prefer it for its cultural offerings: performances, installations, vintage markets, and more. Check the website for upcoming events, and you can probably catch one of their weekends where the whole square comes alive with vendors, shoppers, families, and live music.

ANCIENT THEATER OF EPIDAURUS

Epidaurus; tel. 275/302 2026; www.gtp.gr/TheatreofEpidaurus; €12

About two hour's drive outside of Athens, the 4th-century Epidaurus Theater is perhaps the best-preserved example of the classical amphitheater. In the summer months, the theater puts on all sorts of performances, from theater to music. If you have the time, it's worth a visit. The acoustics here are particularly mind-blowing, especially given the year it was built!

The theater is a two-hour drive from Athens. You can also take the public bus from the central bus depot in Kifisos (west Athens). From June through August, when the Epidaurus Festival runs, there are special buses that travel to and from Epidaurus that coordinate with the performance schedule.

CONCERTS

MEGARON MOUSIKIS (ATHENS CONCERT HALL)

Leof. Vasilissis Sofias and Kokkali; tel. 210/728 2000; www.megaron.gr

This massive concert hall, located in Kolonaki in the heart of downtown, is mostly used for musical performances. There are both local Greek acts as well as international artists.

Festivals and Events

ATHENS JAZZ FESTIVAL

www.technopolisjazzfestival.com; late May-early June

A beloved Athens classic, the Jazz Festival takes place at both the Technopolis and the Onassis Cultual Center. Most of the concerts (which include local and international acts) are free, and there are plenty of vendors at the Technopolis selling food, clothes, ceramics, etc., which gives it a community flavor.

ATHENS PRIDE

www.athenspride.eu; early June

LGBTQ+ tourists from all over the world congregate in Athens for this annual June festival. There's a huge parade that ends in Syntagma. There are plenty of parallel events as well, and Athens becomes more visibly LGBT-friendly during this time.

ATHENS & EPIDAURUS FESTIVAL

www.greekfestival.gr; tel. 210/928 2900; June-Aug.; tickets from €25

This annual festival is the most impressive cultural offering in the city. Performances in theater, ballet, jazz, classical music, opera, and ancient drama are held in some of the most stunning locations in Athens, including the Lycabettus Theater, the Odeon of Herodes Atticus, and Epidaurus. If you can, catch an ancient drama performance in an ancient theater for a once-in-a-lifetime experience.

ART ATHINA

https://art-athina.gr; Sept.

One of the oldest contemporary art fairs in Europe, Art Athina attracts a who's who of curators, artists, galleries, museums, and amateur art lovers who come together to hang out in Zappeion Mansion and ogle this year's selection of sculptures, paintings, mixed media, video, and more.

Shopping

There's some great shopping to be had in Athens, but note that most of what you buy on the islands (leather sandals, scarves, etc.) can also be purchased here, at more or less the same price. So concentrate your sartorial efforts (and your wallet) on local designers who only have shops in Athens.

SHOPPING DISTRICTS

Syntagma

The main thoroughfare that connects Syntagma to Monastiraki is **Ermou,** and the entire area is a pedestrian zone. You'll find all the major high-street brands, like Zara, Cosabella, H&M, and more. There's a nice Korres (beloved cosmetics and skincare brand) here as well, but aside from that, there's no store that you couldn't find elsewhere in another European city.

Kolonaki

As one of the richest neighborhoods in Athens, Kolonaki gives new meaning to the phrase "shop till you drop"; you literally might, given the amount of cardio required to crisscross the hilly neighborhood streets. You'll find some great Greek designers here, as well as luxury brands like Balenciaga and Hermes. If you're a true shopaholic, you'll want to spend a few hours here, occasionally refueling for coffee and food.

Koukaki

In recent years, Koukaki has seen a boom of home-grown designers and artists set up shop in the shadow of the Acropolis. You'll find independent artisans making everything from herb blends to clothes to bicycles.

Monastiraki

Monastiraki is home to Athens' beloved **Flea Market** (Ifestou 2; daily 8am-6pm), where you can find mid-century furniture along with antique objects and old records. Much of it is massively overpriced, but you can occasionally find some gems. Monastiraki is also where you'll find all the tourist shops in a souk-like environment: You can pick up leather sandals, bottles of ouzo, Swarovski crystal jewelry, and other wares. The vibe is very chaotic and skin-on-skin in the summer. It's definitely built for tourists, so keep that in mind as you walk through and are accosted by people trying to usher you into their shops or restaurants.

CLOTHING AND ACCESSORIES

Syntagma

ATTICA

Panepistimiou 9; tel. 211/180 2600; www.atticadps.gr; Mon.-Sat. 10am-9pm

Attica is to Athens what the Galerie Lafayette is to Paris: a catch-all department store with a variety of luxury labels. Tourists can shop tax-free (you'll have to keep your receipts for the airport). Sales happen twice a year, and they always have fantastic window displays.

Koukaki

METHEN ATHENS

Odissea Androutsou 36; tel. 694/752 0477; www.methenathens.com; Tues., Thurs., Sat. 5pm-8pm, Fri 1pm-8pm, closed Sun.-Mon. and Wed.

Support young Greek designers! This is a newish label that's one of the coolest Athens streetwear brands, and it's gender-neutral (though some of the pants definitely weren't made with hips in mind). Methen is the English transliteration of the Greek word for "zero," and tote bags, baseball caps, and T-shirts are all emblazoned with the tongue-in-cheek logo.

LAZY D

57 Falirou Street; tel. 210/921 4649; Tues.-Fri. 11am-8pm, Sat 11am-4pm

Love vintage but want something even more

unique? Check out Lazy D, where two women are designing and hand-sewing unique, vintage-inspired dresses. The cuts are feminine, the inspiration is mid-century, and the shop is a delightful throwback to the 1950s. They also design their own shoes and make wedding dresses.

Kolonaki

CALLISTA CRAFTS

Voukourestiou 11; tel. 210/364 7989; Mon., Wed. and Sat. 10am-5pm, Tues., Thurs.-Fri. 10am-8:30pm

In 2013, at the height of the Greek crisis, most designers were leaving the country, but Eleni Konstantinidis and Celia Sigalou stayed and created Callista Crafts, an homage to Greek leatherwork and macrame technique. Their bags are timeless, classic, and extremely high quality. They've also recently expanded into a small sandal line. Pick up a satchel or backpack from their charming Kolonaki location.

PARTHENIS

Dimokritou 20; tel. 210/363 3158

The Greek institution Parthenis, which has been around since the 1970s, has shops across Greece, but its flagship (along with the store in Mykonos) is this airy space in Kolonaki. The clothes are of excellent quality and are made in their Athenian factory. Designs play with ideas around ancient Greece, gender, and minimalism, and are a surprisingly affordable luxury. The store is now helmed by the founder's daughter, Orsalia Parthenis, who sometimes swings by the shop to chat with clients. Women's and men's clothes are sold here, and some of the designs are unisex.

JEWELRY

Kolonaki

FANOURAKIS

Patriarchou Ioakim 23; tel. 210/721 1762; www.fanourakis.gr/el; Mon.-Fri. 10am-9pm, Sat. 10am-5pm

Originally founded in Crete in 1860, this family-owned jewelry business is one of the most beloved in Greece. These are definitely statement pieces, always using high-quality gold, silver, and gemstones.

Syntagma

LALAOUNIS

6 Panepistimiou Ave. and Voukourestiou Street; tel. 210/361 1371; www.iliaslalaounis.eu; Thurs.-Fri. 10:30am-8:30pm, Mon.-Wed. and Sat. 10:30am-4:30 pm

Originally founded in 1969 by Ilias Lalounis, this company is now run by his four daughters. Lalounis is probably the most respected contemporary Greek jewelry designer. The family continues to use old-world techniques, making each piece by hand, and resulting in true works of art. Most of the pieces use 14k or 18k gold, but the shop offers Lucite pieces as well, at a more affordable price point. Visit the **Lalaounis Jewelry Museum** (12 Kallisperi Street; www.lalaounis-jewelrymuseum.gr/en; Tues.-Sat. 9am-3pm) to learn more about the prolific designer's life and legacy.

GIFTS

Plaka

FORGET ME NOT

100 Adrianou Street; tel. 210/325 3740; Mon.-Sun. 10am-8pm, open till 10pm in summer

You won't find anything remotely kitsch at Forget Me Not, a delightful "souvenir" shop that features contemporary Greek designers and, as they call it, "fabulous memorabilia." Here you will find plenty of tongue-in-cheek design objects (my personal favorites are from Greece is for Lovers, whose designs include a skateboard with leather Hermes-style wings). This is the perfect place to pick up some small gifts for friends and family.

FOOD

Koukaki

DAPHNIS & CHLOE

Erechtheiou 19; www.daphnisandchloe.com; Mon.-Fri. 11am-6pm

Greek herbs are considered some of the best in the world. At Daphnis + Chloe, you can find oregano flowers, mountain tea, red chili

1: fish for sale at the Athens' Central Market **2:** nuts for sale at the Athens' Central Market **3:** Monastiraki flea market

5,98€/kg
ΦΑΓΓΡΙΑ
ΕΛΛΑΔΟΣ ΦΡΕΣΚΑ
5.98
1
4.80€
ΦΥΣΤΙΚΙ - ΑΡΑΠΙΚΟ
ΝΕΑΣ - ΕΣΟΔΙΑΣ
ΚΙΝΑΣ
3.80 €
2
3

flakes, and more, all sourced from small farmers around the country and beautifully packaged. In-store visits are by appointment only via their website.

ELLINIKA KALLOUDIA

Chatzichristou 8; Mon.-Fri. 9am-3pm and 5pm-9pm, Sat. 9am-4pm

While every region in Greece has its own specialty, you might not have time to visit them all: Instead, stop by Ellinika Kalloudia. Friendly and knowledgeable owner Stamatis has spent 20 years scouring the countryside for the best dried goods, preserves, dairy products, wine, and oils. It's the sort of store you walk into planning to bring back gifts from friends and family, but then just end up eating everything yourself. It's all delicious, but I'm partial to the tahini from Limnos and dried figs from Kimi. He has two locations (the second is in Exarchia at Kallidromiou 51), so there's no excuse not to visit.

Kolonaki

YOLENI'S

Solonos 9; tel. 212/222 3623; Mon.-Sat. 8am-midnight, Sun. 10am-8pm

With seven stories of culinary goodness, Yoleni's has enough to keep even the pickiest eater interested for at least a few hours. There's a wine bar and cave, a grocery store (where you can pick up such delicacies as gold-flecked honey), deli, and gourmet restaurant. The store organizes cooking classes, wine tastings, and olive oil seminars (check website for times). The staff is incredibly helpful—perhaps too much so—but it's a great place to pick up some fancy products.

MARKETS

Omonia

CENTRAL MARKET

Varvakios Agora between Sofokleous and Evripidou; tel. 229/402 2780; Mon.-Sat. 7am-6pm

The Central Market is a loud, bustling, frenetic assault on the senses: a jumble of producers selling everything, including fish, meat, cheese, olives, spices, preserves, and more. It's been in continuous business since 1886, and many of the shop owners have been selling their goods at the same spot for generations. One specialty of the market is *basterma*, a dehydrated meat (beef, camel, goat, or lamb) that's spiced with a cumin/fenugreek/garlic/hot paprika paste, and is eaten thinly sliced. Look for it at the Miran or Arapian delicatessens on Evripidou Street. Other things worth looking for are herbs from Mt. Olympus, and anything made with *haroupi* (carob). My favorite is haroupi halva, a dense dessert made from tahini and honey and eaten across the Mediterranean and Middle East.

BEAUTY

Syntagma

KORRES

Ermou 4; tel. 213/018 8800; Mon.-Sat. 9am-8pm

Korres is considered a luxury product outside of Greece, but here, the beloved cosmetics and skincare brand is a staple in every Greek home, and sold for dirt cheap. Created in 1996, it's considered the first homeopathic pharmacy product from Greece. Like Apivita, Korres can be found everywhere, but there's a charming stand-alone shop near Syntagma Square where you can pick up cult favorites like wild rose oil and citrus body wash.

Kolonaki

APIVITA FLAGSHIP STORE

6 Solonos Street; tel. 210/364 0560; Tues., Thurs.-Fri. 10am-9pm, Mon., Wed. and Sat. 10am-5pm

The organic Greek cosmetic brand Apivita is beloved for its natural skincare, haircare, and bodycare products. Though Apivita can be found in any pharmacy, beauty lovers should head to this four-story "experience" store located in a chic neoclassical house in Kolonaki. There's a pharmacy, juice bar, library, hair salon, and spa featuring holistic therapies.

Greater Athens

DIMITRA GOULA

Tsocha Street 18-20; tel. 210/642 1031; www.dimitragoula.gr/en; Tues., Thurs.-Fri. noon-8pm, Wed. 2pm-10pm, Sat. 10am-6pm

Dimitra Goula is the skincare queen of Greece, specializing in all-natural organic skincare products; the majority of her potions, like wild chestnut oil, come from the holy monastery of Mount Athos in northern Greece. Visit her for a superb facial, and buy some of her products, which are custom made on the spot, post-treatment. All of her goods must be refrigerated to preserve their potency, but if you get hooked, she ships internally, on dry ice. Call ahead for appointments. The shop is located in Ambelkopi, about 2 km (1.25 mi) north of Kolonaki.

BICYCLE GEAR

Koukaki

48X17

2 Veikou, Makriyanni; tel. 210/922 5488; Tues.-Thurs. 11am-8pm, Fri. 11am-late, Sat. 11am-4pm

You're probably not going to buy a bicycle while in Athens, but the delightful 48x17 is still worth checking out. They sell custom bikes and bike parts from Tokyo, San Francisco, and Milan, but the real charm are the accessories and cycling apparel, all created by young Greek designers.

Food

There's no shortage of dining options in Athens, though in my humble opinion, it doesn't have the best food on the mainland. A plague that often befalls other capital cities has also descended on Athens: too many tourists, too many shortcuts, and plenty of uninspired, overpriced restaurants. That being said, there are gems in this city, too.

In general, avoid eating in areas like Plaka and Monastiraki, which caters specifically to tourists and usually serves microwaved, premade food. If you head to more neighborhood-y places, like Pangrati, Mets, and Exarchia, you'll have better luck at stumbling across a good meal. My rule of thumb for eating in Athens: if there's a waiter standing outside urging you in, if there's an English/Italian/Chinese/Russian language menu visibly displayed out front, if the banter inside the restaurant is in any language but Greek, avoid it. Use your ears and nose: Does the food smell good? Can you hear plenty of chattering Greek? If so, then it's probably a good restaurant.

SYNTAGMA

Greek

TZITZIKAS KAI MERMIGAS

Mitropoleos 12; tel. 210/324 7607; www.tzitzikasmermigas.gr/en; daily 12:30pm-1am; from €8

This solidly decent taverna in the heart of downtown attracts a steady clientele of locals and tourists. Classic taverna fare is offered with a few modern twists and thoughtful presentation. Try the arugula salad with shaved parmesan, pomegranate, and bacon bits. There's plenty of outdoor seating for the summer months, and service is fast and reliable.

International and Fusion

★ NOLAN

31 Voulis Athina; tel. 210/324 3545; www.nolanrestaurant.gr; Mon.-Sat. 1pm-midnight; from €10

You won't find a ton of fusion food in Greece, but at Nolan, the Japanese-Greek chef is opening up the city's palates. The food is fresh and creative, drawing on both Japanese and Greek ingredients and techniques; think soba noodles in tahini, marinated mackerel, and potato bread. The atmosphere is sleek and modern, with floor-to-ceiling glass windows and plenty of marble details.

ATTIC MOON

Xenofontos 10; tel. 210/322 7095; http://atticmoon.gr; daily 11:30am-11:30pm; from €8

The fact that Attic Moon is probably the best Chinese restaurant in Athens has been confirmed to me by several Athens-based Chinese

Best Restaurants

★ **Heteroclito:** Sip Greek wines and nibble on cheese plates at this lively downtown bar (page 61).

★ **Nolan:** Here you'll find creative fusion cuisine from a Greek-Japanese chef (page 69).

★ **Sushimou:** This tiny restaurant serves the best sushi in Greece, hands down (page 70).

★ **Kosta's:** Head to this popular spot, which serves the best sandwiches in Monastiraki (page 71).

★ **Zisis:** The excellent seafood here is a local favorite (page 71).

★ **Funky Gourmet:** Go on a culinary journey at this fantastic Michelin-starred restaurant (page 72).

★ **Prigkipas:** My favorite restaurant in Exarchia serves excellent kebabs and souvlaki (page 73).

★ **Nice n Easy:** This spot offers healthy food with a California flair (page 74).

★ **Olympion:** A no-frills, truly local *estiratorio* (restaurant) serving traditional Greek specialties (page 75).

friends. There's a pretty extensive menu, and if you know what's what, you can try to order something off the menu. Service is efficient, and the waiters are happy to recommend specific items. They also, bless them, can make actually spicy dishes.

★ SUSHIMOU

Skoufou 6; tel. 211/407 8457; mid-Sept.-mid.-Aug. Mon.-Fri. 6:30pm-11:30pm; menu €60

What happens when Mediterranean fish meets with Japanese knife skills? The bite-size Sushimou is without doubt the best sushi restaurant in Greece, run by Japanese-trained Andonis Drakoularakos, one of the top 100 chefs in the world chosen by Chef World Summit. Reservations are recommended to snag one of the 14 seats.

Cafés

ZONARS

Voukourestiou 9; tel. 210/325 1430; coffee from €5

Relive Athens' bourgeoise past at Zonars, a gorgeous art deco bar, café, and restaurant built in 1939 that was once the stomping ground of Sophia Loren, Melina Merkouri, and Anthony Quinn. It was recently refurbished but retains its original charm, down to the fur-clad old ladies eating chocolate ice cream out of metal bowls. There's a lot going on at Zonars: You can get sushi, martinis, and salads. But the best choice is to come for a coffee and a chocolate mint (Queen Sofia's favorite, apparently).

Bakeries

ARISTON

Voulis 10; tel. 210/322 7626; pies from €1.30

You'll smell the aroma of baking pies wafting through the doors of Ariston before you see the bakery itself. This place is an institution in Athens. They have dozens of sweet and savory pies that you can take away by the slice (the chicken pie and the pumpkin pie are quite good), but their real specialty is *kourou*, a salty cheese pie with a flaky, buttery crust. The bakery is takeaway only.

PLAKA

As you walk around Plaka, you'll notice many, many restaurants, most of which are crowded with tourists. The food is…fine, but it's overpriced, service can be less than stellar, and there's nothing about the run-of-the-mill tavernas that I would go out of my way to recommend. That being said, if you're starving and can't wait to head to another neighborhood, you'll have an adequate, if unmemorable, meal here.

Greek

SENSE FINE DINING

5 Dionysiou Areopagitou Street; tel. 210/920 0240; Tues.-Sun. 6pm-1am; from €30

While your eyes feast on the Acropolis glittering in the background from SENSE Fine Dining's rooftop, you'll be literally chomping down on ancient Greek pillars—albeit gastronomic ones—made of frozen chocolate. Chef Thodoris Papanikolaou has created a stunning menu based on traditional Greek plates and carefully sourced ingredients, with a playfully contemporary twist. Reservations are recommended.

MONASTIRAKI

Greek

★ KOSTA'S

Pl. Agias Irinis 2; tel. 210/323 2971; Mon.-Fri. noon-6pm; from €2.50

This is where you'll find the best sandwich in Monastiraki. Kosta and his family have been grilling it up for 65 years. Souvlaki or kebabs (go for the latter) come with tomato sauce, sliced tomatoes, and onions: a bit atypical for the Greek pita, but absolutely delicious. It's definitely not a secret, so be prepared to stand in line. They usually run out around 3pm.

★ ZISIS

Athinaidos 3, tel. 210/321 1152; daily noon-midnight; from €3.80

Despite being located on a touristic street, this excellent little fish spot is full of locals. The takeaway cones—for under €4—are an excellent deal. You get a gigantic cone filled with vinegar-y slaw and topped with an impressive amount of fried seafood (my favorite is the calamari). You can also sit down to a full spread that will have you thinking you're on a Greek island.

International and Fusion

MAMA ROUX

48 Aiolou Street; tel. 213/004 8382; daily 9:30am-12:30am; from €8

A cheerfully decorated (the roof is covered in umbrellas) and eclectic eatery, Mama Roux offers a mish-mash of global flavors on the food and drinks menus. If you're craving Mexican, Middle Eastern, and Japanese all at the same time, this one's for you.

KOUKAKI

Greek

OLA STA KARVOUNA (THE GIRLS)

16 Drakou, Koukaki; tel. 210/922 5648; mains from €2

According to local lore, the owners never got around to naming their little souvlaki joint, so everyone just started calling it The Girls. That's only sort of true; the official name is Ola Sta Karvouna, but if you need directions, ask for Ta Koritsia (Greek for "The Girls"). The name stuck, and this bare-bones, fluorescent-lit, picture-menu restaurant remains a great neighborhood place to pick up a burger or souvlaki.

Cafés and Coffee Shops

BEL REY

88 Falirou; daily 10am-2am; coffee from €2

Despite what you might hear, Athens isn't the new Berlin, but you'll be forgiven for thinking that at Bel Ray, an uber-hip café housed in a former garage. With vaulted ceilings, monochromatic murals, and a rotating cast of beautiful hipsters, it's a great place to people-watch while brunching and knocking back espressos.

★ LITTLE TREE BOOKS & COFFEE

Kavalloti 2; tel. 210/924 3762; Tues.-Thurs. and Sun. 9am-11pm, Fri.-Sat. 9am-11:30pm; drinks from €2

Part bookstore, part café, Little Tree Books &

Coffee is a charming place to spend a leisurely afternoon. Grab a seat on the tree-shaded terrace and order an expertly executed coffee or the house specialty, hot lemonade. They also have a small selection of sandwiches and pastries. It gets very crowded on weekend afternoons.

DRUPES & DRIPS

Zitrou 20; tel. 697/030 0404; daily 7am-10pm; from €2

Across the street from Takis bakery you can grab a coffee at Drupes & Drips, Koukaki's third-wave coffeehouse and a neighborhood favorite. The baristas brew excellent coffee and serve fresh-pressed juices (try the pomegranate). Like all good cafés, the place slowly morphs into a bar as the day goes by, with an emphasis on Greek wines, prosecco, and small bites.

Bakeries

O FOURNOS TOU TAKIS

14 Misaraliotou; Mon.-Fri. 7am-8:30pm, Sat. 7am-4pm; breads from €1

Athens isn't really known for baked goods—that distinction belongs to the northern city of Thessaloniki—but O Fournos Tou Takis is an exception, in part because the owner was born in Thessaloniki. There's usually a long line of people waiting to buy carrot cake (their house specialty), *lipsopita* (a honeyed sweet bread), or cookies. They also make excellent whole wheat breads.

GAZI AND WEST ATHENS

Greek

KANELLA

Leof. Konstantinoupoleos 70; www.kanellagazi.gr; daily 1pm-2am; from €10

A longtime neighborhood favorite, Kanella is a classic taverna with home-cooked food. It's gotten increasingly popular with tourists in recent years, and prices reflect that, but it's still a great restaurant for a fun night out. Try the *kokkinisto* (slowly braised meat in tomato sauce) and round it out with any of the salads.

ALERIA

Meg. Alexandrou 57; tel. 210/522 2633; www.aleria.gr/en; Mon.-Sat. 7:30pm-11:30pm; tasting menu from €55

Located in a neoclassical villa with a romantic courtyard, Aleria is all about elevated and elegant Mediterranean food. The food is both cozy and delicate: a tricky balance to strike. Choose from meat, fish, or vegetarian tasting menus for the full experience. There are a la carte options as well.

SEYCHELLES

Keramikou 49; tel. 211/183 4789; daily 10am-2am; from €8

This is a hipster-ish taverna that serves authentically delicious Greek staples, with slight twists. Order a variety of mezes, but be sure to get the handmade pasta with pulled lamb. It gets quite crowded, so call ahead for reservations.

Fine Dining

★ FUNKY GOURMET

13 Paramithias Street and Salaminos; tel. 210/524 2727; www.funkygourmet.com/en; closed for reservations until 2020; tasting menu from €145

One of the best fine dining restaurants in Athens, the Michelin-starred Funky Gourmet is more of an art experience, or a culinary voyage, than it is a simple meal. The food is both playful and cerebral: a chocolate bonbon that's actually Roquefort cheese, a pile of granita that has all the tastes of a classic Greek salad. This restaurant is a gourmet must-visit, and it's pretty affordable compared to other European Michelin restaurants. Reservations are required; dress sharp.

EXARCHIA

Greek

AMA LAXEI

Kallidromiou 69; tel. 210/384 5978; Tues.-Sun. 1pm-1am, Mon. 7pm-7am; mains €6-11

Tucked away on a charming side street, Ama Laxei is housed in a converted neoclassical house and features a lovely inner courtyard for al fresco dining. The location is nicer than the

Kafeneio: Greek Café Culture

If the Brits are known for their affinity for tea, then the Greeks must be recognized for what can only be described as a run-away love affair with coffee. You'll notice that every neighborhood (and in some neighborhoods, every block) has a ***kafeneion,*** where old men and women sit drinking thick Greek coffee. The men hold *komboloi* (worry beads) and play backgammon while the women finger their handkerchiefs and keep a watchful eye on the neighborhood kids.

Stepping into a *kafeneion* means stepping out of time: Athenians can drink their coffee over several hours, as they discuss everything from the state of political affairs to the week's latest squabble with the in-laws. Sitting and drinking coffee for such a long period of time is an art form in my book, and you should try it at least once.

summer morning with *freddo cappuccino,* a Greek cold coffee drink

There are two coffees you should try while in Greece: Turkish coffee (called **Greek coffee** here, for obvious reasons of national pride) and ***freddo espresso,*** which is the best iced coffee you'll ever have. Greek coffee is made in a small copper pot called a *briki* and boiled three times over an open flame; a *freddo* is an iced espresso shaken with the intensity of a martini. Both can be ordered with different levels of sweetness (*glyko* for very sweet, *metrio* for a little sweet, *sketo* for plain). *Freddo* can be ordered with milk, but milk is never added in Turkish coffee.

food, which is classic Greek taverna, though the grilled pork belly is a particular standout.

KYMATOTHRAFSTIS

Char. Trikoupi 49; tel. 213/030 8274; Mon.-Sat. 1pm-11pm, Sun. 1pm-8pm; from €5.50

A neighborhood favorite, Kymatothrafstis serves Greek-style fast food. You'll find a long buffet of prepared, hot meals: plenty of stews, roasted vegetables, and meats, plus a variety of salads and grains. It's cheap, and there are two options for plate sizes.

GIORGOS MANOS

Themistokleous 39; tel. 210/381 5442; Mon.-Fri. 10am-5:30pm; from €2

Don't tell the Athenians, but their souvlaki is the worst in Greece. There are only a handful of places making palatable meat sticks, and one of those is at Giorgos-Manos. The meat (pork, chicken) is marinated all day before being expertly grilled, and served with lemon wedges and slices of baguette. There are a few seats, but it's better to order takeaway and walk a few blocks to Exarchia Square. It's a neighborhood institution, so arrive early as they usually sell out each day.

OUZERI LESVOS

Emmanouil Benaki 38; tel. 210/381 4525; daily 10am-1am; from €7

This is a fantastic little slice of the Greek islands here in Athens. Grab a table on the sidewalk and start slinging back shots of ouzo, accompanied by a fantastic selection of meze. The focus is on seafood. The tiny fried shrimp are especially good, but you can't go wrong ordering a selection of the menu.

★ PRIGKIPAS

Char. Trikoupi 23; Mon.-Sat. noon-midnight; 211/405 0070; from €3

This is my favorite restaurant in Exarchia, and for good reason: Friendly owner Kostis is making farm-to-table food easily, and cheaply, available. The best dishes are the kebabs. The meat is brought in daily from his hometown, the northern city of Florina, and grilled to perfection and dipped in *boukovo* (red pepper flakes). Excellent souvlaki, nicely grilled pitas made with corn flour, perfect potatoes, and tangy salads round out the menu. There are a few tables outside, or you can call for takeaway.

Cafés and Coffee Shops

★ LUXUS

Valtetsiou 27; tel. 213/004 7353; Mon.-Sat. 8am-3am, Sun. noon-3am; from €2

This is my favorite café in Exarchia, located on a pedestrian street (good for people watching), with plenty of tables outside in the shade of an awning or in the sun if you're working on your tan. The design inside is art deco–inspired, and as night falls, it turns into a bar. There's always an interesting bohemian crowd, and nice music throughout the day.

PSYRRI

International and Fusion

GOSTIJO

10 Aisopou, Esopou; tel. 210/323 3825; summer Sun.–Thurs. 1pm-11pm, winter Mon.-Thurs. 4pm-11pm, Fri. (Shabbat) reservations only; from €8.50

The only kosher restaurant in Athens, Gostijo serves up Sephardic-style Greek and Middle Eastern food. Much like the Jewish diaspora itself, the menu brings together dishes from Tunisia, Syria, Lebanon, Greece, Turkey, and Morocco. You can order meze-style (go for the leek fritters) or get a big, warm plate of moussaka.

Cafés and Coffee Shops

ISLAMIC ART MUSEUM CAFE

Koumpari 1, Keramikos; tel. 210/367 1000; www.benaki.org; Wed. and Fri. 10am-6pm, Thurs. 10am-11:30pm, Sun. 10am-4pm; from €3.50

Even if you're not interested in the museum, head here anyway and take the elevator straight up to the top floor. This sunlight-filled café is one of my favorite spots in Athens, and is nearly always empty. The interior of the café is covered in a fantastically colorful floor-to-ceiling mural by local artist Navine Khan Dossos. You can also head outside, where you can enjoy tea, coffee, sandwiches, and light snacks with a full view of Keramikos and the Acropolis.

KOLONAKI

Greek

KALAMAKI KOLONAKI

Ploutarchou 32; tel. 210/721 8800; Mon.–Sun. 1pm-midnight; mains €2-7

The interior of Kalamaki Kolonaki is so tiny that most of the seats are located on the sidewalk, but it serves up some of the freshest food in the area. Order some pork steaks or skewers (sold individually), and supplement with a few of their innovative salads. Be sure to order the grilled bread to mop up all the juices from your plate.

International and Fusion

★ NICE N EASY

Omirou 60 and Skoufa; tel. 210/361 7201; www.niceneasy.gr; Sun.-Fri. 9am-1:30am, Sat. 9am-8pm

The Athenian branch of the Mykonian outpost, Nice n Easy is a fantastic modern eatery with a focus on fresh and healthy food. The owner, unsurprisingly, worked in restaurants in LA, and there's definitely a California flair to the menu and decor: Chia seeds and husked cannabis seeds make an appearance, and each dish tracks macros and calories. Try the buffalo meatballs and finish off with a scoop of olive oil ice cream. The name is inspired by the Frank Sinatra song, and his likeness, along with some other old-school Hollywood stars, decorates the interior.

ALEX'S FRESH PASTA BAR

Plateia Dexamenis 3; tel. 210/364 4142; Wed.-Sun. 1pm-8pm; from €8

A new addition on the streets of Kolonaki (they opened in 2018), this tiny eatery specializes in, well, pasta! It's all handmade, topped with a variety of sauces, and served in cute ceramic bowls. Enjoy pure comfort food in a restaurant that attracts a hip, young crowd.

Cafés

PHILOS ATHENS

Solonos 32; tel. 210/361 9163; Mon.-Sat. 9am-5pm; drinks from €1.80, mains €5-12

Everything is chic in Kolonaki, but Philos Athens stands out as something unique. Located in a lovingly restored neoclassical building that used to belong to the famed art collector Koutlidis, Philos is as much a feast for the eyes as it is for the taste buds. There's a great brunch—the pumpkin sandwich and avocado toast are particularly delicious—and nice salads and sandwiches for lunch.

Deli

KOSTARELOS DAIRY

30-32 Patriarchou Ioakim Street; tel. 210/725 9000; Mon.-Sat. 8am-11pm, mains from €5

The Kostarelos family has been churning out (pun intended) dairy products for three generations. The most recent generation has opened Kostarelos Dairy, a restaurant with full-day service and a deli to bring home some delicious cheeses and yogurts. It's not for the lactose intolerant: nearly everything on the menu is dripping in delicious, oozy cheese.

PAN

Greek

ND METS

★ OLYM

Anapafseos 9; te ; daily 7am-1am; from €5

This is one of thos when I have to choose between my and my fear that sharing too many ecret spots might inadvertently ruin This is my favorite *estiratorio* (restaura cooked food) in Athens, offer h home- nation of nostalgia and really excell combi- food. Walk to the back (there's a constant ro on of old men playing backgammon) to check out the foods that have been cooking all day. If you're lucky, they'll have stuffed cabbage leaves. Otherwise, order from the grill (I'm partial to the liver with oven potatoes) and don't skip dessert. The atmosphere is totally no frills, the staff is slightly brusque, and aside from the confused tourist who occasionally wanders in, it's a pretty local setup. They also offer special foods during the Orthodox holidays, like fried cod with garlic sauce during Easter.

MAVRO PROVATO

Arrianou 31; tel. 210/722 3466; Mon.-Sat. 1pm-1am, Sun. 1pm-7pm; from €3

freshly prepared Greek salad at Olympion restaurant

Mavro Provato ... eep in English, and this atmos... oploeio (a restaurant specializ... snacks, meze) sets itself apart ... ck with thoughtful meze and ... rder a bottle of *tsipuro* and a selec... all plates. The menu is divided int... cold dishes, and hot dishes. To be sa... at least one off each.

Café...

OHI...

Arc... ou 32; tel. 211 183 8340; daily 8:30am-11pm; from €3

This charming café in the heart of Pangrati offers excellent coffee and a very tempting selection of baked goods, including vegan and gluten-free options. They have some savory choices as well, including sandwiches and quiches, but I'm partial to a mid-afternoon sugar pick-me-up. There are a few tables outside, and it draws a painfully cool-looking crowd.

International and Fusion

MYSTIC

Ferikidou 2; tel. 210/959 2092; www.mystic.com.gr/en; daily noon-12:45am; from €9

This pizza parlor, inspired by the '90s Julia Roberts film *Mystic Pizza*, is a colorfully decorated and relaxed spot with unique pizza offerings. The dough is made from organic cannabis flour and spelt, making this a good low-gluten option. They also have a spot in Exarchia (Benaki 76).

SPONDI

Pirronos 5; tel. 210/756 4021; www.spondi.gr/spondi; daily 8pm-11:45pm; tasting menu from €79

Spondi offers a truly elegant fine dining experience, and it's one of the most awarded and beloved restaurants in Athens. Come for a romantic evening, or for a truly unique culinary adventure. I suggest the tasting menu, which includes Spondi's special *foie gras* dish, and be sure to follow the sommelier's recommendation for accompanying wines. Spondi attracts a chic crowd, and it's usually full of couples holding hands across the table. Call ahead for reservations.

BABA GHANOUSH

Empedokleous 25; tel. 212/105 0351; babaghanoush.gr; daily noon-midnight; from €4.50

At this great little Middle Eastern eatery you can sample both hummus and baba ghanoush (which are not Greek, contrary to popular belief), plus plenty of other tasty dishes, like falafel wraps and tabouleh salad. There are lots of vegan and vegetarian options. The decor is quite cool, with floor-to-ceiling windows and beautiful ceramic tiles.

Bakeries

PNYKA

Pratinou 13; tel. 210/324 5162; Mon.-Sat 7am-8pm; from €2

All the loaves at this Athenian institution are thoughtfully made with special grain varieties. Try the rye bread or the whole wheat loaf. There's an outpost in Syntagma (Petraki 24), too, and they've even spread their flour-dusted gospel to Vienna. The Pangrati option is the coolest, though, because they have their own flour mill on-site.

Accommodations

There's no shortage of hotels in Athens, from the most luxurious accommodations to hovels ...r backpackers on their last few euros. Most ...rists choose to stay in either Syntagma or ...nd Acropolis (in Plaka), which is close to all the major sights and transportation, but it can be a bit hectic and loud throughout the day.

Since 2018 a startling amount of Athenian property has been turned into Airbnbs. It's

Best Accommodations

★ **InnAthens:** This great budget option is located in a neoclassical building (page 77).

★ **Zillers Boutique Hotel:** A wonderful mid-range choice in an architectural gem (page 77).

★ **Grande Bretagne:** This historic hotel is a worthy splurge in Syntagma (page 78).

★ **Electra Palace:** In this luxury hotel, you'll be situated so near the Acropolis you'll feel like you can touch it (page 79).

a controversial topic in the city, as landlords have started to evict tenants and some Greeks feel pushed out of their own city by tourists; yet, for many other Greeks, it remains the only way they can make money since the crisis. There are plenty of nice apartments for rent around the city, in any event, and it's a good option if you are staying longer-term; try looking for a place in Koukaki.

Hotels in Athens generally have en-suite bathrooms (the exceptions being hostels and guesthouses), and breakfast is typically included in the room fee unless otherwise noted.

SYNTAGMA

Under €150

★ INNATHENS

Souri 3; tel. 210/325 8555; www.innathens.com; from €110 d

Before it was InnAthens, the neoclassical building that now houses one of Athens' best hotel deals was a refugee center, a girls' school, and a hostel. It's been lovingly restored with an emphasis on bespoke elements: marble slabs, wrought-iron balconies, stone walls. Rooms are modern and minimal, and there's a lovely interior courtyard. A 5-minute walk south from Syntagma, the hotel is located in a covered arcade, so it's blissfully quiet.

€150-300

★ ZILLERS BOUTIQUE HOTEL

54 Mitropoleos; tel. 210/322 2277; www.thezillersathenshotel.com; from €150 d

Located in the heart of Plaka, the charming Zillers Boutique Hotel is housed in a renovated neoclassical building and is a favorite with well-heeled Athenians. Rooms are modern and bright, if a bit small, and the staff is wonderfully accommodating. The undeniable standout is the roof garden, with a view of the Parthenon.

PALLADIAN HOME

Farmaki 2; tel. 210/300 8044; from €160 d

Named after the mythical guardian Athena Pallas, the boutique hotel Palladian Home is a wonderful pick for those looking for old-world charm in a modern setting. Palladian Home offers 13 sun drenched rooms in a restored neoclassical building from 1830; the building has retained much of its original charm, updated in contemporary taupes and beiges. There are stunning views, of course, of Acropolis; try to book a room with balcony.

NEW HOTEL

16 Filellinon Street; tel. 210/327 3200; www.yeshotels.gr/hotel/new-hotel; from €270 d

Athens' hippest new address is the aptly named New Hotel, where the focus is on art and design. The owner is famed art collector Dakis Jannou, and the award-winning Brazilian design duo Fernando and Humberto Campana designed the 79-room boutique hotel. There's decor culled from the Venice Biennale, a collection of 2,000 art book titles, and a wonderful rooftop.

Over €300

★ GRANDE BRETAGNE

1 Vasileos Georgiou A Street, Syntagma Square; tel. 210/333 0000; www.grandebretagne.gr; from €400 d

The Grande Bretagne has been a longtime haunt of the jet set since it was first built in 1842, and it underwent an intense restoration in 2013. It has a bit of a checkered past: Nazis used the hotel as their headquarters during their occupation of Athens. Resistance forces dug tunnels under the hotel to ferry secret messages. Still, it remains Athens' most desirable address, and features a stunning baroque bar, rooftop garden, a lovely spa, and sumptuous rooms. Prices drop significantly in winter.

KING GEORGE

3 Vasileos Georgiou A; tel. 210/322 2210; www.marriott.com/hotels/travel/athgl-king-george-a-luxury-collection-hotel-athens; from €380

The sister hotel to the Grande Bretagne, the King George, is something of a boutique offering—just as sumptuous, but with fewer rooms and a more hushed vibe. The penthouse suite, with its own rooftop pool, is to die for; spring for it if you can! Guests have access to all the amenities (spa, gym, etc.) at the Grande Bretagne.

PLAKA AND ACROPOLIS

Under €150

ALICE INN

9 Tsatsou Street; tel. 210/323 7139; www.aliceinnathens.com; from €90

A funky little "micro-boutique" housed in an old neoclassical building on a quiet street near Plaka, Alice Inn is a great budget choice with a surprising amount of luxury. Named after the Greek-British owner's grandmother, the inn has four rooms, each with its own vibe (the best one is the suite with rooftop access). There are communal rooms on the ground floor.

ATHENSTYLE

Agias Theklas 10; tel. 210/322 5010; www.athenstyle.com; beds from €18, private double room from €70

For the budget-conscious traveler with a sense of style, book a bed at AthenStyle Hostel, where the rooms are cheap but the amenities are good: views of Acropolis, a cozy lounge area and communal kitchen, and a rooftop bar. It caters to a younger crowd and is a great place to meet fellow travelers. Rooms are very basic but cheerfully decorated (orange and lime green are their preferred colors).

€150-300

AVA HOTEL

Lisikratous 9; tel. 210/325 9000; www.avahotel.gr; from €220

This is a beautiful little jewel of a boutique hotel; the rooms are all actually suites of different sizes and come styled like apartments. It's one of the best options for Plaka, and has a stunning view of Acropolis.

HERODION HOTEL

Rovertou Galli 4; tel. 210/923 6832; www.herodion.gr; from €165

A fantastic four-star hotel that's slightly more affordable than its competitors, this is a hotel designed for the business traveler, which means everything is streamlined and easy. Rooms are a bit on the small side, but beds are comfortable, the toiletries are nice, and the views (Acropolis, of course) are fantastic.

Where to Stay If...

- It's your first time in Athens: **Syntagma** or **Plaka**
- You're on a budget: **Psyrri** or **Exarchia**
- You love nightlife: **Monastiraki**
- You want a neighborhood feel: **Koukaki** or **Exarchia**
- You're looking for Acropolis views: The **top floor** of almost any building in Athens! (Though it does depend on the direction your room faces.)

Over €300

★ ELECTRA PALACE

18-20 N, Navarchou Nikodimou Street; tel. 210/337 0000; www.electrahotels.gr; from €350

One of the best known luxury hotels in Athens, Electra Palace is a stalwart on the hospitality scene. The bathrooms are marble, the furniture is customized, and the views are fantastic. You're so close to the Acropolis you feel like you could reach out and touch it. Needless to stay, there are also excellent staff and amenities, including a rooftop pool.

PSYRRI

Under €150

ATHENS STYLE HOSTEL

Makri 12; www.backpackers.gr; dorm from €27, private rooms from €40

As far as backpacker options go, this is the best one: There are colorful and airy rooms, a rooftop area with views of Acropolis (!) and cheap drinks, a barbeque in the courtyard, and a communal kitchen. It's got quite the social scene, and it is blessedly clean. Dorms have private bathrooms and lockers with bedding. Breakfast is included. Private rooms (including studios, rooms with views of Acropolis, or singles) are also available.

CITY CIRCUS

Sarri 16; tel. 213/023 7244; https://citycircus.gr; dorms from €55, private rooms from €90

City Circus bills itself as an "alternative travelers space," and for a hostel, it's pretty freaking cool. The prices match the cool factor—you'll pay about twice what you'd pay elsewhere—but the colorful and well-designed rooms are a welcome change from the drab hostels of Europe. Free breakfast is included if you book via their website. Private rooms are available.

EXARCHIA

Under €150

ATHENS QUINTA HOSTEL

Methonis 13; tel. 694/228 2270; http://athens-quinta.hotelsathens.org; dorms from €30, private rooms from €50

This is a cute little boutique hostel in Exarchia, located on a quiet pedestrian street inside a neoclassical house. The furniture is slightly old school, but in an intentional sort of way, and you can choose from single, three- and six-person dorms, all with shared bathrooms. This place is a lot cozier than your average hostel, and there's a nice garden area. Pets are allowed, but smoking is not.

RADISON BLU PARK HOTEL

Leof. Alexandras 10; tel. 210/889 4500; www.radissonblu.com; from €130 d

This is the best of the luxury hotels in the area, if you don't mind being a short walk from the center. It's a classic business traveler hotel, with 153 rooms set across the sleek glass building. There's a nice fitness center and spa, and rooftop views of the Acropolis for half the price you'd pay in Plaka.

KOLONAKI

€150-300

COCOMAT

36 Patriarchou Ioakeim Street; tel. 210/723 0000; from €195 d

Wouldn't you want to sleep atop one of Europe's best mattresses? The acclaimed mattress company Coco-Mat, which makes award-winning, all-natural mattresses, has its own hotel for a veritable "Princess and the Pea" experience. The rooms are a bit of a squeeze (their special "Sleep Tight" rooms are positively miniscule) but you're guaranteed to get a good night's sleep. There's an excellent breakfast, and you can rent one of the company's cute wooden bikes for a cycling tour of the city.

ST GEORGE LYCABETTUS

Keomenous 2; tel. 210/714 6000; www.sglycabettus.gr; from €170

For those looking for a bit of respite from the hustle of Athens, St. George Lycabettus, located up a hill in Kolonaki, is a good bet. To be honest, rooms are a little worn down—this used to be the best hotel in the city—but it's still got plenty of posh charm and the service is excellent. There's a great rooftop pool with views of Acropolis.

Transportation

GETTING THERE

Air

Athens is served by the **Eleftherios Venizelos International Airport (ATH),** which underwent a renovation in 2017. All major airlines fly through Venizelos, with many airlines now offering direct flights from the United States, Asia, and the Middle East. Located 27 km (17 mi) east of the city center, the airport offers all the modern amenities and more: 24-hour luggage service, a children's playroom, a small archaeological museum, and several bank branches and ATMs. There is a 24-hour **Athens Airport Information Desk** with friendly staff giving out booklets and free Athens Spotlighted discount cards, and answering any questions.

AIRPORT TRANSPORTATION

To get to the city center from the airport, you can take a taxi, metro, or bus.

There is a police-manned **taxi** queue outside of the arrivals gate; even if the line is long, it goes quickly. Taxi rates to the center are fixed at €38, but note that between midnight and 7am, the tariff is doubled.

For the **metro,** exit through the arrivals area and walk across the street, up the escalator, and through the hallway to the station. Tickets costs €12 per person, and rides come every 20 minutes.

The **bus** is the most economical way to leave the airport, with lines departing every 30 to 60 minutes, depending on the route (€6). The X95 goes to **Syntagma,** the X96 to **Piraeus,** the X93 goes to the **Kifousia intercity bus station,** and the X97 connects with the **Elliniko metro station.** Visit www.athensairportbus.com/en for timetables.

GETTING AROUND

The most convenient way to get around Athens is **on foot,** as many of the main sights and neighborhoods are within an hour's walk of each other. Walking is not always an enjoyable experience, as Athenian sidewalks are tiny and often full of parked cars, and they have at least three different textured tiles on each street. If you are traveling in a wheelchair or with a stroller, be aware that maneuvering may be difficult or nearly impossible in some neighborhoods.

Metro

Athens has a clean and somewhat comprehensive three-line metro. The **Green Line,** which serves Kifisia to Piraeus, was built in 1869, making it the second oldest in the world after the London Underground. It passes through Piraeus, Omonia, and Monastiraki. The **Red Line** goes from Anthoupoli to Eliniko, passing through the Athens railway station, Omonia, Syntagma Square, and Acropolis. The **Blue Line** goes from the airport to Aghia Marina, stopping in Syntagma and Monastiraki.

A 90-minute ticket costs €1.40, and a five-day pass is €9 (you can buy both from the automated kiosks in any metro station). Some gaps on the metro are filled in by the **tram,** which connects the city center to the southern seaside with three lines.

You buy metro **tickets** directly in the metro from the machines (English-language options available) and validate your ticket at the turnstiles before going into the wagon. The metro runs from 5:15am to 12:30am, Monday through Sunday.

Taxi and Ride-Hailing Apps

Taxis are affordable (minimum ride is €3, double at night), though Athenian cabbies have a bit of a—ahem—reputation in Greece: They're known to be overly chatty and often smoking, and they can take advantage of tourists by driving them in circles and overcharging for baggage. You can mitigate unfair service by running Google Maps on your phone at the same time, though in all likelihood, you'll be okay.

Taxis are clearly marked—they are all yellow and say TAXI on them—and you can hail them in the street. If you're leaving very early in the morning, it's helpful for your hotel to call ahead. Rates are fixed between the airport and the center (€38 during the day, €54 midnight-5am). To Piraeus, rates are €50 during the day, €60 at night.

There's no Uber in Greece, but you can download the **TaxiBeat** app on your phone (www.thebeat.co.gr); it is actually more reliable than most of the taxi services. You can also try **Welcome Pickups** (www.welcomepickups.com) to prebook a ride somewhere; most of the drivers speak English.

Athens Ports

PIRAEUS
(Πιραεύς)

Islands served: *Santorini, Mykonos, Folegandros, Milos, Naxos, Anafi, Karpathos, Rhodes, Kalymnos, Ikaria, Lesvos, Crete*

Piraeus, located 10 km (6 mi) southwest of central Athens, is a city unto itself: This is the biggest port in the Mediterranean, with 20 million people passing through each year. It has its own character, and a long history stretching back to ancient times; the area has been inhabited since the 26th century BC. Piraeus began to be built up during the time of King Otto, and it quickly became a bustling metropolis, as thousands of immigrants and refugees from Asia Minor settled along the port. If you have some time to kill, there are two nice areas worth visiting for a nice stroll along the water: **Zea Marina** and **Mirkolimano.** City bus number 904 or 905 connects the pretty neighborhood of Zea Marina to the metro, and from there you can walk to Mirkolimano.

Purchasing Ferry Tickets

I highly recommend buying your ferry tickets beforehand, and from a tour agency in the center. **Piraeus Port Authority** (tel. 210/455 0000; www.olp.gr) has information but charges for calls. Ferry schedules change yearly, but you can find up-to-date timetables and buy tickets online (www.greekferries.gr, www.openseas.gr, www.ferries.gr). Tickets can be purchased at the port two hours before sailing, but in the rush of summer, this can end up being a very stressful situation. I prefer to buy directly from travel agents, who are the most knowledgeable and can find you the most convenient routes, especially if you're visiting multiple destinations. In Athens, I buy my ferry tickets from the husband-and-wife run **Priority Travel & Tourism** (Sofokelous stoa inside the alley; tel. 210/331 4476; www.prioritytravel.gr).

Bring plenty of snacks and water, as the prices on the boats are more expensive. If you're taking a long-haul ferry, I recommend springing for a cabin or staking out a corner of a sofa (prime real estate).

Food

Along the harbor you'll find plenty of uninspiring fast-food joints and sad souvlaki spots. There are more worthwhile spots along the backstreets.

MANDRAGORAS

Gounari 14; tel. 210/417 2961; Mon., Wed., Sat. 7:45am-4pm, Tues., Thurs., Fri. 7:45am-8pm

A great place to pick up some snacks before your trip, this little delicatessen offers cheeses, mezes, olives, crackers, and other beloved food products.

VAROULKO

Akti Koumoundourou 52; tel. 210/522 8400; www.varoulko.gr; daily 12:30pm-1am; from €40

If you're a fancy sort of traveler, enjoy a

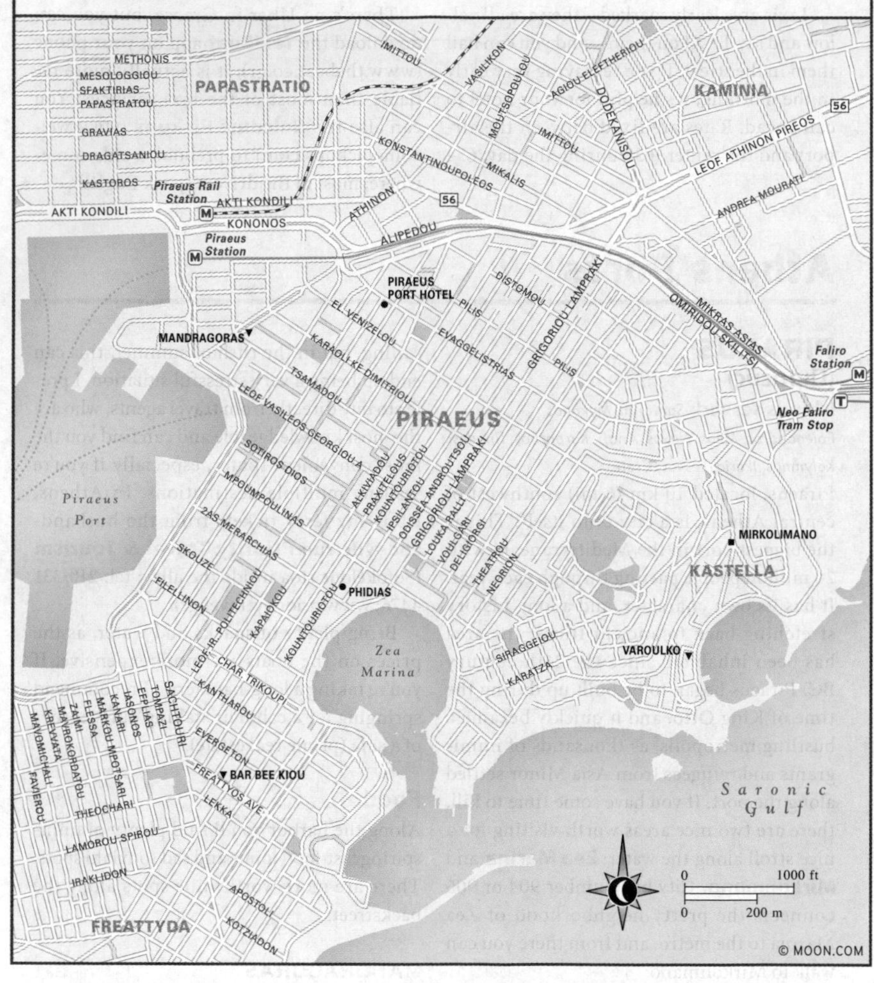

Michelin-starred meal at Varoulko before your boat departure. The chef's father was also a chef, on a ship, and the food is contemporary Greek cuisine with a nod to Piraeus.

BAR BEE KIOU

Leof. El. Venizelou 18; tel. 210/933 3318; www.mparmpeekiou.com/en; Sat.-Sun. 1pm-1am, Tues.-Fri. 6pm-1am; from €7

Consistently voted the best burger in Athens, Bar Bee Kiou serves up gigantic meat patties (there are some vegetarian options as well) with a variety of toppings, from avocado to blue cheese.

Accommodations

Most tourists don't choose to stay overnight in Piraeus (it's really not so far from Athens) unless the ferry time is inconvenient.

PIRAEUS PORT HOTEL

Evaggelistrias 12; tel. 210/412 1112; https://piraeusporthotel.com/en; from €70

If proximity is paramount, try this newly refurbished hotel within walking distance of the metro and port—the cleanest and nicest option of the bunch.

PHIDIAS

Kountouriotou 189; tel. 210/429 6480; www.hotelphidias.gr; from €80

This property is a lot nicer than most of the other port hotels. Though it's a 20-minute walk from the metro and the port, there's a free shuttle service. Rooms are simply decorated but clean, and staff is friendly.

Getting There

Piraeus is definitely hectic, and you should budget at least one hour beforehand to find your dock and minimize stress. The most convenient, cheapest way to get to the port from Athens is via the **metro** (Green Line; 30 minutes, every 10 minutes, 5am-midnight; €1.40). The **X96 Piraeus—Athens Airport Express bus** (Plateia Karaiskaki; 5 euros) stops at the airport and drops you off in front of the Piraeus metro stop.

When arriving in Piraeus, make sure to look at the departure dock on your ticket; the port is massive, and boats leave from different sections of the port. That is the most important piece of advice I can give you. There's a free **shuttle bus** that regularly runs between the ports from gate E7 to E1, the bus leaves from the metro. To get to gate E9, you'll need to take the buses outside of the port (any that starts with the number 8). You can also take a **taxi** between the gates; it's easier to hail a taxi in the rush of Piraeus than to call one.

RAFINA
(Ραφήνα)

Islands served: *Santorini, Mykonos, Crete*

This is the second port for boats headed to select Cycladic islands. It's pretty small and calm, and a good option for people who wanted to avoid the hectic bustle of Piraeus. Note that Rafina was terribly damaged in a fire in summer 2018 that killed 100 people. As of spring 2019, major reconstruction still needed to be done. That said, it's a good idea to contribute financially to Rafina by staying in its hotels and eating at its restaurants.

Purchasing Ferry Tickets

You can purchase your ferry tickets from any travel agent in Athens or the ticket booths directly on the port. For information on ferries try the **Rafina Port Authority** (tel. 22940/28888; www.rafinaport.gr).

Food

TA KAVOURIA TOU ASIMAKI

Directly on the port; tel. 22940/24551; 24/7 in summer

This is the first restaurant on the harbor, and the oldest. Grab a seat on the open-air top floor, and munch on marinated anchovies, a delicious fish soup, and crunchy salads while you watch the boats come in and out of the port.

Accommodations

AVRA HOTEL

3 Arafinidon Alon; tel. 22940/22780; www.hotelavra.gr; from €80

Just 200 meters (656 feet) away from the port, this large hotel is practical and comfortable. Rooms are simple and clean, with sea-facing balconies. It's located at the end of the port.

Getting There

From the Mavromateon bus terminal in central Athens, there are frequent **KTEL** buses to Rafina port (1 hour, 5:45am-10:30pm; €2.60). From the **airport,** buses leave in front of the arrivals hall (4:40am-10:20pm; €3.45, tickets can be purchased onboard).

LAVRION
(Λάβριων)

Islands served: *Santorini, Mykonos, Folegandros, Milos, Naxos*

Located 60 km (37 mi) southeast of Athens, Lavrion port has high-season catamarans to

Naxos, Milos, and Mykonos, as well as other western Cycladic islands. Despite a rich industrial past, it's a bit of a snooze today and not worth spending the night if you can avoid it.

Purchasing Ferry Tickets

There are ferry company kiosks on the port. Call the **Lavrion Port Authority** (tel. 229 202 5249) for ferry information, or visit www.openseas.gr. You can also buy tickets at a travel agency in Athens in advance.

Food

TO STEKI TOU MINA

Ermou 36; tel. 22920/24449; daily noon-midnight

This is a great little restaurant in an old stone building, where everything is homemade. They specialize in fish (grilled, fried, stuffed), and there's a nice variety of salads. The staff is friendly, and this is a worthwhile stop for a filling lunch before a long boat ride!

Accommodations

NIKOLAKAKIS ROOMS

Kon/nou Plioni 29; tel. 22920/27182; from €60

The best budget option that's close to the port, Nikolakakis Rooms is mostly worth staying at for convenience's sake. Rooms are small and a bit threadbare, but they're clean and the staff is friendly. Breakfast is included, but it's not that great.

Getting There

KTEL buses from Mavromateon bus station in central Athens run every 30 minutes to Lavrio (two hours; €5.30). From the **airport,** the buses park in front of the arrivals hall, but you'll have to change in Markopoulo. Don't fret—it's included in the price and time.

Santorini (Σαντορίνη)

Santorini (pop. 15,000) is even more beautiful than you've imagined, with strange red rock formations rising dramatically out of the sea, whitewashed blue-domed villages precariously perched on the island's edge, the depressed caldera, a smattering of colorful beaches, those glowing sunsets, and sprawling archaeological sites.

Santorini is an island born out of catastrophe: a devastating volcanic eruption and tsunami in 1400 BC that wiped out the Minoan civilization—and behind its obvious beauty, it has a strange, almost dark energy. Though it might seem unfathomable now, for much of its modern history, Santorini was a place of extreme poverty. Ironically, it's this hardship that created some of the island's most unique features:

Highlights

Look for ★ to find recommended sights, activities, dining, and lodging.

★ **Sunrise in Oia:** The best time to see Santorini's jewel is before the crowds have woken up, when the streets are mostly empty and bathed in a soft pink light (page 99).

★ **Manolos Village, Therasia:** The best views of Santorini are actually from the cliffside village of Malolos on Santorini's tiny sister island, Therasia, just a short boat ride from Oia (page 104).

★ **Wineries:** Sample the mineral-y assyrtiko and vinsanto varieties around the village of Exo Gonia; both are only found in Santorini (page 106).

★ **Tomato Industrial Museum:** This old tomato canning factory has been turned into a fantastic contemporary art space (page 109).

★ **Ancient Akrotiri:** This well-preserved ancient ruin is Santorini's version of Pompeii (page 111).

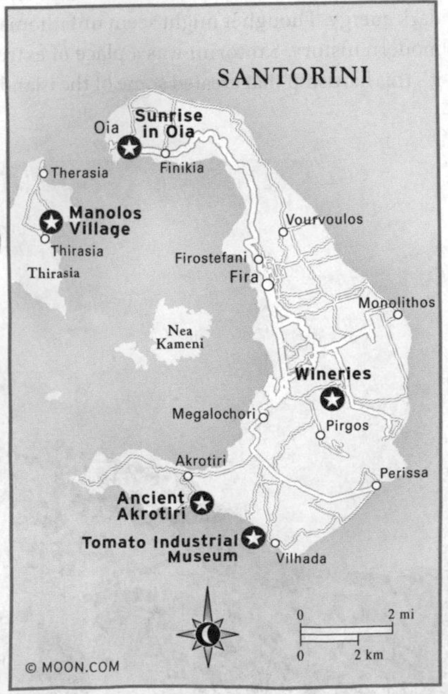

the volcanic soil that allows assyrtiko and vinsanto varieties to flourish, and the sweetly curved bioclimatic dwellings intended to protect the environment and shield homeowners from the harsh sun. Tourism slowly trickled in starting in the 1980s, and today, it's one of the most visited places in the world.

For many tourists, especially honeymooners, Santorini is the dream destination, and there can be a feeling that you need to do everything at once because it's a once-in-a-lifetime trip. I urge you to slow down and remember that the true charm of Santorini lies in its simplicity. No meal, museum, or shopping experience is going to compare with taking a moment (without your phone in your face, please!) to marvel at the incredible view from the caldera (from the Spanish for "cooking pot," a caldera is the depression that happens after a volcano eruption). The first time I saw it—at night, with the twinkle of the stars and the fuzzy light coming from the various hotels and restaurants on the island's lip—I audibly gasped. It's really something else.

PLANNING YOUR TIME

Unlike visiting other Greek islands, the best (and perhaps only) way to have a good time in Santorini is to **plan ahead.** It's not an island for introverts, but with some careful planning, you can have a great time and experience the softer side of Santorini.

You'll need at least two, preferably three, days on the island. Although some places are open year-round, the majority close for **January** and **February,** and/or have altered hours from **November** to **March.** My first tip is to avoid summertime, especially **July** and **August.** The crowds are intense, and the prices are astronomical. Santorini has a long season, and the best time to visit is in **April** or **October.** The weather is mild, the crowds have thinned out (though they never completely go away), and you can get great deals at even the most luxurious hotels. For those who really want privacy, **winter** is even better: the weather is usually mild, only the locals are around, and to be honest, you won't miss out by foregoing any beaches.

Most visitors will want to spend at least one night in **Oia** or **Fira**—the views alone are worth the high costs and crowds. If you want something more quiet, consider staying in **Pirga.**

INFORMATION AND SERVICES

There is no shortage of **banks** and **ATMs** around the island, particularly in Fira, Oia, and any of the coastal resort towns. Almost every place accepts credit and debit cards. The main **health clinic** is on the east side of Fira. It's open 24 hours for emergencies and has enough facilities to treat even major injuries (tel. 22860/21728; www.santorini-clinic.gr). There's a **police station** (tel. 22860/22649) in the center of Fira and a post office on Dekigala; the seasonal **information kiosk** is also in the center and open 9am-9pm weekdays.

GETTING THERE

I recommend arriving in Santorini by boat. The view of the red caldera as you approach the island from the sea is truly fantastic. If you're short on time, you can fly in.

Air

Santorini is one of the easiest islands in the Cycladic islands to get to. The **Santorini Airport** (JTR; tel. 22860/28400; www.santoriniairport.com), located on the central-east side of the island, has flights year-round from Athens with **Olympic Air** (www.olympicair.com), **RyanAir** (www.ryanair.com), and **Aegean Airlines** (www.aegeanair.com). You can find very cheap deals in the wintertime; during the high season there are regular connections from other European cities including London, Edinburgh, and Rome.

Previous: Oia in Santorini, Greece, famous for romantic and beautiful sunsets; Santorini is born of a volcano, and the lip of a caldera looks like a slice of cake; donkeys are a traditional way to get around.

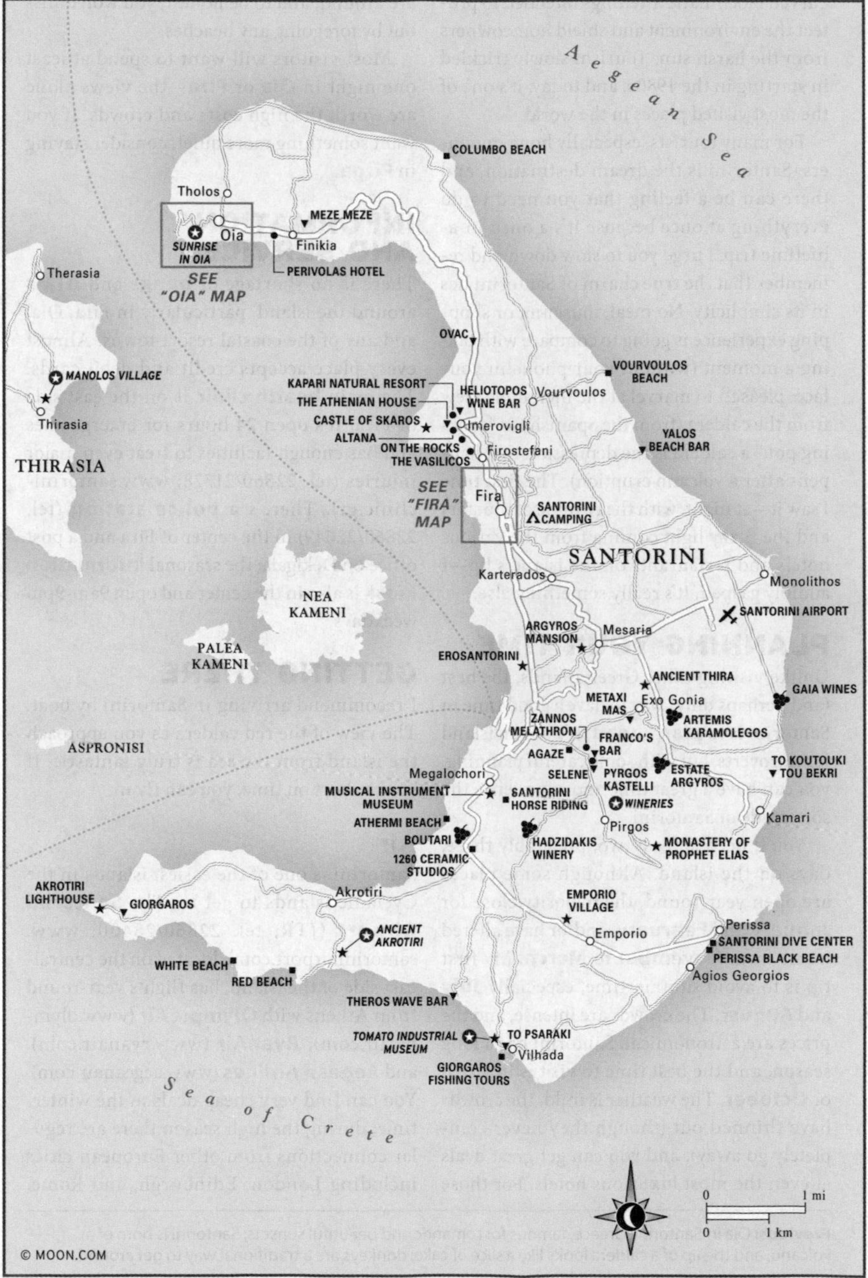
Santorini
Aegean Sea
COLUMBO BEACH
Tholos
MEZE MEZE
SUNRISE IN OIA
Oia
Finikia
PERIVOLAS HOTEL
SEE "OIA" MAP
Therasia
MANOLOS VILLAGE
Thirasia
THIRASIA
OVAC
VOURVOULOS BEACH
KAPARI NATURAL RESORT
HELIOTOPOS WINE BAR
Vourvoulos
THE ATHENIAN HOUSE
CASTLE OF SKAROS
Imerovigli
ALTANA
ON THE ROCKS
THE VASILICOS
Firostefani
YALOS BEACH BAR
SEE "FIRA" MAP
Fira
SANTORINI CAMPING
SANTORINI
Karterados
Monolithos
SANTORINI AIRPORT
NEA KAMENI
ARGYROS MANSION
Mesaria
PALEA KAMENI
EROSANTORINI
ANCIENT THIRA
GAIA WINES
METAXI MAS
Exo Gonia
ARTEMIS KARAMOLEGOS
ZANNOS MELATHRON
FRANCO'S BAR
ASPRONISI
AGAZE
SELENE
PYRGOS KASTELLI
ESTATE ARGYROS
TO KOUTOUKI TOU BEKRI
Megalochori
MUSICAL INSTRUMENT MUSEUM
SANTORINI HORSE RIDING
WINERIES
ATHERMI BEACH
Pirgos
Kamari
BOUTARI
HADZIDAKIS WINERY
MONASTERY OF PROPHET ELIAS
1260 CERAMIC STUDIOS
AKROTIRI LIGHTHOUSE
GIORGAROS
Akrotiri
EMPORIO VILLAGE
Perissa
ANCIENT AKROTIRI
Emporio
SANTORINI DIVE CENTER
PERISSA BLACK BEACH
WHITE BEACH
RED BEACH
Agios Georgios
THEROS WAVE BAR
TOMATO INDUSTRIAL MUSEUM
TO PSARAKI
Vilhada
GIORGAROS FISHING TOURS
Sea of Crete
0
1 mi
0
1 km
© MOON.COM

Crowd Control

In many ways, Santorini is a victim of its own success. Construction has continued at a neck-breaking speed, and in many areas convenience has trumped quality. The endless throngs of people means zero privacy along the caldera; you're often looking at something through someone else's camera. A few tips to help make the most of your stay:

- Avoid visiting in **summer,** especially July and August.
- Visit **Fira** and **Oia** early in the morning, and avoid the sunset hour in Fira—especially in the summer. To be honest, you can also skip Fira altogether.
- Avoid traveling with a big **rolling suitcase** if you're staying in Oia, unless you've booked a hotel on the edge of town. It already takes an eternity and a lot of cursing to navigate the crowded streets and stairs of Oia in the middle of the day at the height of summer—add a giant suitcase and you're just asking for a bad introduction to the village.
- Escape Oia and Fira. Most of the crowds congegate in these towns, but there's a whole island out there to explore! Get out of these hot spots and head to the lesser-known parts of the island: **Emborio, Finikia, Colombo Beach,** and **Pyrgos** all showcase the charm of Santorini without the packs of people.
- For the views and sunsets without the crowds, you could skip Santorini and head to **Anafi** instead.

Note that the crush of visitors extends to the airport, and you should arrive early as the terminals can be chaotic.

There are regular buses to and from Fira's main bus station and the airport (20 minutes, 7am-9pm; €1.80) and most hotels can help you arrange a taxi or airport transfer. A taxi from Fira or Oia to the airport costs around €45.

Ferry

There are frequent ferries, including high-speed ferries, leaving from **Piraeus** and other **Cycladic islands** (4 hours for the high-speed, 9 hours for regular ferry). The main port in Santorini is **Athinios,** located on the western coast, a 20-minute drive from Fira. The first part of the drive consists of dizzying switchbacks up the cliff. Athinios is a surprisingly well-managed panic of neon signs, buses, taxis, and travel providers. Most hotels arrange for transportation up the crazy switchbacks to Fira (from around €10).

GETTING AROUND

Santorini is a bit tricky to negotiate. A **car** is your best option, especially if you want to visit the less explored parts of the island, although driving in Santorini is incredibly hectic.

Bus

The island is serviced by **KTEL Santorini Buses** (http://ktel-santorini.gr; tel. 22860/25404), with regular departures to Oia, Fira, Akrotiri, Kamari, and Perissa, as well as the port and airport. Tickets can be purchased directly on the bus (between €1.80 and €2.40, depending on the destination). Check the KTEL website for up-to-date schedules and prices. Bus service thins out at night, and during the summer, it's as crowded as the subway in Tokyo.

Car

Santorini's roads are narrow, the traffic is heavy, especially around Fira and Oia, and finding **parking** requires a mix of luck, prayer, and sheer skill. Also note that local drivers, likely exasperated by all the confused tourist drivers, can be incredibly aggressive.

In the high season, **car rentals** start from €50 per day, and **scooters/four-wheelers** can be rented from €25 a day. It can be useful to book ahead of time, especially if you are coming in the summer months. In addition to the international companies, try **Nomikos Travel** (tel. 22860/24940; www.nomikostravel.gr) in Fira. Parking, at least, is usually free.

Taxi

Taxis are relatively affordable, though there can be a lengthy waiting time in the summer. The main **taxi stand** in Fira is around the corner from the **bus station** (tel. 22860/23951, 22860/22555). If you're staying at a high-end hotel, they can usually arrange transport for you around the island.

Itinerary Ideas

DAY 1

There are a few moments in life worth splurging on, and getting a room in Oia or Imerovigli with a view of the caldera is one of them. An entire day can (should) be spent lounging poolside and marveling at the view. I have few other recommendations for you on this day: just relax, enjoy the view, and swim in the pool. When you feel the need to stretch your legs:

1. Go for a walk in Oia, stopping at **Kyrkos Art Gallery** or the Musical Instrument Museum.
2. Head to Fira and walk the 600 **Stairs to Fira Skala** for a picturesque view of boats bobbing in the sea, then take the Santorini Cable Car back up the hillside.
3. Have dinner in Fira at the eccentric **Koukoumavlos** (or slink back into your hotel and order room service).

DAY 2

An early morning can be spent quietly walking around Oia, before driving to the island's center to visit archaeological ruins, visit some of Santorini's finest wineries, and catch the sunset from a Venetian castle.

1. Wake up early in the morning to stroll through **Oia** (mostly uninterrupted). Return to your hotel for breakfast.
2. Head to **Ancient Akrotiri** for a walk through Santorini's answer to Pompeii.
3. Stop for lunch at **Metaxi Mas** in Exo Gonia for cuisine that's a mix of Crete and Santorini.
4. Fortified, visit at least two of the area's wineries, starting with **Artemis Karamolegos.** Make sure to sample assytriko and vinsanto.
5. Drive up to nearby Pyrgos for an evening stroll. Afterward, catch the sunset from the top of the village at **Pyrgos Kastelli.**
6. Stay in Pyrgos for a fantastic dinner at **Selene.**

Itinerary Ideas

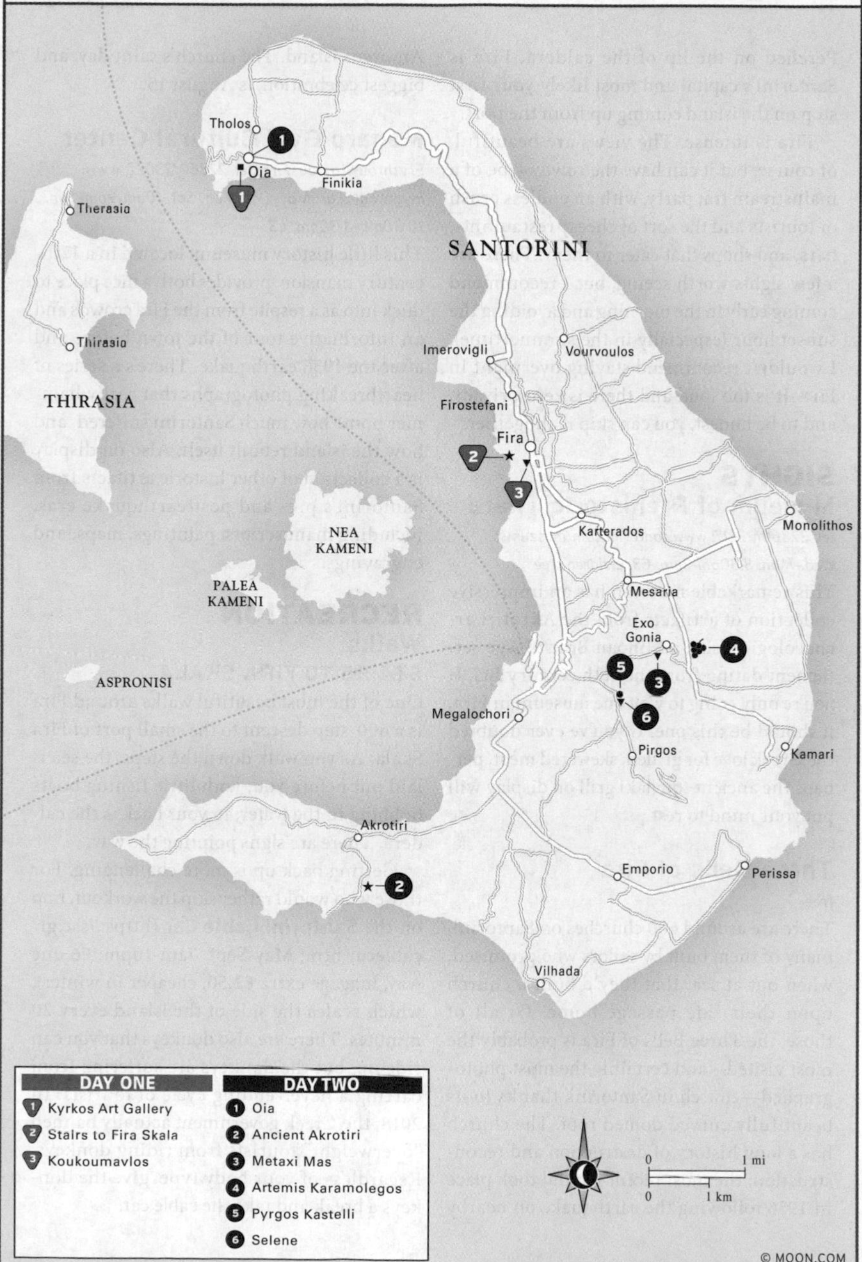

Fira

Φηρά

Perched on the lip of the caldera, Fira is Santorini's capital and most likely your first stop on the island coming up from the port.

Fira is intense. The views are beautiful, of course, but it can have the rowdy vibe of a mainstream frat party, with an endless crush of tourists and the sort of cheesy restaurants, bars, and shops that cater to them. There are a few sights worth seeing, but I recommend coming early in the morning and avoiding the sunset hour (especially in the summertime). I wouldn't recommend staying overnight in Fira. It is too loud and there is zero privacy, and to be honest, you can skip it altogether.

SIGHTS

Museum of Prehistoric Thera

tel. 22860/22217; www.santorini.com/museums; Wed.-Mon. 8:30am-3pm; €3, children free

This remarkable museum has an impressive collection of artifacts from the Akrotiri archaeological site: a Minoan Bronze Age settlement dating from the 16th century BC. If you're only going to visit one museum in Fira, it should be this one. If you've ever doubted the Greek love for grilled, skewered meat, perhaps the ancient souvlaki grill on display will put your mind to rest.

Three Bells of Fira

free

There are around 600 churches on Santorini, many of them built by sailors who promised, when out at sea, that they'd built a church upon their safe passage home. Of all of those, the Three Bells of Fira is probably the most visited—and certainly the most photographed—church in Santorini, thanks to its beautifully curved domed roof. The church has a long history of destruction and reconstruction; the most recent rebuild took place in 1956 following the earthquake on nearby Amorgos island. The church's saint day, and biggest celebration, is August 15.

Megaro Gyzi Cultural Center

Erythrou Stavrou, Fira; tel. 22860/23077; www.mygarogyzi.gr; May-Oct. Mon.-Sat. 10am-9pm, Sun. 10:30am-4:30pm; €3

This little history museum, located in a 17th-century mansion, provides both a nice place to duck into as a respite from the Fira crowds and an informative tour of the town before and after the 1956 earthquake. There's a series of heartbreaking photographs that really hammer home how much Santorini suffered, and how the island rebuilt itself. Also on display is a collection of other historic artifacts from Santorini's pre- and post-earthquake eras, including manuscripts, paintings, maps, and engravings.

RECREATION

Walks

STAIRS TO FIRA SKALA

One of the most beautiful walks around Fira is a 600-step descent to the small port of Fira Skala. As you walk down the steps, the sea is laid out before you, with little fishing boats bobbing in the water; to your back is the caldera. There are signs pointing the way.

Getting back up is more challenging. For those who would rather skip the workout, hop on the **Santorini Cable Car** (https://ssc.gr/cablecar.htm; May-Sept. 7am-10pm; €6 one way, luggage extra €2.50, cheaper in winter), which scales the side of the island every 20 minutes. There are also donkeys that you can ride up, but the donkeys are suffering from carting a never-ending cycle of tourists. In 2018, the Greek government actually banned "overweight" tourists from riding donkeys. Regardless of your body type, give the donkeys a break and take the cable car.

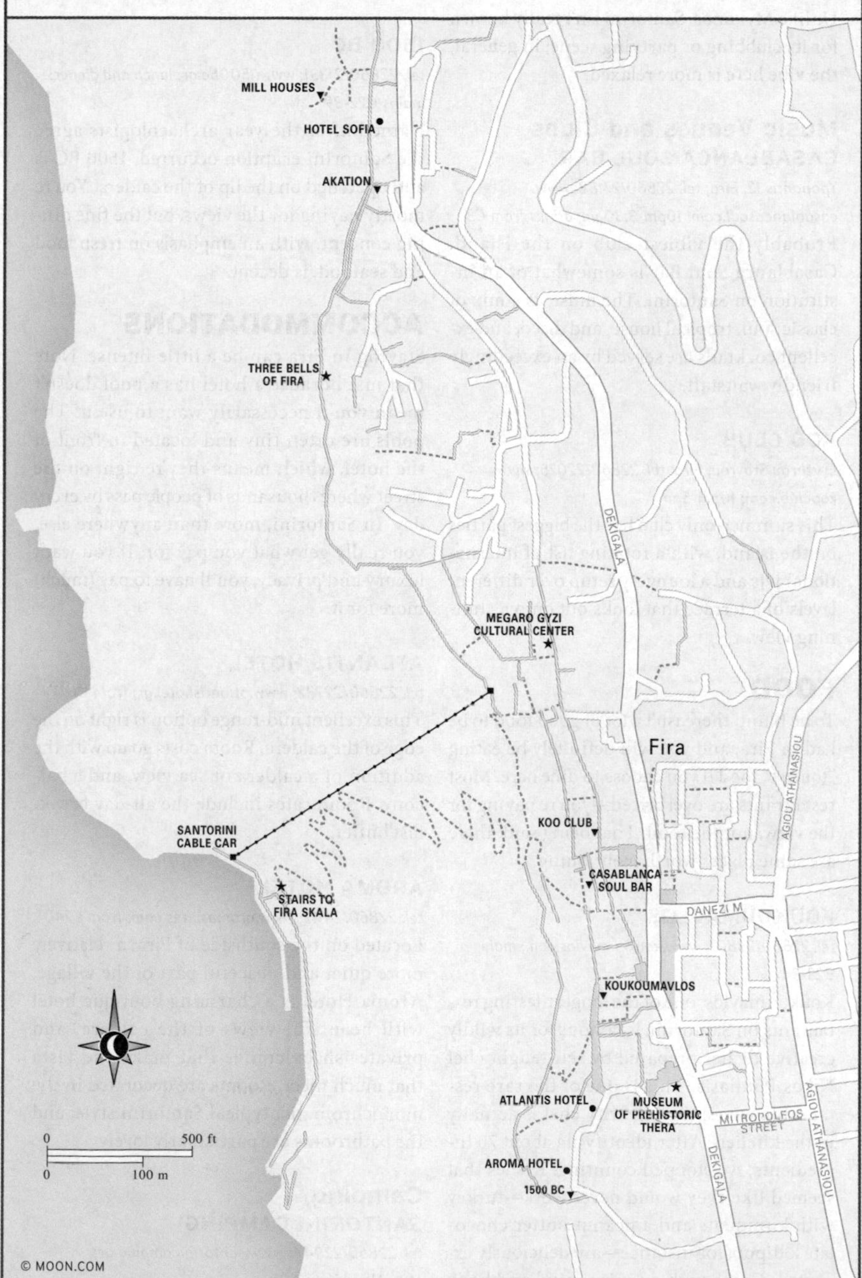
Fira
MILL HOUSES
HOTEL SOFIA
AKATION
THREE BELLS OF FIRA
DEKIGALA
MEGARO GYZI CULTURAL CENTER
Fira
AGIOU ATHANASIOU
KOO CLUB
SANTORINI CABLE CAR
CASABLANCA SOUL BAR
STAIRS TO FIRA SKALA
DANEZI M.
KOUKOUMAVLOS
ATLANTIS HOTEL
MUSEUM OF PREHISTORIC THERA
MITROPOLEOS STREET
AGIOU ATHANASIOU
DEKIGALA
0
500 ft
0
100 m
AROMA HOTEL
1500 BC
© MOON.COM

NIGHTLIFE AND ENTERTAINMENT

Unlike Mykonos, Santorini isn't really known for its clubbing or partying scene; in general, the vibe here is more relaxed.

Music Venues and Clubs

CASABLANCA SOUL BAR

Ypapantis 12, Fira; tel. 22860/27188; www.casablancasoul.com; 10pm-3:30am; drinks from €3

Probably the vibiest club on the island, Casablanca Soul Bar is somewhat of an institution on Santorini. The music is a mix of classic soul, tropical house, and disco, and excellent cocktails are served by an exceedingly friendly waitstaff.

KOO CLUB

Erythrou Stavrou, Fira; tel. 22860/22025; www.kooclub.com; 10pm-5am

This summer-only club has the biggest parties on the island, with a rotating list of international DJs and a lounge-y setup over different levels of a terrace that looks out onto a stunning view.

FOOD

To be blunt, there isn't a lot of good food to be had in Fira, and you will definitely be eating "tourist" food if you choose to dine here. Most restaurants are overpriced—you're paying for the view, not the food. That being said, there are some places worth mentioning.

KOUKOUMAVLOS

tel. 22860/23807; www.koukoumavlos.com; mains €28-34

Koukoumavlos, one of the longest-lasting restaurants on Santorini, is famous for its wildly creative dishes prepared by self-taught chef Nikos Pouliasis. This is one of the rare restaurants where the celebrity chef is actually in the kitchen. After identifying about 70 ingredients, we stopped counting. Dishes that seemed like they would never work—turkey with kumquats and a peanut butter chocolate lollipop, for instance—are deliciously executed. Come with an open mind and book the €74 tasting menu—an excellent value. Reservations are required.

1500 BC

tel. 22860/21331; www.1500bc.gr; lunch and dinner; mains €22-39

Named after the year archaeologists agree the Santorini eruption occurred, 1500 BC is aptly perched on the lip of the caldera. You're mostly paying for the views, but the fine dining concept, with an emphasis on fresh food and seafood, is decent.

ACCOMMODATIONS

Staying in Fira can be a little intense. Note that just because a hotel has a pool doesn't mean you'll necessarily want to use it. The pools are often tiny and located in front of the hotel, which means they're right on the street where thousands of people pass by every day. In Santorini, more than anywhere else, you really get what you pay for: If you want luxury and privacy, you'll have to pay (much) more for it.

ATLANTIS HOTEL

tel. 22860/22232; www.atlantishotel.gr; from €120

This excellent mid-range option is right on the edge of the caldera. Room costs go up with the addition of a caldera or sea view, and a balcony. Room rates include the all-day breakfast buffet.

AROMA HOTEL

tel. 22860/24112; www.aromasuites.com; from €240

Located on the southside of Fira, a relatively more quiet and peaceful part of the village, Aroma Hotel is a charming boutique hotel with beautiful views of the caldera, and private-ish balconies that make the vista that much nicer. Rooms are decorated in the monochromatic, typical Santorini style, and the bathrooms are particularly lovely.

Camping

SANTORINI CAMPING

tel. 22860/22944; www.santorinicamping.gr; Mar.-Nov.; from €10

If you're looking to do Santorini on a budget, the cheapest deal you can get is with Santorini Camping. You can park your car or RV here, sleep in a double bed in a tent (€20), or get a bed in the dorms (€30). Big spenders can spend €60 for a private double room. It's popular with backpackers, who congregate around the poolside bar. Located 700 meters (2,300 feet) east of Fira's main drag.

GETTING THERE AND AROUND

Bus

KTEL Santorini Buses connects Fira with the port, the airport (20 minutes, 7am-9pm; €1.80), Oia (two buses per hour), Akrotiri, Kamari, and Perissa. Fira's **main bus station** (tel. 22860/23951, 22860/22555) is on Mitropoleos Street between Dekigala and Agiou Athanasiou.

Car

By car, the port in Athinios is 20 minutes from Fira; the drive starts with climbing a series of switchbacks up the cliff. Traffic is heavy around Fira, but parking is usually free, although finding and fitting into a suitable spot can be tricky.

Taxi

A taxi from the airport to Fira costs around €45. Most hotels can help you arrange a taxi. The main **taxi stand** in Fira is around the corner from the bus station.

Near Fira

As its popularity has grown and construction has sprawled outward, Fira has merged with the two neighboring villages of Imerovigli and Firostefáni (both within walking distance).

FIROSTEFÁNI (Φηροστεφάνι)

Firostefáni may once have been a separate village from Fira, but these days, the tourist sprawl has encroached into Firostefáni, and there's no distinction between it and its larger neighbor to the south. You'll continue to see the same beautiful, quintessential architecture, but it's a bit quieter than Fira, which can make it a nicer place to stay.

Food

AKATION

Firostefáni shore promenade; tel. 22860/22336; aktaionsantorini.com; Mar.-late Oct. noon-3pm and 7pm-midnight; from €10

Around since 1922, this family-run tavern (now on its third generation of owners) is considered the oldest on the island. For nearly a century, Akation has resisted the allure of tourist-trap food, and dutifully churns out affordably priced, delicious taverna food with a focus on fresh and local ingredients. Try the *skordomakarona* (pasta with garlic), octopus with fava and sweet capers, or anything else that showcases the best of Santorini's produce (tomatoes, fava, arugula). Note that the owners are quite strict about their opening and closing times.

Accommodations

HOTEL SOFIA

tel. 22860/22802; www.sofiahotelsantorini.com; from €100

Located just 700 meters from Fira, the small Hotel Sofia is a good budget option (by Santorini standards), featuring clean, spacious rooms with four-poster beds. There are no caldera views, but there's a small pool (big enough for a half lap, though not entirely private) and a lounge café bar, and Fira is just a short walk away.

MILL HOUSES

tel. 22860/27117; www.millhouses.gr; €350

If you want caldera views, private pools, and Bulgari toiletries, the elegant studios of Mill

Houses are right for you. It's got the white-on-white luxury typical to Santorini, with enough romance to lure honeymooners. Medium sized, but there's enough privacy to make it feel smaller than it is.

IMEROVIGLI (Ημεροβίγλι)

Farther up north from Firostefáni, but still largely an extension of Fira, is Imerovigli. Standing at the highest point of the island, it's considered "the balcony of Santorini" for its fantastic views of the caldera.

Sights

CASTLE OF SKAROS

always open; free

Skaros was a medieval town fortified in the 13th century by the Byzantine Empire. Located on a steep cliff just a short walk from Imerovigli, all that's left of the town, which was deserted by its residents in the 18th century, are the ruins of the castle. It's a great sunset viewing point and has stupendous views, but it's also a very popular hiking and photography spot with tourists—try to come very early in the morning during the high season.

Nightlife and Entertainment

HELIOTOPOS WINE BAR

tel. 22860/23670; https://winebar-santorini.gr; 6pm-10:30pm

Snuggly located inside of a typical caldera cave, Heliotopos Wine Bar serves up a great variety of Santorini's most famous wines (the food, which is mainly pizza, is much less inspiring). In addition to the atmospheric cave lounge, there's a beautiful terrace with lovely views of the caldera.

Food

THE ATHENIAN HOUSE

tel. 22860/36420; www.theathenianhouse.com; 6pm-12:30pm; from €25

Like the name suggests, The Athenian House evokes all the splendor of a neoclassical Athenian house, though built into a cave and perched on the caldera. The menu is nouveau Greek (think deconstructed moussaka, tzatziki with truffle), and the attentive staff takes good care of guests, occasionally offering up free glasses of digestif and adorable keychains. It's also one of the few restaurants that helpfully accommodates those eating gluten-free or vegan.

OVAC

tel. 22860/28900; ovac.gr; 11am-midnight; from €16

The all-day Ovac (breakfast-dinner) is actually a glitzy pool lounge where iced coffee slowly morphs into sushi and cocktails as the sun goes down. At the fine dining restaurant, the emphasis is on Mediterranean fusion and fresh fish; the raw bar is their signature.

Accommodations

ALTANA

tel. 22860/23240; www.altana.gr; €320

Occupying a series of converted wine cellars from the 1800s, this boutique hotel oozes charm and history. It's perched on the caldera with an infinity pool, and rooms come with an indoor or outdoor jacuzzi. Founded by twins with a great sense of kindness and hospitality, they mix a mean cocktail in their on-site *kafeneio*.

ON THE ROCKS

tel. 22860/23889; www.onrocks.net; from €400

This small white and blue hotel, perched on the caldera is charming and luxurious, with a great spa, pool, and beautiful balconies. A nice perk is the free breakfast delivered to your room, so you can enjoy with privacy.

THE VASILICOS

tel. 22860/23143; www.thevasilicos.com; from €405

Once the private hideaway of an art collector, The Vasilicos (the name is a play on both basil and reference to Greek royalty) is a design-forward boutique hotel. There are only a handful of rooms to choose from, all with Cocomat bedding and Apivita products, and

1: Old Greek church and caldera over the Aegean Sea **2:** view of beautiful Firostefáni village with typical Greek white architecture

1

2

featuring terraces, plunge pools, or jacuzzies (or some combination of the three). Be sure to request breakfast in bed.

KAPARI NATURAL RESORT

tel. 22860/21120; www.kaparisantorini.gr; from €500

This environmentally friendly natural resort is the essence of Santorini distilled. Everything is curved, white, and natural-looking. It has all the amenities you'd expect of a luxury hotel, plus extras like a pillow bar and an organic kitchen. With only 14 rooms, this resort never feels overly crowded.

MESSARIA
(Μεσσαρια)

Located 3 km (1.75 mi) south of Fira, the small town of Messaria was built up in the 17th century and became an important landmark during the 19th century, when it served as the island's center of winemaking. The old wealth of the village is still apparent in the crumbling mansions, some of which are open to the public.

Sights

ARGYROS MANSION

tel. 22860/31669; www.argyrosmansion.com; May-Oct. Mon.-Thurs. 10am-6pm

Peak into what life was like for the Santorini aristocracy in the past. Built in 1888, this was the home of George Argyros, an important winemaker at the time. Though part of the home was destroyed during the earthquake, it's been lovingly restored. Tilt your head backward to admire the fantastically painted ceilings. They offer hour-long guided tours in English and Greek. Either call ahead to reserve or just show up, though you might have to wait a little.

Accommodations

★ EROSANTORINI

tel. 211 012 9116; www.erosantorini.com; from €670

If you're looking for true privacy, look no further than this uber-exclusive four-room villa, situated on a two-acre plot of land with stunning views. It feels more like a stay at a friend's house than a hotel, albeit a very fancy friend with impeccable taste. It's named after Eros, the god of love, for a reason: The vibe is very sexy, and there are mirrors over the beds and private Jacuzzis.

EXO GIALOS
(Έχω Γιαλός)

This small beach town is the closest beach to Fira (2.5 km/1.5 mi away). It's a blackish sand beach (the black sand is mixed with red pebbles) and it's easy to access from the coastal road. The beach is mostly organized, with lawn chairs and beach bars.

Nightlife and Entertainment

YALOS BEACH BAR

Exo Gialos; tel. 22860/25816; yalos-santorini.com; all day

This upscale beach bar features a gastronomic menu, yoga classes, DJ events, and yacht services, plus the usual lounge chairs and umbrellas.

VOURVOULOS BEACH
(Βουρβούλου)

This is one of the more secluded beaches on the island, and is mostly used by locals. It's a black pebble beach, and there's not a whole lot to do here, which is the point. If you're looking to escape the crowds and go swimming, check out this spot. From Fira it's 5.4 km (3 mi, 10 minutes) northeast; from Exo Gialos you'll have to cut back up to the main coastal road and then back down to the beach (4 km/2.5 mi, 7 minutes).

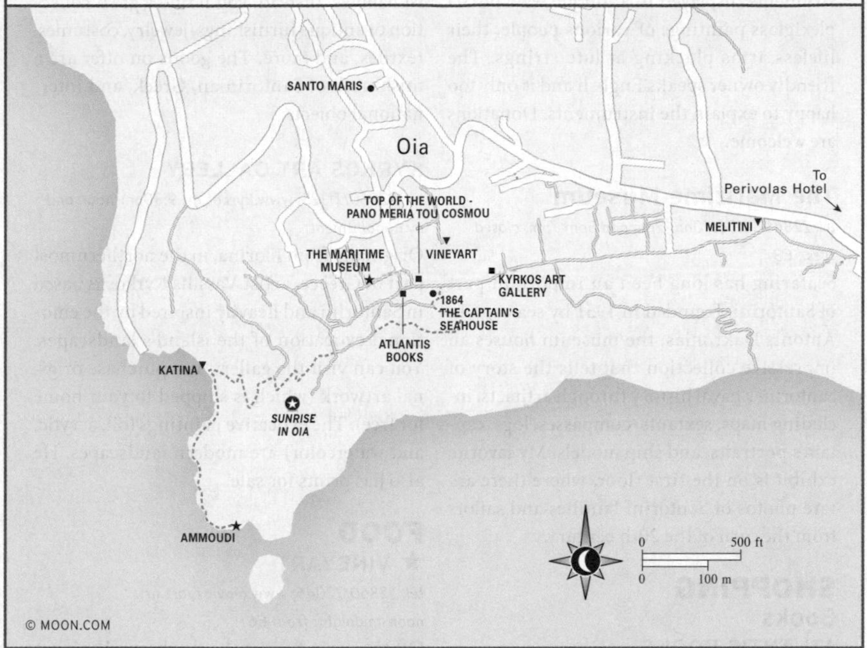

Oia

Oía

Surrounded by water on the northwestern tip of Santorini, Oia lives up to the hype. This might be one of the most beautiful villages in the world. The whitewashed houses carved into the red caldera, the sparkling blue hotel pools, and the tiny alleyways snaking through the village make for a truly unique place.

★ SUNRISE IN OIA

Oia can be overwhelmingly packed, and the throngs of tourists do diminish the vibe, especially along the town's main street, Nikolaou Nomiko and it's hard to appreciate quite how beautiful the village is. If you are visiting in the summer, I suggest wandering through Oia in the very early morning, when everyone else is still asleep and everything is bathed in a soft pink light. You'll be able to walk through the main thoroughfare with room to breathe.

SIGHTS

Ammoudi

Located 200 steps down from the Oia (you can either walk up the stairs or take a donkey ride), this colorful fishing port is nestled around a small bay. It's a lovely place to visit for a meal of fresh fish, and to relax while soaking up the view.

Museum of Ancient, Byzantine Musical Instruments

Megalochori, Oia; tel. 22860/72000; 10am-8:30pm, closed Mon.; free

Located in the old community storehouse

of Oia, this is a great little collection of Byzantine and post-Byzantine Cycladic instruments displayed in a unique way: on 3D plexiglass paintings of various people, their lifeless arms plucking at lute strings. The friendly owner speaks English and is only too happy to explain the instruments. Donations are welcome.

The Maritime Museum

tel. 22860/71156; 10am-2pm and 5pm-7pm, closed Tues.; €3

Seafaring has long been an important part of Santorini. Founded in 1951 by sea captain Antonis Dakronias, the museum houses an impressive collection that tells the story of Santorini's naval history through artifacts, including maps, sextants, compasses, logs, captain's portraits, and ship models. My favorite exhibit is on the first floor, where there are rare photos of Santorini families and sailors from the turn of the 20th century.

SHOPPING

Books

ATLANTIS BOOKS

tel. 22860/72346; http://atlantisbooks.org; summer Mon.-Sun. 10am-10pm

This is definitely the coolest bookstore in Santorini, and it's up there with the most interesting ones in the world. It's an enchanting "hobbit cave" of a shop, filled with quality books in a half dozen languages—the antidote to all those airport paperback thrillers. Opened in 2004 by a group of expat friends, Atlantis Books is somewhat of an eccentric community gathering spot that attracts bohemian personalities. If you're the sort of nice, respectable tourist who understands the vibe of Atlantis, the in-the-know owners might even give you a few secret Santorini tips.

Gifts

TOP OF THE WORLD - PANO MERIA TOU COSMOU

tel. 22860/71587; www.santorini-greek.gr; summer Mon.-Sun. 10am-10pm

This delightful *cabinet de curiosités* is the only shop on Oia's main streets not selling tourist baubles. Instead, you'll find a great collection of antique furnishings, jewelry, costumes, textiles, and more. The goods on offer are a mishmash of Santorinian, Greek, and international objects.

KYRKOS ART GALLERY

tel. 22860/71325; www.kyrkos.gr; 9:30am-noon and by appointment

Originally from Florina, in the northernmost part of Greece, artist Vassilis Kyrkos is based in Santorini and heavily inspired by the emotional evocation of the island's landscapes. You can visit the gallery and purchase original artwork (which is shipped to your home for free). The evocative paintings (oil, acrylic, and watercolor) are modern landscapes. He also has prints for sale.

FOOD

★ VINEYART

tel. 22860/72046; www.oiavineyart.gr; noon-midnight; from €6

Off the main tourist thoroughfare, Vineyart opened in 2015 and is a favorite of locals. It's quiet and spacious, which is rare in Oia, and offers an extensive menu of local meze dishes and the best wines in Santorini. There's no view; instead, the focus is on good food, good drinks, and good people. Let the sommelier guide your drink choices, and try the meat and cheese plate, eggplant salad, and other mezes. Dessert (like pistachio *halva*) is also excellent.

MELITINI

tel. 22860/72343; https://melitinioia.com; Mar.-Nov.; from €6

This spot offers family-recipe Greek tapas (spicy sausages, aubergine salad, *saganaki*) served in a beautiful Cycladic white villa with a rooftop terrace. Service is friendly, but the

1: the sunset over Oia **2:** The kooky Musical Instrument Museum has unique 3D plexiglass paintings. **3:** caldera sunset

place can fill up in the summer, so call ahead to book a reservation.

KATINA

Ammoudi; tel. 22860/72343; https://fishtavernkatina.gr; Mon.-Sat. noon-10:30pm, Sun noon-9pm; from €9

There are several fish tavernas to choose from in Ammoudi, but Katina, which has been around for more than 30 years, is a favorite of both locals and tourists. You can order fresh fish and seafood by the kilo, and wash it down with a Santorini wine. Call for reservations.

ACCOMMODATIONS

It's worth splurging on a luxury hotel in Oia, if only for a night. After all, the best thing about Oia is the view, and it's marvelous to spend a day lounging on a terrace doing nothing but staring into the horizon. Note that even the most private hotels are still not, uh, exactly private—you can hear people laughing from halfway across the caldera—and because the rooms are built on terraces, it's also very easy to spy on people accidentally. At one fancy hotel, I looked up to see that a woman had removed all her clothes and was posing for her partner (and her selfie stick) in front of what she assumed was her private terrace. Most people, ironically, come to Oia for romance, but just know that unless you're indoors, there are several dozen people witnessing your romantic moment.

Over €300

1864 THE CAPTAIN'S SEAHOUSE

tel. 22860/71983; www.sea-captains-house.com; €400

As the name suggests, this former captain's sea house has been transformed into a luxury boutique hotel with four suites. There are beautiful views out onto the caldera, and breakfast is included.

SANTO MARIS

tel. 211 234 0692; www.santomaris.gr; from €500

Located in the northwest corner of Oia (and connected to the village by a 5-minute walk on the hotel's private path) this is one of the more private hotels around. The design is a mix of Cycladic sensibility with boho-chic touches, and between the four swimming pools, spa center, two bars and restaurants, and private jacuzzis, there's enough to do in the hotel that you won't want to leave for a couple of days.

★ PERIVOLAS HOTEL

tel. 22860/71308; perivolas.com; from €600

There's a reason Perivolas Hotel is featured in the book *1,000 Places to See Before You Die*. This was one of the first hotels in Oia, and it remains the most private; it's located just outside the village. This cluster of white cave dwellings is absolutely sumptuous, and everything, from the bed to the couch to the shower, is harmoniously built in. It's a family-run hotel, and while the service is always impeccable, it's also friendly and human in a way other hotels aren't. Some rooms feature private pools; there's also an excellent restaurant with delicious breakfast, a free bottle of vinsanto upon arrival, and an infinity pool with stunning views.

GETTING THERE

There are two **buses** per hour between Fira and Oia. You won't need a car if you are planning to spend the day just in Oia.

1: the view of Oia from the Perivolas Hotel **2:** Next to Oia, the charming village of Finikia is a locals-only spot.

1
2

Near Oia

THERASIA

(Θηρασια)

Visiting the tiny neighboring island of Therasia feels a bit like stepping back in time 50 years, as it's exactly like Santorini, with all the wildness and beauty, and a fraction of the tourists. Electricity came in 1980, drinkable water in 1999, the first paved road in 2008, and an ATM machine most recently. Therasia was actually once part of Santorini; before the volcanic eruption of 1700 BC wrenched the island into pieces, the whole thing was called Strongyli. For most of its history, Therasia was ignored and sparsely inhabited; the 19th century saw an interest in and exploitation of its pumice. It still only boasts a tiny population (160 people) and just a handful of buildings, but it's got the best views of Santorini and makes for an excellent day trip.

★ Manolos Village

Head to the village of Manolos, which is located on the cliff and has the best views of Santorini: you'll see the brick-red layers of Santorini, sandwiched between the azure Aegean on the bottom and the sugar cube white houses at the top.

Getting There

Therasia is just a short 20-minute **boat ride** away from Santorini. The fastest way is to take a boat from **Ammoudi port** near Oia (€5). Check the hours at the port; there are 2-3 boats per day in the summer. The last boat back to Santorini departs at 5pm.

FINIKIA

(Φινίκια)

Just a short walk (approximately 1.5 km/1 mile) east from Oia and off the caldera is the charming little settlement of Finikia. It's home to one of the island's best restaurants, and remains a very local place. If you can, the best time to visit Finikia is in October for their annual *panigiri,* which attracts locals from all over the village and remains one of the island's best kept secrets.

Festivals and Events

AGIA MATRON PANIGIRI

Village center, Finikia; Oct. 20; donations welcome

On October 20, locals from across Santorini (and even neighboring islands like Anafi) come to Finikia to celebrate Agia Matron. You'll hear church bells ringing at 7pm, which signals the start of evening prayers and services. The party really gets started after 10pm though: Big cauldrons of meat and rice bubble away, the instruments come out (as does the wine), and everyone starts dancing till 7am. It's really a locals-only event—by the end of autumn, most tourists are gone anyway—but if you happen to be here, it's one of the best *panigiri* on Santorini.

Food

★ MEZE MEZE

Village center, Finikia; tel. 22860/72242; May-early Oct. 1pm-11:30pm; cash only, from €10

A small restaurant in the village center with a charming terrace, Meze Meze serves up traditional Santorini dishes, like tomato fritters, all made with local ingredients. There's no caldera view, and that's the point: The focus is on fresh and delicious food. In the summer months, it's best to call early for a reservation.

COLUMBO BEACH

Columbo, considered the most secluded beach in Santorini, is about as secret as something can be on this island. It's close to the active part of the volcano so water can get really warm, and the water is clear enough that it's good for snorkeling. There's no bus route here, and you can only access the beach by car or motorbike. It's located 9 km (5.5 mi) northeast of Oia; a taxi will also drop you off.

Pyrgos Πύργος

If you're looking to find a side of Santorini that hasn't been completely dominated by tourism, come to Pyrgos. The former capital of Santorini, Pyrgos is probably the best preserved medieval settlement on the island. Though it's becoming more of a tourist destination, Pyrgos is still under the radar and doesn't draw nearly the same crowds as Fira and Oia. It's a joy to walk through the village alleyways, stop in a *platea* (village square) for a cup of coffee and some people watching, and to see actual Santorini locals go about their business. Pyrgos is perched on a hill, and the view is just as spectacular as Oia. Thanks in part to efforts by locals to revamp the cultural and culinary offerings in their town, a number of excellent restaurants have opened up here.

SIGHTS

PYRGOS KASTELLI

free; daily

The best preserved of the five Venetian castles dotting Santorini, this castle is located at the top of Pyrgos. You can't miss it; lace up your sneakers and just start climbing upward. It was built in the 13th century, originally as a monastery, growing in size to become a fortress. Keep your eye out for the so-called "murder hole" (*fonissa,* in Greek) above the door, where boiling water or oil was poured over the head of would-be intruders.

WINERIES

HADZIDAKIS WINERY

tel. 697 001 3556; www.hatzidakiswines.gr; by appointment

This organic winery is almost entirely run by women (a welcome break from the male-dominated wine world). Opened in 1996, Hadzidakis Winery is particularly strong in assyrtiko and aidani varieties. Tastings take place in the deliciously briny-smelling cave, and the helpful staff are only too willing to answer any of your oenological questions.

NIGHTLIFE AND ENTERTAINMENT

FRANCO'S BAR

tel. 22860/33957; all day

This old-school cocktail bar (they also have a menu of milkshakes, fruit drinks, and light snacks) is a café-bar done up in the traditional Greek style with a great view of the sea (and incidentally, the sunset) from the terrace. The music is retro and disco, and it feels more like you're hanging out at Mr. Franco's very chill house than a bar.

FOOD

SELENE

Pyrgos village, far end of main car street; tel. 22860/24395 (bistro), 22860/22249 (fine dining); restaurant daily 7pm-11pm, café daily noon-11pm; bistro from €14, fine dining from €36

There are two sections to the award-winning Selene: a "meze and wine" bistro downstairs and a fine dining section upstairs, both located in an charming old house. Unless you're celebrating something very special, the bistro—which has the same views, and an equally impressive menu—is a good (and more affordable) choice. Dishes in the fine dining restaurant include "tomato in a can" (about 5 different tastes of Santorini tomatoes), roasted pigeon, and fava foam on a "seabed." At the wine bar, try the grilled octopus with fava and smoked tuna.

AGAZE

tel. 22860/31003; agazesantorini.com; all day; from €8

This adorably colorful and sunny café is full of dreamy details—there's even an olive tree growing inside! It's a great place for a coffee, hearty breakfast (if you're missing eggs or French toast, this is the place to come), or light lunch. At night it morphs into a cocktail lounge.

ACCOMMODATIONS

If you aren't married to a caldera view, then Pyrgos is an absolutely fantastic place to stay for a few nights. There are nice hotels around here, and it's more of an "authentic" Santorini experience than you might have in more touristic towns.

ZANNOS MELATHRON

Pyrgos Kallistis; tel. 22860/28220; www.zannos.gr; from €270

Located in a beautifully refurbished 19th-century mansion perched on the island's highest hilltop, Zannos is a great luxury choice for those who want views of the Aegean but the (relative) tranquility of village life. Rooms are sumptuously decorated, and service is impeccable.

East of Pyrgos

SANTORINI'S WINE COUNTRY

Exo Gonia (Έχω Γωνιά) and **Episkopi Gonias** (Επισκοπή Γωνίας) are the heart of wine country in Santorini. Before the devastating 1956 earthquake, there were at least 10 wineries here. Located a bit east of Pyrgos, this area is a mix of old buildings that survived the quake, and newer construction. There isn't a lot of tourist infrastructure around here, and it's fun to drive through the green valleys in (relative) peace. You'll notice signs pointing to the different wineries. Most wineries have their own tasting menu, and will guide you through the process. You'll definitely sample assytriko, and should ask for vinsanto if they have it.

★ Wineries

In the summer months, call ahead for a reservation, as the places can be packed. Some places have a tasting fee, though most do not.

ARTEMIS KARAMOLEGOS

Exo Gonia; tel. 22860/33395; www.artemiskaramolegos-winery.com; call for reservations

This is the place to try the sweet, lip-smackingly good vinsanto wine, a dessert variety native to Santorini. At Karamolegos, you can try a vinsanto that has been aged for 60 months!

GAIA WINES

Exo Gonia; tel. 22860/34186; www.gaia-wines.gr; call for reservations

Gaia's claim to fame is the delicious thalassitis, a local assyrtiko variety introduced in 1996 that has won over Greek-wine skeptics around the world. In recent years, Gaia has also been selling bottles of "submerged wine," which are battered by the sea. Tastings are held in their shop near Black Beach; the best is to grab a table outside and sample under the sun.

ESTATE ARGYROS

Episkopi Gonias; tel. 22860/31489; www.estate-argyros.com; call for reservations

This brand-new, uber modern winery is a sleek mix of chrome, glass, and cement. It's a bit of a cold environment for wine tasting, but they do make an excellent vinsanto, and they have a vinsanto-infused chocolate bar to go along with it.

Food

METAXI MAS

Exo Gonia; tel. 22860/31323; santorini-metaximas.gr; 1pm-late, closed January and February; €12

Located inside an old house (you can either sit on the terrace, with a view of Anafi island, or inside the vaulted rooms), Metaxi Mas is a delicious mix of Cretan and Santorini dishes. *Dakos* (Greek bruschetta), boiled wild greens, and raki are served alongside fava puree and

Wine on Santorini

Santorini's mineral-rich soil, a result of the volcanic activity on the island, has produced a considerable number of mouth-watering products: tomatoes, capers, arugula, white eggplants, delicate yellow fava beans—but to me, the most unique taste of Santorini is its wine.

You can't leave Santorini without tasting the sweet local wine, vinsanto.

GROWING METHODS

Around the island you'll notice woven vines, their circular shape hugging the ground—very different from the upright vineyards you see anywhere else. Called ***kouloura,*** or "ring" in Greek, these forms allow the grape growers to extract as much humidity as possible from the earth. The climate here is extremely arid, and it's only thanks to the caldera that any dew forms on the island at all. Ironically, humidity is the enemy of most wine-makers around the world! In Santorini, the *koulouri* system produces only a very small amount of grapes, although each one is packed with a super concentrated flavor.

VARIETIES

Assyrtiko

Assyrtiko is not a fruity wine at all. It fills your mouth with an explosive taste of minerality, and it's considered the best white wine in the Mediterranean. It's been dubbed "chablis on steroids."

- **Where to taste:** Gaia Wines

Aidani

A medium bodied white whine with bold hints of fruit and florals. This is an easy-drinking wine for those who like crisp, lemon-colored white wines.

- **Where to taste:** Hadzidakis

Vinsanto

This dessert wine is emblematic of Santorini: sweetness born out of hardship. Vinsanto (also made from assyrtiko grapes) comes in thin, elegant bottles, and is served at the end of dinner (it's also great with cheese). You'll find different "ages" of vinsanto, and the price goes up with the years. Vinsanto can actually be kept for 100 years; you'll likely taste it at 4 years, 10 years, and 25 years.

- **Where to taste:** Artemis Karamolegos

TASTING AT WINERIES

Most tourists come to wineries wearing flip-flops and looking to get drunk. If you do even the *minimum*—ask a thoughtful question, wear a slightly nicer outfit—you will make the winery owners very happy (or at least, feel respected).

You can also organize half and day tours to a variety of wineries, with transport included. Try **Santorini Wine Adventure** (tel. 22860/34123; www.winetoursantorini.com; from €100) or **Santorini Wine Tour** (tel. 22860/28358; www.santoriniwinetour.com; from €100).

white eggplants. Portions are copious, especially the salads, and though the mains tend toward the meat, there are plenty of vegetarian options.

KAMARI AND VICINITY (Καμάρι)

Kamari is a small beach town and resort area that's mostly worth visiting because it's close to two important sights: the ruins of ancient Thira, and the monastery of Prophet Elias. You can stop for lunch at the old-school taverna recommended below after seeing the sights.

Kamari is located at the foot of Mesa Vouno mountain, 5 km (3 mi) east of Pyrgos. Regular buses from Fira (20 minutes) serve Kamari.

Sights

ANCIENT THIRA

tel. 22860/23217; http://odysseus.culture.gr; Tues.-Sun. 8am-3pm; €4, children free

You can either hike (from Perissa, one hour) or drive up switchbacks from Perissa and Kamari to reach Thira, the archaeological site first settled by Dorians in the 9th century. There are layers of Hellenistic, Roman, and Byzantine architecture here, and you can walk through the ancient *agora,* theater, gymnasium, and houses, some of which are still decorated with colorful mosaics. The expansive views make Thira particularly atmospheric.

MONASTERY OF PROPHET ELIAS

5 km (3 mi) from Pyrgos; tel. 22860/31210; daily; free

Built by two monks in 1711, the Prophet Elias monastery is one of the oldest and biggest churches on the island. It's actually a complex of four churches and chapels surrounding a bell tower. Perhaps the most impressive thing about the monastery is its height: It's built on the highest point in Santorini, and both the view and the drive up to the monastery are unparalleled. Follow the main road south out of Pyrgos; the road veers up into switchbacks to reach the monastery; all signposted).

Food

TO KOUTOUKI TOU BEKRI

corner of Ermoú and Agíou Nektaríou; tel. 22860/30574; Apr.-Nov. noon-late; from €10

From the outside, To Koutouki Tou Bekri looks like a beachside tourist trap, but it has a great selection of old-school Greek hangover cures, like *pacha* (a soup made with intestines). You don't have to be hungover to eat here, of course; most of the patrons aren't. At night, the music comes out, as does the plate smashing.

Megalochori and Vicinity

MEGALOCHORI (Μεγαλοχώρι)

The picturesque village of Megalochori dates back to the 17th century, and has a long history of serving as a base for the wealthy merchants who would export vinsanto wine. It's nice to walk around the village center, taking in the old neoclassical mansions and visiting some of the nearby wineries.

Megalochori is located 6.2 km (just under 4 mi) south of Fira.

Wineries

BOUTARI

tel. 22860/81011; www.boutariwinerysantorini.gr; Mon.-Fri. 10am-3pm, in summer call for reservation; tour and tasting €15

This modern-looking winery was built in 1989 and is full of sleek glass and black pebbles. It actually belongs to the fourth generation of the Boutari family, who are known around Greece for their contributions to contemporary wine making. Schedule a tour and tasting and make sure to get a bottle of PDO kallisti reserve, which is the first dry white Santorini wine aged in barrels and bottled.

Horse Riding

SANTORINI HORSE RIDING

tel. 22860/30596; www.santorinihorseriding.gr; from €45

This family-run equestrian club offers riding enthusiasts, from beginners to advanced, different riding options through Santorini. There are trails through the countryside and along the beach, and tours generally last two hours. Book your plan online.

Shopping

1260 CERAMIC STUDIOS

tel. 22860/82423; www.1260ceramicstudio.com; 10am-7pm

Run by artisans Marina Taliadourou and Giannis Vlantonopoulos Source, 1260 Ceramic Studios has a great collection of hand-thrown contemporary ceramic artworks and more functional objects, like bowls and cups. Their forms are more organic than traditional ceramic work, and the pieces make beautiful gifts. The name refers to the high temperature at which the ceramics are fired.

EMPORIO VILLAGE (Εμπόριο)

If you're in the area, make a detour to Emporio village for a half hour walk through its streets. Built in the lowlands at the foot of Profitis Ilias mountain, Emporio derives its name from "trade" in Greek; this village was once an important and easily accessible trading center. It's a very charming village to walk around, and it's mostly inhabited by local Santorinians. There might be a couple of other tourists walking around, but it's far enough off the beaten track that you'll get an element of authenticity you could never find in Oia or Fira. It's located 4 km (2.5 mi) east of Megalochori.

PERISSA BLACK BEACH

This is the longest and most party-like of the three beaches on Santorini's south coast (Red and White Beach being the other two), with plenty of beach bars and loud music making it a favorite of the backpacker crowd. In the summer, the black sand can get incredibly hot, so a towel and umbrella are very necessary! It's 6.7 km (4 mi) east of Megalochori, and is served by regular buses.

VLYHADA (Βλυχαδα)

Easily accessible by bus or car, the small fishing village of Vlyhada, 5.4 km (3.25 mi) south of Megalochori, boasts a very long beach backed by strange white rock formations, created by millennia of rain and wind. There's enough space for a beach bar, and for getting far enough away that you can't notice the beach bar.

Sights

★ TOMATO INDUSTRIAL MUSEUM

tel. 22860/85141; www.santoriniartsfactory.gr; 10am-6pm; €5

Around Greece, Santorini is known for producing the most delicious tomatoes, particularly the tiny cherry tomatoes. In 2014, the D. Nomikos tomato factory was turned into an industrial museum, where you can learn about the history of tomato production and what industrialization did to the island. You'll see the giant machines where people used to triage tomatoes and turn them into puree, as well as the canning procedures, and the photos at the end of the exhibit really hammer home just how hard life was for the working class on Santorini.

There's also a contemporary art space, the **Santorini Arts Factory,** which has rotating exhibits that change yearly. There's a small café where you can sample tomato paste and tomato juice, and the knowledgeable staff can answer any questions you have on labor and art in Santorini.

Recreation

GIORGAROS FISHING TOURS

tel. 693 671 6348; www.santorini-fishing-tours.com; summer; from €130, including lunch

1

2

3

ΠΟΛΤΟΣ ΤΟΜΑΤΑΣ
Δ. Νομικός
TOMATOPASTE
D. NOMIKOS S.A.
Δ. ΝΟΜΙΚΟΣ Α.Ε.

For a hands-on day of sailing around Santorini and learning how to fish, spend the day with the family team at Giorgaros Fishing Tours. You'll set off on a traditional wooden boat, learning all about the marine life around Santorini and eating all your freshly caught fish. Traditional Greek fisherman's cap not included.

Nightlife and Entertainment

THEROS WAVE BAR

tel. 22861/12015; https://theroswavebar.gr; all day

This surprisingly cool beach bar is a favorite among locals and tourists. It's a classic coffee shop during the morning, and serves cocktails by night, with a comfy lounge vibe. In the summer, they host plenty of parties with DJs; check their website for up-to-date offerings.

Food

TO PSARAKI

Vlyháda seafront, Vlyhada; tel. 22860/82783; www.topsaraki.gr/joomla; Apr.-Oct., daily noon-late; from €12

This charming seafood restaurant is perched up on a cliff, and so it offers beautiful views to enjoy while stuffing yourself with prawns. There are all the usual grilled seafood offerings, as well as raw dishes like fresh fish carpaccio and ceviche.

Akrotiri and the Southwest Beaches

If Oia is the head of crescent-shaped Santorini, then Akrotiri (Ακρωτήρι), 6.4 km (3.75 mi) south of Megalochori, is its curled up feet. This side of the island gets a steady stream of tourists looking to check out the famed southwestern beaches, but it's much more relaxed than the north, and there's an equally gorgeous sunset from here.

SIGHTS

Akrotiri Lighthouse

Akrotiri; daily 24 hours

Built in 1892 by a French company, the Akrotiri lighthouse is one of the oldest on the island. It's okay as far as lighthouses go, but what's much more impressive is the amazing view from the rocky cliff, taking in the whole island up to Oia. If you walk out onto the cliff (carefully!) you'll notice up on your left side a rock that looks like a profile of a face. Locals call it "The Indian Rock" because they think it looks like a Native American man's profile. I thought it looked like a very grumpy Winston Churchill. From the town of Akrotiri, drive 5 km (3 mi) west to the edge of the island, where the lighthouse is located.

1: a beautiful church in the traditional village of Emporio **2:** The Akrotiri Lighthouse was built in 1892. **3:** old-school labels at the Tomato Factory, which now is an art space

★ Ancient Akrotiri

Akotiri; tel. 22860/81366; http://odysseus.culture.gr; Apr.-Oct. 8am-8pm; Nov.-Mar. 8am-3pm; €12, children free

Akrotiri is Santorini's version of Pompeii: At once destroyed and preserved by a massive volcanic eruption in 1450 BC, Akrotiri is a living reminder of the stunning contribution of the ancient Minoan civilization. The site was only uncovered in 1860, when the volcanic ash was dug out to be used for construction in the Suez Canal.

Take your time walking through the streets of the ancient city. There are also guided tours available. You'll see the crumbled walls of homes and shops, but also some objects—bed frames, pots, tiled floors, windows—that demonstrate just how alive this place was before the volcano erupted.

SOUTHWEST BEACHES

People seek out the southwest beaches mostly due to their colorful sands. They are otherwise crowded in the summer months, and aren't always terribly relaxing.

RED BEACH

Red from the volcanic minerals in the sand, Red Beach is a small and often very crowded slice of real estate. You'll have to walk down from the main road to get here, and be careful, as there are often falling rocks! From Akrotiri, it's 5 km (3 mi) south.

WHITE BEACH

Right next to Red Beach is a small cove called White Beach, a novelty mostly because the majority of Santorini beaches are black. (If you're driving, you'll need to head back into Akrotiri, as there is no connecting road between the two beaches.) It's less busy than Red Beach, and there's (usually) enough room to spread your towel if you don't want to splurge on a beach chair (€10).

Diving

SANTORINI DIVE CENTER

tel. 22860/83190; www.divecenter.gr; from €30

With programs for both certified and noncertified divers, this dive center will take you on some memorable dives (and snorkeling tours!) around Santorini, including to spooky underwater shipwrecks. There's a central office in Perissa, with a dive station in Akrotiri. All equipment is new, and staff is friendly and PADI-certified.

Food

GIORGAROS

just before lighthouse, Akitori; tel. 22860/83035; Jan. 15-Oct. noon-midnight; from €9

This is one of the cheapest places to get fresh fish in Santorini. The quality is still very high, portions are large, and there's a glassed-in terrace that offers stunning views of the caldera from a distance. They have everything from sardines to lobster, which can be ordered grilled or fried, plus classic taverna dishes.

Getting There

Akrotiri (Ακρωτήρι) is located 6.4 km (3.75 mi) south of Megalochori. **KTEL Santorini Buses** run regularly between Akrotiri and Fira.

Mykonos (Μύκονοσ)

Mykonos' (pop. 15,000) reputation precedes it:

It's the Greek capital of bikini-clad *joie-de-vivre*, sensational hedonism, and eye-watering prices. The marina is full of multimillion-euro yachts, and the beaches are crowded with oiled-up partiers hoping to catch a glimpse of the celebrities who call Mykonos paradise. It's not for the faint-hearted or those on a budget, and in the summer months, expect to pay double for everything. But the white cubist architecture of Mykonos, the craggy landscape dotted with domed churches, and the exquisite fine dining make this island worth a visit, particularly in the off-season. This is also the most common base for visiting the stunning archaeological site of Delos.

Highlights

Look for ★ to find recommended sights, activities, dining, and lodging.

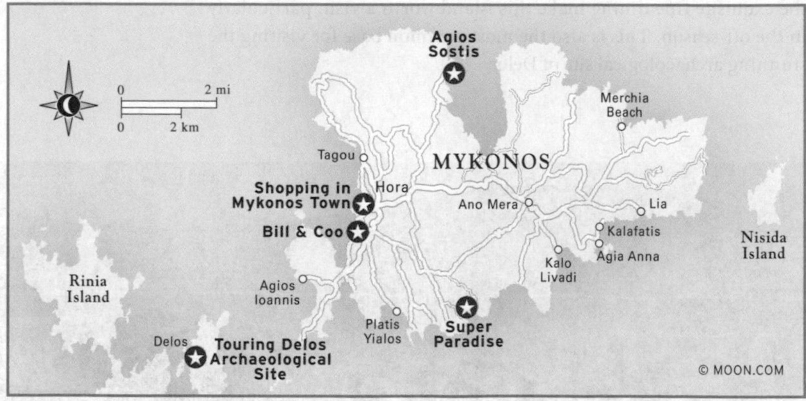

★ **Shopping in Mykonos Town:** Greeks joke that Mykonos Town is like walking through a fashion show. Join the crowd by picking up some chic outfits from local and international designers. My favorite is Parthenis (page 123).

★ **Fine Dining:** Mykonos stands out for its fine dining scene. Enjoy a fantastic meal at **Bill & Coo,** where Greek culinary culture is elevated to the next level (page 124).

★ **Nightlife:** You can't come here without spending at least one entire night out dancing in the beach clubs or one of Hora's many bars. If you only choose one, make it a *nuit blanche* at **Super Paradise** (page 130).

★ **Agios Sostis:** This bohemian beach is one of the last sandy places on Mykonos to not have any lounge chairs or beach bars (page 132).

★ **Touring Delos Archaeological Site:** One of Greece's most stunning mythological sites, the island of Delos is the birthplace of Apollo and Artemis (page 134).

PLANNING YOUR TIME

Mykonos is a year-round destination, and everything will be open at least **April** through **October.** Many restaurants and shops will stay open throughout the year, sometimes closing just for a few weeks in the winter. **July** and **August** are peak season, so expect to pay high prices, wait in line to take photos of the windmills, and make restaurant reservations weeks in advance during those months. If you're here for the partying, high season is also your best time to come, when the clubs have the biggest-name DJs and the parties are the most fun. **September** and **October** are more subdued: Most of the nightlife has ebbed out, and you'll get more of a taste for the local way of life. The weather is still mild enough to swim, and you can find great discounts on hotels. The glitz and glamour will have substantially thinned out, though.

Four days is sufficient time to spend in Mykonos, factoring in at least one day lost to a devilish hangover.

There's no shortage of sleeping options on the island, but you'll have to **book in advance** to get what you want. During the peak season, you'll be incredibly lucky to find anything below €100 for a basic double room with private bathroom; the price for luxury accommodations is tear-jerking, starting at €350. Personally, I wouldn't recommend staying directly inside Hora during July and August, as the partying and noise are relentless. There are plenty of places just outside the Hora and along the southern coast that are quieter.

If you're visiting Mykonos in the high season, I strongly recommend making **reservations** for every night you go out. Trust me—you can eat very well on this island, but only if you plan ahead. Otherwise, you're going to be stuck waiting in line for three hours or eating a sad pita gyro on the corner of the street. Everything is more **expensive** here; a coffee is usually around €5, a beer can cost €15 in a club, a cocktail is €25 or €30. Entry fees for the bigger clubs are €25-50, depending on the DJ and the party (check the club's website ahead of time). For a meal in a fancy restaurant, expect to pay around €70-100 per person (with a drink); if you're trying to save your money, buy sandwiches (around €6) and groceries (the prices are only slightly jacked up from the mainland).

INFORMATION AND SERVICES

Mykonos is a touristic island, and has all the facilities you'll need, though that being said, there's no official tourist office. Check out www.mykonos.gr for tourist information or try the **Mykonos Accommodation Center** (Enoplon Dynameon 10; tel. 22890/23408; daily 9am-1pm and 4pm-9pm) for in-person tourist questions.

The **public health center** (tel. 22890/23994) in Argiana is free. The **police** station is located on the road from the airport (tel. 22890/22716).

There are plenty of **banks** and **ATMs** in the Hora and Ano Meria, as well as smaller villages. Most bars and clubs (especially the larger ones) have ATMs on-site. Still, it's good to bring extra cash: With so many people coming to Mykonos each summer—to both take out and spend money—there are complaints that ATMs run out of cash, or that new restaurants/bars haven't yet set up their credit card systems. In general, though, most places take cards.

GETTING THERE

Air

Mykonos is serviced by an airport, **Mykonos International Airport** (JMK; tel. 22890/79000; www.mykonos-airport.com), located 2 km (1.25 mi) south of the Hora. Throughout the year you'll find daily flights to Athens and Thessaloniki with **Sky Express** (www.skyexpress.gr), **Aegean**

Previous: Delos Archaeological Site; the view of Mykonos port; a beautifully preserved mosaic on Delos.

Airlines (www.aegeanair.com), and **Astra Airlines** (www.astra-airlines.gr). During the summer, there are plenty of cheap flights from other European cities like London, Milan, Berlin, and Paris.

There are plenty of public **buses** waiting at the airport to take you into Hora (€1.60). A **taxi** into town costs €10 and takes about 5 minutes (if there's summer traffic, it can be twice as long), but check with your hotel; many offer free or discounted transfer to/from the airport.

Ferry

Mykonos has regular and year-round ferry service. There are two ports in Mykonos, the **Old Port** 400 meters (0.25 mile) north of Hora, and the **New Port** 2 km (1.25 mi) north of town, where most of the bigger boats dock. Boats leave from **Piraeus** and **Rafina** in Athens up to three times a day (fast and slow ferries; 2.5-4.5 hours; €32-65). During the summer, you can easily connect to neighboring islands like **Santorini, Folegandros,** and **Naxos.**

GETTING AROUND

It's a bit difficult to get around Mykonos (which is 105 sq km/50 sq mi) in the summer. Having a **car** or **motorcycle** is definitely the easiest solution, so you don't have to rely on crowded public buses and taxis, which might not be easily available, but note that **parking** can be difficult, even outside of the high season.

Bus

Mykonos has a decent network of buses (KTEL; www.mykonosbus.com; tel. 22890/22890) that service most of the island. There are two main bus terminals both located in Hora: **Terminal A** (Fabrika Square), which serves the southern end of the island; and **Terminal B** (behind the OTE office), serving the northern end of the island. There are also buses between the ports and the terminals, and in the summer there's a bus directly from the Old Port to Paradise Beach for those who are not messing around.

Car

Car rental agencies are a dime a dozen at the airport and all over the island, including the Hora, the ports, and the bus terminals. Expect to pay at least €45 per day for a car in the high season, and at least €20 per day for a scooter. Note that if you're going to rent a car, parking is a frustrating task that will cause you a lot of grief. If you're alone or in a couple, it's more practical to rent a scooter or motorcycle, though remember that most of the people around you are probably a little tipsy, so drive with caution. I encourage you not to get a quad, as Mykonos is full of eighteen-year-old tourists driving them without the slightest clue of how to properly maneuver them.

There are car and scooter rental places at the **airport,** near the **port,** and at the **bus stations.** All the international car agencies are available (you can book ahead to get a slightly better deal), or if you'd like a local provider, try **Apollon** (Epar. Od. Mikonou near the southern bus station in Hora; tel. 22890/24136; www.apollonrentacar.com; daily 9am-8pm).

Taxi

Taxis (tel. 22890/23700 or 22890/22400) can be found at Hora's **Plateia Manto Mavrogenous** (helpfully called **Taxi Square**), and at the **bus stations** and **ports.** Expect to wait a long time during the high season, and even longer if you call one ahead of time. Fares start at €3.50 and phone bookings have a surplus charge of €3.30.

Itinerary Ideas

For the first day of this itinerary, you can use public transportation, but it's ideal to rent a car for the second day so that you can explore the island's interior on a scenic drive. Advance reservations for Bill & Coo (your dining suggestion at the end of Day 2) are a must.

DAY 1

1 Take the 9am boat to the **Delos Archaeological Site** and spend your allotted four hours wandering around this amazing piece of living history. Make sure to check out the Terrace of the Lions, the bonkers mosaic at the House of Dolphins, and the Sanctuary of the Foreign Gods.

2 Your boat will be back in time for lunch. Have a quick and healthy meal at **Nice n Easy** in Hora Mykonos. Snag a table with a view of the windmills.

3 From the Old Port, you can take a water taxi directly to **Super Paradise Beach** and spend the afternoon sipping champagne and dancing with beautiful people.

4 You'll want to head back to the hotel to change clothes before heading out to dinner. Go for upscale Greek at **Eva's Garden.**

5 Now fueled up, head to **Scorpios** for a wild night of dancing and drinking. You'll probably come home some time in the wee morning.

DAY 2

1 You've probably felt better, huh? If you're in the Hora, pick up some much-needed coffee and pastries from **Popolo.**

2 Rent a car to take a leisurely drive through the island's interior and head to **Fokos** beach, where you can have lunch at Fokos Tavern. Alternatively, head by bus to Ano Mera to schedule a ride with the nice people from Yummy Pedals. They'll take you on a bicycle tour of the island's secluded country roads, and you'll end the afternoon with homemade snacks and a dip in the sea.

3 Back in Hora, get yourself cleaned up and head to **Bill & Coo** in Hora for dinner. Spring for the tasting menu, and let the sommelier guide your evening.

4 From Hora, grab a taxi to **Jackie O** on the South Coast to catch the nightly drag queen show, and to dance and drink some more with all your new friends. Collapse into bed sometime late, again.

Mykonos

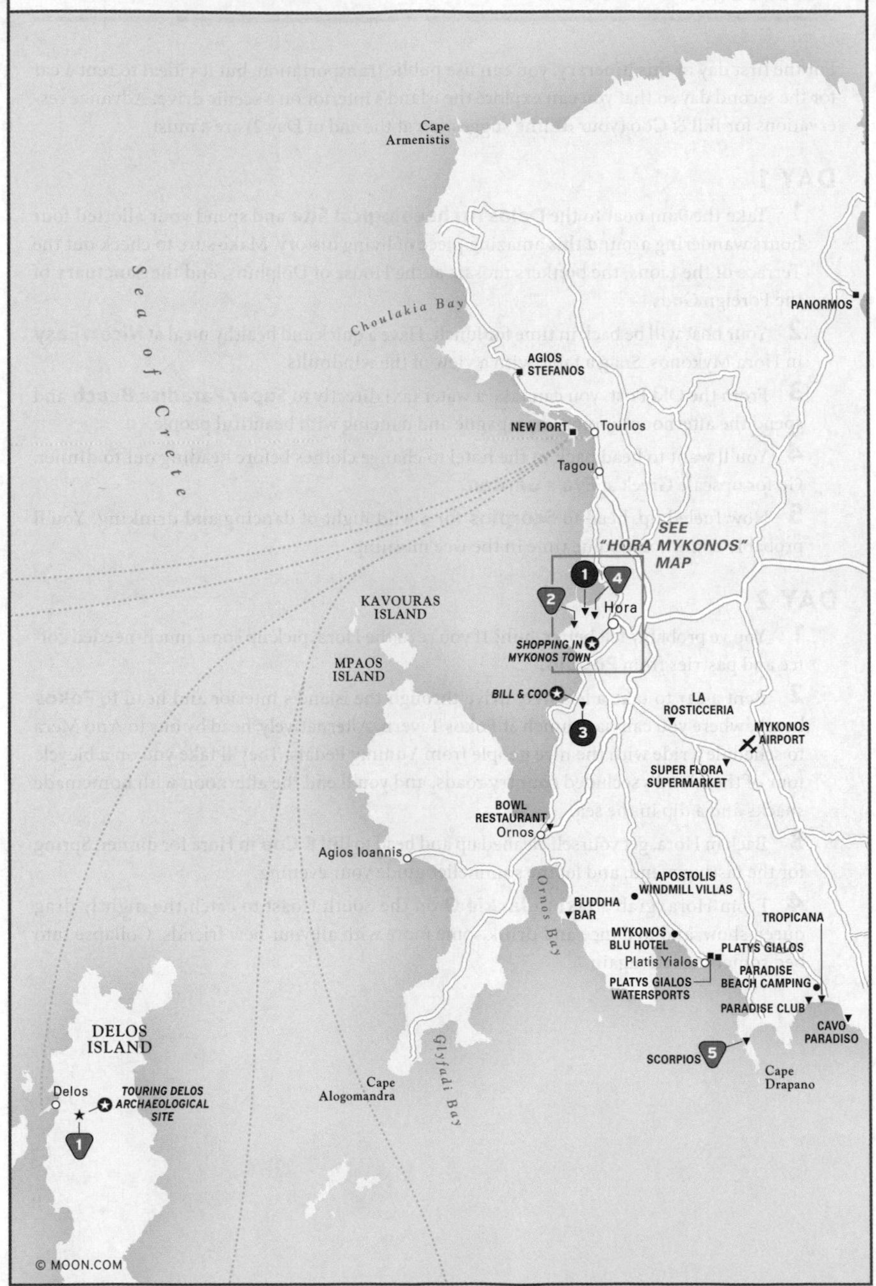

Cape Armenistis
Sea of Crete
Choulakia Bay
PANORMOS
AGIOS STEFANOS
NEW PORT
Tourlos
Tagou
SEE "HORA MYKONOS" MAP
1
4
2
Hora
SHOPPING IN MYKONOS TOWN
KAVOURAS ISLAND
MPAOS ISLAND
BILL & COO
3
LA ROSTICCERIA
MYKONOS AIRPORT
SUPER FLORA SUPERMARKET
BOWL RESTAURANT
Ornos
Agios Ioannis
Ornos Bay
APOSTOLIS WINDMILL VILLAS
BUDDHA BAR
MYKONOS BLU HOTEL
TROPICANA
PLATYS GIALOS
Platis Yialos
PLATYS GIALOS WATERSPORTS
PARADISE BEACH CAMPING
PARADISE CLUB
CAVO PARADISO
5
SCORPIOS
Cape Drapano
DELOS ISLAND
Delos
TOURING DELOS ARCHAEOLOGICAL SITE
1
Cape Alogomandra
Glyfadi Bay
© MOON.COM

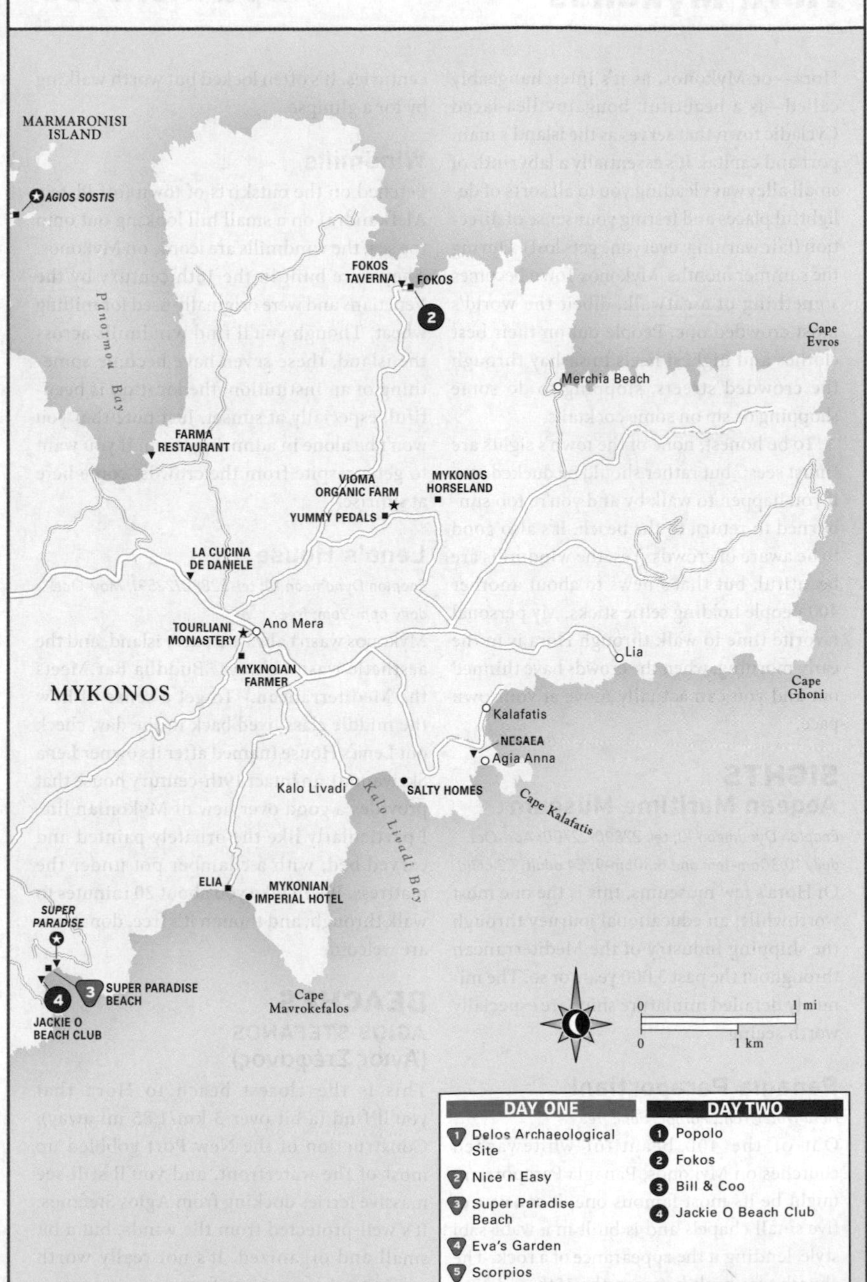
MARMARONISI ISLAND
AGIOS SOSTIS
FOKOS TAVERNA
FOKOS
2
Panormou Bay
Cape Evros
Merchia Beach
FARMA RESTAURANT
VIOMA ORGANIC FARM
MYKONOS HORSELAND
YUMMY PEDALS
LA CUCINA DE DANIELE
TOURLIANI MONASTERY
Ano Mera
MYKNOIAN FARMER
Lia
MYKONOS
Cape Ghoni
Kalafatis
NESAEA
Agia Anna
Kalo Livadi
SALTY HOMES
Cape Kalafatis
Kalo Livadi Bay
ELIA
MYKONIAN IMPERIAL HOTEL
SUPER PARADISE
3
SUPER PARADISE BEACH
4
JACKIE O BEACH CLUB
Cape Mavrokefalos
0
1 mi
0
1 km
DAY ONE
1 Delos Archaeological Site
2 Nice n Easy
3 Super Paradise Beach
4 Eva's Garden
5 Scorpios
DAY TWO
1 Popolo
2 Fokos
3 Bill & Coo
4 Jackie O Beach Club

Hora Mykonos Χώρα Μυκόνου

Hora—or Mykonos, as it's interchangeably called—is a beautiful, bougainvillea-laced Cycladic town that serves as the island's main port and capital. It's essentially a labyrinth of small alleyways leading you to all sorts of delightful places and testing your sense of direction (fair warning: everyone gets lost). During the summer months, Mykonos Town becomes something of a catwalk, albeit the world's most crowded one. People put on their best clothes and highest heels to sashay through the crowded streets, stopping to do some shopping or sip on some cocktails.

To be honest, none of the town's sights are "must sees," but rather should be ducked into if you happen to walk by and you're too sunburned to return to the beach. It's also good to be aware of crowds. Yes, the windmills are beautiful, but that's news to about another 400 people holding selfie sticks. My personal favorite time to walk through Hora is in the early morning, when the crowds have thinned out and you can actually move at your own pace.

SIGHTS

Aegean Maritime Museum

Enoplon Dynameon 10; tel. 22890/22700; Apr.-Oct. daily 10:30am-1pm and 6:30pm-9; €4 adult, €2 child

Of Hora's few museums, this is the one most worthwhile: an educational journey through the shipping industry of the Mediterranean throughout the past 3,000 years or so. The minutely detailed miniature ships are especially worth seeing.

Panagia Paraportiani

Hora Waterfront, Paraportiani; free

Out of the 400 beautiful whitewashed churches on Mykonos, Panagia Paraportiani might be its most famous one. It consists of five small chapels and is built in a wabi-sabi style, lending it the appearance of a rock. The church was built between the 15th and 17th centuries. It's often locked but worth walking by for a glimpse.

Windmills

Perched on the outskirts of town (off Plateia Alefkandra) on a small hill looking out onto the sea, the windmills are iconic on Mykonos. They were built in the 16th century by the Venetians and were originally used for milling wheat. Though you'll find windmills across the island, these seven have become something of an institution; the location is beautiful, especially at sunset. Just note that you won't be alone in admiring them. If you want to get a respite from the crowds, come here at sunrise.

Lena's House

Enoplon Dynameon 10; tel. 22890/22591; May-Oct. daily 6pm-9pm; free

Mykonos wasn't always a party island, and the aesthetic wasn't always "Buddha Bar Meets the Mediterranean." To get a sense of how the middle class lived back in the day, check out Lena's House (named after its owner Lena Skrivanou), an intact 19th-century house that provides a good overview of Mykonian life. I particularly like the ornately painted and carved bed, with a chamber pot under the mattress. It will take you about 20 minutes to walk through, and though it's free, donations are welcome.

BEACHES

AGIOS STEFANOS (Άγιος Στέφανος)

This is the closest beach to Hora that you'll find (a bit over 3 km/1.85 mi away). Construction of the New Port gobbled up most of the waterfront, and you'll still see massive ferries docking from Agios Stefanos. It's well-protected from the winds, but a bit small and organized. It's not really worth coming out of your way for.

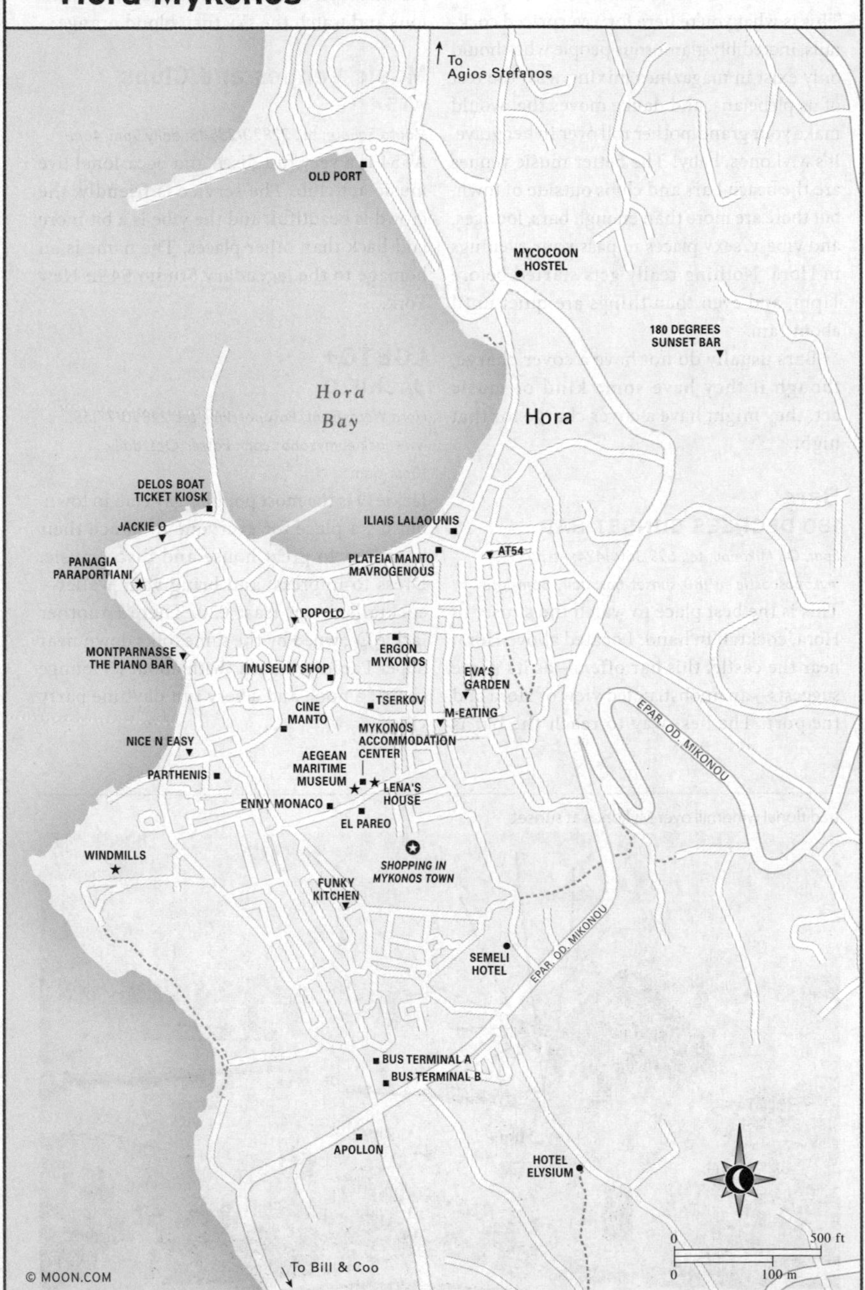
Hora Mykonos
To
Agios Stefanos
OLD PORT
MYCOCOON
HOSTEL
180 DEGREES
SUNSET BAR
Hora
Bay
Hora
DELOS BOAT
TICKET KIOSK
JACKIE O
ILIAIS LALAOUNIS
PANAGIA
PARAPORTIANI
PLATEIA MANTO
MAVROGENOUS
AT54
POPOLO
ERGON
MYKONOS
MONTPARNASSE
THE PIANO BAR
IMUSEUM SHOP
EVA'S
GARDEN
TSERKOV
CINE
MANTO
M-EATING
EPAR. OD. MIKONOU
NICE N EASY
MYKONOS
ACCOMMODATION
CENTER
AEGEAN
MARITIME
MUSEUM
PARTHENIS
LENA'S
HOUSE
ENNY MONACO
EL PAREO
WINDMILLS
SHOPPING IN
MYKONOS TOWN
FUNKY
KITCHEN
SEMELI
HOTEL
EPAR. OD. MIKONOU
BUS TERMINAL A
BUS TERMINAL B
APOLLON
HOTEL
ELYSIUM
0
500 ft
0
100 m
© MOON.COM
To Bill & Coo

NIGHTLIFE AND ENTERTAINMENT

This is what you're here for: overpriced cocktails, incredibly glamorous people who should only exist in magazines mixing with the rest of us plebeians, and dance moves that would make your grandmother roll over in her grave. It's Mykonos, baby! The better music venues are the beach bars and clubs outside of town, but there are more than enough bars, lounges, and vibe-y, sexy places to pass your evenings in Hora. Nothing really gets started before 11pm, and even then things are quiet until about 1am.

Bars usually do not have a cover charge, though if they have some kind of music act, they might have a cover charge for that night.

Bars

180 DEGREES SUNSET BAR

Epar. Od Mikonou; tel. 699 360 1424; http://mykonoscastle.eu/180-sunset-bar; daily 5pm-late

This is the best place to watch the sunset in Hora, cocktail in hand. Located above Hora, near the castle, this bar offers—as its name suggests—an unobstructed view of Hora and the port. The best way to reach the bar is on foot (a steep, though short walk from the Hora). Sit on one of the kilim-covered cushions and watch the sky turn blood orange.

Music Venues and Clubs

AT54

Manto Square; tel. 22890/28543; daily 9pm-4am

AT54 is a very fun disco and occasional live music act club. The service is friendly, the crowd is beautiful, and the vibe is a bit more laid-back than other places. The name is an homage to the legendary Studio 54 in New York.

LGBTQ+

JACKIE O

Hora Waterfront, Paraportiani; tel. 22890/77168; www.jackieomykonos.com; Easter-Oct. daily 10pm-6am

Jackie O is the most popular gay club in town, but it's a place for everyone to dance their heart out to great house and disco music. Dress to impress, and bring your wallet—cocktails are at least €20. There's another Jackie O owned by the same folks down near Super Paradise Beach (with about 75 lounge chairs, a pool, and a very fun daytime party vibe).

traditional windmill over Mykonos at sunset

Jackie Kennedy's Visit to Mykonos

In 1961, Jackie Kennedy—apparently gripped by the so-called "Greek Fever" that had swept the United States following the release of Melina Mercouri's Oscar-winning film *Never on Sunday*—planned an unofficial visit to Greece with her sister and brother-in-law.

Jackie visited the Athenian Riviera and Hydra, but her trip to Mykonos is forever entrenched in the collective Greek memory. Wearing a sleeveless sundress, her hair tucked under a kerchief, Jackie stepped off the boat and was immediately greeted by a pelican. "Is he wild?" she reportedly asked the island's mayor. Wild only in spirit, because this pelican, nicknamed Petros, was already famous on the island and became Mykonos' official mascot a few years later.

Jackie apparently bought a wooden boat for her son, John Jr., and, to the amazement of the villagers, walked up the hill to her designated villa. There, she had lunch with the island's only newspaper writer, Helen Vlachos. Vlachos would later say that under the flowering trees of her garden, Jackie told her "This is the greatest trip in the world. I couldn't be happier."

Mykonos' famous pelican stands in front of a door.

MONTPARNASSE THE PIANO BAR

Agion Anargyroun 24, Little Venice; tel. 22890/23719; www.thepainobar.comp

An institution on Mykonos, Montparnasse is a gay bar that has been around for more than three decades. It's perfect for a pregame sunset cocktail (shockingly affordably priced for Mykonos, at just €8). There's always cabaret and live music after sunset.

Cinema

CINE MANTO

tel. 22890/26165; www.cinemanto.gr; June 1-Sept. 30 evenings; €8, €6 child

Located in a lovely, palm-tree fringed garden in the center of Mykonos Town, Cine Manto is a great place to relax and watch a flick. The films are usually of the Hollywood blockbuster variety (always with subtitles if not in English), and there's a restaurant on-site as well. Check the website for screenings. They also have snacks and full meals available for sale.

★ SHOPPING

Among the Greek Islands, Mykonos stands out for its shopping. Granted, your wallet may cry real tears afterward, but there are enough elegant and chic boutiques in Hora that you can easily spend an afternoon bouncing from one to the other. Mykonos attracts a lot of big spenders, and brands have followed suit. You'll find Louis Vuitton and Balenciaga here. I've highlighted Greek designers that I find particularly interesting, but you can wander around the Hora and discover some more as well.

Clothing and Accessories

PARTHENIS

Alefkandra Square; tel. 22890/22448; www.orsalia-parthenis.com; daily 10am-10pm

Parthenis is the uber-cool, Greece-in-the-1970s, unisex clothing look we should all be wearing. Designed and handmade in Athens, this clothing label was founded by Dimitris Parthenis; his daughter Orsalia now runs the company. Parthenis is an institution on

Mykonos, and you should budget for a small shopping spree here.

ENNY MONACO

Tria Pigadia; tel. 22890/77100; daily 10am-2am

A one-stop shop for curated fashion designs from Greece and around the world, Enny Monaco has excellent (luxury) offerings of clothing, accessories, and shoes for the discerning shopper. Under warm yellow light and in a cocoon of white stone, choose from men and women's designer clothes.

EL PAREO

Enoplon Dinameon and Malamatenia Alley; tel. 22890/22015; daily 10am-10pm

Pareo, sarong, wrap: whatever you call it, this piece of fabric is one of the most versatile beachwear items out there. At El Pareo, most of the pieces are imported from Bali and South Africa, and come in a delightful spectrum of colors and patterns. If you want to look like you were born and raised on Mykonos, this is the place to make that happen.

TSERKOV

Nikou Kalogera 30; tel. 22890/77161; daily 10am-midnight

This high-end clothing brand is only sold on Mykonos and in… Zurich. It's a one-stop shop for a curated collection of international and Greek designers (including cult favorite Zeus + Dione). Definitely a fashionista's store, they have both men and women's clothes, and a beautifully manicured space, full of marble furniture and floating staircases.

Jewelry

ILIAIS LALAOUNIS

14 N. Polykandrioti; tel. 22890/22444; www.iliaslalaounis.eu; daily 10am-8pm

Greek jewelry pioneer Ilias Lalaounis first established his label in 1969 in Athens. He utilizes ancient jewelry-making techniques and is inspired by Greek mythology to create one-of-a-kind pieces. Those on a budget can pick up one of his lucite bracelets. Jackie Onassis was a regular customer here.

Gifts

IMUSEUM SHOP

Dilou 8; tel. 22890/77370; daily 10am-10pm

Do you hate museums but love museum gift shops? Or perhaps you don't have the time to visit all the museums but still want a memento? Enter iMuseum, a new concept shop that brings together replicas of objects from archaeological sites and museums from around Greece. They've got everything from facsimile paintings to ceramic vases to jewelry.

ERGON MYKONOS

Floroi Zoiganeli 23; tel. 22890/28674; www.ergonmykonos.com; daily 11am-1am

This lovely concept store fuses fashion, art, and culture to create an eclectic offering of goods. You'll find everything from ceramics to dresses to tea towels. Their prices are a little more palatable than some, too. Pick up a pair of bedazzled espadrilles, complete with fabric tassels and gold coins, for €60.

FOOD

Greek

EVA'S GARDEN

Goumenios Square; tel. 22890/22160; www.evas-garden.gr; daily 6:30pm-midnight; from €12

For laid-back Greek taverna fare at moderate prices, head to Eva's Garden, which is located in Goumenio Square. Grab a table on the rooftop, which is covered in vine leaves, and dig into some classics like baked lamb with lemon sauce, grilled pork souvlaki, or grilled fish.

Fine Dining

★ BILL & COO

Paralia Megali Ammos; tel. 22890/26292; www.bill-coo-hotel.com/gastronomy-project; daily 8pm-1am; 4-course tasting menu from €140

Of all the delicious meals to be had on Mykonos, Bill & Coo's might be the best. Chef Ntinos Fotinakis is part storyteller, part historian, and part cook: Each detail in his dishes is meant to reflect something about Greek traditional life. The homemade bread comes with a little "brush" made out of rosemary

Dining on Mykonos

Mykonos has some fantastic food, but to enjoy it, you need to do your homework ahead of time. The food here is usually expensive, and because so many people who come to Mykonos are jet-setters, there are lots of fine dining options. The food in these places (including **Bill & Coo, M-Eating, Buddha Bar,** and **Funky Kitchen**) is absolutely delicious, but can break the bank. I recommend choosing one really great restaurant to try, and then sticking to lower-cost options for the rest of your time on the island.

Also, **reservations are essential.** That goes for lunch as well as dinner, especially at any place in town during the summer.

that you use to dab olive oil; it's reminiscent of how Greek priests perform religious rituals. Everything is deliciously executed, but unlike in some other fine dining restaurants, you can really feel the love in the food. The wine list is superb, and service is incredible; if you squint, they will bring a clip light for your menu. Do spring for one of the tasting menus, and follow the sommelier's recommendations.

M-EATING

Kalogera 10; tel. 22890/78550; www.m-eating.gr; daily 7pm-1am; from €17

It's worth splurging on a romantic dinner (reservations recommended) at this luxurious restaurant that combines creativity with fresh, Mediterranean ingredients. It's really one of the best restaurants on the island, and everything from the service to the imaginatively plated dishes is a treat. Try the smoked quail or the sous vide pork meat served with celeriac puree. The decor is classic Mykonian, with curved white, exposed-stone floors and flowering trees.

International and Fusion

NICE N EASY

Little Venice; tel. 22890/25421; www.niceneasy.gr; daily 9am-1am; from €15

The food at Nice n Easy is California-inspired with a Greek twist. (It's an outpost of their Athenian branch.) The focus is on healthy, organic fusion dishes, such as power bowls with quinoa and vegetables, and grilled sea bream. Grab a table outside with a view of the windmills and try the water buffalo meatballs, which are locally farmed.

FUNKY KITCHEN

tel. 22890/27272; www.funkykitchen.gr; daily 6pm-1am; from €18

This creative fusion restaurant brings together Mediterranean flavors with seriously stellar execution and presentation. It's a beloved dining experience on Mykonos and something of a pilgrimage for foodies. The vibe is relaxed and casual, but the food is fine dining kicked up a notch. Be sure to try the feta rolls and don't miss dessert. (I recommend the Turkish Delight ice cream or the chocolate nirvana.)

LA ROSTICCERIA

Drafaki (Road Mykonos Town - Airport); tel. 22890/28750; www.larosticceria-mykonos.com; from €16

A cute little Italian trattoria that's open all day, La Rosticceria serves up Italian specialties for any meal: marmalade-stuffed croissants and espresso for breakfast, sandwiches overflowing with prosciutto and mozzarella for lunch, or homemade tagliatelle or saffron risotto for dinner.

Health Food

POPOLO

Drakopoulou 8; tel. 22890/22208; www.popolomykonos.com; daily 8:30am-2:30am

This adorable and cozy café serves up some excellent coffee, as well as sandwiches, salads, eggs, and other brunch options. There are plenty of vegetarian options, and for the truly hungover, they can deliver to your hotel.

Supermarket

SUPER FLORA SUPERMARKET

Airport; tel. 22890/23509; www.mykonos-flora.gr

Honestly, this supermarket might be the most insane place in all of Mykonos. It's not just a market: there are origami and glass art installations, pulsating techno music, giant TV screens playing Fashion Week videos, and one of the most impressive alcohol sections on the island. You can casually buy a €10,000 bottle of whiskey, rolls of toilet paper, caviar, your probiotics, and a €2 pack of gum all at once. It's conveniently located next to the airport, making it an amazing place to kill time before your flight home.

ACCOMMODATIONS

Under €150

MYCOCOON HOSTEL

Kaminaki; tel. 22890/23168; www.hostelmykonos.com; from €50

A cut above your usual backpacker hostel, MyCocoon is a stylish, affordable option near the Old Port. Bunk beds have been custom built to mimic Cycladic houses and give a good deal of privacy to sleepers. Bathrooms are largely clean and you shouldn't have to wait too long to use it. The smallest dorm size is four people, with a private bathroom; the largest communal dorm sleeps 46 and has five shared bathrooms. If you're traveling with a group, spring for a quad, as it's the cheapest option with the most privacy.

€150-300

HOTEL ELYSIUM

School of Fine Arts District; tel. 22890/23952; www.elysiumhotel.com; Apr.-Oct., from €260

Mykonos' preeminent gay hotel (they call themselves "str8 friendly") is not a place for relaxing, per se. In Greek mythology, Elysium refers to the playground of the gods, and Hotel Elysium is just that: a nonstop party featuring cabaret acts at sunset, poolside cocktails, and really fun dancing and music. Of course, this being a place fit for the gods, the rooms are nice, too, all done up in white and glass, with comfy beds. This medium-sized hotel is located on the edge of Hora, but attracts quite a lot of people at the bar and pool.

Over €300

SEMELI HOTEL

off Rohari; tel. 22890/27466; www.semelihotel.gr; from €460

This is probably the most affordable of the high-end luxury hotels around Hora (prices dip drastically starting in September). Rooms come with marble bathrooms and balcony views to the sea, and there's a wonderful pool area, garden, and spa.

BILL & COO

tel. 22890/26292; www.bill-coo-hotel.com; from €900

A seriously classy boutique hotel located on the edge of Hora, Bill & Coo gives you all the views and none of the noise. With just 32 suites, it has something of a cozy feeling. Though the emphasis is really on sexy luxury, this place is all infinity pools, floor to ceiling glass windows, and lounge chairs. Prices fall by 70 percent in the off-season.

Ano Mera

There's plenty of action outside of Hora, if you know where to look. The only other comparable town (at least in size) is Ano Mera, a picturesque village in the middle of the island about 8 km (5 mi) east of Hora. It's a welcome break from the bustle of Hora: Many locals live here, and there are a couple of sights worth visiting. There is no beach here (it's landlocked), but there's plenty of green farmland around Ano Mera that gives the town a village vibe.

SIGHTS

Tourliani Monastery

Mon.-Sat. 9am-1pm and 3:30pm-7pm, Sun. 3:30pm-7pm; €1

This lovely little church is worth a visit if you're in the area. Built in the 1500s and restored in the 1700s, it's a whitewashed chapel full of treasures like wooden *iconostasis* (portable icon stands) carved by Florentine artisans. It's located on Ano Mera's town square.

Vioma Organic Farm

tel. 22890/71883; www.mykonosvioma.com; daily 11am-4pm

Located in an old monastery's vineyard, Vioma is a stellar example of what Mykonian like was like back in the day. The farm was revived in 1994, when an Athenian bank inspector decided to escape the trappings of city life and return to his roots. A visit is a very nice, chilled out way to spend an afternoon. Call ahead to make an appointment to visit the farm and do some wine tasting. The farm also organizes bike tours under the name Yummy Pedals. Located 2.7 km (1.7 mi) northeast outside of Ano Mera, (7-minute drive).

RECREATION

Cycling

YUMMY PEDALS

tel. 22890/71883; www.yummypedals.gr; 2-hour tour from €40

A lot of Mykonos is actually farmland, though you wouldn't know it if you spend your days between Hora and Scorpios bar. Yummy Pedals, located 2.7 km north of Ano Mera,

Tourliani Monastery in Ano Mera

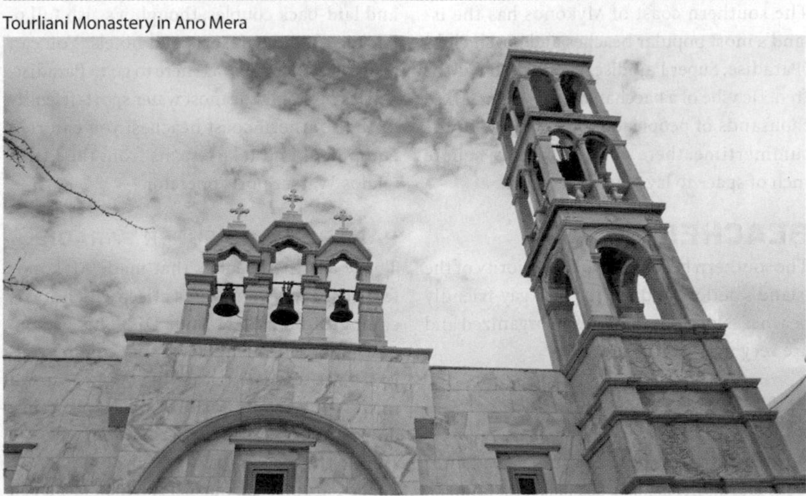

offers mountain-biking tours through the backroads of Mykonos. In addition to riding through the countryside, you'll learn about Mykonos' religious and cultural heritage. Rides end with a dip at the beach, and the team takes plenty of underwater photos for you to bring back home. If you like to mix your fitness with food, book the "Picnic on the Beach" tour (€50), which includes a much-deserved glass of wine.

Horse Riding

MYKONOS HORSELAND

tel. 694 577 8962; www.mykonoshorse.com; from €80

No need to change out of your bikini to ride a Mykonian horse through the azure blue waters of the Mediterranean. You'll be accompanied by an expert guide who will take you on different rides around the island, depending on your skill level. They can organize special packages like photoshoots with horses and picnic lunches. Most of the horses are rescue animals. Located 900 meters (2,953 feet) east of Yummy Pedals.

FOOD

★ LA CUCINA DE DANIELE

tel. 22890/71513; daily 6pm-1am; from €25

This is one of the best (and most established) Italian restaurants on Mykonos, and it's easy to see why: Chef and owner Daniele was born and raised in Tuscany, where he sources some of his ingredients and wines. Everything is delicious, but you can't go wrong with the home-made pastas. Save room for the sorbet.

GETTING THERE

Without traffic, it takes about 15 minutes to drive from Hora to Ano Mera. The view is not particularly scenic—it gets more and more filled with shops and restaurants with each passing year—but you'll start to see more of Mykonos' landscape. Parking can also be difficult in Ano Mera, especially in the main parking spot next to the church.

There are regular buses from Hora to Ano Mera. The last bus from Hora to Ano Mera leaves at midnight in the high season.

South Coast

The southern coast of Mykonos has the island's most popular beaches and beach clubs (Paradise, Super Paradise, Jackie O). It has the frenetic vibe of a bacchanalia; here you'll find thousands of people looking to party. In the summertime, there's barely an extra square inch of space to lay your towel down.

BEACHES

The southern beaches have the majority of the island's action, and are the best gay-friendly beaches. Note that these are all organized and are very much party spots.

PLATYS GIALOS (Πλατύς Γιαλός)

A beautiful sandy beach around 5 km (3 mi) from Hora, this is more popular with families and laid-back couples, though it's also full of package-holiday resorts and hotels. You can also catch the water taxi here to go to Paradise. This is probably the most water sport–friendly of the southern coast beaches; you can rent equipment and take lessons from the Platys Gialos Water Sports operator.

PARADISE AND SUPER PARADISE

These are the beaches that made Mykonos famous. First comes Paradise, which has a campground and 24-hour DJs. This used to be a gay beach, but it's now a very commercialized place that's popular with a younger crowd into mainstream music. Walk 1 km (.6 mi) down an access road on the left side (as you're facing the beach) and you'll come across Super Paradise (or Super P), which has a full gay section, a nudist section on the left-hand side (again, facing the beach), and the Jackie O beach club. The vibe here is a bit funky and bohemian. You must visit both at some point for a Mykonian experience. Located 1 km (.6 mi) south of Platys Gialos.

ELIA
(Ελιά)

This is the longest beach on Mykonos and has become pretty commercialized in recent years. Most of the beach has been taken up by lawn chairs and umbrellas. There's plenty of public transportation (both buses and water taxis) that come to the beach, and there's a good amount of parking space if you have a rental car. There are hourly buses from the Old Port in Hora to Elia (20 minutes; €2). Elia is a "mixed" beach (both gay- and straight-friendly). Located 12.7 km (30 minutes; about 8 mi) east of Paradise.

RECREATION

Water Sports

PLATYS GIALOS WATERSPORTS

tel. 697 727 9584; www.mykonoswatersports.gr; from €30 for classes, Apr. Oct. daily 9am-9pm

For all the water sports your heart could desire, check out the retailers at Platys Gialos Water Sports. There's everything from water skiing, wakeboarding, banana boats, jet skis, wakesurfing, sea kayaks, and standup paddleboards to the truly horrifying looking flyboard. But maybe it's your thing to be shot up 15 meters (49 feet) into the air on a pressurized stream of water?

NIGHTLIFE AND ENTERTAINMENT

Due to size and sound limits, the biggest clubs in Mykonos are actually located outside of Hora. Most of the action happens around the island's southern coast. Sand and surf meet unbridled hedonism to create some of the best entertainment on the island.

You can call ahead to reserve tables and lounge chairs. Keep in mind that the closer you are to the water's edge, the more expensive your chair will be—up to €500 in the poshest places. Most places start their fees at €20, and that's per chair, not per family. And even though most of these places are beachy, don't think the attire is laid-back: This is as much a fashion show as anywhere else on the island. You'll see people in designer bikinis, fringed shawls, huge Jacquemus hats, high-end jewelry, and fancy sandals. All the beach bars are open from April (usually around Easter) till October.

Unlike bars, clubs do have a cover charge. This can go from €25 to €50, depending on the night's DJ.

Bars

SCORPIOS

Paragas; tel. 22890/29250 or 22890/29250; www.scorpiosmykonos.com; daily 11am-late

Perhaps the chicest of the beach bars, Scorpios is where you come if you want to catch a glimpse of one of the Hadid sisters and any other model/celebrities of the moment. It has more of a Coachella/glamping vibe, and a delicious restaurant serving everything from sashimi to meatballs. There are good (albeit expensive) cocktails and a nice roundup of DJs spinning records all day and night.

TROPICANA

tel. 22890/23582; www.tropicanamykonos.com; daily 9am-late

More men in thongs than you've seen in your entire life, all in one place: that's one way to sum up Tropicana, a no-holds-barred hedonistic den by the sea. It's also just a really, really fun place. It's a bit calmer during the daytime (though the music pulses nonstop), and at night it turns downright bacchanalian.

Music Venues and Clubs

PARADISE CLUB

tel. 694 946 8227; www.paradiseclubmykonos.com; daily 8pm-5am

This intense place is actually the island's biggest club, bringing the most famous international DJs and heart-attack inducing crowds. You'll want to dress sexy-chic to fit in. The music and vibe are mainstream club, popular with the 20-30 crowd. There are smoke machines and a small pool that I would discourage you from jumping into. (Let's just say it's not the cleanest water in Mykonos.)

CAVO PARADISO

tel. 22890/26124; www.cavoparadiso.gr; nightly 11:30pm-7am

This might be Mykonos' premier open-air nightclub outside of Hora. It's a gorgeously designed outdoor space, located on the left-hand side (as you're facing the beach) of Paradise bay. Crowds swell during the summertime, when partygoers flock to catch big international DJ acts. The vibe is intense—this is a techno and house club after all—but a good time is basically guaranteed. Check their website for parties.

★ SUPER PARADISE

tel. 698 591 9002; www.superparadise.com.gr

An all-day (and night) beach club that's been around since the 1970s, Super Paradise won't disappoint the hedonists among us. It's known as the party place in Mykonos and has all-day and night events. It attracts an eclectic crowd (basically, anyone with money and an itch to scratch), but it can also be a lot of fun if you're in the right mood. Regular transport from the Old and New Port by water bus and regular bus is available (hourly, 15 minutes; €2).

JACKIE O BEACH CLUB

tel. 697 301 0981; www.jackieomykonos.com

This multilevel space, complete with cocktail bar, restaurant, lagoon, pool, and boutique, is perched on a rocky outcrop overlooking the Aegean. It's difficult to overstate the importance of queer culture in Mykonos, and in many ways, it's sad to see how this history has been overwritten. Enter Jackie O, which is keeping it real with daily evening drag shows, an LGBT- friendly space, and some truly excellent people-watching.

SHOPPING

MYKNOIAN FARMER

Agios Lazaros; tel. 22890/23970; http://mykonosfarmers.com; Mon.-Thurs. 8am-1pm and 4pm-7pm, Fri.-Sun. 8am-5pm

Mykonos has a rich agricultural tradition that's on full display at Mykonian Farmer, a farm and cheese-production site that also offers tours and cooking classes. It's a family business (now in their third generation) that preserves the traditions of Cycladic cheese making with state-of-the-art technology. They offer some cheese tastings, and you can buy a number of products to bring home. It's located 8 km (5 mi) east of Hora.

FOOD

Greek

NESAEA

Agia Anna; tel. 22890/72130; http://niceneasy.gr/nesaea/about-us; daily 9am-2am; from €15 euros

From the owners of Nice n Easy comes a delicious farm-to-table restaurant away from the bustle of Hora. Nasaea is more of a gourmet restaurant than their flagship location in Hora, so expect to find lots of deconstructed (and then thoughtfully reconstructed) Greek classics, like lamb shank and zucchini fritters. Lunch hours call for casual comfort food; by night the elegant dining room transforms into a chic den, and it's worth springing for the tasting menu.

AVLI TOU THODORI

Platys Gialos; tel. 22890/78100; www.avlitouthodori.gr; daily noon-12:30am; from €17

For a lot of Greeks, summer means the start of the world's greatest salad: watermelon mixed with feta. Confusingly, most restaurants don't offer this dish, which is why Avli Tou Thodori has a special place in my heart. In addition to their fruit and feta mix (fortified with mint leaves and *dakos*), they've got a great selection of homey Greek plates, like fried eggs with grated potatoes, plus local dishes like onion pie and Mykonian sausage.

Renting a Private Villa

If there's one place to spring for a private villa with all your friends, it should be Mykonos—and you should do it with **White Key Villas** (tel. 210 721 5530; www.whitekeyvillas.com; from €5,000 per week), consistently voted one of the best villa agencies in Europe. They specialize in luxury villa properties, some of which can sleep up to 22 people, and all of which feature beautiful infinity pools and Cycladic architecture. The villas come with concierge service and maid service—definitely more swanky than an Airbnb!

International and Fusion

BUDDHA BAR

Santa Marina; tel. 22890/23220; www.santa-marina.gr/restaurants-bars/buddha-bar-beach-mykonos; daily 1pm-7pm and 8pm-1am; from €20

What's a tropical vacation without a Buddha Bar? Mykonos of course has one, located in the elegant Santa Marina resort. It's an incredibly chic restaurant, full of billowing gauze and hanging, hammered metal lamps. The focus is on Asian cuisine with a Greek twist. The sushi and sashimi are particularly delicious, and you should definitely spring for a delicious (and fantastically overpriced) cocktail. Reservations are recommended.

Health Food

BOWL RESTAURANT

Peripheral Road, Ornos; tel. 22890/77659; https://bowlmykonos.co; Mon.-Sat. 9am-6pm; from €9

Leave it to a cool Australian couple to create one of the island's most beloved healthy eating spots. The food, clearly, comes in bowls: smoothie bowls, yogurt bowls, poke bowls, Thai noodle bowls. Ingredients are locally sourced whenever possible, and you'll find plenty of vegan and gluten-free options. There's also a great selection of juices and "shots," including the "reviver shot" made with ginger and turmeric, specifically designed to help with a hangover.

ACCOMMODATIONS

Like in Hora, prices are slashed dramatically in the off-season—as much as 80 percent in some cases. If your dream is to stay in one of these hotels but you can't afford the peak season prices (listed below), then come in April or October. The quality doesn't change.

Under €150

PARADISE BEACH CAMPING

tel. 22890/22852; www.paradisemykonos.com; from €15

For the cheapest sleeping option, pitch a tent here; there are also beach cabins and apartments. It's a self-sustaining campground, so you'll find bars, mini markets, a swimming pool, a clothing shop, etc. This is the sort of campground that is more reminiscent of a music festival than anything else, so be prepared for the relentless noise and partying—there's a rotating cast of DJs playing throughout the summer.

€150-300

APOSTOLIS WINDMILL VILLAS

Agios Lazaros; tel. 22890/24606; http://apostoliswindmill.com; from €200

Mykonos' defining features are its windmills—so how about staying in one? This small collection of traditionally built rooms features private terraces or balconies with views of the sea, and charming architectural details. The furniture is a bit lacking, but all in all, it's a great mid-range option. There's a public bus stop 5 minutes away, and two beaches close by, so it's perfect for those without a car.

Over €300

★ SALTY HOMES

Kalo Livadi; tel. 22890/72421; https://saltyhouses.gr; from €450

This beautiful hotel consists of only seven Mykonian-style homes, spread out around a garden (there's a separate pool area with a bar). The beds are obscenely comfortable, and the staff is exceedingly helpful (and dressed very cool, I have to add). A fresh and copious breakfast is served daily on your terrace, and all villas have a view of the sea.

MYKONIAN IMPERIAL HOTEL

Elia Beach; tel. 22890/79500; www.myconianimperial.gr; from €550

This large, five-star hotel and thalassotherapy spa is an institution on Mykonos. It bills itself as "barefoot luxury," which is true; everything is covered in silver or velvet, but all the guests pad around the pool area without shoes. Double rooms can be a bit on the small side, but there's a gorgeous outdoor area with a fantastic pool.

★ MYKONOS BLU HOTEL

Psarou Beach; tel. 22890/27900; www.mykonosblu.com; from €730

If you've ever dreamed about Mykonos, it probably looked like Mykonos Blu, a stunning (and huge, resort-sized) collection of rooms, bungalows and apartments, all done up in creamy white and covered in gauzy mosquito nets, with small bohemian details throughout. There are two beach bars attached to the hotel, and two lovely restaurants as well. Of course, there's also a next-level concierge service that can take care of your every whim.

GETTING THERE

Because the south coast is the most popular part of Mykonos after the Hora, all the destinations are serviced by buses, water buses, and taxis. If you're planning to stay at a beach bar drinking all day, I urge you to opt for public transportation or a private taxi. You can take **Mykonos Cruises' sea taxis** (tel. 697 883 0355; www.mykonos-seabus.gr; every half hour, 7am-11:30pm; one-way €2.50) to reach Platy Gialos, Elia, Paradise, and Super Paradise.

North Coast

The northeast and north parts of Mykonos are quieter, and between Fokos Beach and Agios Sostis, you can get an idea of what Mykonos was like a mere 50 years ago. This is probably the most wild part of Mykonos: The roads are largely unpaved, farmers till the land, and the beaches and landscape are windswept.

Because the North Coast is more deserted and difficult to access, the best way to get there is by car. Taxis won't take you to Fokos beach, for example, which has a bad road and requires a good car (though I rolled fine, albeit cautiously, in my Fiat Panda). The drive from Mykonos Town to Agios Sostis and Panormos is particularly beautiful, as you'll drive through Marathi lake.

BEACHES

The north coast beaches are the island's most tranquil, though they can be exposed to the harsh *meltemi* (seasonal northern winds). Panormos and Agios Sostis are both easily accessible, and are a bit sheltered. I particularly like Fokos, which is the hardest to reach (you'll find a lot of people choose to drive 4WDs out here) but is the most secluded.

★ AGIOS SOSTIS (Άγιος Σώστης)

One of the last (mostly) untouched beaches on Mykonos, Agios Sostis draws the more bohemian, though still young and beautiful, crowds of Mykonos. It's unorganized (bring your towel and umbrella!), and there is no

Backroads of Mykonos

empty Agios Sostis beach in Mykonos

Most people have a very specific idea of Mykonos: hedonistic, jet-setting, full glitz and glamour. While that's definitely accurate, for most of its history Mykonos was an agricultural island, and that's a legacy that you can still find today, if you know where to look.

If you've rented a car or motorcycle for a day, spend an hour or two crisscrossing the island's few roads (it's difficult to get lost) and checking out the interior of the island, where shrubby brown hills and sugar-cube houses make for a magical landscape, and the (almost) forgotten northern coast, where you'll find bohemian beaches and farmers tending to their sheep.

Driving northeast out of Mykonos Town on country roads to beaches like **Agios Sostis** and **Panormos,** you'll pass little farms with happy-looking goats, gruff farmers with walking sticks in hand, and donkeys leading the way. The drive through **Marathi Lake** is particularly beautiful, but I most enjoyed pressing east past **Ano Mera** to **Profitis Ilias** and **Fokos Beach.** There are no crowds, only locals; the houses are squatter and smaller but just as beautiful, and the landscape feels more open, dotted with tiny churches and abandoned construction. You can *hear* things out here: the wind whistling over the waves, the gentle clinking of the farm animals' bells, your own thoughts. You do need to rent a car to have this experience, but I think it's worth it.

music, which is something of a miracle, especially for such a sandy beach. Note that the beach is a bit exposed, and can be exposed to the *metlemi*. If you get hungry, there's a very decent taverna called **Kiki's** up the hill. The beach is located 8.3 km (5.2 mi, 20 minutes) north of Mykonos Town.

PANORMOS (Πάνορμος)

Located on the north end but still easily accessible by public transport, Panormos is a long sandy beach that's nowhere near as busy as its southern counterparts. There's a luxury hotel here, but the rest of the waterfront is unorganized. It's popular with families, but be careful—the winds up here are pretty harsh. Located 1.4 km (.9 mi, 5 minutes) south of Agios Sostis.

FOKOS (Φώκος)

This unspoiled beach (no DJs, no €150 beach umbrellas) is located 13 km (8 mi) northeast of Hora. You'll need to rent a car to come here, but I promise you, if you want a day of rest and relaxation, this is worth it. The roads from Hora or Panormos (12.6 km/7.8 mi, 25 minutes) are a bit rough, so proceed with caution. There's also a fantastic taverna, **Fokos Taverna,** up the hill (about 5 minutes' walk).

FOOD

★ FARMA RESTAURANT

Ftelia Beach; tel. 22890/72361; daily 1pm-1am; from €11

The first farm-to-table restaurant in Mykonos, located in an old farmhouse under the full bloom of *platanos* trees, Farma is a labor of love. The food is all local and seasonal, and the menu is inspired Greek. Must tries include the *ladenia* pie (olive oil pie originally from the island of Kimolos) the *kotosouvli* (giant pork skewer), and the smoked eggplant salad. The meal usually ends with shots of mastica liquor and fried *loukoumades* (doughtnut holes). It's located 20 minutes north of Hora (8 km/5 mi), and 20 minutes east of Fokos (6 km/3.75 mi).

FOKOS TAVERNA

Fokos Beach; tel. 694 464 4343; daily 1pm-7pm; from €10

As you're lounging on Fokos Beach, you'll probably get hungry from all the smells of barbecued meats wafting over from this lovely little beach taverna. The menu is always fresh, featuring grilled fish and seafood, caught fresh daily and other seasonal ingredients. There's also a nice list of Greek wines.

GETTING THERE

If you're not driving, there are five buses from Mykonos Town (Old Town) to Panormos from 10:30am to 6:30pm; the last bus back into town leaves Panormos at 6:55pm. There are no buses to Fokas or Agios Sostis.

Delos Archaeological Site

TOP EXPERIENCE

Of all the beautiful and awe-inspiring archaeological sites in Greece, Delos might be the most important. It's the birthplace of twins Apollo and Artemis and is a UNESCO World Heritage site. The whole emergence of the Cycladic—which comes from the word "circle"—is centered around this spiritual and sacred island, which is now totally uninhabited.

Delos is a dewdrop of an island, just 5km (3 mi) long and 1.3 km (.8 feet) wide. You won't be allowed to spend more than four hours at a time on Delos, so make the most of it. As you explore, you'll be walking the whole time, in full sun, so bring good shoes, water, hat, sunscreen, and sunglasses.

★ TOURING DELOS ARCHAEOLOGICAL SITE

tel. 22890/22259; Apr.-Oct. 8am-8pm, Nov.-Mar. 8am-3pm; museum and site visit €12, children free

There is much to see in Delos. When you arrive at the ticket office, you'll be given a map of the whole site, with three different **self-guided walking tours.** They range from 1.5 to 4 hours, depending on the trail you take (if you have the time and the stamina, I recommend the biggest loop).

The **Sacred Harbor** will be the first thing you see as your boat docks. As you follow the marked path past the ticket office through the site, you'll find the **South Stoa** (complex of houses and ateliers), the **Sanctuary of Apollo,** and the **Sacred Way** path that takes you into the temple complex of **Propylaia.** Here is a fantastic concentration of temples dedicated to Apollo, and a smaller sanctuary

Delos Archaeological Site

for Artemis. Continuing north, you'll find the **Terrace of the Lions.**

For a taste of how the better half lived, head to the **Theater Quarter,** where the wealthiest people of Delos resided. Some of the houses—with courtyards and mosaics—are better preserved than others; the best are the **House of Dionysos** and the **House of Cleopatra.** There are two more fantastic mosaics to be seen at the **House of Dolphins** (which includes an improbable scene of mythical griffins, land-stuck lions, and aquatic dolphins) and the **House of the Masks.**

Interestingly, Delos was also a sacred place for non-Greeks, and their temples—including shrines to the Samothracian Gods, the Syrian Gods, and the Egyptian Gods—are found in the far end of the site in the **Sanctuary of the Foreign Gods,** next to the **Temple of Hera** and **the Grotto of Heracles.**

GETTING THERE

From Mykonos, boats leave the Hora up to four times a day in the high season. The first boat leaves at 9am and the last leaves at 5pm, and the boat ride takes 30 minutes each way. Tickets can be purchased at the **Delos Boat Ticket Kiosk** (www.delostours.gr; €20 adult, €10 child), from their physical location on the Old Port or online. I recommend taking either the first boat or the last boat—you'll want to avoid being stuck on Delos in the middle of the afternoon, when the heat is the strongest.

As soon as you disembark your ferry, you'll be mobbed by **tour guides.** If you really want to learn more about the site, grab a friendly-looking guide (prices are around €10 per person).

Folegandros (Φολέγανδροσ)

Folegandros (pop. 765) is blink-and-you-miss-it small: just 13 km (8 mi) long and 5 km (3 mi) wide, this rugged dew drop of an island is an hour from Santorini, with the same spectacular sunsets and none of the crowds.

Well, that's not exactly true; to experience the wild, unspoiled beauty of Folegandros, you'd better hurry up and visit now. It used to be completely off the tourist grid until, in 2005, *Conde Nast Traveler* published an article proclaiming it the best "undiscovered" island in the Cyclades. Since then, the island has attracted a steady stream of tourists, though they tend to be of the chic and laid-back variety, content to do nothing but lounge topless on beaches and eat grilled fish for lunch. It's become a bit of a scene-y place, particularly among the Athenian crowd,

Highlights

Look for ★ to find recommended sights, activities, dining, and lodging.

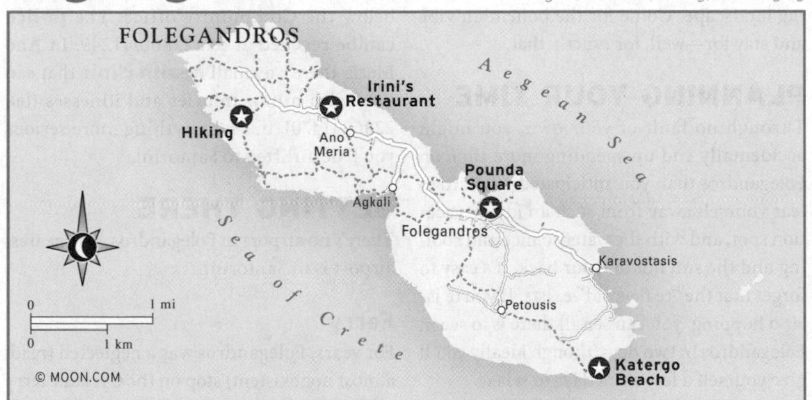

★ **Katergo Beach:** The most beautiful beach in Folegandros is also the hardest to reach. Take a boat to visit this secluded, wild spot, with the cleanest waters on the island (page 141).

★ **Pounda Square:** One of the best-preserved traditional villages in the Cyclades, the Hora is the defining jewel of Folegandros, and where you'll spend most of your nights: make a beeline to the bougainvillea draped Pounda Square, the heartbeat of the Hora (page 142).

★ **Irini's Restaurant:** At this uber-kitsch restaurant, an adorable grandmother prepares handmade pasta, including *matsata,* the island's local specialty (page 146).

★ **Hiking:** Some of Folegandros' best spots are located on unpaved roads, so lace up your hiking boots. A meandering 5.5 km (3.4 mi) hike from Ano Meria to Aspropounta Lighthouse offers stunning views and can be finished off with a swim in the sea (page 147).

but on the bright side, that means there's good people-watching in July and August.

With only three villages, there's not a whole lot to do in Folegandros, which is exactly the point for the modern vacationer. For centuries, though, this was a bane of the island's existence: The harsh land made it difficult to grow crops, and the barren landscape made it impossible to hide from pirates, or the Turks, who regularly attacked the island through the Byzantine and Medieval ages. It has long been a place defined by its isolation; in the 1st century BC, Romans banished prisoners to Folegandros. From 1900 through the 1970s, the island was again used as a place of exile for political prisoners.

Today, nothing of the island's bloody past remains, and instead it's a place for exploring coves, lazily swimming in turquoise waters, and walking miles across the island's bewitching landscape. Come for the bohemian vibe and stay for—well, for exactly that.

PLANNING YOUR TIME

Through no fault of your own, you might accidentally end up spending more time on Folegandros than you anticipated. It's hard to tear yourself away from such an idyllic vacation spot, and with the water so nice and cooling and the sun hot on your back, it's easy to forget that the "real world" exists. If you're island hopping, you can see all there is to see in Folegandros in two days, though ideally you'll give yourself a few extra days to relax.

Aside from scheduling a few dinner reservations, Folegandros is not the sort of island that lends itself to an itinerary. Plan to spend at least **one evening** exploring Hora, and reserve one whole day for a **beach day.** You can combine a **hike** from Ano Meria with a visit to any number of beaches; another option is to take a **boat tour** around the island; tours can be booked at Diaplous Travel.

Unless otherwise noted, businesses on Folegandros operate from **May** to **September.** Most tourists base themselves in **Hora**—there are plenty of good hotel options there. If you want something a bit quieter, consider staying in **Ano Meria.**

INFORMATION AND SERVICES

There are a couple of tourist agencies and information booths at both the port and the Hora, but **Diaplous Travel** (Hora and Port; www.diaploustravel.gr; year round Mon.-Sun., all day) is the only one worth visiting, and the staff are friendly and helpful. You can book air and ferry tickets, transfer money, change your hotel, book a car, rent a helicopter if you feel so inclined, and even plan a wedding with the help of Diaplous. You can also rent motorbikes and book boat tours here.

There's no **bank** on Folegandros, but Alpha Bank and Eurobank have **ATMs** below the Community office. The **police** can be reached at tel. 22860/41249. In Ano Meria there's a small **health clinic** that can help with minor injuries and illnesses (tel. 2286041470), but for anything more serious you'll be airlifted to Santorini.

GETTING THERE

There's no airport in Folegandros. The nearest airport is in Santorini.

Ferry

For years, Folegandros was a neglected (read: almost nonexistent) stop on the Cycladic ferry line. That's a thing of the past now; there are regular ferries from Athens and the nearby islands, and the island is a regular stop on the Piraeus-Milos-Santorini line. During the summer months, boats leave from **Piraeus** to Folegandros 4-5 times a week (6-10 hours, depending on the speed of the boat; €39 for the slow boat, €59 fast). There are also regular ferries to the nearby islands, including **Milos** and **Santorini.** Tickets can be bought directly at the port or through Diaplous Travel.

Previous: Folegandros has some of the most beautiful waters in the Cyclades; a horse prowls the beach; the Church of Panagia, with its long winding walk to the top, is the jewel of Hora.

GETTING AROUND

Tiny Folegandros is only 32 sq km (12 sq mi). If you are so motivated, you can get around Folegandros **on foot;** the legions of French hikers that descend on the island each summer certainly do. It's not necessary to be motorized here, but it is one of the safer islands for driving. You can drive the whole island in around an hour.

Car and Scooter

Cars can be rented at **Diaplous Travel** (up to €60 per day in high season). With only a few roads, it's more practical to rent a motorbike than a car, unless you have a large family. You can rent a scooter from **Donkey Scooters** (from €20 per day), located right before the Hora on the main road from the port.

Bus

The public transportation is pretty good on the island, with regular buses between **Karavostasis, Hora,** and **Ano Meria.** There is usually at least one bus per hour, but the schedule can change from year to year. Check the **blackboard** outside of the bus stops. Bus tickets cost €1.80-2.20.

Taxi

There's one **taxi service** on the island (tel. 694 469 3957). From Hora to the port it costs €7-10; a longer distance, such as to Angali Beach, can cost up to €14.

Itinerary Ideas

DAY 1

1 Book a boat tour leaving Karavostasis at 11am to explore some of Folegandros' secret swimming spots, including **Katergo Beach.**

2 You'll be back in time to head to the Hora and climb to the top of the **Church of Panagia.** Try to time it just as the sun is setting.

3 For dinner, grab a souvlaki from **Souvlaki Club** in Hora and eat it under the shade of the *platanos* trees.

DAY 2

1 Spend the morning at **Galifos Beach** before the summer crowds arrive, swimming in the clear waters and climbing its rock formations.

2 Drive up to Ano Meria to dine at **Irini's Restaurant.**

3 Knock back a coffee after lunch, then head off, by foot, on a 5.5-km (3.5-mi) hike from Ano Meria to **Aspropounta Lighthouse,** which will take you past several churches and Livadaki Beach.

4 Clean off at your hotel and head to the romantic **Eva's Garden** in Hora.

5 Finish your evening with drinks at the raucous **BaRaki** (also in Hora).

Folegandros

Karavostasis Καραβοστάσης

If you're approaching Folegandros by boat, you'll dock at Karavostasis, the island's port, where, seemingly the entire village congregates to greet and bid farewell to ferry passengers. Little fishing boats bob on the water; in the summer they're joined by the larger ferry boats and the increasing number of sleek yachts carrying mysterious celebrities. In the summer, nearly all the white houses that line the port are rented out as rooms to tourists. It's not the most beautiful part of Folegandros, but there are a couple of nice hotels, some decent beaches for swimming, and, should you find your ferry delayed, a few spots to have a final Cycladic meal.

BEACHES

LIVADI (Λιβάδι)

Follow the main road south from the port (you can't get lost) for a little over a mile to find this large, tranquil bay. The island is protected from the strong northern winds, even late in the season. In the summer the campgrounds are open, if you want to pitch a tent.

★ KATERGO BEACH (Κατεργο)

Katergo is Folegandros' most stunning beach, and the most difficult to access. It has both sandy and pebble shores, amazing turquoise water, and a wildness that makes you feel lost in time and space. From Karavostasis, you can take a boat in the summer to reach the beach; those with strong legs can hike 30 minutes south from Livadi to reach the beach. Note that there's no shade and no canteen, so bring your own supplies!

In the summer, there are regular boats running between the beaches. For official tours, a six-hour boat tour costs €40 and includes lunch; and it leaves from Karavostasis at 11am and includes a stop in Katergo. For a cheaper option, grab one of the regularly departing boats (€8) from the port (they're marked).

FOOD

MELTEMI

tel. 22860/41287; Easter-Oct. 9am-late; from €7

There are a few places around the port to grab a bite to eat. Though I'd suggest going to Hora for most of your meals, the family-run Meltemi has a beautiful terrace with views of the ferries coming in and out, and classic taverna food (plus grilled meats and fish) that is reliably good.

ACCOMMODATIONS

★ ANEMI HOTEL

tel. 22860/41610; www.anemihotel.gr/en; Easter-Oct.; from €350

Anemi is the island's only five-star hotel, and as such, it's the most luxurious. There are 12 suites done up with careful attention to detail, all in the traditional Cycladic style with a slight aesthetic twist. There's the requisite infinity pool, daily yoga classes, and a sophisticated clientele. Each year, they also host a music festival. The only drawback is the location; the port really isn't the most charming part of the island.

Hora Χωρα

Folegandros' Hora, 4 km (2.5 mi) northwest of the port, has the honor of being recognized as one of the most beautiful villages in the Cyclades. From a distance, with the village at the bottom and a long, twisting road leading up the mountain's back to the Church of Panagia, it looks a bit like a necklace that's fallen off someone's throat. The Hora itself is a jumble of snaking, white-washed alleyways occasionally interrupted by tree-filled squares full of busy cafés and tavernas, all perched on the edge of a cliff. Add a good dose of the purple bougainvillea that casually hangs from every corner, and a couple of (surprisingly) well-behaved stray cats, and you've got a settlement that looks like it was lifted from a postcard. All of Hora is blissfully vehicle-free; park your wheels at the large parking lot outside the entrance of the village.

Hora is a beautiful place to visit, and you're likely to spend most of your evenings here, after spending all day at the beach, as this is where most of the island's bars and restaurants are located. That being said, if you're looking for total peace and quiet it's better to stay in a hotel outside of the village. There are not really street addresses in Hora, but that shouldn't be a problem: The place is small

Cave of Chrisospilia (Palaiokastro)

Hidden on the northeast side of the island below the **Panagia Church** in Hora, the cave of Chrisopilia (Golden Cave) is one of the largest in Greece, with two main chambers that reach a length of 300 meters (984 feet). Any spelunker would be happy to explore the cave's exceptional stalactite formations, and history buffs will be pleased to visit here: Inside the cave's first chamber, nearly 400 names dating back to the 4th century BC are inscribed on the walls. Archaeologists, who are still uncovering the cave's secrets, believe these names were part of some religious coming-of-age ceremony.

Access to the cave on foot is dangerous and not recommended. If you are interested in seeing parts of the cave (sections of it are off limits), you can hire a boat to take you to the mouth of the cave. Boats can be hired from the port from €20 euros, or ask at **Diapolous Travel**—they organize daily boat tours around the island that include a swimming stop here.

enough that with one walk around, you'll get your bearings.

SIGHTS

★ Pounda Square

The best way to experience the Hora is by walking around and spending some time relaxing in Pounda square. Village life is centered here, and there are several bars and cafés full of locals knocking back cups of Greek coffee and playing backgammon. It really comes alive at night, as kids play under the giant plane tree and people enjoy lingering dinners in tavernas.

Kastro

One of the most inspiring areas of the Hora is the village's oldest section, called Kastro (castle), located at the northern end of the city. Kastro was established in 1212 by the Naxos-based Venetian duke Marco Sanudo, in order to fortify the island and protect inhabitants from frequent pirate attacks. Some houses in the Kastro area are more than 1,000 years old and are still inhabited.

Church of Panagia

Built at the top of a hill, overlooking Hora to one side and the Aegean to the other, the Church of Panagia is the largest church on the island and is dedicated to the Virgin Mary. It's a beautiful whitewashed church with typical Orthodox ornamentation inside. It's believed that the Virgin Mary would offer protection from all those frightening pirates; to this day, during the Easter festivities, the icon of the Virgin is carried around the whole island. As of autumn 2018, the Church was under reconstruction and it was not possible to visit inside, but the view from the site is stupendous.

From a distance, the path from the Hora's central Pounda Square leading to the church looks like a much longer and steeper walk than it actually is; definitely brave it if you're able! At a leisurely pace, with frequent stops to marvel at the view, it will take you about 25 minutes. It's not possible to drive up to the church.

RECREATION

Scooter Rentals

DONKEY SCOOTERS

tel. 22860/41628; www.donkeyscooters.gr; 9:30am-8:30pm; from €20 per day, €40 in high season

Until pretty recently, most inhabitants got around their small island on donkeys. Now there are only a few farmers still riding bareback. For tourists, Folegandros is one of those rare Greek islands where it's pretty safe to drive a scooter, in part because there are only

1: You'll arrive by boat at Karavostasis Port, where locals come out to greet passengers. **2:** a view of Hora with the Church of Panagia at the top **3:** the sugarcube homes of Hora **4:** Some locals still use the traditional method of transportation: donkeys.

1
2
3
4

a handful of roads. Donkey Scooters is your one-stop shop for scooters or AVs. Prices are seasonal, peaking in August. Donkey Scooters is located right before the Hora on the main road from the port.

Diving and Snorkeling

SEA-U

tel. 22860/41624; https://sea-u.com; daily 9am-7pm; single dive with full equipment €60, snorkeling package €30

Much of Folegandros' natural beauty can be found under the water. Head to Sea-U, the island's only PADI-certified dive center, to pick up some gear and go on organized scuba diving excursions around the island. They also rent snorkeling equipment and organize boat excursions, as well as free diving. Anywhere there's a beach, there's the possibility to snorkel, but Sea-U will help you find the best out-of-the-way spots, in a safe environment.

NIGHTLIFE AND ENTERTAINMENT

Bars

BARAKI

tel. 22860/41461; daily 6pm-late

Folegandros doesn't have much of a party scene, but if you're looking for some good music and maybe even a small dance party, you'll find it at BaRaki. As the name implies, the bar is best known for its raki, a Turkish liquor that's similar to ouzo, and particularly for its *rakomelo,* raki that's warmed up with honey and will sneakily make you very, very drunk.

LAOUMI

7pm-late daily; Easter-Oct.

Laoumi feels a bit like a bar from a TV show, where all the characters know each other and the bartender acts as a sort of wise man, doling out drinks at exactly the right moment. The vibe is fun, the owner is very kind, and the music is great. It's a bit more local than the other bars in Hora, although this distinction is thrown out the window during the peak summer months, when barefoot tourists mingle with locals. Located at the entrance of the village right next to the car park.

Wine Bars

WINE BAR MERKOURI

tel. 693 604 9661; daily 7pm-late

Merkouri is the island's only wine bar, and a pretty good one at that. It has a wide selection of more than 40 different Greek wines. It's located outside of the Hora, across from the parking lot, which means you'll find a quieter atmosphere and a startlingly good view of the Church of Panagia.

SHOPPING

Clothing and Accessories

ALWAYS SUMMER

tel. 22860/41104; Easter-Sept. 10am-2pm and 6pm-10:30pm

This cute shop features a good roundup of the usual trendy accessories: embroidered caftans, minimal gold-plated jewelry, strappy leather sandals decorated with silver motifs, fringe shawls, and Aegean-blue inspired clutches and beach bags. This is also a good place to pick up a bathing suit if you've forgotten yours.

FOOD

Tavernas

TO SIK RESTAURANT

tel. 22860/41515; daily 6pm-late; from €12

Also referred to as Chic, To Sik is a very decent taverna in Pounda Square, offering a lot of vegetarian and vegan options (including hummus—despite what foreigners think, not a Greek dish!). During the peak summer season, the service can seem a bit rushed and the crowds relentless. It's best to reserve a table for dinnertime in August.

EVA'S GARDEN

tel. 22860/41110; daily 7pm-late; from €10

Considered the most chic restaurant in Folegandros, Eva's Garden is as much about the clientele (sophisticated, smartly dressed) and the atmosphere (romantic) as it is about the food. Everything is fresh and local. The food is grown at the owner's farm in Livadi.

Local Specialty: *Matsata*

For centuries, Folegandros natives have been hand-rolling *matsata,* a wheat and semolina-based pasta that's boiled and served with rabbit ragu and grated cheese. *Matsata* is prepared fresh and dropped into boiling, salted water almost immediately. It's a very typical "home" food, meaning you won't be able to take any home with you (though if you ask nicely, a culinary-minded local might give you the recipe). *Matsata* is on the menu at almost all the local tavernas, but the best can be found at **Irini's Restaurant** in Ano Meria.

menu in front of a tavern

It's a sort of upmarket taverna menu, with international flavors and techniques woven throughout. Reservations are required in summertime, especially if you want a spot in the lovely garden, though a sidewalk table isn't bad, either.

Souvlaki

PITOKAMOKATA

year-round, daily lunch and dinner; from €3

For cheap eats, head to this cute souvlaki restaurant located off the main square. Be sure to order the fried potatoes; they're particularly excellent. More impressively for a souvlaki spot, they have a nice sandwich option for vegetarians with melted cheese, honey, and grilled veggies. There are a handful of tables outside, but watch out for the shockingly fat cats who will meow for your attention and a bite of your dinner. It's also one of the few Hora restaurants open all year.

SOUVLAKI CLUB

year-round, daily lunch and dinner; from €3

Is there any better name for a sandwich restaurant then Souvlaki Club? I made Mean Girls–style jokes for the entire time it took me to eat a pita (done up in the Folegandros way, which means the tzatziki goes on top of the meat, not on the bottom). The service is great, the location is under a *platanos* tree in the square, and their confidence is inspiring: Their tablecloths read "best in the universe." It's not, but who cares? If you want to take the joke further, buy a "Souvlaki Club: Best in the Universe" baseball cap from the owner.

Breakfast

POUNTA

tel. 22860/41063; www.pounta.gr; Easter-mid-Oct. 8am-3pm and 6pm-midnight; from €7

Owned by a Danish family that's been in Folegandros for over two decades, Pounta is an all-day restaurant that particularly shines at breakfast. There are all your favorite egg dishes, plus crepes, and don't miss the homemade bread, warm from the oven and slathered with a variety of marmalades and jams. Arrive early to snag a table in the beautiful garden.

After you finish your breakfast, lovingly arranged on handmade plates, make sure to pick up some ceramics. Pounta's owner is also a ceramicist and throws beautiful cups, bowls, and mugs.

ACCOMMODATIONS

FATA MORGANA

tel. 22860/41237; www.fatamorgana.gr; Easter-Oct.; from €100

A good mid-range option located just outside of the Hora, Fata Morgana (the name comes from the mirage that forms above a horizon) has several apartment-style suites arranged around a pool and snack bar. It's a particular favorite among Italian tourists.

ANEMOMILOS APARTMENTS

tel. 22860/41309; https://anemomiloshotel.com; Easter-Oct.; from €270

This lovely family-run villa-style hotel is your best bet for lodging in Hora. It's classic Cycladic architecture, but perched at the edge of the Hora's cliffside, with a spectacular view of the sea, plus a pool and a decent restaurant. The staff is particularly warm and welcoming, and the hotel has a loyal band of followers who return each year.

Ano Meria and the Northwest Coast

ANO MERIA (Άνω Μεριά)

The agricultural village of Ano Meria, located in the middle of the island 6 km (3.75 mi) northwest of Hora, is Folegandros' third largest village, which means it's actually pretty small. The views up here are spectacular, and the village is a patchwork series of farmland interspersed with olive trees and crumbling stone walls. The wind is stronger up here, and you'll notice a curious trick that villagers use to protect their citrus trees: they build large, circular stone fences, high enough to block the wind but low enough to let sunlight in. It's a typical Mediterranean construction, also found in Italy, where it's known as *giardino pantesco.*

Food

★ IRINI'S RESTAURANT

tel. 22860/41436; daily, morning-late; from €8

Eating at Irini's is like dining inside of a movie set. This taverna is located inside of a robin's egg-blue mini-market on the main road of Ano Meria, 500 meters (1,600 feet) west of the town. The grandmotherly Mrs. Irini cooks different traditional foods each day (be sure to try her hand-rolled pasta called *matsata),* which you can sample under a canopy of toilet paper rolls and canned tomatoes. It's a very kitsch experience that's not to be missed.

Accommodations

★ PROVALMA

tel. 22860/41132; www.provalma.gr; Easter-Oct.; from €260

inside Irini's Restaurant

This cluster of Cycladic-style studios, organized around a lovely pool with incredible views of Folegandros, is the nicest hotel option in Ano Meria. Rouse yourself out of the incredibly comfortable bed to enjoy the homemade breakfast delivered each morning to your studio; then meander around the grounds and drink up the panoramic view. It's a family-run hotel, and the service is warm without being intrusive. They'll also pick you up and drop you off at the port, and patiently answer any questions you have about the island.

THE NORTHWEST COAST

Scenic Drives

Ano Meria is the last main village in the northwest tip of Folegandros, one of the wildest parts of the island. From here, there are several hikes and drives you can take around the northwest coast. In this area, the villages have completely thinned out, and there are only a few houses and farms scattered around. As you drive along the coast, you'll notice several little coves and pebbled beaches where you can rest your head. Note that there aren't any restaurants or snack stations around here, including on the beaches, so come prepared.

You can follow the one and only paved road northwest from Hora for 8 km (5 mi) up all the way to Merovigli (the farthest town on the map). The road is high enough that you'll see over the bluffs onto the blue sea, and it's usually pretty quiet, especially in the off-season. Once you pass to Merovigli the road becomes dirt, and it's a bit tricky to drive as you navigate down the beaches. The whole drive shouldn't take more than an hour, and that's only if you're driving at a snail's pace.

★ Hiking

These hikes are signposted around Folegandros.

ANO MERIA TO ASPROPOUNTA LIGHTHOUSE

Distance: *5.5 km (3.4 mi)*
Duration: *2 hours one way*
Effort level: *easy*

Built in 1919, when it used to guide ships to safety solely using a wick, the Aspropounta lighthouse now runs on solar energy and is mostly known for the nice hiking trail you take to reach it.

From Ano Meria Myloi (windmills) head south; the hike takes about two hours to cover 5.5 km (3.4 mi) down a well-marked and paved road. You'll pass the **Stavros church** and **Tzanis gorge** before reaching the lighthouse; cut north once you reach **Livadaki Beach** and hike up toward Ano Meria Taxiarhis.

ANO MERIA TO AMPELI BEACH

Distance: *2 km (1.25 mi)*
Duration:*30 minutes one-way*
Effort level: *moderate*

The fastest hike from Ano Meria will take you west, first along a paved path to the **Agios Panteleimonas church,** before the road splits in two. Follow the southern hike down (it will suddenly steeply descend) to reach the beach of **Ampeli,** a small cove with turquoise waters and a strip of sand that's accessible only on foot or by boat. Bring water and snacks!

ANO MERIA TO ZOODOCHOS PIGI

Distance: *4 km (2.5 mi) loop*
Duration: *75 minutes*
Effort level: *moderate*

Starting at the church of **Agios Andreas,** on the west side of Ano Meria, this loop will take you past the church of **Agios Giorgos** to **Lygaria Beach** (where you should stop for a swim) before ending in **Zoodochos Pigi church.** The path is well-marked and often used by shepherds; you'll have an excellent views of the sea and the Kyparissi Cape. Bring water and snacks, as there's nothing here in terms of shops.

Agali and Galifos Beaches

Located in the Vathi Bay on the southwest side of the island, both of these beaches are just a short five-minute drive west of Hora. Follow the main road from Hora to Ano Meria and after 1 km (.6 mi) you'll see the signpost for Agali Beach; it's just a few hundred meters down (the road is paved the whole way, and there's parking). Agali Beach is popular with families because it's easy to access, and it attracts a large crowd in the summer.

AGALI BEACH
(Αγάλι)

The large sandy beach of Agali is the first thing you'll see after following the road downhill the main "highway." It's backed by cliffs on one side and is the most accessible beach in the area, which means it can get quite crowded in the summertime. There are several tavernas and rooms for rent around here, as well as a parking lot.

Food

O PSAROMILIGKAS

Agali; tel. 22860/41116; daily lunch and dinner; from €8

Right at the entrance of Agali beach, you'll find this cute fish restaurant that's open year round. It's perfect for taking a midday break on the shaded terrace from the hard work of lounging beachside all day. The fish is particularly good, and it's freshly grilled to order; be sure to complement it with a glass of raki (you're on vacation, after all!).

GALIFOS BEACH
(Γαλιφός)

You'll notice a walking path on the right-hand side (as you're facing the ocean) of Agali beach. Follow it up the mountain and continue walking. It will take 7-10 minutes to reach Galifos; at times it can be a little steep and rocky, so it's better to walk in sneakers than sandals. You'll find a beautiful little pebbled beach cove that's a favorite among the locals. Though the sign says "No Nudism," this is the de facto nudist beach on this part of the island. If you walk a little into the sea and to the left, there's an even more private cove; on the right side of the beach is an old garage that was used to house fishing boats. The water is incredibly clear, making it perfect for snorkeling, and the cliffside is perfect for rock climbing and diving.

Accommodations

GALIFOS ROOMS

Galifos Beach; tel. 697 613 1295; Easter-Oct.; about €35

As you walk toward Galifos beach, you'll see a hand-painted sign post that reads "Galifos rooms to rent. In a very low price. There is not electricity. They are lighted by gas lamps." For camping with only some of the amenities, rent one of the handful of charming, (super) old-school rooms. There are showers and toilets, but don't expect any further amenities. There's a beautiful view of the beach, and you're well off the beaten path. Note that no electricity means no outlets; embrace the vibe and forget about your phone and Instagram for a while. There are mosquitos at night, so bring some citronella candles.

1: the large sandy beach of Agali **2:** The nudist beach of Galifos is the best secret spot in Folegandros.

1
2

Milos (Μήλοσ)

Ancient volcanic activity shaped Milos (pop. 5,000) into what it is today: a physically quirky, incredibly colorful, geographically insane island. There are more than 70 beaches scattered around this croissant-shaped bit of land, ranging from the moon-like Sarakiniko to the rose and gray-colored Agia Kyriaki. Most of them are inaccessible on foot or by car and can only be visited by boat. Tiny Crayola-colored fishing villages hug the coastline, strange rock formations poke out of the turquoise sea, and abandoned stone houses rise out of the reddish soil like reared heads.

In all honesty, it's not the prettiest of the Cycladic islands—whole sections have been used for mining, and mining plants still dot the island—but it has retained a special charm and character. Much of the island's population was working class, toiling away in the mines or

Highlights

Look for ★ to find recommended sights, activities, dining, and lodging.

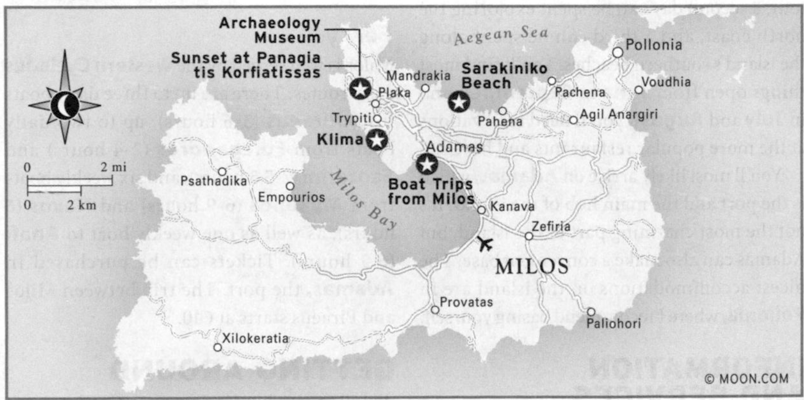

★ **Boat Trips:** A *gyros tis Milos,* or round about the island, is the best way to access most of the island's otherwise inaccessible beaches (page 156).

★ **Archaeology Museum:** Most of the artifacts from the islands' archaeological digs reside here, including a facsimile of the Venus de Milos (page 159).

★ **Sunset at Panagia tis Korfiatissas:** This adorable church is one of the best places for sunset views (page 160)

★ **Klima:** Imagine opening the door of your house and being able to just walk into the sea! This line of colorful houses hugging the coastline is best viewed by boat, but you can also hike down from Trypiti (page 163).

★ **Sarakiniko Beach:** Of Milos' seventy beaches, Sarakiniko is maybe the most remarkable, and the closest thing you'll find to the moon on Earth (page 164).

working farmland for generations, and the locals retain a salt-of-the-earth character. In recent years, Milos has become more of a tourist destination, as travel magazines and fashion photographers have picked up on the island's beauty. But there's still plenty of charm and quiet corners of the island to explore.

In ancient times, Milos was an important and prosperous island in the Minoan civilization, largely thanks to its mineral wealth, including obsidian. The ruins on the island are well-known, from the catacombs to the ancient theater, though its most famous artifact, the 2-meter (6-foot 8-inch) statue of Venus, lives in the Louvre Museum in Paris.

PLANNING YOUR TIME

Milos is pretty sizeable, and it's worthwhile to spend at least **three days** on the island: One day can be spent doing a daylong boat tour, a second day can be spent exploring the north coast, and a third can be spent along the island's southern beaches. You'll find most things open from **June** to **September,** and in **July** and **August,** you'll need reservations at the more popular restaurants and hotels.

You'll most likely arrive on **Adamas,** which is the port and the main hub of the island. It's not the most charming part of the island, but Adamas can also make a convenient base. The nicest accommodations on the island are in **Pollonia,** where I recommend basing yourself.

INFORMATION AND SERVICES

In Adamas, you'll find the **Municipal Tourist Office** (tel. 22870/22445; www.milos.gr; June-Sept. 9am-5pm and 7pm-11pm). There's a **post office** by the main square, as well as several **banks** and **ATMs.** Plaka also has a post office near the archaeological museum, and there are ATMs located throughout the island. You'll find **police** (tel. 22870/23360) at the port and in Plaka (tel. 22870/21204). There's a 24-hour **health clinic** in Plaka (tel. 22870/22700) and plenty of pharmacies, dentists, and private doctors' offices in the island's major towns.

GETTING THERE

The most common way to arrive in Milos is by **ferry**—most visitors will arrive in the port of **Adamas,** located in the northwest part of the island.

Air

Milos has a small airport (**MLO**) located 4.7 km (3 mi) south of Adamas. **Sky Express** (www.skyexpress.gr) has daily flights between Athens and Milos (45 minutes; €80).

There are no buses from the airport, so you'll have to take a **taxi** if you're not renting a car. Taxis cost €13 to Adamas, plus a charge of €0.38 for every piece of luggage that weighs more than 10 kg (22 lbs).

Ferry

Milos is well served by the **western Cyclades** ferry routes. There are up to three daily boats from **Piraeus** (3-6 hours), up to two daily boats from **Folegandros** (2-4 hours) and **Santorini** (2-5.5 hours), and six weekly boats from **Mykonos** (6-9 hours) and **Naxos** (6 hours), as well as one weekly boat to **Anafi** (6.5 hours). Tickets can be purchased in **Adamas,** the port. The trip between Milos and Piraeus starts at €40.

GETTING AROUND

At 160 square km (61 square mi), Milos is one of the larger Cyclades islands, so it's worthwhile to **rent a car.** Note that most of the western part of the island is **off limits** to rental cars due to the exceedingly poor quality of the roads. To visit that part of the island, either rent a **4WD** vehicle or **hike;** no taxis or buses will take you there.

Car

All sorts of wheels can be hired at **Milos**

Previous: A *gyros tis milos* will take you around the island, including to Kleftiko; a fisherman's island, Milos is filled with bobbing boats; the moon-like Sarakiniko.

Rent (tel. 22870/22352; www.milosrent.gr), which has offices in the airport, Adamas, and Pollonia. **Parking** is relatively easy around the island, and Pollonia and Adamas have designated parking lots. However, parking spots can fill up quickly in the summer, and you may have to park on the side of the road. In the high season car rentals start at €35 (from €60 for a 4WD).

Bus

Milos has a pretty decent bus system. Check out **Milos Buses** (www.milosbuses.com) for an up-to-date timetable. Fares are around €1.80, and in the summer, there are hourly buses for **Plaka, Trypiti, Paliochori,** and **Achivadolimni Camping.**

Taxi

Plenty of taxis (tel. 22870/22219) congregate outside the **main square** in **Adamas.** From there to Plaka, it's about €8, and €15 to Pollonia. It costs €1 more if you leave from the harbor of Adamas, and if you call a taxi ahead, that's an extra €2.

Itinerary Ideas

If you're traveling during high season, book your boat trip from Milos on Day 1, or the evening before, if possible. Rent a 4WD for your second day on the island. You'll need it to reach Triades Beach, which is located down an unpaved road at the far western end.

DAY 1

Most of Milos' stunning beaches and landscapes are best viewed from a distance, so it makes sense to take a boat tour on your first day. Bring a towel, bathing suit, sunglasses, and sunscreen. If you insist on bringing your phone or camera, make sure to wrap them in a plastic bag beforehand. Many an electronic device has died on a *gyro tis Milos.*

1 Board a **boat trip from Milos** (*gyros tis Milos*) leaving from Adamas port around 10am. You'll spend the day jumping off the boat into clear waters, sailing past picture-perfect Klima, and swimming in secret coves.

2 By the time you arrive back on dry land (around 6pm or 7pm), you won't have energy to do much more than enjoy a fantastic dinner at **O! Hamos** near the port.

DAY 2

1 Milos' moon-like beach, **Sarakiniko,** a 15-minute drive from Pollonia, is best enjoyed in the early morning before the tourists descend on its lunar surface. Spend a few hours here exploring the strange landscape.

2 When you're done at the beach, drive southwest towards Plaka, stopping at **Mouratos** bakery along the way to stock up on supplies for lunch (I recommend the fried cheese pies).

3 Take some time to explore **Plaka** before driving south around the beautiful curve of Milos toward the western part of the island.

4 Spend the afternoon relaxing at **Triades Beach,** located on the remote western part of the island down an unpaved road. (It'll take you more than an hour to drive here from Plaka.)

5 Drive back toward Empourios to enjoy a dinner at one of the best tavernas on the island, **Empourio.**

Milos

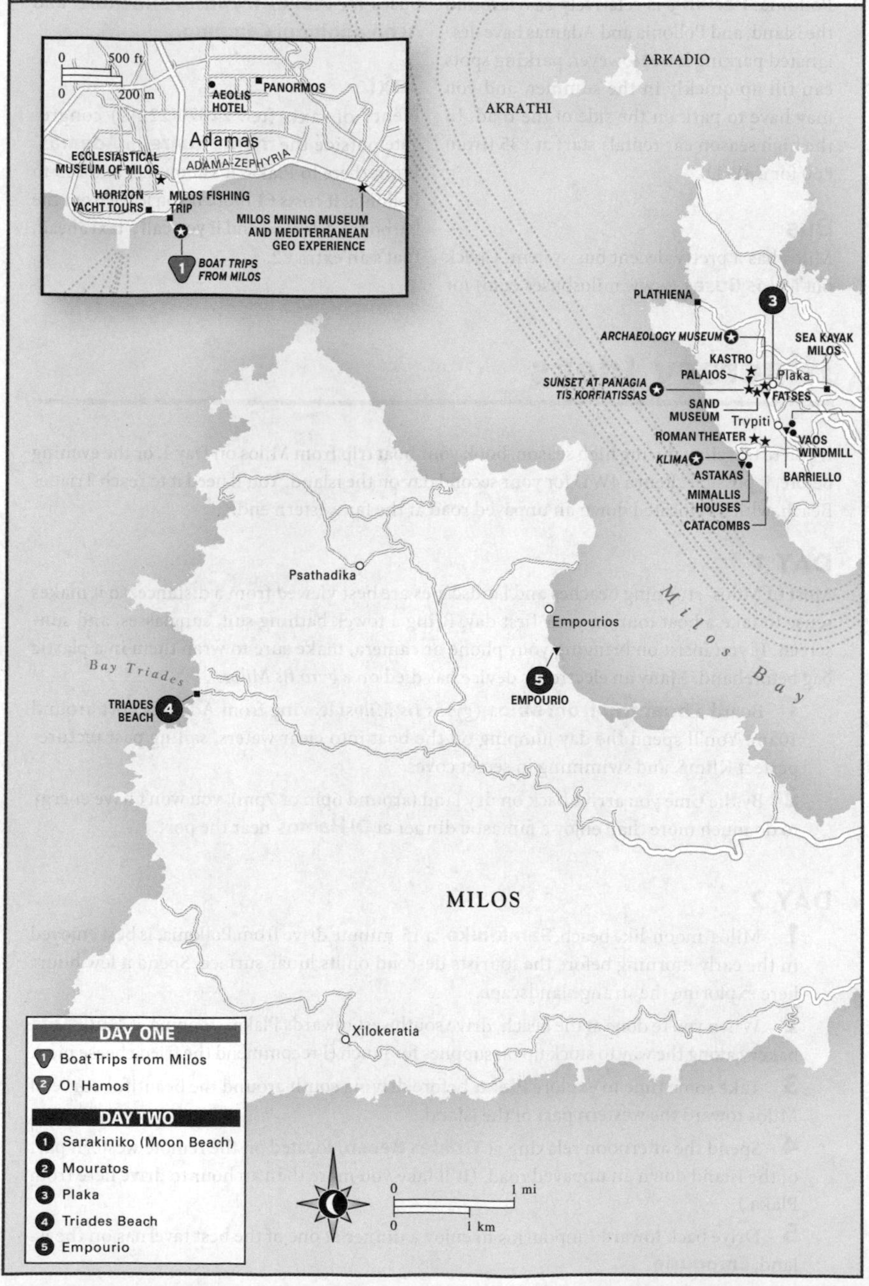

0 500 ft
0 200 m
AEOLIS HOTEL
PANORMOS
Adamas
ECCLESIASTICAL MUSEUM OF MILOS
ADAMA-ZEPHYRIA
HORIZON YACHT TOURS
MILOS FISHING TRIP
MILOS MINING MUSEUM AND MEDITERRANEAN GEO EXPERIENCE
BOAT TRIPS FROM MILOS
ARKADIO
AKRATHI
PLATHIENA
ARCHAEOLOGY MUSEUM
SEA KAYAK MILOS
KASTRO
PALAIOS
Plaka
SUNSET AT PANAGIA TIS KORFIATISSAS
FATSES
SAND MUSEUM
Trypiti
ROMAN THEATER
VAOS WINDMILL
KLIMA
ASTAKAS
BARRIELLO
MIMALLIS HOUSES
CATACOMBS
Psathadika
Empourios
Milos Bay
Bay Triades
TRIADES BEACH
EMPOURIO
MILOS
Xilokeratia
DAY ONE
Boat Trips from Milos
Oi Hamos
DAY TWO
Sarakiniko (Moon Beach)
Mouratos
Plaka
Triades Beach
Empourio
0 1 mi
0 1 km

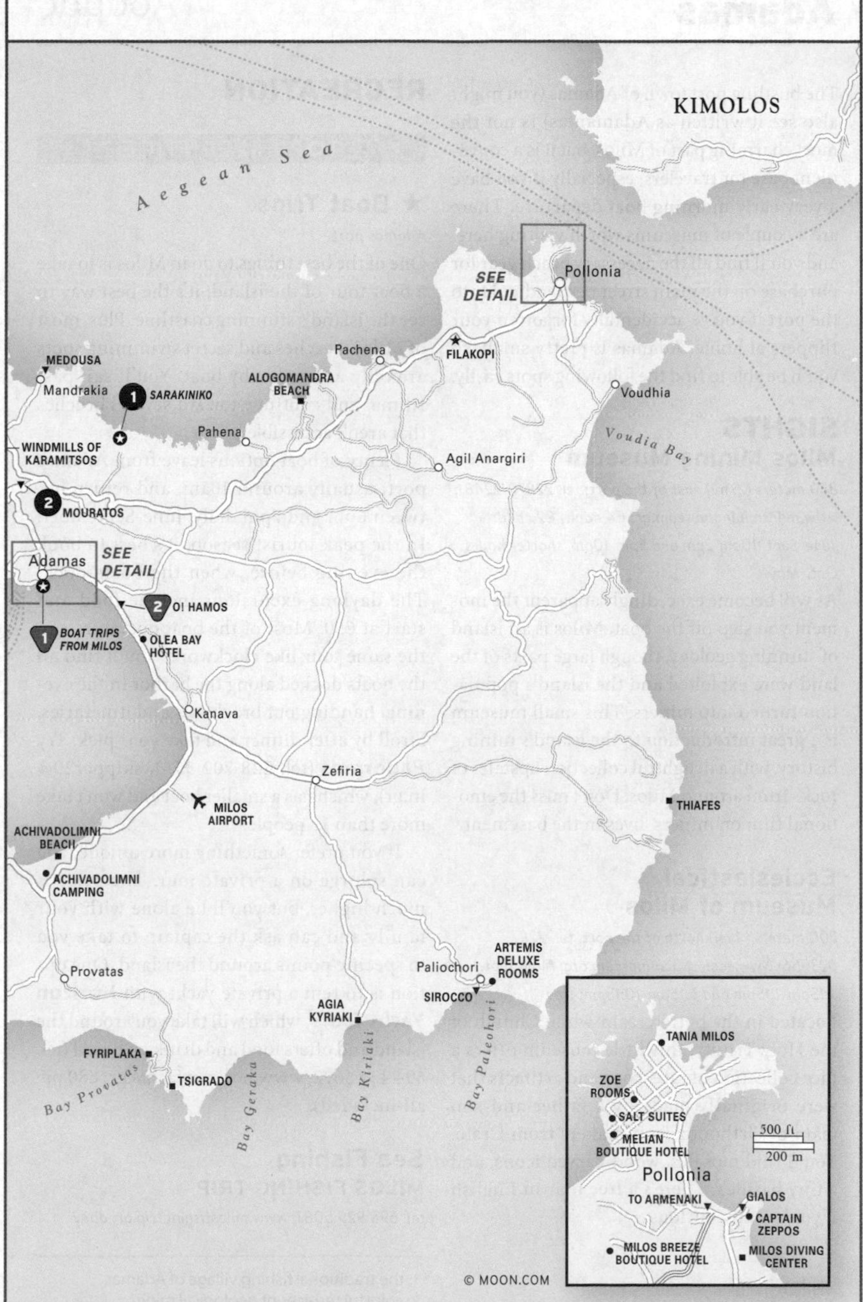
KIMOLOS
Aegean Sea
SEE DETAIL
Pollonia
Pachena
FILAKOPI
MEDOUSA
Mandrakia
SARAKINIKO
ALOGOMANDRA BEACH
Voudhia
Pahena
Voudia Bay
WINDMILLS OF KARAMITSOS
Agil Anargiri
MOURATOS
Adamas
SEE DETAIL
O! HAMOS
BOAT TRIPS FROM MILOS
OLEA BAY HOTEL
Kanava
Zefiria
MILOS AIRPORT
THIAFES
ACHIVADOLIMNI BEACH
ACHIVADOLIMNI CAMPING
Provatas
ARTEMIS DELUXE ROOMS
Paliochori
SIROCCO
AGIA KYRIAKI
FYRIPLAKA
TSIGRADO
Bay Provatas
Bay Geraka
Bay Kiriaki
Bay Paleohori
TANIA MILOS
ZOE ROOMS
SALT SUITES
MELIAN BOUTIQUE HOTEL
500 ft
200 m
Pollonia
TO ARMENAKI
GIALOS
CAPTAIN ZEPPOS
MILOS BREEZE BOUTIQUE HOTEL
MILOS DIVING CENTER
© MOON.COM

Adamas

Αδάμας

The bustling port town of Adamas (you might also see it written as Adamantas) is not the most charming part of Milos, but it is a convenient base for travelers, especially if you have a very early morning boat departure. There are a couple of museums worth visiting here, and you'll find all the necessary beach gear for purchase on the main street perpendicular to the port if you've accidentally forgotten your flippers at home. Adamas is pretty small, so you'll be able to find the following spots easily.

SIGHTS

Milos Mining Museum

850 meters (.5 mi) east of the port; tel. 22870/22481; www.milosminingmuseum.gr; €4 adult, €2 child; June-Sept. 10am-2pm and 5pm-10pm, shorter hours Oct.-May

As will become exceedingly apparent the moment you step off the boat, Milos is an island of stunning geology, though large parts of the land were exploited and the island's population turned into miners. This small museum is a great introduction to the island's mining history, with a delightful collection upstairs of rocks from around Milos. Don't miss the emotional film on miners' lives in the basement.

Ecclesiastical Museum of Milos

200 meters (.1 mi) north of the port; tel. 2287 023956; www.ecclestiacalmuseum.org; May-Sept. 9:15am-1:15pm and 6:15pm-10:15pm; free

Located in the buttercream-white Church of the Holy Trinity, this little museum offers a nice collection of rare icons and artifacts that were originally made by a father-and-son team of Orthodox icon-makers from Crete. You'll find mosaics, wood-carved icons, and a tiny basilica. There's a free tour in English if you're extra curious.

RECREATION

TOP EXPERIENCE

★ Boat Trips

Adamas port

One of the best things to do in Milos is to take a boat tour of the island; it's the best way to see the island's stunning coastline. Plus, most of Milos' beaches and secret swimming spots are only accessible by boat. You'll sail past Klima, and continue toward several beaches that aren't accessible by car.

Plenty of boat options leave from Adamas port, usually around 10am, and return between 6pm and 7pm daily, June-September. In the peak tourist season, it's best to book the evening before, when the boats dock. The daylong excursions include food and start at €50. Most of the boat operators run the same tour like clockwork. You'll find all the boats docked along the harbor in the evening, handing out brochures and itineraries. Stroll by after dinner and take your pick. Try **Panormos** (tel. 228 702 3533, skipper20@in.gr), which has a smaller boat and won't take more than 15 people.

If you prefer something more unique, you can splurge on a private tour. The price is much higher, but you'll be alone with your family and can ask the captain to take you to specific points around the island. One option is to rent a private yacht with **Horizon Yacht Tours,** which will take you around the island and offers food and drink on board (tel. 694 454 6692; www.horizonyachts.gr; €80 pp, all-included).

Sea Fishing

MILOS FISHING TRIP

tel. 698 929 5087; www.milosfishingtrip.gr; daily

1: the traditional fishing village of Adamas
2: colorful terraces of geological mine

1

2

If you'd like to combine your *gyros tis milos* with a bit of sweat, join the father-daughter team at Milos Fishing Trip. Aboard the fishing boat *Anna Maria* you'll get to see some of Milos' most beautiful beaches while also pillaging its seas for lunch. You'll throw a line into the sea (if you don't know anything about fishing, they'll show you the ropes), and cook what you catch; they make a Greek-style bouillabaisse called kakavia onboard. Trips last 6-8 hours, the company caters small groups of up to 15.

Geo Walks

MEDITERRANEAN GEO EXPERIENCE

Adamas; www.miloterranean.gr; daily June-Sept.

Inquire at the Mining Museum about their Mediterranean Geo Experience program: a series of well-detailed maps that provide great half-day "geo" walk options around Milos, to get a more tangible feel for the island's rich geological history.

FOOD

You'll find plenty of food options in Adamas, with a string of restaurants on the port. They are a bit overpriced and serve the kind of standard tourist fare you'd expect, but you can't really go wrong.

★ O! HAMOS

Papikinou Beach; tel. 22870/21672; www.ohamos-milos.gr; Easter-Oct. noon-11pm; mains from €7

My Greek husband proclaimed this one of his favorite restaurants of all the islands he's visited: that's quite a hefty compliment. As we sat down to lunch in the tree-covered courtyard, we sampled fantastic dishes like goat baked in parchment paper, olive oil-covered feta, and fresh chopped salads. Everything, including the meat, comes from the family's farm and livestock, and they make all their own dairy products. Wash it all down with some local beer or wine. Located 1.5 km (1 mi) east of Adamas.

ACCOMMODATIONS

AEOLIS HOTEL

tel. 22870/23985; www.hotel-aeolis.com.gr; from €58 d, breakfast additional €6

A tastefully decorated sugar-white cube of a hotel, with simple lines and twelve breezy rooms that feature tiled floors and balconies, Aeolis is a great budget choice just behind the main square in Adamas. Two of the rooms are handicapped-accessible. It's also one of the few hotels that's open year-round; in summer, there's a two-night minimum stay.

OLEA BAY HOTEL

tel. 22870/31003; www.oleahotel.gr; from €130

Olea is a designer-y boutique hotel, all white (careful with your glass of wine) and minimal design with a pool that's ideal for lounging. Service is top-notch, and they offer plenty of nice amenities, like free loaner bicycles and a great breakfast buffet.

Achivadolimni Αχιβαδολιμνη

Located 7.5 km (4.5 mi) southwest of Adamas, this beach is popular for windsurfing, as it's exposed to the *meltemi* winds in the summer months. The wind is strong and the waves can be quite high (at least by Greek standards) so it's not always the best for swimming. In Greek, *achiavo* means clam, and *limni* means lake: Behind the beautiful beach of Achivadolimni, there's (you guessed it) a small lake where there are thousands of clams.

In the summer, there are hourly buses from Adamas (€1.60) for Achivadolimni Camping.

Camping

ACHIVADOLIMNI CAMPING

Achivadolimni; https://miloscamping.com; from €22

A popular choice with families, windsurfers, and backpackers, this campsite offers both bungalows (with half or full board) and spots to pitch your tent (they also rent tents) or park your caravan. There's a pool, minimarket, and restaurant on-site, and the local bus stops in front of the campground. This is probably the cheapest option in Milos, especially for the tents. The bungalows are actually quite chic, and come with sheets, towels, and cute little terraces.

Plaka Πλάκα

Picturesque Plaka, 5 km (3 mi) northwest of Adamas, is everything you'd want from a Greek island town: white-washed, with tiny alleyways and tumbling bougainvillea, and entirely car-free. It's both the oldest and the highest settlement in Milos; it was built on the site of Ancient Milos, which went through a typical cyclical Cycladic destruction (by the Athenians) and reconstruction (by the Romans).

In the summer, there are hourly buses from Adamas for Plaka.

SIGHTS

★ Archaeology Museum

tel. 22870/28026; Mon.-Tues. 9am-4pm; €2 adult, €1 child

This old-school museum—think glass cases and middle-aged guards following you around—is actually well worth a visit, largely due to its plaster facsimile of the Venus de Milos, which was taken by the French and is considered an art theft here on the island. It'll take you 90 minutes to walk through the whole museum, which boasts an impressive collection of artifacts from digs around the island; some of the pieces date as far back as 1400 BC.

Kastro

free

Originally built on the ancient acropolis of Plaka, the *kastro* (castle) was the town's hilltop fortress. Much of it now lies in ruins, with a small church erected in the 13th century inside the crumbled walls. The best thing about the *kastro* is its stunning panoramic views across Milos, some of the island's best. You can either hike up the endless stairs (signposted from Plaka's center) or take the €1 elevator that's located at the bottom of the hill. Try to come up around sunset.

Sand Museum

tel. 693 826 6860; summer 9am-late, winter 9-4; free

This kooky little museum is a gem. The very sweet geologist Asteris (English speaking) runs the tiny Sand Museum, with sand and rocks from all over the world on display. He's super knowledgeable and can give you a great overview of the geology of Milos. Ask him to show you the magnetic sand. There's also some sand art and other objects for sale.

★ Sunset at Panagia tis Korfiatissas

free

This little church in Plaka is best known for another kind of religious experience: it's one of the best places on the island to catch the sunset. Get here a little bit before sundown to marvel at nature's beauty. You can even discreetly BYOB, if you're so moved.

BEACHES

PLATHIENA

Located 3 km (just under 2 mi) north of Plaka and accessible by car, Plathiena is a long, sandy beach (something of a rarity on rocky Milos!). It's somewhat secluded, making it an ideal choice for those looking for privacy, but there aren't many facilities close by, so make sure to bring food and water.

RECREATION

Kayaking

One of the best ways—at least for the athletes among us—to explore Milos' incredible coastline is to rent a kayak and circumnavigate parts of the island.

SEA KAYAK MILOS

Triovasalos; tel. 694 647 7170; www.seakayakgreece.com; daily 9:30am-5pm; €80

At Sea Kayak Milos (1.7 km/1 mi east of Plaka) you can take guided day trips to all sorts of hidden spots in Milos, from sea coves to secluded beaches, coasting the waves as the wind picks up. They'll teach you to kayak if you know nothing, but as excursions last eight hours, you should have a moderately good level of physical fitness. The price includes a snack, lunch, equipment (including snorkeling gear), photos, and an experienced English-speaking guide.

FOOD

FATSES

tel. 22870/21740; daily 10:30am-1am; from €6

This traditional Greek meze restaurant is located under a giant tree, and local musicians are often around, playing local tunes. It's an ideal place to while away a starry evening, chowing down on *saganaki* (fried snacks) and cured olives. Most of the ingredients are organic, and everything is homemade.

PALAIOS

tel. 22870/23490; Apr.-Oct. daily 8am-9pm; from €4

A cavernous café with a decidedly old-school clientele (it's full of white-haired locals slowly stirring sugar into their coffee cups), this is the perfect place for an afternoon pick-me up. They've got all sorts of cakes, cookies, frozen treats, and caffeinated beverages on offer. If it's available, try *karpouzia* (a watermelon pie, where jam-y watermelon is lodged between two buttery pieces of crust). For those with less of a sweet tooth, they also have savory options and egg-y breakfast choices.

★ MOURATOS

Triovassalos; tel. 22870/22800; daily, early to late

Located a short 7-minute drive southeast of Plaka on the main road from Plaka to Adamas, Mouratos is (in my humble opinion) the best bakery on the island. For the past thirty years, the Mouratos family has been making all kinds of carb-y, yeasted delicacies. Try the *pittarakia* (deep-fried cheese pies, perfect for your beach body), *ladenia* (Greece's answer to focaccia), and the totally delicious bacon roll.

1: the cute church of Panagia tis Korfiatissas **2:** the dimly lit, slightly macabre catacombs of Milos **3:** Bougainvillea fills the streets in Plaka village.

1

2

3

Venus of Milos

The goddess Aphrodite is the patron saint of love and beauty in Greek mythology, her counterpart in Roman mythology is Venus. At some point between 300 and 100 BC, the sculptor **Alexandros of Antioch** took a whack at reproducing the goddess: He carved supple breasts, ripping abs, and a holier-than-thou facial expression (to be fair, she is) into a giant block of marble.

The 2-meter (6-foot 8-inch) statue, known today as Venus de Milo, is one of the most impressive and poetic works of ancient Greek art, and in 1820 the peasant Yorgos Kentrota found the sculpture in Milos, buried in the ground in the ancient Minoan city near Trypiti. Aphrodite was nearly intact, save for her two arms, which remains one of the greatest mysteries in art history. Kentrota enlisted the help of a French naval officer, which led to Marquis de Rivière presenting the masterpiece to King Louis XVIII, who bestowed it on the **Louvre Museum.**

Venus still lives in Paris, but the mayor of Milos has launched an ambitious campaign to bring Venus back to her home by 2020. You'll notice posters of a forlorn Venus against the text "Take me home" scattered throughout villages.

Trypiti and Klima

TRYPITI (Τρυπητή)

A mere 2 km (1.25 mi) south of Plaka is the small village of Trypiti. The name means "holes" in Greek, and is a nod to the soft soil on which Trypiti was built. It was a city of relative importance in the Classical and Hellenisitic periods. It's the home of some very important archaeological sites, and it's worth spending the night at one of the village's converted windmills. You can also hike down to the picturesque village of Klima from here.

In the summer, there are hourly buses from Adamas to Trypiti.

Sights

CATACOMBS

tel. 22870/21625; Tues.-Sun. 9am-7pm; €4 adult, €2 child

Trypiti is home to Greece's only Christian catacombs, which date from the 1st century and are considered one of the most important sights on the island. Over the years, up to 5,000 people were buried in underground tombs. These days, they are mostly empty (all the artifacts are in the Archaeology Museum) but make for an eerie fifteen-minute tour, all backlit with a golden glow. Note that the tours are mandatory in order to visit the caves, but the tour guides are less than enthusiastic.

ROMAN THEATER

This well-preserved theater is dramatically (get it?) situated above Klima and overlooks the port. The horse-shoe shaped arena was built in the 3rd century BC and could seat up to 700 people. It's particularly lovely in the spring, when bright red poppies and other colorful wildflowers pop up in the cracks.

Food

BARRIELLO

tel. 698 421 8360; www.barriello.com; 7pm-3am; from €15

Dishes covered in edible flowers: That's the main vibe at Barriello, one of the more romantic (and thus, pricier) restaurants on Milos. Barriello stands out for its staff, who provide top-notch service and will guide you through the small, but delicious menu. It's an organic restaurant, and everything you eat has been raised on the owner's farm. The menu changes seasonally but you can expect dishes like saffron pear salad and squid stuffed with tomato puree.

Accommodations

You'll notice that there are plenty of windmills in Trypiti. Back in the day, these served agricultural purposes; these days, most of them have been turned into hotels.

VAOS WINDMILL

tel. 261 032 1742; from €80

Three floors, connected by an inner stone staircase, sleep up to four people in this lovingly converted hotel. There's a small terraced garden that offers views across the Aegean, and you'll catch the sunset every night. It's located behind Tryptiri's main church.

WINDMILLS OF KARAMITSOS

tel. 694 556 8086; www.windmillmilos.gr; Apr.-Oct.; from €200

The same concept as Vaos Windmill applies here, too: three floors, with the ground floor used as a living space, and bedrooms upstairs. It was built in 1859 for grinding wheat and was converted in 2010. The decor is more modern and chic than Vaos, and that's reflected in the price.

★ KLIMA

(Κλήμα)

About 1.8 km (1 mi) below Trypiti is this beachfront cliff where a row of white houses, with doors and windows each painted a different color, seem to tumble directly into the Aegean. Klima is a stunning example of Milos syrmata architecture: traditional fishermen's workspaces and dwellings. The ground floor is used for storing boats, which can be directly rolled into and out of the water, while the family lives upstairs. People still live in these houses, most of which are built into the rocks. If you choose to walk through the town's "road," note you will very likely get sopping wet from the endless barrage of waves that break on the harbor!

The best way to see Klima is by boat—all boat tours leaving from Adamas sail past here—but it's also nice to hike down from Trypiti. The 1.8 km (1 mi) hike (40 minutes; easy to moderate) leads past the catacombs, the ancient Roman Theater that hosts the island's Milos Festival each summer, all the way down to Klima Village, with stunning views of the sea the whole way. The path is well marked. As you descend the path to the catacombs, you'll also notice a dirt track (signposted), which leads to the spot where a farmer found the Venus de Milo in 1820. Note that it's easy to walk down, but uphill is a bit more strenuous.

Food

★ ASTAKAS

tel. 22870/22134; daily 9am-midnight; from €12

Opened in 2015, Astakas is one of the best restaurants on Milos, both in terms of view (it's hard to beat dining in Klima) and food. Must-try dishes include the lobster pasta, squid risotto, tomato fritters, and fried baby shrimp. Reservations are recommended in summer.

Accommodations

MIMALLIS HOUSES

Klima; tel. 697 280 8758; www.mimallis.gr; Apr.-Oct.; from €200

If you've ever wanted to live (and sleep) like a fisherman, book the Mimallis House in Klima. The small apartment sleeps up to five, and comes with a canoe (!) in case you want to explore the waves around your house. They have another two houses for rent in Plaka.

Northern Coast: Plaka to Pollonia

The northern curve of Milos, which can be easily driven from Plaka all the way to Pollonia, is home to some excellent scenery and stunning beaches. There's a coastal-ish road (you'll see the sea for most of it) that will take 20 minutes to drive. If you want to spend a bit more time in the car, turn left (coming from Plaka) at the Eka Livanios gas station; the road takes an extra 10 minutes and goes through the interior of the north. Bus service is available to Sarakiniko and Pollonia.

Note that this is the north coast of the island, so you are exposed to the Cyclades' notorious *meltemi* winds.

MANDRAKIA
(Μανδρακία)

The beautiful little fishing port of Mandrakia, 3 km (just under 2 mi) east of Plaka, is like an even tinier, cuter version of Klima. Small fishermen's dwellings and boat storage are built into rocks and open directly onto the sea. Park your car and take some photos from the top before walking down the steps to see the fishing village up close.

Food

MEDOUSA

tel. 22870/23670; June-Sept. daily noon-11pm; from €7

If you weren't already convinced of the fishing prowess of the inhabitants of Mandrakina, then this excellent seafood taverna will certainly do the trick. Start with an order of marinated anchovies or grilled sardines, and don't miss the freshly caught, sun-dried grilled octopus. The bill will come with a shot of alcohol and some fresh fruit (think whole apricots).

★ SARAKINIKO BEACH (MOON BEACH)
(Σαρακινικο)

The otherworldly, lunar-like landscape of Sarakiniko (Moon Beach), 5 km (3 mi) east of Plaka, is composed of volcanic rocks that have slowly been eroded by salt and sea over millennia. Park your car at the lot before the beach, and then head down to walk around the beach. You'll climb up and down stone-white grooves and marvel at the whole place, which looks like one of those drip-drab wet sand castles kids make on the beach, but solidified and in huge proportions. It honestly feels like you are walking on the moon. There's a small beach where people swim, but it gets horribly crowded in the summer. Come early in the morning or at dusk to beat the crowds. There are five daily buses to Sarakiniko from Adamas in the summer high season (15 minutes, €2).

ALOGOMANDRA BEACH
(Αλγκομάντρα)

Alogomandra, 8 km (5 mi) east of Plaka, is actually a small cove right next to the larger sandy beach of Agios Konstantinos, but Alogomandra is a bit more quiet, and has pure white sand and is backed by white rocks. It's good for swimming, snorkeling, and sunbathing. Both beaches lack services.

1: the view from above Mandrakia village
2: Sarakiniko Beach

1

2

Pollonia Πολλώνια

Located in a little islet on the northeastern part of the island, a 20-minute (12 km/7.5 mi) drive from Plaka, Pollonia has in recent years become an increasingly touristic destination; it's also the island's second port. It's remained a picturesque little fishing village, though, with a lovely cluster of hotels and restaurants along the pebbled shoreline. There is a bus terminal in Pollonia with six daily buses in the high season to and from Adamas (30 minutes, €2 euros).

SIGHTS

Filakopi (Φυλακωπη)

8am-3pm Tues., Thurs., and Sat.; €2

Just a three-minute drive from Pollonia is the ancient Minoan city of Filakopi, which was an important and prosperous city during the Bronze Age, thanks to its healthy trade in black obsidian. Most of the city is now in ruins, and the findings are on display at the Archaeological Museum in Plaka.

RECREATION

Diving

MILOS DIVING CENTER

Pollonia waterfront, tel. 697 611 4846; www.milosdiving.gr; daily, 9:30am-3pm; single dive from €40

There's as much to discover underwater in Milos as there is on the island. Join the fine folks at Milos Diving Center for guided dives around the island, including sites of shipwrecks. This is the first dive school in the area, and it's very trustworthy. You'll find a sea teeming with wildlife, and strange formations thanks to Milos' volcanic history.

FOOD

There are plenty of nice tavernas along the harbor in Pollonia, most of them serving freshly caught fish. They'll have it on display outside the restaurant. Look for fish that has clear eyes, and healthy, bright pink gills.

TO ARMENAKI

tel. 22870/41061; Apr.-Oct. lunch and dinner; from €7

Located by the harbor, To Armenaki is a beloved fish restaurant that can get quite crowded in the high season. Try to book ahead in July and August. What sets this place apart from other fish tavernas in the area is an extensive Greek wine list and knowledgeable oenophile owner. The restaurant even does wine tastings in the afternoon with cheese and charcuterie. For dinner, order any of the freshly caught fish; if you're extra hungry, try the seafood pasta with a half lobster.

GIALOS

tel. 22870/41208; Apr.-Oct. lunch and dinner; from €8

This is another fine fish taverna with friendly staff and breezy views. Fish is brought in daily from the sea, and you can choose what you'd like grilled. It's a cut above the other seafront tavernas, thanks to its contemporary twist on fish. The menu changes daily, with offerings like scallops with mashed pumpkin, and squid with couscous. Reservations are recommended.

ACCOMMODATIONS

While there are hotels over the whole island, Pollonia has the highest concentration of designer, boutique hotels that will make your stay on Milos feel special. In the off-season (April, May, October) prices are slashed in half.

Under €150

ZOE ROOMS

tel. 22870/41235; www.zoe-milos.gr; from €100

Zoe Rooms are basic apartment-like units that are good for longer-term visitors—it's one of the cheapest options in Pollonia. None of the decor is particularly inspiring, and the mattresses are a bit thin, but most of the rooms come with a kitchenette and sea view and, most importantly, air-conditioning.

€150-300

★ CAPTAIN ZEPPOS

tel. 22870/41327; www.captainzeppos.com; from €160

This totally charming boutique hotel was inspired by the owner's father, a certain Captain Zeppos. It's located in an old neoclassical-style house, and breakfast is served in your room each day. Honeymooners should spring for the penthouse suite, which offers the most arresting views of the harbor. Helpful staff will assist you with anything you need on the island. The owners also have a car company, and free rental cars are offered with bookings during the off-season.

TANIA MILOS

tel. 210 779 2795; www.taniamilos.gr; from €175

This small Cycladic-style hotel offers rooms that each have a private balcony with a view of the Aegean, and comfortable beds. Breakfast is taken quite seriously here, with big portions of homemade food, and the staff is friendly and generous.

★ SALT SUITES

tel. 22870/41110; www.salt-milos.com; from €200

Probably the chicest of the hotels in Milos, Salt Suites is an homage to the clean, simple lines of Cycladic architecture—think polished cement floors, sculpted showers, and expansive wooden terraces. Ten suites are nestled around the pebbled bay and look out onto the sea; some rooms come with hot tubs, and a general air of romance surrounds the place. This property has all the amenities you'd expect from a five-star hotel, including breakfast basket delivery.

MILOS BREEZE BOUTIQUE HOTEL

tel. 22870/41085; www.milosbreeze.gr/en; from €300

This hotel possesses an inviting mix of traditional architecture and luxury touches, with a jaw-dropping infinity pool. All of the rooms have sea views, and the honeymoon suite comes with a private plunge pool. Note that the hotel only accepts kids over the age of 14.

Over €300

MELIAN BOUTIQUE HOTEL

tel. 22870/41150; https://melianhotel.reserve-online.net; from €320

This lovely hotel and spa is all sleek and white, with just sixteen rooms to keep everything cozy. Suites come with private hot tubs and hammocks, and most rooms have a view of the Aegean. There are plenty of nice amenities, like a pool, complimentary breakfast, and babysitters.

South Milos Beaches

The southern curve of Milos has some fantastic beaches that suit every taste: organized, nudist, windsurfing, etc. There's no direct coastal road connecting these beaches; instead, there's a network of smaller paved roads that cut through villages, and you'll have to strike out to reach each beach individually.

From Adamas, it takes 20 minutes to reach Paliochori, 25 minutes to reach Thiafes, 18 minutes to reach Fyriplaka, 15 minutes to reach Agia Kiriaki, and 17 to reach Tsigrado.

In the summer, there are hourly buses from Adamas for Paliochori and Fyriplaka. Thiafes can only be reached by car.

THIAFES
(θειαφες)

About 11.5 km (7 mi) east of Adamas, this beach is located next to an abandoned sulfur mine. Thiafes is half relaxation spot, half history lesson: During the first half of the 20th century, miners would spend the week sleeping here before walking hours back to their villages for their day of rest on Sunday. Around 300 workers toiled here under harsh conditions, exporting 125,000 tons of sulfur in total. Now abandoned, the beach makes for an arresting site.

PALIOCHORI
(Παλαιοχώρι)

Paliochori lies 10.6 km (6.5 mi) south of Adamas, and it is the most organized beach in Milos, in large part thanks to its length and the fact that it's well-protected from the strong northern winds. You'll feel the volcanic energy of the island in the waters here; it's not uncommon to swim across a bubble of warm water! The local tavernas here also use the volcanic sand to cook some of their food.

Food

SIROCCO

Paliochori; tel. 22870/31201; Apr.-Oct., breakfast, lunch, and dinner; from €10

Lamb and fish are covered in foil and baked in hot sand for hours at Sirocco, a cozy, all-day café-restaurant located on the harbor of Paliochori. You'll watch the chefs rake sand over the pots of food, and then unearth them as customers order. The taste is pretty much the same as with other cooking methods, but it's very cool to see.

Accommodations

ARTEMIS DELUXE ROOMS

Paliochori; http://artemismilos.gr; from €225

A mere 50 meters (165 feet) from Paliochori beach is this luxury complex, which features a collection of five different Cycladic-style rooms (some of which can fit up to 16 people). Each room has a private balcony or veranda, and friendly staff are on call 24/7.

AGIA KYRIAKI
(Αγία Κυριακή)

Considered one of the most beautiful beaches in Milos, this is a lovely sandy beach with clear waters and strange rock formations. It's also relatively isolated. There are several private coves around Agia Kyriaki that are used for nudism.

From Adamas, drive to Zefyria village (9.7 km (6 mi) south), then follow the signs after Zefyria village to get to Agia Kyriaki.

TSIGRADO
(Τσιγκράδο)

If you're looking for a hidden beach that's an adventure and a half to get to, Tsigrado is a good bet: it's easiest reached by sea, but there is a very steep passageway, cut into the rocky cliff, where you can (at your own risk) climb down, aided by the rope system. There's a wooden ladder for the last few steps. You'll be rewarded with a secluded turquoise cove. Most of the boats from Adamas stop here; it's 11 km (just under 7 mi) south of Adamas by car. There are four daily buses to Tsigrado in the summer season from Adamas, with a stop in Fyriplaka.

FYRIPLAKA
(Φυριπλακα)

This lovely sandy beach is backed by imposing volcanic rocks. There are actually two parts to the beach: The first part is organized with chairs and a beach bar, but if you walk around the large rock you'll find a more quiet, unorganized part to the beach. It's a 600-meter stretch between the two, and you can walk between them. There are four daily buses from Adamas to Fyriplaka in the summer season, with a stop in Tsigrado. Fyriplaka is an 18-minute drive (11 km/7 mi) south of Adamas.

West Milos

If you really want to explore this part of the island, you'll need to rent a 4WD car. (Most car rental companies won't let you drive deep into west Milos unless you have a 4WD. While the roads here are unpaved, you can drive relatively easily, even with a basic rental car, to Emporiou.) I recommend splurging on one for a day, as this part of Milos is still wild and empty of tourists. Certainly don't do what I did, which is to drive my decidedly city-tire car through the red mud, wheels spinning for most of the drive. A car rental company can rent you a 4WD for the west coast; no taxis or buses will take you out there.

EMPOURIOS

Food

★ EMPOURIO

Empourios; tel. 22870/21389; daily, lunch and dinner; from €6

For a meal on the edge of the world, it doesn't get more remote (or delicious) than Empourio, a seasonal taverna built around an old flour mill from the 1850s. Everything is homemade, including the feta cheese. On Sunday they make their specialty, goat stew baked in the oven. From Adamas, Empourio village is a 21-km (13-mi) drive west (it will take about an hour). At the Agia Marina church in the village, follow the dirt road left (the restaurant is signposted).

TRIADES BEACH (Τριαδες)

Triades ("trinity" in Greek) Bay is composed of three sandy bays: Cliffs stick out of the land, creating a natural barrier that cuts the beach into three distinct beaches. It's best to drive with a 4WD to this beach, as the road is unpaved, but you'll be rewarded with a secluded stretch of coastline. It's a 21-km (13-mi) drive from Adamas, but count at least an hour on the roads.

Naxos (Νάξοσ)

When Anthony Bourdain's travel show *Parts*

Unknown came to Greece in 2015, the original plan was to visit a couple of islands. Then the team arrived on Naxos (pop. 18,000), and they ended up staying here for the entirety of the production time.

Let that be your first lesson: Naxos will seduce you and hold onto you for longer than you anticipated. First, there's the sheer size of the place—this is the largest and loftiest island in the Cycladics, greener and more fertile than its neighbors. This has created a rich farming and culinary tradition, emitting some of the best produce in Greece. Naxos is particularly famed for its cheeses and potatoes. You could easily spend a week just eating, but take some time to explore the island, from its beautiful beaches to its pine tree forests, Byzantine churches,

Highlights

Look for ★ to find recommended sights, activities, dining, and lodging.

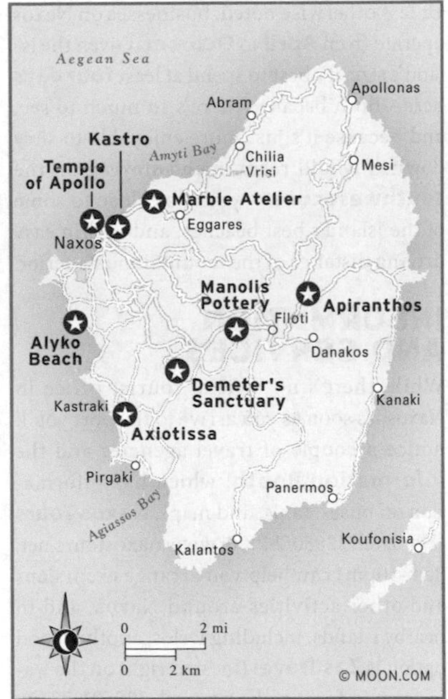

★ **Kastro:** The 13th-century neighborhood in the heart of the Hora is a well-preserved reminder of the island's Venetian past (page 175).

★ **Temple of Apollo:** This stunning temple, built to honor the god Apollo, is a breathtaking sight at the edge of Hora (page 176).

★ **Alyko Beach:** The main attraction at this beach is the abandoned beachside hotel that's been covered in frescoes and turned into an open-air art museum (page 182).

★ **Axiotissa:** Hands down the most delicious restaurant on the island, Axiotissa serves up the best Naxian products and cuisine with love and careful attention to detail. Reservations are required (page 182).

★ **Marble Atelier:** A roadside attraction missed by most, this is a fantastic collection of marble statues, chiseled into kooky forms (page 183).

★ **Demeter's Sanctuary:** This beautiful marble sanctuary is dedicated to the goddess of grain (page 186).

★ **Manolis Pottery:** Manolis, a third-generation pottery maker, creates fantastic traditional pottery out of his studio (page 186).

★ **Apiranthos:** Among Naxos' many beautiful mountain villages, Apiranthos stands out for its stunning marble architecture and fascinating intellectual history (page 188).

and Venetian towers. Along the coast you'll discover turquoise clear waters, but don't miss the island's interior mountains for stunning hikes and tiny villages perched in the clouds.

For decades Naxos was mostly a family destination, but its popularity has erupted in recent years, making certain parts of the island feel like anything but a vacation during the high season in July and August. On the plus side, it means that a slew of very good restaurants and hotels have opened up, and competition has increased quality. More importantly, despite the tourist onslaught, Naxos has held onto its culture: food is still planted, harvested, and cooked in the same traditional way, villages are still full of musicians playing local folk songs, and the island's intellectual, leftist history is still an important part of people's daily lives.

PLANNING YOUR TIME

Unless otherwise noted, businesses on Naxos operate from **April** to **October.** Given the island's size, it's best to spend at least **four days** here—both because there's so much to see, and because it's just more enjoyable to slow down. I would recommend staying on the **southwest coast**—you'll be close to some of the island's best beaches, and within easy driving distance of the mountainous interior.

INFORMATION AND SERVICES

While there's no official tourist office in Naxos, as soon as you arrive to the port you'll notice a couple of travel agencies and the **Information Booth,** which has information on buses, taxis, and maps. **Naxos Tours** (Hora; tel. 22850/24000; www.naxostours.net; 8am-10pm) can help you arrange excursions and other activities around Naxos, and to nearby islands, including Delos; another good option is **Zas Travel** (located right on the waterfront in front of the port; tel. 22850/23330).

There are **ATMs** around the island, and the National Bank of Greece and Alpha Bank both have branches with ATMs in Hora. The **police** station (tel. 22850/22100) is located on the southeastern edge of town and, unlike some other places in Greece, someone actually picks up the phone when you call. The main **hospital** (tel. 22850/24000) is in Glinadou on the eastern side of Hora. Because it serves a large island, it's quite well equipped to handle most emergencies and accidents.

Stuart, a travel photographer, has been living in Naxos for the better part of the decade and knows all the secret, local spots. He organizes both trekking tours (including to Mount Zas) with **The Hidden Naxos** (tel. 694 880 9142; www.hiddennaxos.com; from €35) and minibus tours of the islands. Prices include lunch.

GETTING THERE

It's very easy to get to Naxos by ferry, and it's a beautiful ride from Piraeus. Flying is another popular option.

Ferry

As the largest of the Cycladic islands, Naxos is one of the best-connected ferry hubs, with daily boats (high-speed and normal) to **Piraeus, Crete,** and many **Cycladic** and **Dodecanese** islands. Boats dock in Naxos Hora.

Air

Naxos is served by a small airport (**JNX**), which has daily flights to/from Athens (45 minutes; from €95) with **Olympic Air** (www.olympicair.com).

Though there are no shuttle buses from the airport to the Hora (3 km/1.85 mi from airport), there are **buses** to Agios Prokopios Beach and Agia Anna, both of which are close to Hora. **Taxis** from the airport start at €10 and increase if you have excess luggage.

Previous: the port of Naxos; one of Naxos Hora's beautiful private residences; the beach next to Naxos Hora on a blustery day.

GETTING AROUND

At 429 square km (165 square mi), Naxos is the largest of the Cycladic islands. If you plan on moving around a bit, your best bet is to rent a **car** or **motorcycle,** at least for a day. It's definitely a good idea to rent one for a day to drive through the interior mountain villages, making a necessary stop along the way for *galaktoboureko* (a dessert of custard in crispy phyllo) and shots of *kitron* (citron liqueur). A car will also allow you to see some of the more inaccessible parts of the island, particularly the southeast coast.

Car

In the high season, daily rates for cars start at €45. There are several car rental places along the port, or you can book ahead from **Naxos Auto Rent** (Galanado Village, 5.5 km/3.5 mi from Hora; tel. 22850/41350; www.naxosautorent.com).

Bus

The bus is quite reliable in Naxos and regularly used by locals. The main **bus station** is opposite the main dock in the port (tel. 22850/22291; www.naxosdestinations.com). Note that you have to buy your ticket from the **bus information office,** which is kitty-corner to the bus stop, or from the machine outside. Tickets cost €1.60-3.10 one-way, depending on your destination.

From the main bus station, there are 10 daily buses to Agios Prokopios-Agia Anna-Plaka; 7 daily buses to Filoti-Halki; and 10 daily to Plaka. Printed **timetables** are available next to the bus stop. Check them regularly as they change each month and from year to year.

Taxi

Given the size of the island, taking taxis can be expensive, though should you wish to do so, you can flag one down at the **port** or call tel. 22850/22444.

Itinerary Ideas

You'll need a car for this itinerary, and make sure you make reservations for Axiotissa Taverna (covered here at the end of Day 1) in advance.

DAY 1

For your first day on Naxos, start in Hora, one of the best-preserved villages in the Cycladic, and explore nearby Alyko Beach.

1. Make a beeline for the **Temple of Apollo.** If you make it early enough, you can watch the sun's rays pass through the temple.
2. Walk around **Kastro,** the historic hilltop neighborhood in Naxos Hora.
3. When you tire of wandering Kastro's steep streets, have lunch at **Yema Agapis,** an unforgettable soup kitchen in Hora. (Alternatively, take your order to go for your drive down to the beach.)
4. Drive down to **Alyko Beach** at the southwestern end of the island. Explore the beach's coves, and don't miss the abandoned hotel that's been plastered with frescoes.
5. Finish off the day with a late dinner at **Axiotissa** Taverna, which serves up the best food on the island.

Naxos

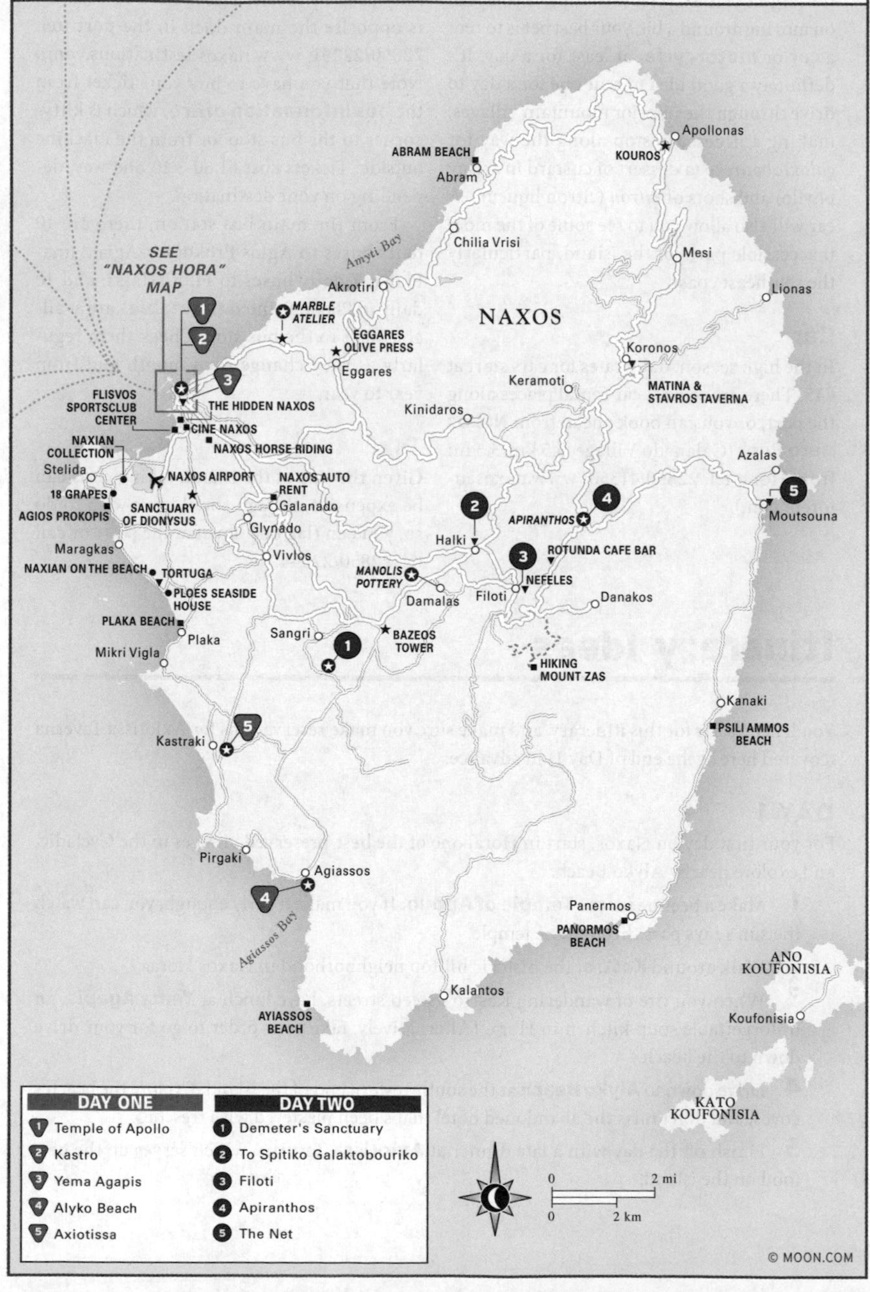
SEE "NAXOS HORA" MAP
NAXOS
Apollonas
KOUROS
ABRAM BEACH
Abram
Chilia Vrisi
Amyti Bay
Mesi
Akrotiri
Lionas
MARBLE ATELIER
EGGARES OLIVE PRESS
Eggares
Koronos
Keramoti
MATINA & STAVROS TAVERNA
FLISVOS SPORTSCLUB CENTER
THE HIDDEN NAXOS
Kinidaros
CINE NAXOS
NAXIAN COLLECTION
NAXOS HORSE RIDING
Azalas
Stelida
NAXOS AIRPORT
NAXOS AUTO RENT
18 GRAPES
Galanado
AGIOS PROKOPIS
SANCTUARY OF DIONYSUS
Glynado
APIRANTHOS
Moutsouna
Halki
Maragkas
ROTUNDA CAFE BAR
NAXIAN ON THE BEACH
TORTUGA
Vivlos
MANOLIS POTTERY
NEFELES
PLOES SEASIDE HOUSE
Damalas
Filoti
Danakos
PLAKA BEACH
Plaka
Sangri
BAZEOS TOWER
Mikri Vigla
HIKING MOUNT ZAS
Kanaki
PSILI AMMOS BEACH
Kastraki
Pirgaki
Agiassos
Agiassos Bay
Panermos
PANORMOS BEACH
ANO KOUFONISIA
Kalantos
Koufonisia
AYIASSOS BEACH
KATO KOUFONISIA
DAY ONE
1 Temple of Apollo
2 Kastro
3 Yema Agapis
4 Alyko Beach
5 Axiotissa
DAY TWO
1 Demeter's Sanctuary
2 To Spitiko Galaktobouriko
3 Filoti
4 Apiranthos
5 The Net
0 2 mi
0 2 km
© MOON.COM

NAXOS
ITINERARY IDEAS

DAY 2

Spend the day driving through the mountainous interior of Naxos, ending with a memorable meal on the island's east coast.

1 First, drive to **Demeter's Sanctuary** to pay homage to the goddess of fertility.

2 Drive to Halki to stroll the atmospheric streets and to sample the best the best *galaktoboureko* on the island at **To Spitiko Galaktobouriko.**

3 Stop next in **Filoti,** beloved for its panoramic mountain views. Grab a coffee in the village square and relax a bit.

4 Stop in **Apiranthos** and explore the backstreets for a slice of local life. Avoid eating here, though—better to drive on to your next stop for a better, more authentic, meal.

5 In the evening, continue on to Moutsouna for a beachside seafood dinner at **The Net.**

Naxos Hora Νάξος Χώρα

Situated on the western coast of the island, Hora is a lovely, bustling place that is best approached by boat. The town is flanked by the Temple of Apollo at the edge of the port and topped with the Kastro. Past the port is a maze of twisting streets with steep stairs, heavy with bougainvillea and full of stray cats. Hora was founded by Marco Sanudo, a 13th-century Venetian who also established the Duchy of the Aegean, and the old town is still divided along its historical faultlines (at least visually): the Bourgos, home to the Greeks; and the Kastro, where the Roman Catholics set up camp. Both are right behind the waterfront; Bourgos is the first section in the north, and Kastro is in the center of Hora. These days, the old town is full of shops, restaurants, and little galleries; there's all the usual tourist kitsch plus a few more refined locales. Don't bother bringing a map into the old town; you'll get lost no matter what! All roads will eventually lead to the Kastro; the rest of the time, just embrace the wandering.

SIGHTS

★ Kastro

free

Though Kastro literally means "castle" in Greek, in Naxos it refers to the hilltop neighborhood established by Marco Sanduo back in 1207. Enter through the north gate (Trani Porta, or Majestic Gate in English) where you'll find old Venetian mansions and adorable narrow streets, though be aware that it's not the easiest place to walk, with lots of high, steep steps.

The crowning jewel of the Kastro, so to speak, is the rectangular **Tower of Sanoudos,** the remnants of one of the 12 defense towers built by Sanduo. Other sites include the restored **Catholic cathedral** and the **French Commercial School,** one of the first schools in Ottoman Greece, opened by Jesuits in 1627. Their most famous pupil was author Nikos Kazantzakis. The school is also home to the **Archaeological Museum** (tel. 22850/22725; Tues.-Sun. 8:30am-3pm; €3), with exhibits on the Ionic and Doric eras, as well as some Early Cycladic marble statuettes. All sights are signposted.

Della Rocca-Barozzi Venetian Museum

tel. 22850/22387; www.naxosfestival.com; daily 10am-10pm; €5

In its heyday, Naxos was full of beautiful old mansions where nobility sauntered about. The aristocrats are gone, but the mansions remain; one of the best preserved has since been turned into the Venetian Museum. You'll glimpse into the lives of the original Italian owners, from what they wore to how they

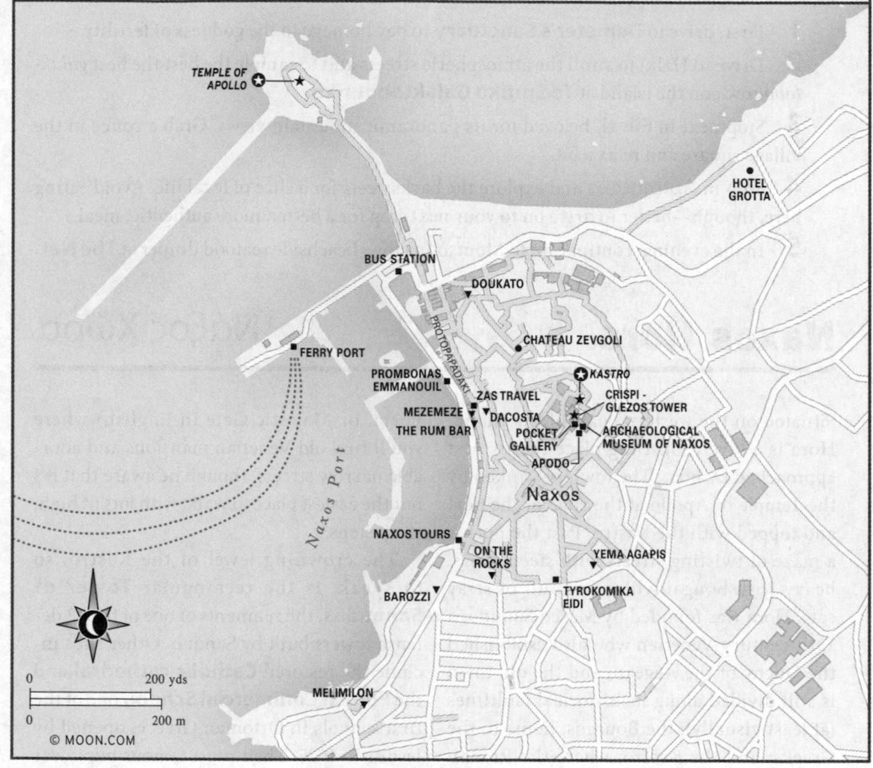

decorated their living spaces. Check the website for concerts (both Greek and international music, as well as classical), which frequently happen in the summertime. Located within Kastro.

Crispi-Glezos Tower

tel. 22850/22525; daily in summer 10am-7pm; €3

Of Kastro's original 12 towers, only the Crispi-Glezos Tower is still standing. The Tower was originally the home of Jacobo, the illegitimate son of 15th-century Duke Guillermo II Crispo. Jacobo had no hereditary rights to the dynasty, but he did have a pretty sweet home, which has since been turned into the **Byzantine Museum.** As of writing, part of Glezos Tower was under construction, and there was only one exhibit inside; curiously, text was only available in French and Greek.

★ Temple of Apollo

free

On an island full of beauty, the Temple of Apollo (also called Portara, or "door" in English) might be one of the more arresting sites. Built in 530 BC by Lygdamis, a tyrant who, true to form, wanted to build the highest building in Greece, the Portara is believed to be a tribute to Apollo, the god of music and poets. The doorway faces Delos, Apollo's birthplace. The temple was originally supposed to be 100 feet tall, but after war broke out between Naxos and Samos, and Lygdamis was overthrown, plans were abandoned.

Today, the temple stands as a beautiful ruin, made even more magnificent by negative space. During high season, the archway is most crowded at sunset. You can walk near the temple, but don't cross the barrier to take a selfie please!

Sanctuary of Dionysus

10am-5pm; €2

A few kilometers behind the Naxos airport is the well-preserved Sanctuary of Dionysus, which includes a small museum with artifacts from the excavation. Dionysus, god of good times and libations, was universally beloved by ancient Greeks, and especially so in Naxos, which historically had a strong tradition of wine production; locals believed Dionysus lived in the forests of Naxos. According to myth, when Theseus abandoned Ariadne on Naxos en route to Crete, Dionysus was captivated by her beauty and immediately fell in love. Ariadne didn't reciprocate the feelings; instead she tried to flee and hide in the forest. Eventually—by force or by true love—Dionysus and Ariadne married. In the 6th century BC, locals built this temple in honor of Dionysus. You can walk around the whole area and get up close to the ruins; because it's not a popular tourist stop, you'll likely have the place to yourself.

RECREATION

Horseback Riding

NAXOS HORSE RIDING

tel. 694 880 9142; www.naxoshorseriding.com; from €45

Equestrians can plan a fun excursion with Naxos Horse Riding, where expat British instructors will take you on fun rides through dirt roads into the sea. They tailor their tours for everyone, from beginners to advanced riders. Their physical office is located just outside of Naxos Hora, in Kokkino Spitia.

Kite Surfing

FLISVOS SPORTSCLUB CENTER

Naxos; www.flisvos-sportclub.com; May-Oct., all day

There are dozens of water sports centers in Naxos, but Flisvos is one of the more comprehensive ones: They've got basic rooms for rent, a surf shop, and when you are done working up a sweat either windsurfing, kite surfing, mountain biking, or catamaran sailing, there's a bar for a much-needed drink. Flisvos organizes lessons for beginners and can help you plan a sailing or yachting trip around the island. Prices range from €18 for bike rental

the stunning Temple of Apollo

up to €600 for multiweek sports packages. It's best to reserve ahead of time; prices increase by at least 5 percent if you book on the spot. They're located just outside of Naxos Hora (10 minutes' walk south).

NIGHTLIFE AND ENTERTAINMENT

Most of Hora's nightlife is located around the port; as you walk around in the evening you'll notice plenty of bars with pulsing music.

Bars

DACOSTA

tel. 697 593 9104; May-Sept. from 9pm

More of a bar than a club, DaCosta is still considered one of the better dancefloors in Naxos. It draws a younger, crowd, who flirt and grind around the bar's chic Grecian white design. During the summer, there are nearly daily parties with local and international DJs; check their Facebook page to see who is playing.

THE RUM BAR

tel. 694 859 2718; from 8pm

One of the few places open year-round, The Rum Bar is known for two things: great views of the sunset overlooking the port, and original, tropical cocktails, some of which feature a heavy handed gurgle of locally produced *kitron*. The music is usually classic rock; they sometimes have live acts (check their Facebook page).

ON THE ROCKS

tel. 22850/29224; May-Sept.; 7pm-3am

This well-stocked bar with friendly owners is frequented by tourists and locals alike. The menu is almost overwhelmingly extensive; as if that isn't enough, there's a catalogue of hookah and cigars to choose from as well. There's a small terrace that's usually packed; arrive early to secure a seat.

Cinema

CINE NAXOS

tel. 22850/22088; https://cinenaxos.gr/en; May-Sept., after dusk; €7.50

There's something extra special about watching a movie outside under the stars. Get your romance on and catch an al fresco film at Cine Naxos (in the winter, they move to the municipal building across the way). Check their website for showtimes and viewings; most of the films are in English. Located on the main road just outside of Hora on the way to the airport. The outdoor seats are crowded with families and canoodling teenagers.

SHOPPING

Gifts

POCKET GALLERY

year-round, daily 10am-3pm and in summer 6pm-late

This is a beautiful little gallery space that has expanded to include a larger shop right across the cobblestone street. Pocket Gallery offers a curated selection of local and foreign artists and designers. It's run by an Australian expat and artist, and there's nothing kitschy or touristy here. Instead, expect to find ceramics, paintings, jewelry, and cards. It's the perfect place to shop for a gift for friends back home or, let's be honest, for yourself.

APODO

year-round, daily 10am-3pm and in summer 6pm-late

This cultural gift shop/concept store is a hidden spot in the Hora, chock full of local delights. The shop itself is beautiful, with old tiles, exposed stone walls, and a little courtyard. It's got a bit of everything, including food products (marmalades and spreads) as well as ceramics and art, much of it featuring designs of fish.

Local Produce

TYROKOMIKA EIDI

year-round, daily 10am-3pm and in summer, daily 6pm-late

This old-school family store is a veritable *cabinet de curiosite* of local products: sausages and woven baskets dangle from the ceiling, giant vats of olives brined in salt give a pungent odor to the shop, wheels of cheese are piled precariously on top of each other. This is the place to buy everything from honey to copper pots, olive oil soaps, and distilled bottles of ouzo and raki.

PROMBONAS EMMANOUIL

year-round, daily 10am-3pm and in summer 6pm-late

Located on the waterfront, this is the best place to buy any kind of citron product your sour heart could imagine: candies, spoon fruit, jams, liquors, chocolates, etc. The lumpy fruit looks like a lemon on steroids, and the *kitron* liqueur it produces is unique to Naxos. It's a family-run business and they have their fields just outside of Hora; ask if you can visit. October is when the large, lumpy fruit is harvested for distillation.

FOOD

Greek

★ YEMA AGAPIS

year-round, lunchtime; free

If you do one thing in Greece, and I mean this from the bottom of my heart, you should go to Yema Agapis (literally: "love food" in English) to bask in the unbelievable energy of Mrs. Nicoletta, who is possibly the kindest person I've ever met. Yema Agapis is a soup kitchen supported by the church across the way. Each morning, Mrs. Nicoletta arrives to cook vats of food for anyone who walks in, whether they are financially in need of a free meal or not. The food is Greek home cooking and, unlike other soup kitchens, always includes a healthy helping of protein. Don't bother trying to give Mrs. Nicoletta money (a hug will do), but if you do feel moved to donate, you can leave some money at the church.

DOUKATO

Old Town; tel. 22850/27013; summer only, daily 6pm-late; from €8

Location, location, location: Doukato is housed in a space that has already seen three lives (a monastery, a church, and a school); the superb dining experience at Doukato is the location's fourth iteration. The cuisine is typical Greek with a focus on local ingredients and specialties including *gouna* (sun-dried mackerel).

Seafood

★ MEZEMEZE

tel. 22850/26401; year-round, daily noon-late; from €6

Given MezeMeze's prime location along the touristic part of the port, it wasn't until several locals recommended this place that I finally caved. It's a good reminder that looks can be deceiving; this is one of Hora's best restaurants, with an excellent mix of Naxian and Cretan cuisine. This place is best known for its seafood, so go ahead and order a variety of grilled fish and dishes: mackerel and octopus are particularly good. The decor is nautical chic. Like elsewhere in Greece, anything frozen is marked on the menu.

Fine Dining

BAROZZI

tel. 22850/27672; Apr.-Oct., daily 6:30pm-3am; from €15

Perhaps the most upscale restaurant in Naxos, Barozzi is a new addition that elevates Naxian cuisine and ingredients to a fine dining level. Even *horta,* the ubiquitous wild greens long eaten by peasants, get the star treatment: here, they're served with watermelon infused with wasabi. There is also a unique selection of cocktails and an extensive wine list. Reservations are recommended.

Breakfast

MELIMILON

tel. 694 490 7102; www.melimilon-naxos.gr; daily 9am-3pm; from €3

This adorable café located next to the town hall derives its name from the ancient Greek word for marmalade, which at Melmilon is of the homemade variety and served up as part of an incredibly tasty breakfast. Located in a quiet corner of the Hora, with a beautiful garden, the restaurant also offers cheeses, omelets, red pepper spread, breads, and coffee cooked over embers. Marmalades and spreads are also available for purchase.

ACCOMMODATIONS

CHATEAU ZEVGOLI

tel. 22850/26123; chateau-zevgoli.gr; from €60

Located in a converted medieval mansion in the Bourgos, Chateau Zevgoli is decorated in an old-school Naxian style, heavy on the charm with great views of the Hora and sea. The hotel is small, with only six rooms, and two nearby self-catering apartments that are better for families or those staying for longer periods. There's a bit of bohemian charm, aided by the attentive staff and the fact that since no taxis can reach this part of Hora; only those with limited amounts of luggage make it here.

HOTEL GROTTA

tel. 22850/22215; www.hotelgrotta.gr; year-round; from €70

This chicly designed boutique hotel is a family-run affair, with a wonderfully attentive staff and great amenities, including a Thalassotherapy (sea water therapy) pool, hammam, sauna, and whirlpool. Breakfast is included, and it's a particular standout; expect copious amounts of baked goods. The hotel is an excellent value for money, even in the high season.

Southwest Coast

The coast of Naxos south of Hora is home to some of the island's best beaches. You'll find beachgoers from kite surfers to nudists taking advantage of the coastline's superb sand and, in some places, intense wind and waves. Immediately south of Hora and the airport is an intense cluster of tourist attractions; here you'll find plenty of hotels, restaurants, bars, beach bars, cafés, sports centers, bakeries, etc. The area around Agios Prokopis and Agia Anna is the most heavily touristic, and in the peak summer season, the crowds can be overwhelming. Agios Prokopis—regularly voted as one of Greece's most beautiful beaches—is particularly crowded. But drive down the main road and continue farther south, where you'll be flanked by the blue sea on one side, and fertile green hills dotted with sheep and goats on the other. The coast becomes more rugged and less crowded down here, and the road ends around Alyko beach. The beaches here are more bohemian, without lawn chairs or bars, and several of the beaches are nudist (this can change from season to season).

From the main bus station in the port, there are 10 daily buses to Agios Prokopios-Agia Anna-Plaka, and 10 daily buses to Plaka. You will need a car or taxi ride to reach Alykos and Ayiassos beaches.

AGIOS PROKOPIS
(Άγιος Προκόπης)

Agios Prokopis is one of the more popular tourist spots in Naxos, thanks to its strip of hotels and family-friendly beach. It's located 6 km (3.75 mi) south of Hora.

Beaches

AGIOS PROKOPIS

One of Naxos' best-known beaches, Agois Prokopis is a long strip of sandy beach with clear, calm waters. It draws big crowds, and is the center of the tourist industry. Here you'll find plenty of beach bars, places to rent sea kayaks for around €10, cafés, hotels, and more. It's best for families, as there are plenty of activities for kids, but if it's privacy you're seeking, you won't find it here.

Food

There are plenty of touristic places to eat in Agios Prokopis. Honestly, there are none that I would go out of my way to recommend, but the **Naxian Collection hotel** below has a fantastic restaurant that's open to non-guests.

Accommodations

18 GRAPES

tel. 22850/44194; www.18grapes.com; from €200

This lovely boutique hotel, with 18 Cycladic-style rooms, is run by a local family of wine-makers (hence both the numerical and oenological references in the hotel's name). There's a lovely pool, though you're 200 meters (650 feet) from Agios Prokopios beach. An attentive and friendly staff will take care of everything from arranging helicopter tours to beauty treatments. It's got all the luxury perks, like Nespresso machines and Korres products. A special touch is the welcome package, complete with a bottle of wine.

★ NAXIAN COLLECTION

Stelida, Naxos; tel. 22850/24300; www.naxiancollection.com; from €300

This gorgeous hotel is an example of traditional Cycladic architecture fully dialed up, creating a luxurious oasis. The rooms, decorated in creamy minimalist tones, are equipped with steam showers or soaking tubs; should you need more water, head out to the private or semi-private pool that comes with each bungalow. The grounds are lovely, and touches such as hand-carved marble statues lend a peaceful, artistic feeling to the place. The staff is exceedingly helpful and professional; they'll even organize a cooking class for you with the woman who cooked for Anthony Bourdain. The owner is a wine and whiskey connoisseur; ask for a tour of the impressive cave. Naxian Collection is located 1.2 km (.7 mi) north of Agios Prokopis.

PLAKA BEACH
(Πλάκα)

The 5-km (3-mi) stretch of Plaka has something for everyone: At the southernmost end of the beach is an area called Orkos, which attracts windsurfers and kite surfers; other parts of the beach are reserved for nudists. Plaka is heavy on the nature, too: There are dunes where, in the fall, little white flowers will pop out and the sand is backed by green vegetation.

Plaka is around 4 km (2.5 mi) south of Agios Prokopios Beach; most people drive or take the bus from Hora. There's plenty of parking, and the beach is backed by plenty of restaurants, hotels, shops, etc.

Food

TORTUGA

tel. 22850/24300; www.tortuganaxos.com; May-Oct. 9am-midnight; €30

Fine dining, but with your bathing suit on (though it helps if it's one of those uber-chic embellished bathing suits with the oddly placed slits). Tortuga is an all-day beach bar that offers exquisite food and an extensive wine list under boho-chic bamboo pergolas. Grab a lounge chair, start your day with a light breakfast, and finish with the sous-vide beef.

Accommodations

PLOES SEASIDE HOUSE

tel. 694 821 2775; www.ploesnaxos.gr; from €60

This complex of nine rooms—including doubles and cottages—is a good choice for families and groups looking for a self-service vacation. Like most island hotels, Ploes Seaside House sticks to traditional Cycladic design; here, all the rooms have views of the Aegean and a private terrace. It's a brand-new hotel, so everything is exceedingly clean and staff are eager to help.

NAXIAN ON THE BEACH

tel. 22850/24300; www.naxianonthebeach.gr; from €415

If you're here purely for the beach, but you still want a taste of luxury, head to Naxian on the Beach. Owned by the same people who own Naxian Collection, Naxian on the Beach offers a similar level of hospitality, this time 30 feet from the beach and in a more bohemian environment. The rooms are slightly more rustic (though still achingly chic), with views of Plaka Beach. It's a bit like glamping, with lots of hammocks and raffia, but it's not suitable for families.

★ ALYKO BEACH (Αλυκών)

At the southwestern end of the island, about 24 km (15 mi) south of Hora, is Alyko beach, a cedar forest and series of coves that create semi-private beaches before stretching out into a long strip of white sand beach. One of the beach's best attractions isn't the sea at all, but rather a hotel from the 1960s that was abandoned midway through construction. A few years ago, an Athens-based graffiti artist came and painted incredible frescoes on the abandoned structure; the result is a stunning piece of free art. This is an unorganized beach, so you won't find any cafés or beach bars; bring your own snacks and water. Alyko is also the last place in Naxos where you can do free camping.

Food

★ AXIOTISSA

15 km (9 mi) south of Hora, Alyko; tel. 22850/75107; Apr.-Oct. 2pm-late; from €8

As soon as you decide to visit Naxos, pick up the phone and reserve a spot for every night you're on the island to dine at Axiotissa. And when you get there, take a moment to say thank you to the lovely Sophia, who runs the front-of-house with a contagious energy, and her partner in the kitchen, Yannis. This family-run taverna consistently serves up the best food on the island, with a focus on fresh, local products, sourced with the utmost care from farmers employing the best industry practices, and that's reflected in the modern, innovative approach to classic Greek dishes. We had the grilled whole fish and a variety of salads, and it was the best thing I'd eaten in a long time. You can't go wrong with anything you order, whether it's meat, fish, or vegetables. The ambience is like being at a very cool, bohemian dinner party. Seriously, reservations are required.

★ F.B.I.

23 km (14 mi) south of Hora - Alykos; tel. 698 277 2053; May-Sept. daily noon-7pm

This little food truck is parked outside of Alykos beach from May-September. The name stands for Food Beverage Ice Cream, and the brothers helming the truck do all three fantastically: they have black angus burgers, pancetta tacos, "live" ice cream (the cream is frozen on a plancha in front of you), and aloe vera juice. They also host parties during the summer months.

Alyko beach

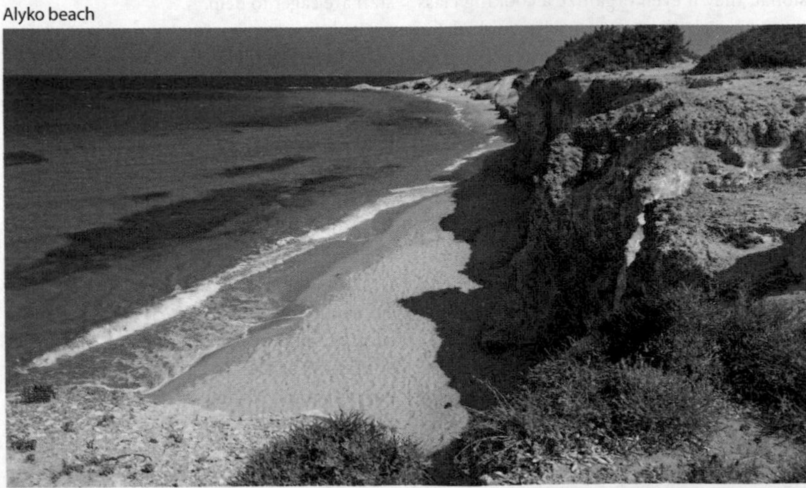

AYIASSOS BEACH
(Αγιάσος)

For 4 km (2.5 mi) beyond Alyko the road is unpaved and will take you to Ayiassos beach, a place of historical importance: it's here where our old Venetian friend Marco Sanudo, of Kastro fame, landed in 1207 to conquer the islands and take them from the Byzantines. It's a huge sandy beach with wind, and it's usually pretty empty.

Northern Naxos

From Hora, take the road north toward Eggares and continue all the way up the coast to Apollonas (36 km/22 mi). The road is very atmospheric and relatively easy to drive, with just a few hairpin turns along the way. The northern part of the coast is battered by strong winds, making it, aside from a few spots, less than ideal for sunbathing, but there's a number of cool sites worth checking out. On the drive, you'll notice massive piles of discarded marble scraps, left over by the companies that mine the marble quarries farther inland from the coastline. It is technically not illegal to grab one as a souvenir while thinking to yourself, "It is wild that in some countries they leave piles of garbage on the side of the road and in Naxos they have trash piles of *marble*."

In the summer, there are daily buses from the port to both Eggares and Apollonas. Check www.naxosdestinations.com for time schedule, or the schedule at the port (it changes yearly). Note that the food is not the best here, and most of the tavernas are quite expensive.

EGGARES
(Εγγαρές)

Located a short 9-km (5.5-mi) drive from Hora, Eggares is a charming traditional village with Cycladic appeal: Think whitewashed houses and cobblestone streets. It's a small farming village nestled in the green plains, and is responsible for a large portion of the island's agricultural production, thanks to the village's healthy and plentiful water sources. Inside the village is a main square with two churches.

Sights

HILL OF THE NATIVITY

For the best view in Eggares, head east of the village for 1 km (.6 mi) toward the Hill of Nativity, where ancient Greeks built a sanctuary dedicated to water nymphs. The sanctuary is no longer standing but there's a stellar view of the countryside. You can walk, but since it's just a quick stop and you'll continue on your way, I recommend driving. Nearby **Galini village** is also worth a quick walk around, for its traditional architecture and quiet streets.

EGGARES OLIVE PRESS

May-Sept., daily 11am-6pm; www.olivemuseum.com; free

Although there are more than 90 olive press plants in Naxos, few have been as lovingly restored (or are as easily accessible) as the Eggares Olive Oil Press, located on the main road on the outskirts of the village as you're entering or leaving Eggares from Hora. It features a comprehensive overview of traditional methods of olive oil production, and includes a tasting of different oils, baked goods, and olives at the end. Admission is free, and the guided tour is included.

★ MARBLE ATELIER

tel. 694 262 2366; free

As you drive into Eggares, you'll pass by a sign advertising a marble workspace. Please do pull over; this is an amazing, blink-and-you-miss-it outdoor artist's workshop full of beautiful, wonderfully weird sculptures made out of marble and wood. It's a constantly evolving space. On a recent visit, there was a table full of lovely Cycladic-inspired busts, but I certainly hope for your sake that the exquisitely sculpted marble penis (complete with perfectly formed marble testicles) will still be on display by the time you visit.

APOLLONAS (Απόλλωνας)

This seaside hamlet, 27 km (17 mi) northeast of Eggares, has gotten the touristic treatment in recent years, and is the most developed village in north Naxos. There are two main beaches in town, a small sandy one and a larger pebble beach. Beyond the beach is the usual strip of restaurants, tavernas, cafés, minimarkets, rooms for rent, and hotels, making it a useful pit stop but not the most relaxing of places in the high season.

Sights

KOUROS

free

Easter Island has its Moai statues, and Naxos has its kouros. These 10-meter (32-foot) long rock statues are somewhat haphazardly laid down on the ground, like they suddenly got tired and stopped to have a quick nap. Naxos' kouros are scattered across the island. There's one in Flerio (another village in Naxos, 11 km/7 mi east of Hora) that's better maintained and accessible by taxi, but my favorite is the one of Apollo (weighing a whopping 80 tonnes/88 tons) just outside of Apollonas. Archaeologists believe it's a likeness of the god Apollo, dating back from the 7th century BC. To reach him, it's best to drive, as it's located just off the main road.

Beaches

ABRAM (Αβραμ)

Situated in a small cove 15 km (9 mi) west of Apollonas, Abram beach is one of the most tranquil and secluded on the north coast. The back of the beach is full of thick, lush vegetation, and to one side there's an adorable whitewashed church. It's relatively easy to drive here from Apollonas; just note that the last 300 meters (980 feet) of the road aren't paved. It's an unorganized pebbly beach, but there are a few tavernas and rooms for rent.

Inland Naxos

As you drive from the coast or Hora into Naxos, everything starts to change. The land seems to shoot up around you, forming hills and mountains and cliffs that poke into the clouds. Little villages pop up, some of them seemingly built into the sides of mountains. The character of the people changes, too: There's something about living in mountains that makes you more gregarious, more hospitable—a warm humanness wrapped up in a slightly gruff exterior (one must survive the hardship of mountain life, of course). There are more than two dozen villages dotting the interior of Naxos; some are no more than a few streets and a couple of inhabitants, while others are sprawling mini-towns with hundreds of people. It's a joy to drive through the twisting mountain roads, stopping every now and again on the side of the road to gasp at the natural beauty around you. A good trip is to go from Sangri to Halki to Apiranthos, before stopping in Koronos for lunch. Consult the map beforehand; the most circuitous route is often the safest and best paved road to travel.

It's best to rent a car to explore this area, but from the main bus station, there are seven daily buses to Filoti-Halki (€2.30). Five daily buses also serve Apiranthos (€3.10 on the Filoti-Halki route), and two stop in Apollonas (€6.20).

1: Pottery has been the mainstay of Manolis' family for four generations. **2:** the delicious custard pie at To Spitiko Galaktobouriko **3:** A local artist carves marble sculptures in his open-air studio.

1
2
3

SANGRI
(Σαγρή)

Made up of two settlements, Ano Sangri and Kato Sangri (they're divided by a couple of kilometers), Sangri (11 km/7 mi south of Hora) is a protected village from medieval times. The quiet, well-preserved town is full of cobblestone paths and beautiful houses, though note that there are not a lot of good options for food or coffee. It's a rather tiny village, and its real draw is that it's part of the archaeological region of Gyroula, home to Demeter's Sanctuary. There's a lovely view from the village, which is perched up on a hill, down to the rolling green fields below and the ruins of Demeter's Sanctuary. Stop along the 6-minute drive down from the village to the ruins to take a few photos.

Sights

BAZEOS TOWER

Ano Sangri; tel. 22850/31402; www.bazeostower.gr

Of the 30 still-standing towers built on Naxos by feudal Venetians, who used them as bases of operation for their fields, Bazeos is one of the better-preserved ones. The tower was originally a monastery in the 17th century, before it was bought by the Bazeos family. As Naxos becomes increasingly recognized for its arts and culture scene, the Bazeos Tower is an important landmark. The descendents of the original owners have since turned the tower into a cultural center, with atmospheric concerts, readings, art exhibits, and festivals taking place during the summer months. The annual Naxos Festival is held here each year in July and August. Check their website for events.

★ DEMETER'S SANCTUARY

Drimalia 843 02; tel. 22850/42325; Tues.-Sun. 8am-3pm; €2

Surprise: one of the island's best attractions isn't a beach at all, but rather the stunning ruins of Demeter's Sanctuary, which have been so thoughtfully preserved that it's easy to imagine yourself actually in ancient Greece, laying down an offering for Demeter, the goddess of fertility. This Ionic temple was constructed in 530 BC (another project of Lygdamis; unlike the Temple of Apollo, this one was fully constructed). Most of the original columns are still standing, and the way they frame the sky makes an arresting sight, even on a cloudy day.

Aside from the temple, there are several facilities that point to the daily working lives of ancient Greeks, including pottery, wine, and olive oil workshops. Demeter was also goddess of grain, and looking out onto the rolling green hills of Naxos spread out below, it's easy to see why this spot was chosen in her honor. The sanctuary was transformed into a church and later plundered, laying in ruins until relatively recently, when it was restored by a group of German and Greek archaeologists. It's also possible to walk from Sangri to the sanctuary.

DAMALAS
(Δαμαλάς)

The teeny town of Damalas, 6 km (3.75 mi) east of Sangri, is one of the smallest villages in Naxos. It's just a few streets at the foot of Lagos hill in the valley of Tragea. While most of the inhabitants have left, there are still a few who've preserved the traditions of the village, namely olive oil production and pottery (the whole Tragea valley has a special soil that's used in the pottery).

Sights

There's a small **olive oil museum** (in the center of the village, free) that opened in 2000, showcasing how the townspeople used to collect and grind olives into an oil, though the most interesting bit about the museum is the smell: a musky, pungent odor from centuries of producing and fermenting olives. There's also a small parish church built in 1800, **Agia Irini**, that's worth a quick peek inside for a whiff of rural worship.

Shopping

★ MANOLIS POTTERY

tel. 22850/32820; year-round Mon.-Sat. 8am-7pm

The four-generation Manolis Pottery store

Hiking Mount Zas

Standing tall at 1,004 meters (3,280 feet), Mount Zas is the highest mountain in the Cyclades. It's also known as **Mount Zeus,** as it's thought to be where Zeus was brought to be birthed in order to escape the wrath of his father. Zeus went on to become king of the Olympians. It's a place with very strong energy!

There are two popular routes for hiking Mount Zas. One is the well-marked, relatively easy 8-km (5-mi) loop from the church of **Agia Marina:** Drive from Filoti toward Apiranthos for 3.3 km (2 mi), and at the junction turn right to head to Danakos. Continue for 800 meters (2,600 feet), and Agia Marina is the second church on the right-hand side. The other is the 6-km (3.75-mi) loop from **Arai Spring** next to Filoti. The first half is well marked; beyond the cave you'll just follow the beaten foot path. At some points, the walk can be steep, so make sure to bring sturdy shoes and plenty of water, and if you're hiking in the summer, use sunscreen. The views alone are worth the hike up here—you'll feel like you're floating above Naxos. For more information, see www.naxostrek.com.

and workshop is Damalas' finest example of traditional pottery. On the main road (Naxou-Aparanthou) right before the entrance of the village, you'll find the vast shop, where you can pick up bowls and cups, though the coolest thing in the shop is a bird-shaped whistle that, when dipped in water, warbles as loud and sharp as any sparrow. If you have children, purchase at your own risk; they won't be able to put it down. Pieces start at around €5 for a small, simple cup. At the entrance of Damalas you'll find the workshop where Manolis is throwing pots in the corner, while his adorable 90-year-old mother sits outside. If you're lucky, he'll show you the cup of justice.

The cup of justice—or the Pythagorean cup—is the BC-philosopher's idea of a practical joke. It's shaped like a normal wine cup, but inside there's a central column; it's shaped like a miniature version of a Bundt pan. There's a hole at the bottom of the cup's stem that reaches almost the top of the central column, creating a sort of open space. When the cup is filled so that the top of the column is still visible, the cup performs the normal duties of a cup. As soon as you pour a little extra wine, though, everything comes spilling out. According to Manolis, the cup of justice was meant to be shared among a group of people, to see who was trustworthy and who was greedy. Interestingly, some modern toilets utilize the same siphon technology. You can buy one from Manolis, who makes them by hand.

HALKI (Χάλκη)

As soon as you arrive in Halki (16 km/10 mi southeast of Hora), you'll notice that you're in an exceptionally beautiful place. Halki used to be the capital of Naxos, and the wealth of its past still lingers: The outskirts of the village have faded Venetian facades, while the interior of the village is a labyrinth of white-washed houses and cobblestone streets, all draped in a blanket of hot pink bougainvillea. Halki is best for strolling through its atmospheric streets and stopping to eat some sweets (the restaurants are of very standard tourist quality). There's some good shopping to be done in Halki as well, not to mention the best *galaktoboureko* on the island.

Sights

If you have time, check out the **Panagia Protothronos** church located in the village center. The first frescoes in the church date back to the 7th century; the church was later renovated in 1052 and several additional decorative layers were added through the centuries.

Shopping

FISH & OLIVE

tel. 22850/31771; www.fish-olive-creations.com; May-Oct. 10am-9pm

I didn't realize that I needed, with an utmost urgency, a multi-thousand euro giant marble statue until I visited Fish & Olive, the stunning gallery and boutique of Naxian potter Katharina Bolesch and her partner, artist Alexander Reichardt. Taking advantage of Naxos' rich marble sources, the pair do exquisite work, usually around the motifs of fish and olives (two themes tied to life in the Aegean). They have smaller (and more affordable) works too, including bowls, jugs, and dishes, but the real stars of the gallery are the wabi-sabi-style marble statues.

Food

★ TO SPITIKO GALAKTOBOURIKO

Summer 8am-last customer, winter 8am-3pm; from €2

As you drive up the road into Halki, you'll notice a blue *kafeneio* on the side of the road. Park your car and make a beeline for To Spitiko Galaktobouriko, where Mrs. Katerina makes the best *galaktoboureko* (custard pie) on the island, maybe all of Greece. It's been a hallmark of the village for more than 60 years. She makes other things as well, including a delicious baklava, but her specialty is custard pie. Wash it down with an expertly made Greek coffee. Unsure when to stop by? "I'm here all day," Mrs. Katerina told us, rolling her eyes with a smile.

Accommodations

ONAR - THE OLIVE GROVE VILLA

tel. 690 845 9327; www.villaonar.com; from €100

For those looking to stay in the mountains, the small Onar is a lovely choice. This newly renovated complex offers simply furnished rooms with sweet views of the olive groves around the villa, and the mountains; they also have self-service apartments. There's a daily breakfast and the staff can help you organize excursions and transfers.

FILOTI (Φιλώτι)

Located on the slopes of Mount Zas, 3 km (just under 2 mi) northeast of Halki, Filoti is one of the largest villages in Naxos. It's actually composed of three smaller settlements, Liiri, Klefaro, and Rachidi, which now act as neighborhoods. The main heart of the village is Gefyra (bridge, in English), an atmospheric square with little cafés and tavernas where you can sit, grab a coffee, and people-watch under the shade of the giant *platanos* trees. (I wouldn't recommend eating at these tavernas, though, as they cater to the tourist crowd and can be overpriced and underwhelming.) Filoti is particularly beloved for its panoramic views of the mountains, often dotted with at least a few of the 60,000 sheep that are reared and graze around the village.

Sights

Filoti is well known for its **Tower of Barozzi,** built in 1650 by the feudal lord of the same name, and for its beautiful Byzantine-era churches. Nearby the tower is the **Church of Panagia Filotissa,** a sumptuously decorated Orthodox church dating back to the 1700s. The church is also the main base during one of the best times to visit Filoti, their August 15 *panagiri,* a three-day feast with drinking, dancing, music, and plenty of food.

Food

NEFELES

tel. 22850/31455; Apr.-Oct. noon-late; mains from €12

This modern Greek taverna is the best of Filoti's dining scene. The small menu focuses on local flavors and traditional dishes. Since you're in the mountains, it's better to order meat than fish here. Make sure to try the tomato marmalade. The service is exceedingly hospitable and friendly, and they'll occasionally organize live music concerts.

★ APIRANTHOS (Απειρανθος)

Apiranthos (7.4 km/4.5 mi north of Filoti),

Manolis Glezos and Naxos' Radical Academic Scene

For a small island village, Apiranthos is the birthplace of a disproportionate amount of intellectuals and politicians, including Petros Protopapadakis, who served briefly as prime minister of Greece for the summer of 1922. But the prodigal son of Apiranthos is the great Manolis Glezos, a left-wing politician and guerilla fighter who was actively involved in the resistance against the Nazi occupation of Greece during World War II. Glezos shot to infamy in 1941 when he, along with another activist, climbed to the top of the Acropolis to tear down the Nazi flag, emblazoned with a swastika.

He was imprisoned as a dissident and spy by the Nazis and later during the Greek Civil War and the military junta. Since then, he's appeared on a Soviet postage stamp, was a member of Greek parliament, was tear gassed at the age of 91, joined Syriza and quit (making him the oldest member of EU parliament), and invented a way of combating floods through a process of building micro dams. He has written six books and has three more in the works. Now in his mid-90s, Glezos still regularly visits Apiranthos, especially in the summer. Glezos is a living legend, and the optimal example of Greek anti-fascism; ask the locals about him, or If you're extra lucky, you might even spot him walking around town.

built at the foot of Mount Fanari, is 600 meters (1,968 feet) up in the clouds and exudes a very special vibe. From a distance, it almost looks like the village is part of the mountain itself. Nicknamed the "marble village" for the amount of local marble that's gone into the village's architecture, its name actually means "many flowers" in Greek.

Apiranthos has gotten quite touristic in recent years, but it's still a joy to walk through the marble-paved streets, duck under archways, and marvel at the preserved houses. As you walk into the village, the main road is full of cafés, restaurants, and shops. Don't bother eating in Apiranthos; the restaurants all cater to tourists and are underwhelming. It's better to continue the drive to Moutsouna and eat some fresh fish on the coast. The cluster of museums at the entrance to town isn't particularly interesting either. Instead of visiting these, follow the road and turn to your right to explore the backstreets. Not a lot of tourists wander off the central path, and you'll be rewarded with scenes of local life: a man making a delivery of canned goods on the back of a donkey, kids running around with a soccer ball, the sounds of pots banging and the smell of onions frying from the open kitchen windows—this is a purely residential area.

Nightlife and Entertainment

ROTUNDA CAFÉ BAR

tel. 22850/61254; https://rotondanaxos.gr/; Mon.-Sun. 10am-midnight

Located just outside of Apiranthos, Rotunda Café Bar is the best place to grab a drink or coffee for sunset. It's perched on the side of the road and is seemingly suspended in the mountains.

KORONOS
Κορωνος

Steeply built into the side of a ravine, Koronos (9 km/6 mi north of Apiranthos) is an achingly quaint village to spend an hour or so exploring. Comprising five neighborhoods, it's a labyrinth of stairs, terraces, and little squares. It's also mostly a village of old people, the vast majority of them over the age of 70, lending a calm air to the place. As you walk through, you'll notice different wells; until the 1960s, there was no central water supply in Koronos, and locals relied on the local wells.

Food

MATINA & STAVROS TAVERNA

year-round, summer 1pm-late; from €8

The infectiously kind and friendly Matina oversees this uber-local taverna. All the

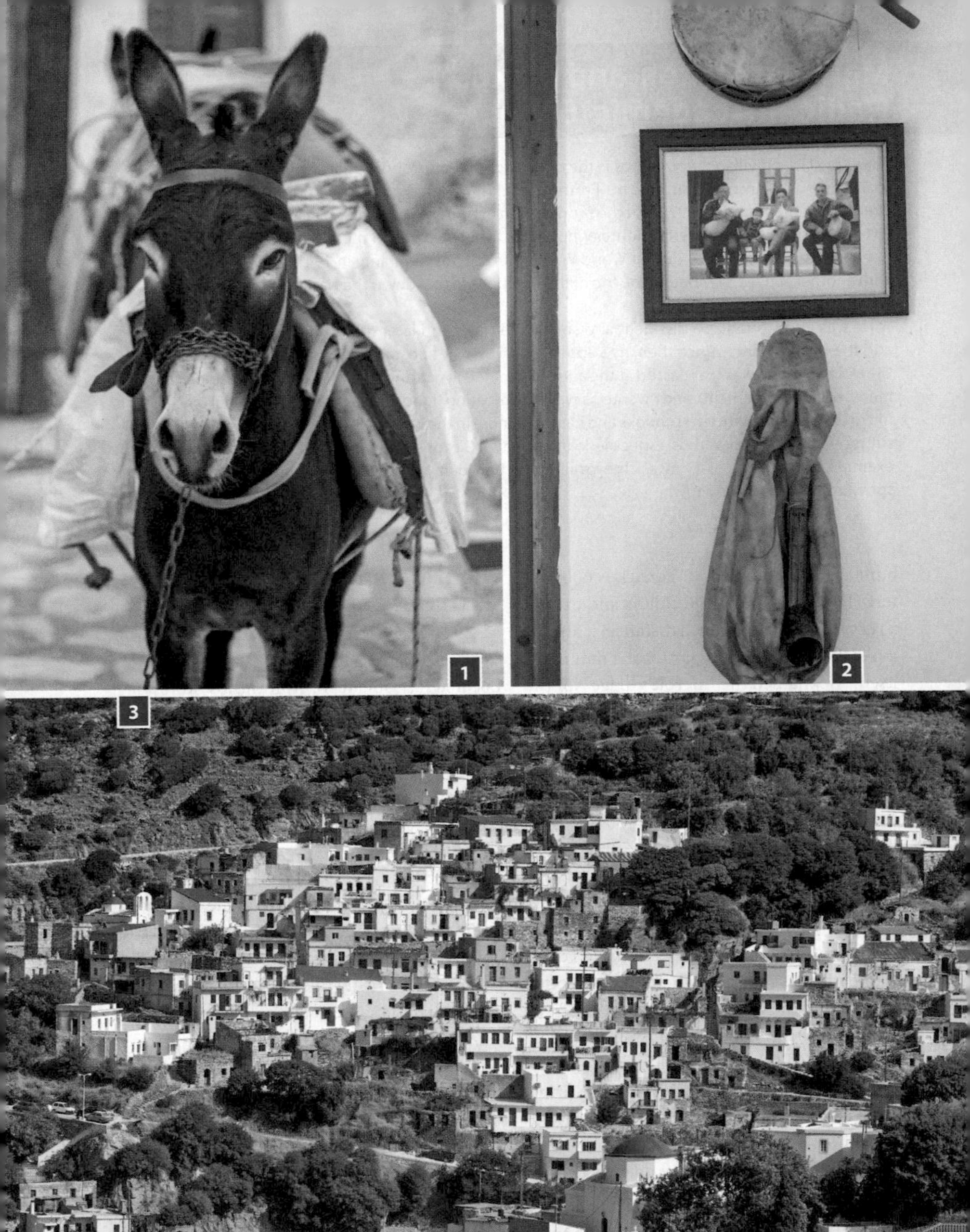
1
2
3

produce is grown by the family, the meat comes from their livestock, and the water comes from a well next to the restaurant. It's a typical joint, with no menu—just whatever happens to be cooked that day. It used to be a locals-only spot, but word got out and now tourists know to come here, too. Matina and Stavros are trying to make small adjustments to accommodate foreigners; there's a new waiter who speaks a few words of English. Definitely try some of the Naxian cheeses, and save room for the shot of raki and dessert that are always complimentary at the end. They also have a few rooms for rent (from €60).

The Southeast Coast

Most visitors don't make it far down the eastern coast of Naxos; even fewer head down to Panormos. The roads aren't as good here (and after Kleido, 5 km/3 mi north of Panormos they are non existent), and the winds are quite strong, making it occasionally unpleasant, but if you are open to a bit of adventure, you'll be rewarded with empty beaches, charming local encounters, and excellent grilled fish. This part of the island is full of wild beauty and rugged charm. Your best option for visiting is to rent a small fishing boat from the harbor of Panormos (around €20 euros) to take a tour of the wild southern tip of Naxos.

MOUTSOUNA (Μουτσουνα)

The cozy seaside village of Moutsouna is picture-perfect. It's a small hamlet hugging the sea, with colorful fishing boats bobbing in the water, and octopus drying under the sun. The atmosphere is calm, and there is a series of small coves with little beaches that you can check out (once you walk a little bit away from the small port, the water is more clean for swimming). Moutsana was an important part of Naxos' stone trade; emery (a dark granular rock composed of different minerals) and marble were loaded onto ships at the port after being brought from the mountains via a rope funicular.

The fastest way to get to Moutsouna from Hora is to drive through the interior of the island, through the villages of Halki, Filoti, and Apeiranthos. It's a distance of 37 km (23 mi) that takes well over an hour because of all the twisting mountain roads.

Food

THE NET

Summer, 7am-11pm; from €10

There's something about fresh fish, grilled over open coals, served with a cold beer and, best of all, a view of the sea, that just screams summer. The Net has all of those things, plus a very good stuffed calamari and friendly service. It's a typical no-frills beachside restaurant, but what else could you ask for? If you're still searching for meaning, turn your gaze and lose it in the Aegean—or have another beer.

PSILI AMMOS BEACH (Ψηλή Άμμος)

Located 25 km (15.5 mi) south of Moutsouna, Psili Ammos is a beautiful sand beach, perfect for those looking for an escape from the more hectic beaches of the west coast. This beach offers clear views to the teardrop island of Donousa, part of the "smaller Cyclades."

1: a donkey shows off his face in Koronos Village **2:** instruments and photographs hanging in Matina & Stavros Taverna **3:** the view of Koronos Village nestled in the mountains

PANORMOS BEACH (Πάνορμος)

Panormos is the last easily accessible beach on the southeast coast. It's a closed bay, which means it's sheltered from the strong winds, and it's a wonderful place to unwind. It's also an unorganized beach, but there's a small canteen selling snacks and drinks. One of the best things to do in Panormos is to find a local who'll take you on a boat ride toward the southern tip of the island to see all the beaches that aren't accessible by foot or car, for around €20. (Ask around for Giannis the fisherman.)

Anafi (Ανάφη)

Tiny Anafi (pop. 150), shaped like a little fish

swimming westward toward its much better known neighbor, Santorini, is perhaps the Cyclades' best-kept secret. This Greek island is reminiscent of a time when nary a lawn chair nor an umbrella touched a beach, and the tourists who stumbled upon the island were the sort of people who would hike up mountains to do sunrise sleepovers and treat the locals with respect.

In short: If you want isolation and pure relaxation, with a healthy dose of hippie bohemia, this is the place for you. There's not a lot to do, which is exactly the point. Plan your days around the sun, lose yourself in the waves, and make new friends. According to Greek mythology, Apollo made Anafi emerge out of the sea as a safe haven for the

Highlights

Look for ★ to find recommended sights, activities, dining, and lodging.

★ **Hora:** One of the most beautiful villages in the Cyclades, Anafi Hora is a great place to while away an afternoon, lost in the labyrinth of streets (page 196).

★ **Sunset:** Be sure to be looking west as the sun goes down—Anafi's sunsets are amazing and you can enjoy them in total privacy (page 198).

★ **Kalamos Rock:** The second-largest monolith in the Mediterranean makes for an absolutely stellar view of the sea and the sunrise—if you're courageous enough to brave a nighttime hike (page 198).

★ **Megalos Roukounas:** This beach is awash with free campers and bohemian spirits, plus a truly excellent family taverna (page 200).

Argonauts on their return passage from the Golden Fleece; it was literally a beacon of light in the sea of darkness. Jason and his followers dubbed the island "Anafi," which means "to appear" in ancient Greek; it also explains the island's devotion to Apollo.

During the winter months, Anafi is home to only its 150 permanent residents—some of the classes at the local school have only one or two students per class! In the summer, thousands of tourists roll through, many of them free camping and spending their days naked around the various beaches.

PLANNING YOUR TIME

You might accidentally pass three months here and not realize it until you wake up, deeply tanned and enlightened, rapidly blinking your eyes at some point in mid-September. Because there's nothing to "do" in the traditional, capitalist sense of the word, you could spend **one day** in Anafi or **several weeks,** depending on your love of vacation and beach time. Most visitors, who return year after year, usually spend a few weeks here.

For those seeking privacy with warmth, come in **June. July** and **August** are the busiest time of the year, with the population swelling to around 5,000. The crowd is fun in a hippie-bohemian way, and the energy of the tourists is completely different from the feel of neighboring Santorini. If you come in **late spring** or **early fall,** you'll be alone on the island, and be aware that many restaurants and accommodations may be closed. Unless otherwise noted, all shops, restaurants, and accommodations mentioned here are open from **May** to **September.** During the **summer** season, everything is open daily.

Anafi is very small. Most tourists, if they're not free camping, congregate in the **Hora.**

INFORMATION AND SERVICES

There are two **ATMs** on the island, one in Agios Nikolaos port and another in the quasi-post office of the Hora. There's no **police** station, and there's one **general practitioner clinic** right outside of Hora that also dispenses medicine. The staff at the clinic are exceedingly kind and will help you out with most minor-to-moderate injuries and illnesses. Patients with serious injuries are helicoptered out of Anafi to Santorini. For tourist information and to buy ferry tickets, head to Hora's main street to find **Roussou Travel** (tel. 22860/61220).

GETTING THERE

Ferry

Anafi's been off the grid for so long in part because it's so difficult to get to. There's no airport, and though it lies only 22 km (13.5 mi) from Santorini, not all ferry lines stop here. During July and August, there are pretty decent, twice-weekly connections from **Piraeus;** the trip passes through **Santorini** and takes 9-11 hours. You can also go directly from Santorini (1.5 hours). In addition, there are 1-2 weekly ferries from **Crete** (4-8 hours), **Folegandros** (4.5 hours), **Karpathos** (10 hours), **Milos** (7 hours), **Mykonos** (5 hours), **Naxos** (8 hours), **Rhodes** (19 hours), and other **Cycladic islands.** Hours change each year, so consult www.ferries.gr for the most current information. You can buy your tickets directly from the kiosk at the harbor one hour before ferries arrive, or from **Roussou Travel** (tel. 22860/61220) in the Hora's main street.

The **port** of Agios Nikolaos is 1 km (.6 mi) from Hora, up a very steep road. Buses meet the arriving ferries to take you to Hora (€1.80), or to the monastery (€2.60).

GETTING AROUND

The island is only 38 square km (14.5 square mi), and with only two main roads on the

Previous: view of Hora village; the port of Anafi where fishermen are based; Anafi is a walking island.

island, you don't really need a car or motorbike in Anafi; most people just **walk** everywhere. Most travelers congregate in the Hora. There's a **bus** that regularly meets ferries at the port (€1.80), and another route that takes you to Zoodochos Pigis monastery on the east of the island (€2.60). **Hitchhiking** is common here, and taxis are nonexistent, but if you do want to rent a car or motorcycle, try **Moto Manos** (tel. 22860/61430; www.rentacarmanos) in the Hora.

Itinerary Ideas

DAY 1

1. Drop your things and head straight to **Megalos Roukounas** beach. Spend the whole day relaxing, making new friends, and swimming in the impossibly blue sea.
2. When you're feeling peckish, eat at the beach's namesake taverna, **Ktima Roukounas.**
3. As the sun starts to dip, head up to **Hora Village** to watch the stars come out.

DAY 2

Pack plenty of snacks and water, and head out from Hora on the 9-km (3.5-mi) hike up to Kalamos Rock. Along the way, you'll pass through the winding coastal roads that cut through beaches and ruins.

1. From Hora, follow the signs toward Roukounas beach. Visit the well preserved temple at the **Sanctuary of Apollo,** right before Zoodochos Pigis Monastery.
2. Make a pit stop at the **Zoodochos Pigis Monastery.** Walk around the grounds at the monastery, and if one of the monks is in, you can visit inside.
3. Continue your climb up to **Kalamos Rock.** The bravest among you can spend the night at the rock, waking up in the morning to see the most glorious sunrise.

Sights

HORA AND VICINITY

★ Hora (Χώρα)

If you need any convincing that this is one of the most stunning settlements of Cycladic architecture, know that the Athenian neighborhood of Plaka, easily the city's most beautiful, was mostly built by Anafians. Wander through the labyrinth-like alleys, occasionally stopping to enjoy the 360-degree view of the sea. Village life congregates in the *platia* (square), which especially comes alive during *panagiri* (saints' days) and other festivals.

Kastelli Archaeological Site

www.anafi.gr; Tues. and Thurs. 10am-2pm

Kastelli is the ancient capital of Anafi. You can walk around the ruins, noticing the outline of the city's defensive walls. There are a few carved tombs and marble statues that are still at the site; the rest is housed in the on-site archaeological museum.

The ruins are about a 1.5-km (1-mi) walk east of Hora.

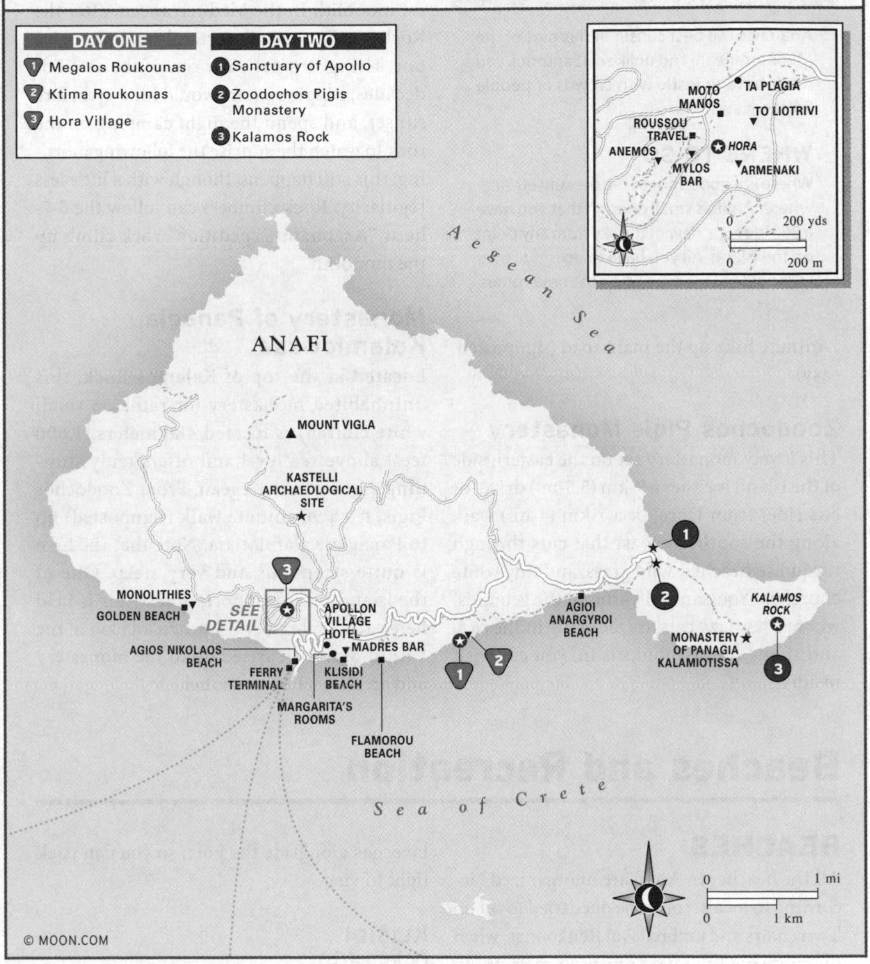

EAST COAST

Those with strong legs can take the 7km (4-mi) hike from Hora along the southern coast to the eastern end of the island. It's a beautiful walk that leads through ruins and beaches. The whole walk to the Zoodochos Pigis monastery will take you around two hours. All sights listed below are free to visit. There is also a bus, which leaves from Hora, to the Zoodochos Pigis monastery.

Sanctuary of Apollo

Right before the Monastery of Zoodochos Pigis you'll find the ruins of the Sanctuary of Apollo. The origins of the sanctuary stem from Jason and the Argonauts, who is said to have founded the cult of Apollo in Anafi. The sanctuary, which includes a well-preserved temple, is made from a glinting quartz rock. If you're hiking from Hora, it's worth it to stop at the sanctuary for a small tour. It's about a

★ Sunsets in Anafi

Anafi has the best sunset in this part of the Mediterranean, and unlike on Santorini, you don't have to jostle with crowds of people for the view.

WHERE TO GO

Where is a good spot to see the sunset? Anywhere! Anafi is small enough that you have a 360-degree view of the sky from any point on the island. All you have to do is pull over to the side of the road when the time comes.

7-minute hike up the main road (signposted, easy).

Zoodochos Pigis Monastery

This lovely monastery set on the eastern side of the island is either a 9-km (5.5-mi) drive (or bus ride) from Hora, or a 7-km (4-mi) walk along the southern coast that cuts through turquoise beaches, wild grass, and tiny white churches. You can walk around the grounds, where a few lazy cats are lounging in the sun, and if one of the monks is in, you can visit inside.

★ Kalamos Rock

Locals claim that Kalamos is the second highest monolith in the Mediterranean, after the Rock of Gibraltar. It's certainly an impressive one, rising dramatically out of the sea. For decades, hippie visitors would hike up before sunset, and spend the night camping on the rock to watch the sunrise the following morning; this still happens, though with a little less regularity. Rock climbers can follow the 5-7-hour "Argonaut Expedition" rock climb up the monolith.

Monastery of Panagia Kalamiotissa

Located at the top of Kalamos Rock, this uninhabited monastery (or rather, a small white church) is located 480 meters (1,600 feet) above sea level and offers truly stunning views of the Aegean. From Zoodochos Pigis, it's a 90-minute walk (signposted) up to Panagia Kalamiotissa. Note that the hike is quite strenuous and very steep. One of the island's most important festivals is held here each September 7-9, when an icon of the Virgin Mary is carried up to the monastery and an all-night party is held.

Beaches and Recreation

BEACHES

All the beaches in Anafi are unorganized (according to locals, someone once tried to set up lawn chairs and umbrellas at Roukounas; when they returned the next morning, everything had been dumped into the sea). Bring your own provisions, especially water! They're also all nudist-friendly, whether they're secluded, like Flamorou, or more popular, like Roukounas.

AGIOS NIKOLAOS (Άγιος Νικόλαος)

This long stretch of sandy beach is the closest beach to the port. As you exit the ferry, you'll notice it on your left. There are a couple of rooms to rent here, and there are a few tavernas alongside the port, so you can pack light to visit.

KLISIDI (Κλεισίδι)

This beach, 2 km (1.2 mi) south of Hora, is one of the closest ones to Hora, and is accessible from the port. It's a long, sandy beach capped by huge rocks; come early to grab a spot under one, so you can have some shade throughout the day. It's also one of the few places where

1: You'll find these beautiful sugar cube buildings scattered around Anafi. **2:** Anafi's sunsets are as beautiful as those in Santorini—with a fraction of the crowds. **3:** The red Roukounas beach turns into a hippie paradise in the summer.

1
2
3

non-nudists outnumber nudists on the island. There are a lot of rooms for rent here, as well as some easily accessible tavernas, making it a popular spot for tourists.

★ MEGALOS ROUKOUNAS (Μεγαλοσ Ρουκουνασ)

Accessible by bus from the Hora, Roukounas (4.2 km/2.6 miles east of Hora), with its long stretch of golden sand, is one of the biggest beaches in Anafi. In addition to the excellent taverna, Ktima Roukounas, there are also some shower facilities, so in July and August, Roukounas is very popular with free campers who pitch their tents along the beach. While it's not the most private, it's quite lively and you'll be sure to meet plenty of interesting people.

FLAMOROU (Φλαμόρου)

One of the most beautiful beaches of the island, Flamorou (3 km/1.9 mi southeast of Hora) is a small cove hidden beneath the scrubby, barren landscape of a Cycladic mountain. This beach is quite secluded and doesn't receive a lot of tourists, making it the perfect secret spot for those looking for isolation.

ÁGIA ANÁRGYRI

Walking up to this beach (4 km/2.5 mi east of Hora), with its beautiful, windswept chapel of the same name at the top of the cliff, is a really special moment. The beach can either be reached by boat from the port (€10), or, for those with good hiking and climbing skills, down the rather precarious path to the sand below. Very private!

HIKING

There are 18 km (11 mi) of well-marked hiking trails around Anafi. You can't really get lost on the trails, but note that aside from some beachside tavernas, there are no shops or markets, so pack your provisions and put on plenty of sunscreen before heading out. For more information, including maps, check out www.anafi.gr.

Katikies of Anafi

On your hikes throughout the island, you'll notice these small structures in various stages of array (and disarray). *Katikies* are farmhouses, and were long the backbone of Anafi's agricultural society. Like all Cycladic architecture, *katikies* were designed to blend in harmoniously with the landscape, and their neutral color and irregular shape make them barely discernible from a distance. Most *katikies* consist of eight structures that housed a family, their animals, and their various farming activities.

A few of the *katikies* are still inhabited today, but most, though protected by Anafi, are abandoned, and are great fun to (respectfully!) walk around and inspect. The whole island is dotted with these, so wherever you go, keep your eyes peeled.

HORA TO KALAMOS ROCK

Distance: *9 km (5.5 mi)*
Duration: *4 hours*
Effort level: *Easy/moderate*

One of the most popular routes goes from Hora all the way to the Kalamos Rock, stopping at the monastery of Zoodochos Pigis on the way.

Just outside of Hora, at the intersection between the monastery and the port, follow the signs toward Roukounas beach. You'll pass along the coastal beaches; follow the upper paths, most of which are paved, till you reach the monastery of Zoodochos Pigis (7.8 km/5 mi; 2.5 hours; easy).

From there, you'll continue 460 meters (1,500 feet) up the signposted path toward Kalamos Rock. The second part of the hike is harder, as it's a steeper incline and will take longer. Be careful in case of strong winds.

Phenomenon Festival

Anafi isn't so underground that the art world hasn't heard of it, but that's not a bad thing. About a decade ago, two scientists from France and Italy who shared a passion for contemporary art dreamed up the idea of using the wild beauty of a Greek island as a sort of visual "terra incognito" that could be rediscovered and reimagined by artists.

In 2015, that idea was given life on Anafi, and **every two years** since, the Phenomenon Festival (www.phenomenon.fr) brings contemporary art to the island. For **two weeks,** usually in **July,** the island buzzes with performances, artist residencies, lectures, and screenings, drawing an international and distinctly chic crowd. Each edition brings a different theme, usually around themes of collective memory, history, and political urgency. If you're planning to visit Anafi in the summer, it's worth it to catch a few days of the festival.

The festival takes place at various locations around the island, and the next one is scheduled for **2021.**

Nightlife and Entertainment

Most nightlife on Anafi is concentrated around Hora proper and Klisidi Beach, just a few kilometers away. In July and August, Roukounas also becomes a round-the-clock party spot, though of the pretty chill variety.

HORA AND KLISIDI

MADRES BAR

Klisidi; tel. 22860/61237; daily, all day

A popular spot on a hill overlooking Kleisidi beach, Madres Bar is the most happening spot on the island. In the summer, everyone congregates here for raucous parties where guest bartenders serve up creative cocktails and guest DJs spin tunes until the early morning hours.

MYLOS BAR

daily, 10am-late

Located inside a converted windmill at the entrance of Hora, Mylos is one of the most atmospheric bars around. Grab a seat at the terrace and sip your cocktail under a velvety blanket of night stars.

MONOLITHIES

Hora; tel. 697 487 4407; daily, all day

A newish spot done up in the minimal, millennial-approved style, this is part shop (selling works by Greek designers), part art gallery, part café, and part bar. Pick your poison, or spend an afternoon and evening indulging. It's located in the center of Hora.

Shopping

YAKINTHOS FASHION SHOP

June to September; daily, 10am-2pm, 6pm-2am

This chic little shop in Hora sells bikinis, jewelry, and other beach accessories, and it doubles as a sort of pharmacy in the European sense of the word (you can buy beauty products, sunscreen, etc.). They also have a very chic collection of sunglasses.

Food

Because Anafi is such a tiny island, a lot of provisions are imported from the mainland; this is especially true for meat. You're best off ordering fish, which is wildly fresh and tastes as briny as the sea.

Nearly all the restaurants in Anafi are family-owned, and that's reflected in the generous service and friendliness of staff. You can't really have a bad meal here!

HORA

ANEMOS

tel. 22860/61289; daily, lunch and dinner; from €7

This family restaurant in the Hora specializes in incredibly fresh fish and seafood dishes (they catch everything themselves). The extensive menu includes copious portions of lobster pasta, freshly grilled or fried fish, and Anafi's special fish soup. It's a no-frills restaurant with great, friendly service and excellent food. It's also one of the few places open year round.

TO LIOTRIVI

tel. 22860/61209; daily, 10am-12pm; from €10

Housed in one of the island's oldest oil producing mills, Liotrivi is a cozy taverna serving up traditional Greek classics with fresh ingredients from the sea and from the family's garden. Grab a seat on the terrace, which boasts stunning views of the Aegean.

ARMENAKI

tel. 22860/61234; daily, 10am-1pm; from €10

Start your day with a *freddo espresso,* a prickly pear and orange juice, and a bowl of Greek yogurt drizzled with local honey at this family-run taverna, which first opened in 1999. For dinner, try the owner's twist on moussaka, made with eggplant and minced tuna. In August, there's often music and dancing to accompany your meal.

ROUKOUNAS

★ KTIMA ROUKOUNAS

tel. 22860/61206; daily, 10am-late; from €7

This lovely family-owned beach taverna has been a fixture in Anafi for the past 15 years. Much of the food is grown in the family's garden, and you can't go wrong with anything on the menu; it's all cooked by the family matriarch! In July and August, dinner regularly transitions into a quasi-music festival, with plenty of dancing and partying. The infectiously warm and gregarious Irini, the owner's daughter, will immediately make you feel at home.

Accommodations

While free camping (pitching your tent and just hanging out for a while) is technically illegal in Greece, this is more in the theoretical sense of the law than in practice, especially on islands like Anafi. It's quite popular among young Greeks. In July and August, Roukounas turns into a veritable music festival landscape of tents with clothes hanging out to dry.

In addition to free camping, there are several rooms for rent around the port and Hora. In July and August, it's better to book ahead, but for the rest of the season you can show up without any planned reservation.

HORA

TA PLAGIA

tel. 22860/61308; http://taplagia.gr/en; Apr.-Oct.; from €60

Located on the eastern edge of Hora, this family-run bed-and-breakfast (€5 extra) is a

Nudism in Greece

While it's technically illegal in Greece, nudism is practiced by locals and tourists alike, and you'll see everyone from children to grandparents nude at the beach.

Contrary to what you might think, there's nothing sexual about it, and for many people, it's a way to experience the sea and sun and to have total freedom. I find that Americans seem particularly uncomfortable with nudism compared to Europeans. (I've heard 30-somethings shriek and giggle like tweens.) But if it's something that interests you, there's no better place to try it than Anafi.

ETIQUETTE

There is, uh, an etiquette around nudism. If you do stumble upon some nudists, just politely nod and carry on your way. There's no need to stare, or point and laugh. If you're a straight man, please don't do anything that a woman would already find creepy with clothes on. If you want to join in, be observant of your surroundings—if everyone on the beach is clothed, you probably want to try a different beach where more people are nude.

good place to crash with friends. Rooms and studios can sleep up to four people. There's no air-conditioning, but the ceiling fans will keep you cool and there are kitchenettes and balconies. Note that there's an additional charge to use the Internet, should you need it.

KLISIDI BEACH AND VICINITY

MARGARITA'S ROOMS

tel. 22860/61237; www.margarita-anafi.gr; May-Sept.; €60

Anafi is full of these little family-run rooms that offer only basic amenities but are heavy on the charm. Margarita's Rooms is a great choice for those looking for an affordable vacation. The rooms are located on Klisidi beach, which can be a bit isolated, but you really don't need much else besides beach, shower, and an excellent restaurant, which is luckily on-site, offering all meals.

APOLLON VILLAGE HOTEL

www.apollonvillagehotel.com; May-Sept.; €95

Twenty Cycladic units are scattered on the hillside overlooking Klisidi beach, and you can choose from studios, apartments, or individual rooms. Each offers stupendous views, and friendly staff and a few thoughtful touches make it a great value for money. There's an adjacent café-bar that serves up refreshments and turns into something of a party in the evening.

WEST OF HORA

★ GOLDEN BEACH

Kameni Lagada; tel. 22860/28856; https://goldenbeachresort.reserve-online.net; Apr.-Oct.; €215

The only large(ish), luxury hotel on the island, Golden Beach is a brand new addition to Anafi—it opened in 2018. Sixteen Cycladic-inspired rooms are nestled around a pool, all with their own private hot tub and balcony that offer truly jaw-dropping, unobstructed views of the sea. There's a little path that descends down to two different beaches, and they're starting to offer sea sports like canoe and kayak. The hotel is a bit out of the way (a few kilometers west of Hora), and while staff will happily pick you up from the port and occasionally ferry you around, if you prefer to be autonomous you will want to rent a vehicle.

Karpathos (Κάρπαθοσ)

The craggy island of Karpathos (pop. 8,000), the second-largest of the Dodecanese, has long lived in the shadow of its neighbors Crete and Rhodes. In antiquity, it was dismissed by Homer (he famously referred to it as "Krapathos"), and when modern Greece unified in 1843, mainlanders considered Karpathos as distant as France. It's not, obviously, but that's still good news for the contemporary traveler who braves the 16-hour boat ride from Piraeus (or the much more manageable 1-hour flight from Athens) to find an island precariously stuck in time.

Karpathos is wild, with 107 beaches, winds so strong they move objects and clothing with a comical ferocity, and a shrubby landscape that allows for a 360-degree view of the sea and sky. It's an island ruled

Highlights

Look for ★ to find recommended sights, activities, dining, and lodging.

★ **Windsurfing:** Even beginners will have a blast riding the waves in Karpathos' famous Southern Coast bays, where blustery winds send you skimming across the sea (page 213).

★ **Apella Beach:** Spread a towel out at one of Europe's most beautiful beaches, where pure white sand is backed by fragrant green cliffs (page 217).

★ **Olympos Village:** Time seems to stands still in Olympos, one of Greece's oldest villages (page 218).

★ **Panigiri of Vroukounda:** The church of Agios Ioannis comes alive every August 28-29, as locals walk from Olympos to the deserted ruins of Vroukounda for a massive sleepover party with raucous dancing, eating, singing, and drinking (page 221).

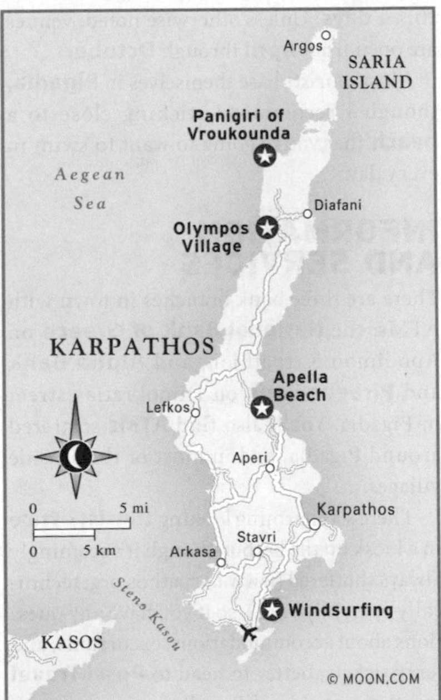

by the compass: The north is green and fertile; the south is parched. The western side of the island is battered by blustery winds, making it an ideal place for windsurfers, while the eastern side is calmer. In the middle lie mountains, sitting like giant mounds of rumpled laundry. The island has a peculiarly large number of Americans; thousands of Greeks left the island in the middle of the 20th century for the United States and have since returned each summer. This means many Karpathians speak English, and even in the most remote village, you'll be able to communicate.

PLANNING YOUR TIME

Given how out of the way Karpathos is, you'll want to spend at least **five days** on the island, making up for the journey. If you're already planning a trip around the Dodecanese, you'll see everything you want to see in about **three days.** Unless otherwise noted, venues are open from **April** through **October.**

Most tourists base themselves in **Pigadia,** though I recommend sticking close to a **beach** that you're going to want to swim in every day.

INFORMATION AND SERVICES

There are three bank branches in town with ATMs: the **National Bank of Greece** on Apodimon Karpathion, and **Alpha Bank** and **Piraeus Bank** on Dimokratias street in Pigadia. You'll also find **ATMs** scattered around Pigadia, and in most of the seaside villages.

There's a charming looking **tourist office** in a kiosk on the harbor, though it's seemingly always shuttered (www.karpathos.org; technically open July-Aug.), so if you have any questions about accommodations, excursions, and ferry tickets, better to head to **Possi Travel** (on the east side of Pigadia, two streets up from the waterfront; tel. 22450/22235), the town's main travel agency.

For any health issues, head to the **Hippocrates Health Clinic** on Dimokratias. Nearby, you'll find the **police station** (tel. 22450/22224) and the **post office.**

GETTING THERE

Planes are the fastest and easiest way to get to Karpathos.

Air

If you travel to Karpathos by plane, you'll arrive at **Karpathos Island National Airport** (AOK), at the southwest end of the island, and you'll fly over blue seas dotted with racing windsurfers as you land. There are 2-4 daily flights from Athens, served by **Olympic Air** (www.olympicair.com; tel. 210/355 0500). Flights take about one hour and cost €50-70 one way, though prices can fluctuate in the high season.

There are also flights to and from other islands, run by **Sky Express** (www.skyexpress.gr; 2810/223 800). There are daily flights between Karpathos and **Rhodes International Airport** "Diagoras" (RHO; 40 minutes; €60). During the summer months, there are direct flights from select European countries, including Italy, Germany, and Sweden.

Buses to/from the airport only operate from late July to September on a very spartan schedule (11:30am Thurs., 10:30am Sat., return 5pm; €2.50). **Taxis** cost a flat rate of €25 to take you into Pigadia, 14 km (8.5 mi) from the airport.

Ferry

Blue Star Ferries (tel. 210/422 2440; www.bluestarferries.com) serves the island's main port in **Pigadia,** including a stop in the northern village of **Diafini.** There are ferries twice weekly from **Piraeus** (17 hours; €44), once weekly from **Milos** (16 hours; €38), three

Previous: The view of the oldest village in Greece, Olympos; an old woman walks the street in Olympos; a tourist boat leaving Apella Beach.

times weekly from **Rhodes** (6 hours; €21), and once weekly from **Santorini** (8 hours; €27).

GETTING AROUND

Because Karpathos is quite big (302 square km/115 square mi), the bus service is so spotty and taxis so expensive, your best bet is to rent a car.

Driving in Karpathos is not for the faint-hearted. The **mountain roads** only fit one and a half cars, but are somehow two-lane. Around Pigadia there's free street **parking** and the roads are manageable, but as soon as you start to go up toward the beaches or into the mountains, the roads are full of twists and turns, and at night, there are no lights. Exercise caution and drive defensively.

Car

During the high season, you won't find a basic car for less than €45 euros per day (with insurance). All major car rental companies have outlets at the airport, and there are several more local providers in town. Recommended operators include **Budget Rentacar** (www.budget.gr) and **Gatoulis** (www.karpathosgatoulis.com; the name means "kitten" in Greek, and all cars come with an image of an adorable cat). You need to spend more to rent a car with 4WD if you're planning to visit certain beaches.

Bus

Local buses are run by **KTEL** (www.karpathosbus.wordpress.com) all across the island; the main **bus station** is in Pigadia (M Mattheou, Pigadia; tel. 22450/22338). Arrive a bit early to pay for your round-trip ticket (€4-15, cards accepted).

Taxi

Taxis are wildly expensive (around €40 from Pigadia to the west coast); prices are posted at the central **taxi rank** (Dimokratias, Pigadia; tel. 22450/22705).

Itinerary Ideas

This itinerary has you based in Pigadia. On Day 1, you won't need a car unless you're planning on going back to Sofia's Taverna in Kyria Panagia for dinner; if you want to be carless, skip that and have dinner back in Pigadia. You'll want a car for Day 2. Pack a swimsuit for both days. On Day 2, bring a good pair of walking shoes, too.

DAY 1

1 Grab a coffee and a freshly baked doughnut for breakfast from **Prateriou Artou Zaxaroplasteio** and stroll along the backstreets of Pigadia.

2 From Pigadia's harbor, take a boat ride on **Sofia My Love.** You'll hit all the best beaches just north of town: Achata, Kyria Panagia, and Apella. You'll eat lunch on the boat and be back by early evening.

3 Have dinner at **Sofia's Taverna** on Kyria Panagia Beach.

4 Still have energy? Have an evening cocktail at **Anoi Bar** in Pigadia before hitting the sack.

DAY 2

1 Best to leave by 8:30am to head to **Olympos Village** to beat the crowds. Have a coffee near the windmills, and spend several hours exploring the streets of Olympos and talking

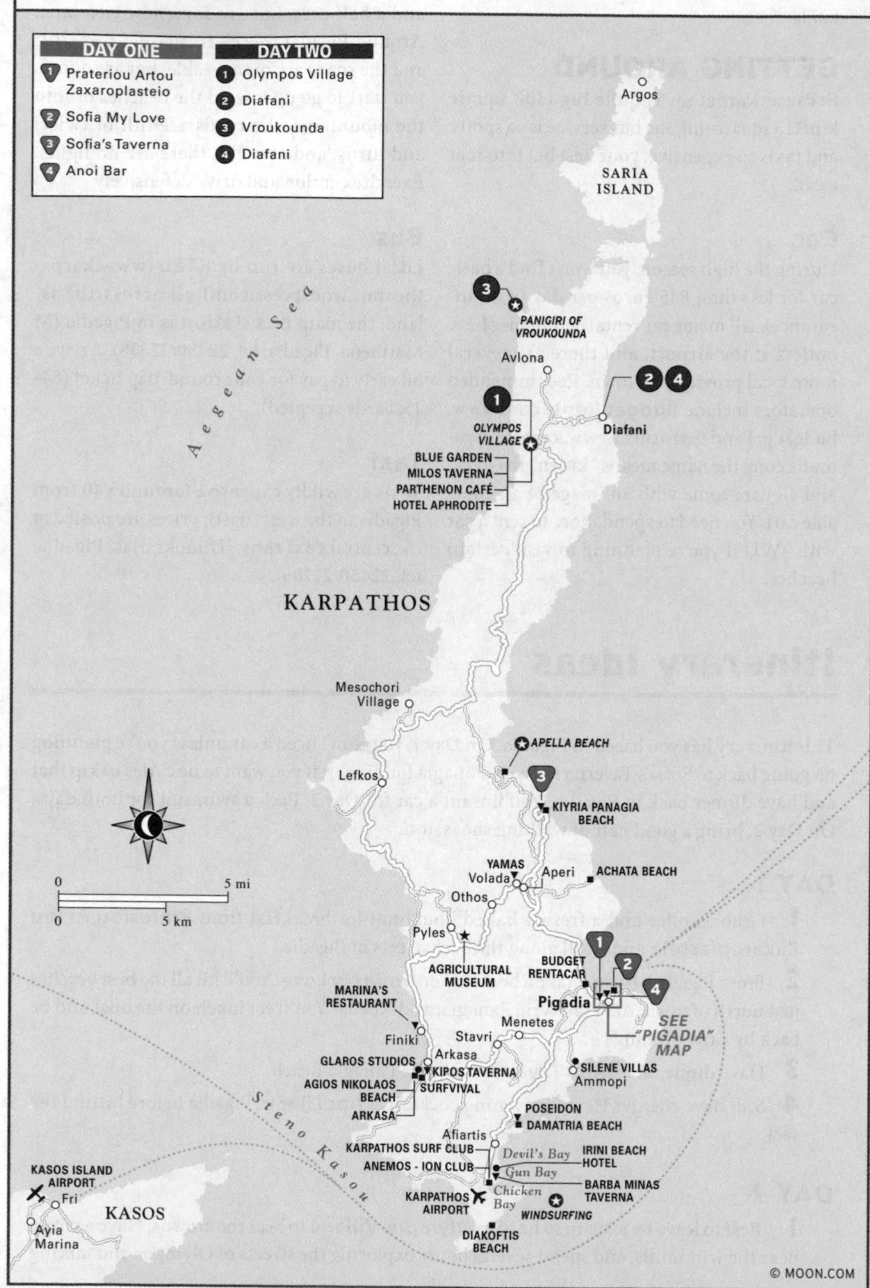
Karpathos
DAY ONE
1 Prateriou Artou Zaxaroplasteio
2 Sofia My Love
3 Sofia's Taverna
4 Anoi Bar
DAY TWO
1 Olympos Village
2 Diafani
3 Vroukounda
4 Diafani
Argos
SARIA ISLAND
Aegean Sea
PANIGIRI OF VROUKOUNDA
Avlona
Diafani
OLYMPOS VILLAGE
BLUE GARDEN
MILOS TAVERNA
PARTHENON CAFÉ
HOTEL APHRODITE
KARPATHOS
Mesochori Village
APELLA BEACH
Lefkos
KIYRIA PANAGIA BEACH
YAMAS
Volada
Aperi
ACHATA BEACH
Othos
0
5 mi
0
5 km
Pyles
AGRICULTURAL MUSEUM
BUDGET RENTACAR
MARINA'S RESTAURANT
Pigadia
SEE "PIGADIA" MAP
Menetes
Finiki
Stavri
Arkasa
GLAROS STUDIOS
KIPOS TAVERNA
SILENE VILLAS
Ammopi
AGIOS NIKOLAOS BEACH
SURFVIVAL
ARKASA
Steno Kasou
POSEIDON
DAMATRIA BEACH
Afiartis
KARPATHOS SURF CLUB
Devil's Bay
IRINI BEACH HOTEL
ANEMOS - ION CLUB
Gun Bay
BARBA MINAS TAVERNA
KARPATHOS AIRPORT
Chicken Bay
WINDSURFING
DIAKOFTIS BEACH
KASOS ISLAND AIRPORT
Fri
KASOS
Ayia Marina
© MOON.COM

to locals. You can have lunch at the Blue Garden, or, if you're feeling especially Greek, just some ouzo and meze at the local *kafeneion*, Parthenon Café.

2 Drive down to **Diafani** for a dip in the sea.

3 Refreshed from your ocean swim, walk half an hour to explore the ruins of **Vroukounda.**

4 Head back to **Diafani** for a seaside dinner at one of the fish tavernas lining the harbor.

Pigadia Πηγάδια

Pigadia is the capital and main port of Karpathos, and while it's a good base for the island, it's not exactly the most architecturally pleasing town; you won't find any whitewashed hamlets here. The town has the usual collection of shops and restaurants clustered around the harbor, and a small amphitheater where there are outdoor concerts during the summer months. Take some time to wander the port's bougainvillea-laced backstreets, where you'll find some more interesting elements, including bakeries churning out cumin-studded dried breads, and locals hawking giant watermelons out of truck beds.

Pigadia is small enough that a quick walk through the town will have you oriented. The waterfront is the heart of the town, and the handful of backstreets are easy enough to navigate.

SIGHTS

The Archaeological Museum of Karpathos

Pigadia harbor; tel. 22450/23441; Tues.-Sun. 9am-2pm; €2

Located in a 1930s art deco building that served as the provincial headquarters under Italian rule, The Archaeological Museum of Karpathos is a three-room journey through the island's ancient history, from the Neolithic to the Byzantine periods. Most of the items on display are pottery pieces from excavated ruins.

RECREATION

Diving and Snorkeling

The water is so clear in parts of Karpathos that you can see down 30 meters (98.5 feet), rendering goggles an unnecessary accessory. But if you do grab a pair, you'll be dazzled by beautiful marine life, underwater labyrinths, and strange rock formations. Indeed, the best snorkeling spots are the rocky ones, like **Apella, Achata,** and **Ammopi Beach.**

KARPATHOS DIVING CENTER

Pigadia harbor; tel. 22450/22860; www.divingkarpathos.gr; single dive €60, guided dive €85

If you're a first-time diver, get started with the guidance of qualified trainers from PADI-certified Karpathos Diving Center. They also do night dives, and you can rent equipment here.

Boat Tours

Boat tours leave on daily excursions from Pigadia's harbor, taking a circuitous route around the beaches of Ahata, Kiria Panagia, and Apella. Boats leave at 8:30am and return at 5pm daily; during the peak season, you should buy your ticket the evening before (the captains wait outside the boat). Boats moor near the beaches, so you can jump off (or walk off the plank) and explore the beach.

SOFIA MY LOVE

Pigadia Harbor on the waterfront; €25, including lunch

The creaking pirate ship Sofia My Love is the most popular choice with tourists for boat tours, in part because it goes to a secret beach only accessible by boat: Vasilis Paradise is a beautiful little cove with a strip of pebble beach and fantastically clear sand, plus,

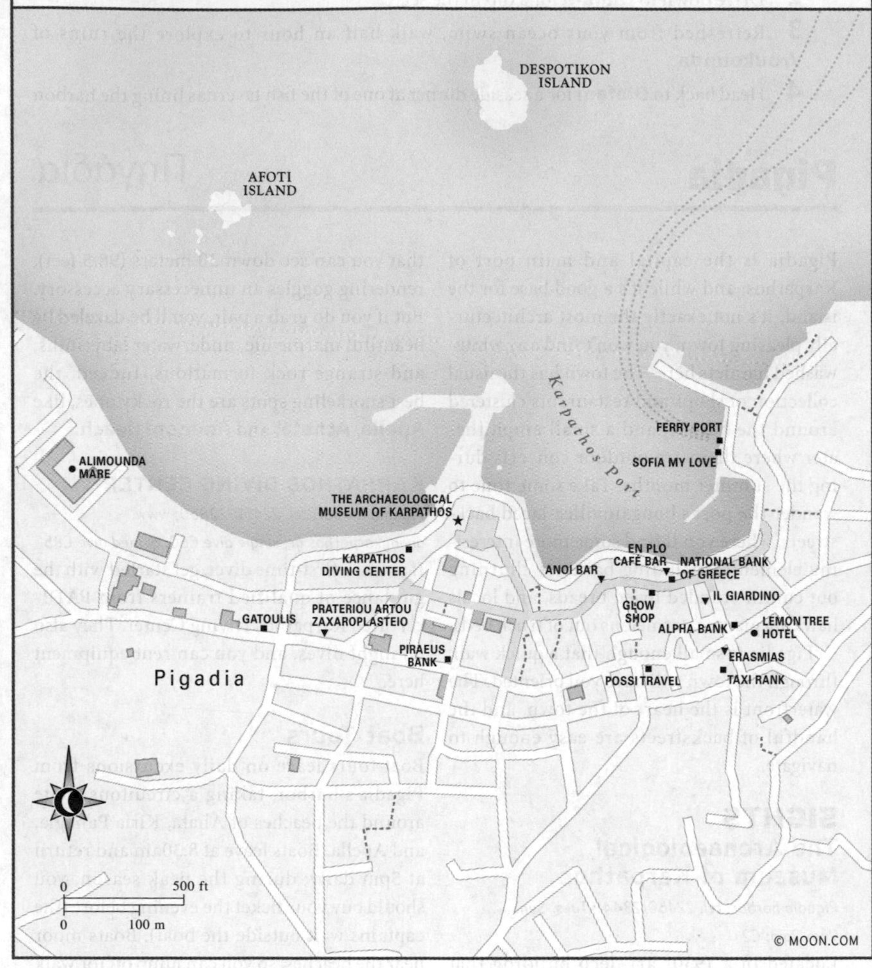

you'll be alone (albeit with the rest of the boat guests). The included lunch comprises grilled souvlaki, salad, and bread.

NIGHTLIFE AND ENTERTAINMENT

Pigadia is the nightlife center of Karpathos, but things never get too crazy on this island.

ANOI BAR

tel. 22450/23960; 8am-late; drinks €2-12

Settle down for a drink at Anoi Bar, an all-day café and bar that really picks up in the evenings. Grab a pillow and sit on the wide back steps, where you'll have a beautiful view of the harbor.

SHOPPING

GLOW SHOP

tel. 22450/23869

Head to Glow Shop to pick up bohemian fashion styles with a Greek flair, including lacey caftan dresses, straw hats, and jewelry and clutches emblazoned with the evil eye.

FOOD

Greek

ERASMIAS

tel. 22450/22222; lunch and dinner; from €2

A meat-heavy sandwich isn't so out of place in Karpathos, where a depleted fishing industry means most mainstream restaurants serve the frozen stuff. At Erasmias—mostly a takeaway restaurant with a few plastic tabletops—order a pita gyro stuffed with french fries, tzatziki, and onions. If you're extra hungry, order the gyro plate.

Italian

IL GIARDINO

tel. 22450/22866; lunch and dinner; mains from €12

With so many Italian tourists in Karpathos, it's no wonder several Italian restaurants have popped up across the island. In Pigadia, Il Giardino is a particularly nice one, housed in an old neoclassical building with a beautiful interior garden. It's a sumptuous setting to indulge in thick steaks and squid ink risotto.

Breakfast and Bakeries

PRATERIOU ARTOU ZAXAROPLASTEIO

tel. 22450/81332; daily 7:30am-5pm; from €1.50

Karpathos is known for its hard-as-a-rock crackers studded with cumin seeds. They're meant to be soaked in water and oil before eaten (otherwise you'll break your teeth), and they make for a perfect tomato salad topping for the beach. This bakery sells plenty of salty pies, as well as delicious cream-stuffed doughnuts and other sweet treats.

EN PLO CAFÉ BAR

Apodimon Karpathion 12; tel. 22450/23990; daily 7:30am-2:30am

One of the best breakfast spots on the island, En Plo is a laid-back spot perfect for reading your morning newspaper and digging into a giant stack of pancakes. They have delicious juice, like blackberry, and specialty coffee sweetened with local honey. At night, they dish out cocktails till late.

ACCOMMODATIONS

Under €150

LEMON TREE HOTEL

Papanastasiou 2; tel. 698 031 5885; €70 d

A stay at the Lemon Tree Hotel, located in a renovated neoclassical building 200 meters (656 feet) from the port, makes a good base for a budget traveler. The dozen or so rooms are simple but clean, with a friendly staff. There's Wi-Fi throughout, and some rooms feature kitchenettes and/or balconies. The hotel is located in a renovated building from the 19th century, and there are lovely neoclassical details throughout.

Over €300

ALIMOUNDA MARE

tel. 22450/23902; www.alimounda.gr; €253 d with breakfast, junior suite €368 with breakfast

With 266 rooms each featuring a balcony, Alimounda Mare is the largest luxury hotel on the whole island. Located right on the beach (albeit a slightly rocky one) just a few minutes' walk from downtown Pigadia, Alimounda Mare boasts a lovely infinity pool, gym, spa, two restaurants, and two bars. It's popular with couples and families, as they have plenty of kids' entertainment.

The Southeast Coast

As you drive south out of Pigadia, you'll leave all the hustle and bustle of town behind. This part of the island is battered by winds and beloved by windsurfers, who have little use for streets full of shops and museums. Visitors are drawn to the three consecutive bays that increase in difficulty for windsurfers; they're not the best places for relaxing, but there are plenty of sparkling blue coves where you can spread your towel and lounge in peace.

Note that there are dozens of beaches that can only be reached in a 4WD vehicle (marked signs indicate this); exercise extreme caution when driving down these roads. There are buses to Ammopi, but otherwise, you'll need a car here.

AMMOPI (Αμμοπη)

Located 8 km (5 mi) south of Pigadia, Ammopi is the main town in the Amfiarti region of the south. There's not a lot going on here. Though the area is supposed to be a resort, there's only a handful of hotels, and no commercial center or stripmall area to speak of. It's a good place to stay if you want to be windsurfing all day, or exploring any of the little coves that are along the coast.

Accommodations

IRINI BEACH HOTEL

Gun Bay; tel. 22450/91000; www.karpathos-windsurfing.gr; from €60

If you're here to windsurf every day, shack up at Irini's Beach Hotel, where the rooms are breezy and big enough to store your windsurfing equipment. They also have rentals available, as well as instructors to take you out for lessons. There's a pool too, should you tire of the salty sea.

SILENE VILLAS

Ardani, Ammopi; tel. 697 273 7743; silenevillas.com; villas from €160

If you prefer to stay as close to Ammopi beach as possible, book a room at Silene Villas. Located on the beautiful Ammopi Bay, this cluster of six villa-style lodgings features bright and contemporary decor, stunning views of the sea, and access to a private pool.

DAMATRIA BEACH (Δαματριά)

Located 20 km (12.5 mi) southwest of Pigadia, Damatria Beach is a long golden beach with pebbles and fantastic turquoise water. It's 6 km (3.75 mi) past the airport, and the road is unpaved, so be careful when driving. You won't need a 4WD, but you will need some patience. The beach is unorganized.

AFIARTIS (Αφιάρτης)

Afiartis is actually a collection of three different bays. This is the best windsurfing beach in Karpathos, and it draws appropriately sized crowds. The coolest surfers—all bronzed skin and golden haired—congregate at Devil's Bay, which has the strongest winds and attracts the most daredevil antics. Then there's Gun Bay for intermediates, and Chicken Bay for beginners. None of these beaches is particularly agreeable for swimming and sunbathing; the wind is too strong, and they're full of windsurfers anyway. There are dining and refreshment options on the beach, as well as places to organize lessons and rent equipment.

Beaches

DIAKOFTIS BEACH (Διακόφτης)

Near the airport you'll find the lagoon of Karpathos, an enchanting series of turquoise coves with soft white sand. From Pigadia it's an 18-km (11-mi) drive south to Diakoftis. When you turn after the airport, the road becomes unpaved, but it's worth it: With a few umbrellas and a small canteen, this spot is quite relaxing and features unique rock formations teeming with marine life.

★ Windsurfing

From May to mid-October, windsurfers from around the world come to Karpathos to take advantage of the island's brutal winds, congregating in Afiartis on the southern coast. There are three bays to choose from, corresponding to skill level: the aptly named **Chicken Bay** for beginners, **Gun Bay** for intermediates, and **Devil's Bay** for pros, where the winds reach up to 45 knots. They are all located next to each other, separated by natural boundaries of the cliffs. As you're driving down from Pigadia, the first bay you'll see is Devil's Bay, followed by Gun Bay and Chicken Bay.

ION CLUB

Gun Bay; www.ion-club.net/en; tel. 22450/91061

You can rent equipment and get lessons from the folks at ION Club. On Sundays at 8pm, surfers also hold barbecue parties that are open to people who take lessons.

KARPATHOS SURF CLUB

Chicken Bay; tel. 697 347 4816; www.karpathossurf.com

Located on Chicken Bay, Karpathos Surf Club is a favorite thanks to its professional yet laid-back instructors, and wide range of programs and packages. Three hours of beginner's lessons, plus two hours of rental, costs €100.

Food

POSEIDON

1.7 km (1 mi) north of Afiartis, Damatria Beach; tel. 697 869 4482; http://poseidon-karpathos.com/restaurant/; cash only

Have you ever wanted to dine with a local reality TV star? Then don't miss out on the chance to eat at Poseidon, a beachside restaurant run by Angela Papavasiliou. She placed fifth in the first edition of Greece's MasterChef, and has been churning out modern Greek food with an international twist since. This isn't your traditional taverna: You'll find gazpacho, shark meat, and John Dory with mushrooms. (Shark meat is more commonly consumed in the Mediterranean than in the United States, and is not as taboo.)

BARBA MINAS TAVERNA

Chicken Bay; tel. 697 322 6624; daily 11:30am-10pm; from €7

This taverna serves very good, classic fare, with an emphasis on fresh seafood: whole grilled dorade with lemons, seafood spaghetti, and stuffed calamari are all on the menu, and dessert is a big bowl of fresh fruit. There's a nice view of the sea, and the staff is friendly.

ANEMOS ION CLUB

Gun Bay; tel. 22450/91061; www.ion-club.net/en; 9am-late; from €7

Surfers and instructors hang out at Ion Club, which also doubles as a surf shop offering lessons and rental equipment. The menu is mostly salads, sandwiches, and burgers, and at night everyone congregates on the terrace for cocktails.

Central and Southwestern Karpathos

West across Pigadia you'll cut through mountainous villages filled with oddly constructed homes, relics of American tastes mixed with Greek construction. Along with the north, the west is the less touristic part of the island, with plenty of little towns and charming villages, like Arkasa, Finiki, Lefkos, and Menetes. There are beautiful beaches here, too; indeed, some of the beaches on the southwest coast are some of the most stunning in Greece, but be careful with the winds. On the western side of the island, wind batters the beaches even more than on the east coast. Though there aren't as many windsurfing options here as on the southeast coast, there are still plenty of places to feel yourself blown across the waves by the wind.

There's a bus line from Pigadia that makes stops in Menekes, Arkasa, and Finiki.

MENETES
(Μενετές)

Driving west out of Pigadia (8 km/5 mi), the first village you'll come across is Menetes, a colorful settlement perched in the green-brown mountains. It's worth a stop for the fantastic views across the mountain and toward the sea. It's a bit difficult to walk here, as there are no sidewalks, but you can drive around slowly to admire the pastel-colored facades of the houses and the balconies covered in flowers. There's a big *panigiri* here on August 15 that you can check out if you're in town.

ARKASA
(Αρκάσα)

Coastal Arkasa (on Google maps you'll see it written as Arcesine) is the largest city on the west coast, built into the cliffs and on the ruins of the ancient city of Arkesia. The local population is 600, but the number swells in the summer, as this is a popular place for surfers and families to spend their vacation. This town caters to tourists, and you'll find plenty of amenities. The best beach here is Agios Nikolaos; when you tire of sunbathing, follow the track along the beach (signposted) for 500 meters (1,640 feet) to the Basilica of Agia Sophia, where you'll find mosaics, chapels, and an amphitheater from the 5th century.

Surfing and Windsurfing

SURFVIVAL

tel. 698 980 5037; www.surfvivalschool.com; 1-hour class €55

The very cool folks at Surfvival (get it?) in Arkasa offer surf lessons, as well as gear and clothes to help you look the part. They also organize surf camps, as well as some windsurfing classes, which practice at Agios Nikoloas beach.

AGIOS NIKOLAOS BEACH
(Άγιος Νικόλαος)

Drive down the winding roads of Arkasa to reach Agios Nikolaos beach, a sleepy cluster of homes with a few small cafés and tavernas. The main beach is to the left of the parking lot and is partly organized (sun beds cost €8) with a canteen and volleyball nets. But the real gem of Agios Nikolaos is a tiny pebbled beach on the right of the parking lot. There's only room for a few bathers, so arrive early to grab a spot. There's excellent snorkeling around the rock formations and very clean waters. From Arkasa, it's a 2-km (1.25-mi) drive down to the beach.

Food

KIPOS TAVERNA

Arkasa; tel. 697 815 9843; from €5

With a thatched roof terrace that lets in filtered columns of gold light, Kipos Taverna has all the allure of a traditional Greek taverna. The food here is classic fare, with an emphasis on grilled seafood and meat. They also have a few menu items with tourists in mind, like moussaka.

Accommodations

GLAROS STUDIOS

Agios Nikolaos Beach, Arkasa; tel. 22450/61015; www.glarosstudios-karpathos.com; €50-55

As the only hotel on Agios Nikolaos beach on the southwest side of the island, the small Glaros Studios stands out as a cozy and economical home base. The rooms are decorated in a traditional Karpathian style, with mattresses atop raised wooden platforms. Studios feature small kitchenettes, so you can prepare breakfast and small meals at home, and if you're feeling lazy, head to the adjoining taverna, which serves reasonably priced Greek classics.

FINIKI

(Φινική)

Colorful Finiki is the best-known fishing village on Karpathos. It was built by fishermen and, until 1900, it was known as the island's commercial port. The town is built around the beach, which acts as both a port and a local swimming spot. Behind the beach are rows of palm-fringed houses, tavernas, and snack bars. There's a nice pale blue church on the bluff that overlooks the town, which is 2 km (1.25 mi) north of Arkasa.

Food

You can't go wrong with any of the restaurants in Finiki. They all catch and grill their own fresh fish.

MARINA'S RESTAURANT

Finiki waterfront; tel. 22450/61100; daily 8am-11:30pm; from €7

Sometimes you're just really in the mood for an all-American breakfast. I get you—and so does Marina, the jovial owner of her namesake restaurant. She lived in Florida for a decade, and churns out pancakes, waffles, hash browns, and sunny-side-up eggs with all the aplomb of a seasoned diner cook. Should you choose to come for lunch or dinner, you can't go wrong with any of the freshly caught and grilled fish options.

PYLES

(Πύλες)

The tiny mountain village of Pyles is located 14 km (8.7 mi) northwest of Pigadia, through mountain roads. There's not much to see or do here, but if you're driving through, it's worth a stop at the Agricultural Museum.

Menetes is an isolated village on the east coast of Karpathos.

American Culture in Karpathos

I had never heard fluent Greek spoken in a thick New York accent before coming to Karpathos. The effect is momentarily jarring, but you'll get used to it quickly. Karpathos is the most "American" of the Greek islands, thanks in part to a massive exodus after World War II that saw Karpathian men and women leaving the islands to try their luck in the United States. Most settled along the eastern seaboard, opening up restaurants and businesses, and industriously saving their money through years of hard work.

These Greeks have been returning every summer, building summer homes across the island (you'll notice some distinctly American touches to the houses in the interior villages) and generally supporting the local economy. Many diaspora children have returned to Karpathos and permanently live here; others simply return for the warmer months. You'll hear endearing mash-ups of the language: "Artemis, *poulakimou* [my chicken]!" screeched one woman at the beach, "Stop throwing sand at your brother!"

Sights

AGRICULTURAL MUSEUM

tel. 22450/23441; Mon.-Sat. 10am-1pm and 6pm-8pm; €2

Historically minded foodies should head to the mostly outdoor Agricultural Museum in Pyles, where you'll find a cute little farm, exact replicas of a period wine press, a farmhouse and dairy, a wood-fire oven churning out local biscuits, and a fully operational windmill. Karpathos is sadly no longer known for its gastronomy; most of the fish sold in restaurants is bought frozen from Italian and Egyptian fishermen, and local production is limited to individual families. This museum is a nice reminder of what life used to be like.

VOLADA (Βωλάδα)

Located 10 km (6.25 mi) northwest of Pigadia and 12 km (7.5 mi) northeast of Finiki, the small settlement of Volada is a typical Greek mountain village. Most of the homes here are summer places for expat Karpathians, and you'll likely drive through here once (make sure to crane your head around; there's a nice view of Pigadia).

Nightlife and Entertainment

YAMAS

tel. 22450/31123; noon-late; drinks €2-12

In the town of Volada you'll find a roadside bar called Yamas, serving up giant, colorful cocktails against a stunning view of Pigadia and the harbor. It's mostly popular with locals, who flock here on Wednesdays for Tropical Night, and there are plenty of live music acts and DJs throughout the summer. Most nights culminate in several rounds of Greek circle dancing.

North End

North out of Pigadia, you'll come across some of the most beautiful beaches on Karpathos. The farther up you go, the more magical the landscape gets: Seemingly suspended in time is the fantastic Olympos village, where sugar cube houses hold traditionally dressed grandmothers and plenty of secrets. The wind here is quite strong, and there's a different energy on this side of the island. Most tourists come to see Olympos and skip the rest, which is a shame. There's a lot to see and do around here.

Most of the beaches in North Karpathos are unorganized, secluded, and a bit difficult to get to. If you don't have a 4WD, don't drive down the dirt roads, as cars can easily get stuck! Of the destinations listed here, Achata, Kyria Panagia, Apella, and Olympos are accessible by bus. I recommend renting a car for a day to visit this part of the island at your own pace.

ACHATA BEACH (Αχατα)

This rocky beach is an idyllic cove on the east side of the island. There's a nice tavern near the parking lot and a few umbrellas for rent in the middle of the beach. Waters are clean and cool, and it's a bit isolated from the winds. It's located 12 km (7.5 mi) north of Pigadia, but it will take you 30 minutes through the winding mountain roads along the coast.

KYRIA PANAGIA BEACH (Κυρία Παναγία)

Half organized, half unorganized, Kyria Panagia is a pebbly beach with clear waters backed against crumbling rock formations located on the southeast side of the island. There are a few caves and diving spots, and it's a great beach for families. As you swim, you'll notice the beautiful red-domed church of Kyria Panagia on the bluff overlooking the ocean.

Kyria Panagia is located 11 km (6.75 mi) north of Achata. Again, allow 30 minutes due to the winding roads. Buses depart from Pigadia for Kyria Panagia twice a week (30 minutes; €3).

Food

★ SOFIA'S TAVERNA

Apr.-Oct. all day; mains from €8, rooms €60 in high season without breakfast

Located up the main street from the stunning, pebbled beach of Kyria Panagia, the family-run Sofia's Taverna is a welcome respite from the tourist traps dotting the coastline. All the food is homemade, from the bread to the tiny deep-fried shrimp; produce is local, and the proprietor catches fresh fish each morning (a surprising rarity in Karpathos). Standouts include their riff on a traditional Greek salad featuring caper leaves, and grilled calamari. It's very much a family business; expect to be cajoled into conversation by the proprietors' daughter, and get ready to coo over their infant baby.

★ APELLA BEACH (Απέλλα)

Locals will proudly tell you that the European Union voted Apella the most beautiful beach in Europe. It's only a slight exaggeration; the European Best Destination website *did* list Apella as one of the most beautiful. Down a winding mountain road 13 km (8 mi) from Kyria Panagia, you'll find turquoise waters and white sand, backed against a red cliffside dotted with pine trees on the island's eastern coast. There are umbrellas for rent (€8 with two lawn chairs) and a small taverna at the top of the beach. For ultimate relaxation, walk 100 meters (328 feet) down the beach, and then follow the goat path up the mountainside. About 250 meters (820 feet) on the other side you'll find a nearly empty beach used mostly by nudists.

Buses depart from Pigadia for Kyria

Panagia three times a week (45 minutes; €3.30).

MESOCHORI VILLAGE
(Μεσοχώρι)

One of the most beautiful villages in Karpathos is the Mesochori Village, 34 km (21 mi) north of Pigadia. Park your car at the top of the village and walk down the rambling whitewashed streets; there are no sidewalks, per se, as all the roads cut through homes and backyards. There's a beautiful church built on the three natural springs of the Panaghia Vrysiani monastery, which is worth a visit for the well-preserved frescoes inside. Finish off your visit with a Turkish coffee from the local *kafeneio* called Skopi Café, located just above the church where, if you ask nicely, you'll be given a traditional Karpathian *baklava* (it's made with olive oil, not butter).

TOP EXPERIENCE

★ Olympos Village
(Όλυμπος)

From a distance, Olympos looks like a collection of Lego blocks stacked precariously on a crumbling cliff. But this village has survived intact since the 7th century and is in no danger of going anywhere. The village was built by the residents of Vroukounda, who were attracted to this cloistered spot nestled in the mountain range after a barrage of relentless pirate attacks. Since then, Olympos has remained cut off from the rest of the outside world, which allowed it to preserve its past. An asphalt road now connects the village to the rest of Karpathos, but the village remains a living testament to its past.

Olympos is best appreciated by a slow stroll: Sip a coffee at the windmills, wander through the curving streets, or try on some handmade leather sandals at the village's last shoemaker. Residents dress in traditional costumes, a unique dialect of Dorian Greek is spoken, and an ancient musical culture still exists. The village is best experienced during a *panigiri* (the most important one is on August 29). You can also catch musicians riffing at the Parthenon Café, across from the main church.

This traditional village is not a gimmick, though locals definitely take advantage of the tourist season: Prices increase, and you'll find a carnival-like vibe as buses and boats drop off tourists each day. To avoid the crowds, visit in the early mornings or late afternoons after the public transportation has left—or better yet, visit during the bookends of the summer season.

Olympos is isolated, and while there is bus service (€6 each way) from Pigadia to the village a few times per week, the schedule is limited (Mon. 8:45am departure from Pigadia, return at 4pm.; Wed., Fri., and Sat. 9:15am departure from Pigadia, return at 4pm). A cab takes about an hour and costs €75, which is more than the price of a daily car rental. Olympos is located 43 km (27 mi) north of Pigadia (1 hour 15 minutes by car).

Shopping

J. PREARIS

Olympos (main road); tel. 22450/51310; 10am-9pm

Though the village of Olympos was once self-sufficient, a lot of products have been outsourced. It's simply too time-consuming to produce such intricate handicrafts. One exception is J. Prearis, the last shoemaker in the village, who is still crafting handmade leather sandals, boots, and traditional clogs out of his workshop. Sandals start at around €20.

ART FROM KARPATHOS

St. Barbara; daily 10am-8pm

Spend enough time in Olympos and one of the older women wandering around will grab your hand to tie a traditional scarf around your head. The scarves look like the flowered Russian shawls, but they have been bedazzled within an inch of their lives. They take a week to make by hand, so nearly all of the shops sell fake versions made on the mainland—all

1: Olympos village **2:** a tourist woman outfitted with a scarf **3:** Apella Beach, the prettiest slice of sea in Karpathos

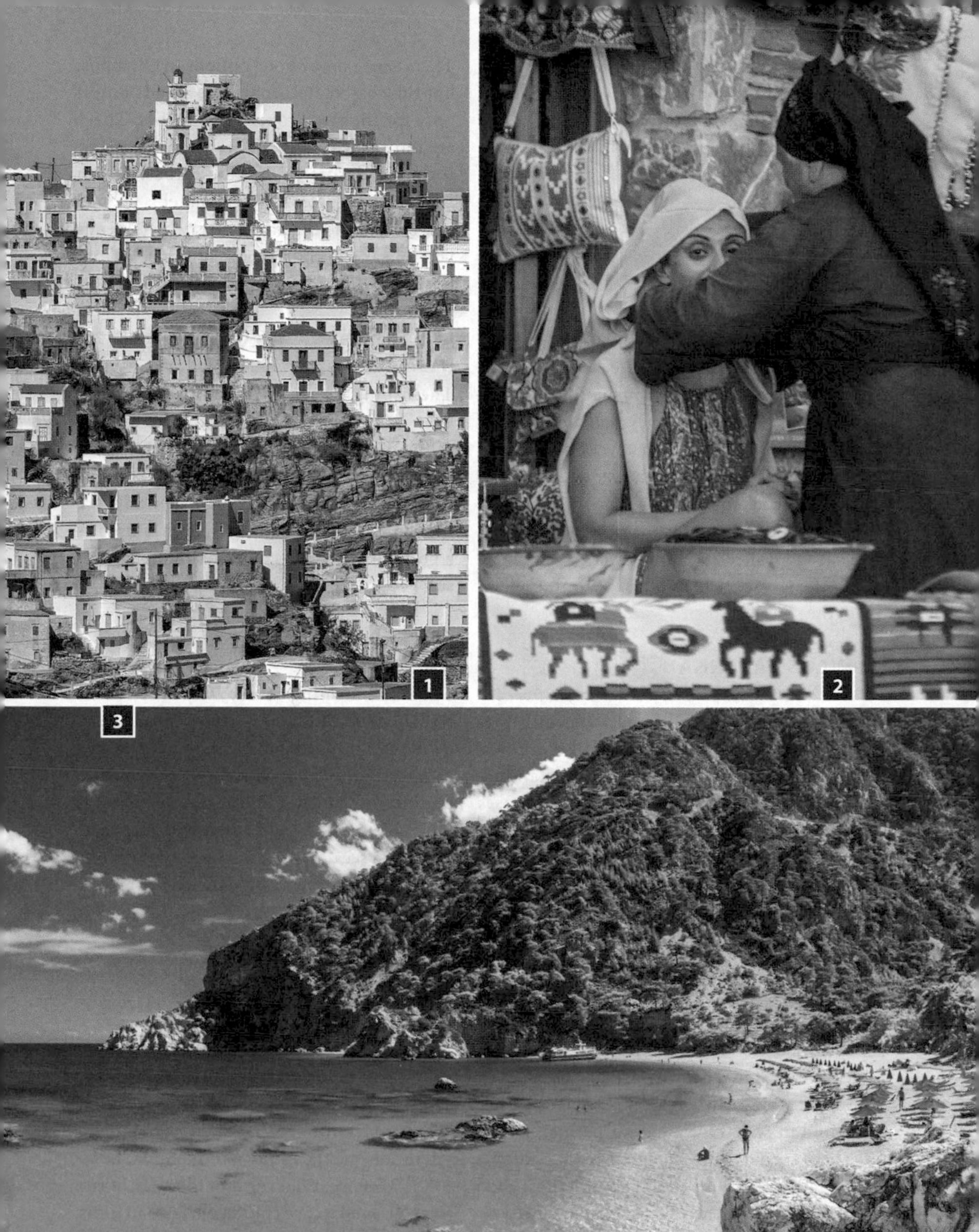

except for the very first shop on St. Barbara, which only sells vintage wares, starting from 30 euros. The shop is owned by artist Kalliopi Pavlidou, who also sells beautiful oil paintings of Karpathian scenery.

Food

BLUE GARDEN

tel. 22450/51101; Apr.-Oct. 10am-midnight; dinner for 2 with drinks around €25

Tired of reading menus? Head to the Blue Garden in Olympos village, a small rooftop restaurant run by husband-and-wife team Nikos and Popi (they both speak great English). You'll drink whatever Nikos pours into your glass and eat whatever Popi has happened to cook that day, based on the local, seasonal produce. In July, that might be stewed goat and stuffed zucchini flowers. Snag a table on the terrace, which offers stunning views of the sunset.

MILOS TAVERNA

tel. 22450/51333; Apr.-Oct. 10am-midnight; from €10

There are 80 windmills and watermills that used to operate in Olympos until the 1950s. These days, head to one of the last standing ones, which is 300 years old and now houses Milos Taverna. With stunning views of the sea (come here at sunset), much of the food is cooked in a wood-burning oven, like bread, *horta* (wild greens) pie, and goat. This is also a fantastic place to have a coffee.

PARTHENON CAFÉ

tel. 22450/51307; all day

This *kafeneion* located at the top of Olympos village, next to the town's main square, is best visited at night, when local musicians gather round to play traditional Karpathian tunes. There are old photos hanging on the wall, the room is thick with the smell of hand-rolled cigarettes, and the raki is supplemented by little plates of meze.

Accommodations

HOTEL APHRODITE

Olympos; tel. 22450/51307; from €45

There aren't many hotel options in Olympos, but the cozy Hotel Aphrodite stands out, if only for the jaw-dropping sea views. There are only four rooms, all of which are nicely, if simply, decorated, but the real attraction is the private balconies. The hotel is located just behind the central square, which means you'll hear the church bells and music from the local *kafeneio.*

DIAFANI (Αυλώνα)

The fishing village of Diafani is the "beach town" of Olympos. It's located 8 km (5 mi) east of the mountain village. It's a cute little resort town with a curve of restaurants hugging the pebble bay. Take your pick; they all serve the same fresh seafood. The beach is used as a port but also has a couple of umbrellas and sun beds for rent.

AVLONA (Αυλώνα)

The small farming community of Avlona is located 48 km (30 mi) north of Pigadia, and 6 km (3.75 mi) south of Olympos. It's located in a fertile valley sandwiched between two mountains, and though it doesn't have as much life now as it did a hundred years ago, you'll still see dozens of stables with threshing floors where farmers would thresh their grain.

Hiking

AVLONA TO VROUKOUNDA

Distance: *11 km (6.75 mi)*
Duration: *2 hours*
Effort level: *moderate*

There are some wonderful hiking trails around Olympos. The most beautiful is a 2-hour, 11-km (6.75-mi) walk through the village of Avlona and to Vroukounda, home to the 3,500 year old ruins of the ancient city Vrykous, and a cave church of Agios Ioannis. The path is mainly cobbled, and bright blue and red indicators mark the way. Bring your own water and food, as there are no facilities (though in the spring months, there's plenty of fresh thyme and mountain tea to pick). The trailhead at Avlona is located 50 km (30 mi) north of Pigadia (1.5-hour drive).

VROUKOUNDA (Βρουκούντα)

Vroukounda is a place for adventurous explorers: 3,500 years ago, the area was an important and populated area on Karpathos; these days, it's a site full of craggy cliffs you can jump off of into clear water, and what's left of the ruins (some long fallen down walls, a couple of staircases). There's also the cave church of **Aglos Ionnnais,** which is visited by locals on the saint's name days, August 28-29, when people walk in traditional costumes from Olympos all the way to Agios Ioannis and camp out overnight. You can join them; just make sure to bring a pillow and sleeping bag.

To get here, you can hike from Avlona (see above) or Diafani. (From Diafani, head north on foot for 30 minutes to reach Avlona, and continue for two hours.) You can also take a boat ride from Diafani port to Vroukounda. Catch a ride on the tourist boat "Nikos" (departs every day at 10am and returns at 6pm from the port); you'll spend the day in Vroukounda exploring little coves that can only be reached by boat. The excursion costs €25, lunch and snack included.

Festivals and Events

★ PANIGIRI OF VROUKOUNDA

Throughout the summer, there are several *panigiria* across the island, but the most famous is the *panigiria* of Vroukounda on August 28-29. It's totally unique in Greece, taking place outside in the cave chapel of Aghios Ioannis, before the party moves to the beach. Women and men dress in traditional costumes and dance to local music for hours. It's all-night revelry, and no one sleeps much during the two-day affair, though you can bring your own sleeping bag and camp out al fresco with everyone else. Note that Karpathians are quite tied to their traditions, and during specific local dances, outsiders aren't allowed to join in. *Panigiria* are free to attend, and you'll eat and drink gratis.

SARIA ISLAND (Σαρία)

At the very northern tip of Karpathos, separated by a thin stretch of sea, there's a small (20 square km//7.75 square mi), volcanic drop of an island called Saria. The island attracts history buffs as well as nature lovers. It's the site of the ancient Nisyros settlement, which served as a home base for Saracen pirates. The ruins and their six chapels (including a temple dedicated to Apollo) are accessible to visitors via a moderate 1-kilometer (.6-mi) one-hour hike. Your boat captain will point you in the right direction.

The island is also famous for its wildlife: it's a breeding ground for Eleonora's falcon, long-legged buzzards, the Mediterranean monk seal, and 2,500 goats, which you'll see all over the island. The beaches are beautiful, but better to wear shoes—those goats don't clean up after themselves. The island is uninhabited, and there are no restrooms or restaurants.

Boats leave from Pigadia's harbor to Saria daily in the morning and return in the late afternoon (from €50 round-trip, including lunch). Show up the evening before to put your name down on the list for the following morning.

Rhodes (Ρόδοσ)

Rhodes (pop. 90,000) is the largest Dodecanese island, and the most historically important: Minoans, Mycenaeans, Greeks, Romans, Byzantine, Ottomans, and Italians have all passed through here at some point, leaving behind a wealth of monuments, architecture, ruins, and relics. History is palpably important here, and much of Rhodes Town has been incredibly well preserved, to the point that you can easily find accommodation in a Medieval-era knight's house.

It's become one of the most touristic islands in Greece: An average 2 million tourists pass through here each year. It's gained a reputation for being a party destination for package tourists from England and Northern Europe, and it's a preferred location for hen nights and

Highlights

Look for ★ to find recommended sights, activities, dining, and lodging.

★ **Medieval City of Rhodes:** Feel all the historic influences—Jewish, Ottoman, Italian, Byzantine—at once by wandering through the Old Town's atmospheric, cobblestone streets (page 228).

★ **Street of the Knights of Rhodes:** This well-preserved Medieval-era street is a passageway through time (page 228).

★ **Palace of the Grand Master:** This is the most beautiful of the buildings erected by the Knights of Rhodes. Your time is best spent gazing at its façade (page 229).

★ **Acropolis of Lindos:** This beautiful ruin is perched on a cliffside with stunning views of the sea (page 237).

★ **Western Rhodes:** For a more off-the-beaten-track experience, drive through the wild, windy western coast where you'll find (relatively) empty beaches and a more local vibe (page 240).

bachelor parties. Still, much of the cheesy nightlife can be avoided, and there's plenty to explore in the western and southern part of the island, where few tourists wander. Windsurfers will have a great time in the southern tip of the island, where strong winds make for excellent sporting.

PLANNING YOUR TIME

With so much sightseeing, you'll want to budget at least **four days** on Rhodes—more if you want to take a break from all the fabulous ruins and museums with lazy days on the beach. I recommend spending at least two days in **Rhodes Town,** where you can sleep in a historic stone house, before basing yourself in **Lindos** for another two days to explore the southern part of the island.

The island's economy is heavily dependent on tourism, and everything runs from **April** to **October.** During the off-season, you may find some standard places open (there is a large population to support, after all!), but some establishments may be closed.

INFORMATION AND SERVICES

You'll find everything you need on Rhodes. **ATMs** are a dime a dozen in the Old Town and New Town, as well as the coastal resorts, and most places take **credit cards.**

There's a general **hospital** (Andreas Papandreou; tel. 2241/360000; always open) but it's underfunded and understaffed, unfortunately. If you have insurance, better to go to the private **Euromedica Clinic** (Koskinou; 2241/045000; www.euromedica-rhodes.gr; always open). Staff are English-speaking, and it's the largest private health clinic on the island.

Tourist offices can be found in the New Town (Plateia Rimini; tel. 2241/035495; www.rhodes.gr; Mon.-Fri. 7:30am-3pm) and the Old Town (Platanos and Ippoton; tel. 2241/035945; www.rhodes.gr; Mon.-Fri. 7am-3pm); both have helpful staff and useful brochures, street maps, and leaflets. The **National Tourism Office EOT** (Greek Tourist Information Office, Makariou and Papagnou; tel. 2241/044335; www.ando.gr/eot; Mon.-Fri. 8am-2:45 pm) also has maps and transport information.

The main **post office** is at Mandraki Harbor (tel. 2241/035560), as is the port **police** (tel. 2241/022220). Tourist police can be reached 24/7 (tel. 2241/027423); for **emergencies** and ambulances call 166.

GETTING THERE

Rhodes is the best-serviced Dodecanese island, but given how far away it is from the mainland, most tourists choose to fly here from Athens.

Air

The **Diagoras Airport** (RHO; tel. 2241/088700; www.rhodes-airport.org) is located on the western coast between Paradisi and Kremasti. There are regular flights via **Aegean Airlines** (tel. 2241/098345; www.aegeanair.com), **Olympic Air** (tel. 2241/024571; www.olympicair.com), and **Sky Express** (tel. 281 022 3800; www.skyexpress.gr) from the mainland (Athens and Thessaloniki), as well as neighboring islands and Crete.

There are **taxis** waiting at the airport (€29.50 into town, 25-percent surcharge after midnight). Rhodes' **Eastern Bus Service** goes regularly to the airport (€2.20 euros; 40 minutes).

Ferry

As Rhodes is the Dodecanese's main port, there's no shortage of ferry options. The two main ferry companies are **Blue Star Ferries** (111 Amerikis; tel. 2241/022461; www.bluestarferries.com; daily 9am-8pm), which takes care of long-haul, slower services to Crete and Piraeus; and **Dodekanisos Seaways** (Afstralias 3; tel. 2241/070590; www.12ne.

Previous: a panoramic view of Lindos Bay; the Street of the Knights of Rhodes; Butterfly Valley in Rhodes.

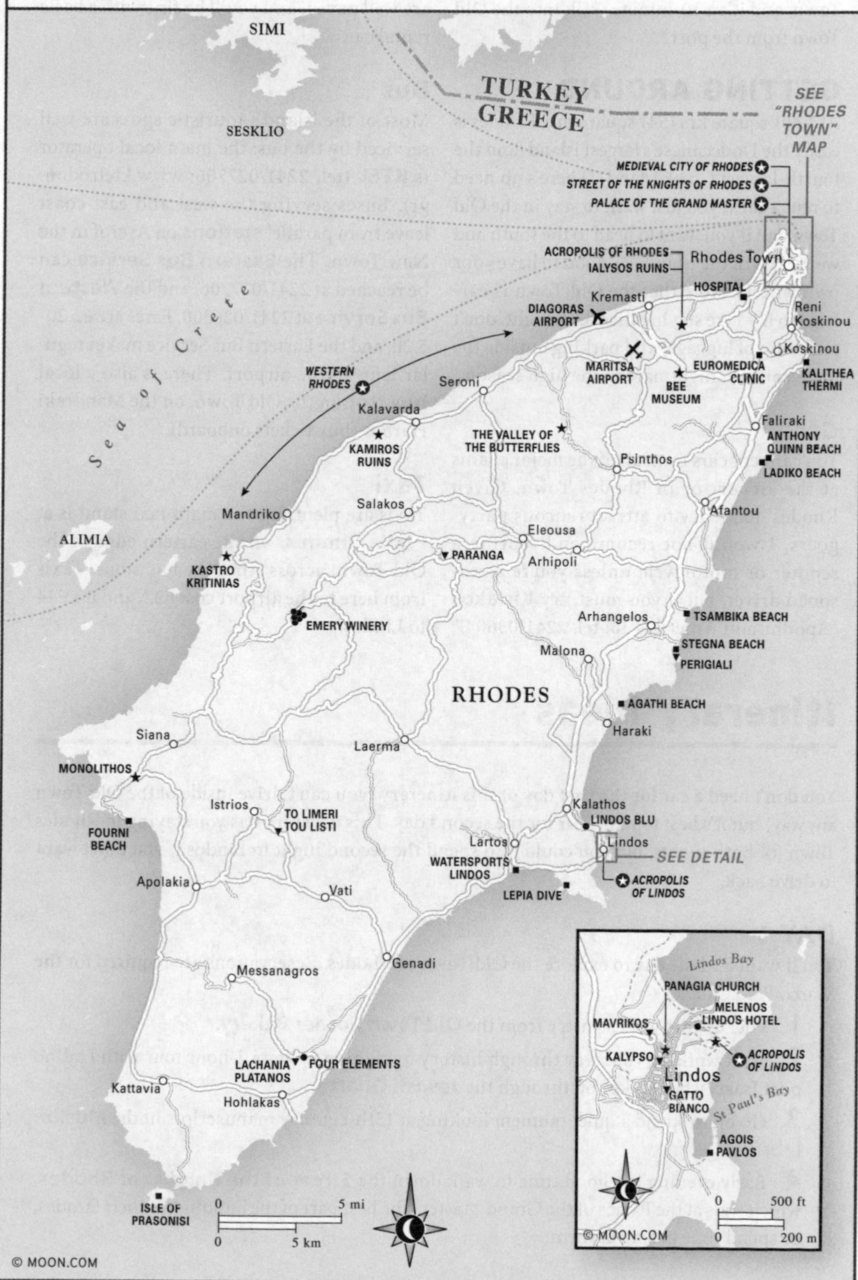
Rhodes
SIMI
TURKEY
GREECE
SESKLIO
SEE "RHODES TOWN" MAP
MEDIEVAL CITY OF RHODES
STREET OF THE KNIGHTS OF RHODES
PALACE OF THE GRAND MASTER
ACROPOLIS OF RHODES
IALYSOS RUINS
Rhodes Town
HOSPITAL
Kremasti
DIAGORAS AIRPORT
Reni Koskinou
Koskinou
MARITSA AIRPORT
EUROMEDICA CLINIC
KALITHEA THERMI
BEE MUSEUM
WESTERN RHODES
Seroni
Kalavarda
Sea of Crete
KAMIROS RUINS
THE VALLEY OF THE BUTTERFLIES
Faliraki
ANTHONY QUINN BEACH
LADIKO BEACH
Psinthos
Salakos
Afantou
Mandriko
ALIMIA
Eleousa
PARANGA
Arhipoli
KASTRO KRITINIAS
EMERY WINERY
Arhangelos
TSAMBIKA BEACH
STEGNA BEACH
PERIGIALI
Malona
RHODES
AGATHI BEACH
Haraki
Siana
Laerma
MONOLITHOS
Istrios
TO LIMERI TOU LISTI
Kalathos
LINDOS BLU
FOURNI BEACH
Lartos
Lindos
SEE DETAIL
WATERSPORTS LINDOS
ACROPOLIS OF LINDOS
Apolakia
Vati
LEPIA DIVE
Genadi
Messanagros
LACHANIA PLATANOS
FOUR ELEMENTS
Kattavia
Hohlakas
ISLE OF PRASONISI
0
5 mi
0
5 km
© MOON.COM
Lindos Bay
PANAGIA CHURCH
MELENOS LINDOS HOTEL
MAVRIKOS
KALYPSO
ACROPOLIS OF LINDOS
Lindos
GATTO BIANCO
St Paul's Bay
AGOIS PAVLOS
0
500 ft
0
200 m
© MOON.COM

gr), which has high-speed catamarans to the northern islands. Ferries dock in Rhodes Town, and it's a 10-minute walk into the Old Town from the port.

GETTING AROUND

At 1,401 square km (541 square mi), Rhodes is easily the Dodecanese's largest island (and the fourth-largest Greek island). There's no need to rent a car if you just want to stay in the Old Town, but if you want to head to the south and west parts of the island, it's good to have your own wheels. Note that the Old Town is car-free (so if you're staying there overnight, don't pack a lot of luggage) and parking outside the town can be a nightmare in the high season.

Car

You can rent cars from all of the major chains at the airport or in Rhodes Town. Given Rhodes' tendency to attract raucous party-goers, I would not recommend renting a scooter or motorcycle unless you're a seasoned driver, but if you must, try **Kiriakos** (Apodhimon Amerikis 16; tel. 2241/036047; www.motorclubkiriakos.gr), who delivers to the Old Town. Most of the roads in Rhodes are well paved, and you'll be fine with a basic rental car.

Bus

Most of the island's touristic spots are well serviced by the bus; the main local operator is **KTEL** (tel. 2241/027706; www.ktelrodou.gr). Buses serving the west and east coast leave from parallel **stations** on Averof in the New Town. The **Eastern Bus Service** can be reached at 2241/027706, and the **Western Bus Service** at 2241/026300. Fares are €2.20-5.20, and the Eastern Bus Service makes regular trips to the airport. There is also a local **bus stop** in the Old Town, on the Mandraki Harbor (buy tickets onboard).

Taxi

Taxis are plentiful; the main taxi stand is at **Platia Riminis,** on the eastern edge of the Old Town, across from the bus stops. Taxis from here to the airport cost €22, and it's €44 to Lindos.

Itinerary Ideas

You don't need a car for the first day of this itinerary (you can't drive inside of the Old Town anyway) but it's best to rent a car for the second day. This itinerary has you staying in Rhodes Town for both nights, but you could also spend the second night in Lindos if you don't want to drive back.

DAY 1

You'll want a whole day to explore the Old Town of Rhodes. Reservations are required for the Marco Polo Cafe.

1. Fuel up first with a pastry from the **Old Town Corner Bakery.**
2. Start working your way through history by signing up for a 2-hour tour with Ladino poet Isaac, who'll take you through the **Jewish Quarter.**
3. Go off to spend a quiet moment looking at 15th-century manuscripts in the **Muslim Library.**
4. Early evening is a good time to walk down the **Street of the Knights of Rhodes,** which ends at the Palace of the Grand Master. The best part of the buildings is their facades, so spend time gazing at them.

Itinerary Ideas

PAPAGOU
Rhodes Town
DIMOKRATIAS
VIRONOS
0 1,000 ft
0 250 m
TURKEY
GREECE
SEE DETAIL
Rhodes Town
Kremasti
Reni Koskinou
Koskinou
Sea of Crete
Seroni
Kalavarda
Faliraki
Psinthos
Mandriko
Salakos
Afantou
ALIMIA
Eleousa
Arhipoli
Arhangelos
Malona
RHODES
Haraki
Siana
Laerma
Istrios
Kalathos
Lartos
Lindos
SEE DETAIL
Lindos Bay
Lindos
St Paul's Bay
0 1,000 ft
0 400 m
Apolakia
Vati
Genadi
Messanagros
Kattavia
Hohlakas
0 5 mi
0 5 km
DAY ONE
1 Old Town Corner Bakery
2 Jewish Quarter
3 Muslim Library
4 Street of the Knights of Rhodes
5 Marco Polo Cafe
6 Raxati Café
DAY TWO
1 The Valley of the Butterflies
2 Gatto Bianco
3 Acropolis of Lindos
4 Isle of Prasonisi
5 Lachania Platanos
© MOON.COM

5 You've earned a three-course meal at the **Marco Polo Cafe,** inside the namesake mansion's courtyard.

6 Finish your day with a cocktail at one of Rhodes' many watering holes, such as **Raxati Café.**

DAY 2

1 Beat the crowds and head out early to the **Valley of the Butterflies,** a 45-minute drive from Rhodes Town. You'll walk around the resin-scented gorges and watch as thousands of butterflies flutter around you.

2 Drive across the island's wild interior, till you reach Lindos (an hour from the Valley). Fill up on pizza and pasta at **Gatto Bianco.**

3 After lunch, work your way up to the city's **Acropolis,** which boasts stunning views of the coast.

4 By now it's late afternoon. Drive an hour south to the **Isle of Prasonisi** (located at the southern tip of the island) for a quick swim and lounge in the sand.

5 Finish the day with dinner at **Lachania Platanos,** a 40-minute drive north of Prasonisi.

Rhodes Town Ρόδος

Rhodes Town is actually made up of two distinctly separate entities: the Old Town (the Medieval City of Rhodes), where some of the island's most impressive sights lie, and the so-called New Town, which is actually at least 500 years old (everything is relative). The Old Town is a walled medieval city within the New Town, which started to grow toward the waterfront in the 1500s. One of the best things to do is wander the Old Town without a map, allowing yourself to get lost and to stumble across the amazing layers of history as you stroll. However, during the summer rush, it can get unbearably crowded, so try to avoid the midday hours.

SIGHTS

★ Medieval City of Rhodes

The whole Old Town—the Medieval City of Rhodes—is a UNESCO World Heritage Site, where you can feel the history wafting in the air as you walk through its cobbled streets. The town came about when the Knights of Saint John, the Catholic military order of monks fighting in Jerusalem, arrived on Rhodes in 1309. The knights came from all over Europe, and were divided along linguistic lines known as "tongues": France, Aragon, Auvergne, Provence, England, Germany, and Italy. They were a Christian holdout in an Ottoman Turkish–dominated island. The knights remained on Rhodes until 1523, when they were granted safe passage out of the island along with 5,000 Orthodox Christians.

The walled city of the Old Town has a population of 6,000, who come in and out of the city through the seven gates that line the walls. The Old Town is roughly divided into three areas: the northern part, which includes the Palace of the Grand Master and the Street of the Knights of Rhodes; the Jewish quarter; and the southern part where non-Jewish commoners lived.

★ STREET OF THE KNIGHTS OF RHODES

Ippoton; always open; free

Take some time to stroll down the most important street in the Old Town, the exceedingly well-preserved Street of the Knights of

Rhodes. You'll notice seven different facades on this 200-meter-long street, meant to represent the seven countries that the Knights hailed from, though the architecture has a general French flair. This street can get intensely crowded during the summer, so try to come very early in the morning, when you'll be easily able to identify the street's most charming details, like Gothic doorways, fountains, and stone sculptures representing the flags of each country. The street stretches all the way to the Palace of the Grand Master, the most impressive of the buildings.

★ PALACE OF THE GRAND MASTER

tel. 2241/365270; Apr.-Oct. Mon.-Sun. 8am-8pm, Nov.-Mar. Tues.-Sun. 8am-3pm; €6

In a city full of prominent buildings, this is perhaps the most noteworthy monument in the Old Town. Founded in the early 14th century over 7th-century Byzantine ruins, this architectural landmark was the administrative seat and residence of the Grand Master of the Order of the Knights Hospitaller. There are two permanent exhibits in the Palace covering ancient Rhodes downstairs and a random assortment of artwork upstairs; however, the residences—with walls and floors decorated with stunning mosaics—are more interesting. The exterior of the building looks like a set from *Game of Thrones*: all turrets and tiny windows and a beautiful courtyard.

ARCHAEOLOGICAL MUSEUM

Plateia Mousiou; tel. 2241/365200; Apr.-Oct. Mon. 9am-3pm, Tues.-Fri. 8am-8pm, Sat.-Sun. 8am-3pm, Nov.-Mar. Tues.-Sat 9am-4pm; €8

Located inside the stunning former Knight's hospital, complete with beautiful walled gardens, this museum holds treasures that date back 7,000 years. Many of the archaeological museums around the islands can be dusty and forgotten, but this one certainly is not: some of its most impressive pieces include the bathing Aphrodite, drunken Dionysus, and the headless statue of Artemis. Budget at least a few hours to walk through the museum, and to spend a bit of time relaxing in the gardens.

JEWISH QUARTER

Rhodes used to have a sizeable Jewish population; the majority were Sephardic Jews, originally from Spain, who spoke Ladino. By the 1930s, there were more than 4,000 Jews living in Rhodes. Tragically, the majority of its residents were murdered during World War II, and today there are only two dozen Jews left.

The Jewish quarter has the distinction of being the least touristic part of the Old Town, which in my book, makes it doubly worth checking out. Two-hour **tours** (€10) of the Jewish Quarter can be arranged through the Synagogue museum's website with Isaac Habib, a Ladino poet from South Africa, or by calling Isaac at tel. 2241/022364.

SYNAGOGUE MUSEUM

Dosiadou; tel. 2241/022364; www.rhodesjewishmuseum.org; May-Oct. Sun.-Fri. 10am-3pm; free

Pay your respects and learn more about the important Jewish history on Rhodes, and the community's contribution to the island, with a visit to the Synagogue Museum. The museum is next to the **Kahal Shalom Synagogue;** built in 1577, this is the country's oldest synagogue and is still used for religious services.

MUSLIM LIBRARY

Sokratous; Mon.-Sat. May-Oct. 9:30am-3pm; free, donations welcome

Rhodes' Ottoman history is on full, literary display at this cute little library that acts as an oasis of calm in the busy old city. It's opposite the Mosque of Suleyman, and was built in 1794. It houses more than 2,000 books in Persian, Arabic, and Turkish. Included are rare illustrated copies of religious texts dating back to the 15th century, and complete Ottoman historical tomes. I love the little maps and engravings that decorate the walls, and it's a peaceful spot to pop into for a half hour.

New Town

MUSEUM OF MODERN GREEK ART

Plateia Haritou; tel. 2241/043870; www.mgamuseum.gr; Tues.-Sat. 8am-8pm; €3

Tired of all the ancient history? Stop by the Modern Greek Art Museum, where the main gallery at the northern end of the New Town has a nice collection of paintings, drawings, engravings, and sculptures by some of 20th-century Greece's best artists. Highlights include sculptures by Theodoros, and paintings by Tsarhouis Giannis and Gaitus Giannis (not related). Unfortunately, the museum is underfunded, and outside of the permanent collection, they don't really host new exhibits.

ACROPOLIS OF RHODES

Monte Smith; always open; free

Athens doesn't have the only Acropolis in Greece. This beautiful ruin is the site of the ancient Hellenistic city of Rhodes, dating from the 2nd century BC. Renovated buildings include the stadium, the theater (that was used as a lecture hall), and the Temple of

---

1: detail of the Rhodes Acropolis **2:** the view of Rhodes Old Town **3:** the medieval building of the Hospital of the Knights of Rhodes

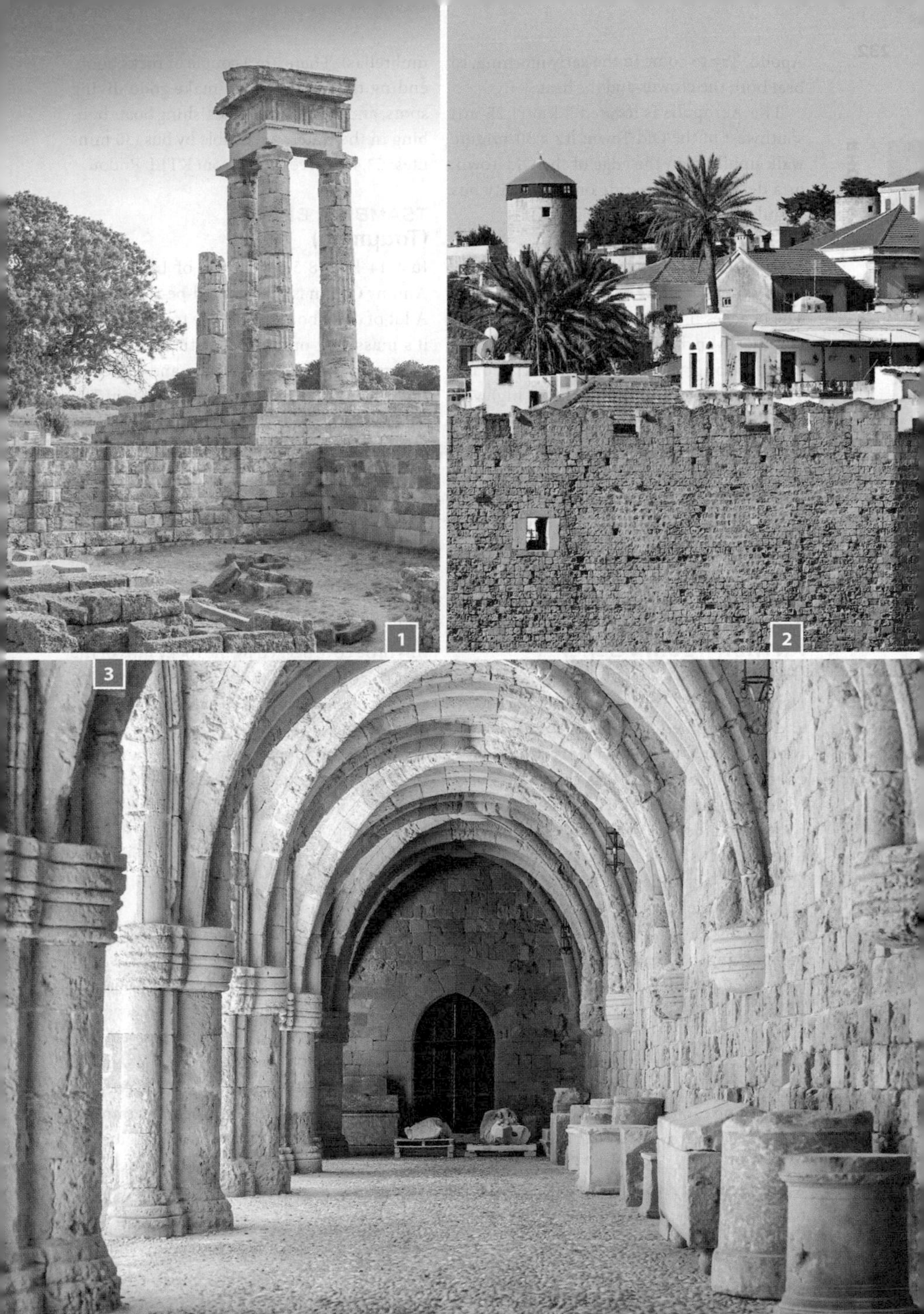
1
2
3

Apollo. Try to come in the early morning, to beat both the crowds and the heat.

The Acropolis is located 2 km (1.25 mi) southwest of the Old Town. It's a 30-minute walk uphill from the edge of the Old Town, or a decidedly easier ride on the #5 city bus (regular buses throughout the day).

BEACHES NEAR RHODES TOWN

The beaches listed below are organized geographically in descending order from Rhodes Town, along the island's eastern coast. They're all connected along the 95 highway, and though you can take the bus to different beaches, I'd recommend a car so you can arrive at some of the more popular ones earlier in the morning. All of these beaches are organized, which means you can rent umbrellas (from €8). If you take the bus, note that the KTEL Rodou services the eastern part of the island.

ANTHONY QUINN BEACH (Άντονυ Κουνν)

Drive 17 km (10.5 mi) south of Rhodes Town and you'll come to Anthony Quinn Beach. Named after the famous actor who supposedly fell in love with this emerald cove a while filming Guns of Navarone, this tiny rocky beach is one of the most popular on the island. It's unbelievably crowded in July and August, and despite its rocky topography, cafés have managed to organize half the beach with umbrellas. Try to get there early in the morning to stake out your spot. Accessible by bus (30 minutes, €2.40; three daily) from KTEL Rodou.

LADIKO BEACH (Λαδικο)

If there's no room on Antony Quinn, try your luck at the nearby cove of Ladiko, located a few hundred meters south. The color of the water here is truly unreal, but there's scant real estate on the sand (and it's all covered in umbrellas). There are a couple of rocks bookending the beach, which make good diving spots, and several adorable fishing boats bobbing in the water. Accessible by bus (30 minutes; €2.40; three daily) from KTEL Rodou.

TSAMBIKA BEACH (Τσαμπικα)

Just 14 km (8.5 mi) south of Ladiko and Antony Quinn is this see-and-be-seen beach. A lot of daily boat tours leave from here, and it's massively organized, with hundreds of umbrellas, beach sport arenas, and canteens. If you want a beach with activity, this is it! The water is quite shallow here, making it good for kids, and the sand is soft and fine. Accessible by bus (40 minutes, €3.90; two daily) from KTEL Rodou.

STEGNA BEACH (Στεγνά)

Travel 7.5 km (4.5 mi) south of Tsambika, and 500 meters from the village of Archaegalos, this little cove backed by the rocky hills of the east coastline is a family-friendly affair. It's not the most beautiful beach on the island, but it is one of the more relaxed ones, as evidenced by the number of locals who head here to swim during the tourist season. Accessible by bus (45 minutes; €4.90; two daily) from KTEL Rodou.

AGATHI BEACH (Αγαθή)

Agathi Beach is 13.5 km (8 mi) from Stegnas and close to the village of Charaki. This long sandy cove is one of the more relaxed beaches on Rhodes (though there are still canteens and it is partly organized). One of the best features is a 700-year-old cave church at the end of the beach (you'll notice the rocks), which you can go inside and explore. Some people camp out around the church. Charaki is accessible by bus (50 minutes; €4.90; two daily) from KTEL Rodou.

1: the expanse of blue waters along surprisingly modern Rhodes Town **2:** the tiny cove of Anthony Quinn's Beach

1

2

RECREATION

For better or worse, Rhodes caters to tourists, and that means that all kind of activities, no matter how un-Greek they are, are available, from escape rooms to Segway tours.

Boat Tours

Along the Mandraki Harbor in Rhodos Town (where the bus stop is), you'll find plenty of boats advertising day trips to beaches around the island, to Turkey, and to Symi island—some of them are glass-bottomed. They all offer the same daylong excursions (from €30, no food or drink included), which take you to the colorful Symi island and leave you there for a few hours to explore at your own pace. It's worth it if you absolutely want to visit Symi and only have a day to spare; otherwise, they can be aggressively touristic.

Spa

KALITHEA THERMI

tel. 2241/037090; www.kallitheasprings.gr; daily 8am-8pm; €3 for access to the springs

This fun art deco spa, built in 1923 by an Italian architect, was renovated after years of neglect. The healing properties of Kallithea Springs are well known, but the real attraction is the aesthetics of the spa itself—it's beautiful enough that weddings are hosted here.

NIGHTLIFE AND ENTERTAINMENT

Rhodes has no shortage of bars, clubs, music venues, casinos, and other forms of nocturnal hedonism to satisfy your inner party animal. While a lot of the popular places fall more into the category of "22 year olds double fisting Jaeger bombs" (no offense if that's your thing), there are some quieter places as well that have a more relaxed vibe. Most bars and other nocturnal activities are concentrated in the backstreets and along the harbor of the New Town.

RAXATI CAFÉ

Sokokleous 1-3; tel. 2241/036351; daily 10am-late

One of the most bohemian options in the Old Town, this lovely bar and coffee house overlooks the Pasha Mosque and serves drinks in a jovial setting. It's a good mix of tourists and locals, and you can easily strike up a conversation.

MACAO BAR

Plateia Aronas; tel. 693 640 0305; www.macaobar.gr/en; Apr.-May Fri. and Sat. 8pm-6am, June-Sept. nightly 9pm-4am

Macao Bar is a very sleek and chic bar/mini club in the Old Town. There are occasional DJs who spin house music, the crowd is polished and well dressed, and the expertly shaken cocktails are pretty affordable (from €9).

ROGMI TOU KRONOU

Plateia Aronas; tel. 2241/025202; Tues.-Sun. 7pm-4am, closed Mon.

This is a very fun, gothic-inspired cocktail bar in the Old Town that has theme nights (locals come decked out) in the summer and plenty of live music. The proprietors are rock 'n' roll fans, so the music is usually more of the rollicking variety. All in all, there's a laid-back environment with friendly patrons. The name translates as "A Crack in Time."

COLORADO CLUB

tel. 2241/075120; Apr.-Oct. 10pm-dawn

This warehouse club is one of the newer ones on the scene in the New Town, but it seems poised to last: There's a rotating list of international DJs, plenty of strobe lights and fog machines, and enough dancing 20-somethings to keep the vibe going till the wee morning. As far as nightclubs go, it's one of the better ones on the island.

SHOPPING

You'll find typical tourist souvenirs in Rhodes Old Town and New Town: sandals, scarves, jewelry, bathing suits, baskets embellished with "RHODOS," etc. The Old Town has more Ottoman-inspired goods of varying quality for sale, like religious icons, Arabian-style lamps, and olive-wood products. The

New Town has high-street fashion brands, including shops like Sephora, United Colors of Benetton, and Zara. During the summer months, shops are open every day at least 10am-9pm; most will stay open even later.

MINISTRY OF CULTURE MUSEUM REPRODUCTION SHOP

Ippitou Street, New Town

Transporting back illegal antiques will land you with a hefty fine, or even jail time. It's much better to drop by this official Museum Reproduction Shop, which sells facsimiles of ancient Rhodian tiles, friezes, sculptures, and more. Prices are quite affordable, and they sell small enough reproductions to snugly fit into your luggage.

KALOGIROU ART

30 Panetiou St., Old Town

For a (much) heftier price tag, you can pick up some (still legal) antiques from Kalogirou Art, which sells a fantastic assortment of kilims, pots, wooden furniture, paintings, and more. The breezy courtyard garden, complete with a banana tree, and the pebbled mosaic floors all lend an incredible atmosphere that will make you want to pull out your wallet.

FOOD

Souvlaki

★ KELLIDES

96 28th Oktovriou, New Town; daily 11:30am-1am; from €3

For food on the go in the New Town, you can't beat Kellides, which makes the best souvlaki in town. Try yours with the freshly baked pita bread and the tzatziki that comes mixed with parsley. This is definitely a no-frills place: The service is fast, the grill is hot, and there aren't a lot of places to sit and eat, but the quality of the sandwich more than makes up for it.

Greek

GRINIARIS

Platía Agíou Ioánni 176; tel. 2241/034005; lunch and dinner; closed Sun. in summer, Mon. in winter; from €5

Located just beyond the walls and within walking distance of the Old Town, Griniaris is a classic *mezedopolio* (restaurant serving meze, small tapas-style dishes ordered with beer or ouzo), and the photos on the wall will give you a visual history of the building (it's always been some sort of meeting hub). The beer is overpriced, so stick to ouzo and any number of the warm appetizers. The seafood dishes are particularly good. Cash only.

Bakeries and Sweets

STANI

Agias Anastasias 28, New Town; tel. 2241/031991; daily 7am-1:30am; from €2

What's a vacation without gorging yourself on ice cream? This bakery in New Town serves excellent frozen treats, as well as pastries and savory pies. All of their sweets are Turkish, including baklava, *kataifi,* plus *masticha* ice cream (made from tree resin). The service isn't the most charming, but you'll leave smiling with a sweet treat in hand anyway.

OLD TOWN CORNER BAKERY

Omirou 88, Old Town; tel. 2241/038494; daily 8am-9pm, from €2

Arrive early at this lovely and atmospheric bakery to buy their pastries, which tend to sell out quickly in the morning. They also have healthy fruit and vegetable juices to counterbalance all the buttery croissants, and excellent drip coffee. If you're headed to the beach later, stop by to pick up some sandwiches and sweets for an afternoon picnic.

Seafood

DINORIS

14 Mousio Square, Old Town; tel. 2241/025824; Apr.-Oct. daily noon-midnight, Nov.-Mar. Sat.-Sun. only; from €8

Dinoris is a lovely fish restaurant in an atmospheric, cave-like setting with vaulted ceilings. Free appetizers are usually included, and the service is friendly without being overbearing. This place has been expertly churning out seafood dishes, like marinated anchovies, and grilled fish options for the past half century.

PERIGIALI

Stegna Beach; tel. 2244/023444; daily lunch and dinner; from €10

Perigiali, a lovely seaside taverna located on Stegna Beach near to Rhodes Town, focuses on freshly caught fish. It's family run, so the service is warm and reliable, and the dishes are copious. Everything is good; I recommend the fish soup (if the weather isn't too hot for you to enjoy it).

Fine Dining

★ MARCO POLO CAFE

40-42 Aghiou Fanouriou, Old Town; tel. 2241/025562; Apr.-Oct. 8pm-11pm; €40 for three courses

If you're not staying at the Marco Polo Mansion, do yourself a favor and book a reservation in the lovely, fragrant courtyard, where a creative, changing menu plays on the agricultural and culinary traditions of Rhodes. This is semi-fine dining, so spring for the three-course menu (dessert is a must!), or order dishes like black pork or hazelnut-crusted shrimp a la carte. Menus can be changed for vegetarians. Reservations are required.

ACCOMMODATIONS

History is everywhere in Rhodes, so you might as well lean into it all the way, and rest your weary head at one of the fabulously atmospheric guesthouses. I highly recommend spending at least one night at an Ottoman-era hotel. After all, It's not every day you can stay in a 600-year-old mansion! Note that if you're staying in the Old Town, your taxi can't drive you up to your hotel's door (most of the city is pedestrian-only), so take that into account when packing your luggage.

Under €150

MARCO POLO MANSION

Agiou Fanouriou 40, Old Town; tel. 2241/025562; www.marcopolomansion.gr; Apr.-Oct.; from €80

Marco Polo Mansion used to be the home of a pasha (a high-ranking Ottoman officer) back in the 15th century, complete with a harem. These days it's decidedly less hedonistic, though the regal and glamorous air still linger. Rooms are at once rustic and refined—the bathrooms are particularly charming—and it's a lovely option for couples. Breakfast, as at other boutique hotels, is served in the courtyard. The Mansion is also home to the **Marco Polo Café** (open to non-guests).

★ KOUKOS TRADITIONAL GUESTHOUSE

Nikiforou Mandilara 22, Old Town; tel. 2241/073022; www.koukostraditionalguesthouse.reserve-online.net; from €120

This is as Greek as it gets! Situated above a lively taverna, this quirky guesthouse is done up in the traditional Rhodian style (think wooden ceilings, raised beds with mini ladders, *komboloi*). This is not the type of hotel for the introvert; the owner is incredibly jovial, and you'll have to walk through the taverna to get to your room. For the right person, though, this hotel is a ton of fun.

★ IN CAMERA ART BOUTIQUE HOTEL

Sofokleous 35, Old Town; tel. 224 107 7277; www.incamera.gr; from €140

Though the Old Town is full of stunning boutique hotels, In Camera might be the one to top them all: The renovations of this majestic guesthouse took more than 16 years, and the results are four exquisite suites. If you can, spring for the Nike of Samothraki suite, which is set across three floors and has fantastic views of the Old Town, or the Nymph of Helio, which has a 16th-century hammam. There's also a delicious buffet breakfast, and friendly staff who will help you organize any number of activities and excursions.

€150-300

SPIRIT OF THE KNIGHTS

Alexandridou 14. Old Town; tel. 2241/039765; www.rhodesluxuryhotel.com; from €160

In this lovely six-suite boutique hotel, the heavy brocade curtains, stained-glass windows, and dark wood will make you feel like a monk in the Middle Ages. Though it's located in the Old Town, it's on a quiet side street. Perks include a library and lovely courtyard where breakfast is served daily.

ALLEGORY BOUTIQUE HOTEL

Antifanous 11 and Ippodamou, Old Town; tel. 2241/037470; www.allegoryhotel.com; from €220

Unlike other boutique hotels in the area, this one will pick up your luggage with an electric golf cart! This restored family home has been stunningly renovated, and every detail shows in the common spaces and the five individual suites: from the original artwork from the Benaki Museum hanging on the walls, to the Korres products, to the private courtyards (some suites come with hammams or hot tubs). It's located within the Old Town's walls, so it can be a bit noisy at night.

EFCHI 1904

Marias Konstantaki 11, Old Town; tel. 694/539 9911; www.efchi1904.gr; from €240

This small guesthouse features five rooms situated around an inner courtyard. It's a very family-friendly place (its run by a family, and you'll be given a key to the front door), and the whole vibe is rather low-key and intimate. Each room is painted in a different color scheme—sometimes aggressively, so unless you are color blind, make sure you know ahead of time which room color you're getting! Breakfast is included. This property is open year-round, and prices are drastically reduced during the off-season.

TRINITY BOUTIQUE HOTEL

Perikleous 31-39, Old Town; tel. 2241/030303; www.trinityboutiquehotel.gr/home/gr; from €250

Another beautiful guesthouse that was originally a Knights of St. John's residence, Trinity Boutique Hotel is located within the walls of the Old Town. Six lovingly restored rooms are nestled around a quiet courtyard where you'll eat a delicious breakfast under the bougainvillea. The decor is Ottoman-chic, rooms have their own private balconies, and mattresses come from Coco-Mat.

KOKKINO PORTO ROSA

Archiepiskopou Efthimiou 24, Old Town; tel. 2241/075114; www.kokkiniporta.com; from €300

This is another charming boutique hotel located on a quiet side street in the Old Town. A lot of thought has gone into the decor, which features antiques and a baby grand piano in the entrance. There's a delicious restaurant on-site where you'll eat your morning eggs and *halloumi* (cheese) in the courtyard, and you'll get a free pass to the neighborhood's gym and sauna.

Lindos Λίνδος

Lindos, 47 km (29 mi) south of Rhodes Town, is considered one of the most beautiful towns on Rhodes, and it's not difficult to see why: The first thing you see is the stunning Acropolis, perched on the cliff and dominating the white, Cycladic-style homes that cluster around the base of the hill. Originally established 4,000 years ago, Lindos has changed hands many times: the Dorians, Byzantines, Franks, and Turks have all passed through here, leaving their mark on the village's architecture. There are multiple buses departing from Rhodes to Lindos, and the ride takes about an hour.

SIGHTS

★ Acropolis of Lindos

tel. 2241/365200; Apr.-Oct. Mon.-Sun. 8am-8pm, Nov.-Mar. Tues.-Sun. 8am-3pm; €12 adult, €6 child

This stunningly well-preserved Acropolis rivals the one in Rhodes Town. The walls were built by the Knights of St. John, forming a protective barrier around the Temple to Athena Lindia and the Hellenistic-era stoa (market).

The view up here is dramatic out onto the sea and the city—take your time to enjoy it. Note that there's a 116-meter climb to the top of the Acropolis, and there are no barriers up here to prevent you from falling off the cliff's many edges.

Panagia Church

always open; free

As you're walking up the road to the Acropolis, you'll notice the heavenward-pointing Church of Panagia, originally built in the 1300s. Since then, it has undergone numerous renovations, the most recent of which was done by the Italians in 1923. The Knights of St. John also had a hand in some of the remodeling. The most impressive features are inside the church, including the detailed mosaic on the floor and the frescoes from the 19th century.

BEACHES NEAR LINDOS

AGOIS PAVLOS (Άγιος Παυλοσ)

The closest beach to Lindos (it's a 12-minute walk south from the city center), this beautiful stretch of sand is mostly famous for its stunning view of the Acropolis of Lindos. The beach is totally organized, with every available inch of space taken up by umbrellas. It's not very comfortable if you have kids (there's not a lot of room for them to play), but it's perfect for couples looking to lounge with a nice vista. There are canteens and tavernas nearby.

ISLE OF PRASONISI (Πρασονήσι)

At the very southern tip of Rhodes, 52 km (32 mi) south of Lindos, you'll find Prasonisi, one of the most impressive beaches on the island, where two sandy coves come together to form a small sort of islet that you can reach by walking or swimming. This beach is very popular with windsurfers, particularly at the end of the summer, and you'll have jumping athletes in your viewpoint the whole time. There are a couple of rooms for rent here, with some tavernas. Two buses run daily from Rhodes (Ktel Rodou) to Prasonisi (3.5 hours; €10.90)

RECREATION

Diving

Rhodes has some great diving and snorkeling spots. As the largest of the Dodecanese islands, it has a long coastline teeming with wild sealife, including octopus, starfish, and lobsters. Soft coral, rock caves (especially the **Cleotobus Tomb** in Lindos), and shipwrecks

staircase of the Propylaea and Church of St. John on the Acropolis of Lindos

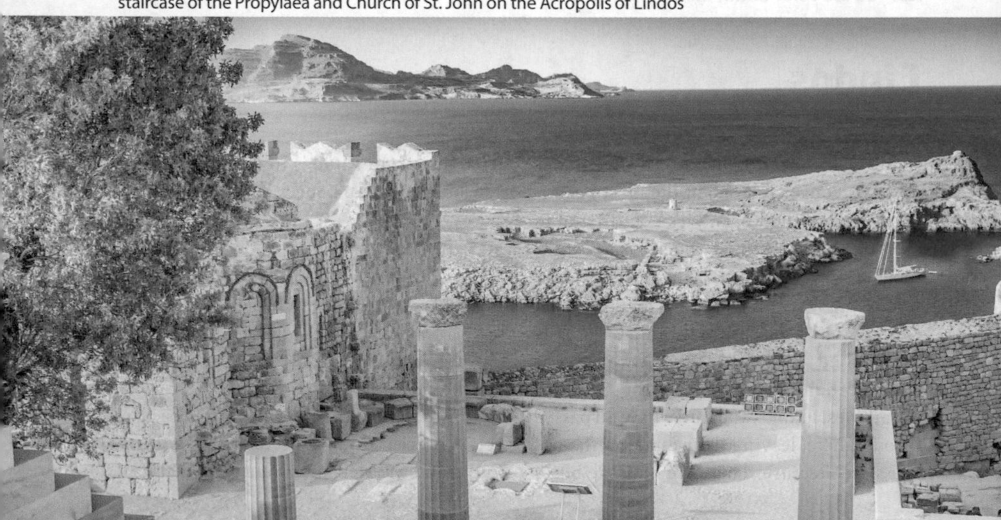

round out the underwater sights. The most interesting places to dive are around Lindos and Kallithea.

LEPIA DIVE

Pefki; tel. 693 714 7970; www.lepiadive.com; recreational courses from €280, beginner courses from €60

What sets this diving company apart is its thoughtful inclusiveness: There are packages and dive certifications here for people with disabilities, and the whole center is adapted for wheelchairs. It's difficult to overstate how impressive this is in Greece, a country that is notoriously difficult for disabled people to navigate. There are also PADI courses for children and advanced courses; dives will take you to caves or underwater wrecks, or through reefs. They're located 5 km (3 mi) outside of Lindos, in the southern village of Pefki.

Windsurfing

Battered by winds, the southwest coast of Rhodes has some of the best windsurfing in the Dodecanese. Surfers come from all over the world to fly across the waves; there are dozens of waters ports shops specializing in windsurfing gear and classes across the southern coast.

WATER SPORTS LINDOS

tel. 694/572 2263; www.watersports-lindos.com; from €10

For everything from windsurfing to banana boats to snorkeling, this outfitter has it all, for different age levels and at different price points. Families can try their special "fun program" where the whole group can ride together in something ominously called The Twister (an inflatable half sphere tugged along by a motorboat). Located 8 km (5 mi) west outside of Lindos in the seaside village of Lardos.

FOOD

Greek

MAVRIKOS

tel. 2244/031232; Apr.-Oct. daily noon-late; from €12

Mavrikos, located in Lindos, is something of the granddaddy of Rhodes restaurants: It was founded by an actual grandpa back in 1933, and it's always been considered the island's more cutting-edge restaurant, offering modern twists on Greek classics. Think *horta* (greens) with carob syrup, or lamb liver marinated in wine. To be honest, this restaurant's glory days are a bit in the past, but it remains an atmospheric restaurant with an extensive Greek wine list. Service can be a bit touch and go; reservations are recommended. Expect to pay at least €40 for three courses with wine.

KALYPSO

tel. 2241/032135; www.kalypsolindos.gr; 11am-midnight daily; from €13

Located inside a former captain's private home in Lindos (the decor still matches—think lots of heavy wood furniture and ironed white tablecloths), Kalypso is a delicious restaurant specializing in fresh seafood and Dodecanese recipes like *makarounes* (handmade pasta). They have two terraces; call ahead for reservations during summer months.

LACHANIA PLATANOS

Lachania; tel. 694/419 9991; daily 10am-11:45pm; from €8

This family-run taverna features all the Greek classics, under a green *platanos* tree. You'll have to beat out the locals for tables (best to make a reservation) and for some of the taverna's more beloved dishes, like pastitsio and zucchini fritters. Finish your meal with a slice of baklava and a syrup-y coffee. It's located 33 km (20 mi) southwest of Lindos, in the village of Lachania.

Italian

GATTO BIANCO

tel. 693 456 2253; daily 10am-midnight; from €12

Getting tired of Greek food? For a brief time, Italians controlled Rhodes, and you can have a culinary taste at Gatto Bianco, located in Lindos. Here you can sample exquisitely prepared Italian food. The pizzas are delicious, as are the pastas and seared steaks. The service is friendly, but it's a bit on the expensive side. Reservations are suggested.

ACCOMMODATIONS

There are far fewer hotels and guesthouses in Lindos than in the northern part of the island, so be sure to book ahead. Note also that a lot of hotels advertised online might not be in Lindos proper, but along the coast, which requires some sort of vehicle to get around. The benefit of staying here is that you're closer to the southern and western parts of the island, which are a long drive from Rhodes Town.

In Lindos

LINDOS BLU

Vlycha Beach, Lindos; tel. 2244/032110; https://lindosblu.gr; from €260

This is an elegant, modern-style luxury hotel and resort, complete with an infinity pool (is there anything better than gazing out at the infinite vastness, cocktail in hand?), sensational service, and a pillow menu. This is an adults-only hotel, and it definitely has a sexy, resort-like feel to it—perfect for couples looking for a romantic getaway. You'll want to book one of the 74 rooms months in advance, as a repeat clientele keep this place busy all season long.

MELENOS LINDOS HOTEL

tel. 2244/032222; www.melenoslindos.com; from €370

One of the most luxurious accommodations in Lindos, Melenos offers Ottoman-style elegance in a breezy palace. Billed as an "arts and culture" hotel, this property has both of those: There are craft details all over the hotel, from the pebbled mosaic floor to the Lindian-style wooden ceilings. Make sure to eat at least once in the rooftop restaurant, which has stunning views of the bay. Book one of the 12 luxury suites ahead; this place has gotten a lot of press in recent years.

Outside Lindos

FOUR ELEMENTS

Lachania; tel. 693 945 0014; www.bnbthefourelements.com; from €110

As the name suggests, there are only four apartments, so-called after the four elements of earth, air, fire, and water. The fully equipped apartments, which come with kitchens and are wheelchair-accessible, are perfect for families looking for an affordable vacation in the quiet countryside. You can make use of the communal pool, barbeque, and garden. There's a two-night minimum. Located 33 km (20 mi) southwest of Lindos, in the village of Lachania.

★ Western Rhodes and the Interior

The interior of Rhodes and its western coast are among the less touristy parts of the island. There's an excellent network of paved roads crisscrossing the interior; if you've rented a car or scooter, I strongly encourage you to head off and explore this pine-scented corner of the island, with little plan or sense of direction. There are plenty of restaurants in Monolithes and in the interior villages—you'll find lots of traditional local tavernas; I've highlighted my favorite but feel free to explore others that look (and smell!) good to you. While there are some buses that reach towns on this side of the island, the service is not frequent.

Beachgoers, especially those traveling with small children, should note that the beaches of western Rhodes are more exposed, making them very windy and the current much stronger.

The following sights are listed in geographical order from Rhodes Town, heading south. Several are ruins, and if you're going to visit just one in the area, I'd make it Kamiros.

IALYSOS RUINS

tel. 2241/040037; May-Oct. 8:30am-8pm, Nov.-Apr. 8:30am-3pm

Just 7 km (4 mi) from Rhodes Town lies Ialysos. Along with Kamiros (and Lindos), Ialysos was one of the major cities of Rhodes: it's biggest claim to fame was birthing Diagoras, the Olympic champion. The town was repeatedly conquered and rebuilt, and what's left is a veritable historical layer cake, with Doric, Byzantine, and medieval layers of architecture—it's not particularly well preserved, so it will likely be of interest to only the most die-hard history buffs, but you can see the restored **Chapel of Agios Gerogios** from the 14th century, and a second chapel from two centuries earlier, which houses a few preserved frescoes.

BEE MUSEUM

5th km Tsairi- Airport Road, Pastida; tel. 2241/048200; www.beemuseum.gr; Mon.-Sat. 8:30am-5pm; €3

Technically a museum, this is an excellent place to learn about bees and then buy the many amazing products that bees make: honey, propolis, pollen, etc., all the more important as bees are dying at alarming rates across the world. You'll learn about the history of beekeeping and honey in Rhodes (and in Greece in general—honey was the nectar of the Olympian gods!), and you can go for a stroll in the garden, which is full of Rhodian herbs and buzzing bees. You can also purchase some traditional Rhodian products made from bees, like *melekouni*, a honey-sesame sweet that's typically given away during weddings and christenings. The museum is 14 km (8.5 mi) south of the Old Town in Rhodes Town; the fastest way is to drive.

THE VALLEY OF THE BUTTERFLIES (πεταλούδα)

tel. 2241/08 2822; daily 9am-5pm; €5

Petalouda means "butterfly" in Greek, and 7 km (4 mi) inland from the coast you'll find this gorgeous forest, full of streams and little pools and trodden paths, where in July and August the tiger moths mature. If you go outside of these months, you'll be alone—without other tourists, and without the butterflies, too. If you go during their season, please remember that butterflies are beautiful, delicate creatures, so don't be like the hordes of other tourists who stomp their feet and clap loudly in the hopes that it will scare the butterflies into flying out of their hiding spots. If you're

Valley of the Butterflies

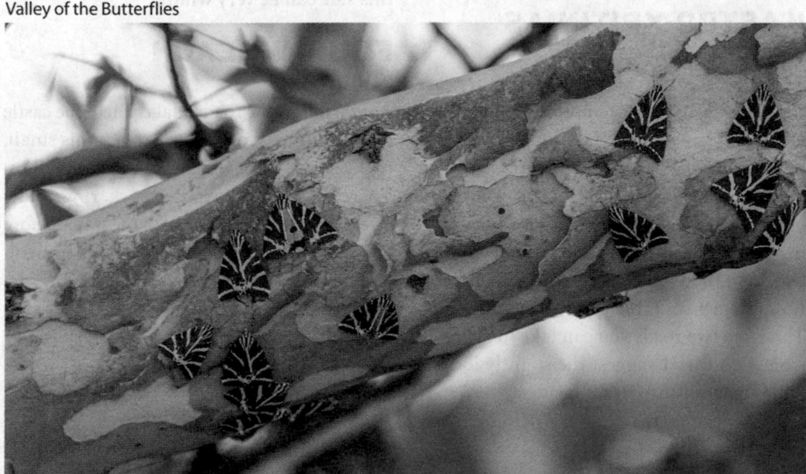

visiting in the summer season, come early in the morning, when the butterflies are everywhere, and you can stroll around the network of short paths at your leisure.

The Valley of the Butterflies is located 30 km (18.5 mi) south of Rhodes Town. There are twice daily buses from the West Side Terminal in Rhodes to the Valley of the Butterflies (€5.40).

KAMIROS RUINS

tel. 2241/040037; May-Oct. 8am-7:40pm, Nov.-Apr. 8:30am-3pm; €6

Located 42 km (26 mi) south of Rhodes Town, on the western coast (and 19 km/12 mi south of the Valley of the Butterflies) are the ruins of the Kamiros. There were three great cities in ancient Rhodes, and Kamiros was one of them. As an agricultural epicenter, the Doric city of Kamiros flourished, peaking in the 7th century. It was overtaken by Rhodes, and then several earthquakes decimated the city. In 1859, the ruins of Kamiros were uncovered, surprisingly well-preserved. You can stroll around the ruins, including the partially intact Doric temple, a stoa, and another temple dedicated to Athena. This is worth a visit if you're in the area, though most of the ancient city's artifacts are in the Louvre and British Museum.

KASTRO KRITINIAS

Attavyros; always open; free

This time, the ruins are of a 16th-century castle, though what's most impressive is the vista around the castle, and the stunning views of the sea and the castle's fortifications as you drive toward it (south of Skala Kamirou, right off the main road, signposted). It's worth driving past, but not going too far out of your way for—though it's worthwhile if you're in Kamiros, which is only 28 km (18 mi) away. There are two roads you can take to get here; from Kamiros, I suggest the slightly longer, but more beautiful coastal road.

EMERY WINERY

Embonas; tel. 2246/041208; Apr.-Oct. 9:30am-4:30pm; free visits and tasting

Embonas, this tiny mountain village perched on Mt. Attavyros, is the island's de facto wine region. Come to Emery Winery to sample some delicious Rhodian wines, and to get a comprehensive overview and tour of Rhodian wine production. I love that this winery opens up at 9:30am, offering free samples to anyone hardy enough to drink that early. You can double down here on visiting the winery and Kastro Kitinias.

MONOLITHOS

About 20 km (12 mi) from the Kritinia Castle lies one of the most beautiful villages in Rhodes, nestled between olive groves and rolling green hills. Its crown jewel is the 15th-century castle perched on a 240-meter high rock. It's definitely worth the hike to the top, to pay your respects in the little **castle church** dedicated to Saint Paneleimon, and to take in the stupendous views. There are two weekly buses from the West Side bus station in Rhodes to Monolithos (€5.20).

Beaches

The current is much stronger on the exposed western flank of Rhodes, and the beaches on this side can be very windy.

FOURNI BEACH (Φουρνι)

As you follow the road to take you to the castle of Monolithos, you'll come across this small, rocky beach, 7 km (4 mi) south of Monolithos. There's a beautiful exposed rock, ringed like layers of a cake, coming out of the water before ending in a gentle slope (a good place to swim to, and then sunbathe). The beach is unorganized, but there is a small canteen that sells refreshments.

Food

★ PARANGA

Appollonas; tel. 2246/091247; www.paraga-apollona.gr; Sat.-Sun. 1pm-8pm; from €9

A Greek "cookhouse" in Apollonas, Paranga serves up classic Greek fare under vaulted ceilings. Much of the food, like goat with beans or stifado with beef, is cooked in traditional wood-burning ovens, and though the decor errs a bit on the side of kitsch, the food is excellent and the service is warm. The menu changes, so take your waiter's recommendation! Reservations are encouraged.

TO LIMERI TOU LISTI

Epar.Od. Apolakias-Profilias; tel. 2244/061578; daily 8am-midnight; from €7

Tucked inside a family-run stone guesthouse, this restaurant (open to non-guests) serves up delicious homemade Greek food that's cooked over open flames. The menu offers more traditional "mountain food," so expect hearty portions. The eggplant salad and pork leg are particularly delicious, and the service is top notch. It's located 25 minutes east of Monolithos but is well worth the drive.

Kalymnos (Κάλυμνοσ)

Kalymnos (pop. 30,000) is something like the wild child of the Dodecanese: dramatic mountainscapes, deep stony crags plunging into blue seas, green valleys bursting with flowers, and displays of farm life. All that natural drama has attracted a bevy of attention seekers from all over the world; Kalymnos is renowned for having some of the most enticing morphology around, and in the early autumn, the island is literally crawling with climbers ready to scale the island's giant vertical rocks and slippery slopes.

Despite the grandeur of its skyline, most of the island's history was made underwater. This is the center of Greece's sponge-diving industry. Unfortunately, plant diseases have largely wiped out the growth of sponges in the eastern Mediterranean, and most of what remains

Highlights

Look for ★ to find recommended sights, activities, dining, and lodging.

★ **Maritime and Folklore Museum:** Learn how fishing and diving shaped the island of Kalymnos (page 250).

★ **Kalymnos Scuba Diving Club:** The folks at this center will get you outfitted for snorkeling, diving, and boat rides across the island, with a bit of history tagged on for free (page 251).

★ **Kalymnos Sponge Factory:** The last sponge factory on the island is a great place to learn about the production of "Kalymnian gold" and to purchase a few sponges (page 252).

★ **Platis Gialos:** This black-sand beach is a fantastic place to catch the sunset (page 254).

★ **Rock Climbing:** Kalymnos has some of the best rock climbing on the Mediterranean, with a variety of grades to scale. Most climbers hang out on the western coast, near the towns of Masouri and Myrties (page 255).

★ **Kalymnos Trail:** This impressive 100-km (62-mi) trek circumvents the entire island. You can also walk half-day portions of the trail (page 255).

★ **Telendhos Island:** Take a 10-minute boat ride across the western coast of Kalymnos to this dewdrop of an island, where there are no cars, only 50 inhabitants, and a whole lot of charm (page 256).

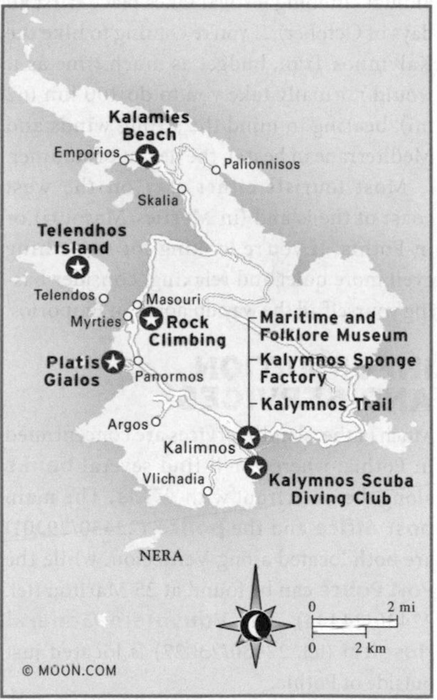

★ **Kalamies Beach:** This secluded little spot near the sleepy village of Emporios is one of the most peaceful beaches on the island (page 258).

in Kalymnos is memories of bygone days, artifacts in museums, and stories shared in coffee shops. That being said, you can still buy sponges along Pothia's quay (the price increases with the quality of the sponge; the cheaper they are, the more likely you are to use them for dishes instead of in the shower), but know that most of these otherworldly looking objects are imported from Asia.

PLANNING YOUR TIME

Kalymnos' season is generally from April to October, though you might find some shops closed during the bookends of the season. Budget at least three days to spend on the island; if you're here for the rock-climbing, you'll probably want to spend a week. Note that the climbing season goes from March to mid-November, with the busiest season being from September to October, when the annual climbing festival takes place (first 10 days of October). If you're coming to hike the Kalymnos Trail, budget as much time as it would normally take you to do 100 km (62 mi), bearing in mind the strong winds and Mediterranean heat in the height of summer.

Most tourists either stay on the west coast of the island (in Myrties/Masouri) or in Pothia. If you're looking for something even more quiet and relaxing, consider basing yourself all the way up north in Emporios.

INFORMATION AND SERVICES

Much of the island's services are concentrated in Pothia, where you'll find several **banks** along the waterfront with **ATMs.** The main **post office** and the **police** (22430/29301) are both located along Venizelou, while the **Port Police** can be found at 25 Maritou (tel. 22430/24444). The **Vouvaleio General Hospital** (tel. 22430/23027) is located just outside of Pothia.

Pothia has a remarkably good **Municipal Tourist Information** office (tel. 22430/29299; www.kalymnos-isl.gr; Mon-Fri 8am-3pm; entrance where ferries dock), where you can find all the up-to-date information on buses and ferries, information on rock climbing and festivals, and other basic info and tips. The island's main travel agency is **Magos Travel** (near where ferries dock; tel. 22430/28777; www.magostours.gr), which has a convenient 24-hour travel ticket machine outside.

GETTING THERE

If you are short on time, I recommend flying to Kalymnos, as the ferry ride is quite long from the mainland. If you're coming from Rhodes, hop on the boat.

Air

Kalymnos has a small airport, **Kalymnos Island National Airport** (JKL), 6 km (3.75 mi) northwest of Pothia that's serviced by daily **Olympic Air** flights (www.olympic-air.com) to and from Athens (from €140; 1 hour). There are plenty of taxis and buses waiting to meet flights during the summer months. A taxi from the airport to Pothia costs €10.

Ferry

Most boats arrive at the main ferry port of **Pothia. Dodekanisos Seaways** (tel. 22410/70590; www.12e.gr) connects the island with Rhodes and other neighbors. **Blue Star Ferries** (tel. 22410/22461; www.bluestarferries.com) connects Kalymnos with Piraeus and Rhodes three times a week. From **Rhodes,** boats can take 3-6 hours and cost €40-20; from **Piraeus** boats take up to 11 hours and cost €52.

GETTING AROUND

At 111 square km (43 square mi), Kalymnos is one of the more manageable Dodecanese islands. Taxis are pretty affordable, and if you don't want to rent a car for your whole

Previous: Kalymnos port at sunrise; Kalymnos has a particularly rich history of sponge diving; the reflection of the port.

Kalymnos

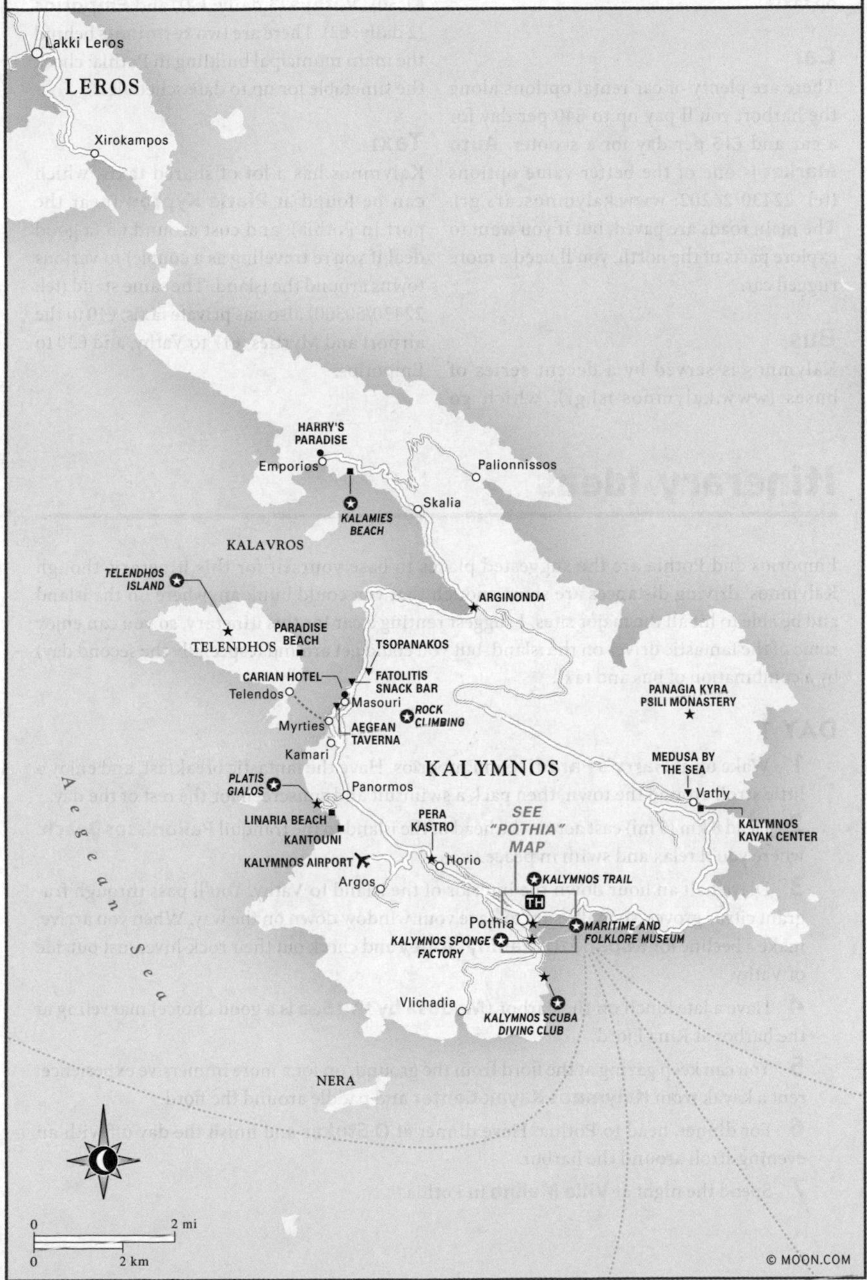

Lakki Leros
LEROS
Xirokampos
HARRY'S PARADISE
Emporios
Palionnissos
Skalia
KALAMIES BEACH
KALAVROS
TELENDHOS ISLAND
ARGINONDA
PARADISE BEACH
TELENDHOS
TSOPANAKOS
CARIAN HOTEL
FATOLITIS SNACK BAR
Telendos
Masouri
ROCK CLIMBING
Myrties
AEGEAN TAVERNA
PANAGIA KYRA PSILI MONASTERY
Kamari
KALYMNOS
MEDUSA BY THE SEA
PLATIS GIALOS
Panormos
Vathy
LINARIA BEACH
PERA KASTRO
SEE "POTHIA" MAP
KALYMNOS KAYAK CENTER
KANTOUNI
KALYMNOS AIRPORT
Horio
Argos
KALYMNOS TRAIL
TH
Pothia
MARITIME AND FOLKLORE MUSEUM
KALYMNOS SPONGE FACTORY
Aegean Sea
Vlichadia
KALYMNOS SCUBA DIVING CLUB
NERA
0
2 mi
0
2 km
© MOON.COM

trip (especially if you are hiking or just planning on chilling in one spot), you can get by on taxis.

Car

There are plenty of car rental options along the harbor; you'll pay up to €40 per day for a car and €15 per day for a scooter. **Auto Market** is one of the better-value options (tel. 22430/24202; www.kalymnoscars.gr). The main roads are paved, but if you want to explore parts of the north, you'll need a more rugged car.

Bus

Kalymnos is served by a decent series of buses (www.kalymnos-isl.gr), which go from **Pothia** port to **Myrties, Masouri,** and **Armeos** (just north of Masouri; 7 daily; €1.50), **Vathys** (3 daily; €2), and **Emporios** (2 daily; €2). There are two **terminals** behind the main municipal building in Pothia: check the timetable for up to date schedules.

Taxi

Kalymnos has a lot of shared taxis, which can be found at **Platia Kyprou** (near the port in Pothia), and cost around €5 (a good deal if you're traveling as a couple) to various towns around the island. The same stand (tel. 22430/50300) also has private taxis: €10 to the airport and Myrties, €17 to Vathy, and €30 to Emporios.

Itinerary Ideas

Emporios and Pothia are the suggested places to base yourself for this itinerary, though Kalymnos' driving distances are short enough that you could bunk anywhere on the island and be able to hit all the major sites. I suggest renting a car for this itinerary, so you can enjoy some of the fantastic drives on the island, but you could get around (especially the second day) by a combination of bus and taxi.

DAY 1

1 Wake up at **Harry's Paradise** in Emporios. Have the fantastic breakfast, and enjoy a little stroll around the town, then pack a swimsuit and sunscreen for the rest of the day.

2 Head 8 km (5 mi) east across the head of the island to the tranquil **Palionissos Beach,** where you'll relax and swim in peace.

3 Drive half an hour down the interior of the island to Vathy. You'll pass through fragrant citrus groves, so make sure to have your window down on the way. When you arrive, make a beeline for **Kopanezos Family Honey** and check out their rock-hives just outside of Vathy.

4 Have a late lunch on the harbor (**Medusa by the Sea** is a good choice) marveling at the harbor at Rina Fjord.

5 You can keep gazing at the fjord from the ground, or, for a more immersive experience, rent a kayak from **Kalymnos Kayak Center** and paddle around the fjord.

6 For dinner, head to Pothia. Have dinner at **O Stukas** and finish the day off with an evening stroll around the harbor.

7 Spend the night at **Villa Melina** in Pothia.

Itinerary Ideas

DAY 2

You'll want to bring a swimsuit and a good pair of walking shoes today.

1 Start your day on a sweet note by picking up a *galaktoboureko* (custard pie) from **Michalaras** café in Pothia.

2 Fortified, spend an hour learning about Kalymnos' sponge diving history at the **Maritime and Folklore Museum.**

3 Head west toward Panormos, making a stop in Horio at **Pera Kastro,** where you can poke around an abandoned village with churches and frescoes.

4 Continue along the western road to Myrties. From there, take the boat to **Telendhos Island** (a 10-minute ride) and spend the late afternoon walking around the island and sunbathing at Paradise Beach. Have dinner at Zorba's in Telendhos, before catching a boat back to the mainland.

5 Have a nightcap at **Linaria** (there are three bars in the village; all of them are a lot of fun) before returning to your hotel for the night.

Pothia Πόθια

Pothia is the capital of Kalymnos and will also be your likely first stop upon arrival, if you're coming by boat. It's the biggest settlement on the island and has a vague metropolitan vibe, with all the things that go along with it: traffic, gruff people, etc. While there are some worthwhile museums and restaurants to try here, it's perhaps not the best option for the nature-seeking traveler. The town is small enough that you'll get your bearings eventually. The harbor is the main reference point for directions.

SIGHTS

Archaeological Museum

A lot of Kalymnos' most beautiful features are underwater: like the 2-meter (6.5-foot) tall gold bronze statue of a robed woman, carved sometime in the 2nd century BC. Found in 1994, the robed woman now lives in the Archaeological Museum and is known as "Our Lady of Kalymnos." Other discoveries, including those found above water, like gold, pottery and jewelry, are also on display. Allow one hour to explore the museum. The museum is located at the right end of the harbor, a few streets back. It's located on the back streets on the north side of Pothia.

★ Maritime & Folklore Museum

Central Waterfront; tel. 22430/51361; mid-June-mid-Sept. daily 9am-5pm; €3

Kalymnos' social and economic fabric was formed by the seas surrounding the island. It's difficult to overstate just how much fishing and diving have contributed to the island. The best place to learn about this—through the impressive collection of photographs, diving costumes and apparati, salvaged shipwreck goods, and more—is at the Maritime Museum. You'll learn how people dived and how sponges are collected. Diving is incredibly difficult work; it's severely debilitating to the human body, and divers are paid little. It's sobering to realize the amount of blood, sweat, and tears have been put into this labor.

Traditional Kalymnian House

on the road for Monastery of Saint Savva; tel. 22430/51653; daily 8:30-3pm and 5pm-8pm; €5

This privately owned home has been turned into a small museum dedicated to the folk lifestyle of Kalymnos. The museum is run by Faneromeni Skylla-Halkidou, the daughter of a sponge diver. She is generous with her time, and shares both personal stories and the history of the island and its people, including

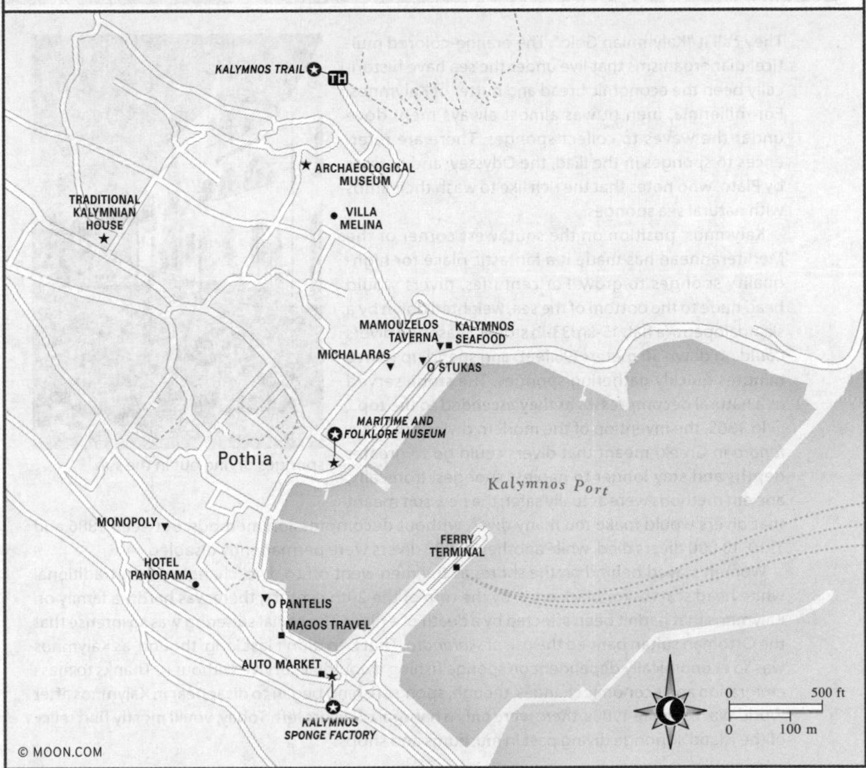

what diving was like from the perspective of the women who stayed on the shores while their husbands went underwater.

RECREATION

Diving

★ KALYMNOS SCUBA DIVING CLUB

tel. 697 464 6413; www.kalymnos-diving.com; from €50

If you're a certified diver, be sure to book a one-day dive to see the underwater world of Kalymnos, complete with volcanoes, caves, and shipwrecks. Here, you'll also learn about the history of diving in Kalymnos, and they'll demonstrate the traditional techniques of *skandalopetra* (stone and rope freediving) on boat trips that leave from the shop and go around Kalymnos. They also have PADI open-water certification courses that can be done over three days (€350). This is a dive shop, but you'll learn so much that it will feel a bit like a museum.

NIGHTLIFE AND ENTERTAINMENT

MONOPOLY

tel. 22430/59963; daily, 11am-late

A sleek little café bar perfect for recovering from the bends (just kidding—don't get drunk if you get the bends!). It's open all day, like most Greek cafés, and seamlessly transitions from morning coffee to evening cocktails. There's also a cute little outdoor space.

The Sponge Industry

sponges drying out in the sun

They call it "Kalymnian Gold": The orange-colored multicellular organisms that live under the sea have historically been the economic bread and butter of Kalymnos. For millennia, men (it was almost always men) dove under the waves to collect sponges. There are references to sponges in the Iliad, the Odyssey, and in texts by Plato, who notes that the rich like to wash their limbs with natural sea sponges.

Kalymnos' position on the southwest corner of the Mediterannean has made it a fantastic place for high-quality sponges to grow. For centuries, divers would head nude to the bottom of the sea, weighted down by a skandalopetra (a flat, 15-kg/33-lb stone). Seasoned divers could go down 30 meters (98 feet) and spend up to five minutes quickly gathering sponges. The stone served as a natural decompressor as they ascended to the top.

In 1865, the invention of the modern diving suit (*skafandro* in Greek) meant that divers could go to greater depths and stay longer to harvest sponges. Ironically, ancient methods were actually safer; the new suit meant that divers would make too many dives, without decompression methods. Between 1886 and 1910, 10,000 divers died, while another 20,000 divers were permanently disabled.

Women stayed behind on the shores as the men went off to dive, changing their traditional white head scarves for black ones. By the turn of the 20th century, there was hardly a family on Kalymnos that hadn't been affected by a death of a diver. The social suffering was so intense that the Ottoman sultan banned the use of *skafandro*. That ban didn't last long, though, as Kalymnos was so economically dependent on sponge fishing it couldn't survive without it. Thanks to mass emigration and economic changes, though, sponge fishing began to disappear in Kalymnos after World War II. By the 1980s, there were only a handful of divers left. Today, you'll mostly find relics of the island's sponge diving past in museums and shops.

SHOPPING

KALYMNOS SEAFOOD

tel. 697 473 6282; daily 7am-4pm

Though men are often at the forefront of Kalymnos' diving culture, women have always been part of the scene. While the men fish for the goods underwater, it's usually the women who turn the fish and seafood into delicious meals. At Kalymnos Seafood, a women's co-op, their skills are put on display. You'll find their canned seafood and other recipes, including tuna smoked with herbs and inky black octopus paste. Note that the owners don't speak great English.

★ KALYMNOS SPONGE FACTORY

Potami Kalimnou; tel. 22430/28501

You'll obviously want to buy a sponge in Kalymnos—they're used for everything from scrubbing down the kitchen sink to tenderly washing a baby's bottom, and the prices reflect the quality and size. At the Kalymnos Sponge Factory, the only factory left on the island (serving the 80 sponge divers left on Kalymnos), you'll not only learn about sponge diving and production, and see workers in action, but you'll also be able to buy a few authentic Greek sponges. Unfortunately, a lot of sponges in other places might not be from Kalymnos (tourist shops tend to bulk up their stock with sponges from Asia).

FOOD

In addition to any freshly caught fish, Kalymnos has two local specialties: *fylla* (vine leaves stuffed with rice and ground meat) and *mououri* (goat loaded with giblets and rice and slowly cooked in a sealed clay pot). Along the harbor you'll find plenty of tavernas; most offer at least a moderate quality of food.

O STUKAS

tel. 697 080 2346; lunch and dinner daily; from €6

This small waterfront taverna makes excellent meze and has an unbeatable three-course meal for €9 (vegetarian) or €10 (fish or meat). Given the views of the sea and the surroundings, it's best to choose fish, which is freshly caught.

MICHALARAS

tel. 22430/29446; daily 9am-midnight; from €3

This lovely waterside café/pastry shop has some of the best desserts on the island. Be sure to try the *galaktoboureko,* a custard pie made with fresh milk.

O PANTELIS

tel. 22430/51508; daily lunch and dinner; from €7

If you're tired of the port, and fish, head one street up to this cozy taverna that specializes in meat dishes. This is the place to try *fylla* and *maououri.* Their generous, fresh salads come loaded with fruits and nuts.

MAMOUZELOS TAVERNA

Panormos; tel. 22430/47809; daily lunch and dinner; from €9

This family-owned seafood taverna has excellent views of the sea, along with the quintessential line of octopus hanging out to dry. Be sure to try the sea urchin salad, seabass carpaccio, and, if you're lucky, the squid ink risotto. Reservations are recommended.

ACCOMMODATIONS

HOTEL PANORAMA

tel. 697 342 0269; www.panorama-kalymnos.gr; from €40

This cute, 13-room, family run hotel makes an excellent budget option. Each room has a balcony and comes equipped with an air-conditioner, though the furnishings are rather bare-bones. There's a wonderful view of the port from the rooftop, though, and the staff is friendly and attentive.

VILLA MELINA

tel. 22430/22682; www.villa-melina.com; from €65

Housed in a neoclassical building from the 1930s, this shabby chic hotel is a great option for those who like eccentric, slightly worn around the edges style. It's seen better days, but the place is charming and the proprietor is extremely hospitable. Plus the swimming pool and well-thumbed library add to the villa's character. There are a handful of rooms, and the guests are usually as kind as the jovial English-speaking owner, Antonis.

Western Kalymnos

Most of the tourist facilities and the highest density of foreigners are concentrated on the west side of the island. This is also where there's the best rock-climbing. Note that the northwest head of Kalymnos after Emporios is mostly inaccessible to visitors; there's not a good road system up here, so don't try to brave it with your rental car.

Buses go from Pothia port to Myrties, Masouri, Armeos just north of Masouri (7 daily; €1.50), and Emporios (2 daily; €2). There is no bus to Panormos; you will have to take a taxi if you don't have a car.

HORIO

Sights

PERA KASTRO

always open; free

Sea Urchins

Locals in Kalymnos are pretty proud of the fact that Andrew Zimmerman, the exuberant host of the Discovery Channel's TV show *Bizarre Foods*, chose to highlight Kalymnos' rich seafood cuisine. By most American standards, sea urchins are considered a bizarre food, though as Zimmerman points out, the orange, custard-like filling inside the spiky shells is considered a delicacy across the Mediterranean. There are more than 700 varieties of sea urchin, and the most common two found in the Mediterranean are called *Paracentrotus lividus* and *Arbacia lixula*. You'll also notice plenty of sea urchins when you're swimming in the sea; be very careful not to step on them, and don't be tempted to harvest them unless you know what you're doing.

EATING SEA URCHIN

Sea urchin is often eaten raw, with maybe a little bit of lemon, and it's one of the most delicious things you can eat on Kalymnos. In Greek, sea urchin is αχινός (achinos), and you'll often see it served as a "salad," though there are no greens or vegetables in it—just pure sea urchin. They are also fantastic in pasta. **Mamouzelos Taverna** is the best place to try sea urchin on Kalymnos, and it has a particularly good sea urchin salad.

This island truly loves its seafood, and that doesn't stop with sea urchin. The most popular way to eat octopus here is to dip it in your glass of ouzo; supposedly, both taste better that way!

Driving west out of Pothia, you'll first come across Horio, the former capital of Kalymnos. It's worth stopping here to check out Pera Kastro (4 km/2.5 mi from Pothia), an old village built into the hills to avoid detection from the pirates. Now abandoned and mostly in overgrown ruin, it has nine little 15th-century churches with original frescoes, all in varying states of disarray.

PANORMOS
(Πάνορμος)

It's worth making a little stop in the beachside hamlet of Panormos, 2.6 km (1.5 mi) west of Horio, where you'll find a strange little archaeological site that isn't open to tourists, though you can—and should—peak through the fence: You'll see the fragments of a 5th-century church of Christ of Jerusalem, mosaics, remains of the ancient city, and temples of Delian Apollo and Asclepius.

Beaches

★ PLATIS GIALOS (Πλάτης Γιαλός)

Located close to Panormos, Platis Gialos is considered one of Kalymnos' most beautiful beaches, thanks to its fine black sand and clear waters. There are some tavernas and kiosks here to buy snacks, but remember to bring a towel because the black sand gets extra hot during the summer. Platis Gialos also has a fantastic view of the sunset

KANTOUNI (Καντούνι)

Kantouni is also located a short walk from Panormos, and is more of a resort-y and organized beach. But the real draw here is the hiking route up to Aghios Fotis church. From the left (southern) side of Kantouni, hike 3 km (1.85 mi) along the marked trail up the mountain to Aghios Fotis; the whole route there and back will take 1.5 hours. The route runs parallel to the sea, and you'll have great views of the coastline. The church is a typical island Greek church, and it's beautiful against the backdrop of the sea. Be sure to bring water!

LINARIA
(Λιναριά)

Linaria is the first large beach town you'll come across out of Pothia on the western route. It's just a kilometer (.6 mi) west out of Panormos, and is an easy walk if you don't have a car. It's a bit of the nightlife hub of the island, and it's nice to come here during or after sunset for a drink.

Beaches

LINARIA BEACH (Παραλία Linaria)

This cute sandy beach backed by mountains is something of a social hangout. There are several tavernas, bars, and rooms for rent backing the beach. The water is clear and the sand is fine, and it's a nice sunbathing spot.

Nightlife and Entertainment

There are three bars on Linaria, all equally popular, and it's worth hopping from one to the other. Check out **Domus** (tel. 22430/47760; daily 9am-2am), which runs from morning coffee to sunset cocktails; **Albus** (tel. 693 759 4898; daily 7pm-3am), which has great music, an extensive food menu, and cocktails; and **Rock & Blues** (tel. 22430/47533; daily 2pm-midnight), a Hard Rock Café-esque beach bar.

MYRTIES AND MASOURI (Μυρτιές, Μασούρι)

Named after the myrtle bushes that surround the area, Myrties is a little coastal settlement that has a nice sandy beach. A little farther north is Masouri, another coastal village with a nicer (read: longer, sandier) beach than Myrties. It's also the main haven for climbers, who base themselves here to conquer the cliffs and crags around the coastline and across the water on Telendhos Islet. It's located 6 km (3.75 mi) north of Linaria and Panormos.

★ Rock Climbing

Kalymnos attracts climbers from around the world, thanks to its seemingly endless abundance of strange rock formations, fjords, slabs, roofs, and caves. Add on top the beautiful views of the Dodecanese sea, a bright orange sunset, and the sweet air of a Greek island, and you've got yourself a truly impressive place to climb.

Aris Theodoropolous, the co-founder of two climbing websites, **Climb Greece** (www.climbgreece.com) and **Climb Kalymnos** (www.climbkalymnos.com), should be given credit for his contribution to putting Kalymnos on the world map. He co-wrote the *Kalymnos Rock Climbing Guidebook* (for sale online, and in Myrties and Pothia). Serious climbers should consult this guide as well as the Climb Kaymnos website before heading out here.

SIMON MONTMORY

Myrties; tel. 698 367 4162; www.kalymnosclimbingguide.com; from €220

If you want a climbing guide, Simon Montmory offers multiday climbing courses, including private guides and multi-pitch climbs. He's developed several new pitches across Kalymnos and Telendhos, and trains climbers in French and English. An intro to rock climbing class will teach you all the basic skills. Half-day beginner lessons for 1-3 people cost €220 euros, while an all-inclusive five-day course will set you back €585.

Hiking

★ KALYMNOS TRAIL

Distance: 100 km (62 mi)
Duration: 10 days
Effort level: strenuous

Kalymnos is quickly establishing a reputation as an important hiking destination. The most interesting route on the island is the 100-km (62-mi) trail that circumvents the island and makes a stop in Telendhos as well. It includes a rest on the ferry, though if you're very hardcore, you could brave the swim across. You'll have to pass through difficult mountain terrain and engage in some "rock-scrambling" to complete the trail, but serious hikers rave about it.

If you do it all at once, it will take around 10 days, but you can also hike portions of the trail on full- or half-day excursions. I recommend consulting the Kalymnos maps published by Terrain Maps (www.terrainmaps.com) or Topo Guide (www.topoguide.com); all the maps are found in a book published by Terrain Maps that is available in Pothia and Myrties.

Festivals and Events

If you come to Kalymnos at any point during the year, you'll find rock climbers (though the intense sweat of summer makes it a bit more difficult to grasp holds properly), but the place is really bursting at the seams during the annual rock climbing festival in October (https://climbingfestival.kalymnos-isl.gr). Climbers from all over the world make the pilgrimage; the most popular spots for climbing on the island are Odyssey, Grande Grotta, Arhi, and Spartacus. There are different grades on the island, and even beginners can try their hand at climbing. It's also a great treat just to watch people scamper up rocks.

Food

AEGEAN TAVERNA

tel. 22430/47146; daily 2pm-midnight; from €8

Aegean Taverna is known for its generous portions, with a quality to match. The focus is on fresh seafood, often drizzled in some sort of sauce. Try the stuffed calamari, and take your time eating while you enjoy sunset views across the sea.

TSOPANAKOS

tel. 22430/47929 daily noon-11pm; from €8

This family-owned restaurant is as authentic as it gets: The owner is a farmer who supplies all of his own meats and cheeses. The bread is homemade, the goat is local, and everything is delicious.

FATOLITIS SNACK BAR

tel. 22430/47615; 9am-late; from €5

This vine-covered roadside café is the unofficial club of the climbing gang, who usually hang out here before and after climbs, sharing adventure (and misadventure) stories over classic café fare like toasts, sandwiches, and ice cream.

Accommodations

CARIAN HOTEL

tel. 22430/47700; http://carianhotel.gr; from €130

This new (as of 2018) four-star hotel offers 34 rooms with stunning views of Telendhos, exceedingly comfortable beds on which to rest your weary climbing muscles, and sleek, modern furnishings. Breakfast is included, and there's also a hotel spa and pool.

★ TELENDHOS ISLAND

Tiny Telendhos used to be connected to Kalymnos, until a huge earthquake in the 6th century splintered it off, creating this semicircle-shaped islet. Home to around 90 people and completely car-free, it's swimming distance from Kalymnos, but most people take the 10-minute boat from Myrties (every 30 minutes 8am-midnight; €2). There's excellent rock climbing and scuba diving here (there are rumors of an ancient sunken city off the islet's western flank), and the sunset views here are stupendous. You can either come for a day trip or stay overnight. Be sure to check out **Paradise Beach,** a peaceful nudist beach located on the northeast coast, and take a short 1-km (.6 mi) hike around the islet's southwestern corner, where you'll come across some preserved 6th-century tombs (follow the signs marked Early Christian Necropolis).

You'll find a row of tavernas and cafés along the jetty. If you only have time for one, make it **Zorba's** (tel. 22430/48660; lunch and dinner; from €8), where the owner catches fresh fish and seafood every day and grills it in the kitchen.

EMPORIOS (Εμπόριος)

Emporios (20 km/12 mi from Pothia) was the first merchant center in Kalymnos and was an important point of fishing and farming. Nestled between two valleys, it's now just a sleepy little hamlet made of white, Cycladic-looking cube houses that hug a pebble beach. Emporios feels a bit like the end of the world (it's literally the last village of the island), and it's worth visiting for its laid-back vibe and crystal-clear waters.

There's a daily bus from Pothia up to

1: the most popular rock-climbing spot on the island, with a view of Telendhos **2:** the view of Telendhos island from Kalymnos

1

2

Emporios, and you'll also find day trips by boat to Myrties (they have no fixed schedule, so ask around at the waterfront). A paved, 7.7-km (5-mi) road connects Emporios with Palionissos beach on the island's east coast. It's a lovely route if you don't want to drive back down south to get back to the port.

Sights

ARGINONDA

A nice stop along the way to Emporios is the inlet of Arginonda, equally stunning and not nearly as busy as the similar fjord in Vathy. It's located 6.5 km (4 mi) south of Emporios. You can see the fjord from the beach.

Beaches

★ KALAMIES BEACH (Καλαμιές)

One of the more secluded beaches on the island, Kalamies is located just 1.3 km (.8 mi) before Emporios (it's not signposted—you'll just notice a sharp curve in the street and a road leading downward). It's sometimes referred to as "Pirate Beach" because of the **Exotic Ambeli** taverna on the beach; the owner's family dresses up as pirates. The beach has a bit of a bohemian vibe, thanks to the laid-back air and the friendly hippies who hang out by the sea, and it's a great place to spend an afternoon. It has nice golden sand and calm waters.

EMPORIO BEACH (Εμπόριο)

Emporio is far enough out of the way that its beaches are relatively empty, and the village's pebbled main beach doesn't disappoint in terms of tranquility. The beach is flanked by strange rock formations, and there are fragrant green pine trees where you can catch a bit of shade. In the center of the beach, there are a few chairs and umbrellas; snacks can be bought back in the village.

Food and Accommodations

★ HARRY'S PARADISE

tel. 22430/40062; www.harrysparadise.gr; from €50

This little bohemian hotel is well-known around the island. As the name suggests, there's a slice of heaven to be found here, with a private garden absolutely bursting with aromatic flowers. This is one of the rare places where the garden is nicer to look at than the sea! Rooms are well-equipped and come with large terraces that feature rocking chairs. There's also a restaurant attached to the hotel that's open to non-guests. The menu changes daily, but the food is always fresh (many of the ingredients are locally grown), with plenty of vegetarian options and fun riffs on Kalymnian cuisine (from €10).

Vathy and Eastern Kalymnos

The northeast coast of Kalymnos is rather barren, but as the kilometers pass by between Pothia and Vathy (13 km/8 mi), the cliffs give way to valleys and the area becomes lush. This is the citrus-growing center of Kalymnos, and it's an olfactory joy to drive through with the windows down, your head half stuck out. The fabulous Vathy Fjord is also located here.

You can take the bus from Pothia to Vathy (3 daily; €2), but you'll need a car to access destinations north of Vathy. The roads above Vathy aren't all paved, so drive with caution.

VATHY (Βαθύ)

The area around Vathy was traditionally the agricultural basin of the island, and you'll notice the heavenly scent of citrus from the orchids around the area. It's somewhat of a surreal contrast: the industrial, mineral grays of the rocky landscape with the bright orange and yellow of the citrus groves.

Vathy is located 15 km (9 mi) east of Pothia, a 30-minute drive.

Sights

VATHY FJORD

Rina Harbor

Like a little bit of Norway here in Greece, this strange little inlet is a geographical wonder and brings hordes of day tourists from neighboring Kos. Two gray cliffs dotted with fragrant pine trees cut away to reveal a thin, turquoise blue bay that unrolls like a long tongue. Fishing boats bob in the water, and behind the dock, there is a row of tavernas and cafés, perfect for drinking in the view. There are several ways to experience the fjord: You can rent kayaks, climb up the cliffs (I would recommend this only if you're a seasoned climber), or just sit back and crane your neck up.

Kayaking

KALYMNOS KAYAK CENTER

tel. 22430/31132; from €10

One of the nicest ways to enjoy Vathy Fjord is by kayak, which you can rent from the Kalymnos Kayak Center. You'll paddle out in the tranquil water, the cliffs on either side enveloping you. If you kayak out around sunset, the sky will be a fantastic purple color. You can also kayak toward the Daskalio caves (guides will point you in the right direction), which lends a great air of adventure as you duck your head under stalactites.

Shopping

AMFIPETRAN YOUTH CLUB

tel. 694/160 5006

Call ahead to meet the guys running this Youth Club, which sells citrus products like spoon sweets, jams, and liquors from the Vathy valley, which is the citrus-production heart of Kalymnos.

KOPANEZOS FAMILY HONEY

Vathy; tel. 22430/29446

The Kopanezos family, who have run an organic bee-keeping production out on the rocks since the 1950s, make a damn good thyme honey and treat their bees kindly. They preserve traditional nomadic methods of bee-keeping.

Food

Vathy is one of the best areas to eat seafood on the island, and you can't really go wrong at any of the little tavernas hugging the harbor. Order anything that's been freshly caught—grilled or fried. Octopus dipped in ouzo is a particularly good choice.

AIGIA PELAGOS RESTAURANT

tel. 22430/31408; daily lunch and dinner; from €7

This lovely seafood restaurant is right on the harbor, where you can order freshly caught fish (grilled or fried) as well as oven-fish dishes, like shrimp *saganaki.* You'll find a mix of tourists and locals, and nights occasionally end with impromptu Greek dancing and music.

MEDUSA BY THE SEA

tel. 697 279 2482; daily lunch and dinner; from €7

Medusa by the Sea uses exceedingly fresh ingredients and boasts a super friendly staff, helped by English-speaking Kaliopi. You'll find traditional taverna dishes and fresh seafood, plus things that are a cut above the classic taverna fare, such as mushrooms with feta baked in the oven, or spinach with blue cheese sauce. They have a great view of the fjord.

PANAGIA KYRA PSILI MONASTERY

free

A few different origin stories exist for this stunning cave monastery built into the facade of a mountain, but this one is my favorite: A shepherd looking for his lost goat stumbled upon a cave with an icon of the Virgin Mary inside. The shepherd tried to bring the icon to his village, but each time, it magically returned to the cave. Eventually the villagers gave in and built a monastery there (though it no longer functions as one today). Inside, the monastery is full of curves, and there are shelves and seats hacked into the walls of the cave. There's a big *panagiri* (religious festival) at the church each year on August 15; if you're in Kalymnos at this time, definitely join in the celebration.

To get here from Vathy, follow the signs clearly pointing toward the church on foot; at the end of the dirt road you will reach the path that takes you on a 1-km (.6-mi), 30-minute hike. There's a nice view down toward Rina fjord and the Vathy harbor. To get to the start of the path, you can either walk through Vathy (about 3 km/1.75 mi) or drive to the northeast end of the town (everything is signposted).

PALIONISSOS (Παλιόνησσος)

At the north end of the island, there's a beautiful bay backed by three cliffs. This remote beach is becoming increasingly popular with rock climbers, but it also remains a tranquil oasis with clean waters for swimming.

From Vathy it's a lovely 23-km (14-mi) drive north (40 minutes) through the island's interior. If you're going to or coming from Emporios, there's a good paved road (6 km/3.75 mi) that can take you between the two without having to drive back down to the port. It's also a really beautiful route, full of goats and heady with the scent of oregano, and on a clear day you can easily see the Turkish coastline.

Samothrace (Σαμοθράκη)

Since Samothrace is so difficult to get to, it remains the domain of a small, devout following, and new initiates looking for adventure in a hippie paradise. Tucked away in the northeast corner of the Aegean, Samothrace (human pop. 3,000, goat pop. 100,000) is marked by dramatic granite ridges, exceptional hiking trails, and hidden waterfalls. This isn't a beach-y island; most of Samothrace's beauty is found in its lush, mountainous interior, which is more reminiscent of New Zealand than the Mediterranean. Here, a network of streams and rivers provides stunning vistas, and you'll stumble across natural rock pools and increasingly grand waterfalls. Since Samothrace is so difficult to get to, it remains the domain of

Highlights

Look for ★ to find recommended sights, activities, dining, and lodging.

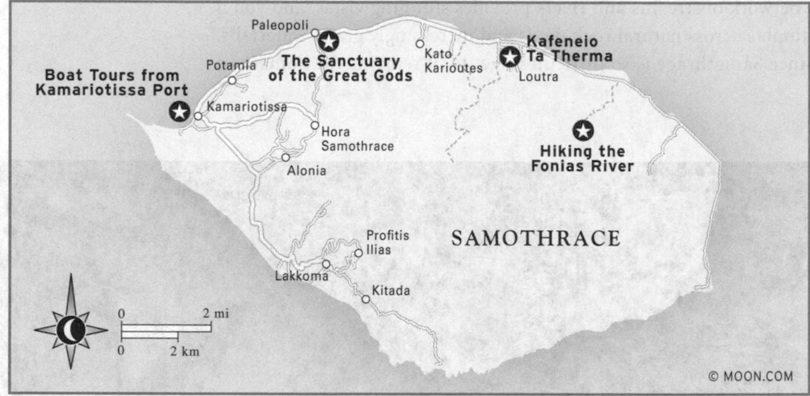

★ **The Sanctuary of the Great Gods:** The site of this ancient Thracian cult remains one of Greece's most mysterious and important religious ruins (page 267).

★ **Boat Tours From Kamariotissa Port:** Visit some of Samothrace's most beautiful (and least accessible) beaches with a boat tour leaving from the port (page 269).

★ **Hiking the Fonias River:** Hike at least the first 40 minutes of the trail from Loutra. This impressive river feeds some of the island's most beautiful rock pools and waterfalls (page 271).

★ **Kafeneio Ta Therma:** The most happening of the bars in Loutra doubles as a dance hall, cultural space, and general meeting spot for Samothrace's locals and devout visitors (page 273).

a small, devout following, and new initiates looking for adventure in a hippie paradise. People tend to free camp around the island, and are often found hiking and lounging in varying states of undress. It's not for everyone, but if it is for you, you'll want to stay forever.

PLANNING YOUR TIME

Samothrace is best visited from **June** to **September.** In the **winter** much of the island is frozen over, and the warmth of **spring** causes the river to thaw and flood the mountainside, making hiking and camping impossible.

Given how troublesome (and expensive, depending on where you're coming from) it is to visit, I suggest budgeting at least **one week** to chill on the island. All venues should be open **June-August,** with some opening earlier in **May** or staying open through **September.** In **June** and early **July,** it can still be chilly at night, so pack layers for when the sun goes down.

Most travelers stay in either Loutra or Kamariotissa. Samothrace is manageable enough that you can stay in either and still get around easily.

If you're planning on **camping** on Samothrace, bring a tent, sleeping bag, comfortable pillow, a small gas stove, and some basic provisions. The most die-hard Samothrace visitors show up with only a hammock, which they sling between two trees; you can go this route as well. Note that free camping is technically illegal on Samothrace, although it is widely practiced. If you're not camping, book a room at the port of **Kamariotissa,** where most of the hotels are, or in **Loutra** (less touristic and more bohemian).

Given Samothrace's reputation as a hippie hangout, port **police** can be very intense with drug searches, particularly during July and August when there are reggae festivals around the island. Several friends of mine have been strip-searched by police upon arriving at the port. You are significantly better off traveling without any drug paraphernalia, even if Greece has relatively relaxed laws around marijuana consumption.

INFORMATION AND SERVICES

You'll find port **police** (tel. 25510/41305) at Kamariotissa, where you'll also find two of the island's **banks with ATMs,** and an internet café. There are **pharmacies** around Hora and Kamariotissa, and the island's main **health center** is in Hora (tel. 25510/50700).

The only travel agency on the island is **Samothraki Travel** (tel. 698 490 8254 or 25510/89444; www.samothraki-tourism.gr). They offer excellent guided trekking tours (from €15) and canyon tours (from €40) across the island, as well as diving tours (€50 per couple). Tours usually happen in August and September. Because so little of Samothrace's hiking is marked, unless you are a very seasoned hiker you really should go on a guided tour.

GETTING THERE

Getting to Samothrace is a journey. There is no airport, and the island is only accessible from the port town of **Alexandroupoli** (an hour-and-a-half flight from Athens; a half hour from Thessaloniki); your only option is the ferry. **SAOS Lines** (www.saos.gr) runs twice daily ferries between the mainland and Samothrace (2 hours; up to €14.50). Ferries are pretty regular in the summer, but timetables vary widely outside those months.

GETTING AROUND

At 178 square km (69 square mi), Samothrace is a pretty manageable island, but only the north part is served by **bus.** If you're planning on camping, you'll be **walking** most of the time. If you want to spend time in the south or east, you'll need to rent a **car. Hitchhiking**

Previous: Waterfalls of Vathres; the looming mountain of Samothrace; goats are the mascot of Samothrace.

Samothrace

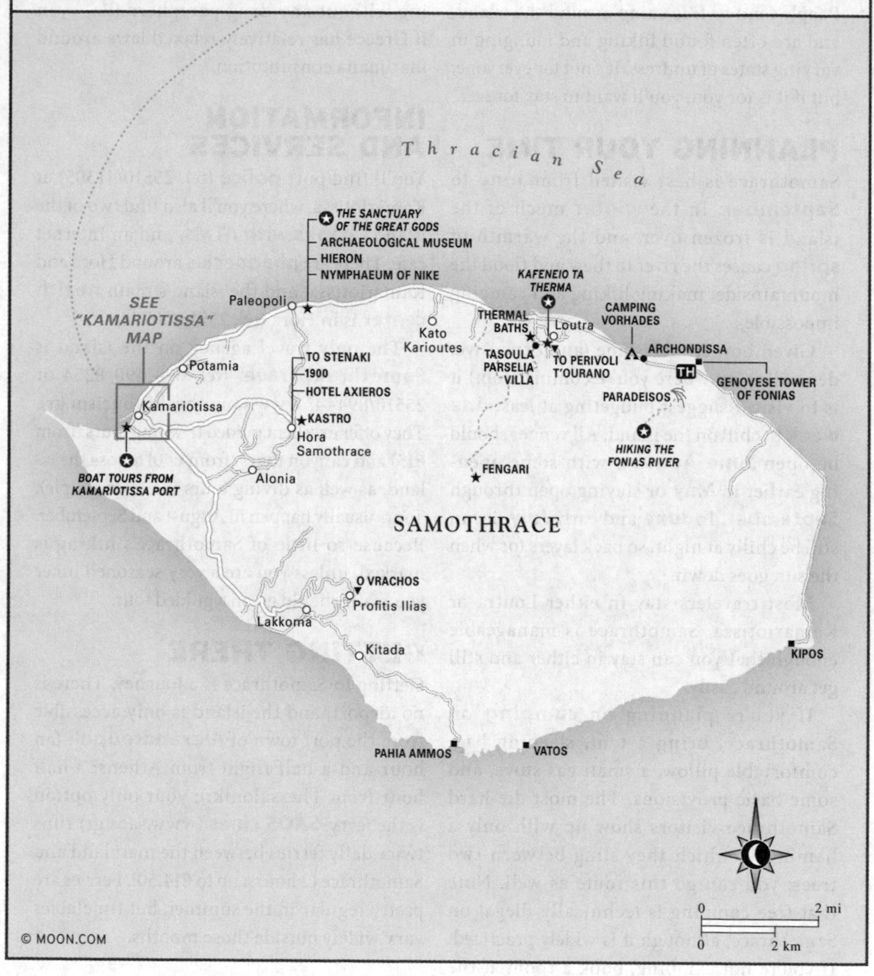

SAMOTHRACE

is also a viable way to get around the island and is practiced by both locals and tourists.

Bus

Six to seven buses (2 euros) leave **Kamariotissa** along the northern part of the coast to **Loutra** (20 minutes), and there are 5-6 daily to **Hora** (10 minutes). Buses run much less frequently during the winter.

Car

Niki Tours (Kamariotissa; tel. 25510/41465) and **Kyrkos Rent-a-Car** (Kamariotissa; tel. 25510/41620) both offer small jeeps, motorcycles, and sedans. Note that there's only one **gas station** 1 km (.6 mi) above Kamariotissa on the way to Hora, and you'll need to book ahead in July and August. Most of the roads in Samothrace are paved, and the most inaccessible parts of the island are better reached by boat or walking.

Taxi

There's a **taxi station** at the port, and one of the three (!) available taxis is waiting for customers just before the municipal **bus station.** There aren't taxi companies, but try giving Nikos (tel. 697 288 3501) or Panagiotis (tel. 697 238 1762) a call. The longest trip won't cost more than €20.

Itinerary Ideas

I definitely recommend renting a car for this itinerary. Bus service is spotty, and you'll want to spend time lingering in each spot.

DAY 1

Spend your first morning exploring this magical island's most mystical offering: the **Sanctuary of the Great Gods.** Spend a few hours walking through the ruins, making sure to visit the sanctuary's most famous sites.

1 Learn more about the Sanctuary's history at the **Archaeological Museum.** There's a plaster cast of the Winged Victory of Samothrace, now in the Louvre after it was stolen by the French diplomat Charles Champoiseau in 1863.

2 Next, visit the **Hieron,** a site of initiation rituals, and the theater located opposite.

3 Follow the path down to the **Nymphaeum of Nike** monument, which, though it now stands in the Louvre, was originally here, facing out towards the sea. The energy is incredibly strong!

4 In the evening, head to the Hora for a stroll and dinner at **1900.**

DAY 2

In general, Samothrace's hiking trails are not for the faint-hearted, but most people will be able to manage the trek along the Fonias River. The first 40 minutes are easy, and you can stop at that if you aren't a seasoned hiker. Bring a hat and bathing suit!

1 Pick up some provisions in **Loutra** at a mini-market (there are several, you'll easily find one!), including snacks and water.

2 To start the hike, drive 4.7 km (3 mi) east from Loutra to the **Fonias River** trailhead (next to the ticket booths).

3 The first part of the hike is easy and well-marked, and after 40 minutes will take you to a 12-meter-high (40-foot) waterfall called **Paradeisos.** Go for a swim, then turn around and head back to Loutra. (It's possible to continue farther on the trail, but note that the paths from here are not well marked, so it's best to consult with Samothraki Travel before heading farther.)

4 Spend the evening knocking back beers with your new pals at the **Kafeneio ta Therma** in Loutra.

Itinerary Ideas

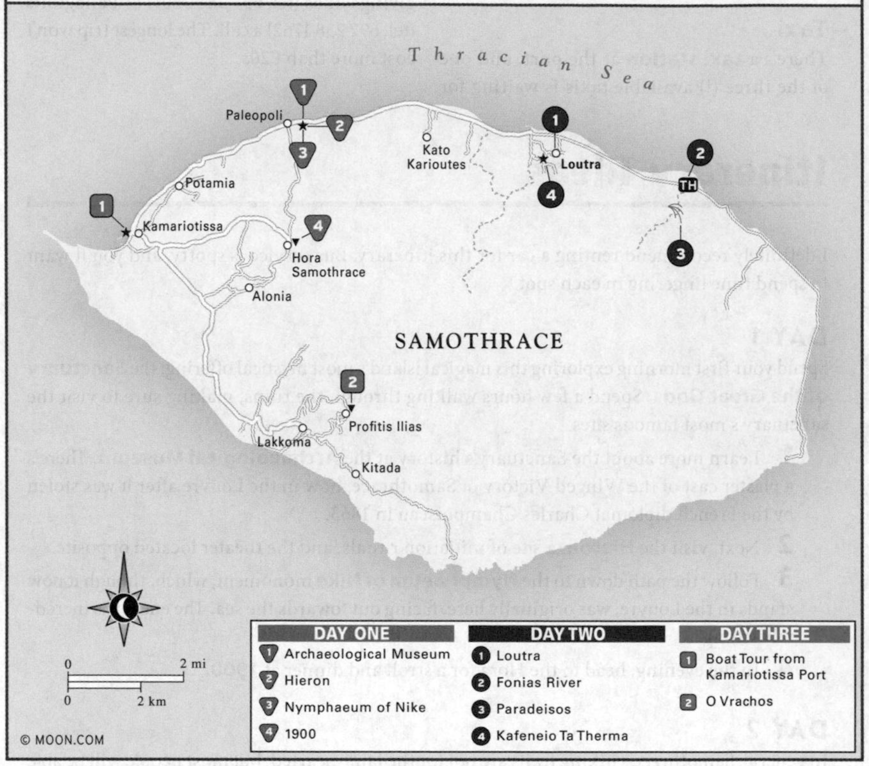

DAY 3

The island's best beaches are located on the southern coast, which is best accessed by boat.

1 Take a **boat tour from Kamariotissa** (departing 10am) and spend the day swimming and ogling the strange rock formations and waterfalls. Book at the port beforehand, or just show up early in the morning to secure a spot. You'll be dropped back off, all bronzed and salty, around 6pm.

2 After your boat drops you back off at the port, drive for 15 minutes to reach **O Vrachos** in the mountain village of Prophet Ellias, where you can finish your day with a roasted goat dinner (the local specialty).

Hora Samothrace Χώρα Σαμοθράκη

Hora (also, somewhat confusingly, called Samothrace), 6km (3.75 mi) east of the port in Kamariotissa, is the island's capital. Snugly constructed between two sheer cliffs to avoid the detection of pirates, it was ruled by both the Byzantines and the Genoans. It's an adorable little town, and quite a colorful one: Most of the homes are roofed with terracotta, and the whole town is awash in a reddish glow. It's a great place to stroll through the twisted, cobble-stoned lanes, and enjoy a nice dinner.

SIGHTS

Kastro

Wed., Fri.-Sun. 11am-2pm; free

Built in 1431-33 by the Genovese noble Palamede Gattilusio, the *kastro* (castle) is probably the most imposing monument in Hora. It's been recently converted into a proper sightseeing spot, with signs and plaques in English. There are great views from here across Hora and to the sea, as well as some gory details, like a so-called murder hole used to execute any dissenters of Genovese rule. It's located in the center of town.

TOP EXPERIENCE

★ The Sanctuary of the Great Gods

tel. 25510/41474; daily 8am-3pm, museum Tues.-Sun. only; €6

Forget about the Olympian gods; those guys are squabbling nymphs compared to the Great Gods of Samothrace. This sanctuary to them is one of the most mysterious and important archaeological sites in all of Greece, constructed by the Thracians around the 4th century BC (although religious activity was detected as early as the 7th century BC). This sprawling temple complex will take your breath away. Columns soar skyward, and you'll find remnants of altars, rotundas, temples, and more, all in various states of ruin.

Archaeologists are still trying to understand why this temple complex was built, and for what purpose. It's believed that the main deities to which the temple is dedicated are the fertility goddess Alceros Cybele (the Great Mother) and her consort Kadmilos (god of the phallus). The Thracian cult worshipped these

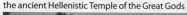

the ancient Hellenistic Temple of the Great Gods

Goat!

goats stand to attention

Goats are an island fixture on Samothrace: There are about 33 goats (*katsika*) for every individual human on the island. They roam free, and none belong to a specific person: When someone wants to kill one for dinner, they just register the number. You'll see them absolutely everywhere, so watch out for their excrement, and be aware that goats are apt to walk all over cars—that's why it's always a good idea to get full insurance with the rental company! There's no real way to avoid it ... so just embrace it, should an errant goat try to walk across your trunk. With such abundance, it should be no surprise that goat is the most famous dish on Samothrace.

WHERE TO TRY

When cooking goat, it's traditionally prepared in the **oven,** but you'll also find it **grilled** and **stuffed.** Any restaurant you go to will have at least one goat specialty for you to taste, and unless you're a vegetarian, you absolutely should. Here are some suggestions of places to try:

- **1900** (Hora Samothrace, page 268)
- **Taverna Klimataria** (Kariotissa, page 270)
- **O Vrachos** (South Coast, page 275)

A sad note: Tourists often litter on the island, and the goats then eat plenty of things that are decidedly not for consumption (plastic wrappers, bags, etc.) leading some people to avoid eating goat on Samothrace.

Megaloi Theoi (Great Gods) by building impressive monuments, but it's also been a historically important meeting point: Alexander the Great's parents met here and the Trojan race was sired here.

You can get a more extensive overview of the site and its history at the **Archaeological Museum,** which includes images and descriptions of the secretive nocturnal rituals that took place at the sanctuary, and a plaster facsimile of the Winged Victory of Samothrace; the real one, sadly, was taken by the French and now resides in the Louvre. Other unmissable sites include the **Nymphaeum of Nike** (where the Winged Victory used to live), and the **Hieron,** a Doric building that hosted the higher levels of initiation rites.

People from Samothrace and devoted visitors alike speak in hushed tones about the spiritual energy of this place. It's undeniable that this ruin possesses an immense ability to hold onto you.

The temple is located about 3 km (2 mi) north of Samothrace. Allow yourself at least several hours to wander around the 5 hectares (12 acres) of densely wooded area, stumbling across the various monuments.

FOOD

1900

tel. 25510/41222; mid-May-mid-Sept. daily noon-1am; from €6

This charming little taverna offers great views of the *kastro* and its surrounding valley. Be sure to grab a table on the vine-leaf-covered terrace. The food is classic Samothrace, which means lots of goat marinated in herbs and stewed vegetables.

TO STENAKI

tel. 25510/42032; daily 9am-11pm; from €3

Sometimes you just need to satisfy your sweet tooth. Enter To Stenaki, an adorable, all-day café that has a great, if somewhat random, assortment of food. The crepes are delicious, and this is a great place to grab breakfast, but you can also come for some meze (appetizers) and beer in the early evening.

ACCOMMODATIONS

There aren't a lot of good sleeping options in Hora. You're better off finding a spot in Loutra or around the port.

HOTEL AXIEROS

tel. 25510/41416; www.axieros.gr; from €50

This is a good budget option with nice views of the villages, and surprisingly decent furniture (the rooms are all traditionally decorated). Rooms sleep up to four people and come with kitchenettes, making this property ideal for families or people looking to save a few bucks.

Kamariotissa Καμαριώτισσα

Your first stop in Samothrace will be Kamariotissa, the island's port and its largest town. There's not a lot here to keep an intrepid traveler interested, but if you need to rent a car, use an ATM, or organize any other logistics, it's a useful stop.

BEACHES

NIKI BEACH (Νίκη)

Niki Beach is the port's main beach. It's a pebbled affair with decent swimming and a cluster of beach bars and tavernas. It's not the nicest beach on the island, and it makes no sense to go out of your way to swim here, but if you're one of those people who needs to swim immediately upon arrival, Niki Beach is a good choice.

RECREATION

★ Boat Tours from Kamariotissa Port

At Kamariotissa port, you'll notice several boats that are docked, waiting to take tourists on day tours around the island. Because much of the island's southern coast is unreachable by car, this is an excellent way to see all the hidden gems, such as Kremasto Waterfall, Vatos beach, and Tis Grias Ta Pania hanging rock. You'll get a brief history lesson from the boat's captain, and stop at several swimming holes along the way. Lunch is typically included, and boats stop along the southern coast.

Boats require at least 10 people before the trip will start. Tours depart at 10am, returning at 6pm. You can either book at the port the evening beforehand, or show up early in the morning. These are typical tourist boats, but they're smaller in size than the pirate schooners on other islands. If you prefer to explore alone, you can rent a private boat through **Euplous** (tel. 693 703 0168).

SAMOTHRAKI CRUISES

Kamariotissa; tel. 22510/95359; www.samothrakicruises.com; from €15

These boats will zip you around the island, including stops along the southern coast like Kremasto Nero and Vatos Beach. They offer two routes: a shorter tour for €15 and a day-long tour for €25, plus a family package for €75 euros. It's an old-school fishing style boat, and you can sunbathe on the bow while the captain circumnavigates the island.

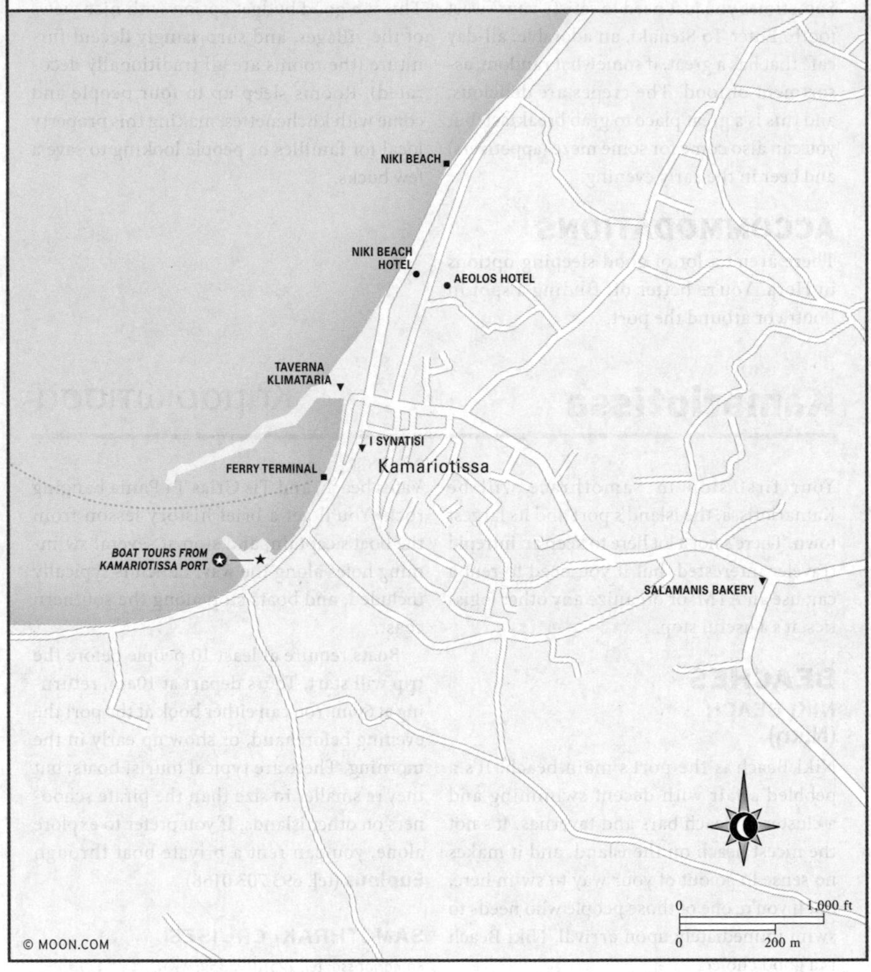

FOOD

Along the northern coast from Kamariotissa to Loutra, you'll find plenty of fish tavernas. The fish is fresh, the seating is outdoors, and there's not a whole lot that can go wrong, so don't feel married to the below suggestions (all located in Kamariotissa itself).

TAVERNA KLIMATARIA

tel. 25510/41535; daily 9am-10pm; from €5

With nice seating under a platanos and a couple of grape vines, this atmospheric taverna with waterfront views makes an excellent dinner choice. The specialty (as in most of Samothrace) is goat, but they also have excellent oven-baked dishes, fresh fish, and large salads.

I SYNATISI

tel. 25510/41308; lunch and dinner; from €6

This cozy restaurant is run by a spear diver who catches fresh fish daily. Whether you order it fried or grilled, you'll watch the chef prepare it from the open-plan kitchen. There's also a selection of meat dishes, and the Samothrakian dessert *chaslamas,* a syrupy dessert with a Turkish name.

SALAMANIS BAKERY

Kamariotissa; tel. 25510/4 1259; Mon.-Sat. 6:30am-2pm; from €1

At this delicious bakery, all of the creations are handmade, and all of the ingredients are local from the island. Mrs. Eleni (who speaks a little English) is the warm-hearted woman at the helm of this family operation; she dishes out spinach pie, cheese pie, custard pies, and *koulouri* (sesame rings that are originally from Turkey).

ACCOMMODATIONS

In Kamariotissa, you'll find several rooms to let and one-star hotels offering only the most basic accommodation.

NIKI BEACH HOTEL

tel. 25510/41545; www.nikibeach.gr; from €55 (breakfast included)

In operation since 1982 and renovated in 2007, this spacious hotel manages to keep an intimate feeling, thanks to the gracious and welcoming hosts. Rooms are decently sized with modern amenities, and face either the sea or the inner courtyard. As the name suggests, it's located just across from Niki Beach. It's a medium-sized hotel (large by Samothrakian standards) and offers a great homemade breakfast that you can eat outside or by the fireplace in the large entrance hall.

AEOLOS HOTEL

tel. 22510/41595; from €45 (breakfast included)

Perched on a hill with views of Mt. Fengari, Aeolos is a little guesthouse with nice owners and a swimming pool. Rooms are basic but clean and comfy, with private balconies, air-conditioning, and little kitchenettes. The beach of Kamariotissa is 20 meters (66 feet) away.

Loutra Λουτρά

Loutra (also known as Therma, thanks to its hot water springs) is located 14 km (9 mi) east of Kamariotissa, and is the island's most popular place to stay, with a very decent selection of hotels and tavernas. It's a lush, green village, full of trees and little creeks. Everyone seems to descend on Loutra during the night—if you're camping around the area, it's the only place with viable electricity—and the cafés fill with people singing, dancing, and drinking: good vibes all around.

SIGHTS

Thermal Baths

Loutra bus stop; tel. 25513/50800; June-Sept. 7am-10am and 6pm-9pm; from €4

You can't miss the big white building next to the bus stop. Here you'll find therapeutic mineral-rich springs that offer an ancient method of treating a bevy of health problems. Though the Thermal Baths are not as potent as the springs in Ikaria, this is still a delightful way to soothe sore joints after all that hiking. A bit farther uphill from the bath house are two small outdoor baths that are free.

HIKING

★ FONIAS RIVER

Distance: 5km (3 mi)

Duration: 45 minutes one way

Effort level: Easy

Fonias means "murderer" in Greek, and this river is so named because, outside of the docile summer months, serious flooding transforms the water into a gushing cascade. The river starts about 4.7 km (just under 3 mi) east of Loutra, near the **Genovese Tower of Fonias,** built in 1431. You'll notice ticket

Free Camping

a tent in the green landscape of the island of Samothrace

"Free camping" is exactly what it sounds like: camping without paying. Essentially, it means you pitch your tent up anywhere your heart desires, and that you follow the universal rules of camping: no open fires, leave the place cleaner than you found it, respect nature.

Here's the thing about free camping: It's technically **illegal,** carrying a maximum penalty of three months in prison and a €150 fine. But given how common it is in Greece—especially in the current financial climate—it's actually the preferred, low-budget way for young Greeks to spend their travel holidays, and it's generally overlooked by police. There are certain islands that are more conducive to free camping than others, and Samothrace is probably the best place to pitch a tent. Most people free camp a bit outside of the trails, near waterfalls. You'll notice tents and hammocks slung up around the woods and sometimes directly on the beach.

If you decide to buck the law and free camp, there are a few things to keep in mind:

- Don't set up camp on a walking trail; it's very annoying for all the hikers who have to go around you.
- Some people set up on the beach, but finding a bit of shade may be more comfortable.
- Pack up everything if you leave camp for the day; otherwise, the goats will likely trample all over your camp and maybe eat a nylon bag or two.
- Pack up trash and take it back with you to town. In general, respect the environment.
- You'll have to bring your own water, a small gas cannister (which can be bought at any Greek supermarket), and food provisions.

You can also pitch your tent at the **Municipal Camping** (tel. 25513/50800) in Loutra. These paying campgrounds under the trees offer very basic facilities. This is very legal camping, and you'll have to pay a small fee (from €3).

booths that are open only in the summer—this is the starting point. Still standing (relatively) tall at 12 meters (39 feet), it was built out of stone, plaster, and tiles, as part of a defensive line by the Gattilusi family. There's no reason to go out of your way to see this, but if you're hiking up Fonias River, it makes a nice pit stop (accessible by car). You can also drive from Loutra to start of the trailhead and park your car in front of the tower and then continue walking.

The path meanders along the river heading into the interior of the island. The first 40 minutes (about 1.5 km/.9 mi) are well-marked, at which point you'll come across a large rock pool perfect for a dip and a 12-meter (39-foot) waterfall called Paradeisos. The second pool is another two hours' walk, but unfortunately, the paths to it and the other five waterfalls and pools are not marked. To find them, consult with Samothraki Travel before hiking farther. Each year, a lot of hikers get temporarily lost in the wilderness.

FENGARI

Distance: *8 km (5 mi)*
Duration: *6 hours one way*
Effort level: *Strenuous*

Standing tall at 1,611 meters (5,285 feet) in the center of the island, Fengari (moon) is the highest peak in the Aegean islands, and the top of the Saos mountain. Most hikers start the six-hour climb (it's a pretty tough trail) from Loutra. The path starts at the top of the village, next to the concrete water tank. The trail passes first through a dense fern forest, then through thick oaks, before thinning out. You'll cross small streams and waterfalls along the way, too. Bring plenty of water and snacks.

You'll want to leave very early in the morning to have a full day of sun, and definitely don't hike up if there's any sort of bad weather. Some people (especially those who believe the local lore that reaching the summit on a full moon means your wish will come true) get stuck when they miscalculate the amount of time it takes them to go up and down the summit, so it's advisable to tell your hotel or campground owner that you're headed up the trail before you leave.

FOOD AND NIGHTLIFE

★ KAFENEIO TA THERMA

tel. 698 499 4856; daily 8am-2am; from €3

Of all the happening spots in Loutra, this one has the most energy. It's the town's central attraction, and has been for more than 20 years. Sit down at any time for a coffee, a more fortified beverage, or something sweet, and enjoy the plethora of human activity before you: artists, singers, dancers, musicians, wild conversations, etc. It especially comes alive at night.

TO PERIVOLI T'OURANO

tel. 25510/98313; June to mid-Oct. daily 11am-2am; from €6

Just on the northeast edge of Loutra, on the way to the nearby village of Gria Vathra, you'll find this cute, shaded taverna. The name translates to "Heaven's Orchard." They have a great selection of mezes, salads, pasta, and *saganaki* (pan-fried appetizers), and a grill cooking up plenty of meat (including goat). Wash it down with wine, and unwind to the traditional live music that plays regularly.

ACCOMMODATIONS

CAMPING VORHADES

tel. 25510/98258; July-Aug. only; from €3

This is the primary municipal campground on the island, just 3 km (under 2 mi) east of the village. Less hard-core campers flock here: There's a minimarket, restaurant, hot water, and other facilities that add a touch of glam to camping. There are toilets and showers, and for an extra €4 you can tack on electricity. You can also rent a caravan here for the full season for €550.

TASOULA PARSELIA VILLA

tel. 25510/98318; www.samothraki-studios.gr; from €50

These little bungalows, each with its own yard or balcony, are strewn across a lush and peaceful forested setting that is reminiscent of an Italian *agriturismo* (farm accommodation). Each studio has air-conditioning and comfy beds; there's a communal kitchen in the main living area. There are only a handful of bungalows available, so book in advance.

★ ARCHONDISSA

tel. 25510/98090; www.archondissa.gr; from €75

Undoubtedly the nicest option on the island, this property offers Cycladic-inspired architectural cubes featuring colorful interior designs, little kitchenettes that are nicely tucked away behind wardrobes, and a beautiful flower garden. The sea is a mere 30 meters (100 feet) away, and the staff is friendly and attentive. If camping fills you with dread but you still want to be close to nature, this is a great pick. It's a medium-sized hotel with different-sized rooms and apartments (the largest sleep up to five guests).

South Coast Beaches

The southern part of the island is in many ways Samothrace's least explored. There's no road between Pahia Ammos and Kipos Beach, so the beaches (other than Pahia Ammos, accessible by car from Kamariotissa) are reachable only by boat or, in the case of the seriously athletic and agile, by doing some intense hiking and climbing through the island's wild interior. Note that around Samothrace, but particularly in the interior, hiking trails are usually not well marked. It's always best to let someone know where you're going, and to consult with Samothraki Travel. It would take hours to get from Loutra to some of the southern beaches, so don't do it unless you're planning on either leaving at the crack of dawn, or spending a few days camped out on the beach.

One boat operator in Loutra used to serve the southern beaches, but unfortunately the boat burned down in 2018. As of the writing of this book, it was unclear if the boat was repaired, or if there was another official operator in town, but it's possible (and common) to convince a fisherman to take you on a trip (€25-30); you can also take a boat from the port.

BEACHES

Note that all these beaches are nudist-friendly, probably have some campers out on them, and lack beach bars or restaurants. It's a good idea to bring your own food, water, and umbrella if you're going to be spending the whole day.

KIPOS (Κήπος)

This long, golden sandy beach is most easily accessed by boat from the port, although some brave souls do take the (unmarked) hiking trails through the interior to reach it.

VATOS (Βατός)

Only accessible by boat from Loutra or the port, Vatos is a very unique pebbled beach. Its most impressive feature is the **Kremasto Waterfall**, which dumps directly into the sea. It's a breathtaking view when you arrive by boat.

a long, sandy beach

If you take the boat toward Vatos, you'll come across the strange natural rock formation Tis Grias Ta Pania (The Old Woman's Sails) along the way. According to local legend, one day an old woman left her laundry out to dry on a rock, but a strong wind blew it away. Annoyed, she did what any of us would do, and put a hex on the laundry so it became petrified. The oddly shaped gray rock is the cursed laundry.

PAHIA AMMOS (Παχιά Άμμος)

This is considered one of the most beautiful beaches on the island, and luckily it's accessible by car from Kamariotissa (though some people also like to walk the moderate 8 km (5 mi) from the nearby village of Profitis Ilias). If you're driving, you'll take the southern road from the port for 15 km (9 mi), passing through interior villages. There's a little bar and restaurant, and the sandy, expansive beach has plenty of room for everyone.

FOOD

★ O VRACHOS

Profitis Illias; tel. 25510/95264; daily 10am-11:45pm; from €6

O Vrachos means "the rock" in Greek, and this little taverna tucked away in the mountain village of Prophet Ellias, located 11 km (8 mi) southeast of Kamariotissa, is the perfect place for a lazy lunch. The specialty is goat (though they tend to run out of goat early on and sometimes you have to wait for them to finish roasting it) marinated with plenty of herbs. The eggplant smoked on coals and turned into a salad is also delicious, and you'll find friendly service and decent wine. It's located in the village proper, and if you're hiking from Pahia Ammos beach (8 km/5 mi), it makes the perfect reward after a few hours of walking.

Ikaria (Ικαρία)

Ikaria (pop. 8,600) might be the strangest (and thus, coolest) of the Greek islands, and depending on how down you are with studied eccentricity, left-wing politics, and a poetic nonchalance for the concept of time, it might also become your favorite.

This is the birthplace of Dionysus, god of wine. His legacy lives on in the island's nocturnal lifestyle and truly wild *panigiri* (religious festivals); it was also, for most of the first half of the 20th century, used as a place of exile for communists and other political dissidents. For a couple of years, from 1946 to 1949, communist exiles actually outnumbered the locals, and since then, Ikaria has been dubbed "the red rock." The most famous exile was composer Mikis Theodorakis, who is considered a national treasure in Greece.

Highlights

Look for ★ to find recommended sights, activities, dining, and lodging.

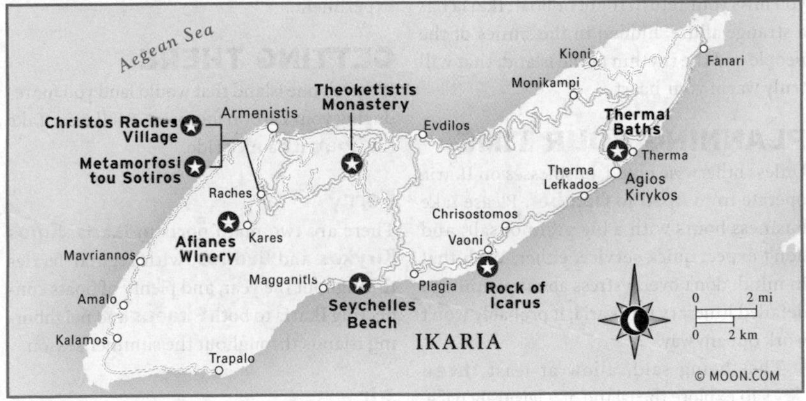

★ **Thermal Baths:** Soothe any aching limbs or sore muscles in Europe's most radioactive water (page 284).

★ **Rock of Icarus:** When Icarus flew too close to the sun and fell to the sea, a rock popped up in his place—according to legend, anyway (page 286).

★ **Seychelles Beach:** So-named because it resembles a Caribbean beach, this is the best seaside on Ikaria (page 286).

★ **Theoketistis Monastery:** A rock-hewn monastery with stunning frescoes from the 16th century (page 289).

★ **Christos Raches Village:** The so-called "village that never sleeps" is the best place to learn about Ikaria's unique concept of time (page 294).

★ **Metamorfosi tou Sotiros:** If you're in town on August 6, head to the mountain village of Christos Raches to witness the island's most raucous Orthodox feast day (page 294).

★ **Afianes Winery:** Head to this family-run winery to sample some of the island's best wine (page 295).

Though it's not the most beautiful island—there are only a few beaches worth visiting, and some roads in the south are completely inaccessible by car—one of the best things about Ikaria is just how little people care about tourism. Unlike on other islands, the local economy doesn't *depend* on tourism, so no one is aggressive, the towns are void of overt tourist infrastructures, and the summer season is just a continuation of normal life. The locals are kind and hospitable, and the other types of visitors you'll run into are similarly down to earth. The island is also home to some of the most therapeutic waters in Europe; the thermal baths have incredible healing properties that locals use on a regular basis (probably another reason why they live so long!).

This is a magical place. Don't try to come here with a schedule, and don't be alarmed if you miss your return flight or boat: Ikaria has a strange allure, hidden in the smiles of the people and the rhythm of the island, that will truly warm your heart.

PLANNING YOUR TIME

Unless otherwise noted, businesses on Ikaria operate from **April** to **October.** Please take business hours with a big grain of salt, and don't expect quick service, either. With that in mind, don't overly stress about planning a detailed itinerary for Ikaria; it probably won't work out anyway.

That being said, allow at least **three days** to explore the island at a leisurely pace. Another way to organize your time is to plan a visit during one of the island's massive ***panigiria*** (in summer: June 24 and 29; July 1, 17, and 27; August 6 and 15-20; and September 17). The *panigiria* happen around the island, but the most raucous ones are located in **Raches.** You'll get a taste of local life and the nocturnal hedonism unique to Ikarians.

Unless you're in Ikaria solely to visit the hot springs, it's nice to base yourself on the northern side of the island, between the coast of **Evdilos** and **Nas** (including **Armenistis**) or in one of the central villages, such as **Raches.**

INFORMATION AND SERVICES

You'll find **ATMs, banks, pharmacies,** and **police stations** in both Evdilos and Agios Kirykos. Police are located above the Alpha Bank in Agios Kirykos (tel. 22750/22222); the main **hospital** is also located here (tel. 22753/50201). In some villages, like in Raches, you won't find these state systems. Some years ago, the residents of Raches got together and decided they didn't need a police force; they would self-police their own community. This won't have any particular impact on you as a tourist, unless you're inspired to go back to your own hometown and try a self-policing experiment.

GETTING THERE

If there's one island that would laud you for reducing your carbon footprint, it's Ikaria. Take the **boat;** it's a nice ride.

Ferry

There are two main ports in Ikaria, **Agios Kirykos** and **Evdilos**, with regular ferries throughout the year, and plenty of boats connecting Ikaria to both **Piraeus** and neighboring islands throughout the summer season.

Air

Ikaria has a small airport at its eastern tip, in the town of Faros. **Ikaria Island National Airport** (JIK; tel. 22750/32216); the island is serviced by **Aegean Air** (www.aegeanair.com), **Astra Airlines** (www.astra-airlines.gr), and **Olympic Air** (www.olympicair.com). There's a **bus** that goes from Agios Kyriykos to the airport (20 minutes; €2.60), stopping in Evdilos, Armenistis, and Christos Raches. If you don't want to wait, there are **taxis** waiting

Previous: The view of Dracano Archaeological Site; the stone church of Theoketistis Monastery; relax on Armenistis before going to grab a goat milk ice cream across the street.

outside when flights arrive (from the airport to Evdilos it costs €55, to Armenistis €60, and to Agios Kirkos €15).

GETTING AROUND

At 252 square km (97 square mi), Ikaria is a decently serviced island, but if you'd like to venture outside the bus circuit, you should rent a **car** or **motorcycle. Hitchhiking** is normal among locals; we picked up some people and had no problems. It's a cool way to meet people, but if you are easily creeped out by people, or are yourself very creepy, don't do it!

Car

There are several car rental places in Evdilos and Agios Kirykos and at the airport, but it's wise to reserve ahead during the summer rush. Try **Mav Cars** in Agios (tel. 22750/31036; mav-cars@hol.gr) or **Aventura** in Evdilos (tel. 697 228 4054; aventura@otenet.gr). Car rentals start from €35 in the high season.

Bus

The **main bus route** goes between Rahces, Armenistis, Evdilos, Agios Kirykos, Faros, and the airport (multiple times per day). There are additional **smaller routes** from Agios Kirykos to Therma and Faros, and another route from Agios Kirykos to Evdilos, Armenistis, and Raches. These are all the comprehensive stops on the island; to get anywhere else you will need a car.

Note that during weekends and holidays, hours can vary. For a more scenic journey, there's a daily **water taxi** (€3) from Agios Kirykos to Therma. Note that the bus changes yearly, so you'll have to check on site in the summer when you arrive.

Taxi

Taxis congregate outside the port and waterfront promenade but are rather expensive (at least €55 from Agios Kirykos to Evdilos). On www.island-ikaria.com you will find a comprehensive list of each taxi driver on the island, with their name and phone number.

Itinerary Ideas

This itinerary has you based in or around Evdilos. For both days, you'll want to have a car to have the flexibility to drive whenever you want.

DAY 1

1 After a relaxing breakfast in your hotel, strike out for the hippie paradise of Nas, 15.3 km (9.5 mi) west of Evdilos. Spend the morning relaxing on the beach and checking out the ruins of **Artemis Temple.**

2 For lunch, try any of the excellent seaside tavernas—though I'd suggest going for the freshly grilled fish at **Anna.**

3 Spend the afternoon sampling wines at **Afianes Winery** (call ahead for driving directions) and talking to the friendly owners about the importance wine has in Ikaria's social and cultural sphere.

4 Once it's dark, head to the nocturnal village of Christos Raches. Have dinner at the **Taverna Platanos** as late as you can possibly stand. Take the time to chat with a few locals and get a taste of what makes Ikaria so special.

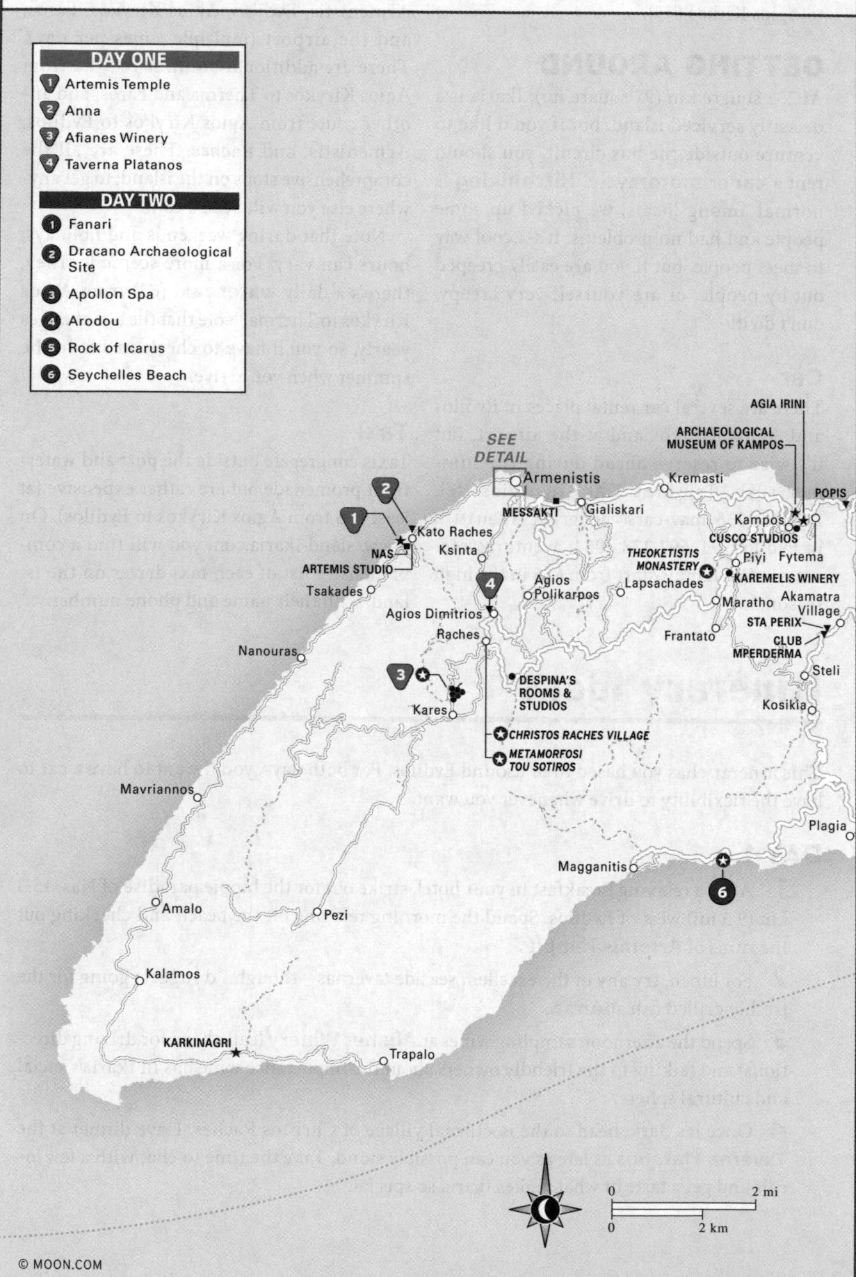
Ikaria
DAY ONE
1 Artemis Temple
2 Anna
3 Afianes Winery
4 Taverna Platanos
DAY TWO
1 Fanari
2 Dracano Archaeological Site
3 Apollon Spa
4 Arodou
5 Rock of Icarus
6 Seychelles Beach
SEE DETAIL
Armenistis
Kremasti
AGIA IRINI
ARCHAEOLOGICAL MUSEUM OF KAMPOS
POPIS
MESSAKTI
Gialiskari
Kampos
CUSCO STUDIOS
Fytema
Kato Raches
NAS
ARTEMIS STUDIO
Ksinta
THEOKETISTIS MONASTERY
Piyi
KAREMELIS WINERY
Tsakades
Agios Polikarpos
Lapsachades
Akamatra Village
Maratho
Agios Dimitrios
STA PERIX
CLUB MPERDERMA
Raches
Frantato
Nanouras
Steli
DESPINA'S ROOMS & STUDIOS
Kares
Kosikia
CHRISTOS RACHES VILLAGE
METAMORFOSI TOU SOTIROS
Mavriannos
Plagia
Magganitis
Amalo
Pezi
Kalamos
KARKINAGRI
Trapalo
0
2 mi
0
2 km
© MOON.COM

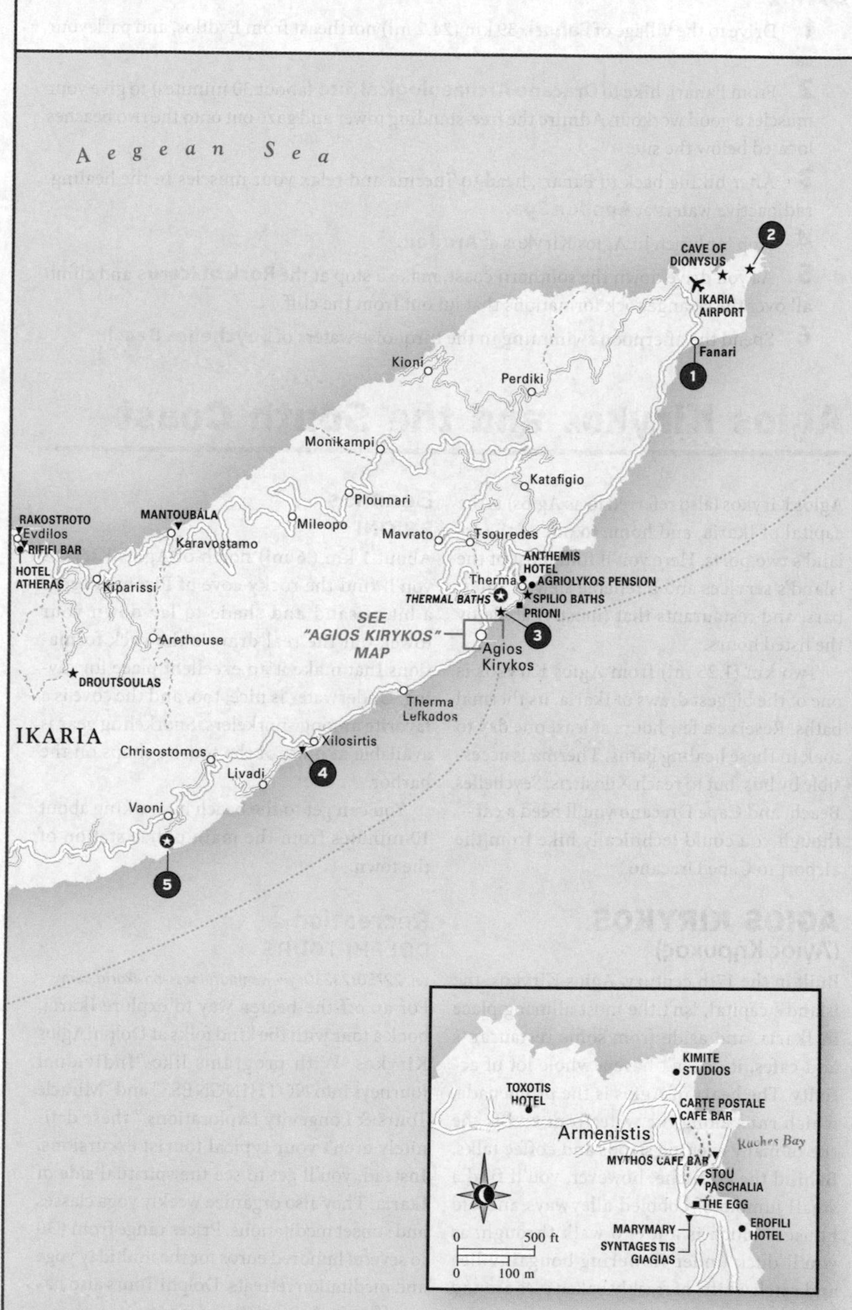
Aegean Sea
CAVE OF DIONYSUS
IKARIA AIRPORT
Fanari
Kioni
Perdiki
Monikampi
Katafigio
Ploumari
Mileopo
Mavrato
Tsouredes
RAKOSTROTO
Evdilos
RIFIFI BAR
HOTEL ATHERAS
MANTOUBÁLA
Karavostamo
Kiparissi
ANTHEMIS HOTEL
Therma
AGRIOLYKOS PENSION
THERMAL BATHS
SPILIO BATHS
PRIONI
SEE "AGIOS KIRYKOS" MAP
Agios Kirykos
Arethouse
DROUTSOULAS
Therma Lefkados
IKARIA
Xilosirtis
Chrisostomos
Livadi
Vaoni
1
2
3
4
5
KIMITE STUDIOS
TOXOTIS HOTEL
CARTE POSTALE CAFÉ BAR
Armenistis
Kaches Bay
MYTHOS CAFÉ BAR
STOU PASCHALIA
THE EGG
MARYMARY
SYNTAGES TIS GIAGIAS
EROFILI HOTEL
0
500 ft
0
100 m

DAY 2

1 Drive to the village of **Fanari,** 39 km (24.2 mi) northeast from Evdilos, and park your car.

2 From Fanari, hike to **Dracano Archaeological Site** (about 30 minutes) to give your muscles a good workout. Admire the free-standing tower and gaze out onto the two beaches located below the site.

3 After hiking back to Fanari, head to Therma and relax your muscles in the healing, radioactive waters at **Apollon Spa.**

4 Stop for lunch in Agios Kirykos at **Arodou.**

5 As you drive down the southern coast, make a stop at the **Rock of Icarus** and climb all over the strange rock formations that jut out from the cliff.

6 Spend the afternoon swimming in the turquoise waters of **Seychelles Beach.**

Agios Kirykos and the South Coast

Agios Kirykos (also referred to as Agios) is the capital of Ikaria, and home to one of the island's two ports. Here you'll find most of the island's services and a reliable slew of cafés, bars, and restaurants that (mostly) abide by the listed hours.

Two km (1.25 mi) from Agios Kirykos is one of the biggest draws of Ikaria, its thermal baths. Reserve a few hours at least one day to soak in these healing baths. Therma is accessible by bus, but to reach Xilositris, Seychelles Beach, and Cape Dracano you'll need a car—though you could technically hike from the airport to Cape Dracano.

AGIOS KIRYKOS (Άγιος Κήρυκος)

Built in the 17th century, Agios Kirykos, the island's capital, isn't the most alluring place in Ikaria, and aside from some restaurants and cafés, it doesn't have a whole lot of activity. The heart of Agios is the promenade, which runs along the waterfront and is the site of many evening strolls and coffee talks. Behind the corniche, however, you'll find a small jumble of cobbled alleyways and old houses, which is a joy to walk through, as you'll duck under flowering bougainvillea and catch whiffs of freshly baked pies around every other corner.

Beaches

PRIONI

About 1 km (.6 mi) north of Agios Kirykos you'll find the rocky cove of Pironi. There's a bit of sand and shade to lay down your towel, but the real draw is the rock formations that make it an excellent place for diving. Underwater is nice, too, and the cove is a favorite among snorkelers. Snorkeling gear is available at most of the tourist shops on the harbor.

You can get to the beach by walking about 10 minutes from the main police station of the town.

Recreation

DOLPHI TOURS

tel. 22750/23230; www.mindfulness-on-ikaria.com

For an off-the-beaten way to explore Ikaria, book a tour with the kind folks at DolphiAgios Kirykos. With programs like "Individual Journeys into NOTHINGNESS" and "Miracle Tours & Longevity Explorations," these definitely aren't your typical tourist excursions. Instead, you'll get to see the spiritual side of Ikaria. They also organize weekly yoga classes and sunset meditations. Prices range from €30 to several hundred euros for the multiday yoga and meditation retreats. Dolphi Tours also has an office in Armenistis.

Agios Kirykos

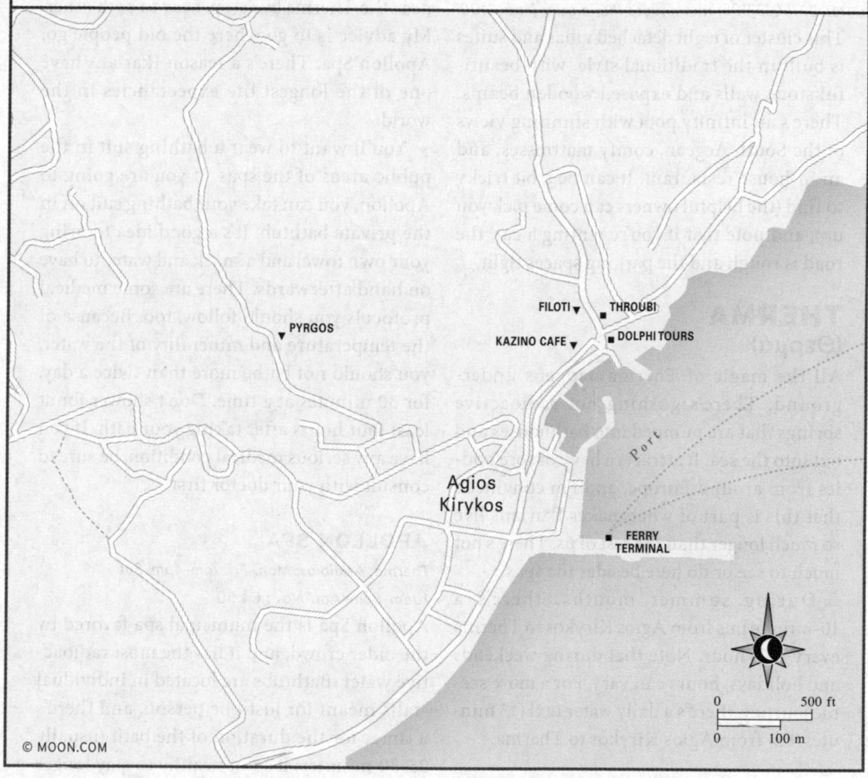

Shopping

THROUBI

tel. 22750/22383; www.throubi.gr; Mon.-Sat. 9am-3pm and 6pm-9pm

Located a few meters off the main promenade, Throubi is a sort of upscale grocery store that offers a good selection of Ikarian products, including herbs, preserves, and cosmetics. You can try most things before you buy them; make sure to stock up on the creamy local honey.

Food

KAZINO CAFÉ

tel. 22750/23290; 8am-midnight; from €2

Of the several cafés that line the waterfront promenade, Kazino Café, housed in a large 1850s building, is perhaps the most atmospheric. It's a good place for people watching and coffee sipping, either of which should be accompanied by one of their excellent sweets (especially the rice pudding). There are savory snacks on offer as well.

FILOTI

tel. 22750/23088; lunch and dinner; from €5

This pizza parlor has become something of an institution in Ikaria, with people coming from all over the island to grab a slice. They're done in the Greek style, which means a thicker crust than the Italian version, and a sweeter sauce. If that's not in your taste, there's also pasta, salads, and grilled meats. Prices are low and portions are generous.

Accommodations

PYRGOS

tel. 22750/22105; www.pyrgos-ikaria.com; from €100

This cluster of eight detached villas and suites is built in the traditional style, with beautiful stone walls and exposed wooden beams. There's an infinity pool with stunning views of the South Aegean, comfy mattresses, and an in-house restaurant. It can be a bit tricky to find (the helpful owners can come pick you up), and note that if you're renting a car, the road is rough and the parking spaces tight.

THERMA (Θερμά)

All the magic of Therma happens underground: There's gushing hot radioactive springs that are pumped into bathhouses and out into the sea. It attracts a bevy of sore bodies from around Europe, and I'm convinced that this is part of what makes Ikarians live so much longer than the rest of us. There's not much to see or do here besides the spas.

During summer months, there's a 10-minute bus from Agios Kirykos to Therma every half hour. Note that during weekends and holidays, hours can vary. For a more scenic journey, there's a daily water taxi (15 minutes; €3) from Agios Kirykos to Therma.

★ Thermal Baths

Ikaria's thermal waters, some of the most radioactive in the world, are so renowned that Greek doctors prescribe specific hours in the water to treat their patients' aches and injuries. I was admittedly skeptical, but after a half-hour soak, my husband's knee, which was stuck at an awkward angle and painful after days of continuous driving, was somehow cured. "Unbelievable!" he shouted as we left, ecstatically flexing his leg.

There are three main "spas" within Therma, though as of summer 2019, one was undergoing extensive renovation. All three are very bare-bones and void of decoration, but aesthetics are beside the point: people come from across Europe to stay in Therma and just visit the baths every day. Many Greeks come to Ikaria specifically to experience the thermal waters, too. All three spas are located near the Therma bus stop, near to each other. My advice is to go where the old people go: Apollon Spa. There's a reason Ikarians have one of the longest life expectancies in the world.

You'll want to wear a bathing suit in the public areas of the spas. If you are going to Apollon, you can take your bathing suit off in the private bathtub. It's a good idea to bring your own towel and a snack and water to have on hand afterwards. There are some medical protocols you should follow, too. Because of the temperature and minerality of the water, you should not bathe more than twice a day, for 30 minutes at a time. Don't shower for at least four hours after taking your bath. If you have any serious medical condition, be sure to consult with your doctor first.

APOLLON SPA

Therma, Asklipios; Mon.-Fri. 7am-4pm, Sat. 10am-6pm, Apr.-Nov.; €4.50

Apollon Spa is the municipal spa favored by the older crowd, and it has the most radioactive water. Bathtubs are located in individual stalls meant for just one person, and there's a timer for the duration of the bath (usually 25-30 minutes; it's not healthy to stay longer in one sitting).

SPILIO BATHS

Therma, Asllipios; tel. 22750/24048; daily 8am-5pm; €3.50

Spilio is the "coolest" of Ikaria's thermal baths. It's built inside a cave and has a hammam and jacuzzi, but it's quite small and can get crowded. Spilo is preferred by young people but has the least healing water.

Accommodations

ANTHEMIS HOTEL

Epar.Od. Ditikon, Therma; tel. 698 145 7304; www.anthemishotelikaria.com; from €25

1: the harbor of Agios Kirykos village on Ikaria island in Greece **2:** Therma village

1
2

This no-frills two-star hotel is one of the best deals in Therma. You get what you pay for: furnishings are straight out of the 1970s, as are the electronics, but there's Wi-Fi and a surprisingly vast breakfast buffet. The owners are especially kind without being overbearing, though their English is limited. This is a style of hotel favored by Greeks coming to Ikaria to take advantage of the waters.

AGRIOLYKOS PENSION

Therma; tel. 22750/22433; www.agriolykos.gr; May-Oct.; from €70

Built onto a cliff with stunning views, Agriolykos Pension is a good base if you're in Ikaria to visit the hot springs. The rooms are very basically furnished, and the TVs are anything but modern, but the vibe is friendly and open, and breakfast is served daily in the charming garden. They organize a lot of events during the season (yoga workshops, meetings, exhibits, etc.), which has its pros and cons: lots of interesting people to meet, but not always the most peaceful place.

XILOSIRTIS (Ξυλοσυρτης)

The small village of Xilosirtis, located 5 km (3 mi) west of Agios Kirykos, is a lush, seaside town. The village's main attractions are a blue domed church and a hot spring. It's nice to stop in the village if you're driving to the Rock of Icarus and want to stretch your legs, but neither warrants going out of the way. Not far from Xilosirtis, you'll also find the Rock of Icarus, supposedly the point where Icarus fell into the sea according to Greek mythology.

Sights

★ ROCK OF ICARUS

The story of Icarus is well known: the golden boy who believed himself stronger than the gods and flew too close to the sun, which melted his wax wings and sent him plunging to a watery death in the sea. You can actually visit his grave, in a manner of speaking. As you veer off the Agios Kirykos-Magganitis road at the village of Vaoni, to start driving down towards the rock, you'll find a landscape full of strange rock formations and giant slabs of marble that drop straight into the sea. There's an amphitheater and a small stone monument facing the sea, and in the distance, the rock of Icarus rises dramatically out of the sea. It's a fantastic area to explore: The rocks have little pools and steps and arches, all carved out by years of relentless sea waves. Note that there are no protective barriers, so be careful if you're with kids.

The Rock of Icarus is located 14 km (8.75 mi) west of Agios Kirykos and 7 km (4.3 miles) west of Xilosirtis.

Food

ARODOU

Agios Kirykostel; tel. 22750/22700; lunch and dinner; from €6

This family-owned restaurant is run by matriarch Eleftheria, who speaks minimal English but dutifully churns out mouth-watering Greek taverna classics, including house specialities *pitarkia* (small cheese pies) and *kolokythokeftedes* (fried zucchini balls). Be sure to sit in the courtyard, which is shaded by trees and offers stunning views of the nearby islands of Patmos and Samos.

★ SEYCHELLES BEACH (Σευχελλες)

On an island not known for its beaches, the aptly named Seychelles stands out as a unique tropical paradise. Around 30 years ago, a landslide revealed this pebbled cove. It's not a secret anymore, and there's not a lot of space to pitch umbrellas and lay out towels, so head there early in the day in July and August.

It's easiest to access Seychelles beach from Agios Kirykos, as the roads west of the beach are either rough or nonexistent. From Agios Kirykos, follow the route west to Magganitis for 25 km (15.5 mi) until you reach a tunnel. Right after the tunnel you'll notice a hand-painted sign (directly on the road) for Seychelles. There's a car park to your left; you'll have to foot the rest of the 300-meter

TOP EXPERIENCE

Time in Ikaria

When our boat arrived in Ikaria on a chilly October morning, a few hours after midnight, we were too excited to fall asleep. We drove for a bit through the mountain villages above Evdilos, and were shocked to find, at 2am, a car mechanic fully open, the owner tinkering away on a motorcycle under fluorescent lights. The next morning, at the much more reasonable working hour of 11am, the mechanic was completely closed. So was the village *kafeneio,* where we were hoping to get a coffee. "He got too drunk last night and is still sleeping," explained a woman sweeping her porch.

Time in Ikaria is seemingly presented as a philosophical concept: What is it, *really?* Why does it matter? A brief explanation:

HISTORY

Pirates lived on the nearby island of Fourni, and Ikaria tried to pass itself off as an uninhabited island in order to skirt invasions. One of the most successful ways to do this was to suspend daytime activity and do everything under cover of dark. To this day, a lot of Ikarians, particularly in the interior and west of the island, still observe nocturnal behaviors that partly stem from this era.

WHAT IT MEANS FOR VISITORS

Don't be surprised to find businesses that operate at night and close during "regular" daytime business hours. Listed opening hours are meant to be taken with a grain of salt. Don't expect prompt service, either: My Greek father-in-law has a story about sitting at a café in Ikaria one morning, waiting for a coffee. It took three hours to arrive.

On Ikaria, life is not a race that should be governed by materialism and the ticking clock of capitalism: it's meant to be lived slowly, and savored. I personally fell in love with this way of thinking about time, and was never bothered by slow service or quirky hours. The trick is not to take it personally! If you start getting antsy, just take a deep breath and remember: Time is just a social construct, and we are all but tiny flecks of matter on a blue water balloon hurtling through the universe.

You can get a feel for Ikaria time anywhere on the island (maybe less so in Agios Kirykos), but the best place to release yourself from the bounds of time is **Chirstos Raches Village** on the western end of the island.

(984-mi) walk down. Note that it's quite slippery and uneven, and you'll have to slide down a rock to get to the beach at the end. It's unorganized, so bring your own drinks and snacks.

CAPE DRACANO AND VICINITY

The very eastern tip of Ikaria is not a widely visited area, aside from those leaving and entering the island by plane. However, behind the airport you'll find a couple of sights and beaches worth visiting.

Fanari (Φανάρι)

In the little town of Fanari (10 km/6 mi northeast of Agios Kirykos) you can purchase some snacks and coffee. The roads on this part of the island are unpaved, full of potholes, and generally tricky to navigate unless you've got a 4x4. If you don't mind walking, I suggest leaving your car in Fanari to walk to the Dracano Archaeological site; you can double back to pick it up and drive to the Cave of Dionysus.

Dracano Archaeological Site

9am-3pm in summer; free

This beautiful old fortress (which is partially

preserved, and partially in ruins), was open for business as of summer 2018, though you should check the municipality website to make sure it's open when you're visiting. The main attraction is a free-standing tower, which was built during the time of Alexander the Great. Dracano is built on a cliff, and looks out onto two lovely beaches (Paraligia Gymiston, a nudist beach, and Agios Giorgos).

Dracano is located 2.5 km (1.5 mi) north of Fanari. The road to Dracano is unpaved; I drove it anyway, and you can too if you exercise extreme caution. You can also hike from Fanari village (about 30 minutes).

Cave of Dionysus

To reach the Cave of Dionysus, drive behind the airport, past the military camp, and continue till you reach a small beach called Iero. You can park at the beach. To the right of the beach you can hike up some rocks before you reach a big cave that, according to local legend, was the place of nurture and worship of the god Dionysus. It's a bit underwhelming, to be honest, though it still has an interesting, slightly spooky energy. If you're either going to or coming from the Dracano ruins, there's a well-indicated walking path that you can follow. It's no more than 400 meters (1,312 feet) from the beach up to the cave.

Evdilos and Around

Evdilos is a fairly new settlement. It was built in 1830, after piracy was eradicated from the island, and became the temporary capital during the second Turkish occupation, from 1834 to 1912. Evdilos means "eye-catching" in Greek, and this second port city is certainly a charming one, full of old houses, small cafés, fishing boats bobbing in the harbor, and winding streets. It's a convenient and central base for exploring the island. There's not a whole lot to keep you here, though, and your time is better spent exploring the nearby villages and beaches. Kampos, Theoketistis Monastery, Piyi, Karavostamo, and Akamatra are not accessible by bus.

EVDILOS (Ευδηλος)

Evdilos is 41 km (25 mi) from Agios Kirykos; it's a wonderful drive along the sea and through the mountainous interior on well-paved roads. There are daily buses from Agios Kirykos as well.

Beaches

One kilometer (.6 mi) west of Evdilos is the seaside village of **Fytema.** There's a beach in the village; it's not worth going out of your way for, but if you want a dip before lunch, it's fine. The sand is coarse and the water can be a bit rough.

Nightlife and Entertainment

RIFIFI BAR

Evdilos; tel. 22750/33060; daily, all day

Located right on the port—perfect for people watching—Rififi is a classic harbor café that easily makes the transition from day (good coffee) to night (draught beer and plenty of snacks).

Food

RAKOSTROTO

Evdilos; tel. 22750/32266; May-Oct. daily 8am-5am; from €10

Located in the center of Evdilos, this taverna serves up island classics with Ikarian hospitality. All veggies and herbs are sourced locally, the seafood is fresh, and the French fries are hand cut. This is a good choice for families, and there are plenty of vegetarian options, too.

POPIS

Fytema; tel. 22750/31928; May-Oct. daily 11am-late; from €7

Popis is Ikaria, distilled to its essence: good

taverna food, a leftist owner (that would be Popi), a well-shaded terrace with an ocean view, plus curiously (sometimes frustratingly) slow service. Don't come here rushed, but do come to enjoy their various pies and grilled seafood. Popis is located on the main coastal road in the seaside village of Fytema, 1 km (.6 mi) west of Evdilos.

Accommodations

HOTEL ATHERAS

tel. 22750/31434; www.atherashotel.gr; from €45

The most popular of budget hotels in Evdilos. This casual spot is just a four-minute walk from the beach. There's a pool and hot tub, and rooms are clean and basic, albeit with somewhat strange decor choices. Most of the rooms have private balconies that look out onto the pools.

KAMPOS (Κάμπος)

Two km (1.25 mi) east of Evdilos is the ancient town of Kampos, which used to be the Ikarian capital back when it was called Oinoe, a reference to the town's winegrowing, which was revered throughout the ancient world due to the wine's particularly strong alcohol content. Today Kampos is more of a sleepy hamlet, but an incredibly lush and green one, with a few interesting sights.

Sights

The small **Archaeological Museum of Kampos** (tel. 22750/31300; Tues.-Sun. 8:30am-3pm; €2) has a nice collection of artifacts from the Oinoe archaeological dig. Next door you'll find the twelfth-century church **Agia Irini** (free); walk a bit farther and you'll find the ruins of an abandoned **Byzantine palace.**

Accommodations

★ CUSCO STUDIOS

tel. 22750/31381; www.ikariautopia.com; Apr.-Nov.; from €50, breakfast additional €5

This small, family-run set of studios is unbelievably peaceful, with spacious rooms with private terraces that overlook the wooded hills and the sea. Guests receive a bottle of house wine upon arrival, and the service is top-notch Icarian hospitality, but the real draw is the artistic component: There's a small gallery downstairs featuring work from both local and foreign artists, and at the time of writing the owners had plans to set up artist residencies and art symposiums.

★ THEOKETISTIS MONASTERY

no official hours, always open

This remarkable medieval monastery 4 km (2.5 mi) west of Kampos features a main church with wonderfully preserved frescoes dating back to 1688. However, most fascinating are the small churches and buildings on the grounds that are built into hanging rocks and cracked slabs of granite, forcing you to stoop and twist and gasp in awe as you work your way around the monastery. Theoketistis means "covered by God," and the monastery was designed as much for worshipping God as for hiding from the pirates who used to regularly attack Ikaria. These days there are no pirates—only the charming Mrs. Maria (no English), who keeps the grounds scrupulously clean, pours fresh oil into the church candles, and sells homemade pastas and preserves.

PIYI (Πηγή)

Accommodations

★ KAREMELIS WINERY

tel. 22750/31151; www.ikarianwine.gr; May-Sept.; from €70

This wonderfully atmospheric *agriturismo* (farm accommodation) in Piyi, 5 km (3 mi) southwest of Evdilos, is a family-run winery and restaurant, where, if you book far enough in advance, you'll be lucky enough to stay in one of the charmingly restored stone houses. This is ideal Ikarian living at its best: a sun-dappled terrace, lovely owners, and food so delicious and local that even a piece of bread and an olive will make you feel warm inside. The owners organize small excursions for the guests, as well as airport pickup and transfers, and meals (breakfast is already included). If you can't stay there, you can email or call to try to schedule a cooking course with dinner (€60).

KARAVOSTAMO (Καραβόσταμο)

The cute seaside village of Karavostamo, 8 km (5 mi) east of Evidilos, is pretty far off the tourist radar, despite being located on the beach. The village is divided into two parts: the upper part, with stupendous views of the sea, and the lower part along the harbor, which is nice for a walk. It's a good stopover on the hour-long drive between Agios Kirykos and Evdilos.

Food

MANDOUVALA

tel. 22750/61204; May-Oct. daily noon-late; €10

For those who insist on seaside dining while in Greece (you're not wrong!), head to Mandouvala, a beloved taverna perched on a beachside rock. They have a wide variety of fresh seafood and fish, as well as good vegetarian options and mezes.

AKAMATRA VILLAGE (Ακαμάτρα)

Akamatra, 4 km (2.5 mi) south of Evdilos, is so cute it looks like the sort of Disney village where the animals can talk and braid human hair. There are hand-painted wooden signs, charmingly constructed whitewashed homes, a cobblestone main square shaded by giant oak trees, a tiny church...There's a traditional *kafeneio* on the town square, a bakery located on the main road up to the square, and a well-marked walking path (3.15 km/2 mi) that will take you to the nearby village of Droutsoulas.

Hiking

AKAMATRA VILLAGE TO DROUTSOULAS

Distance: *3.15 km (2 mi) one way*
Duration: *1 hour*
Effort level: *moderate*

This is a nice hike that starts in Akamatra village; you'll first pass the Alama cave before heading down into the valley. There, you'll pass through the old village of Kseredon, continuing your walk toward the village of Droutsoulas. There's not much to see of the village, but it's a popular spot with climbers who climb the sheet-like rocks. Keep your eyes open for three watermills that you'll pass along the way. Be sure to wear sturdy shoes and carry water.

Nightlife and Entertainment

CLUB MPERDERMA

7pm-late

First, a pronunciation lesson: together the Greek "M" and "P" are pronounced as "B." This hippie bar is less club and more bar with live music acts during the summer, but it's a fun place to hang out where a lot of locals congregate, and the smell of weed often lingers in the air.

Food

STA PERIX

tel. 22750/31056; lunch and dinner; from €3

This lively restaurant is usually packed with locals and tourists, and dutifully serves up both traditional taverna fare and loads of mezes, all of which is best accompanied by a bottle (or two, or three) of *tsipuro* (a strong distilled alcohol). The atmosphere is very laid-back and friendly, and it's a great place to strike up a conversation with your dining neighbors. It also has a great sunset view.

1: the interior of the church of Theoketistis Monastery **2:** Wine production dates back to ancient times on Ikaria. **3:** the stone church of Theoketistis Monastery

Raches and the West End

The western part of Ikaria encompasses some of the best aspects of the island. The mountainous villages, of which Christos Raches is the crowning jewel, have preserved the daily traditions of Ikarian life and host some of the wildest *panigiri;* the mild Cycladic-like weather has created fun beach resorts like Armenistis and its hippie cousin Nas; and the fertile ground hosts some of the island's best wineries and tavernas.

ARMENISTIS (Αρμενιστής)

The little harbor town of Armenistis, 12 km (7.5 mi) west of Evdilos, is the closest thing you'll find to a beach resort in Ikaria, though in the wintertime it quickly converts back into a small, sleepy seaside settlement with around 70 full-time inhabitants. There are two, long sandy beaches, both of which are lined with cafés and tavernas. There are a couple of decent bars here as well, but it remains more of a family-friendly location than anything else.

Daily buses from Agios Kirykos to Christos Raches also stop in Armenistis.

Beaches

MESSAKTI (Μεσσάκτι)

Ikaria's most popular beach, located 1.8 km (1 mi) east of Armenistis, also becomes one of its busiest in July and August. This is a long, sandy coast with clear turquoise waters, and two rivers intersect the beach, creating some freshwater pools. It's an organized beach (umbrellas, bars) with a lot going on: surfing, kayaking, volleyball tournaments, and stand-up paddleboarding. There's a lifeguard present during the summer, and the shallow waters make it ideal for families.

Yoga

THE EGG

www.the-egg-greece.com; May-Aug.

This breezy, wood-beamed retreat center looks like something out of Bali, and so do the classes and workshops they offer, which include yoga, dance, and meditation. The Egg is available to rent (for events, parties, or private workshops), or you can check their website to drop in on some yoga classes, schedule a Thai massage, or learn the traditional local dance. It's located between Evdilos and Armenistis (5 km/3 mi east of Armenistis).

Nightlife and Entertainment

CARTE POSTALE CAFÉ BAR

tel. 22750/71031; all day

Come here for refreshing jolts of caffeine during the daylight hours, and switch to wine or beer after the sun goes down. They organize live music events and parties during the summer, and the terrace offers lovely views of the sea. There are always a couple of groovy people hanging out here, and the blissful lack of wi-fi means it's even easier to strike up conversations with strangers. Carte Postale is located 50 meters north of the church.

MYTHOS CAFE BAR

tel. 22750/71086; 7pm-late

This is as close to a cocktail bar as you'll find in Ikaria, with excellent service, good, stiff drinks, and an energy that turns increasingly rambunctious as the night goes on. Grab a spot on the terrace.

Food

MARYMARY

tel. 22750/71595; lunch and dinner; from €10

This seaside taverna is one of the favorites in Armenistis. It's a mix of freshly grilled seafood, burgers and pasta, and slightly upscale taverna classics. Most things are, in that frustrating hipster fashion, served on pieces of

Scenic Drives on the West End

The west side of Ikaria is perhaps the most remote part of an already remote island—the scenery becomes more rugged, and here you'll find some of the island's most interesting villages. Note that you'll need to exercise caution as you drive here. The road is very twisty, and you'll constantly be swiveling your head to drink in the fantastic landscape.

MOUNTAIN VILLAGES

It's worth renting a car to explore the route from Armenistis into the mountain villages of **Prophet Illias** and **Raches.** The mountainous part of Ikaria is really the heartbeat of the island, and it's a joy to drive through the scented pine forests and come across little stone villages and roadside bakeries with each twist of the road.

COASTAL ROUTE

After **Nas,** the road to **Nanouras** (5.5 km/3.4 mi) is a bit complicated, as it's winding and only partly paved but generally okay to drive. It becomes a paved road again until you reach Karkinagri (18 km/11 mi after Nanouras). This side of the island is wild and generally little visited by tourists, but the drive, through strange rock formations and stunning views of the sea, is very much worth it. Count at least an hour and a half for the whole drive from Nas to Karkinagri. There's a little lighthouse at **Cape Papas,** and then the world seemingly ends at **Karkinagri,** a tiny seaside village seemingly only populated by octogenarians. Note that the road ends at Kargkinagri: From Kargkinagri to Manganitis there is no road.

slate, but the service is reliable and the terrace is breezy and lovely.

STOU PASCHALIA

tel. 22750/71302; lunch and dinner; from €6

Visit Stou Paschalia as much for its decor, in a large, neoclassical-style Ikarian house, as for the food, which includes organic produce exclusively sourced from the family farm, generously bathed in olive oil and freshly cooked. You'll enjoy classic taverna flavors, perfectly executed.

SYNTAGES TIS GIAGIAS

tel. 22750/71150; lunch and dinner; from €2

It's not summer without (multiple helpings of) ice cream, and this local sweet shop, on the second floor of the town's main shopping "complex," has the best flavors. They excel at making goat's milk products (ice cream, custard pie, pudding), and have a tempting lineup of other Greek sweets. You can also bring home some jars of jams and spoon sweets (fruits and vegetables caramelized in simple syrup).

Accommodations

KIMITE STUDIOS

tel. 22750/71545; www.ikariarooms.gr; €60

These six small but modern studios are perfect for couples or families. Most rooms sleep up to four, but some accommodate up to six, and all offer views of the sea. The helpful staff can assist in organizing trips or excursions.

EROFILI HOTEL

tel. 22750/71058; www.erofili.gr; from €90

This is a decent mid-range, mid-sized option located on Amnensitis' main street, with a pool and well-appointed rooms. The views of the beach are lovely, and the real draw is the close proximity to the sea.

TOXOTIS HOTEL

tel. 22750/71570; www.toxotis-ikaria.gr; from €165

Toxotis is probably the smartest hotel in Ikaria. A series of autonomous villas with large verandas, a fireplace you'll hardly have use for, an infinity pool, and seriously comfortable bedding all make for a luxurious place to relax. There are seven villas sprawled out across the grounds.

★ CHRISTOS RACHES VILLAGE

(Χρήστος Ράχες)

Dubbed "the village that never sleeps," Christos Raches is the quintessential Ikarian village. There's a collection of beautiful stone houses nestled around a main square (host to some of the island's most raucous parties, the largest is on August 6), and a couple of nice shops and restaurants with, of course, the quirky hours. Nothing is open before 10am except for the school, post office, and local bakery (after 11am the baker leaves and an honor-system is used to buy loaves of bread). Everything closes during the afternoon for the daily siesta, and the village starts to come alive at night, which is also the best time to visit. There aren't any touristic sights in the traditional sense, but this is the place to come to experience the slowness of Ikarian life. True, it's become more of a tourist hotspot in recent years (especially during July and August) but it's still worth it to come here after the sun has set to walk around the boisterous streets, knock back a drink or two, and strike up a conversation with some friendly locals.

Christos Raches is located 6 km (3.75 mi) south of Armenistis. There are daily buses from Agios Kirykos to Christos Raches (via Evdilos and Armenistis).

Festivals and Events

★ METAMORFOSI TOU SOTIROS

August 6

This is probably the biggest *panigiri* that happens in Raches. The name translates to "Transfiguration of the Savior," and it's a celebration for Jesus Christ. Thousands of revelers fill the main square in Raches, dancing, drinking, and singing in honor of the feast day. The crowds are a bit relentless, but the overall vibe is jovial and inviting. It's best to contribute some money (around €10 per person) to join in the eating and drinking.

Shopping

WOMEN'S COOPERATIVE

tel. 22750/41076; www.tasteikaria.com; hours vary

Founded in 2009, the Women's Co-op original goal was to promote sustainable agriculture, maintain traditional Ikarian recipes, and work with women from around the island. They've done well: This cute shop sells great sweets, liquors, herbs, jams, and preserves; they also have a daily selection of fresh pies.

Food

COUSINA

tel. 22750/41374; lunch and dinner; from €6

Run by two cousins (both trained in France and Italy) and located just off the main square, CousinA is traditional taverna food, with the creativity dialed up. Ingredients are fresh and hyper-local (the cheese comes from their uncle's farm). Standouts include the pasta, eggplant salad, and tomato salad.

TAVERNA PLATANOS

tel. 22750/41374; 5pm-4am; from €10

Unmissable, thanks to its prime location under the blooming *platanos* tree (500 meters/1,650 feet from the center of town), this taverna serves up delicious Ikarian classics with a gourmet twist: think Greek spring rolls and beef stewed in wine sauce. Here you'll find good house wine, copious portions, and kind owners.

Accommodations

DESPINA'S ROOMS & STUDIOS

tel. 22750/41100; www.ikariarooms.net; from €60

Nestled in the hills bordering the village of Raches, the small-sized Despina's is a collection of simply furnished rooms and studios decorated in a traditional Ikarian style. The floors are tiled, the furniture is wood, and every room features air-conditioning, heating, and a private bathroom. In the morning, throw open the windows in to find yourself awash in a field of green.

Blue Zones

At one seaside restaurant on Ikaria, my husband and I were the only diners in attendance under the age of 80. "How old are you?" we curiously asked two friends sitting next to us, who were busy eating pieces of cheese and regularly topping up each others' wine (that they were drinking out of large water glasses). "Don't tell them!" shouted the older of the two (91). His friend excitedly responded, "What! You should be proud to tell your age! I'm 89! I've had a good life … I've traveled, I've had many women, and when I go, I'll go! I'm ready!"

In 2005, National Geographic fellow Dan Buettner coined the term "blue zones" to refer to places where people live much longer than average. Of the five places he identified, Ikaria has the highest concentration of nonagenarians (one out of three people lives to be over 90), almost no cases of dementia, 20 percent lower rates of cancer, and 50 percent lower rates of heart disease than mainland Greece. This is attributed to a combination of factors, including a healthy well-rounded diet rich in local products and accompanied by plenty of wine, lots of regular exercise outside, and incredibly strong social relationships. Plus, no one is really stressed out about time.

★ AFIANES WINERY

Pr. Hlias Rahon; tel. 22750/40008; www,afianeswines.gr; noon-10pm Thurs.-Tues.

A visit to the island of Dionysus would be terribly incomplete without a stop at Afianes, a delightful family-run winery that offers tastings and tours, and has a small museum that showcases the history of Ikarian wine. Oenophiles will appreciate the detailed tours and interesting facts (did you know that in 300 BC, wine was mainly used as medicine?) and will fall in love with the winery's natural, sulfite-free wines. There are two varieties that are indigenous to Ikaria that must be sampled—the dry red, especially.

The winery is located 3.2 km (2 mi) south of Raches. While there are signs pointing the way, it's easy enough to get lost (I did!). It's best to call ahead for directions, as the road is a bit complicated.

NAS
(Νας)

Three km (1.85 mi) west of Armenistis you'll come across the hippie beach enclave of Nas. It used to be a totally free-spirit, nudist paradise, and while it's become somewhat commercialized, it's still one of the cooler places on the island. Nas is well-known for the ruins of an ancient temple dedicated to the goddess Artemis, and a small river that runs through the bay, creating a beautiful and strange landscape. It's particularly magical around dusk. There are no buses to Nas, so you'll need a car.

Sights

ARTEMIS TEMPLE

always open; free

As you're facing the beach, you'll notice the ruins of an old temple on your left-hand side. In the 6th century BC, Ikarians built this temple to the goddess Artemis, patroness of sailors and protector of hunters and wild animals. It's believed that Nas was the first settled area in Ikaria, and this little cove acted as a port. The temple is now in tatters, but it lends a fantastic atmosphere to the beach.

Beaches

NAS
(Νας)

If you continue straight past the restaurants in Nas, you'll get to this beautiful little sandy cove beach. There's enough room for a good dozen or so people to lay down their towels (though more crowd in here during the summer). Behind the beach you can walk back into the valley—about 200 meters in, as you follow the river Chalares, where you'll come across a waterfall and natural pool—though be warned, it's quite rocky and there isn't a well-marked path.

Food

These three tavernas are all of equal standing, and are located in a row next to each other right near Nas beach. They're all family-run, with a focus on fresh and local ingredients, and should you find yourself spending several evenings in Nas, it's worth it to try all three and find your own favorite. Broadly speaking, visit **Anna** for fish (tel. 693 214 9155; lunch and dinner; from €8), **Thea** for meat dishes (tel. 22750/71491; lunch and dinner; from €5), and **Naides** for vegetarian options (tel. 22750/71488; lunch and dinner; from €6).

Accommodations

There's nothing fancy in Nas, but there are several cheap rooms to rent that are ideal if you're planning on spending most of your time at the beach.

ARTEMIS STUDIO

Nas Village; tel. 22750/71485; from €40

These clean, simple rooms are facing out onto the beach—all the better to catch the sunset—and the small hotel features a plant-filled terrace and an on-site restaurant. You're right next to the beach, and the quality of the food is quite high. What more could you want?

Lesvos (Λέσβος)

Greece's third-largest island, Lesvos (pop. 87,000), has been a longtime favorite with the LGBTQ community. Sappho, the archaic lesbian poet, was born here, and western Lesvos in particular caters to LGBTQ visitors. Lesvos offers something for everyone: There are sandy beaches, beautiful old villages, therapeutic hot springs that boast some of the warmest mineral water in Europe, a stunning petrified forest, wetlands, and excellent bird-watching. One of the main attractions lies in the island's agricultural history: 11 million olive trees cover the island in a thick blanket, and 50 percent of the world's ouzo is produced here.

Lesvos is one of the most far-flung Greek islands, and is much closer to Turkey than it is to the Greek mainland. This has had an impact

Highlights

Look for ★ to find recommended sights, activities, dining, and lodging.

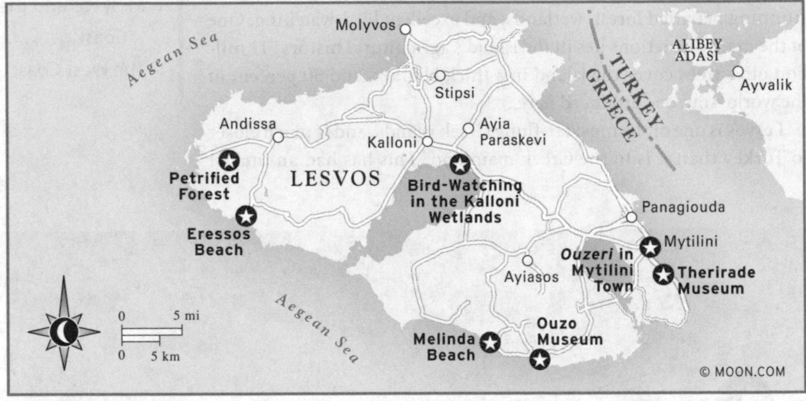

★ ***Ouzeri* in Mytilini Town:** At least one meal should be eaten (er, drunk) in an *ouzeri,* where seafood-based meze accompany little ice-cold bottles of ouzo (page 303).

★ **Therirade Museum:** Peruse a surprising collection of some of Europe's most impressive modernist painters—including Miro, Picasso, Matisse, and Le Corbusier—in a tiny Lesbian mansion (page 307).

★ **Ouzo Museum:** Educate yourself on ouzo in Plomari, a tiny town that's the epicenter for the liqueur. Ouzo is so much more than a drink in Lesvos—it's a way of life (page 310).

★ **Melinda Beach:** Bliss out at my personal favorite beach in Lesvos, where the only reason to leave your towel is to snack on grilled calamari at the excellent seaside taverna (page 312).

★ **Bird-Watching in the Kalloni Wetlands:** Hundreds of species of birds pass through Lesvos each year, and the protected Kalloni Wetlands is the best place to see scores of birds fly overhead as they migrate north or south (page 317).

★ **Eressos Beach:** The main beach of the alternative, bohemian town of Skala Eressos faces west, offering an unbeatable sunset view (page 319).

★ **Petrified Forest:** A geographical wonder, the Petrified Forest is one of the biggest in the world, and features fossilized trees and animals (page 320).

on the island's history (it was occupied by the Ottomans) and the current political crisis. In the past years, Lesvos has become ground zero for refugees fleeing war, political persecution, and economic desperation in their home countries. Although migration has slowed following the controversial 2016 EU-Turkey deal to allow deportations from the islands back to Turkey, there are still thousands of refugees trapped at Moira refugee camp in eastern Lesvos. The horrors most of the migrants have experienced is unimaginable, and most of the islanders responded with an intense humanity. It's always good to exercise kindness, but in Lesvos, even more so.

PLANNING YOUR TIME

Lesvos is not just a tourist island. People live here year-round, and there's a vibrant student population as well as a strong agricultural industry. So, most facilities are open **year-round.** In the winter, many of the beach tavernas and bars are closed, but everything in the towns will be open.

You'll want to spend at least four days on Lesvos: two in the southern end around **Mytilini,** and two more in the north and northwest near **Skala Eressos.** If you're coming for bird-watching or hiking—or if you're just a big fan of lounging on the beach—you could easily spend more, and most people do. I once accidentally spent a month and a half on Lesvos. It was supposed to be a week-long trip!

INFORMATION AND SERVICES

The municipal **tourist office** is located near Gate B at the port in Mytilini (tel. 22510/43255; Mon-Sat 9am-3pm) and can help with maps, brochures, etc. There are several travel agencies on the quay that can help with excursions, rentals, and day trips to Turkey. Try **Mitilene Tours** (Kountourioti 87; tel. 22510/54261; www.mitilenetours.gr).

The **Port Authority** (tel. 22510/40827), **Port Police** (tel. 22510/28827), and **Tourist Police** (tel. 22510/22776) can all be found along the waterfront. The main general hospital is called **Bostaneio** (E Vostani 48; tel. 22510/57700).

Banks and **ATMs** can be found in all the major towns (Mytilini, Molyvos, Plomari, Skala Eressou, etc). Note that in Mytilini, there has been an increase in robberies, so you'll want to exercise slightly more caution when taking out money, especially at night.

GETTING THERE

The easiest way to get here is to fly directly into the Mytilini Airport. Pro tip: if your flight is delayed, go for a dip in the sea; the beach is directly in front of the airport.

Air

Mytilini Airport (MJT; tel. 22510/38700) is located 8 km (5 mi) south of Mytilini. There are regular flights from Thessaloniki and Athens with **Aegean Air** (www.aegeanair.com), **Olympic Air** (www.olympicair.com), **Astra Airlines** (www.astra-airlines.com), and **Sky Express** (www.skyexpress.gr). Flights from both Athens and Thessaloniki take a little under an hour. There are also flights between the islands, including Ikaria and Rhodes. Book a bit in advance to get good deals.

Taxis to town from the airport are fixed at a rate of €10. **Buses** are waiting for flights and cost €1.60.

Ferry

All ferries dock in **Mytilini.** There are daily boats to Piraeus (9 hours) and various Turkish ports, and weekly boats to Thessaloniki and nearby Greek islands. For timetables and to purchase tickets, head to one of the many agencies on the waterfront. **Olive Groove Travel** (11 Pavlou Kountourioti; tel. 22510/37533; www.olive-groove.gr; daily 7:30am-10pm) is a good all-purpose shop, least of all because of its name.

Previous: octopus out to dry in the sun; there are over 11 million olive trees in Lesvos; Melinda beach at sunset.

Lesvos

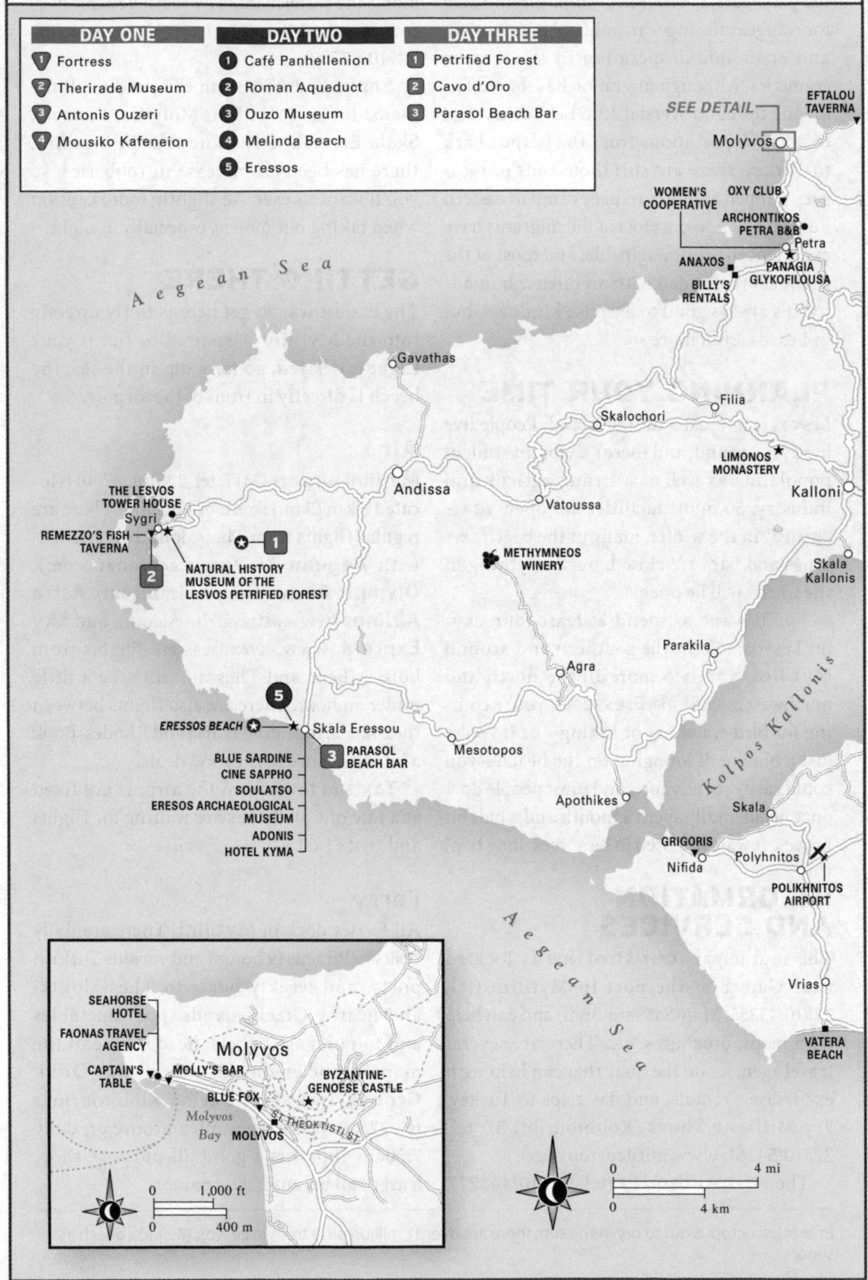
DAY ONE
1 Fortress
2 Therirade Museum
3 Antonis Ouzeri
4 Mousiko Kafeneion
DAY TWO
1 Café Panhellenion
2 Roman Aqueduct
3 Ouzo Museum
4 Melinda Beach
5 Eressos
DAY THREE
1 Petrified Forest
2 Cavo d'Oro
3 Parasol Beach Bar
SEE DETAIL
EFTALOU TAVERNA
Molyvos
WOMEN'S COOPERATIVE
OXY CLUB
ARCHONTIKOS PETRA B&B
Petra
ANAXOS
PANAGIA GLYKOFILOUSA
BILLY'S RENTALS
Aegean Sea
Gavathas
Filia
Skalochori
LIMONOS MONASTERY
Andissa
Kalloni
Vatoussa
THE LESVOS TOWER HOUSE
Sygri
REMEZZO'S FISH TAVERNA
NATURAL HISTORY MUSEUM OF THE LESVOS PETRIFIED FOREST
METHYMNEOS WINERY
Skala Kallonis
Parakila
Agra
ERESSOS BEACH
Skala Eressou
PARASOL BEACH BAR
BLUE SARDINE
CINE SAPPHO
SOULATSO
ERESOS ARCHAEOLOGICAL MUSEUM
ADONIS
HOTEL KYMA
Mesotopos
Kolpos Kallonis
Apothikes
Skala
GRIGORIS
Nifida
Polyhnitos
POLIKHNITOS AIRPORT
Aegean Sea
Vrias
VATERA BEACH
SEAHORSE HOTEL
FAONAS TRAVEL AGENCY
Molyvos
CAPTAIN'S TABLE
MOLLY'S BAR
BYZANTINE-GENOESE CASTLE
BLUE FOX
ST. THEOKTISTI ST.
Molyvos Bay
MOLYVOS
0 1,000 ft
0 400 m
0 4 mi
0 4 km

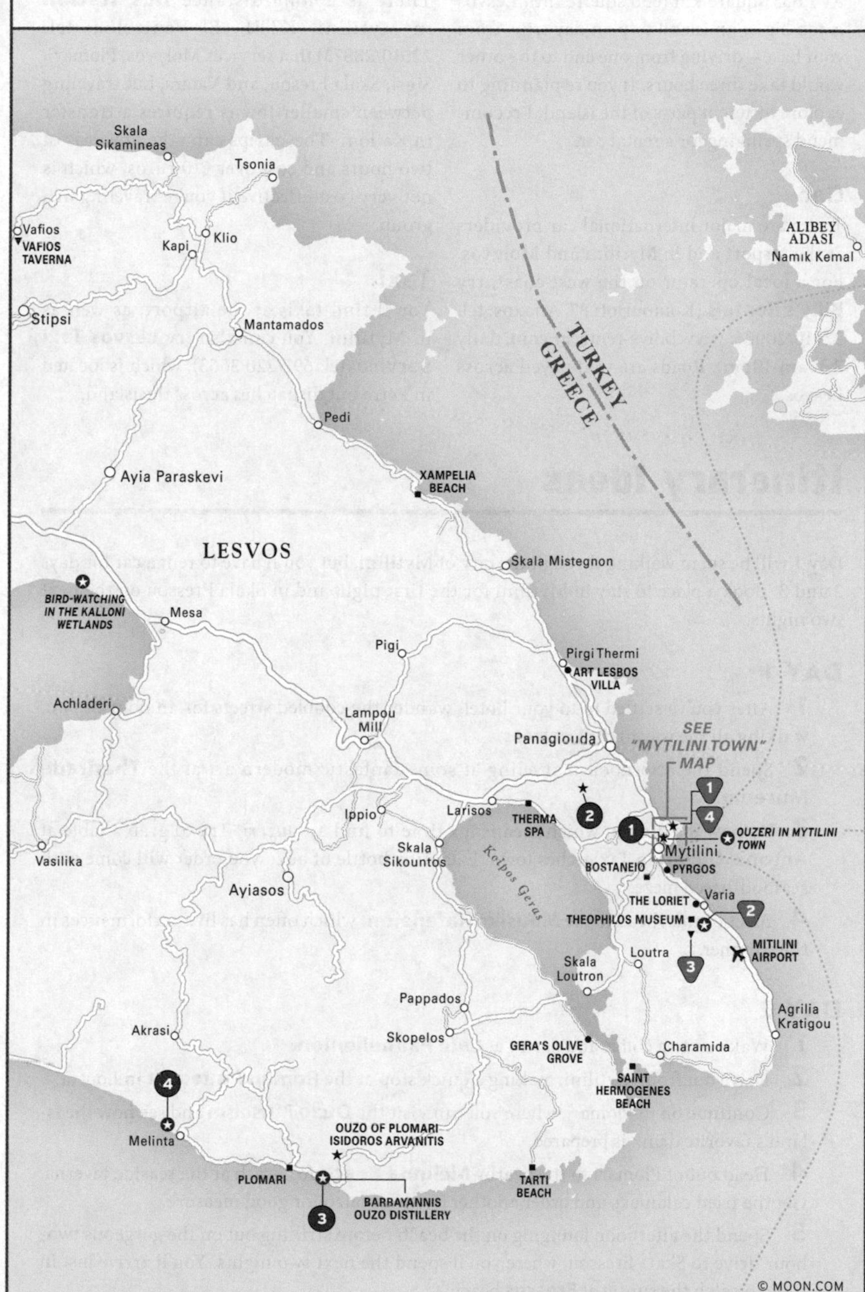
Skala Sikamineas
Tsonia
Vafios
VAFIOS TAVERNA
Klio
Kapi
Stipsi
Mantamados
Pedi
Ayia Paraskevi
XAMPELIA BEACH
TURKEY
GREECE
ALIBEY ADASI
Namık Kemal
LESVOS
Skala Mistegnon
BIRD-WATCHING IN THE KALLONI WETLANDS
Mesa
Pigi
Pirgi Thermi
ART LESBOS VILLA
Achladeri
Lampou Mill
Panagiouda
SEE "MYTILINI TOWN" MAP
Ippio
Larisos
THERMA SPA
OUZERI IN MYTILINI TOWN
Mytilini
Vasilika
Skala Sikountos
Kolpos Geras
BOSTANEIO
PYRGOS
Ayiasos
THE LORIET
Varia
THEOPHILOS MUSEUM
MITILINI AIRPORT
Loutra
Skala Loutron
Pappados
Agrilia Kratigou
Akrasi
Skopelos
GERA'S OLIVE GROVE
Charamida
SAINT HERMOGENES BEACH
Melinta
OUZO OF PLOMARI ISIDOROS ARVANITIS
PLOMARI
TARTI BEACH
BARBAYANNIS OUZO DISTILLERY
© MOON.COM

GETTING AROUND

At 1,633 square km (630 square mi), Lesvos is too big of an island to plan day trips from your base—driving from one end to the other would take three hours. If you're planning to explore different parts of the island, I recommend springing for a rental car.

Car

There are major international car providers at the airport and in Mytilini and Molyvos. For a local operator on the west coast, try **Billy's Rentals** (Kontourioti 87, Anaxos; tel. 22510/20006; www.billys-rentacar.com; daily 7:30am-10pm). Roads are well paved across Lesvos.

Bus

There is a long-distance **bus station** in Mytilini (KTEL, El Venizelou; tel. 22510/28873) that services Molyvos, Plomari, Sigri, Skala Eresou, and Vatera, but traveling between smaller towns requires a transfer in Kalloni. These trips can take upwards of two hours and cost over €10 euros, which is not very cost-effective if you're traveling in a group.

Taxi

You'll find taxis at the airport, as well as in Mytilini. You can also try **Lesvos Taxi Service** (tel. 697/220 3663), which is located in Petra but dispatches across the island.

Itinerary Ideas

Day 1 will be spent walking through the city of Mytilini, but you'll have to rent a car for days 2 and 3. Book a place to stay in Mytilini for the first night and in Skala Eressou on the next two nights.

DAY 1

1 After you've settled in to your hotel, wander the cobbled streets for an hour or two, walking all the way to the **Fortress.**

2 Spend the afternoon marveling at some fantastic modern art at the **Therirade Museum.**

3 By now it's dinner, which means it's time to find an *ouzeri.* Try to grab a table at **Antonis Ouzeri** in Taxiarches town. Each tiny bottle of ouzo you order will come with seafood-based meze.

4 After dinner, head to the **Mousiko Kafeneion,** which often has live performances in the summer.

DAY 2

1 Wake up to a coffee and pastry at **Café Panhellenion.**

2 Drive out from Mytilini, making a quick stop at the **Roman Aqueduct** in Loutra.

3 Continue on to Plomari, where you can visit the **Ouzo Museum** and see how the island's favorite drink is prepared.

4 Head out of Plomari to the nearby **Melinda Beach** for lunch at the seaside taverna. Get the fried calamari, and order another bottle of ouzo for good measure.

5 Spend the afternoon lounging on the beach before striking out on the gorgeous two-hour drive to Skala Eressou, where you'll spend the next two nights. You'll arrive just in time to catch the sunset at **Eressos** beach.

DAY 3

1 From Skala Eressou, it's a short half-hour drive to the **Petrified Forest.** Spend the morning walking through fossilized tree trunks and branches, marveling at this natural history.

2 Have lunch at any of the excellent seaside tavernas in Sigri, such as **Cavo d'Oro,** before driving back down to Skala Eressou.

3 Revel in the bohemian artist vibe of the village at **Parasol Beach Bar,** a friendly café/bar right on the beach.

Mytilini Town Μυτιλήνη

Mytilini does double-duty as the island's capital city and port of arrival; it will likely be your first stop. Lesvos is one of the few islands that can boast a cultural movement year-round, thanks to a bustling student population, and Mytilini is an attractive enough city to spend a few days and use as a base for exploring the southeast coast of the island. Eating and drinking are the staples of Mytilini's lifestyle, and you'll likely spend a few hours each day in a restaurant. But it's also an attractive walking city; wander along the port and through the city's backstreets, which are full of churches, museums, and neoclassical buildings.

SIGHTS

Archaeological Museum

8 Noemvriou; tel. 22510/40223; Tues.-Sun. 8am-3pm; €4

Archaeology buffs will be happy to spend an hour or two walking through this museum, which gives a glimpse of Lesvos life from the 2nd century BC through the 3rd century AD. What used to be two wings has been newly refurbished into one building and houses an impressive collection of mosaics and terracotta figurines, among other finds.

Fortress

tel. 22510/27970; Tues.-Sun. 8:30am-3pm; €2

The imposing fortress (also called the castle) sits at the northern end of the port. Originally built during the Byzantine era and added onto by other conquerors, the fortress is composed of three archaeological sections: the Acropolis, the middle castle (later modified by the Ottomans) and the lower castle, which is the newest part of the fortress, constructed in the 17th century by the Ottomans. You can walk around the decently preserved ruins to find the outline of the Gattilusi palace, a *madrassa* (Koranic school), and a dervish cell. It's a good chunk of Mytilini's history, all in one place.

NIGHTLIFE AND ENTERTAINMENT

Entertainment in Mytilini centers around ouzo, and the line between "restaurant" and "bar" is pretty blurry. Lesvos is the best place to seek out *ouzeri,* places where you drink ouzo and eat lots of little snacks. Think of it like Greek tapas, but be careful—ouzo is a lot stronger than beer!

TOP EXPERIENCE

★ *Ouzeri*

KAFENEION O ERMISI

2 Kornarou; tel. 22510/26232; daily 9am-2am; from €5

This is the oldest restaurant on the island and has been a local favorite for decades. The decor is very old-school Greek *kafeneion* meets *ouzeri*—think oil paintings, classic marble-topped tables, and lots of wooden details. They offer 15 different kinds of ouzo, accompanied by delicious seafood and meat

Mytilini Town

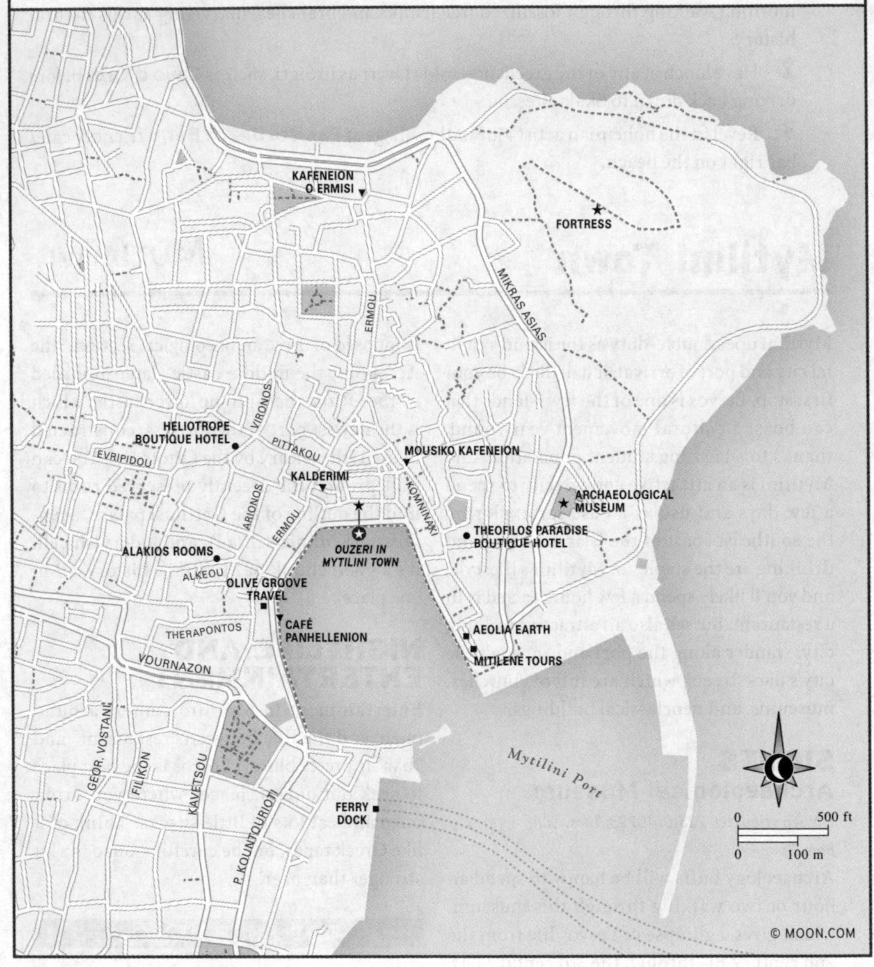

meze. It's full of old folks from Lesvos and a couple of tourists who know what's up.

ANTONIS OUZERI

Taxiarches town; tel. 22510/61951; Mon.-Sat. 9am-midnight; from €5

Located 6 km (3.75 mi) south of Mytilini in Taxiarches town, Antonis Ouzeri is one of the best *ouzeris* around, with a wonderful view of the city and the port. Paired with ouzo are lots of delicious small meze, including fried seafood, *soutzoukakia* (meatballs in tomato sauce), and vegetable salads. There's no parking, but there's a church close by with a lot where you can leave your car.

Live Music

MOUSIKO KAFENEION (ART CAFÉ BAR)

Vernardaki St; tel. 22510/28827; Mon.-Sat. 7:30am-3am, Sun. 8:30am-3am

This music café is something of an arts

cooperative, designed to "bring people together" around good vibes and good tunes. They regularly host live music acts across the spectrum—everything from jazz to electronic music. This venue is popular with students. Check their Facebook page for events.

SHOPPING

The main shopping street of Mytilini is Ermou, where you'll find stores selling everything from sandals to postcards to books to bottles of olive oil. Nearly all of the gift shops sell local food products. Just be sure to wrap up your bottles of oil and ouzo carefully before bringing them back home.

AEOLIA EARTH

P. Kountourioti 87; tel. 22510/54550; daily 8am-9pm

This cute little gift shop sells all kinds of local and organic treats: olive oil, jams, ouzo, spoon sweets, and more. They've also got a collection of wooden toys and souvenirs to bring back home.

FOOD

KALDERIMI

Thasou; tel. 22510/46577; daily lunch and dinner; from €8

This traditional taverna serves a mostly Greek clientele, who duck into the alleyway restaurant to chow down on zucchini flowers stuffed with rice, oven-baked meat dishes, and of course, grilled fish and octopus. There are plenty of local ouzo varieties to choose from.

★ CAFÉ PANHELLENION

13 Pavlou Kountourioti; tel. tel. 22510/21706; daily, all day; from €3

This traditional café has retained many of the same luxurious touches that set it apart when it opened at the turn of the 20th century: vaulted ceilings, brass details, hat boxes, and floor-length mirrors. The café is split into two levels: Originally the bottom was for the aristocrats, and the working class were hidden on the second floor. These days, it's much more democratic, and it's a great place to come for a coffee and pie. It's right next to the church, and on Sundays, all the little old ladies come in (with their own snacks!) to have a post-mass coffee and gossip.

ACCOMMODATIONS

Under €150

ALAKIOS ROOMS

tel. 22510/47737; http://alkaiosrooms.gr; €50

A central location, bright and spacious rooms, and kind staff all contribute to making Alakios a good value. It's a pension-style hotel, located in a renovated building. The furniture is sparse and heavy on the wrought iron, but overall it's quaint and charming and they have a nice breakfast (included) in the morning.

HELIOTROPE BOUTIQUE HOTEL

tel. 22510/45857; www.heliotrope.gr; from €85

"Boutique" is a bit misleading; this place feels more like a mini resort, with all new construction, modern Ikea-style furniture, and a well-lit pool area. It's very close to Vigla beach, which is the closest beach to the city worth swimming in. Most of the 62 rooms have nice sea-facing views.

★ PYRGOS

tel. 22510/25069; www.pyrgoshotel.gr; from €97

This is a very chic and atmospheric four-star hotel located in a neoclassical building that was originally constructed in 1916, and it oozes old-world charm. The furniture is Louis XIV-inspired, and many of the original details of the house (the exposed stone walls, for example) have remained. A yummy breakfast (included) is served in the dining room or on the veranda.

★ THEOFILOS PARADISE BOUTIQUE HOTEL

Skra 7; tel. 22510/43300; www.theofilosparadise.gr; from €130

This is the best of the hotel options in Mytilini. Located in an old neoclassical building and full of shabby-chic design, Theofilos is indeed its own little slice of paradise. It's a medium-sized hotel with special split-level

The Refugee Crisis

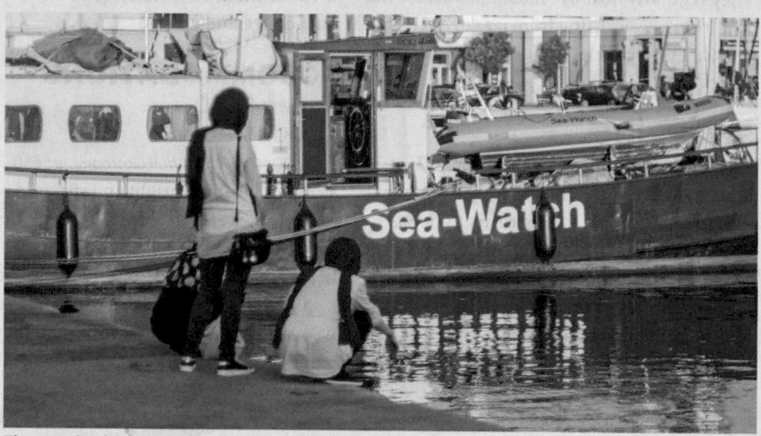

Thousands of refugees have been arriving on Lesvos since 2014.

In 2015, at the height of the so-called refugee crisis, thousands of people fleeing war, poverty, and political persecution arrived daily on the shores of Lesvos on rubber dinghies. Forty-five percent of all asylum seekers arriving in Europe passed through Lesvos. Suddenly this Greek island was thrust into the international spotlight, as orange life vests piled up on the shores and refugee camps filled up. Many people drowned in the unforgiving waters of the Mediterranean. Survivors arrived exhausted and scared on the eastern coast. The people of Lesvos were lauded for their humanitarian reaction (they were nominated for a Nobel Peace Prize), as people already suffering under austerity opened up their homes, hearts, and wallets to these refugees.

While the number of arrivals has slowed at time of this writing (2019), there is still a refugee camp, **Moira,** in the heart of Mytilini that is greatly overcrowded, squalid, and prone to violence and sexual harassment, as desperation over containment grows. The United Nations High Commission for Refugees and Oxfam have decried the camp as "inhumane," and *The New York Times* dubbed Lesvos "Greece's Island of Despair." Unless you willingly turn a blind eye, you will see the impact of the refugee crisis, especially in Mytilini. You'll notice plenty of refugees in the streets trying to have some normalcy in their day to day; you will most likely drive by Moira at some point and see the crowded tents. There's been rising tension between the refugees stuck in the camps and locals in the villages, and there's unfortunately been an increase of rape and robbery in town. Refugees continue to suffer as the Greek government and the European Union fail to take action, and locals feel increasingly burdened by filling in the role they feel the state should take.

If you're coming to Lesvos, I encourage you to spend some of your time either volunteering with local organizations on the ground, donating money, or educating yourself about the crisis. Most organizations prefer long-term, committed volunteers. If that sounds like you, try contacting **Lesvos Solidarity** (www.lesvossolidarity.org, tel. 22510/62000) or **A Drop In The Ocean** (www.drapenihavet.no).

rooms for families, and amenities include a delicious Greek breakfast (included), a hammam and sauna, and a rooftop area with a pool. It's an excellent value for money.

Vicinity of Mytilini Town

VARIA (Βαριά)

The fantastic Therirade Museum and the Theophilos Museum are both located in the suburb of Varia, 4.5km (2.8 mi) south of Mytilini, and it's easy to combine them on one visit.

Sights

★ THERIRADE MUSEUM

tel. 22510/23372; www.museumteriade.gr; Tues.-Sun. 9am-2pm; €3

A far-flung Greek island might seem like the last place you'd find paintings by Miro, Picasso, Matisse, and Le Corbusier, but here we are. This gem of a museum, which was built in honor of Stratis Eleftheriadis, an art critic and native of Lesvos, is well worth a visit. Over two floors, you'll find 16 rooms filled with fantastic modern art by European artists, as well as some Greek painters and sculptors. The museum is located 4.5 km (just under 3 mi) south of Mytilini.

THEOPHILOS MUSEUM

tel. 22510/41644; Mon.-Fri. 8:30am-2pm; from €3

They say artists only get rich after they die. That's sadly the case for Theophilos, a Greek folk art painter from Lesvos whose work was exhibited in the Louvre one year after his death in 1934. This small museum (it looks more like a farmhouse from the outside) has a collection of 86 of his paintings.

Accommodations

THE LORIET

Airport Road, Varia; tel. 22510/43111; www.loriet-hotel.com; €240

Located across two beautiful 18th-century mansions comprising 30 rooms and two villas, The Loriet is one of Mytilini's most established hotels. It has a beautiful garden with a pool in the back, and the front rooms boast lovely sea views. Some of the rooms are very nicely designed (wood floors, Oriental rugs, etc.), while others are completely lacking charm. Located 4 km (2.5 mi) south of Mytilini.

LOUTRA (Λουτρά)

The small village of Loutra is an easy drive (9km/5.5 mi, about 20 minutes) southwest of Mytilini. The area is famous for its hot springs, Roman ruins, and a couple of beautiful beaches, including Saint Hermogenes.

Sights

ROMAN AQUEDUCT

This Roman aqueduct, also known as Kamares ("arch" in Greek) is one of the most special archaeological sights on Lesvos—not to mention, an incredible engineering feat (though I'm not sure how the Greeks feel about the Romans besting them in hydraulic construction). This aqueduct is still undergoing reconstruction, but it is remarkably well-preserved and it's surrounded by olive trees.

From Loutra, the aqueduct is a 25-minute drive north. It's a bit difficult to find; follow the signs for Moria from the Gulf of Gera-Mytilini road.

Beaches

SAINT HERMOGENES BEACH (Άγιος Ερμονίδης)

This beach is situated on a beautiful little bay that has the church of St. Hermogenes, a beautiful little white sugar cube that's carved into the rock and topped with a light blue dome.

It's a small beach, so arrive early to spread out your towel. The strip of sand is backed by rocks that are covered in pine trees, lending the whole area a heavenly scent in the summer. The beach is partly organized with a little canteen selling drinks and snacks. Located an easy five-kilometer (three-mi) drive south of Loutra that will take about eight minutes.

Recreation

THERMA SPA

Km 7 Mitilini-Kalloni Road; tel. 22510/41503 www.thermaspalesvos.com; daily 9am-9pm; from €8

Vacation can be exhausting. It's a good thing Mytilini has an excellent spa to help you relax. This newly renovated complex 7 km (4.25 mi) out of town has an Ottoman-style indoor section and an open-air pool where you can lounge and take in the view of the Bay of Gera. There are plenty of thalassotherapy treatments (body therapies using water; *thalassa* means "sea" in Greek) available, plus Eastern-style massages and techniques. Prices are very reasonable, ranging from €8 for entry to €40 for a massage.

PIRGI THERMI
(Πυργί Θερμή)

Ten km north from Mytilini is the small town of Pirgi Thermi. It's known for its tower mansions (a foundation of Lesbian architecture, first built in the 17th century), which you'll notice, in various states of disrepair, around the outskirts of the village.

Sights

Prigi Thermi is also known for **Panagia Toulout,** a well-preserved 12th-century Byzantine church that's worth seeing. Pirgi Thermi used to be a rich town, thanks to its thermal spas set in gardens along the sea, but those have since been abandoned. If you're into abandoned buildings, you can check it out.

Accommodations

ART LESBOS VILLA

tel. 22510/28633; www.art-lesvosvillas.gr; from €85

Art Lesbos Villa is a good option if you'd like to be a bit outside the city and enjoy the comforts of staying in an apartment. The name is a bit misleading; these are actually separate houses with pretty basic facilities. The complex consists of eight villas.

XAMPELIA BEACH
(Χαμπέλια)

This is a cove beach, 24 km (15 mi) north of Mytilini, with unbelievably clear blue waters. Xampelia is organized. There's also one decent taverna at the end of the beach. It's in the direction of Molyvos, and makes a good pit stop if you're driving up there.

1: the Roman aqueduct among olive trees 2: the Statue of Liberty in Mytilini Town 3: the view of Plomari from the harbor

1

2

3

The South Coast

The towns and beaches below are listed in geographical order along the south coast, from east to west. After Tarti, you'll cut east. It's a coastal road for most of the trip, and the 53-kilometer, 1-hour drive from Tarti to Polyhnitos and Nifida is really beautiful. Unfortunately, there's no bridge that cuts across the bay, so if you're departing Mytilini you'll have to drive along Kolpos Geras Bay to reach the south. Aside from Plomari, the other destinations are not reachable by bus. If you're trying to save money, you can take a taxi from Plomari to Tarti, Melinda, Polyhnitos, or Nifada.

TARTI BEACH
(Τάρτι)

Tarti Beach is one of the more popular beaches on the island, thanks to its crystal-clear waters and long strip of sand. It's half organized, half unorganized (try to snag a shady spot under the trees, if you can) and there are a couple of fish tavernas serving up fresh seafood; they're all good.

Tarti beach is located 40 km (25 mi) south of Mytilini. The drive takes around 50 minutes and has you driving along the Epar. Od. Mitilinis-Kallonis and the Epar. Od. Therma.

PLOMARI
(Πλωμάρι)

The small town of Plomari, 20 km (12 mi) east of Tarti, is famous for being the ouzo capital of the world. It's well worth spending at least a day here, knocking back ouzo at the different museums and distilleries. Each year in early August, there's a big ouzo festival that draws connoisseurs and amateurs from around the island.

Three buses per day depart from Mytiline for Plomari. The ride takes around 75 minutes.

Sights

★ OUZO MUSEUM

tel. 22520/31450; www.theworldofouzo.gr; Mon.-Sat. 9am-4pm; €2

A visit to this six-generation, family-owned museum is more of a factory tour than anything else, but it's an excellent way to get a (literal) taste of Plomari's ouzo-making history. They've been in business since 1894, and still make ouzo the traditional way: it's a labor-intensive, 18-step method with the use of copper distillation. You'll get both a historical overview of ouzo, as well as an olfactory and taste tour; smelling and sampling are integral parts of the ouzo process. Your tour ends with a sample of products.

BARBAYANNIS OUZO DISTILLERY

tel. 22520/32741; Mon.-Sat. 9am-4pm; www.barbayanni-ouzo.com; free

At Barbayannis, you'll get a tour of both the museum (full of family photos and company heirlooms) and the factory, where people still work to make ouzo. You'll learn how ouzo is made, and find out some of the special ingredients the family puts in their ouzo to give it a distinct case. The Barbayannis family doesn't believe in ice; your sample of ouzo at the end will be served with cold water!

Festivals and Events

OUZO FEST

www.ouzofest.gr; July (usually the second week of July)

This annual festival, which usually takes place in July, is organized by the Lesvos Association of Distillers, and is the best time to meet distillers and sample different ouzos all in one place. The streets of Plomari are filled with stalls for tasting ouzo and sampling local cuisine, as well as live music and dancing.

Ouzo: A Way of Life

ouzos for sale at a shop in Mytilini Town

Ah, ouzo. It's not just a drink; it's a way of life here on Lesvos, where the majority of Greece's ouzo distilleries are concentrated. It's an anise-flavored liqueur, usually consumed as an aperitif, and best enjoyed with a couple of meze. This isn't a drink to be consumed at a bar, with pulsating loud music and strobe lights—this is a *conversation* drink, consumed by the sea, though as renowned Greek food writer Christos Zouraris writes, "At ouzo time the participants deliberately avoid weighty issues, knowing full well that they will face them in due time."

HISTORY

In 1989, the European Union gave Greece the right to label ouzo as a purely Greek traditional product. So, while it's often lumped in with raki and pastis, ouzo is something special. On Lesvos, there are 17 distilleries that still produce ouzo using the traditional method, with copper distillation. Interestingly, though ouzo is quintessentially Greek, the name itself is not: When Greece first began exporting ouzo to the rest of Europe in the 19th century, the majority of the crates were shipped to the French port city of Marseille. Custom officials scrawled "Uso di Massalia" (for use in Marseille) on the boxes, and from "uso" came the word ouzo.

HOW TO DRINK OUZO

You first pour the ouzo into a glass, and then add the water and last the ice. When the alcohol comes in contact with the water, it turns a cloudy, milky white color. This very specific order of making a drink allows the flavors to release slowly. You should try as many different bottles as you can in Lesvos; each restaurant or family has its preferred brand. The biggest distillery is **Ouzo of Plomari Isidoros Arvanitis** (Kampos Plagias; tel. 22520/32228)—you'll find their bottles in restaurants and supermarkets across Greece.

You can find ouzo in any café, bar, restaurant, or *ouzeri* on the island—it's practically a law! Some restaurants might have their own house ouzo, it's worth asking your waiter.

Food

There are plenty of good places to eat in Plomari, so don't fret if you don't want to go to Melinda, the highly recommended taverna down the road. Most of the restaurants congregate around the town's main square across the small river, or along the harbor. You can also duck into any of the *kafeneion* that are filled with old men; you'll get meze with your drink.

TO AMMOUDELI

from €10

Located on the western edge of town (300 meters/984 feet from the main square), with stellar views of the sea, To Ammoudeli is a classic Greek island taverna: The octopus is hung up to dry, the vegetables are organic, and everything is doused with a healthy portion of olive oil. Ask for whatever fish is most fresh that day, and get it grilled, or opt for the marinated prawns or fried calamari.

Accommodations

GERA'S OLIVE GROVE

tel. 21094/83533; www.gerasolivegrove.reserve-online.net; from €55

Set across a generous scattering of olive groves—the dense vegetation provides a fantastic backdrop to the sea in the distance—sit four self-catered lodges. The construction is more modern, and the lodges can sleep up to six people. It's best for families who are looking for a longer-term stay.

★ MELINDA BEACH (Μελίντα)

I almost don't want to tell you about this beach because I think of it as *my* beach. As you walk left from Melinda Beach Taverna, you'll come across some friendly hippie free campers who seem to be a summer staple, and farther past that, there's plenty of room to lay down your towel. But see that rock cutting out into the sea? Take off your shoes and wade around it to find a stunning secret beach that has cool rock formations to burrow into for shade, and a huge expanse of sand. You'll be alone—or maybe you'll find me there, too, giving you the stink eye.

Hiking

MELINDA-PALEOHORI TRAIL

Distance: *1.2 km (.75 mi)*

Duration: *30 minutes*

Effort level: *moderate*

This short (but very steep) hike from Melinda beach leads past the chapel of **Panagia Krifti** and some natural hot springs (free to take a dip; signposted) to the small town of **Paleochori.** The road is paved asphalt and marked, so you can't miss it. It's worth exploring both the chapel and the hot springs, and filling up your water bottle with the fresh mountain water that streams out of the stone fountain a few minutes into the hike.

Food

★ MELINDA BEACH TAVERNA

Melinda Beach; tel. 697/821 6054; daily 9am-midnight; from €5

This family-run beach taverna is one of the best I've ever been to in Greece. From the 90-year-old *yiayia* sitting in the corner shucking beans, to the father who dives for octopus and calamari each morning, to the briny seaweed that's thrown on top of the feta-tomato salad, this is a perfect place for lunch or dinner. You can't go wrong with any of the fish options, and you are legally obliged to drink some ouzo. They also have basic rooms for rent (€35) with air-conditioning.

VATERA BEACH (Βατερά)

At just over 9 km (5 mi), this is probably the longest beach on Lesvos, making it ideal for families who have children that need to burn a lot of energy running up and down the beach. The water here is deep blue, and the sand is a bit pebbly. There are several beach bars and organized places along the beach to buy snacks and drinks.

Vatera is 28 km (17 mi) from Melinda, but the drive will take you over an hour given how winding the road is. There are two daily buses that depart from Mytilinie for Vatera. The ride takes around 90 minutes.

Food

AKROTIRI

Agia Focas, Vatera; tel. 22520/61465; daily lunch and dinner; from €6

This is a nice family-run taverna specializing in seafood, served seaside. They have some interesting offerings like smoked mackerel, *lakerda* (marinated raw tuna), fish soup, and even lobster macaroni. The last two have to be ordered a day in advance; call to reserve. The wine is homemade, and the service is friendly.

POLYHNITOS AND NIFIDA (Πολιχνίτος/Νυφιδα)

Drive 11 km (just under 7 mi) north of Vatera, and you'll find the agricultural town of Polyhnitos. It's famous for having some of the hottest thermal waters in Europe (the water starts at 40°C/104°F) and some very excellent food. The area around the bay is also beloved by bird-watchers, who come to catch a glimpse of some of the more than 100 registered bird species that pass through here. Spring is particularly impressive, when swans, herons, flamingos, and other big birds arrive in their yearly migration.

The seaside town of Nifida, 5km (3 mi) west of Polyhnitos, sits at the mouth of the Bay of Kallonis. It's one of the oldest inhabited places of Lesvos, and is a pretty touristic town at this point. There are plenty of facilities here, and it's a good place to grab lunch before bird-watching or after the thermal waters.

Recreation

BIRD-WATCHING

The valley between Vatera and Aghios Fokas (a 4-km/2.5 mi stretch along the beach) is a good place on this side of the island for bird-watching. The southern edge is a natural arrival point for migrating birds, and they'll soar over your head and continue into the valley and onto the Gulf of Kalloni (the wetlands). It's not often visited by bird-watchers, so you'll be able to pull out your binoculars in peace.

POLYHNITOS SPA

Polyhnitos; tel. 22520/41229; www.hotsprings.gr; Mon.-Sat. 2pm-8pm, Sun. 11am-8pm; €4

This small small spa offers access to the hot mineral-y waters. Please note that at the time of this writing the spa was closed for renovation until 2020.

Food

AMETHYSTOS

Polyhnitos; 697/231 6381; from €7

This cozy restaurant located in a stone building serves up hearty Lesbian fare. The décor is charmingly rustic (think burlap sacks for curtains) and the food is delicious: roasted meat and potatoes, bubbling eggplant with tangy cheese, and fried fish. They sometimes have live music acts

★ GRIGORIS

Nifida; tel. 22520/41838; daily in summer noon-midnight; from €8

This truly excellent seaside taverna is run by two brothers who have a serious love for deep-fried patties. They have the usual *keftedakia* (meatballs), made from pork as well as *keftedes* made from tomato, cheese, chickpea, and zucchini. Order them all with a big bowl of tzatziki to dip, and send yourself off to culinary heaven. They also have great fish options.

Molyvos and the North Coast

Northern Lesvos is a rich, green part of the island, covered in olive and pine trees and full of agricultural villages. As you drive up from Mytilini, you'll pass through some small villages that seem stuck in time: old women dressed in black stare out their windows, and men play with their *komboloi* (worry beads) and sip thick coffee in the *kafeneions*. There are several nice beaches here, though this is a more touristic part of the island; you won't find a lot of privacy, but you will find a lot of amenities and people. There's a rich history around here, and well-preserved homes that make it an aesthetically pleasing place to visit.

MOLYVOS (Μόλυβος)

Molyvos (you might also hear it referred to as Mithymna), 60 km (37 mi) northwest of Mytilini, is the most established town in this area. The Ottomans passed through here and left their signature architectural mark. You'll find picture-book perfect winding, twisting streets, sienna-colored stone houses with tiled roofs, and traditional balconies made of carved wood. The town is built along a stony beach, and has great food and nightlife. If you're planning on spending time in the north, Molyvos is an excellent place to base yourself.

If you're driving, there are two roads: an inland route and a coastal road. The inland route is slightly shorter, but the coastal road offers lovely views of the sea. For those without a car, two buses per day depart Mytillini for Molyvos, a 90-minute ride.

Sights

BYZANTINE-GENOESE CASTLE

tel. 22530/71803; Tues.-Sun 8am-3pm; €2

Dominating Molyvos is this fantastic castle, which was built in the 12th century but actually contains stones of an earlier structure besieged by Achilles during the Trojan War (the war happened across the Lesvos strait in ancient Troy). It's a steep climb up the hill to the castle, but the views from the top are stupendous. On a clear day, you can see all the way to Turkey. It's definitely worth a visit; follow the signs posted along the road to reach the castle.

Beaches

MOLYVOS (Μόλυβος)

As far as town beaches go, this is a really good one—all sand, and with clear blue water. It's a very long beach, and you'll find space to chill alone as well as organized sections with umbrellas, chairs, beach bars, and snacks. There are also a couple of restaurants if you want to eat a full meal.

Boat Tours

FAONAS TRAVEL AGENCY

Sea Horse Hotel, Molyvos; tel. 22530/71320; www.seahorse-hotel.com; €20 euros

Inside the Sea Horse Hotel, the fine folks at Faonas Travel Agency will help you organize boat tours from Skala Sikamenas village, (10 km/6 mi) from Molyvos) to Eftalou, the natural thermal springs. You can relax in one of the seven private baths, and cool down with a dip in the sea afterward. Day-long boat rides on small boats start at €20 euros and leave in the morning. They can also help you organize sunset boat tours of the north coast.

Yoga

MOLYVOS YOGA HALL

www.angela-victor.com; by donation

Kind couple Angela and Victor run yoga workshops (dates vary throughout the year) that are wildly popular with foreigners. The focus is more on the healing power of yoga and spirituality than solely on being able to

1: the view from Molyvos Castle **2:** boats bobbing in the harbor of Molyvos

twist your body into a pretzel. The yoga hall doesn't have a physical location; check the website for more information. Classes and workshops are in English. It's donation-based, so give as much as you feel moved to!

Nightlife and Entertainment

MOLLY'S BAR

tel. 22530/71539; daily 6pm-6am

This is probably the most popular bar in Molyvos, and you'll likely end up here at least once for a cocktail. It's a mix of locals and tourists who come for the fun and funky music playlist and the friendly atmosphere. It's got a bit of an English pub vibe, making it popular with Brits, but in truth it's laidback enough to attract everyone. It's also a proper bar, not an all-day café that switches to hard alcohol after 5pm.

OXY CLUB

tel. 697/176 3034; Thurs.-Sun. 11pm-8am, occasional extra days in summer

This club/lounge on the bay picks up late at night and in the warm summer months. Here nice views of the sea come with good music; check their Facebook page for up-to-date information on parties and events (they sometimes have special entrance fees for women). For a while, the club's car park was used as a makeshift reception center for refugees arriving on the island.

Food

There's plenty of good food in Molyvos (and in neighboring Petra). In Molyvos, there are a bunch of restaurants along the harbor. They all look touristy because of their location, but don't worry, they do serve fresh, delicious food.

★ VAFIOS TAVERNA

tel. 22530/71752; daily 10am-11:30pm; from €7

At this delicious taverna with an exhaustive menu, all the recipes are originally from the owner's grandmother. That's very good news for you, as it means lots of clay pot cooking and traditional Lesbian recipes. They have some hard-to-find treats, like stuffed onions and fried zucchini blossoms, and roasted lamb on the spit. You'll need to drive there; follow the main road to Skala Sikimanias, and the restaurant is right before the school.

CAPTAIN'S TABLE

tel. 22530/71005; daily noon-midnight; from €7

At this quintessential family-run restaurant, Maria's father catches the fish every day, while Maria and her husband prepare the food in the morning. Unlike other tavernas, they don't just stick to Greek tastes: When inspiration strikes, they offer curries, satay, gnocchi, and other international dishes. The grilled and roasted meats are also delicious. Located on the harbor, it's a bit touristy but still fun.

BLUE FOX

tel. 694/209 1898; 9am-late; from €3

Enjoy an afternoon pick-me-up in this warm and friendly café with a fantastic balcony overlooking the harbor. Blue Fox is more of a sweets shop than anything else. Portions are huge, though, so don't be put off by the higher than average prices. They have ice cream, waffles, crepes, and a bevy of homemade cakes and pies.

EFTALOU TAVERNA

tel. 22530/71049; daily 10:30am-midnight; from €6

Husband-and-wife team Manolis and Heidi (both English speakers) run this great little taverna on the beach, 6 km (3.75 mi) east of Molyvos in the village of Eftalou. Manolis is in charge of the savory options and the grill. His specialty is grilled fish, which changes depending on the season. Heidi makes all of the pies and cakes.

Accommodations

SEA HORSE HOTEL

tel. 22530/71320; www.seahorse-hotel.com; from €50

Located right on Molyvos' harbor, the Sea Horse Hotel is a lovely stone building that exudes an old-world charm—at least from the inside. Rooms are spacious and clean, with sizable balconies facing the sea, but don't expect fancy decor on the inside; the floors are tiled and the comforters are burnt orange. They also have a good restaurant attached to the property and a travel agency, and the proprietors are very friendly.

PETRA
(Πέτρα)

Petra, 6 km (3.75 mi) south of Molyvos, is definitely a touristic town, but that's not necessarily a bad thing. The town's center was pedestrianized a couple of years ago, and it's nice to walk around the restored traditional houses. It is quite small, though, and there's not a lot to keep you here for a long time. There are plenty of good restaurants to try, but you can skip the souvenir shops. There are six daily buses from Molyvos to Petra, and it takes 15 minutes.

Sights

PANAGIA GLYKOFILOUSA

daily; free

Panagia Glykofilousa literally translates to the "Sweet Kissing Virgin" (or, Our Lady of the Sweet Kiss). This is the main focal point of Petra, under which the rest of the village spans out. It's a large rock (petra actually means rock in Greek) topped by the monastery. You need to climb the 114 steps that are carved into stone to reach the top, at which point you'll be rewarded with great views of Petra and the bay. There's a small church dedicated to Agios Nikolaos at the bottom of the rock, and there's a big *panigiri* here every August 15.

Beaches

ANAXOS
(Αναξος)

Anaxos is another organized sandy beach, 2.7 km (1.5 mi) south of Petra, with a lovely view across the water of Molyvos town. It's becoming something of a beach resort area, so you'll find all the amenities you could need. It can be a bit crowded, so arrive early to secure a spot.

Food

★ WOMEN'S COOPERATIVE

tel. 22530/41238; summer only, lunch and dinner; from €5

I deeply love a women's cooperative, and this one, located on Petra's main square, is no exception. The co-op was founded in 1983 to boost the independence and employment of women, and now boasts 32 members. Everyone in Greece is always saying their mother is the best cook—well, here is a restaurant filled with 32 different people's mothers. Statistically, it has to be amazing, and it is. It's all Greek traditional food, and you can't go wrong on the menu.

Accommodations

ARCHONTIKOS PETRA B&B

tel. 22530/41092; from €103

Originally built in 1821 as a country mansion for a wealthy family, Archontikos Petra was fully restored into this beautiful B&B in 2008. The decor is a mix of Greek antique and English country shabby-chic. There are five rooms on the villa's second floor, each with its own bathroom and view of the garden. You won't get the anonymity of a hotel here, as the ground floor is all a common area, but you will get plenty of charm and history.

SOUTH OF MOLYVOS AND PETRA

Limonos Monastery

Kaloni; tel. 22530/22798; free

This is the largest monastery on Lesvos, and was founded in 1526 by St. Ignatios. It's one of the wealthiest monasteries in the Aegean, and houses an impressive collection of Byzantine-era manuscripts, books, frescoes, and more. Note that it's prohibited for women to enter the church or the courtyard, except on St. Ignatios' feast day on October 14. It's located 20 km (12 mi) south of Petra, and you'll need a car to get here.

Kalloni Wetlands

★ BIRD-WATCHING

www.lesvosgeopark.gr; free

Lesvos is fantastically situated for bird lovers. Between Africa, Asia, and Europe, millions of birds migrate through here each year. The Kalloni wetlands, 40 km (25 mi) northeast of Mytilini is a particularly interesting place for bird-watchers. There are 300 observed bird species here: You'll spot everything from pink flamingos to gray herons and stone curlew. The area itself is full of vegetation and ponds that provide natural habitats for the birds. The best time to visit is during the spring or autumn.

Most amateur bird-watchers would do well to contact English-speaking **Eleni Galinou** (tel. 697 280 9610; https://lesvosbirdwatching.gr) to organize specific excursions (from €90). Though she's based in central Lesvos, her favorite place to bird-watch is in the Kalloni wetlands. She organizes half- and full-day excursions, as well as bird photography courses. You'll need a car to get here.

The West Coast

The west coast of Lesvos is home to some of the island's most stunning landscapes, thanks to a massive series of volcanic explosions that left this place petrified—literally. It's full of jagged rocks and fossilized trees, and it can feel like a real adventure driving or hiking through here.

In addition to natural history buffs, the west coast draws its fair share of LGBTQ travelers; Skala Eressou is the birthplace of the poet Sappho. Considered one of the greatest lyric poets of all time, she is renowned for being a symbol of love and desire between women, and for a lot of people, she's a feminist icon and gay role model (though the Byzantine Church dismissed her as "a sex-crazed whore who sings of her own wantonness"). Scholars are actually divided on how "gay" Sappho was, but that's beside the point. She raised women's voices and sang about the strength, beauty, and resilience of women. The terms "sapphic" and "lesbian" both come from Sappho, and Skala Eressou is full of (usually older) lesbian couples. There's a two-week festival devoted to Sappho in September.

Sigri is the area's other main town, though it's more of a sleepy fishing village that it seems like the rest of the world forgot. It's a collection of white-washed houses around a curving bay, with fishing boats bobbing in the harbor. There's nothing specifically to see in Sigri, but it's a nice, tranquil place to walk around and stop for lunch.

SKALA ERESSOU (Σκάλα Ερεσού)

Considering what a large island Lesvos is, it's a bit surprising—and frustrating—that there's not a quicker way to get to this part of the island. You could take the bus, but I would spring for the rental car and drive, since the interior of Lesvos is so beautiful anyway. It's an 86-km (53-mi) drive west from Mytilini that can be done in under two hours. Two buses per day depart Mytillini for Skala Eressou, and the ride takes around 2.5 hours.

Sights

ERESOS ARCHAEOLOGICAL MUSEUM

Tues.-Sun. 8:30am-3pm; free

Located on the southeast part of Skala Eressou, two blocks behind the sea, this is the quintessential archaeological museum that you will find in a village on a Greek island: small, a bit dusty, with random hours, but with some stunning objects. The mosaics on the floors of the first three halls are superbly restored and are particularly interesting. My favorite is the one showcasing the theatrical masks of Menander; there's also a scene of an athletic Orpheus fighting wild animals.

Beaches

★ ERESSOS BEACH (Ερεσος)

This is one of the best beaches on Lesvos. It's a long sandy strip of beach, and it is imperative that you come here at least once to watch the sunset. The beach has remained largely unspoiled, though there are a few beach bars and tavernas at the entrance of the beach. One thing that makes Eressos so unique is the vibe. This is a special community here in Skala Eressos, and you can definitely feel the relaxed, bohemian energy. There are a lot of local and foreign artists who call this area their home, the tourists who come here are of the "flip-flops are a lifestyle" variety, and everyone is generally friendly and down to earth.

Hiking

SKALA ERESSOU TO TSICHOLONITAS

Distance: *19-km (12-mi) loop*

Duration: *4 hours*

Effort level: *moderate*

This hiking trail leaves northwest from Skala Eressou and ends at the beach of Tsicholonitas. You'll mostly be walking elevated along the coast; reddish colored boulders are the only things marring the grass-covered hills along the sea. Bring plenty of water and food, as there's nothing along the way. It's also a long walk without much shade, so avoid this hike in the height of summer or the middle of the day.

Nightlife and Entertainment

PARASOL BEACH BAR

tel. 22530/52050; daily 9am-2am

An all-day café that morphs into a bar once the sun goes down, this is a funky little beach bar with a music playlist to match. The decor is a bit Caribbean-inspired, and the cocktails are in the same vein. It's a very fun place to spend a few hours with your new friends. During the day, if you're craving international food, stop by for some pizza or noodles.

CINE SAPPHO

This very cute outdoor cinema also has a bar. Movies come subtitled in English, and you can nurse your beer while watching whatever's on the screen. Somehow the cool breeze, night stars, and alcohol make even the worst movie enjoyable. You'll see posters around town advertising the week's screening. There's a mix of Greek and Hollywood movies, and it's family-friendly.

Festivals and Events

THE ERESSOS INTERNATIONAL WOMEN'S FESTIVAL

www.womensfestival.eu; usually mid-Sept.; wristbands €75

This two-week festival is run by women, to celebrate women. There are parties, dancing, workshops, alternative fashion shows, open-air film screenings, art exhibits, excursions, and talks scattered around the town. It attracts an older, white, lesbian crowd, but it's an open and safe space for all women.

Food

There's a lot of really good food in Skala Eressou, so don't be bothered if the restaurants recommended below are full (as they can be in the summer months, it's helpful to call ahead for reservations). There are plenty of good restaurants along the beach and in the small streets behind the harbor.

SOULATSO

tel. 22530/53078; daily lunch and dinner; from €6

With a great raised platform that looks out onto the sea, Soulatso is a worthy choice for a sunset dinner. All the fish is fresh and delicious, but their specialty is mackerel.

ADONIS

tel. 22530/52240; daily lunch and dinner from €10

If you've always wanted to smash plates on the floor or throw napkins in the air—a deeply Greek practice that sadly is increasingly hard to come across—try your luck at Adonis, especially if there's a wedding or baptism happening. It's a classic Greek taverna with excellent food and good music, and the evening often ends up in song and dance. Try the lamb shoulder, which is slowly roasted on the spit and served with veggies from their farm, or the big, juicy prawns marinated in garlic.

★ BLUE SARDINE

tel. 22530/53503; daily lunch and dinner; from €5

Nearly everything at the Blue Sardine is handmade by Alexis, the gregarious owner of this seaside taverna (it's the last one on the beach). The olives are from his own trees, the *kritamo* (wild greens) are picked in the morning, and the anchovies are marinated in his own sauce. Plating and presentation are a notch above your typical beach taverna. He's got an impressive variety of ouzo, and if you're based on the West Coast, you'll probably eat here more than once.

Accommodations

HOTEL KYMA

tel. 22530/53555; from €45

An excellent budget value, this guesthouse affords lovely views from the private balcony—you can almost reach out and touch the sea. It's particularly moving at sunset and sunrise. The hotel is on the smaller side and rooms are simple, but there's regular maid service and air-conditioning. Breakfast is included.

SYGRI

(Σιγρι)

Sigri is 27 kilometers northwest from Skala Eressou. Two buses per week depart Mytilini for Sygri on Monday and Friday, and the ride takes around 2.5 hours.

Sights

★ PETRIFIED FOREST

tel. 22510/47303; www.petrifiedforest.gr; July-Sept. Tues.-Sun. 8am-4pm, Oct.-June Tues.-Sun. 9am-5pm; €2

Formed a mind-boggling 20 million years ago by a volcanic explosion that covered the entire area in a blanket of lava and ash, this is a truly wild park full of trees that have been turned into rocks. It's the second-largest petrified forest in the world, and home to the largest petrified tree in Europe. You'll also come across petrified animal bones! Bring water and wear a hat, and take a couple of hours to wander around. It's also known as the "forest of silence" and is a magnificent place to feel insignificantly tiny in the face of almighty nature. The forest is located at the eastern edge of Sygri (signposted).

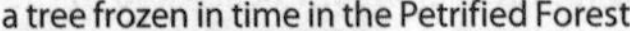

a tree frozen in time in the Petrified Forest

NATURAL HISTORY MUSEUM OF THE LESVOS PETRIFIED FOREST

Sigri; tel. 22530/54434; www.lesvosmuseum.gr

Come to this museum for a succinct overview of Lesvos Petrified Forest, complete with samples, maps, and a couple of petrified branches, logs, and plant fossils from the area. This is a worthwhile stop only if you've visited the petrified forest and are dying to know more about it.

Food

CAVO D'ORO

tel. 22530/54221; daily noon-11pm; from €7

Have you ever wanted to pick your octopus off the clotheslines where it's been drying in the sun for the better part of the afternoon? Well at Cavo d'Oro, an excellent seafood taverna, you can do exactly that. Choose from a variety of fresh seafood, from smoked mackerel to raw clams to mussels in wine. Top it off with some salads, fried potatoes, and ouzo.

REMEZZO'S FISH TAVERNA

tel. 22530/54327; daily noon-midnight; from €7

Specializing in lobster—there's a giant fish tank with dozens of lobsters crawling around—Remezzo's is something of an institution in Sygri. It's really worthwhile to go for the grilled or boiled lobster (especially if you're coming from a country where lobster is prohibitively expensive), but all the seafood is good here.

Accommodations

THE LESVOS TOWER HOUSE

Faneromenis 8, Pedino; tel. 22530/22788; €90

This fantastic apartment-hotel is 20 km (12.5 mi) north of Sygri in the town of Pedino, perfect for any architecture or history buffs. As the name implies, this is a stone mansion with a tower. The decoration is in the same old-school Lesvos vibe. There's a great pool, superb views of the sunset, and a lovely garden. Service can be a bit touch and go, but it's fun to stay for one night. There are only four apartments in the whole hotel. Note that this is a four-star hotel, but it's self-catering.

METHYMNEOS WINERY

Chidiria; tel. 697/208 5371; www.methymnaeos.com; Aug.-Sept. 10am-2pm or by appointment

Organic wine lovers should head to Methymneos, 31 km (19.25 mi) north of Skala Eressou, the first professional winery on Lesvos, to sample some delicious and unique wines. All the wines are made from the *chidiriotiko* grape, a variety that's only grown on Lesvos. Because the wines are grown in the same area as the petrified forest (remember all that lava?), their bottles have a distinct and mineral-y taste. Contact the winery to arrange a tour and tasting. Designate a driver or hire a taxi to get here.

Alonnisos (Αλόννησοσ)

Alonnisos (pop. 4,600) is an island that you smell before you see. It has an astonishing number of endemic herbs and is teeming with wildflowers, lending a fragrant air to the island. As part of the Sporades, Alonnisos is intensely green, and is densely blanketed with oak and pine trees; taking a deep breath in the forest is enough to make your head dizzy. Then there's the crisp, salty smell of the ocean. Residents are very eco-conscious, and everything doesn't just seem cleaner—it *is* cleaner.

The eco-vibe descends into the water, too. Thanks to the National Marine Park, it boasts some of the cleanest water in Greece. The sea is a refuge for dolphins, seabirds, and the endangered Mediterranean monk seal. One new friend excitedly showed me pictures of the monk

Highlights

Look for ★ to find recommended sights, activities, dining, and lodging.

★ **Boat Tours of the National Marine Park of Alonnisos:** Take a boat trip through Europe's largest marine park. If you're lucky, you might catch sight of dolphins and monk seals (page 332).

★ **Chrisi Milia Beach:** Spend a lazy afternoon under the fragrant pine trees of this pebble beach, which has perfect water for snorkeling (page 333).

★ **Hayiati:** The heart of Alonnisos beats loudly in the pedestrian-only village of Palio Alonnisos, where you'll wander around stone houses and soak up the incredible views. Make a beeline for the top to reach Hayiati, a sweets shop with the best views in town (page 337).

★ **Agios Dimitrios Beach:** This beautiful, boomerang-shaped beach is a favorite with both locals and tourists, who come to lounge on the lawn chairs and swim in its cool, calm waters (page 339).

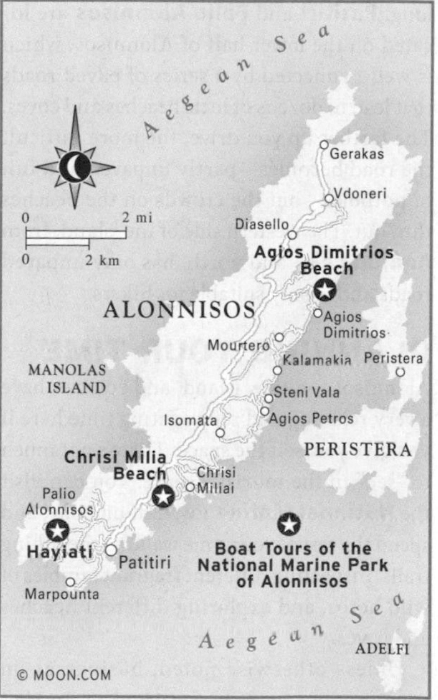

seal that swam alongside him at one beach, something of a Grecian miracle.

I know I shouldn't play favorites, but I am defenseless against the beauty and calmness of Alonnisos, and it is firmly in my top three Greek islands. One of the first inhabited islands in all the Aegean, Alonnisos is surprisingly off the grid for most tourists. The tourists who do come through are of the bohemian variety, which makes it very easy to make new friends, and contributes to the cool vibe of the island. If you're looking to while away a few days (or weeks, I'm not judging) of your summer, hiking, reading, sunbathing, and lazily swimming, you've come to the right place.

ORIENTATION

At 129 square km (50 square mi), Alonnisos is one of the smaller Sporades islands; it's only 4 km (2.5 mi) wide, and 14 km (8.5 mi) long. **Patitiri** and **Palio Alonnisos** are located on the lower half of Alonnisos, which is well-connected by a series of paved roads that lead to dozens of little beaches and coves. The farther up you drive, the more difficult the road becomes—partly unpaved and full of potholes—but the crowds on the beaches thin out. The western side of the island, from **Agalou Laka** and north, has only unpaved roads and is only suitable for hikers.

PLANNING YOUR TIME

Alonnisos is a slow island, and you can have a very relaxing and rejuvenating time here if you give yourself the space. There's not much to "see" in the touristic sense. You can visit the **National Marine Park** in one day, and spend the rest of your time walking the hiking trails, inspecting different fragrant jumbles of wild herbs, and exploring different beaches and coves.

Unless otherwise noted, businesses on Alonnisos operate **May-September.** In May, June, and September, you'll have the island more or less to yourself. July and August can be quite busy, but it's still nowhere near as crowded as other Sporades islands.

Most visitors congregate around **Patitiri** or **Palio Alonnisos.** This is the part of the island with the most restaurants, hotels, and other facilities.

INFORMATION AND SERVICES

You'll find **ATMs** in Palio Alonnisos and Patriti, but the majority of other services are located in the latter. **Police** (tel. 24240/65205, you'll see their cabin on the harbor), the **post office** (tel. 24240/65560), and the island's main **health center** (tel. 24240/65208) are all in Patriti. There is no official government tourist center, but there are several private tourist agencies along the Patriti waterfront that can help you organize tickets and excursions. Try **Alonnisos Travel** (tel. 24240/65188; www.alonnisostravel.gr; daily 9am-10pm) as they also organize snorkeling and swimming trips.

There are plenty of tourist shops in Patitiri selling snorkeling equipment for cheap if you'd like to pick up a mask.

GETTING THERE

There is no airport on Alonnisos. The only way to travel there is by **ferry.** Alonnisos is not accessible from Piraeus port; boats leave from **Volos** and **Agios Konstantinos** on the mainland (about a three-hour drive from Athens), from **Paralia Kymis** on Evia, and during the summer months, from the nearby **Sporades islands** of Skyros, Skopelos, and Skiathos. Ferries dock in Patitiri.

GETTING AROUND

Alonnisos is a big **walking** island, and plenty of people choose to forego buses and car rentals in favor of long hikes and hitchhiking (quite common, especially on the uphill route between Patitiri and Palio Alonnisos).

Previous: an abandoned car on the side of the road; tuna is a delicacy on Alonnisos; Alonnisos island.

Hiking on Alonnisos

Alonnisos has 14 surveyed, numbered, and signposted walks, which include both short walks to hidden beaches, and longer routes. Thanks to the effort to clean and organize these hikes, Alonnisos is a lot easier of an island to hike on your own than, say, Samothrace. Add to that the pure air, the beautiful vistas, and the stunning flora and fauna you'll get to walk through, Alonnisos is truly a hiker's paradise.

Some of my favorite routes are:

- From **Patitiri** to **Palio Alonnisos** (2.5 km/1.5 mi, 40 minutes)
- From **Gerakas** to **Tourkou Mnima** (page 340)

LOCAL GUIDE

If you like to hike with a guide, call **Chris Browne** (organized through Alonnisos Holidays; tel. 24240/65804; www.alonissosholidays.com), an expat resident who wrote a comprehensive walking guide *Alonnisos Through the Souls of Your Feet* and who also organizes treks. All walks leave from Patriti harbor starting at 9:30am. Note that walks are conducted in April, May, June, September, and October.

From Patitiri there are two main roads that lead inland to the rest of the island. These roads don't have official names; locals just refer to them as left-hand or right-hand. Don't worry, though, it's impossible to get lost, and even if you do, a friendly Alonnisosian will help you.

Bus

There is a bus route between Patitiri and Palio Alonnisos (10 minutes; €1.70) that also continues to Steni Vala (25 minutes from Patriti; €1.80). Bus timetables are available at the port. Buses leave frequently in the summer. There's also another **beach bus** (tel. 697/380 5610; €5 roundtrip) in the summer that goes from Patitiri to some of the beaches in the north. The western parts and the most northern part of the island are not accessible by bus.

Car, Motorcycle, and Bicycle

There are several reliable car and bike rental places in Patitiri, on the waterfront. For motorcycles and bikes, try **I'm Bike** (tel. 24240/65010). **Alonnisos Travel** (tel. 24240/66000; www.alonnisostravel.gr) also has car rentals.

Unlike other islands, Alonnisos is safe enough that you can drive a motorcycle without any fear. A car isn't entirely necessary, though, especially if you're a solo traveler or in a couple. Aside from the north and west of the island, the roads are fine to drive. None of the places mentioned in this book require a 4x4.

Taxi

There's always a cluster of taxis on the waterfront in Patitiri, across from the Alykon Hotel. There isn't a taxi company, but try giving **Nikos** (tel. 697/225 0295) or **Spiros** (tel. 697/888 1360) a call. From Patitiri to Palio Alonnisos it costs €6; it's €10 to Leftos Gialos and €13 to Steni Vala.

Itinerary Ideas

It's a good idea to base yourself in Patitiri or Palio Alonnisos for this itinerary—but really, Alonnisos is small enough that you can set your bags down anywhere you'd like.

DAY 1

1 Head to the **Ikos Traditional Products,** a local women's cooperative in Patitiri, to pick up some provisions for an afternoon picnic, including several slices of their excellent, homemade *spanakopita* (spinach pie).

2 Hop in a car and make a beeline to **Chrisi Milia Beach** and spend the morning lounging by the sea and enoying your picnic.

3 In the mid-afternoon, head to Palio Alonnisos (you can either walk from Patitiri or drive up to the village). Spend an hour walking around the town's cobblestone streets before settling into dinner at **Astrofegia**—but don't order dessert.

4 After dinner, continue up the main road to **Hayiati,** where you can enjoy a giant slice of cake and watch the sunset over the island.

DAY 2

1 Your second day in Alonnisos should be spent doing a full tour of the **National Marine Park of Alonnisos** by boat. You'll learn all about the conservation efforts of the island, visit some neighboring, uninhabited islands, and, if you're lucky, spot some dolphins and monk seals! Meet your boat at **Patitiri Harbor.** Lunch will be included.

2 After you return in the afternoon, hike up to the **Agioi Anargyroi** church. You can either walk the whole 4 km (2.5 mi) from Patitiri, or drive and just walk the last 500 meters (1,640 feet) on the dirt path. Watch the sunset from this cliffside Byzantine church.

3 Head back into town and have a boozy, ouzo-filled dinner at **To Kamaki Ouzerie** in Patitiri.

Patitiri Πατητήρι

Patitiri, located on the southeast end of Alonnisos, is the island's largest town. Any services that need to be taken care of happen here. There's a decent number of good restaurants and accommodations, though remember that it's the busiest part of the island, so it's not the quietest, especially in the summer months. The town is small enough that you'll quickly get your bearings—if something isn't on the harbor, it's just one or two streets above.

SIGHTS

Alonnisos Museum

Harbor; tel. 24240/66250; www.alonnisosmuseum.com; May and Sept. 11am-6pm, June-Aug. 11am-8pm; €4

Located at the far end of the waterfront, and at a high enough vantage point that it looks down on the rest of the port, the Alonnisos Museum is a great peek into the island's life, including a very cool collection of pirates' weapons. There's a re-created farmhouse interior downstairs, to give you a taste of what

Alonnisos

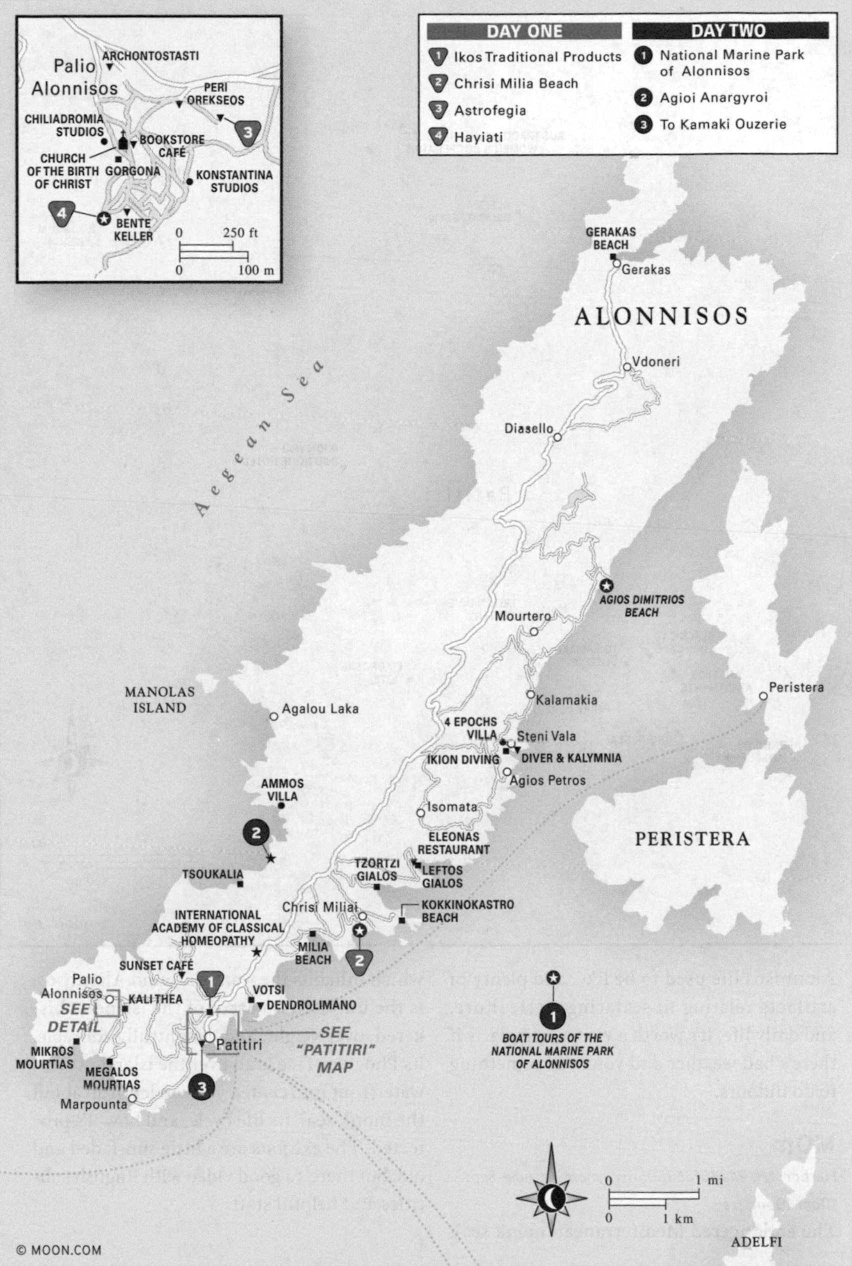

DAY ONE
Ikos Traditional Products
Chrisi Milia Beach
Astrofegia
Hayiati
DAY TWO
National Marine Park of Alonnisos
Agioi Anargyroi
To Kamaki Ouzerie
Palio Alonnisos
ARCHONTOSTASTI
PERI OREKSEOS
CHILIADROMIA STUDIOS
BOOKSTORE CAFÉ
CHURCH OF THE BIRTH OF CHRIST
GORGONA
KONSTANTINA STUDIOS
BENTE KELLER
0 250 ft
0 100 m
GERAKAS BEACH
Gerakas
ALONNISOS
Vdoneri
Aegean Sea
Diasello
AGIOS DIMITRIOS BEACH
Mourtero
Kalamakia
Peristera
MANOLAS ISLAND
Agalou Laka
4 EPOCHS VILLA
Steni Vala
IKION DIVING
DIVER & KALYMNIA
Agios Petros
AMMOS VILLA
Isomata
ELEONAS RESTAURANT
PERISTERA
TSOUKALIA
TZORTZI GIALOS
LEFTOS GIALOS
Chrisi Miliai
KOKKINOKASTRO BEACH
INTERNATIONAL ACADEMY OF CLASSICAL HOMEOPATHY
MILIA BEACH
SUNSET CAFÉ
Palio Alonnisos
KALI THEA
SEE DETAIL
VOTSI
DENDROLIMANO
SEE "PATITIRI" MAP
Patitiri
BOAT TOURS OF THE NATIONAL MARINE PARK OF ALONNISOS
MIKROS MOURTIAS
MEGALOS MOURTIAS
Marpounta
0 1 mi
0 1 km
ADELFI

Patitiri

Alonnisos life used to be like, and plenty of artifacts relating to seafaring, agriculture, and daily life. It's worth a visit, particularly if there's bad weather and you need something to do indoors.

MOm

Harbor; tel. 24240/66350; www.mom.gr; June-Sept. 10am-10pm; free

The endangered Mediterranean monk seal, which inhabits the waters around Alonnisos, is the unofficial mascot of the island: whiskered, overweight, and delightfully adorable, its Phocidae face is all over the island. At this waterfront info center, you can learn all about the monk seal, its life cycle, and how it's protected. The exhibits are a little sun-faded and old, but there's a good video with English subtitles and helpful staff.

HIKING

HIKING TO AGIOI ANARGYROI

Distance: *4.5 km/2.8 mi*

Duration: *35 minutes*

Agioi Anargyroi is a small church perched at the edge of a cliff, meaning that there are spectacular views at the end of this short hike. Starting from Patitiri, follow the paved northwestern road until it ends. Walk an additional 500 meters (0.3 mi) to reach the church.

BARS AND NIGHTLIFE

DRUNK SEAL

Harbor; www.drunkseal.com; 10am-late; from €5

Probably the most happening bar on the island, Drunk Seal is a cocktail and music lounge with a perpetual party in the summer months. If the logo is any indication—a seal balancing a martini glass on its nose and casually flipping a fin—you're in for a raucous time.

SHOPPING

Gourmet Items

ALELMA DELICATESSEN

Epar. Od Patitiri-Gerakas; seasonal, 9am-2pm and 6pm-late Apr.-Oct.

Across Greece, Alonnisos is known for its tuna fish, which is canned and preserved in olive oil. This tuna is particularly low in mercury and rich in omega-3, making it a great healthy food choice. One of the best tuna producers is Alelma, which is headquartered in Patitiri. They also have a great selection of herbs and oils, all of which can be easily packaged and brought home.

IKOS TRADITIONAL PRODUCTS/ WOMEN'S COOPERATIVE

Ikion Dolopon St.; tel. 24240/66270; daily 9am-2pm and 6pm-9pm

Imagine the culinary prowess of a dozen grandmothers with a bevy of local, organic produce, and you have Ikos Traditional Products. Located on the outskirts of Patitiri on Ikion Dolopon street, this local women's cooperative has a great selection of jams, preserves, spoon sweets, and baked goods to take home (or, who are we kidding, immediately eat). They make amazing savory pies, and I advise you to come early in the morning to snag the coveted middle piece.

FOOD

BLACK CAT CAFÉ

corner harbor; tel. 24240/66307; year-round, breakfast, lunch, and dinner; from €6

One of the few places that's open year-round, Black Cat Café is a solid choice for breakfast or lunch. Portions are quite hearty, and the fare is typical café style, with nice salads, pressed sandwiches, good coffee, and free Wi-Fi.

TO KAMAKI OUZERIE

just behind the port; tel. 24240/65245; April-Oct. daily noon-1am; from €4

Opened in 1987, this is one of the first *ouzeri* in Alonnisos, and it remains a favorite amongst both tourists and locals. It's meze-style food: Order a bottle of *tsipuro* and you get a different meze or two with each drink. It's the perfect tapas-style dinner. The octopus *stifado* (stew) is a house favorite, though all the food, especially anything with seafood, which has been bubbling away since the early morning to give the flavors time to concentrate, is delicious. In the summer months, there's live Greek music every Tuesday, Thursday, and Saturday. With your back to the port, head up 40 meters (130 feet); the *ouzeri* is located on your left-hand side.

ZAVALIADIS BAKERY

Epar. Od Patitiri-Gerakas; tel. 24240/66477; Mon.-Sat. 6am-6pm; from €1

If you're a fan of a carb-heavy picnic, look no further than this bakery, which has a great selection of savory pies, sweets, baked goods, and, somewhat inexplicably, a selection of German gluten-free snacks.

ACCOMMODATIONS

★ ANGELOS APARTMENTS

tel. 697/395 5267; www.angelosalonissos.com; Mar.-Oct.; from €30

Run by the charismatic Angelos, this is

1

2

3

International Academy of Classical Homeopathy

Homeopathy is the belief that the body can heal itself. Though homeopathy has its fair share of non-believers, it's a school of thought that attracts a wide-range of individuals. One of the most popular figures in contemporary homeopathy is Dr. George Vithoulkas, a recipient of the Right Livelihood Award (the "alternative" Nobel prize), who opened the **International Academy of Classical Homeopathy** (1.5 km/1 mi north of Votsi; tel. 242 406 5142; www.vithoulkas.edu.gr) on Alonnisos in 1995, though Vithoulkas has been teaching homeopathy on the island since 1980. Those interested in homeopathy can sign up for lectures and workshops in English over the summer, or pick up a book in the bookstore. The stately old house and the grounds are beautiful to walk through, and you'll meet an eclectic group of students from around the world.

hands-down the best budget option on the island—although with so many nice touches like a hand-drawn welcome sign, a good-bye gift, olive oil toiletries, and king size beds, it hardly feels budget at all. They currently have seven rooms, but they plan to expand in 2019. Book well in advance.

LIADROMIA HOTEL

tel. 24240/65521; www.liadromia.gr/en; from €50

This small, family-run boutique hotel is a good mid-range option, especially for families who want to book a studio that comes with a small kitchenette. Liadromia is the Byzantine name for Alonnisos, and there are plenty of nice touches here, like a welcome drink and daily breakfast buffet.

★ IKION ECO BOUTIQUE HOTEL

tel. 24240/66360; www.ikionhotel.gr; from €145

On an eco-conscious island, the medium-sized Ikion Eco is making waves as a truly "green" hotel: non-toxic and energy-efficient, with soap-saving programs and mattresses from CocoMat that are so comfortable you might never want to get out of bed. Each room is equipped with a handy smartphone with GPS, which you can take with you around the island. The spacious rooms have lovely balconies that look out onto a blue expanse, and the sumptuous breakfast, with homemade breads and jams, is a daily treat. Staff, helmed by the charming Mrs. Ioanna, are exceedingly friendly and quick to offer great local tips for the island.

National Marine Park of Alonnisos Northern Sporades

Harbor, Patitiri; www.alonissos.gr/en/marine-park

In many ways, Alonnisos is the eco-warrior of the Greek islands, making it something of an anomaly in litter-friendly and plastic-crazy Greece. One of the island's most impressive eco-contributions is the National Marine Park, established in 1992. It's the largest marine park in Europe and has helped protect countless marine species (especially the monk seal), kept the water and aqua-environment sparkling clean, and brought the implementation of several important protection and research programs. In addition to Alonnisos, the park encompasses six smaller islands (Peristera, Kyra Panagia, Gioura, Psathoura, Piperi, Skantzoura) and 22 uninhabited

1: restaurants in the main street of Hora
2: delicious meze at To Kamaki Ouzerie **3:** live music at To Kamaki Ouzerie

islands and rocky islets. The park encompasses all the area around Alonnisos.

Boat tours and diving are truly the best way to experience the marine park. There's a good chance you'll see dolphins, though they can be a little shy. If you do dive (or snorkel, or even just open your eyes underwater), you'll see the best of what the marine park has to offer: thousands of fish and sea life that you can't spot from your towel on the beach.

★ BOAT TOURS

From the Patitiri harbor, you'll find several tour operators that will take you on day-long boat trips through the marine park. The tours include stops along the way for swimming, a visit to the monastery of Kyra Panagia, where you'll chat with the only monk living on the island, and lunch. You'll also learn about the conservation efforts on Alonnisos. Tours start from €50 a day; it's best to sign up the day before. **Alonnissos Travel** (tel. 242 406 5188, www.alonnisostravel.gr) is a good option.

DIVING AND SNORKELING

Aside from the dolphins and monk seals, the marine park is also home to a number of shipwrecks, including sunken ancient ships. It's a diver's paradise, and it's becoming easier to organize dives in specific parts of the park. You're not guaranteed to see marine life on any of the tours, nor when you snorkel, but if you'd like to do some underwater sightseeing on your own, try **Chrisi Milia** beach.

TRITON DIVE CENTER

Patitiri; www.bestdivingingreece.com; from €65

Even if it's your first time diving, the enthusiastic folks at Triton Dive Center will make your experience enjoyable, fun, and safe. They offer dives in the marine park, where the guides will point out all the sea life and wrecks. Dives include snacks, water, and free transport to the site.

Marine Park in the distance

Flora on Alonnisos

Alonnisos is teeming with fruit trees, wildflowers, and herbs, and each season brings different flora to the island. Winter marks the arrival of saffron crocuses and anemones, and sourgrass blooms sprout up in January. If you peek under the olive trees in February, you'll find the curled Friar's cowls. Spring brings out poppies, orchids, and gladioli; as the weather heats up, you'll spot (and smell) shrubby knapweeds' purple flowers and delicious honeysuckles. As the weather cools down, Alonnisos becomes filled with pink heathers and cyclamens. No matter what time of year you visit, you'll be rewarded with some of nature's most beautiful offerings.

In addition to the usual sage, rosemary, thyme, oregano, and other heavenly scented herbs you can find across Greece, Alonnisos is home to some **medicinal** and **therapeutic** herbs—these herbs are at their most fragrant in July and August.

WHERE TO LEARN MORE

- You can find some different herbs for sale at the **Women's Cooperative** (page 329).
- To learn more about (respectfully) picking wildlife, you can visit the **International Academy of Classical Homeopathy** (page 331).
- Or set out on a hike with a **guide** (page 325) who can advise you on which herbs are safe for picking.

Beaches North of Patitiri

There's one main road leading out of Patitiri to the north, and all the beaches below are accessible by car. In the summer months, buses regularly leave from the station on the harbor to some of the northern beaches (tel. 697/380 5610; €5 roundtrip). Check the timetable, as it changes.

ROUSOUM BEACH
(Ρουσουμ)

The first bay from Patitiri, an easy 1-km (0.6-mi) walk north, is this cute little swimming spot with a rocky beach, clear water, and a few tavernas and family-friendly beach studio room for rent. It's more of a resort-y style beach, and it can get crowded with families in the summer.

VOTSI
(Βότση)

This little, tranquil fishing village a few kilometers north of Patitiri is a great choice for families, thanks to the bevy of facilities and restaurants. The small beach is located right in the town. It is partly organized, and has plenty of restaurants and snack bars. It's a cute pebbly cove with small orange cliffs surrounding it, accessible from the main road. You can walk from Rousoum to Votsi—it's just 650 meters (0.4 mi).

Food

DENDROLIMANO

Votsi; tel. 24240/65252; 6pm-11:30pm; from €10

Dendrolimano means "tree by the harbor" in Greek, and this slightly upscale, beachside taverna is exactly that. It has a romantic vibe, and is great for couples, who come to enjoy the well-crafted cocktails, extensive wine list, and seafood.

★ CHRISI MILIA BEACH
(Χρυσή Μηλιά)

This is one of the best-known beaches on the island, and for good reason. This long, sandy beach is a true paradise on Alonissis. At the parking lot, Chrisi Milia is to the right side—it's somewhat organized, with one taverna at the far end and a snack bar with good lunch options. It's a good spot for snorkeling as well. My favorite part of this beach is to the far left, as you face the water; walk all the way down and you'll notice a hidden-ish grove of pine trees. This is the second part of the beach, known as **Milia.** The water here is so clear that you can see the bottom of the sea, even swimming out dozens of meters. During the peak season, come early in the morning to secure a spot on the beach—it gets busy! It's 2.5 km (1.6 mi) north of Votsi.

KOKKINOKASTRO BEACH
(Κοκκινόκαστρο)

This is one of the more famous beaches in Alonnisos, thanks to the dramatic red cliffs that hug the beach. The left side is organized with a small beach bar; to the right it's all unorganized, and if you walk down far enough, you'll find some pine trees that offer a bit of shade. To be honest, I think this beach is more for sightseeing, as it's the site of the submerged ancient city of Ikos, which can be viewed by diving. For true relaxation, it's not the most comfortable or private place. It's located 6 km (3.7 mi) north of Chrisi Milia.

TZORTZI GIALOS
(Τζώρτζη Γιαλός)

This cute beach is situated in a sizeable cove, protecting it from the elements and making it an ideal spot for snorkelers. It does get crowded in the summer, and surrounded by cypress trees and olive groves, you feel like you're inside a giant chlorophyll hug. There's a nice taverna on the beach called **Paratholas,** where you can eat under the olive trees. It's located 3.5 km (2 mi) north of Kokkinokastro.

LEFTOS GIALOS
(Λεφτός Γιαλός)

This is one of the more popular beaches in Alonnisos, but it's also considered a "tourist" beach. Lots of boats stop here, and there are plenty of beach bars and tavernas, so the vibe feels more like a party than a relaxing vacation. It is beautiful, though, and swimming out into the sea to look back at the mountains is particularly rewarding. It gets quite crowded in the summer. It's located 4 km (2.5 mi) north of Tzortzi Gialos.

Food

ELEONAS RESTAURANT

tel. 24240/66066; www.eleonas-alonnisos.gr/en/; lunch and dinner; from €15

Located on Leftos Gialos beach under the shade of giant olive trees, Eleonas is a breezy and atmospheric seaside restaurant specializing in contemporary Mediterranean cuisine and fresh seafood. During peak summer, it's best to make a reservation for dinner in the olive grove. The restaurant owners also have a couple of rooms for rent.

Palio Alonnisos Παλιά Αλόνησσος

If Patitiri is the brain of Alonnisos, then the achingly lovely Palio Alonnisos (also known as Old Alonnisos and Hora), located 4 km (2.5 mi) east of Patitiri, is most certainly its soul. Perched on a hill, with a beautiful vantage point on the rest of the island, Palio Alonnisos is a traditional village full of stone houses and bougainvillea. The whole area is pedestrian-only (there's a car park at the entrance of the village), and the place really comes alive at night; it's home to some of the island's best bars and restaurants. Come here a bit before sundown to snag a table at the terrace of Hayiati and enjoy the spectacular view.

1: Rousoum Beach **2:** Votsi Beach **3:** a view of Tzortzi Gialos beach

1
2
3

SIGHTS

Church of the Birth of Christ

This small stone church, built in the 17th century, is located right off the main village square. There are the usual Orthodox fineries inside the church, and the air is heavy with the smell of incense and candles. I love small village churches, and entering this one at night, when everything is illuminated by candles and everyone else is drinking it up in the nearby bars, makes for a very special moment.

RECREATION

Beaches and Hiking

From the village, there's a 2-km (1.25-mi) path that leads down to two different beaches: Mikros Mourtias to the west, and Megalos Mourtias to the east. Hiking to both beaches is a popular activity.

MIKROS MOURTIAS

Mikros Mourtias is supposedly a nudist beach. There's a big spray-painted sign saying "NUDISM ONLY," but on a recent visit, everyone was fully clothed and the beach was rather crowded. It's a small sandy beach flanked by stone cliffs.

The walk from Palio Alonnisos to Mikros Mourtias (2 km/1.25 mi, 30 minutes, easy on the way down and brutal on the way back up) is marked #1 on Alonnisos' hiking trail. You'll notice the donkey path from the village (signposted) that leads southwest to this small cove of a beach. (You can also drive your car down here.)

MEGALOS MOURTIAS

From Palio Alonnisos, follow a steep paved road southeast 1.7 km (1 mi, signposted, 30 minutes, easy on the way down but brutal on the way back up) to reach the village's most popular beach. It's a pebbled beach and the water is nice, but with a couple of tavernas and facilities, it gets pretty crowded during the summer.

Yoga and Massage

KALI THEA

www.kalithea.org; from €10 for a class, 1-hour massage €30

If the good food, calm sea, and hours sunbathing still haven't fully relaxed you, let Bibi and Lee, the kind owners of Kali Thea, turn your body into a veritable flesh puddle with hatha yoga classes and massage sessions (starting from just €30 for one hour!). Group classes are drop-in; you can also organize private classes.

BARS AND NIGHTLIFE

There aren't really raucous bars in Palio Alonnisos. In addition to the places listed below, both Hayiati and Archontostasi restaurants are good places for a drink/hangout.

SUNSET CAFÉ

tel. 693/751 8845; all day

As the name would suggest, this is one of the best places in Palio Alonnisos to watch the sunset: the expansive terrace looks out onto the Western coast of the island, and you can even see Skopelos island in the distance. It's also a restaurant, but I would skip the food in favor of a glass of wine and the view.

BOOKSTORE CAFÉ

www.bookstorecafe.gr; 10:30am-3pm, 6:30pm-2am

Holidays can be hard for introverts; there's so much socializing, drinking, partying, etc. If you want to just relax with a book in your hand, head to this very cute café with a selection of literature in English (plus a nice collection of translated Greek works). In classic Greek style, they make the transition from daytime coffee to alcohol as the sun sets.

SHOPPING

BENTE KELLER

www.bentekeller.gr; May-Oct., daily 11am-3pm and 7pm-11pm

Hailing from the Netherlands, Bente Keller is something of an institution on Alonnisos, and at her charming shop in the hora, you can purchase her lovely watercolor paintings and handmade beeswax candles. Keller also wrote a book on hiking trails in Alonnisos, and if you ask nicely, she can give you a few tips.

GORGONA

antiqueshop.elmashouses.com; May-Oct., daily 11am-3pm and 7pm-11pm

After spotting a rack of vintage clothes out of the corner of my eye, I whirled around so hard I nearly gave myself whiplash. It's not often you see quality vintage on a Greek island. This shop has a fascinating mix of antique furniture, objects, accessories, and vintage clothes for women. Gorgona means mermaid in Greek, and Elma, the lovely woman at the helm of the shop, looks a bit like a mermaid herself. Elma also has a couple of rooms for rent, aptly called Elma's Rooms.

FOOD

★ HAYIATI

tel. 24240/66244; https://hayiati.com; 9am-2am; sweets from €4

All roads in Palio Alonnisos lead to Hayiati: Located at the end of the main street, in a beautiful stone villa with a stunning terrace, Hayiati is the go-to spot in Hora. Technically, it's a *glykopoleio,* or sweet shop, and the specialty is cake, creamy puddings, and pies, but let's not pigeon-hole Hayiati. It also offers excellent savory dishes, like handmade pastas and big, crunchy salads, and downstairs there's a fun piano bar and impressive cocktail lounge.

ARCHONTOSTASTI

tel. 242 406 6310; 9am-1:30am; from €7

This gigantic restaurant—there's a sizeable indoor and outdoor area—has plenty of live music concerts during the summer months, and is a great place to unwind with your new friends. They also have food (the portion sizes reflect the size of the restaurant!). The menu veers between Greek (souvlaki, grilled fish) and vaguely international offerings (pizza, chicken with soy sauce). Try the seafood pasta.

PERI OREKSEOS

lunch and dinner; from €7

A standard taverna that's open longer than its seasonal counterparts, Peri Orekseos offers all the classic Greek fare, plus kid-friendly favorites like cheeseburgers. Service is fast and friendly, and while the food is just okay, the atmosphere and view are terrific. You can see all of the Marine Park below you, and the sun sinks just below your eyeballs.

★ ASTROFEGIA

tel. 24240/65182; 7pm-late; from €9

In the busy summer months, make a reservation on the grape-vine-strewn terrace, which boasts stunning views out to the rest of the island. The food is excellent-quality Greek taverna, and it's a favorite with both locals and tourists. Try the *roka* salad (arugula) and the grilled calamari, then wash everything down with the excellent halonouse wine.

ACCOMMODATIONS

CHILIADROMIA STUDIOS

tel. 24240/65814; www.chiliadromia.gr; from €35

These seven quiet and comfortable rooms are located in a traditional Alonnisan house with stupendous views. Each room comes with a private bathroom and balcony, and the décor is simple and country-chic. It's a great budget option and though there's no breakfast, you're close to the cafes in town.

KONSTANTINA STUDIOS

tel. 24240/66165; www.konstantinastudios.gr; from €95

Named after the owner, Konstantina (she'll pick you up from the port!), these well-appointed studios come fully equipped with high water pressure (something of a rarity on islands), balconies, and kitchenttes—though you won't really need it, given how delicious the breakfast spread is.

Western Alonnisos

The western side of Alonnisos is one of the less visited areas of the island, and offers a natural, wild beauty with unparalleled views. The below destinations are all accessible by car from both Patitiri and Palio Alonnisos, but note that the western side of the island north of Agalou Laka is unpaved and only suitable for hikers.

SIGHTS

Agioi Anargyroi

free

This small church dedicated to the Holy Unmercenaries was built on top of the ruins (open to the public) of a monastery dating back to Byzantine times that was destroyed in an earthquake. The building is perched on the edge of a cliff, making the views from up here absolutely stunning. You can drive here, but many choose to hike from Patitiri (4.5 km/2.8 mi). Even if you drive, you'll have to walk about 500 meters (0.3 mi) from the end of the road to the church.

BEACHES

Tsoukalia (Τσουκάλια)

Somewhat of a rarity on rocky Alonnisos, Tsoukalia is a nice (moderately) sandy beach. It's an archaeological site of an old pottery factory, and you might get lucky and find an ancient pottery shard. According to archaeologists, the pottery factory was most likely making *amphorae* (two-handled jugs with long necks) meant for holding wine. You can access the beach from a dirt path off the main road. From Patitiri, head north; after 3.5 km (2 mi) the paved road ends and the dirt road to Tsoukalia starts. It's just a few minutes' walk to the beach.

ACCOMMODATIONS

AMMOS VILLA (VILLA AQUILA)

Megali Ammos; tel. 697 023 8882; www.ammosbeachvilla.com; €995

Run by the same family who owns Ikion Eco, Ammos Villa is a high-end villa perfect for large groups or big families. With a private pool, hot tub, stunning views, and an open plan kitchen, and good access to the beach, it's a nice hideaway. It's located on Megali Ammos beach, which is a 3.5-km (2-mi, 10-minute drive) north of Patitiri.

Steni Vala and the North End

The farther north you venture on Alonnisos, the more likely you are to be isolated. There's only one road reaching the northern tip of the island, and it's often full of potholes. There are some lovely hikes to do around here, and a few beaches worth checking out as well. Steni Vala is accessible by bus but Agios Dimitrios is not.

STENI VALA (Στενή Βάλα)

After Patitiri, Steni Vala is the most populated village on the island. It's a little fishing village sitting on a pretty harbor, and it's a great place to eat some fresh fish while watching the fishing boats bobbing in the water. Located 10.2 km (6.2 mi) north of Patitiri, on a paved road. There's also a bus that continues to Steni Vala from Patitiri that passes through Palio Alonnisos (25 minutes, from €1.80).

Diving

IKION DIVING

www.ikiondiving.gr; Apr.-Oct. Mon.-Sun.; basic dive from €45

This well-regarded diving center is located just on the water, with classes and excursions for both beginners and advanced divers. They have different dive locations around the island, where you'll get to interact with the stunning marine wildlife up close and personal. They also offer snorkeling classes. Make sure to bring an underwater camera!

Food

DIVER & KALYMNIA

lunch and dinner; from €7

With a big terrace looking right out onto the water, Diver & Kalymnia is a classic Greek island taverna. The owner is a fisherman, so the product is always fresh. Ask the waiter for whatever's been caught that day, and supplement the freshly grilled fish with some fried zucchini, tzatziki, and a bottle of ice-cold ouzo.

Accommodations

4 EPOCHS VILLA

https://4epochesalonnisos.com; €60

A riff on the classic Four Seasons, but Alonnisos style, 4 Epochs is about as resort-y as you'll find here on Alonnisos. It's a cluster of villas surrounding a nice pool; they also have a gym, restaurant, bar, children's play area, and rooftop terrace. The design is a bit colorful Ikea, and the rooms are spacious and clean.

★ AGIOS DIMITRIOS BEACH

(Άγιος Δημητρός)

From an aerial perspective, Agios Dimitrios is shaped like a boomerang. The beach juts out and cuts back in, and thanks to its beauty, it's one of the most beloved and popular beaches in Alonnisos. Large swathes of the beach are organized, and you can rent an umbrella and lawn chair. Located 5.4 km (3.25 mi, 12-minute drive) north from Steni Vala. The road is unpaved.

Hiking

AGIOS DIMITRIOS TO KASTANOREMA

Distance: *1.5 km (1 mi)*

Duration: *30 minutes*

Effort level: *easy*

This walk is marked Path #11 and you will see yellow markers for it from Agios Dimitrios beach. You'll follow a steep built-in staircase past the water reservoir and continue downhill for 1.5 km (1 mi). The views of the sea are beautiful. You can combine this hike with

Agios Dimitrios Beach

trail #15, which will loop you back around. The combined walking time of both hikes is 2.5 hours.

GERAKAS BEACH (Γέρακας)

Where the map of Alonnisos ends, you'll find Gerakas beach, a small pebble beach with very calm water. The main attraction here is a small canteen run by a septuagenarian couple out of a truck.

The beach is located 17 km (10.5 mi) north of Steni Vala (about a 40-minute car ride, given the poor state of the road).

Hiking

GERAKAS TO TOURKOU MNIMA

Distance: *2.4 km (1.5 mi)*

Duration: *30 minutes*

Effort level: *moderate*

This short walk goes from Gerakas to the cove of Tourkou Mnima and takes you well off the beaten path. It's not part of the numbered, "official" hikes, but it is marked with red dots so you won't lose your way. From the snack bar on Gerakas, and before the little chapel of Agios Nikolaos, head east along the coast. At some points the vegetation will get quite thick, but it's passable. About 1 km (.6 mi) in, the path ends, and you'll see the pebbled bay of Tourkou Mnima; continue for another 200 meters (650 feet) till the end of the path and go for a dip in the water. Go back the way you came to return to Gerakas.

Food

GIORGOS CANTEEN

Gerakas Beach

I was not expecting to meet the coolest person in the world here, but, here he is: Mr. Giorgos, a former sailor with the homemade tattoos to prove it, runs around in cutoff jean shorts happily pouring out complimentary shots of *tsipuro,* grilling souvlaki, and telling tales of his wild youth. Ask him about the time he accidently ended up in Lagos for half a year at some point in the 1960s. Though the canteen is only open for lunch, you can pre-order a fish dinner for the evening. To pre-order, ask him in person earlier in the day while you're relaxing on the beach. He also occasionally hosts parties, which finish "when the gods decide."

Skyros (Σκύροσ)

Skyros (pop. 3,000) is an island of tradition, not tourism, which is all the better for the intrepid traveler on the hunt for what Greek islands were like 30 years ago. Despite being the largest of the Sporades islands, it's off the beaten path for most tourists. The locals here depend on industries that have been in their blood for centuries: horse breeding, farming, pottery, wood-carving, bee-keeping... There are a few good hotels to choose from, but there are no restaurants that cater specifically to tourists (read: better food for you), and there's an emphasis on quality and freshness everywhere you go.

Perhaps because tourism isn't the backbone of the island, locals here are exceedingly charming. One morning, while exploring Hora, I found myself invited to join an 11am wine-and-cheese session by a couple of

Highlights

Look for ★ to find recommended sights, activities, dining, and lodging.

★ **Hora's Pots:** Skyros' Hora is considered one of the most beautiful towns in the Aegean, and the ceramic pots that are stuccoed around the roofs and chimneys of the whitewashed houses add to the aesthetic (page 345).

★ **Palamari Archaeological Site:** One of the most important Aegean settlements from the early and middle Bronze Aegean period, this fantastic archaeological site is usually empty and it's located right on the beach (page 352).

★ **Mouries Farm:** Learn about the adorable Skyrian ponies, and, if you're an appropriate size, ride one (page 356).

★ **Renes Bay to Cape Lithari Lighthouse:** Hike through the windswept, shrubby landscape of southern Tris Boukes, which feels like the end of the world—and was for British poet Rupert Brooke, who is buried here (page 357).

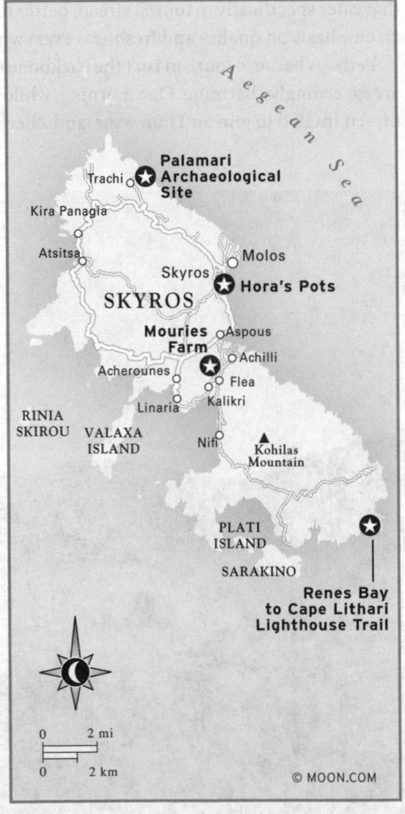

septuagenarian friends. With any luck, you'll have the same experience.

Pinched in the middle by an invisible corset, Skyros is divided in two: The fertile north is green, and full of farmland and pine forests, and the beautiful traditional village of Hora. The south is rockier, hillier, and home to the stunning Bay of Tris Boukes. It seems like every Greek island has a connection to mythology, and Skyros is no exception. It was apparently a hiding place for Achilles, and he is believed to have ridden a Skyrian horse into Troy. The adorable, tiny Skyrian horses are an endangered breed, but local and foreign equestrian enthusiasts have worked tirelessly to preserve the species, and you can now find the horses around the island.

PLANNING YOUR TIME

Three days is enough time to visit all the sites in Skyros, with two days spent exploring the bays of the north and the beautiful Hora, and one day spent hiking through the strange and moon-like south. June to August is the island's busiest period, and if you visit in **May** or **September,** you'll likely have the place to yourself. Outside of the summer months, tourists flock to Skyros for its wild **pre-Lenten carnival** during the winter. Be sure to book accommodations in advance if you'll be traveling at this time.

Unless otherwise noted, businesses on Skyros operate May to September. Most visitors base themselves just outside of **Hora, Magazia,** or **Molos.**

INFORMATION AND SERVICES

Skyros has a great tourism website, www.visitskyros.gr, that provides lots of tourist information and interactive mapping that can be helpful in planning your trip. Otherwise, the **Skyros Travel Agency** (Agoras; tel. 22220/91600; www.skyrostravel.com; 9:30am-1:30pm and 6:30pm-9:30pm) can arrange accommodations, transport, rentals, and excursions.

The **post office** (7:30am-2pm) and national **bank** (with **ATM**) are on the main square in Skyros Town. There's another ATM farther up the main street. Most places accept credit or debit cards. There's also a **police** station in Agoras (tel. 22220/91274). There's a **health center** in Hora (tel. 22220/92222), but for serious emergencies you'll be sent to Evia or the mainland.

GETTING THERE

Air

Skyros is serviced by a small airport, **Skyros Island National Airport** (SKU) 11 km (6.75 mi) north of Hora, also known as Skyros town. There are regular flights to and from Athens (25 minutes; from €28), Thessaloniki (45 minutes; from €50), and Skiathos (35 minutes), and in the summer months, there are occasional charter flights to other western and northern European cities. Local flights are operated by **Aegean** (www.aegean.com) and **Sky Express** (www.skyexpress.com).

There are occasional **buses** for Aegean passengers, but you will most likely either rent a **car** or take a **taxi** from the airport to get to your destination. A taxi from the airport to Skyros Town costs €25.

Ferry

Like Alonnisos, Skyros is not accessible from Piraeus. Ferries, operated by **Skyros Shipping** (www.sne.gr), leave from **Kymi** in Evia daily (1.75 hours; €12). If you are in Athens, you can take the **KTEL bus** from Athens' Liossion bus station (3.5 hours; €16) to catch up with the early-afternoon ferry departure in Kymi. Ferries also link to Alonnisos and Skopelos in the summer months. You can buy your ticket in Skyros Town or at the Linaria port from **Skyros Travel** (tel. 22220/91600; www.skyrostravel.com; daily 9:30am-1:30pm and 6:30pm-9pm).

Previous: view of rocky, green Atsitsa Beach; Skyros has a rich history of producing ceramic tiles; around Skyros Town you'll notice *pithari* (pots) stuck on chimneys and rooftops.

The ticket office on the port opens one hour before departure.

Ferries in Skyros dock in **Linaria,** a 10-km (6-mi) drive from Hora.

GETTING AROUND

Skyros is 209 square km (80 square mi), and its cinched "waist" serves as an indicator of where to go: The **northern** half is populated, while the **southern** part after Kalamitsa is pretty barren. Along the southern coast, there are two **restricted military zones;** you'll notice the outposts and bored-looking soldiers.

The island is relatively well connected by bus, but depending on how much time you spend in Skyros and where you visit, it can be helpful to have a car or motorcycle. The bus services the port in Linaria, Hora, Magazia, Molos, and the airport.

Bus

There are three daily buses that leave from the port of **Linaria** (to coincide with ferry arrivals and departures) and **Skyros Town;** during the summer months buses also regularly go to **Magazia** and **Molos** (€1.80. There are also occasional buses to the airport (€2.70). In Skyros Town, the bus stop is near the bottom of the main street close to the primary school.

Car or Motorcycle

Most of the island is paved, and easy to navigate. If you drive to the southern part of the island, you'll be mostly alone on the roads.

Skyros Travel (tel. 22220/91600; www.skyrostravel.com; daily 9:30am-1:30pm and 6:30pm-9pm) can help organize car rentals for you, or you can rent a car at the Pegasus kiosk at the airport. In town, there are plenty of local and international operators. **Martina's Rentals** (Marchairas 1; tel. 22220/92922) and **Vayos Motorbikes** (near the bus station; tel. 22220/92957) are both reliable local operators. There's also a **Europcar** (www.europcar.com; tel. 22220/92092) in Molos.

Taxi

Taxis (tel. 22220/91666 or 697/289 4088) congregate at the airport, Linaria port, the main square in town, and the bus stop.

a couple ride a motorbike through the winding roads of north Skyros

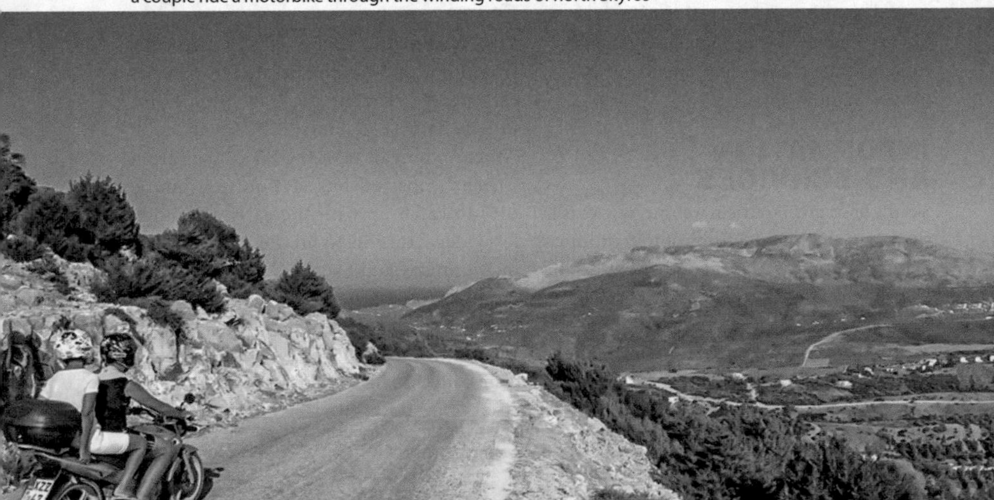

Itinerary Ideas

DAY 1

Explore Hora, Magazia, and Molos, and head up to Palamari archaeological site on your first day on Skyros.

1 Spend the early morning walking around Hora, making sure to grab a pastry from **O Mitsos** bakery.

2 Walk to the top of Hora to the **Monastery of St. George** for spectacular views of Molos and Magazia.

3 Before leaving Hora, grab lunch at **O Pappous Kai Ego** ("Grandpa and Me"), which makes particularly good *dolmades*.

4 Head north toward Molos and Magazia to spend the afternoon relaxing in the sun and splashing in the waves at **Molos Beach.**

5 Continue driving north toward **Palamari.** It's likely you'll have the vast archaeological site all to yourself.

6 On your way back to Hora, grab dinner at one of the restaurants in Molos or Magazia. The sea-facing balcony at **Oi Istories Tou Barba** is one good option.

DAY 2

On your second day on Skyros, drive down to the wild, deserted southern part of the island.

1 Make a pit stop at **Rupert Brooke's Grave** to pay tribute to the poet (and take in beautiful views).

2 Park at Renes Bay, a few kilometers south of the gravesite, and hike the 4.5-km (2.75-mi) Renes Bay to **Cape Lithari Lighthouse** trail. Keep an eye out for endangered Eleonora's falcons along the way.

3 Next, head to **Mouries Farm.** Cuddle an adorable Skyrian pony and then head to their adjacent taverna for an excellent meal.

Hora Χώρα

TOP EXPERIENCE

Skyros' Hora (also interchangeably referred to as Skyros Town) is considered one of the most beautiful villages in the Aegean. With an endless maze of bougainvillea, cobblestone streets and whitewashed houses with flat roofs that you can climb up on, it truly is a magical place. Hora is also a chic town; unlike other island villages, it doesn't have a lot of tourist junk; the shops here sell high-quality products that make for beautiful presents.

The main street of Hora is called Agoras, and it's used as a compass. Hora is on a hill, and Upper Agoras refers to the part of Hora at the top of the hill.

SIGHTS

★ Hora's Pots

Wandering through the bougainvillea-draped streets of Hora, one of Aegean's most beautiful traditional settlements, is a highlight of any trip to Skyros. If you want a focal point

Skyros

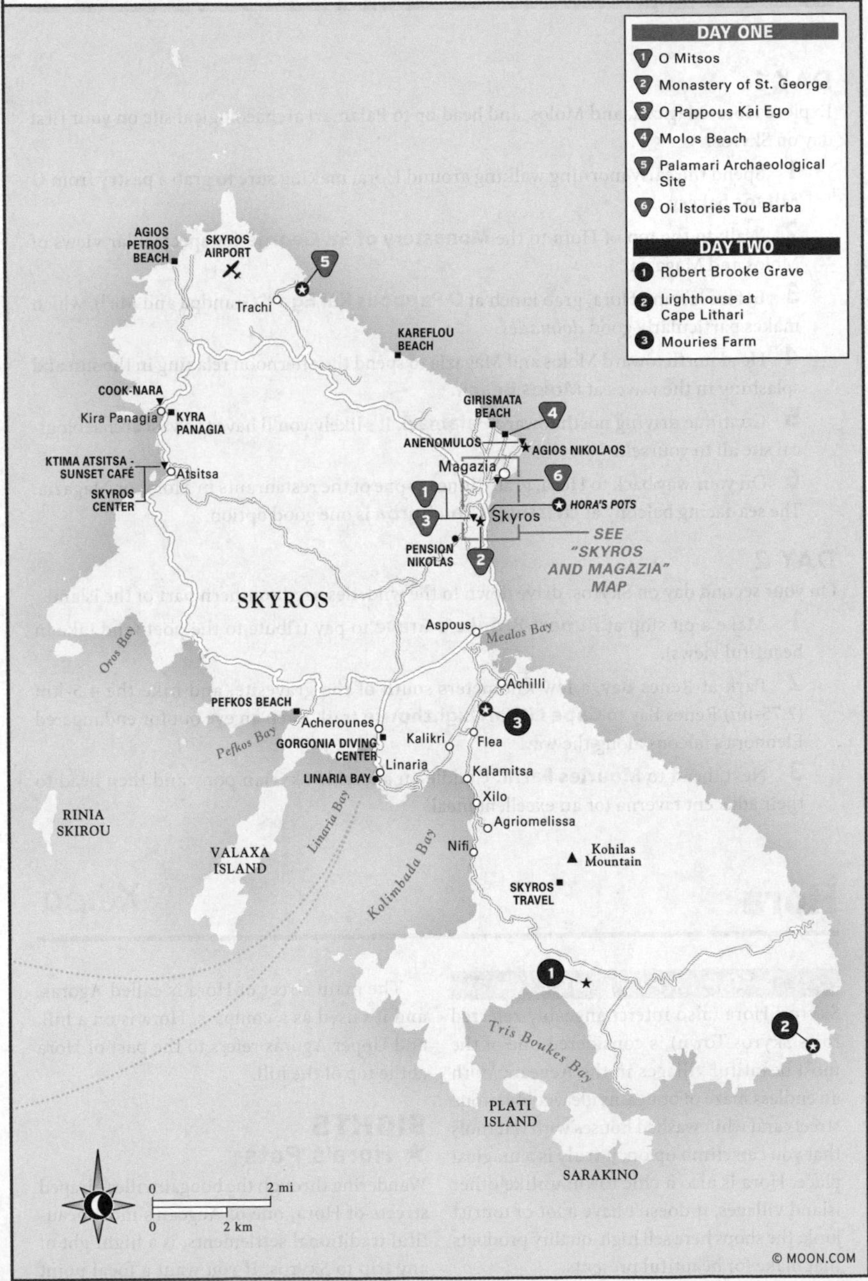
DAY ONE
1 O Mitsos
2 Monastery of St. George
3 O Pappous Kai Ego
4 Molos Beach
5 Palamari Archaeological Site
6 Oi Istories Tou Barba
DAY TWO
1 Robert Brooke Grave
2 Lighthouse at Cape Lithari
3 Mouries Farm
AGIOS PETROS BEACH
SKYROS AIRPORT
Trachi
KAREFLOU BEACH
COOK-NARA
Kira Panagia
KYRA PANAGIA
GIRISMATA BEACH
ANENOMULOS
AGIOS NIKOLAOS
KTIMA ATSITSA - SUNSET CAFÉ
Atsitsa
SKYROS CENTER
Magazia
HORA'S POTS
Skyros
SEE "SKYROS AND MAGAZIA" MAP
PENSION NIKOLAS
SKYROS
Aspous
Mealos Bay
Oros Bay
Achilli
PEFKOS BEACH
Acheroune s
GORGONIA DIVING CENTER
Kalikri
Flea
Pefkos Bay
Linaria
LINARIA BAY
Kalamitsa
Xilo
Agriomelissa
RINIA SKIROU
VALAXA ISLAND
Linaria Bay
Kolimbada Bay
Nifi
Kohilas Mountain
SKYROS TRAVEL
Tris Boukes Bay
PLATI ISLAND
SARAKINO
0 2 mi
0 2 km
© MOON.COM

Skyros and Magazia

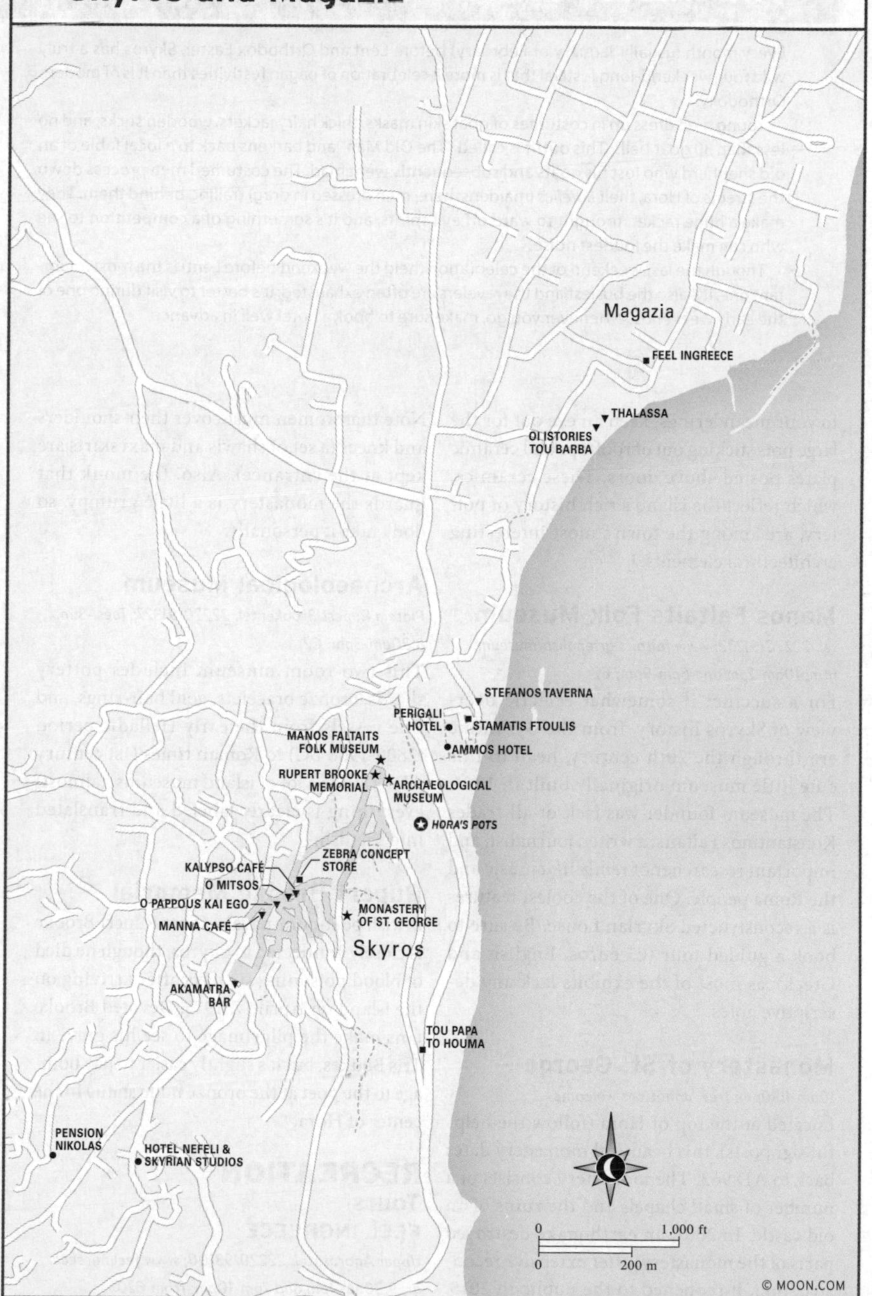

Magazia
FEEL INGREECE
THALASSA
OI ISTORIES TOU BARBA
STEFANOS TAVERNA
PERIGALI HOTEL
STAMATIS FTOULIS
AMMOS HOTEL
MANOS FALTAITS FOLK MUSEUM
RUPERT BROOKE MEMORIAL
ARCHAEOLOGICAL MUSEUM
HORA'S POTS
ZEBRA CONCEPT STORE
KALYPSO CAFÉ
O MITSOS
O PAPPOUS KAI EGO
MANNA CAFÉ
MONASTERY OF ST. GEORGE
Skyros
AKAMATRA BAR
TOU PAPA TO HOUMA
PENSION NIKOLAS
HOTEL NEFELI & SKYRIAN STUDIOS
0
1,000 ft
0
200 m
© MOON.COM

The Wildest Carnival in Greece

Every month (usually January or February) before Lent and Orthodox Easter, Skyros has a truly wild four-weekend-long festival that is more a celebration of pagan festivities than it is of modern Orthodoxy.

Young men dress up in costumes of goat skin masks, thick hairy jackets, wooden sticks, and no less than 30 goat bells: This outfit is called "The Old Man" and harkens back to a local fable of an old shepherd who lost his goats and subsequently went mad. The costumed men process down the streets of Hora, their *korelles* (maidens: here, men dressed in drag) trailing behind them. They make a huge racket, thought to ward off evil spirits, and it's something of a competition to see who can make the loudest noise.

Though the last weekend of the celebration (held the weekend before Lent) is the most important one, it's also the busiest and the revelers are often exhausted; it's better to visit during one of the early weekends. Whenever you go, make sure to book a hotel well in advance.

to your meanderings, keep an eye out for the large pots sticking out of rooftops and ceramic plates posted above doors. These ceramics, which reflect the island's rich history of pottery, are among the town's most interesting architectural elements.

Manos Faltaits Folk Museum

tel. 22220/91232; www.faltaits.gr/english/museum.htm; 10am-2pm and 6pm-9pm; €2

For a succinct if somewhat eclectic overview of Skyros history, from the Byzantine era through the 20th century, head to this cute little museum originally built in 1964. The museum founder was jack-of-all-trades Konstantinos Faltaits, a writer, journalist, and important researcher of *rembetika* music and the Roma people. One of the coolest features is a reconstructed Skyrian house. Be sure to book a guided tour (€5 euros, English and Greek), as most of the exhibits lack any descriptive notes.

Monastery of St. George

10am-1:30pm; free, donations welcome

Located at the top of Hora (follow the helpful signposts), this beautiful monastery dates back to AD 962. The monastery consists of a number of small chapels and the ruins of an old castle. In 2001, an earthquake destroyed parts of the monastery; after extensive reconstruction, it reopened to the public in 2015. Note that women must cover their shoulders and knees (a set of shawls and maxi skirts are kept at the entrance). Also, the monk that guards the monastery is a little grumpy, so don't take it personally.

Archaeological Museum

Plateia Rupert Brooke; tel. 22220/91327; Tues.-Sun. 8:30am-3pm; €2

This two-room museum includes pottery shards, bronze bracelets, gold hair-rings, and fine vessels from the early Helladic period (2800-1900 BC) to Roman times (1st century AD). Unlike a lot of island museums, (almost) everything is clearly labeled and translated into English.

Rupert Brooke Memorial

British poet-cum-naval-officer Rupert Brooke is closely connected to Skyros, though he died of blood poisoning six days after arriving on the island on April 17, 1915. Devoted Brooke fans make the pilgrimage to see his grave in Tris Boukes, but it's slightly easier to pay homage to the poet at the bronze nude statue in the center of Hora.

RECREATION

Tours

FEEL INGREECE

Upper Agoras; tel. 22220/93100; www.feelingreece.gr; 9:30am-1pm and 7pm-10pm; from €20

For sustainable, informative tours that focus on highlighting and preserving the traditions and natural beauty of Skyros, look no further than Feel in Greece. From Skyrian cooking classes to dance lessons (useful if you're planning on coming back for Carnival), to hiking trips to see ponies and falcons, to woodcarving and pottery making, this wonderful tour company has something to satisfy everyone in your family.

NIGHTLIFE AND ENTERTAINMENT

AKAMATRA BAR

tel. 22220/29029; 8am-midnight

This all-day bar makes the transition from coffee to cocktails very easy. They have a lovely terrace in the back, with a great view of the mountains behind Hora. During the summer, they occasionally have parties with DJs.

KALYPSO CAFÉ

Agoras; noon-late

Located inside a beautiful old pharmacy and all done up in marble and dark wood, Kalypso is one of the classier establishments in town. During the day, stop by for a *freddo espresso;* by night, the owner puts on jazz and blues and whisks up very summery beverages like sangria and frozen margaritas.

SHOPPING

ZEBRA CONCEPT STORE

tel. 22220/93053

This hip shop has been around since 1930, albeit with a change in products. You'll find chic caftans, floppy straw hats, ceramics, and small artworks. It's got a great bohemian vibe, and you'll definitely leave with at least one (if not ten) things!

SKYRIANA KERAMIKA

Middle Agoras; tel. 22220/91559

Master potter Ftoulis Stamatios throws and fires his wares at his workshop in Magazia, and sells his plates, cups, pitchers, and other elaborately painted vessels in this cute little shop. There's something to buy at nearly every price point, and it makes a great souvenir.

FOOD

Greek

O PAPPOUS KAI EGO

tel. 22220/93200; lunch and dinner; from €6

The name of this beloved restaurant means "Grandpa and Me," which, honestly, is the ideal dream team. It's full of taverna classics made with local Skyrian products. There's nothing bad on the menu, but they make a particularly mean *dolmades* (stuffed grape leaves).

Breakfast

MANNA CAFÉ

tel. 22220/93042; May-Oct. 8am-noon; from €2

This lovely café is the perfect breakfast spot, with a menu full of smoothies, free-range eggs, and organic products. If you're feeling adventurous, try their traditional Skyrian breakfast options like *gialas* (dried bread rusks with salted goat's milk) and *colivochiles* (wheat porridge with honey and sesame). The café also doubles as a small market, and they sell local jams, spoon sweets, liquors, tomato sauce, and honey.

Bakery

★ O MITSOS

year-round 7am-noon; from €1

My barometer for measuring the quality of a bakery is the number of old people and children who congregate inside. O Mitsos does extremely well with both demographics, so it's no surprise that this old-school café sells the best savory pies and *bougatsa* (cream pie) in all of Hora. It's worth waiting for one coming out of the oven, so you can eat it piping hot.

ACCOMMODATIONS

There aren't many worthwhile places to stay inside of Hora proper (although you can find some nice Airbnbs). Instead, most hotels are just outside of Hora, accessible by car and taxi.

PENSION NIKOLAS

Playia (back road in Hora); tel. 22220/91788; www.nicolaspension.gr; from €40

This is a great budget option just a five-minute walk from Agoras. Don't expect anything uber-chic, but the staff is friendly, and rooms are clean and equipped with air-conditioning and balconies. There's also a lovely garden.

★ HOTEL NEFELI & SKYRIAN STUDIOS

tel. 22220/91964; www.skyros-nefeli.gr; from €75

Located just on the edge of town (practical for those with a car), this is one of the island's smartest hotels. Studio designs veer from traditional Skyrian wood carpentry to more Cycladic-style minimalism. There's a copious breakfast, which is best enjoyed outside by the saltwater pool. The hotel also organizes bike tours around the island (from €20).

Magazia and Molos Μαγαζιά, Μώλος

These villages are just 1-2 km (0.6-1 mi) apart, so you'll often see the two written together on signs, though they technically refer to two different things: Magazia is the cute resort town that encompasses the long beach beside Skyros town, while Molos is 1.5 km (1 mi) to the north—they're close enough to walk together. In recent years, Magazia's tourism has spread to Molos, and the once-sleepy town now boasts a number of bars, rooms for rent, and tavernas. Even though this area is the most "touristic" on the island, it's still pretty relaxed as far as Greek islands go.

During the summer months buses regularly depart Skyros Town and Linaria for Magazia and Molos (€1.80).

SIGHTS

AGIOS NIKOLAOS

Molos; free

This spectacular church in Molos is worthy of a visit. A small sacred space is hewn out of a giant slab of rock, and the effect is something like a mismatched, wabi-sabi puzzle. During ancient times, this area was a quarry. You can still enter the little church, which has an altar and icons, and usually half a dozen scented candles flickering away.

BEACHES

MOLOS (Μωλος)

Undoubtedly the best-known beach on Skyros, Molos is one long, seemingly never-ending strip of golden sand curving around a turquoise sea. Parts of the beach are organized, with beach bars and umbrellas, but the beach is large enough that you can find a corner for yourself. The water is usually calm, and it's a great swimming spot. It's located 2 km (1.25 mi) north of Hora.

TOU PAPA TO HOUMA (Του Παπα/Χουμα)

Toward the southern end of Magazia, underneath the large rock of Hora, is this cozy, sandy beach that's good for swimming. It's a nudist-friendly beach, although plenty of clothes-wearing folks pass through here too. There are no amenities and it's unorganized.

NIGHTLIFE AND ENTERTAINMENT

THALASSA

Molos; tel. 22220/92044; all day

A beautiful Cycladic beach bar, with lots of gauzy white curtains and palm-frond thatched roofs, Thalassa is a lovely beach bar that converts into a cocktail lounge at night. During the summer months, particularly in August, they host parties with live music and DJs.

★ ANENOMULOS

Cape Pouria, 3 km north of Molos; tel. 22220/93656; www.anemomulos.gr; 9am-3am

Anenomulos is the cocktail-companion to Agios Nikolaos. Though the church is built out of a rock, Anenomulos is built out of an old windmill. It's open during the day, serving snacks, coffee, and juice, but this place is most beautiful during the early evening when, cocktail or glass of wine in hand, you can watch the sunset on Skyros Town.

SHOPPING

Ceramics and Sculpture

STAMATIS FTOULIS WORKSHOP

Magazia

In addition to a larger showroom in Skyros Town, ceramicist Stamatis Ftoulis has a sweet little workshop in Magazia. You can pick up traditional Skyrian pottery, including plates, cups, bowls, etc., all colorfully hand-painted. There are two types of Skyrian pottery: simple, unglazed utilitarian objects with white-line drawings, and more intricate ceramics featuring folklore stories.

GIORGOS LAMBROU STUDIO

Magazia; tel. 22220/91334; by appointment only

Sculptor Giorgos Lambrou creates impressive, larger-than-life pieces of artwork. His earlier works are made out of wire; he now works mostly in solid bronze, with a strong slant toward social critique. You can visit his studio in Magazia by calling ahead to his sister Aliki Lambrou (avoid calling during siesta hours between 2pm-5pm; she speaks a little English). If it's not practical to purchase and send home a meter-tall bust, you can always buy a small postcard or watercolor.

FOOD

Even though it's a resort-y area, you can't go wrong eating in Magazia or Molos. There are plenty of delicious restaurants to choose from.

STEFANOS TAVERNA

Magazia; tel. 697/435 0372; breakfast, lunch, and dinner; from €5.50

This classic all-day taverna serves up a delicious range of traditional baked dishes like *kokkinisto* (hearty stuffed vegetables) as well as plenty of lighter options like grilled fish and boiled *horta* (wild greens) generously doused in olive oil and lemon. Snag a seat at the terrace, where you'll have a view of the beach.

OI ISTORIES TOU BARBA

Molos; tel. 22220/91453; lunch and dinner; mains from €4

There are worse ways to while away an afternoon than grabbing a blue chair at the color-matching, sea-facing balcony of Oi Istories Tou Barba and ordering lobster spaghetti off the handwritten menu. They offer both traditional dishes and slightly more creative ones, like crab salad and fish soup.

ACCOMMODATIONS

PERIGALI HOTEL

Magazia; tel. 22220/92075; www.perigali.com; from €60

These comfortable and breezy studios and apartments (there are 27 total), just across from the Magazia beachfront, have a bit of a resort-feel. There are options for half- and full-board, making this an affordable choice for travelers, especially families. There's a pool, a children's play area, and a daily breakfast option. This hotel is open year round.

★ AMMOS HOTEL

Magazia; tel. 22220/91234; www.skyrosammoshotel.com; from €160

This hotel embodies Cycladic architecture at its finest. Ammos offers a beautiful collection of 21 sugar cube rooms that are cleanly and simply decorated (make sure to take a room with a sea-facing terrace for an extra €20). The saltwater pool is the heart of the hotel, and the gym and spa offer personal yoga classes and kinesiology treatments. The staff is attentive and unobtrusive, making Ammos a luxurious and romantic beachside escape. Prices are reduced 50 percent in the off-season.

Northeast Coast

Heading out of Magazia and Molos, the northeast coast of Skyros makes for a fantastic drive. There are plenty of little beaches here, as well as the must-see Palamari archaeological site. You'll follow the interior road for 11 km (just under 7 mi), cutting through the bucolic countryside with occasional glimpses of the blue sea. Technically it takes 18 minutes, but you'll want to drive it slowly to savor the view (and avoid the potholes). There are separate turnoffs for the beaches. There are no buses that run along the northeast coast.

BEACHES

Girismata (Γυρίσματα)

A 5-km (3-mi) drive from Skyros Town, Girismata Beach is a long, sandy beach north of Molos. This is an activity-heavy beach, with plenty of tavernas, restaurants, rooms for rent, and beach bars (though note that as of 2018, there were no umbrellas or chairs for rent). The water is quite shallow, making this beach particularly good for kids.

Kareflou (Καρεφλου)

This long, partly sandy beach, 6 km (3.75 mi) north of Girismata beach, is the local favorite. There's a small white chapel at the far end of the beach, but aside from that, there's nothing going on here: no umbrellas, no beach bars, no tavernas. It's popular with nudists, though clothed people also come here. It's one of the more relaxing spots in Skyros, and the views and water are fantastic.

★ PALAMARI ARCHAEOLOGICAL SITE

free

This fantastically excavated archaeological site 13 km (8 mi) northwest of Skyros Town was once a well-fortified port, and one of the most important Aegean settlements of the early and middle Bronze Aegean period (2500-1800 BC). You'll most likely have the vast site to yourself, and it's an incredible feeling to wander around the ancient rooms and sidewalks, the sea crashing wildly around you. There's a small **exhibit hall** next to the ruins as well, with great photos of the excavation team looking very 1990s (open Mon-Sat 8am-2pm). Most of the artifacts from the site are in the Archaeological Museum.

Northwest Coast

The northwest coast of Skyros, especially the stretch from the pretty little fishing village of Atsitsa down to Kalamitsa, is home to some beautiful coastline, excellent restaurants, and those delightful Skyrian ponies. The coast regularly cuts in and out, giving way to bays and capes. Only Kalamitsa is accessible by bus from Hora (two daily); for the other destinations you'll need a car.

AGIOS PETROS BEACH (Αγιοσ Πετροσ)

Past Palamari and Cape Aloni, you'll notice signs for Agios Petros. This small sandy beach, 9 km (5.5 mi) west of Palamari, is quite private, and favored by nudists who tend to pitch tents and free camp in the pine trees

1: the entrance to a traditional home in Skyros 2: sandals made in the traditional way, with strings of leather, in Skyros Town 3: the view of rocky, green Atsitsa Beach

1
2
3

Skyrian Ponies

tiny and adorable Skyros horses

The adorable Skyrian horse, which never reaches more than 11 hands tall, is a highly intelligent and gentle creature that almost went extinct in the 20th century. Much of their history is unknown, but they are thought to have been brought to the island by Athenian colonists in the 5th to 8th century AD. It's also believed that Alexander the Great rode these horses, and, if you look closely at the frieze on the Parthenon, the horses depicted in stone bear a striking resemblance to the Skyrian pony. There are several nonprofit organizations and farms such as **Mouries Farm** and the **Skyrian Horse Society** (www.skyrianhorsesociety.gr) that have successfully brought the pony back from the point of extinction; it is now a protected breed.

Equestrians should visit Skyros during the three-day **Skyrian Horse Festival** in late June, which features traditional dance, horse parades, and live music. It's not very likely you'll see ponies running wild in the island like in the past. If you want to see them, you should head to Mouries Farm.

that edge around the beach. There's a pretty decent dirt road to the beach, and there's no need for a 4WD.

Food

O KARRAS & O PARNONAS

Agios Petros; tel. 694/763 9270

About 100 meters (328 feet) north before the beach, you'll come across this truly excellent taverna. Ingredients are locally sourced, and though the menu is typical classic taverna, each dish is prepared with care. Anything with fish is particularly good.

ATSITSA (Ατσιτσα)

Situated around Cape Pertitsa, the small port of Atsitsa is one of the most beautiful villages on this coast. If you're driving in from the north, you'll notice the stunning Kyra Panagia church perched on a cliff overlooking the sea just before reaching the village.

Recreation

SKYROS CENTER

Atsitsa Bay; www.skyros.com; UK +44 198/386 5566

This adults-only alternative living and learning space was established in 1979 and put

Skyros on the map as a destination for holistic wellness practitioners. They organize yoga and arts holidays with courses, including life coaching, watercolor painting, and singing classes, all designed to bring out your inner creative child. There's also a center in Skyros Town.

Food

★ COOK-NARA

tel. 22221/00005; lunch and dinner; from €5

Located at a juncture in the road in Kyra Panagia (2 km/1.25 mi north of Atsitsa), this beloved taverna is a favorite on the island. Grab a seat at the sun-dappled terrace and order from taverna classics, or order from the grill.

KTIMA ATSITSA - SUNSET CAFE

tel. 22220/91331; breakfast to sunset; from €2

For views that will make your jaw drop, head to the very aptly named Sunset Café. This little organic spot has the friendliest service and a nice selection of breakfast, lunch, and snack options. They often host weddings in the summer, and are sometimes closed for private receptions.

PEFKOS BAY

This small bay, backed by trees (*pefko* means "pine" in Greek), is a quiet beach, ideal for a lazy afternoon. There are a few fishing boats bobbing in the water, and part of the beach is organized with umbrellas and chairs. There are a couple of good tavernas right on the beach; try **Stamatia** (Pefkos; tel. 697 255 8232; mains from €6), which has been making baked dishes for the better part of half a century.

Pefkos is located 6 km (3.75 mi) northwest of Linaria.

Linaria and Vicinity

LINARIA (Λιναριά)

If you're arriving by ferry, Linaria will be your first sight of Skyros. This cute little port features a jumble of houses on the green hills above the water, and while it's not the most beautiful part of the island, it can make a useful base if you'd rather be close to the port for an early morning ferry departure.

Diving

GORGONIA DIVING CENTER

Aheroúnes; tel. 22220/96007; www.skyros-diving.com; daily in summer 9am-8pm; €120-380

This good diving center 1.4 km (1 mi) north of Linaria offers classes and excursions for both beginner and professional divers. They have a special "scuba ranger" program for children above 8 years old.

Food

MARIGO

Linaria, 22220/96010; from €8

This little restaurant right on the port serves up fantastic fresh-caught seafood that's served grilled, steamed, or fried. For those who prefer a more carnivorous meal, they have plenty of meat options too. They have a really nice and friendly staff as well, and dessert is usually on the house at the end of the meal.

Accommodations

LINARIA BAY

tel. 22220/93274; www.linariabay.gr; from €50

Choose from studios, apartments, or traditional Skyrian rooms at this simple but affordable hotel. Rooms are sparsely furnished, with lots of wood in the classic Skyrian style, but they all feature balconies facing the sea.

PEGASUS

tel. 22220/91600; https://pegasus-studios-apartments-skyros-island.booked.net; from €100

Another affordable option in Linaria Bay, Pegasus studios feature stone fireplaces (though you'll more likely be using the A/C) and balconies with sea views. There aren't a lot of frills here, but it's a down-to-earth place with rooms arranged around a nice garden. Breakfast at the nearby café comes at an extra cost.

★ MOURIES FARM

tel. 694/746 5900; https://skyrianhorses.weebly.com; by appointment; from €10

Adjacent to Mouries restaurant, 5 km (3 mi) northeast of Linari in Kalikri, is a horse farm and conservation center, where you can learn all about the Skyrian horses, and children under 12 can take a ride around the farm (€10). The center also runs volunteer programs, and there are usually half a dozen foreigners working on the farm, having fallen in love with both Skyros and the doe-eyed ponies. Under the watchful eyes of the trainers, you'll get to pet the ponies (be still my heart) and feed them apples or sugar cubes, and watch the trainers brush them down and check their hooves.

Food

★ KTIMA MOURIES

tel. 22220/93555; https://skyrianhorses.weebly.com; lunch and dinner; from €6

Among the wildly good restaurants in Skyros, Ktima Mouries (adjacent to the horse farm) stands out. This excellent taverna serves up authentic Greek food using local ingredients. They're particularly known for their meat dishes, as well as local cheeses. There's a small playground in the back for kids, and parents can relax and get buzzed under the veranda.

Bay of Tris Boukes and South Skyros

"We're selling seashells!" screamed a line of children past Kalamitsa, standing on the side of the road as the sun dipped into the sea behind them, turning the sky a rich, lurid pink. We pulled our car over to the side of the road—I can't resist the entrepreneurial spirit of tweens—and peered into their lunch boxes that were moonlighting as display cases for the shells. On an island like Skyros, the children run just as happily wild as the horses. As we drove off, our pockets considerably lighter, the girls faded away from the rearview mirror, and we didn't see a single other human our whole ride down to Tris Boukes.

The southern part of Skyros is an abrupt departure from the vegetative north. There are no restaurants or hotels here; there are hardly any houses. Half the area is a restricted military zone. The landscape changes dramatically, too: It's all shrubs and rocks and goats, bleating loudly, and an alarming amount of goat skulls and bones. As you drive down, look out for the rock arrangements that have been made by some mysterious artist who comes to Skyros every summer to move the giant boulders into human-like formations.

You're completely on your own out here, so there's no bus, and it's not always easy to get a taxi to take you here. Instead, rent a car for the day to explore everything at your own pace; I promise you, it's worth it!

SIGHTS

Rupert Brooke's Grave

Many visitors to Skyros make the pilgrimage to the grave of Rupert Brooke, who was buried here after his death aboard a French military hospital ship. There's a simple wooden sign on the road in Greek pointing you in the direction of the grave, and the tombstone features an inscription from his famous sonnet "The Soldier." This is a popular sight for Brooke fans, but even if you've never heard of him, the view from here—and the emptiness

Hiking on Skyros

Hiking through Skyros' moon-like south is a special experience. You can hike the **Cape Lithari lighthouse trail** (page 357) yourself, and for maps of all the island's routes, visit **Skyros Life** (www.skyroslife.com). Another option is to join a trip led by one of the local guides listed below.

GUIDED HIKES

Led by local couple Panos and Ariadni (who speak English), **Rediscover Skyros** (tel. 695 548 7024; www.rediscoverskyros.com; by appointment; no fee but donations welcome) is a hiking club that takes you on routes and trips around the island that usually end with a swim. Their approach is eco-conscious, and they are very involved in cleaning and maintaining hiking trails. They don't have a brick-and-mortar shop, so get in touch online about different walking options around Skyros (donation based). **Feel Ingreece** (Upper Agoras, Hora; tel. 222 209 3100; www.feelingreece.gr; 9:30am-1pm and 7pm-10pm) is another option for guided hiking trips.

of the landscape—is stunning. From Linaria, it's 16 km (10 mi) south and will take you 30 minutes.

Lighthouse at Cape Lithari

Originally built in 1864, the Cape Lithari Lighthouse is the only lighthouse in Greece built with a two-story building at its base. It's made of stone and glass, and in 2012, the Ministry of Culture listed it as a historical monument. You can't go inside, but it's a beautiful building and it's fun to stand next to it and imagine yourself as a 19th-century lighthouse keeper. From Linaria it's a 20-km (12-mi) drive that will take you 35 minutes (though note that you won't be able to drive all the way to the lighthouse; the road ends several kilometers before).

HIKING

★ RENES BAY TO CAPE LITHARI LIGHTHOUSE

Distance: *4.5 km (2.75 mi)*

Duration: *1 hour*

Effort Level: *moderate*

Though the lighthouse is nice, what's particularly beautiful is the hike from nearby Renes Bay to Cape Lithari. The 4.5-km (2.75-mi) route will take you along cliffs dramatically plunging into the sea, and from April to October, you'll likely catch sight of Eleonora's falcons. Skyros is home to the largest colony of this endangered bird species. Renes Bay is a few kilometers south of Rupert Brooke's grave; continue down the dirt road.

Corfu (Κέρκυρα)

Thanks to its Italian history, Corfu (pop. 97,000) is probably the least typically Greek of the Greek islands. Here you'll find a Venetian harbor town, Italian-influenced food, and a lilting Greek that has much in common with melodic Italian. Corfu's jewel is its old town, where forts, arcades, cobblestone streets, and pastel-colored buildings make it feel like a lost island of Venice. The island was later ruled by the British from 1815-1864, and you'll feel that legacy in the sights, abundance of ginger beer, and odd game of cricket played in Corfu Town's main square.

Corfu has always been a hospitable place: It was a place of refuge for a shipwrecked Odysseus in Homer's *Odyssey.* In modern times, it was one of the first Greek islands to really open itself up to mass tourism, and unfortunately, much of the island has been heartbreakingly overdeveloped.

Highlights

Look for ★ to find recommended sights, activities, dining, and lodging.

★ **Old Town:** Wander through the cobblestone streets and duck under archways to feel transported to a different time and place (page 365).

★ **Corfu Museum of Asian Art:** This fantastic collection of East and South Asian art is housed in an atmospheric palace (page 365).

★ **Palaio Frourio:** The well-preserved Old Fort offers stellar views of Corfu Town and the sea (page 365).

★ **Palia Perithia:** The oldest and best-preserved village in Corfu has been in existence since Byzantine times, and is undergoing something of a renaissance, with renovated houses and an uptick in traditional crafts (page 375).

★ **Myrtiotissa Beach:** Lawrence Durrell's favorite beach is one of the more pristine on the island, thanks to its difficult-to-reach position (you'll have to hike down). It's also a favorite of nudists (page 379).

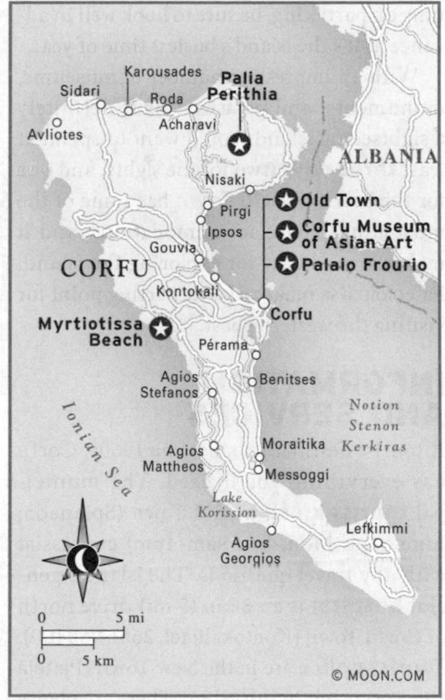

During the summer months, the crowds are relentless. But the island still holds enough mysteries that you can privately uncover on your own. Head to the interior mountain villages of Palia Perithia and the untamed western coast for a taste of authentic Corfu.

PLANNING YOUR TIME

Thanks to a bustling student population, Corfu—or at least, Corfu Town—is alive **year-round,** and it's one of the few Greek islands that makes a worthwhile trip in the middle of winter. Of course, Corfu is nicer under the warm sunshine, and you're best off visiting in **May** or **September.** Avoid the summer months when it becomes unbearably crowded, both in the city center and the beach towns.

Corfu is renowned for its **Easter** celebration (date depends on the Orthodox calendar, but usually in April or May); if you're planning on partaking, be sure to book well in advance as it's the island's busiest time of year.

With an impressive number of museums, monuments, and palaces, this is definitely a sightseeing island. You'll want to spend at least **three days** (two for the sights, and one for the beach). **Corfu Town** has some of the most atmospheric accommodations, and it makes a good base for exploring the island. Paleokatritsa makes a good starting point for visiting the western coast.

INFORMATION AND SERVICES

A tourist destination since the 1960s, Corfu has everything you'll need. The municipal **tourist kiosk** in Old Town (Spianada; June-Sept. Mon.-Sat. 9am-4pm) can assist with any travel questions. The island's general **hospital** is an 8 km (5 mi) drive north of Corfu Town (Kontokali; tel. 26613/60400). **Tourist police** are in the New Town (Plateia San Rocco; tel. 26610/29186). There are plenty of **banks** and **ATMs** around the Old Town, as well as along the New Port harbor, and in the resort areas.

GETTING THERE

The easiest way to get to Corfu is to fly, unless you are already on the western mainland.

Air

Daily local and international flights land at Corfu's airport, **Ioannis Kapodistrias International Airport** (CFU; tel. 26610/89600; www.corfu-airport.com) 2 km (1.25 mi) southwest of the Old Town. **easyJet** (www.easyjet.com), **Ryanair** (www.ryanair.com), and **British Airways** (www.ba.com) offer direct flights between the UK (and other European countries) and Corfu. **Aegean Air** (www.aegeanair.com) has direct flights from Athens and Thessaloniki; **Astra Airlines** (www.astra-airlines.gr) from Thessaloniki; and **Sky Express** (www.skyexpress.gr) from Preveza, Kefallonia, and Zakynthos.

The airport has seen better days; there's chatter of a new one being built, but as of the time of this writing, that hasn't materialized. From the airport, taxis cost around €12 to Corfu Town. Local Bus 15 leaves from the airport to Plateia San Rocco in the New Town, and the New Port a bit farther away.

Ferry

Ferries arrive and depart from **Neo Limani** (New Port), a short distance from the Old Town, and **Lefkimmi,** a town on the southern part of Corfu.

There are ferries to Igoumenitsa, Greece's biggest western port (1 hour, daily; €10). Given the island's close proximity to Italy, it's no surprise **ANEK Lines** (www.anek.gr) connects Corfu with Bari (8 hours, twice weekly; €60) and Ancona (14.5 hours, once weekly; €85) in Italy. There are no ferries from Athens, and service between the Ionian islands is still spotty, even during the summer months.

Previous: beautiful Paleokastritsa Beach; wander Corfu Town to find nice details; the view of Corfu from the Old Fort.

Corfu

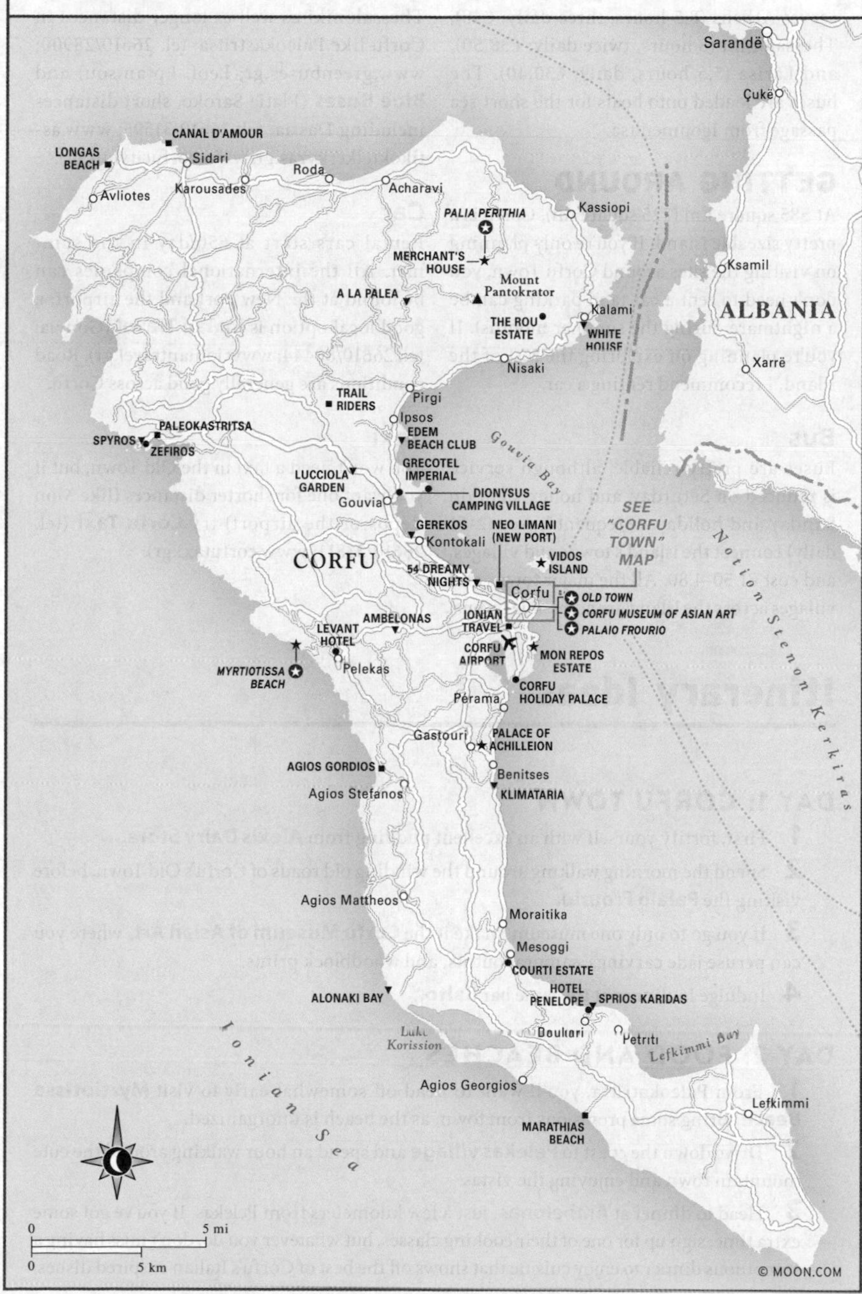

Sarandë
Çukë
Ksamil
ALBANIA
Xarrë
CANAL D'AMOUR
LONGAS BEACH
Sidari
Roda
Acharavi
Karousades
Avliotes
Kassiopi
PALIA PERITHIA
MERCHANT'S HOUSE
Mount Pantokrator
A LA PALEA
THE ROU ESTATE
Kalami
WHITE HOUSE
Nisaki
Pirgi
TRAIL RIDERS
Ipsos
EDEM BEACH CLUB
PALEOKASTRITSA
SPYROS
ZEFIROS
Gouvia Bay
GRECOTEL IMPERIAL
LUCCIOLA GARDEN
DIONYSUS CAMPING VILLAGE
Gouvia
GEREKOS
Kontokali
NEO LIMANI (NEW PORT)
SEE "CORFU TOWN" MAP
CORFU
VIDOS ISLAND
54 DREAMY NIGHTS
Corfu
OLD TOWN
CORFU MUSEUM OF ASIAN ART
PALAIO FROURIO
Notion Stenon Kerkiras
AMBELONAS
IONIAN TRAVEL
LEVANT HOTEL
CORFU AIRPORT
MON REPOS ESTATE
MYRTIOTISSA BEACH
Pelekas
CORFU HOLIDAY PALACE
Perama
Gastouri
PALACE OF ACHILLEION
AGIOS GORDIOS
Benitses
Agios Stefanos
KLIMATARIA
Agios Mattheos
Moraitika
Mesoggi
COURTI ESTATE
ALONAKI BAY
HOTEL PENELOPE
SPRIOS KARIDAS
Boukari
Petriti
Lefkimmi Bay
Lake Korission
Ionian Sea
Agios Georgios
Lefkimmi
MARATHIAS BEACH
0
5 mi
0
5 km
© MOON.COM

Bus

Green Buses (www.greenbuses.gr) serves Athens (8.5 hours, three daily; €48), Thessaloniki (8 hours, twice daily; €38.50), and Larisa (5.5 hours, daily; €30.40). The buses are loaded onto boats for the short sea passage from Igoumenitsa.

GETTING AROUND

At 585 square km (225 square mi), Corfu is a pretty sizeable island. If you're only planning on visiting the sites around Corfu Town, you don't need to rent a car (and parking can be a nightmare during the summer months). If you're planning on exploring the rest of the island, I recommend renting a car.

Bus

Buses are pretty reliable, although service is reduced on Saturday, and nonexistent on Sunday and holidays. Frequent buses (2-11 daily) connect the island's towns and villages, and cost €1.50-4.80. All the major towns and villages across the island are accessible by bus.

There are both **Green Buses** (long distance, on Avramiou and goes to Athens and Thessaloniki as well as longer distances in Corfu like Paleokastritsa; tel. 26610/28900; www.greenbuses,gr; Leof. Eptanisou) and **Blue Buses** (Platia Saroko, short distances including Dassia; tel. 26610/31595; www.astikoktelkerkyras.gr, www.corfucitybus.gr).

Car

Rental cars start at €50/day in the summer. All the international companies can be found at the New Port and the airport; a good local option is **Ionian Travel** (Gouvia; tel. 26610/80444; www.ioniantravel.gr). Road conditions are generally good across Corfu.

Taxi

You won't need a taxi in the Old Town, but if you want one for shorter distances (like Mon Repos or the airport) try **Corfu Taxi** (tel. 26610/33811; www.corfutaxi.gr).

Itinerary Ideas

DAY 1: CORFU TOWN

1 First, fortify yourself with an excellent pudding from **Alexis Dairy Store.**

2 Spend the morning walking around the winding old roads of Corfu's Old Town, before visiting the **Palaio Frourio.**

3 If you go to only one museum, make it the **Corfu Museum of Asian Art,** where you can peruse jade carvings, samurai outfits, and woodblock prints.

4 Indulge in dinner at the wine bar **Salto.**

DAY 2: FOOD AND BEACHES

1 From Paleokatritsa, you'll want to head off somewhat early to visit **Myrtiotissa Beach.** Bring some provisions from town, as the beach is unorganized.

2 Drive down the coast to **Pelekas village** and spend an hour walking around the cute mountain town and enjoying the vistas.

3 Head to dinner at **Ambelonas,** just a few kilometers from Pelekas. If you've got some extra time, sign up for one of their cooking classes, but whatever you do, don't miss having a sumptuous dinner to enjoy cuisine that shows off the best of Corfu's Italian-inspired dishes.

Itinerary Ideas

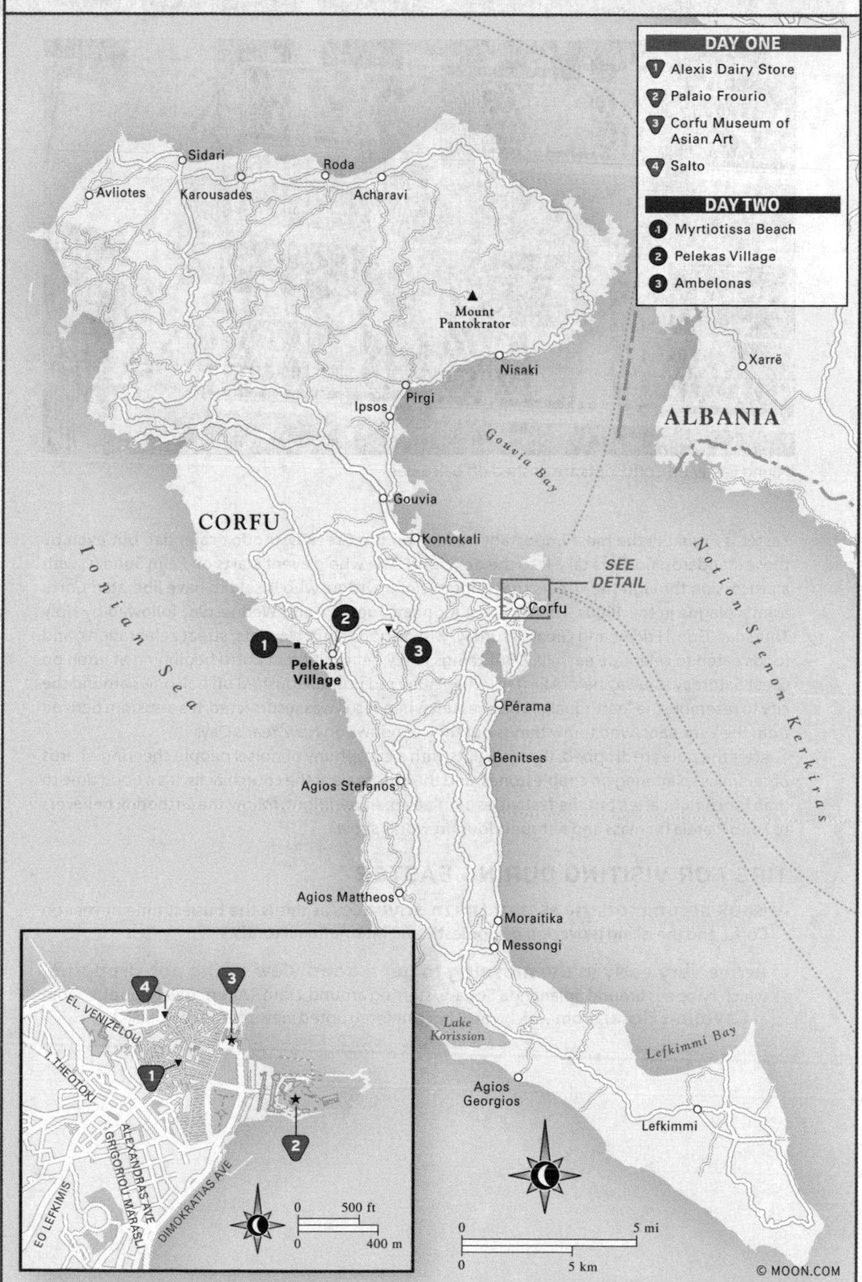

DAY ONE
1 Alexis Dairy Store
2 Palaio Frourio
3 Corfu Museum of Asian Art
4 Salto
DAY TWO
1 Myrtiotissa Beach
2 Pelekas Village
3 Ambelonas
Sidari
Roda
Avliotes
Karousades
Acharavi
Mount Pantokrator
Nisaki
Pirgi
Ipsos
Xarrë
ALBANIA
Gouvia Bay
Gouvia
CORFU
Kontokali
Ionian Sea
Notion Stenon Kerkiras
SEE DETAIL
Corfu
Pelekas Village
Pérama
Benitses
Agios Stefanos
Agios Mattheos
Moraitika
Messongi
Lake Korission
Lefkimmi Bay
Agios Georgios
Lefkimmi
EL. VENIZELOU
I. THEOTOKI
ALEXANDRAS AVE
GRIGORIOU MARASLI
DIMOKRATIAS AVE
EO LEFKIMIS
0 500 ft
0 400 m
0 5 mi
0 5 km
© MOON.COM

Easter on Corfu

During Easter on Corfu, pots are pushed off balconies.

Easter is arguably the most important holiday on the Greek Orthodox calendar, but even by those standards, Corfiots take it to the next level. The whole event starts on Palm Sunday, with a procession through the streets that honor Saint Spyrdon, who is said to have liberated Corfu from a plague in the 1600s. There's Great Monday, Tuesday, and Wednesday, followed by Holy Thursday, Good Friday, and Great Saturday, with various church events, street celebrations, and foods eaten to celebrate each day. But things really get exciting in Corfu beginning at noon on Great Saturday (the day before Easter), when huge red pots are pushed off balconies around the city to resemble the "earthquake" that was felt when Jesus was resurrected. It's a custom derived from the Venetians, who threw things out their windows on New Year's Day.

After the pots are dropped, the air erupts with a cacophony of noise: people cheering, shards of ceramics splintering on cobblestones, and the iron peals of the church bells. It's a good time to grab lunch right after, but the festivities aren't over. At midnight, follow the Orthodox believers to Pano Plateia for mass and a stupendous fireworks show.

TIPS FOR VISITING DURING EASTER

- **Book accommodations months in advance,** as this is the busiest time of year on Corfu, and the island is overrun by domestic and international tourists.
- **Arrive very early in the morning to get a good view of the pot-dropping,** which happens around Spiananda Square, starting around 11am. (Alternatively, book a room at **Cavalieri Hotel,** from which you'll have uninterrupted views of the spectacle.)

Corfu Town Κέρκυρα

Corfu Town is the capital and harbor of Corfu, and the island's beating heart. Known for its Venetian architecture, it can feel more like an Italian city than a traditional Greek island town. Corfu Town makes an excellent base for travelers, especially if you're visiting outside of the brutally hot and crowded sum mer months. The old town is the section of the city that butts up against the coastline and is instantly recognizable by its old-world architecture; the New Town surrounds the older section of the city.

SIGHTS

Corfu Town is heavy on sights. If you want to take them all in, I suggest purchasing a **joint ticket** (€14), which will give you admission to the Palaio Frourio, the Museum of Asian Art, the Antivouniotissa Museum, and Mon Repos. You can purchase it directly at any of the sights.

★ Old Town

Corfu Town is broadly divided between its new and old section. The latter is a UNESCO World Heritage Site and home to some of the island's most interesting architecture, museums, and restaurants. Though the town dates back to the 8th century BC, most of the construction you'll see—neoclassical houses, romantic winding pathways, arcades—is of the Venetian variety.

SPIANADA SQUARE

Welcome to the biggest square in the Balkans: Spianada is the place to see and be seen. A row of restaurants and cafés sit under stone arcades, which form the perimeter of a large green park. There are houses built in the traditional Corfiot style, with plenty of faded pastel colors to add to the atmosphere. Grab a coffee (pricey but worth it) at one of the cafés under the arcade, and watch the world go by.

In the warmer months, there are occasional pickup and semiprofessional games of cricket played on the green. (Interestingly, cricket is the sport of choice on Corfu. It was brought over by the British and quickly adopted.) Locals call cricket *fermaro kai issia* ("block and wallop"), and are just as mad about it as the British. If you are too, head to www.cricketcofru.com for more information.

★ CORFU MUSEUM OF ASIAN ART

Palace of St Michael and St George; tel. 26610/30443; www.matk.gr; 8 daily am-8pm; adult €6, €3 child

Located inside the city's prominent palace, this is the only museum in Greece dedicated to East Asian and Indian art, and it's a good one. You'll find stunning collections of Chinese ceramics, jade carvings, samurai outfits, woodblock prints, and more. The curators couldn't resist bringing in some Greek elements as well: The India section is supplemented with information about Alexander the Great. Be sure to walk through the palace gardens, which offer lovely views to Mandraki lido, the city beach.

★ PALAIO FROURIO

tel. 26610/48310; summer, daily 8am-7.30pm, Nov.-Mar. 8am-3pm; €6

In Greek, Palaio Frourio means "Old Fortress," which should give you a clear idea of what this is: a Venetian-built fortress from the 14th century, built upon a Byzantine city. It's a lovely place to wander around. You'll circle around the fort, and there's a Byzantine museum at the entrance. Walk up to the Land Tower, where you'll be rewarded with fantastic vistas, though be warned it's a favorite make-out spot of Corfu students and you'll probably stumble upon some lovebirds. You can walk up to the lighthouse for a stellar view of Corfu Town; equally nice is a downward stroll to the rocky beaches at the base of the Frourio—both are part of the complex.

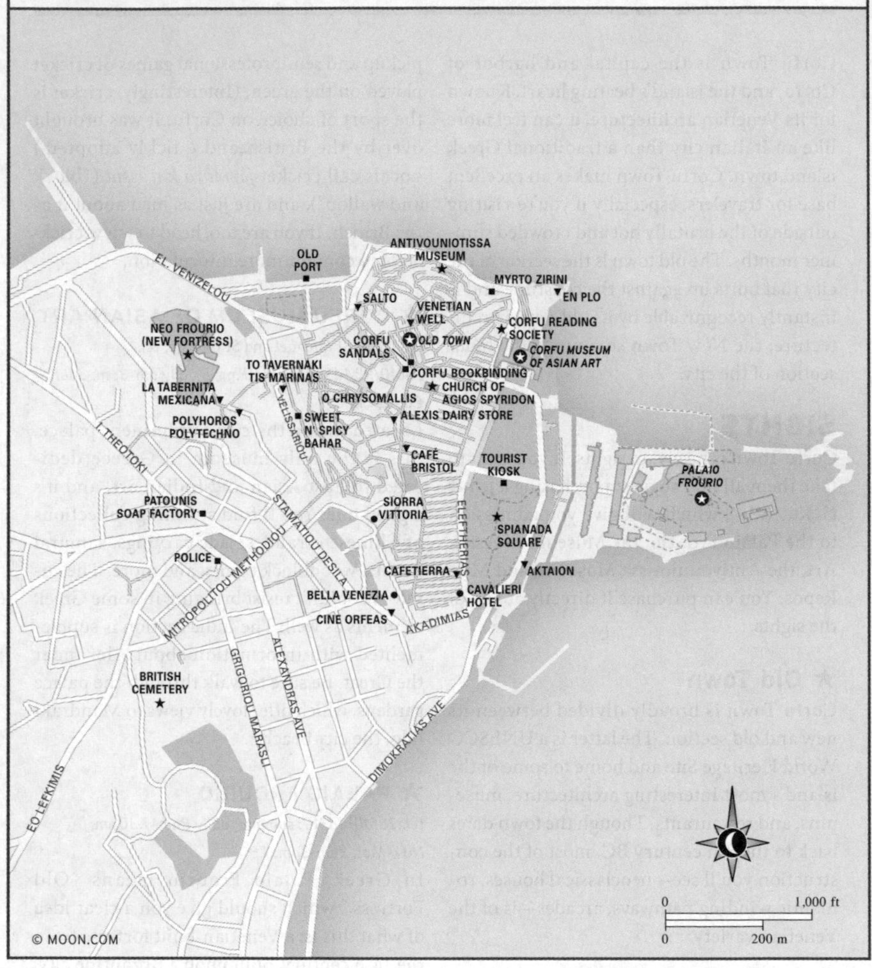

CHURCH OF AGIOS SPYRIDON

Agios Spyridonos; daily 8am-9pm; free

Despite being ruled by Catholics and Protestants for centuries, Corfu has held on firmly to its Orthodox heritage. One of the more beautiful odes to Greek Orthodoxy is this splendid church, full of frescoes and heady with the scent of incense. It's the resting place of Corfu's patron saint, Spyridon. Since 1453, when his corpse was brought here from Constantinople, he's been kept in a silver casket that is paraded through town during important holidays and *panigiri*.

CORFU READING SOCIETY

Kapodistriou 120; tel. 26610/39528; www.anagnostikicorfu.com; Mon.-Sat. 9:30am-1:30pm, afternoon by appointment only; free

Stumbling upon secret reading nooks is the vacation dream of nerdy introverts. Corfu has its own Reading Society (a library), located in a creamy neoclassical villa. Founded in

1836 by 14 noblemen inspired by the Geneva Society, it's now home to some 30,000 volumes of books and is the oldest cultural institution in modern Greece. It's also open to the public (the noblemen were not so democratic). Walk up the external staircase (there's no sign) to browse one of the books on Ionian culture. It's a nice quiet place to spend an afternoon away from the crowds.

ANTIVOUNIOTISSA MUSEUM

Off of Aresniou; tel. 26610/38313; www.antivouniotissamuseum.gr/en; Tues.-Sun. 8:30am-3pm; €4 adult, €2 child

This Byzantine museum is situated inside the beautiful Church of Our Lady of Antivouniotissa, which does double duty as a place of worship and home to an exquisite collection of Byzantine and post-Byzantine artifacts. Notable exhibits include religious iconic paintings and narthexes (traditional Orthodox burial antechambers). The building has undergone extensive renovations and is the best-preserved example of Heptanesian Basilica style (noted for high pews and painted wallpaper) on the island.

NEO FROURIO

Apr.-Oct. daily 9am-3:30pm; free

The Venetian-built Neo Frourio (aka the New Fort) is actually only slightly younger than Paleo Frourio, but it serves as both an architectural and security complement to the other fortress. There are stunning views from here over the red-tiled roofs of Corfu Town.

New Town

BRITISH CEMETERY

off of San Rocco Square; daily; free

First founded in 1814, the British cemetery was regularly used as a place to inter officials, soldiers, and residents. During the first and second World Wars, Corfu was used by Allied soldiers as a military base, and the plots filled up. There are about 500 graves now, all doused in history. The place is so forgotten, there are even tortoises ambling about. The best time to visit the cemetery is during May, when the orchids are in full bloom. If you're asking locals for directions, refer to it as the English Cemetery.

Outside Corfu Town

MON REPOS ESTATE

Kanoni Peninsula; May-Oct. 7:30am-7:30pm, Nov.-Apr. 7:30am-5pm; €3

To feel like royalty for the day, head to the park-estate of Mon Repos, 3 km (2 mi) south of Corfu Town. The neoclassical buildings, built in 1831 by English Commissioner of the Ionian Islands Frederick Adam, as a gift to his Corfiot wife, Nina Palantianou, sit on 104 hectares (258 acres) of wooded land. Prince Philip, husband to Queen Elizabeth II, was born in the villa that now hosts the Museum of Palaepolis. Your ticket gets you access to the museum, where you'll find sculptures and preserved interiors.

The estate is also home to ancient ruins, like the Temple of Artemis and the Early Christian Basilica (both free). As you walk around the perimeter of the estate, you'll notice these spots. You can picnic on the grounds, but be sure to bring your own food and water as there's nothing around.

Athletes can walk the 3 km distance (about half an hour, mostly uphill), or take bus 2a from Spianada (every 20 minutes; €1.70).

VIDOS ISLAND

Old Port; every hour; €5

From the old port, catch a 10-minute boat ride across the bay to Vidos island. There's not much happening on the lush, green island, but if you walk across the island 600 meters (1,968 feet) to the northern part, you'll come across some nice beaches.

NIGHTLIFE AND ENTERTAINMENT

Big clubs and bars are located in the New Town, or along the coastal road north of Old Town. In the Old Town itself, expect to find smaller venues, cozy bars, and some more intimate live music venues. Some tavernas also have musicians come and play inside the restaurant during summer months.

Bars

CAFÉ BRISTOL

49 Evgeniou Voulgareos; tel. 693/666 0101; daily 9am-2am

One of the coolest café-bars in Corfu, Café Bristol is done up with jungle wallpaper, vintage tiled floors, and a massive lightbulb installation. It's something of a cultural hub in Corfu Town, and is always crowded, particularly at night when the bartenders sling expertly crafted cocktails.

Live Music

POLYHOROS POLYTECHNO

Corner of Solomoú and Sholemvoúrgou; tel. 26610/27794; 8:30pm-late daily

In Greek, *polyhoros* means something that has multiple purposes, which exactly describes this little space: It's something of a bar and dance club, with a DJ console, and live events. It's the only place in Corfu to listen to experimental music, and it draws a more interesting crowd than other bars on the island.

Clubs

54 DREAMY NIGHTS

tel. 694/064 5436; http://54dreamynights.com

All done up in chrome, white leather, and glass, this is probably the most pulsating nightclub in Corfu Town. During the summer months, there's a rotating list of local and international DJs who come to play. It's mainstream, so expect to find the same music and club looks that you would anywhere else; during the most hype parties, up to 3,000 people come. It's located behind the new harbor, a 30-minute walk from downtown Old Town.

Cinema

CINE ORFEAS

Aspioti 1; tel. 26610/39769; www.cineorfeas.gr

The Old Town's only cinema also happens to be the best kind: an open-air one. Watch newly released blockbuster films (in their original language, with subtitles) al fresco. Check the website for daily screenings.

SHOPPING

There's plenty of good shopping in Corfu, though you'll also be greeted with the to-be-expected onslaught of tacky tourist shops (mostly concentrated on Philhellinon). The good is mixed in with the bad, though along Arseniou street the shops become a bit more bohemian.

Gifts

MYRTO ZIRINI

5 Arseniou Street; tel. 6973/923 198; www.myrtozirini.gr; Mon.-Fri. 10am-7pm, Sat. 11am-4pm

Local artist Myrto Zirini makes beautiful, handcrafted ceramics in organic oval shapes and earthy glazes, and he takes custom orders. There's also a workshop attached to the showroom, where you can see the ceramic making process; call ahead to visit the workshop.

SWEET N' SPICY BAHAR

Agias Sopfias 12; tel. 26610/33848; www.sweetnspicy.gr; 9am-8:30pm

Though we're far from the bazaars of Istanbul, Corfiots make do with this lovely little spice shop filled with herbs, spice blends, and condiments. Offerings are a mix of Greek and foreign spices.

PATOUNIS SOAP FACTORY

I. Theotoki 9; tel. 26610/39806; Mon., Weds., Sat. 9:30am-2pm, Tues., Thurs., Fri. 9:30am-2pm and 6pm-8:30pm

Since 1850, this little factory has been churning out olive oil soaps. In 2017, their in-house soap-making technique became part of the National Inventory of the Intangible Cultural Heritage of Greece. You can visit the factory, and, more importantly, purchase soap bars on-site. And though it's a factory, you won't be forced to buy wholesale in bulk; individual bars are for sale and make great presents.

1: a small fountain serves as a meeting point in Corfu Town **2:** the old clock tower in the old fort **3:** the view of Corfu from the Old Fort

1

2

3

Sandals

CORFU SANDALS

Philhellinon 9; tel. 26610/47301; 9am-11pm

Pick up a pair of well-made leather sandals in a variety of colors and styles, at reasonable prices. Most sandal shops have flimsy foam soles that wear out easily, but these guys use ergonomic soles that support even the most tired feet. All of the sandals are made in Corfu.

Books

CORFU BOOKBINDING

Maniarizi-Arlioti 27; tel. 26610/31566; www.ionianbookstore.com; Mon.-Fri. 10am-9pm

The aptly named Corfu Bookbinding organizes special bookbinding workshops (call ahead). It's also an old-school bookshop with a variety of new and old books, prints, and frames. Books are mostly in Greek, but of beautiful quality. It's located next to the cathedral.

FOOD

Grocery

★ ALEXIS DAIRY STORE

Spirou Vasiliou 12; www.alexis-corfu.com; tel. 26610/39012; daily from 8am

Is there anything better than going to buy food and coming out with a slice of country bread thickly spread with creamy, salted butter, followed by a cup of rice pudding and for good measure, another bowl of chocolate pudding? That's my ideal lunch, and it should be yours too at Alexis Dairy Store, a family-run spot that produces all their products from their own cows. You'll order at the counter, and can eat either standing up (for the truly impatient), or at one of the little tables. You can also take away, but you'll want to refrigerate the food quickly in the summer heat.

Greek

O CHRYSOMALLIS

Nikiforou Theotoki 6; tel. 26610/30342; daily noon-midnight; from €7

This old-school taverna with modest decor mixes Greek classics with grilled fish options. Try the *sofrito*, meatballs, or any of their pasta dishes. Located in the center of town, O Chrysomallis is a favorite of both locals and tourists.

TO TAVERNAKI TIS MARINAS

Velissariou 35; tel. 21131/15555; daily noon-midnight; from €6

A classic Greek taverna, this one named after Marina (the owner's mother) offers a rotating list of classics. Try the *sofrito* or any of the baked dishes, like eggplant cooked with tomato and topped with feta. They also have some grilled fresh fish options (try the sea bream), as well as seafood plates like pasta with mussels and marinated octopus.

International

EN PLO

Faliraki; tel. 26610/81813; www.enplocorfu.com; Mon.-Sat. 9:30am-11:30pm, Sun. 10am-11pm; from €12

Beloved for its setting—right next to the sea, with great views of mainland Greece—En Plo is a romantic setting for a meal. The menu features pizza and sandwiches alongside more Greek options, including salads and grilled fish. However, to be honest, it's better to come here for a glass of wine and some appetizers rather than for one of the full-course dinners, as they can be overpriced. It's also nice to come here for a mid-morning coffee.

LA TABERNITA MEXICANA

Dionisiou Solomou 31; tel. 26610/42328; https://latabernita.gr; daily 6:30pm-2am; from €10

I get that you did not come all the way to Greece to eat Mexican food. But maybe you're tired of gyros and souvlaki? If so, pull up to a table at the festively decorated Tabernita Mexicana, which is beloved by Corfiots. There's excellent service, and big portions, though the food is more Tex-Mex than Mexican—think nachos, fajitas, Mexican pizza, all to be washed down with margaritas. Also, dishes have been modified for Greek palates; you won't find mouth-numbingly spicy salsas here.

Greek Food with an Italian Accent

The Venetians ruled Corfu for more than 400 years, and one of the few good things to come out of such a long occupation was the food. The Venetians brought over crops like tomatoes, beans, peppers, coffee, and corn that were then unknown to the Corfiots. You won't necessarily find a lot of pure Italian restaurants in Corfu, but there's plenty of Italian influence in the food: Dishes are marinated in oil and tomatoes, pasta is eaten constantly, and there are more spices than in other parts of Greece. Some must-try dishes include:

- ***Sofrito:*** lightly pan fried veal in wine sauce
- ***Fogatsa:*** a brioche eaten during Easter that resembles a *pannetone*
- ***Bianco:*** fish cooked with plenty of garlic and oil

Fine Dining

VENETIAN WELL

Platía Kremastís; tel. 26615/50955; www.venetianwell.gr; June-Oct. daily 7pm-12:30am, Nov.-May 5pm-11pm, closed Sun.-Mon.; from €10

This is one of Corfu's finest dining options, with inspired dishes like caramelized onion tarts, Corfiot wine-marinated meats, pasta with truffles, and ice cream with local kumquats. Try to dine al fresco in the courtyard, where tables are arranged around an old Venetian well. Service is excellent. Reservations are recommended.

Coffee

AKTAION

Agoniston Politechniou; tel. 26610/37894; www.aktaion.gr; daily 9am-2pm; from €3

This is one of the most historic places in Corfu to drink coffee. In ancient Greek, *aktaios* means "seaside," and it's no surprise that this café-bar has unrivalled views of the Palaio Frourio. During World War II, the building was used as an open-air cinema, before it was converted into a restaurant and café. The food is standard, but the coffee and wine list are excellent.

★ CAFETIERRA

Kapodistriou 8; Mon.-Fri. 8am-7pm, Sat. 8:30am-4pm, Sun. 9am-4pm; from €2

The young couple who own this shop lived in Germany for many years, and picked up some fantastic roasting skills along the way. Stop by this micro roastery for a perfectly pulled espresso, or to buy some of their house coffee blends. In my humble opinion, this is the best coffee in Corfu.

Wine Bar and Bistro

★ SALTO

Donzelot 23, Spiliá/Old Port; tel. 26613/02325; daily 6:30pm-midnight, Sept.-Oct. lunch only; from €8

Though Corfu isn't the most productive wine producer in Greece, do yourself a favor and book a meal at Salto, a lovely wine bar and bistro emphasizing quality in small portions. Let the experienced sommelier guide your wine order. You can't go wrong with the charcuterie and cheese plates and a fresh, crunchy salad; if you're more hungry, go for any of the daily specials. They have a few bottles from Corfu and the Ionian islands, as well as other Greek labels. Reservations are recommended.

Seafood

GEREKOS

Kontokali; tel. 26610/91281; daily 6pm-midnight; from €8 euros

This fish taverna serves up the fresh catch of the day. Order a couple of different plates, so you can sample the prawns, calamari, sardines, and fish (either grilled or fried). This is a family-run restaurant, and has been for a while; ask about the historic family photos on the wall. The restaurant is located 6 km (3.75 mi) north of Corfu Town in the town of Kontokali.

Kumquats

bottles of liqueur made from kumquats

The tiny orange kumquat (κουμκουάτ; also pronounced kumquat in Greek) is so strongly associated with Corfu (and has wormed its way into so many preserves, ice creams, jams, pastries, etc.) that you might be surprised to learn that this citrus fruit actually came from a British botanist named Sydney Merlin, who brought the plant over in 1846. These days, most kumquats are produced in northern Corfu, and the bitter fruit has PDO status (European Union quality system certification mark).

There are kumquat farms scattered across the island, and the harvest period is from January-May. The bulk of the harvest is turned into a liquor that is also called kumquat. You can also sample kumquat spoon sweets and jams (nearly every souvenir store in the Old Town sells them), and some restaurants have kumquat desserts on their menu. This fruit is not often eaten raw—it can be quite bitter and hurt the stomach—but if you come across a fresh one, give it a nibble.

Vegetarian

LUCCIOLA GARDEN

12 km (7.5 mi) Palaiokastritsa Road, Sgombou area; tel. 693/438 7701; Thurs.-Fri. 6pm-midnight, Sat.-Sun. 1:30pm-midnight; from €12

As the name suggests, this spot is located in a beautiful garden courtyard of an old building a bit outside of Corfu Town. This organic restaurant has friendly service and plenty of vegetarian options, and the food is all fresh and local.

ACCOMMODATIONS

The Old Town has the most atmospheric accommodations, and I recommend staying at least one night in a restored hotel. However, beauty comes at a price: Rooms are usually noisy, thanks to the constant crush of people outside, and can occasionally have flying cockroaches (sadly a reality across the Ionian in the heat of summer). If you want something more relaxed but still near to the sights, look around New Corfu.

Old Town

BELLA VENEZIA

N Zambeli 4; tel. 26610/46500; www.bellaveneziahotel.com; from €135

This lovely neoclassical villa has a wealth of stories; previous lives include being a bank and a girls' school. Today, Bella Venezia oozes class with decor that matches the villa's past (think grand pianos and plum-colored drapes), and there's a lovely garden for breakfast. Request a room with a balcony for the views of the Old Town. There are 30 rooms, plus one suite.

CAVALIERI HOTEL

4 Capodistriou Street; tel. 26610/39041; www.cavalieri-hotel-corfu-town.com/en; from €140

For those who want to stay in the heart of Corfu Town in a 17th-century nobleman's mansion, Cavalieri Hotel makes a fine choice (especially during Easter, when you'll have uninterrupted views of all the pot smashing). Decor in this 50-room hotel is rather grandmotherly, but there's a great rooftop bar and restaurant with great views.

★ SIORRA VITTORIA

Stefanou Padova 36; tel. 26610/36300; www.siorravittoria.com; from €200

One of the finest boutique hotels in Corfu Town, Siorra Vittoria is located in a lovingly restored 19th-century mansion, where traditional architecture is augmented by sleek modern touches, like marble bathrooms. Beds are exquisitely comfortable, and breakfast is served either in your room (for lazy mornings) or in the leafy garden. There are seven double rooms and two suites.

New Town

CORFU HOLIDAY PALACE

Dimokratias 2; tel. 26610/39485; www.corfupalace.com; from €195

This large resort hotel is something of an institution in Corfu, located on the waterfront 5 km (3 mi) south of the Old Town with a pool, six restaurants, a bowling alley, and tennis courts. Rooms are pretty spacious and bright, and face out onto the bay. Some suites have kitchenettes. With so many activities, services, and amenities, this is a good choice for families.

GETTING THERE AND AROUND

Corfu's airport, **Ioannis Kapodistrias International Airport** (CFU; tel. 26610/89600; www.corfu-airport.com), is 2 km (1.25 mi) southwest of the Old Town. Take **Local Bus 15** to reach Plateia San Rocco (also known as Plateia Georgiou Theotoki) in the New Town, which is just outside the Old Town—a short walk. **Neo Limani** (New Port), where ferries arrive and depart, is west of the Old Town and is also on the Local Bus 15 route from the airport.

Mt. Pantokrator and Northern Corfu

As you drive north out of Corfu Town, you'll immediately hit a row of beach resorts, which cater to package tourists looking for all-inclusive vacations. There's nothing remarkable about these towns (Gouvia, Dassia, Ipsos, and Pyrgi), and during the summer months, the beaches are frustratingly crowded. However, this region is home to the looming Mt. Pantokrator, the highest point on Corfu (you can see all the way to Albania on a clear day!), which is well worth a visit. Palia Perithia, 53 km (33 mi) north of Corfu Town, is another can't-miss. There are buses to Dasia and Ipsos that depart regularly from Corfu Town.

NORTH OF CORFU TOWN: DAFNILA BAY AND VICINITY

Many tourists base themselves around Dafnila Bay, and though it's largely a tourist trap, there are a few places worth checking out.

Nightlife

EDEM BEACH CLUB

Dassia; tel. 26610/93013; www.edemclub.com; daily May-Sept. 11am-5am

This all-day beach club, 14 km (8.5 mi) north of Corfu Town in the town of Dassia, is a favorite on the island. It opens early, serving up coffee and orange juice, but its character really comes out at night, when the music is blasted, the cocktails are shaken, and hundreds of revelers show up to dance the evening away.

Food

A LA PALEA

Strinilas; tel. 26630/72622; Apr.-Oct. daily 10am-11:30pm; from €7

This delightful mountaintop taverna, 16 km (10 mi) north of Dassia (28 km/17 mi from Corfu Town) in Strinilas, next to Petalia village, is located under the shade of a giant tree, and you'll really feel like you're eating in the middle of nature. Dishes are traditional Greek classics, with nice touches like freshly baked bread. You're in the mountains, so go for the meat dishes. This spot is a bit harder to get to, which means it sees more locals than tourists—not always the case in Corfu.

Accommodations

DIONYSUS CAMPING VILLAGE

Dafnila Bay; tel. 26610/91417; www.dionysuscamping.gr; from €7.10

This is probably the best budget option on the island, especially if you have a camper or a tent to pitch. It's also a remarkably nice campsite, sitting in a 400-year-old olive grove and boasting its own pool. Little huts (from €14) are also available for rent. Bus line 7 stops very close by.

★ GRECOTEL IMPERIAL

Tzavros, Kommeno; tel. 26610/88400; www.corfuimperial.com; from €260

One of the most luxurious resorts on the island, the Grecotel Imperial is absolutely luxurious: It's all marble, baroque furnishings, private gardens, plunge pools, and sleek spas. Located on a private peninsula that juts off into the Ionain Sea, it's an incredibly relaxing spot. You'll never want to leave once you arrive; everything your heart desires (including archery) can be arranged for you. Breakfast is included, and rates are slashed in the off-season.

MT. PANTOKRATOR

At 906 meters (2,972 feet), this is the highest point on Corfu and makes a welcome break from the sea. You can drive, hike, cycle, or ride a horse up the switchback roads to the top of the mountain, passing little villages along the way.

Driving to the Summit

You can start the drive at the bottom of the mountain. The most direct route is from the village of Strinylas (27.5 km/17 mi from Corfu Town; 52 minutes); from there you'll follow the signposts up to the summit—it's paved. Once you reach the summit, you'll find the monastery of Moni Pantokrator.

Hiking

MT. PANTOKRATOR LOOP

Distance: 9.3 km (5.8 mi)
Duration: 3-hour loop
Effort Level: moderate

One of the best places to start a hike is Palia Perithia, 53 km (33 mi) north of Corfu Town, where a three-hour loop will take you around the northern back of the mountain. You'll pass through both New and Old Perithia, where Italian architectural influences mix with Greek. As you continue up the road, you'll see splayed out below you the Stroggyli valley and Korission lake. In the spring, wildflowers are in bloom, and in the summer, the smell of herbs will fill your nose. At the top of the summit is a monastery (and an ugly telecommunications tower, which was erected a few years back). The views, with all of Corfu below you, and Italy and Albania in the background, are still unbelievably beautiful. You will pass tavernas along the way, and there's a café at the summit. Still, you should bring water with you for the hike.

Gerald Durrell on Corfu

The Durrells were a British family who lived on Corfu before World War II. One of their sons, Gerald Durrell, a conservationist and animal lover, went on to write several memoirs about his family's often hilarious and crazy adventures in pre-war Greece. The Durrell parents were hippies, and their home welcomed a bevy of bohemian writers and artists, including Henry Miller. The Durrells' life was turned into a wildly popular British TV series, *The Durrells*. While you're on Corfu, you'll likely come across some sunburnt British tourists with a dog-eared copy of *My Family and Other Animals* in hand, waxing poetic about the cultural richness of the Durrell family.

The writer also had a few favorite haunts on the island, including **Myrtiotissa Beach** and **Kalami** on the northeast coast. In Kalami, you can dine at the **White House,** located inside the writer's former home.

Horse Riding

TRAIL RIDERS

Ano Korakiana, Mt. Pantokrator; tel. 694/665 3317; www.trailriderscorfu.com; summer Mon.-Fri. 10am-noon and 6pm-8pm, winter Thurs.-Sat. by appointment

British rider Sally-Ann Lewis spent 10 years rounding up cattle in Wyoming before moving to Corfu to set up Trailriders in 1992. After picking up a horse from the stable 2 km (1.25 mi) south of Ano Korakiana, you'll go on an hour-and-a-half trek (€60) through the village and base of the mountain. Bring apples or carrots to feed your horse! Suitable for ages six and up.

KALAMI (Καλάμι)

Kalami is the more charming of the northern beaches, in my opinion. A sweep of bright green trees hugs the little village, which sits around a sickle-shaped bay. The beach is located 30 km (19 mi) north of Corfu Town. It's a typical little resort town with a couple of residences, tavernas, and shops. Kalami also has the distinction of being one of the Durrells' favorite haunts.

Food

WHITE HOUSE

Kalami; tel. 26630/91040; www.corfu-kalami.gr; daily 9am-midnight; from €10

Dinner with a dash of sophisticated history: The White House is located in the former waterfront home of British writer Lawrence Durrell. You can enjoy a combination of Greek and Italian dishes (the pastas and anything with seafood are particularly delicious) either inside the house or along the quay, where fishing boats bob in the calm sea.

Accommodations

THE ROU ESTATE

Sinies; tel. 020/8392 5858; www.simpsontravel.com; from €700 per week

This former rural cottage has been lovingly restored into a charming villa complex, with all the amenities you'd expect from a luxury hotel. There are 16 villas, each with 2-5 bedrooms; some of the rooms come with private gardens or pools. There's a delicious restaurant on-site, but you'll need a rental car to get out of the complex. The estate is located in Sinies, 9.6 km (5.9 mi) west of Kalami.

★ PALIA PERITHIA (OLD PERITHIA) (Παλιά Περίθεια)

Palia Perithia, 53 km (33 mi) north of Corfu Town, has the double honor of being Corfu's oldest and best-preserved village. The village dates back to at least the 14th century, though in the 1960s, it was largely abandoned. Thanks to the efforts of a couple of entrepreneurs, life is being breathed back into Palia Perithia. Take a stroll through the stone alleyways and feel yourself transported back in time. The houses have been lovingly restored, and now house people busy baking sourdough bread, making jam from the fruit orchards that surround the village, and keeping bees.

Food

O FOROS

tel. 695/595 0459; from €10

An atmospheric taverna (the interior is filled with local artifacts) offering truly warm hospitality, O Foros is the best of Palia Perithia's four tavernas. The food is rustic rural; try the rabbit stew, or the fried zucchini balls with tzatziki. There's usually a free dessert at the end—often a slice of homemade walnut cake.

Accommodations

★ MERCHANT'S HOUSE

tel. 698/871 2885; www.merchantshousecorfu.com; from €195

If not being seaside isn't a deal-breaker for you, book a room in this stunning historic villa that's been painstakingly restored into a boutique bed-and-breakfast. There are no traditional hotel amenities like pools or gyms, which means your fellow guests will be of the same variety as you: historically inclined, curious, and friendly. Proprietors Mark and Saskia take care of everyone with enthusiasm.

KASSIOPI (Κασσιόπη)

Have you ever wanted to party like Nero? Come to Kassiopi, 36 km (22 mi) north of Corfu Town, where the Roman Emperor, in true Julio-Claudian style, had extravagant holidays. These days, Kassiopi is a small resort town nestled along the harbor, with a very respectable beachfront and plenty of good restaurants. The small church, apparently built on the ruins of a temple to Zeus, is worth a visit. On August 15, the village hosts a raucuos *panigiri*.

NORTHWEST BEACHES

It's not particularly worthwhile to drive along the coastal route in the summer, as it's often full of traffic. If you want to reach the northwest, better to cut through the interior (40 km/25 mi, about one hour).

CANAL D'AMOUR (Σιδάρι)

The Love Channel is one of those places that sounds better in name than in practice: Though this rocky little cove is considered the most romantic spot on the island, that's sadly not true in 2019, unless your idea of romance is tourist shops, blaring music, and sitting uncomfortably close to total strangers. The rock strata are impressive—they look like those drippy wet sand castles—and if you visit very early in the morning, you'll be able to have a few moments of privacy.

LONGAS BEACH (Λογγάς)

Located in Cape Drastis, the northwesternmost point of the island, Longas beach is a beautiful stretch of sand backed by reddish cliffs that keep the beach quite cool in the morning. This west-facing beach is one of the best spots on the island to watch the sunset.

Southwest Corfu

The western coast of Corfu is perhaps some of the most beautiful scenery on the island, with (relatively) empty beaches, charming villages, and cliffs. It's a bit tricky to navigate. There's no continuous coastal road that connects the beaches to the towns, so you'll be doing a lot of driving as you explore this region. The southwest part of Corfu is reachable by long-distance Green buses.

1: statues stand to attention outside of Palace of Achilleion **2:** a church on Corfu **3:** Bathers enjoy a dip in Paleokastritsa Beach.

1
2 
3

The Corfu Trail

The Corfu Trail is a 220-km (136-mi) long hike, marked by yellow signposts, that covers nearly all of the island, starting in Kavos and ending at Saint Spiridon beach. If you're physically capable, it's one of the best ways to revel in Corfu's natural beauty and to get away from the hustle and bustle of the island's touristic side.

ROUTES

From Paleokastritsa, serious hikers can follow the Corfu Trail to the villages of **Lakones** (4.6 km/2.85 mi, 1.5 hours, moderate) and **Krini** (7 km/4.3 mi, 2.5 hours, challenging), where you'll find the ruins of the Byzantine fortress of Angelokastro and breathtaking views of Paleokastritsa. As you walk, you'll pass through scented orange and lemon groves, and you'll catch glimpses of the glittering blue sea. You can also drive; it's a beautiful drive along the coast and up through the mountains. From Corfu Town, it's 24 km (15 mi) northwest (35 minutes).

GUIDED HIKES

The folks at **Corfu Trail** (www.corfu-trail.com) have marked off dozens of trails around the island, and can organize week-long walking trips, including options on the Corfu Trail (pricing upon request only) for you. A good way to dip your toe is by hiking one of the routes around Mt. Pantokrator.

PALEOKASTRITSA VILLAGE (Παλιόκαστρο)

Probably the most popular resort on the west coast, this town stretches along for 3 km (1.85 mi), crossing through a series of beautiful little bays; behind the village is a series of mountains covered in fragrant trees. At the end of Paleokastritsa is the village where a bone-tired Odysseus is said to have washed ashore. There's also a nice little monastery from the 13th century, the **Moni Theotokou** (7am-1pm and 3pm-8pm daily; free), which is also home to a small museum (Apr.-Oct., same hours), where you can pick up a couple of homemade treats. There are regular daily buses from Corfu Town to Paleokastritsa (€2.30, 40 minutes). If you're driving, the village is located 22.6 km (14 m) northwest of Corfu Town.

Beaches

PALEOKASTRITSA (Παληοκάστριτσα)

This is the main beach of the Paleokastritsa village, and while it's a bit small, it's considered an island favorite. The water is especially cold, which makes it refreshing at even the hottest times of day. It's obviously not secluded, and there are plenty of amenities to choose from.

Boat Trips

From the small jetty in Paleokastritsa, you'll find a couple of boat operators to cruise you around the bay in glass-bottomed boats (usually the glass is more than a little dinged up, but you'll get the idea). Try **Yellow Submarine** (tel. 697/740 9246; www.yellow-submarinegr; 10am-6pm, 9pm; from €10) or **Paradise Sunset** (tel. 697/227 6442; from €10).

Food

SPYROS

tel. 26630/41030; www.spirostaverna.gr; daily 9am-late; from €7

This local taverna is set apart from the rest by its use of fresh ingredients (from the owner's farm) and a deft hand on the grill (all the meat is local, too). On Tues. and Sat., they host traditional Corfiot barbeques, where the meat is marinated and slowly grilled over an open flame. Wash it down with a glass of Moschato wine, which, you guessed it, the owners also produce.

Accommodations

ZEFIROS

tel. 26610/94942; https://zefiroscorfuhotel.gr; from €90

This family-run hotel is located in a traditional Corfiot-style house right on the beach. It first opened in the 1930s. There are just a handful of rooms, but all are clean and well-appointed, and offer nice views of either the sea or the garden.

★ MYRTIOTISSA BEACH (Μυρωτιωτισσα)

Apparently this beach, 5 km (3 mi) northwest of Pelekas, was one of Durrell's favorite beaches, and it remains one of the least touristic ones on the island (there are no beach bars or hotels here). It's the only place on the island where nudity is tolerated. It's quite difficult to get to; drivers need to leave their cars at the hilltop before walking down a steep, pebbly road, but you'll be rewarded with a pristine, semi-private cove.

PELEKAS AND VICINITY

Thirty minutes from Paleokastritsa is the charming mountain village of Pelekas (Πέλεκας), best known for its observation point of Kaiser's throne (referring to the German Kaiser, Wilhem, who was rumored to have loved this spot for a sunset) and its stunning 360-degree views of the island. It's gotten increasingly popular with tourists in the summer, so come early in the morning to have the views (partially) to yourself.

Food

AMBELONAS

Karoumpatika; tel. 693/215 8888; www.ambelonas-corfu.gr; June-Oct. Wed.-Fri. 7pm-11pm, Dec.-May Sun. 1pm-6pm; mains from €15

This old vineyard estate 5 km (3 mi) east of Pelekas is as multipurpose as it can get. They host weddings, wine tastings, and cooking classes, and they have a beautiful little restaurant. Try the pork roast with kumquat or the Venetian-style beef liver. The space is gorgeous, and you can learn about, taste, and buy traditional Corfiot wines, jams, and other preserves.

Accommodations

LEVANT HOTEL

tel. 26610/94230; www.levantcorfu.gr; May-Oct.; from €100, including breakfast

I love a hotel in a neoclassical building, and the Levant Hotel, with its robin's-egg blue walls, wrought iron balconies, and cream-colored facade, definitely doesn't disappoint. There are just a few rooms available here, so it's got an intimate B&B vibe. There's also an excellent restaurant on-site, with great views of the sunset.

AGIOS GORDIOS BEACH (Άγιος Γόρδιος)

Driving from Pelekas (10 km/6 mi, 17 minutes) down a beautiful country road full of vineyards and olive trees, you'll eventually get to this sandy cove nestled between giant rocks. This is a beach for tourists, so you'll have all the amenities you could want. It's particularly good for families.

Food

ALONAKI BAY

Alonaki; tel. 26610/75872; lunch and dinner daily in summer; from €10

This rustic, family-run taverna in Alonaki (30 km/18.6 mi southeast of Corfu Town), has both delicious food (there's a small menu of ready-prepared meals and grilled items) and stupendous views (it's located at the top of the cliffs). You'll want to follow the dirt road out of Alonaki to Lake Korisson to find it. The family also has a couple of rooms and apartments to rent (from €50).

MARATHIAS BEACH (Μαραθιάς)

This long stretch of reddish sand is revered for its crystalline waters. Though the main part of the beach is inundated with tourist facilities, if you walk just a bit away from all of that, you'll see that the beach extends for 2 km (1.25 mi) and there's plenty of privacy to be had. It's 35 km (22 mi, 55 minutes' drive) south of Corfu Town.

Southeast Corfu

Driving southeast from Corfu Town, you'll immediately be hit by a slew of generic and uninspiring resort towns, popular with package tourists. Press on toward the villages of Boukari, Petriti, and Lefkimmi, where you'll get more of a taste for Corfu without the mass tourism. The following places are a few gems in the tourist trap. There are regular buses from Corfu Town to Messogi and Boukari.

SOUTH OF CORFU TOWN: GASTOURI TO MESOGGI (Γαστουρι/Μεσογγη)

Sights

PALACE OF ACHILLEION

Gastouri; tel. 26610/56210; www.achillion-corfu.gr; Apr.-Oct. 8am-8pm, Nov.-Mar. 8am-4pm; €8

Have you noticed that Corfiots love a good palace? This one was built in the 1890s as a summer residence for Austria's empress Elizabeth, the niece of King Otto of Greece. It's set on a steep hill about 12 km (7.5 mi) south of Corfu Town, and the grounds, which include lovely terraced gardens, offer panoramic views of the island. The interior of the palace is just as beautiful and has been preserved with the original moldings and tiling. If you're pressing on to some more southern towns, it's worth stopping by.

Food

★ KLIMATARIA

Benitses; tel. 26610/71201; www.klimataria-restaurant.gr; Mon.-Sat. 6:30pm-11:30pm, Sun. noon-4:30pm; from €12

One of the most beloved restaurants on the island, this is the sort of place you travel for, regardless of the fact that there's nothing else around. Call ahead for a reservation, as there are only 11 tables. This tiny taverna located inside an old villa is particularly lauded for its fish and meze. Try the *xtapodi ksidato* (boiled octopus marinated with vinegar, lemon juice, parsley, and olive oil) and the *psari bourdeto* (fish in a spicy red tomato sauce, and the chef's specialty!). It's located in Benitses, 13.6 km (8.5 mi) from Corfu Town.

Accommodations

★ COURTI ESTATE

Mesoghini; tel. 697/584 6418; www.thecourtiestate.com; from €200

Sprawled out across 4 hectares (10 acres) of olive groves, Courti Estate is a sumptuous retreat that combines architecture, history, and modern luxuries to deliver a one-of-a-kind hotel experience. There's a restaurant on-site that only uses organic produce, and a dazzling infinity pool. Located in Mesoggi, 22 km (13.6 mi) south of Corfu Town.

BOUKARI (Μπουκάρι)

The old fisherman's harbor of Boukari remains a sleepy little hamlet. Boats bob in the sea, the villagers take afternoon naps, and not a whole lot happens here—which makes it a welcome respite from the bustling resorts of the north. There's a cute pebbled beach that's suitable for families, but note that there are no facilities like beach bars.

Food

SPRIOS KARIDAS

tel. 26620/51205; daily lunch and dinner; from €8

Located under a giant eucalyptus tree, this little seaside taverna serves up whatever was freshly caught that morning, like swordfish or seabream. There are other options too, like fried calamari and mussels steamed in white wine sauce. Service can be a bit slow and gruff, but the food is good and fresh.

Accommodations

HOTEL PENELOPE

tel. 26620/51791; boukaribeach.gr; from €40

This charming, 14-room hotel makes an excellent base for those who just plan on swimming and eating in Boukari's delicious restaurants all summer. Rooms are basic but surprisingly well-equipped, with orthopedic mattresses, and there are free bikes and airport shuttles if you book directly through their website. This is a very good budget option.

PETRITI

(Πετρίτη)

Petriti is the largest fishing village in the southern part of the island. It's slightly less mellowed out than Boutari—there are five tavernas here hugging the waterfront—but the dogs still nap in the shade and the old fishermen still haul up their nets. Across the bay are the salt flats, and you'll notice a tiny islet, whose sole resident has declared it a republic (not legally binding, in case you were wondering).

LEFKIMMI

(Λευκίμμη)

With 5,000 inhabitants, Lefkimmi is the second largest city on Corfu, and the island's second port. Most tourists don't spend much time here. There aren't so many tourist facilities, and the island's construction hasn't been revamped in decades, which lends a sweet charm to the place. There's a small river that cuts through the town (giving it something of a Venetian air) that fishermen use to enter and exit the sea. The narrow streets are lined with merchants' mansions, in varying states of disrepair, and there are a couple of Italianate churches. It's a nice place to walk around for an afternoon if you arrive by boat from the mainland.

Zakynthos (Ζάκυνθοσ)

Zakynthos (pop. 41,000) was nicknamed "Il fiore di Levante" (Flower of the East) by the island's Venetian overlords (later shortened to Zante by the locals), and it is truly a feast for the eyes, with turquoise waters, endless pine tree forests, and stunning caves. It's the southernmost of the six main Ionian islands, and is probably the most touristic. Swathes of the island have become commercialized to the point of becoming a tourist playground, with drunk 20-somethings riding 4WDs barefoot through towns, and the endless clacking sound of beachgoers in their flip-flops, shopping for plastic beach toys and sand souvenirs. However, there's plenty of beauty and idyllic nature still to be found in Zakynthos, and many areas to enjoy the sweet-talking charms of the locals.

Highlights

Look for ★ to find recommended sights, activities, dining, and lodging.

★ **West Coast Scenic Drive:** The sparsely populated western part of the island makes for a beautiful drive. Leaving Zante Town, wind through stone villages and pine forests till you reach the dazzling blue waters of the coast (page 396).

★ **Korakonissi:** This craggy cove features amazing spots for jumping into mind-bogglingly clear blue water (page 396).

★ **Sunset in Kambi:** Catch the last rays of the day high atop this mountainous village on the west side of the island (page 398).

★ **Blue Caves:** Take a glass-bottomed boat ride through glowing blue grottos (page 401).

★ **Volimes Village:** Meander through the stone streets of this traditional mountain village (page 401).

★ **Shipwreck Bay:** This world-famous beach, complete with a rusted schooner, has the bluest water you've ever seen (page 401).

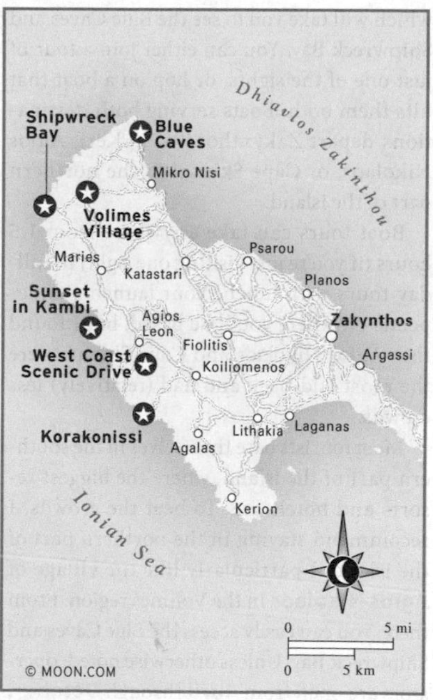

Zante can be divided into three zones: the east and south, where most of the resorts are concentrated; the stunning northwest coast, where limestone cliffs meet wildly unreal blue waters; and center of the island with its rolling green hills. There are excellent tavernas to be found, with the melodic sounds of *kantadhes* (Italianate folk ballads) streaming out the windows. This is also something of an extreme sports lover's island, with plenty of opportunities for BASE jumping, diving, and hang-gliding. Avoid the summer months, when tourism reaches a fever pitch. May and September are just as lovely, and half empty.

PLANNING YOUR TIME

You'll want to spend at least **two days** on Zakynthos, mostly focused on the northwest coast and the interior of the island (including Volimes region and Koilomenos). Reserve one afternoon to do a boat tour of the island, which will take you to see the Blue Caves and Shipwreck Bay. You can either join a tour of just one of the sights, or hop on a boat that hits them both. Boats serving both destinations depart Zakynthos Town, Keri, Agios Nikolaos, or Cape Skinari in the northern part of the island.

Boat tours can take anywhere from 1.5 hours (if you're just visiting one sight) to full-day tours with lunch. Your launch site depends on where you'll be based, but I found that Agios Nikolaos and Cape Skinari were the most laid-back and had (relatively) less crowds.

Most tourists base themselves in the southern part of the island, where the biggest resorts and hotels are. To beat the crowds, I recommend staying in the northern part of the island; I particularly like the village of **Agios Nikolaos** in the Volimes region. From there, you can easily access the Blue Caves and Shipwreck Bay. Unless otherwise noted, operators are open from **April** through **October.**

INFORMATION AND SERVICES

As a well-known tourist destination, Zakynthos has you covered. The main tourist information center, **Zakynthos Info Center** (tel. 26950/33192; www.zakynthosinfocenter.gr; Mon.-Sat., 9am-5pm), is in Lagana, 8 km (5 mi) south of Zante Town. It's a one-stop shop with friendly staff to help you with booking tours, getting tourist recommendations, renting cars and motorcycles, and just about anything else a freshly arrived visitor could want.

In Zakynthos town, you'll find the main **police** station halfway up along the waterfront (tel. 26950/24482; May-Oct. 8am-10pm). There are **banks** in Zakynthos Town and plenty of **ATMs** across the island. Most places accept credit cards.

Iassis Medical Center (tel. 26950/51105; www.iassismedical.gr) has clinics in Laganas, Alykanas, Tsilivi, Argasi, Kalamai, and Vasilikos.

GETTING THERE

Most people arrive on the island by plane.

Air

Zakynthos International Airport (ZTH; tel. 26950/29500; www.zakynthos-airport.com) is located 5 km (3 mi) south of Zakynthos Town. **Taxis** are available at the airport (€16 during the day; €20 at night) and take 10 minutes to reach Zakynthos Town. While there's no direct **bus** from Zante Town to Agios Nikolaos, you can take the bus first to Argasi and then transfer to another bus for Agios Nikolaos (€1.80).

Olympic Air (www.olympicair.com) operates flights from Athens, and **Sky Express** (www.skyexpress.gr) has flights to and from the other Ionian islands, including Corfu. During the summer season, **Air Berlin** (www.airberlin.com) and **Easyjet** (www.easyjet.com) have charter flights from

Previous: the technicolor coral of the Blue Caves; you can't miss Shipwreck Bay; a traditional Zakynthian house in the countryside.

European countries, including the UK, Italy, and Germany.

Ferry

Zakynthos has two ports, **Zakynthos Town** (main port) and **Agios Nikolaos** (in the north). Most Ferries leave for Zakynthos Town from the mainland ports of Kyllini and/or Igoumenitsa (287 km/178 mi and 470 km/292 mi, respectively) northwest of Athens; buses are available from Athens' main bus terminal to the ports). **Ionian Group** (www.ionian-group.com) runs up to seven daily ferries in the summer months between Zakynthos Town and Kylleni. **Ionian Pelagos** (www.ionianpelagos.com) has twice daily seasonal ferries from Agios Nikolaos to Pesada in Kefallonia.

Given its proximity to Italy, there are also occasional international ferries calling to/from Iogumenitsa on the way to Bari and Brindisi in Italy. **Ventrouis Ferries** (www.ventrouisferries.com) connects Zakynthos Town with Italy.

Bus

If you're coming from the mainland, you can also take the bus to **KTEL Bus Station** (Zakynthos Town; tel. 269502/2265; www.ktel-zakynthos.gr). From the KTEL Kifisou bus station in Athens there are four daily buses (6 hours; €28.60); from Thessaloniki two weekly buses (10 hours; €54.40); and four daily from Patras (3.5 hours; €8.70) to the mainland port of Kyllini on the western edge of Peloponnese. The bus goes on the ferry at Kyllini, so factor in an extra €8.90.

GETTING AROUND

At 405 square km (155 square mi), Zakynthos is a pretty sizeable island. There's a comprehensive network of buses, but they can get quite crowded in the summer. It's nice to rent a car, at least for part of your trip, so you can explore some places at your own leisurely pace.

Bus

A comprehensive network of buses radiates out of Zakynthos Town. The KTEL bus main station (tel. 26950/22255; www.ktel-zakynthos.gr) is a 15-minute walk southwest of Plateia Solomou, near the hospital. All the major towns and villages (including the Volimes region) plus resort areas of the island are connected by bus; in the summer months, the service starts early and ends later in the evening.

Car

There are plenty of rental car options at the airport, in larger resort towns, and in Zakynthos Town. Car rentals start at about €40 per day. Try **Europcar** (airport; tel. 26950/43313; www.europcar-greece.com), **Hertz** (Lomvardou 38, Zakynthos Town; tel. 29950/45706; www.hertz.gr; 8am-2pm and 5:30-9pm), or **Diamond Cars** (tel. 26950/65155; www.diamond-carrentals.gr), which will bring a car to you anywhere on the island.

Roads are well-paved and pretty easy to drive in Zakynthos, but given the number of tourists, I advise against renting a motorcycle. There are plenty of accidents in the summer months.

Taxi

Taxis are widely available and can be arranged by calling **Zante Taxi** (tel. 26950/48400). However, it's almost always cheaper to rent a car for the day.

Itinerary Ideas

You will need a rental car for both days, and be sure to reserve a table (by the water's edge if possible!) for Nobelos (day 1). In summer, reservations for Ampelostratos (day 2) are also a good idea. For both days, don't forget your towel, sunscreen, swimsuit, and snorkel mask!

DAY 1

1 Early morning is the best time to take a boat tour (3 hours) of the Blue Caves and Shipwreck Bay, as you'll beat the lunchtime crowds. Take the first boat heading out of **Agios Nikolaos** around 9am.

2 On your first stop on the boat tour, marvel at colorful coral inside the **Blue Caves.**

3 Next up on the boat tour is **Shipwreck Bay,** where you can hop off the boat and explore the famous beach.

4 You'll probably be hungry when you come back to shore! Drive 25 minutes west to Anafonitria to have lunch at the local taverna, **Nintri Café.** Afterward, you can walk to see the view of Shipwreck Bay from the top (this is the best spot for photos).

5 After lunch, drive 10 minutes north and spend an hour walking around the traditional stone village of **Volimes.**

6 Finish the day with dinner at the romantic **Nobelos Bio Restaurant** in Agios Nikoloas, and spring for the sea urchin salad.

DAY 2

1 Spend the morning walking around the colorful streets of Zante Town, starting with morning coffee at **Latas Art Café** in the Bohali District, which has stupendous views of the city and harbor.

2 Fill up your car with gas and head out of town. First drive 11 km (7 mi) west to the village of Lithakia, where you can visit the **Aristeon Olive Oil Press and Museum** and learn about the importance of olive oil production on Zakynthos.

3 Next, head north along the interior road and stop for lunch at **Selene Taverna** in Agios Leon.

4 Spend the afternoon lounging about on **Korakonissi** beach, jumping into the clear blue waters and marveling at the strange rock formations.

5 Catch the sunset in **Kambi** (you can do the small hike to the town's massive cross for great views).

6 Head back inland to Koiliomenos to have a traditional Zakynthian dinner at **Ampelostratos**. Reservations are a good idea in summer.

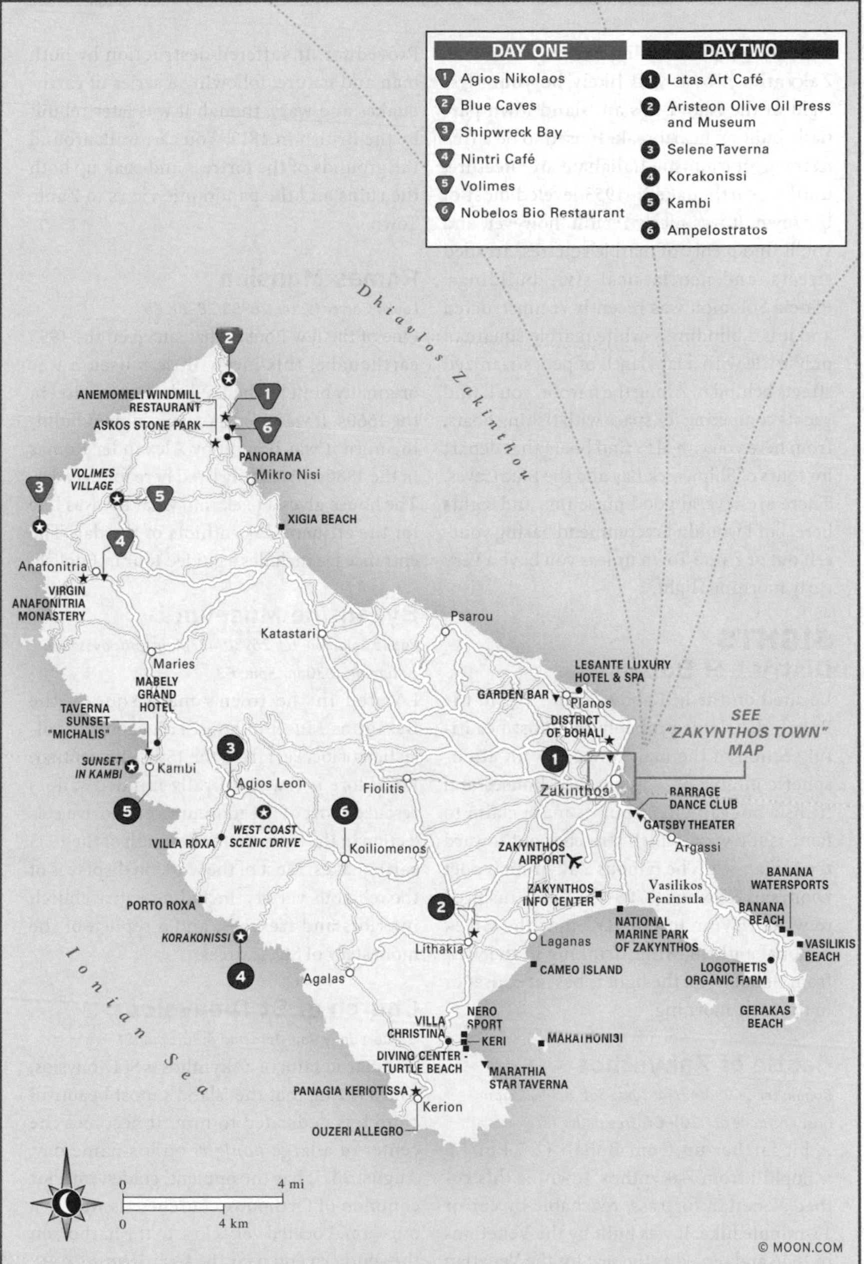
Zakynthos
DAY ONE
1 Agios Nikolaos
2 Blue Caves
3 Shipwreck Bay
4 Nintri Café
5 Volimes
6 Nobelos Bio Restaurant
DAY TWO
1 Latas Art Café
2 Aristeon Olive Oil Press and Museum
3 Selene Taverna
4 Korakonissi
5 Kambi
6 Ampelostratos
Dhiavlos Zakinthou
ANEMOMELI WINDMILL RESTAURANT
ASKOS STONE PARK
PANORAMA
Mikro Nisi
VOLIMES VILLAGE
XIGIA BEACH
Anafonitria
VIRGIN ANAFONITRIA MONASTERY
Psarou
Katastari
Maries
MABELY GRAND HOTEL
TAVERNA SUNSET "MICHALIS"
SUNSET IN KAMBI
Kambi
Agios Leon
WEST COAST SCENIC DRIVE
VILLA ROXA
Fiolitis
Koiliomenos
LESANTE LUXURY HOTEL & SPA
GARDEN BAR
Planos
DISTRICT OF BOHALI
SEE "ZAKYNTHOS TOWN" MAP
Zakinthos
BARRAGE DANCE CLUB
GATSBY THEATER
Argassi
ZAKYNTHOS AIRPORT
BANANA WATERSPORTS
Vasilikos Peninsula
ZAKYNTHOS INFO CENTER
BANANA BEACH
PORTO ROXA
KORAKONISSI
Lithakia
Laganas
NATIONAL MARINE PARK OF ZAKYNTHOS
VASILIKIS BEACH
LOGOTHETIS ORGANIC FARM
CAMEO ISLAND
Agalas
Ionian Sea
GERAKAS BEACH
VILLA CHRISTINA
NERO SPORT
KERI
MARATHONISI
DIVING CENTER - TURTLE BEACH
MARATHIA STAR TAVERNA
PANAGIA KERIOTISSA
Kerion
OUZERI ALLEGRO
0 4 mi
0 4 km

Zakynthos Town Ζάκυνθος

Whether you're arriving by ferry or plane, Zakynthos Town will likely be your first sight of the island. It's an island town partially built on heartbreak: It used to be a fine example of exquisite Italianate architecture, until an earthquake in 1953 leveled most of the town. It was nicely rebuilt, however, and you'll find plenty of marble squares, arcaded streets, and neoclassical-style buildings. Plateia Solomou was recently reconstructed and it is a blindingly-white marble square of public life with a labyrinth of pedestrianized streets behind it. Along the harbor, you'll find yachts competing for space with fishing boats; from here you can also find boats that depart for tours of Shipwreck Bay and the Blue Caves. There are several good museums and sights here, but I wouldn't recommend basing yourself out of Zante Town unless you have a very early morning flight.

SIGHTS

District of Bohali

Located on the hill above Zante Town, the Bohali district is probably the most beautiful section of the main town. It's an atmospheric jumble of whitewashed houses and fuchsia bougainvillea, but its main claim to fame is the view, which stretches out toward the Ionian sea. The famous Zakynthian poet Dionysios Solomos (1798-1857) was inspired to write "Hymn to Liberty," now the Greek national anthem, while drinking in the view from Bohali. Tip: the light is best at sunset or in the early morning.

Castle of Zakynthos

Bohali; tel. 26950/42714; Tues.-Sat. 8am-2:30pm (last entrance at 1:30); €4, free under 18

A bit farther up from Bohali (2.5 km/1.5 mi uphill from Zakynthos Town) is this ruined Venetian fortress, reachable by car or 15-minute hike. It was built by the Venetians in 1646 and served as the seat for the Venetian Proveditor. It suffered destruction by both man and nature, following a series of earthquakes and wars, though it was later rebuilt by the British in 1812. You can walk around the grounds of the fortress and soak up both the ruins and the panoramic views to Zante Town.

Romas Mansion

Louka Carrer 19; tel. 26950/28381; €5

One of the few houses that survived the 1953 earthquake, this lovely little museum was originally built by the English Vice counsel in the 1660s. It was used as a government building until it was bought by Alexander Romas in the 1880s; his family lived here for decades. The house gives a peek into what life was like for the affluent Zakynthiots of the day. The entrance fee includes a guided tour in English.

Byzantine Museum

Pateia Solomou; tel. 26950/42714; http://odysseus.culture.gr; 8:30am-3pm; €3

Located in the town's main square, the Byzantine Museum houses an exquisite collection of local art from the 15th-19th century. Local lore is that culturally minded sailors rescued most of the museum's expansive collection in the immediate aftermath of the 1953 earthquakes. Most of the work on display is of the religious variety, including entire church interiors and frescoes, and a replica of the monastery of St. Andreas.

Church of St Dionysios

Harbor; daily 9am-1pm and 4:30-9pm; €1

The patron saint of Zakynthos is St Dionysios, so it's fitting that the island's most beautiful church is dedicated to him. It becomes the center of a large *panigiri* on his name day, August 24. It has the opulent, golden interior common of Orthodox churches, as well as a museum. Located very close to the harbor, on the southern end near the ferry jetty.

Zakynthos Town

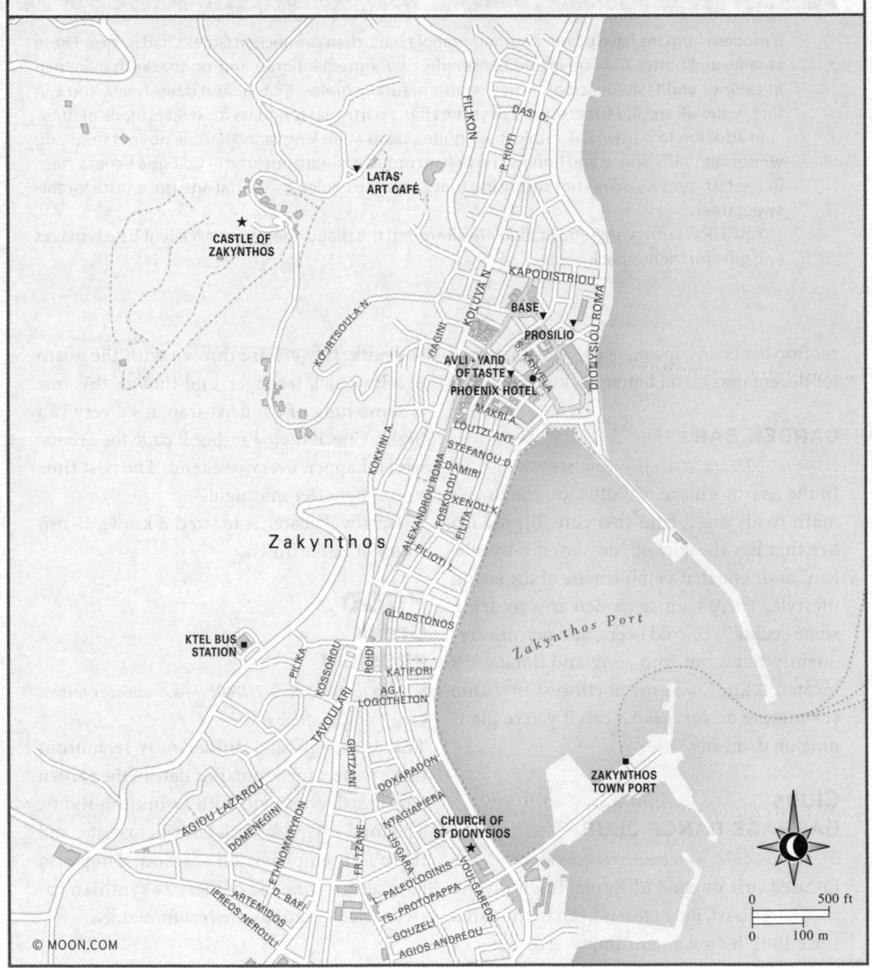

NIGHTLIFE AND ENTERTAINMENT

Zakynthos has a bit of a party reputation, thanks to the loads of package tourists who come to the island each summer on hen nights and stag dos (and just general youthful debauchery). Expect loud music, sugary cocktails, and an enthusiastic crowd of dancers.

Bars

BASE

L Ziva 3; tel. 26950/42419; www.basecafe.gr; 9pm-late

This split-level bar has two personalities: There's a ground floor café, that serves up cold coffees and beers to a local crowd and is ideally situated on Plateia Agious Markou for people watching; and by mid-afternoon, the

Nut Sweets: *Pasteli* and *Mandolato*

If modern humans have power bars and granola bars, then the ancient Greeks had *pasteli.* These sesame and honey bars are incredibly simple, two-ingredient grab-and-go snacks that are rich in calories and taste delicious. (They're also naturally grain-, gluten- and dairy-free!). You can find *pasteli* all around Greece, but Zakynthos has a particular fondness for sweets made of nuts.

In addition to *pasteli,* Zakynthiots are quite skilled at making *mandolato,* a nougat from egg whites, almonds, sugar, and honey. The first recorded nougat appeared in Cologna Veneta, Italy, in the 15th century, so it's not surprising that Zakynthos, ruled by the Italians, got a taste for this sweet treat.

You'll find both *pasteli* and *mandolato* all around the island; they make excellent beach snacks and gifts for friends back home.

rooftop bar opens up and becomes a hip venue for decent music and better cocktails.

GARDEN BAR

Tsilivi; tel. 69756/82708; afternoon-late

In the nearby village of Tsilivi, on the town's main road, you'll find this cute, hippie-ish bar that has the sort of "no shoes, no problem" aesthetic that's emblematic of the island lifestyle. There's a nice garden area to drink some cocktails or cold beers, and patrons frequently burst out into song and dance. It's located 6 km (3.75) mi northwest of Zante (15-minute drive). Take a cab if you're planning on drinking.

Clubs

BARRAGE DANCE CLUB

tel. 69555/86878; www.barrageclub.com

Located just outside of Zante Town on the road to Argassi, Barrage has been in the game since 1991. It's got a semi-impressive roster of foreign DJs who come to spin at summer parties, plus a lovely garden and a VIP section.

Bouzoukia

GATSBY THEATER

Epar. Od. Zakinthou-Vasilikos; Thurs.-Sat. 11pm-6am

If you want a Greek *bouzoukia* night, come one evening to throw flowers at singers at the Gatsby Theater. *Bouzoukia* are nightclubs featuring live *laiko* (urban folk music) performances. The singing is loud, everyone is drunk, flowers are thrown with the gusto of a love-sick teenager, and though this one is something of a tourist-trap, it's a very fun night. Check their Facebook page for events, which happen every weekend. The best time to come is after midnight.

Gatsby Theater is located 2 km (1.25 mi) south of Zante Town.

FOOD

Greek

PROSILIO

A Latta 15; tel. 26950/22040; www.prosiliozakynthos.com; 6pm-late; from €9

This is an upscale, dinner-only restaurant that's perfect for a romantic date in the garden courtyard, complete with twinkling lights. The food is Greek, with gourmet twists, and there's an emphasis on seafood. They also have a nice wine list of local Zakynthian varieties. Reservations are recommended.

LATAS ART CAFÉ

Bochali; tel. 26950/48230; 10am-1am; from €6

At this family-run taverna, the food is decent and the view—a panoramic one from the top of Bochali—is stupendous. Stop by for a coffee in the morning, a drink around sunset, or during lunch or dinner for taverna classics made by hand. In addition to Greek dishes, they've got international favorites like pizza and pasta, plus some truly indulgent desserts, like chocolate soufflé topped with ice cream.

Italian

AVLI - YARD OF TASTE

Rizospaston 15; tel. 26950/29815; www.avlizante.gr; noon-1am; from €8

Given Zakynthos' close connection with Italy, it's no surprise that the food has been influenced by Italian cuisine. One of the best places to sample this fusion is Avli, a quaint restaurant in the center of town done up in a rustic chic style. A large selection of gluten-free, vegetarian, and vegan options are available, and most of the ingredients are organic. Try their signature salad with figs and walnuts, or the spicy "drunken" mushrooms.

ACCOMMODATIONS

PHOENIX HOTEL

Solomos Square 2; tel. 26950/42419; www.zantephoenix.gr; from €120

If you want to be in the center of town, look no further than the ideally situated, medium-sized Phoenix Hotel, located on the town's main square and within walking distance of all the major sights. Though the outside is neoclassical and genteel, the rooms are modern and spacious, and feature balconies that look out onto Solomos Square.

LESANTE LUXURY HOTEL & SPA

Tsilivi; tel. 26950/41330; www.lesante.gr; from €230 d

This five-star hotel choice is located in tranquil Tsilivi village, 4 km north of Zante Town. Surprisingly affordable, Lesante has repeatedly won luxury hotel awards for its swank design, top-notch amenities, and exquisite spa. It has something of a resort-y feel, given its large size, but attentive staff and the lovely pools, plus private balconies, make you forget the other guests. Prices are reduced by half during the bookend months of summer.

Vasilikos Peninsula Βασιλικός

Driving south from Zante Town will take you down to the stumpy little leg of Vasilikos peninsula. Home to some very famous beaches, this is the thumping resort heartbeat of Zakynthos, and it attracts a lot of package tourists and 20-somethings who seem to be perpetually celebrating bachelor parties. Ironically, this is also an area of the island that is home to endangered loggerhead turtles, and parts of it are protected.

The resort town of Vasilikos is favored by families and groups looking for nonstop entertainment. It's a bit jarring to enter the multicolored, capitalist-influenced beach town that's specifically been tailored tourists, and if you haven't purchased a package tour from your home country, there's no particular reason to be here. However, there are still a few pockets of sanity elsewhere on the peninsula, including one of the island's best accommodations.

There are free buses (www.casaplaya.gr) from Langanas, Kalamaki, and Argassi (making stops in the major hotels, resorts, and bars) to Banana Beach. There are no buses from Zante Town—the type of tourist who heads to Banana Beach is most likely staying on a resort.

From Zante KTEL, there are regular buses to Argassi, and from there, to Gerakas (€2-5; up to 2 hours).

BEACHES

BANANA BEACH

One of the most famous beaches on the island, this long narrow sand beach is more of a social hangout spot than anything else. It's usually crowded, and there are plenty of beach bars, restaurants, live music, and umbrellas to keep everyone entertained. It's also the most popular place on the island for hang-gliding. It's located 13 km (8 mi) south of Zante. There are free buses from Langanas, Kalamaki, and Argassi to Banana Beach (making stops in the major hotels, resorts, and bars; www.casaplaya.gr).

National Marine Park of Zakynthos

Established in 1999 in order to protect the marine biodiversity in Laganas Bay, the **National Marine Park** (tel. 26950/29870; www.nmp-zak.org; free) is primarily known as a breeding ground for loggerhead turtles. It's the first national park established for the protection of sea turtles in the Mediterranean. The park stretches over a 90-square-km (35-square-mi) watery surface, from Marathia Cape to Gerakas beach, and encompasses 32 square km (12 square mi) of land. Some parts of the beach are strictly prohibited to visitors (these spots are clearly marked). From May to October, when the turtles are breeding, tourists are barred from sundown to sunrise. Eggs start to hatch in July, and conservationists and volunteers put up signs over the turtle nests to protect them.

VISITING THE PARK

The best way to visit the park is to take a boat tour from Keri that will take you to **Marathonisi Beach** (accessible only by boat), just off Marathia cape, and a place where there are many turtles. Or you can visit **Gerakas Beach** at designated hours during the turtle-hatching season. (The general public is permitted on sea turtle nesting beaches from 7am to sunset.)

TURTLE ETIQUETTE

In spite of volunteer efforts, many of the poor baby turtles never hatch, because visitors damage the nests. To be a good human to the babies:

- Avoid the areas where the turtles are hatching.
- Even during the day, don't set up your sun beds or umbrellas near them.
- Don't play around them (lest you accidentally step in a nest and crack an egg).
- Try to keep the music and voices down, because the noise is disorienting to the hatchlings.

VASILIKIS BEACH (Βασιλικής)

Next to Banana Beach (1 km/.6 mi south) is the equally beautiful Vasilikis beach. It's also organized, with plenty of places to grab food and drink, and it has the same lovely stretch of golden sand, but it's nowhere near as hectic as Banana Beach. This is a good spot for those looking for a little more quiet in the area.

GERAKAS BEACH (Γέρακας)

At the tip of the peninsula is Gerakas Beach, another sandy strip that's considered the island's best beach, thanks to its landscape and the hundreds of baby turtles that hatch and struggle to make it to the sea in the summer. It's an important nesting spot for the endangered loggerhead turtle, and visitor numbers are restricted. This long sand beach ends in a promontory that's made of clay. Sadly, the promontory is now closed off after visitors irreversibly damaged it by pulling off too much clay to make masks, so it must be viewed from afar. There are no tourist facilities here, and it's a wonderful place of nature and quiet. It's located 3 km (just under 2 mi) south of Vasilikis, and 7 km (4.3 mi, 14 minutes by car) south of Zante Town.

RECREATION

Water Sports

BANANA WATERSPORTS

Banana Beach; tel. 69/3703 3178; www.bananawatersports.com; 9am-9pm

If you want to banana while at Banana Beach, this one-stop water sports shop is your best bet, located right on the beach. Pick up rental equipment for a variety of water sports at fairly reasonable prices, like canoes for €5. You can try everything from knee-boarding

(€40) to paragliding (€50) to an inflatable banana boat ride (€10).

ACCOMMODATIONS

★ LOGOTHETIS ORGANIC FARM

Vasilikos; tel. 26950/35116; www.oliveoilfarmshop.com; from €110

If Italy has its *agriturismi*, then Zakynthos has the Logothetis Organic Farm—a delightful, family-run accommodation set in an olive grove. With just half a dozen or so rooms, each furnished in traditional Zakynthian style, you'll feel like you've been whisked away to the most relaxing countryside retreat. There's an oil press on-site, where you can learn all about the family's oil press business, and partake in some cooking classes. Rooms come with a free bottle of wine, and the outgoing owner is only too happy to chat about Zakynthos history.

Keri and Laganas Bay

Driving westward across the Bay of Laganas toward the Keri peninsula, you'll come across a string of beaches and tourist attractions. There are a lot of boat tours that leave from here to circumnavigate the island, including stops in Blue Caves and Shipwreck Bay, and plenty of tour operators congregate around here (it can be a bit overwhelming in the crowded summer months). But Keri itself is a cute little harbor town, and the 35-minute drive (on an easy road) across the southwest landscape is beautiful. You'll be driving through the bucolic green countryside, catching occasional glimpses of the blue sea as you near the coast.

Buses leave Zante Town for Keri on a regular basis, but the other destinations in Laganas Bay are best accessed by car.

LITHAKIA
(Λιθακια)

Sights

ARISTEON OLIVE OIL PRESS AND MUSEUM

tel. 26950/52898; www.aristeon.gr; 9am-7pm; free tours and tastings

Zakynthos has an impressive number of olive trees, their silvery-green leaves twinkling in the sunlight. Learn all about how olives are harvested, and pressed into liquid gold at the Aristeon Olive Oil Press and Museum. There are continuous half-hour tours in English, though the best part comes at the end when you sample freshly pressed extra virgin olive oil.

Lithakia is 12 km (7.5 mi) southwest of Zante Town. You'll need a car to get there, and the drive takes about 20 minutes.

CAMEO ISLAND
(Άγιος Σωστής)

Better known for being an Instagram photo op spot (the queue is mostly full of people looking to pose, not explore), Cameo is a tiny island off the coast of Laganas that is connected to the mainland by a long, rickety bridge. Visually, it's quite arresting, with a bit of a Robinson Crusoe air to it. At the time of writing, the island and bridge leading to it are closed due to legal disputes over ownership. It's unclear when it will be open again, though officials hope it will be in 2020 or 2021. It's located 3.5 km (2 mi) east of Lithakia (a 7-minute drive), and makes a nice stop on the way to Keri.

KERI
(Κερί)

The lovely little village of Keri is tucked away in the south side of the island, and has retained much of its original charm, with stone houses, narrow alleyways, and plenty of fragrant bougainvillea. There's also a nice church with an impressive bell tower (Panagia Keriotissa) and the Keri lighthouse, located on a cliff.

Keri is located 27 km (17 mi) south of Zante Town. Buses leave Zante Town for Keri on a regular basis (20 minutes; €2).

Sights

PANAGIA KERIOTISSA

free

Located on the southern side of Keri, this bright-yellow church with a big bell tower was built in 1745 and is a fine example of the island's Venetian architecture. To be honest, the facade is the best part of the whole thing. There's a small park located around the church where you can take a stroll.

LIGHTHOUSE

free

You can't go inside this small, squat, lighthouse, but why would you want to anyway, when the views out to the sea are so stupendous? This is a great place to watch the sunset (though it gets quite crowded in the summer, especially in August).

Boat Tours to Marathonisi Beach (Μαραθονήσι)

One of the less explored, and thus less touristy, beaches on the island, Marathonisi is a beautiful sandy beach accessible by boat. The beach is known for being the "island of the turtles," and is the heart of the National Marine Park. Daylong tour operators (from Keri, or from Zante Town) that are heading to Shipwreck Bay also make stops at Marathonisi for a few hours (€20-50, depending on time). Many tour operators on the harbor in Keri offer the same deal, but if you want something more intimate, spring for a 3-hour private tour with **Isala Travel** (30 Lomvardou Street Zante Town; tel. 26953/01600; https://isalatravel.com). Small private yachts will take up to eight people (€250 euros) to special swimming spots on Marathonisi.

If you'd rather stay on the mainland, lay your towel down at the equally lovely **Keri Beach,** located on the waterfront of Keri, which offers views of Marathonisi.

Diving and Water Sports

There are more than a dozen dive spots across the southern coast of Zakynthos: You can explore caves, deep walls, wrecks, and reefs, all teeming with fish. If you're planning a diving holiday, it's best to be based near Keri, where you'll find good outfitters at reasonable prices (though it's always cheaper to bring your own equipment). If you only have time for one dive, go to **Lakka** (off the coast of Cape Keri). It's the site of the famous stone arches covered in coral, which curve upward to the light streaming through the water. There's also a big cavern to explore, and it's likely you'll spot a monk seal in the midst of all the breemers and eels.

NERO SPORT

Keri; tel. 26950/28481; www.nero-sport.de; dives from €45 with equipment

Nero Sport is a beloved 30-year institution that specializes in diving, boat trips, and water sports. For diving parents accompanied by little ones, the fine folks at Nero Sport will happily babysit your kids while you explore the underwater world.

DIVING CENTER - TURTLE BEACH

Keri; tel. 26950/49424; http://diving-center-turtle-beach.com; €25 per dive

This is another PADI-certified diving center that will take you on snorkeling and diving excursions around the bay, where you'll see plenty of marine life—and hopefully even a couple of turtles.

Food

There are a lot of good dining options in Keri and the surrounding area. If you don't mind walking a bit or driving a few kilometers, I suggest heading to Marathias (2.2 km/1.3 mi south of Keri), where you'll find good classic Greek meals and stunning views of the Ionian Sea. The village is known for having

1: a boat bobbing in the water in Korakonissi Beach **2:** the bougainvillea-covered Diafokeriko Restaurant **3:** the tiny Cameo Island

1

2

3

some of the best products on the island, including olive oil. If you want to stay in Keri to eat, avoid the restaurants on the harbor and head into the village for dining options.

OUZERI ALLEGRO

tel. 697/926 1627; lunch and dinner; from €6

I wouldn't recommend springing for the ouzo if you're about to go diving, but otherwise, knock back whatever you want at this great local taverna on Keri's main square. The food is classic Greek taverna, all home-cooked and with a rotating daily menu. They have a lot of oven specialties and fresh fish. Ingredients are local, and though the clientele is almost exclusively tourists, don't be turned off! On summer Sundays they have live music.

MARATHIA STAR TAVERNA

Marathias; tel. 26950/45846; lunch and dinner; from €7

This friendly family-run taverna is located in an old stone house with a terrace that has beautiful views of the sea below. You can't go wrong with anything from the grill, whether it's meat or fresh seafood, which is drizzled in local olive oil.

Accommodations

VILLA CHRISTINA

Limni Keriou, Keri; tel. 26950/49208; www.villachristina.gr; from €160

This small, mid-range hotel features a cluster of maisonettes set around a pool. It's perfect for families with kids who want space to lounge about and cook their own meals (there's a minimarket a short walk away). The maisonettes are clean and spacious, and feature their own balconies.

West Zakynthos

The west side of Zakynthos is sparsely inhabited and more wild than other parts of the island. There's no coastal road along the west coast, but there is a series of lovely highland roads that are well paved and easy to drive, leading through the wooded hills slightly inland. Every once in a while, the road veers to the coast, as you climb up cliffs and descend down toward coves.

★ WEST COAST SCENIC DRIVE

There aren't buses to the west side of the island, so your best bet is to rent a car for the day and set off exploring. Spend some time driving in the general direction of Koilomenos (you can take some turns along the way to explore the area), which is a fine place to stop for lunch. Then enjoy an afternoon lazing about Korakonissi or Porto Roxa beach (I prefer the former, though the latter is more popular with tourists). While you're in the area, you should end your day at Kambi, which has the best sunset view on the island. It's 18 km (11 mi) to Koilomenos (about 35 minutes' drive) and a further 14 km (9 mi) to Kampi (20 minutes' drive).

KOILIOMENOS (Κοιλιόμενος)

Located 17 km (10.5 mi) east of Zante Town (30 minutes' drive), the little stone village of Koiliomenos makes a nice stopover for lunch on the way to the beach.

Beaches near Koiliomenos

★ KORAKONISSI (Κορακονήσι)

We saw a small hand-painted sign, turned down an unnamed road, and I found my favorite beach in Zakynthos. About a 7-km (4-mi) drive down from the main road in Koiliomenos is a lovely little cliff marked by a small snack kiosk. Descend to the left of the kiosk (150 meters/492 feet) to a rocky beach full of strange formations and perfect for jumping. On the right side of the kiosk is a more secluded beach (though the path is more difficult to manage). A snack bar is open from 9:30am until sunset every day from June to October.

Food

TO DIAFOKERIKO

5pm-late; from €8

This restaurant, located at the entrance to the village, looks like a postcard: It's a 300-year-old stone house elegantly covered in pink bougainvillea. Landscape paintings by local artists (for sale) adorn the walls. There's a small stone terrace, and you can also dine in the old kitchen of the house, next to the hearth. Their specialty is *sofigadora* (beef stew), though you can't go wrong with any of the homemade specialties.

AMPELOSTRATOS

tel. 698/326 1051; 5pm-late; from €8

An old stone house set in a rustic olive grove, Ampelostratos is a favorite of the locals and it's a bit tricky to get to. From the main road of the village, you need to follow the signs, driving down a bumpy dirt road between two fig trees to get to your dinner. The focus is on local products, including plenty of Zakynthian specialties, like braised rabbit in tomato sauce.

AGIOS LEON
(Άγιος Λέων)

The mountainous settlement of Agios Leon is off the beaten path as far as tourists go, though the village has retained much of its original character, with plenty of red-tiled houses and those requisite twisting village alleyways. The beaches here are mostly full of locals, and while they are rocky, the water is clear and beautiful.

Agios Leon is located 25 km (15.5 mi, 40 minutes) west of Zante Town.

Beaches

PORTO ROXA (Πόρτο Ρούχα)

This sandless, craggy beach has free sun beds and parasols in the organized part, and several cafés/tavernas for food and drink. It's a rocky bay and has a sort of wild beauty, and it's an enjoyable place to while away an afternoon, diving off the specially designed diving board or climbing into the water down the stairs that locals built. It's located 5 km (3 mi) south (10 minutes) from Agios Leon.

Shopping

VIOTEXNIA EPIPLON MARGARIS

tel. 26950/48642; www.epiplamargaris.gr; daily 10am-8pm

Given the plethora of olive trees that populate Zakynthos, it's no surprise that the islanders have created a whole artisanry of olive wood products. This little store, across from the town's gas station on the main road, has a range of olive wood objects (including larger furniture pieces), as well as some traditional textiles for sale.

ELIA SHOP

Kladis Giannis; tel. 69775/99277; daily 10am-8pm

Elia means olive in Greek, and this shop sells just that: bottles and bottles of local olive oil (extra virgin, flavored, you name it), which make wonderful gifts to bring back home.

Food

SELENE TAVERNA

Kladis Giannis; tel. 26950/48610; breakfast, lunch, and dinner; from €7

Located right on the main square of the village, this lively, family-run restaurant serves up hearty portions of Greek classics: hand-cut fried potatoes, barrel feta drizzled with local olive oil, and grilled meat. They also have breakfast options, such as fresh orange juice and omelets.

Accommodations

VILLA ROXA

tel. 69408/14524; www.villaroxa.gr; villas from €370

The newly built Villa Roxa is one of the most luxurious hotels on the island, situated at the top of a cliff with stellar views to the west coast of Zante. Villa Roxa is actually just one villa that's suitable for up to seven guests (there are three bedrooms, three bathrooms, and a private pool). It's perfect for a large family or a group of friends.

★ KAMBI (Καμπή)

This charming, traditional village is famous for having the best sunset views on the island. It's perched on a west-facing hill. Kambi is located 8 km (5 mi) north of Agios Leon (12 minutes) on a curvy mountain road. With only 60 inhabitants in the village, there's not a lot going on here—the village itself is full of abandoned stone houses—but the locals have capitalized on the fantastic views and there's a nice restaurant at the top. If you don't want to pay for the view with a cocktail, just park your car on the side of the road when you're driving from Agios Leon.

Sights

On top of the rock of Shiza, overlooking the village of Kambi, sits a huge cross dedicated to the Greek soldiers who died in battle during the country's civil war, and in World War II. It's located 1.3 km (.8 mi) west of the center of Kambi village (signposted).

A good **hiking path** (marked) leading from the village will take you to the cross. Walking the whole thing will take about 25 minutes. Alternatively, leave your car at Michalis' Taverna and walk the rest of the 800 meters (2,625 feet).

Food

TAVERNA SUNSET "MICHALIS"

tel. 26950/48740; 9am-late; from €9

Michalis has the best view on the island: This taverna is located on an unnamed road atop a cliff just at the edge of the sea. The food is actually quite good as well, as is the service, but you're really here to watch the sky turn a fiery orange while nursing a cold beer. Best to arrive at least an hour or so before sunset in order to snag one of the best terrace tables.

Accommodations

MABELY GRAND HOTEL

Exo Chora; tel. 26950/41302; www.mabely.com/hotel; from €130d

Located just outside of Kambi in the neighboring village of Exo Chora on the cliff of Porto Schiza, this hotel offers 108 rooms, each with a private balcony or terrace that faces the sea (and the sunset). It's a five-star hotel with marble floors and cream-colored furniture, but the prices are affordable. There are two pools, plus a restaurant.

Northern Zakynthos: Agios Nikolaos to Shipwreck Bay

If you want to base yourself somewhere more tranquil in Zakynthos, I recommend spending time in the Volimes region (which encompasses the village of Volimes as well as Agios Nikolaos), located 30 km (18.5 mi) north of Zante Town. There are good restaurants, affordable pensions, tranquil beaches, and enough activities to keep the kids entertained.

This area is also home to the island's two biggest landmarks: Shipwreck Bay and the Blue Caves. It's best to have your own car to explore, as this area is not well serviced by public transportation.

AGIOS NIKOLAOS (Άγιος Νικόλαος)

Agios Nikolaos (you might hear it referred to as Skinari) is a little fishing port and village on the northeast coast of Zakynthos. The harbor looks out onto a tiny dewdrop of an island, and there are regular boat departures in the summer to the neighboring Ionian island of Kefalonia. It's a very laid-back place, with a small strip of restaurants and tour operators along the harbor, and several pensions for rent. It's also a common departure point for boats to the Blue Caves, as well as stops at Shipwreck Bay.

Agios Nikolaos is located 30 km (18.5 mi) north of Zante Town. It's a nice place to stay, close to some of the main attractions but far enough from the touristic part of the south coast to get some peace and quiet. As of this writing, there were no direct buses from Zante Town to Agios Nikolaos. From Zante KTEL, there are regular buses to Argassi, and from there, buses to Agios Nikolaos (€1.88 daily; 1.5 hours).

Sights

ASKOS STONE PARK

www.askos.gr; May-Aug. 9am-7pm, Oct.-Apr. 10am-5pm; €9.50 adult, €6 children 3-12, under 3 free

If your kids are tired of the beach, bring them to this strange little private park. It's sort of like a petting zoo on steroids, with animals like racoons and deer roaming around. After September, it's impossible to go inside the park because it's the time of year when the male deer are growing in their horns and fighting with each other to compete for the ladies. Located 2 km (1.25 mi) south of Agios Nikolaos (5 minutes by car).

Beaches near Agios Nikolaos

XIGIA BEACH (Χίγια)

You'll smell this beach before you see it, but don't let that deter you. Xigia beach has a high sulfuric content in the water, giving the water some therapeutic qualities: Sulfur is good for alleviating pain from arthritis, and can also help reduce cellulite. It's actually the nearby caves that house large quantities of sulfur. If the smell doesn't bother you, you can rent an umbrella, grab some food at one of the beachside bars, and spend a whole day here. The beach is located between Zante Town and Agios Nikolaos.

Food

★ NOBELOS BIO RESTAURANT

tel. 26950/41330; www.nobelos.gr; 8am-late; from €16

This elegant family-run restaurant is one of the best places to eat in Zakynthos. Reserve a table on the waterfront and indulge in delicious dishes like sea urchin salad (which arrives, somewhat embarrassingly, on a bowl of dry ice) and shrimp *saganaki*. There's also an innovative cocktail menu and a wonderfully extensive wine list of bottles from across Greece (stay local and try the Zante Robola). If you eat at just one restaurant in Zante, make it this one. Reservations are a must in the summer months.

ANEMOMELI WINDMILL RESTAURANT

Askos, tel. 26950/31555; noon-late; from €6

The big draw here is the location. As the name implies, this restaurant is situated inside of a converted old windmill (there's also a terrace extending outside). You'll find reliable Greek taverna classics, in a restaurant run by a local family. Located 3 km (2 mi) south of Agios Nikoloas.

Accommodations

Agios Nikolaos is peaceful and family-friendly. It's a great, tranquil place to stay, especially if you're able to get a reservation at Nobelos. I recommend staying in Agios Nikolaos if you want the beauty of Zakynthos with much less of the noise and commotion.

NOBELOS SEASIDE LODGE

tel. 26950/31400; www.nobelos.gr; from €200

Adjacent to the restaurant is this small boutique hotel (there are only four rooms) run by the same family. The rooms are set up in an old stone house typical of Zakynthian architecture, and decorated with antique furniture.

1
2

It's a lovely place to stay if you can manage to snag a reservation.

PANORAMA

tel. 26950/31013; from €50

A great little budget option, this small family-run pension has about half a dozen rooms that are simple, clean, and spacious. There's a nice breakfast in the morning, which you can enjoy in the garden or the terrace.

★ BLUE CAVES

The blue caves are a series of underwater caves and grottos that have translucent, practically bioluminescent water and are covered in colorful pink and purple coral. The caves are located 4 km (2 mi) north of Agios Nikolaos.

There is no charge to visit the caves, but the easiest way to see them is by boat (€10). (You could also swim here from the shore, but it's quite a rocky way down and you'll have to be very careful not to get run over by a boat.) Glass-bottomed boats dip into the caves, and the jovial sailors who man the boats are all too happy to point out the best photo spots and the bright purple coral.

There are multiple operators offering boat trips from both Agios Nikolaos and Cape Skinari (the northern most point of Zakynthos), to take you to both Shipwreck Bay and the Blue Caves. There are also boat trips for the caves from Zakynthos Town and Keri too, but these take much longer. There's time for jumping off the boats into the water, so I encourage you to bring a snorkel mask (they don't rent them on the boats) to be able to best appreciate the caves. A trip to just the Blue Caves takes around an hour and a half to two hours; allow three hours for an additional stop at Shipwreck Bay. There's not much difference between leaving from Agios Nikolaos or Cape Skinari.

1: a bowl of olive oil in Nobelos restaurant
2: Thousands of people visit the beach in the summer.

★ VOLIMES VILLAGE

Until the 1980s, the only way to get to the northern part of the island was in a boat, which means that the village of Volimes was one of the last places on the island to be developed for tourism. It remains one of the most beautiful villages on the island: a traditional settlement with plenty of charm. It was the embroidery capital of Zakynthos, and there are still shops selling tiny embroidered fabrics.

Shopping

TSOUKALAS SHOP

Volimes (entrance to the village); tel. 69709/52419; daily 10am 7pm

This old-school shop is stocked with traditional Zakynthian products, including handmade textiles like scarves, tablecloths, napkins, and more, which are woven on the loom or hand-embroidered. They also have food products like nougat, olive oil, and cheese.

★ SHIPWRECK BAY

Anafonitira, Elation

You've undoubtedly seen the pictures: a rusted old schooner marooned on a golden sand beach, backed by sky-high cliffs surrounding a sea that is a completely unreal blue color. I'm here to tell you that it's even more stunning in person, with water so blue it looks Photoshopped, and that you will not be alone in your quest to see this beauty.

There are two ways to get to Shipwreck Bay: by boat, on tours that operate out of Zante Town, Agios Nikoloas, Cape Skinari, or Keri in Laganas Bay; or by car, if you drive to the top of the cliff and peer down over the edge. You can't get to Shipwreck Bay itself by car, and you can't get to the top by boat, so choose one, or do both for the photos.

Boat Tours

If you're taking a boat, the best time to leave is either very early in the morning to beat the lunchtime rush of tourists or just before sunset (again, the crowds have thinned out, plus there's the added bonus of the sunset views).

BASE Jumping

Zakynthos has something of a reputation for being an adrenaline junkie's playground. Perhaps the most heart-stopping sport is BASE jumping: leaping into the void with nothing but a bicycle helmet and a onesie made out of parachute material to protect you. (Did your stomach drop just thinking about it? Mine did!) The acronym refers to the four major categories one can jump off of: building, antenna, span, and, most troublingly, earth.

BASE jumping is not for beginners, but if you're someone who loves to be amped up on dopamine, you can check out the Facebook page for **BASE Jump Greece,** which organizes one big event every summer, attracting BASE jumpers from around the world. It's the only time that there's a safety rescue team present for BASE jump operations in Zakynthos. And if it's not your bag, just look up the videos of humans flying in the air, suspended above Shipwreck Bay. It's enough excitement for me.

There are dozens of tour operators that offer trips to Shipwreck—the farther away you are from the site, the longer the tour takes. Boat tours from Zante (€45) take up to 8 hours and include lunch. The closest departure point is Agios Nikolaos (tours cost €25 and take around 2.5 hours). Bring a swimsuit and towel, as the tours include a long stop in Shipwreck Bay.

Driving to Shipwreck Bay

We humans with our phones have all but ruined the second option: Everything at the top of the cliff seems to have been designed for taking selfies. After a couple of people fell to their deaths trying to take a selfie, the municipality built a fenced-in plank that sticks out of the cliff, where you can wait in line for hours to take a picture. If you're facing the water, you'll notice a hiking path to the right of the plank; you can follow that down the mountain ridge as the people thin out and the view is equally stupendous. If you want to take photos from the top, the best time is at 1pm when the sun rises from Skopos Mountain and the lights and shadows are just perfect, according to locals. However, if you want to be alone, you should arrive around sunrise.

ANAFONITRIA (Αναφωνήτρια)

A nice little traditional village, Anafonitria is best known for being home to Shipwreck Bay. It's also famous for its icon of the Virgin Mary, which, according to local lore, was found by sailors in a shipwreck; they heard a faint call and saw a flickering light emitting from the icon. You can see the icon at the monastery. The village is located 14 km (9 mi) southwest of Agios Nikolaos.

Sights

VIRGIN ANAFONITRIA MONASTERY

Built in the 15th century, this Byzantine relic is one of the few religious sites on the island to withstand the 1953 earthquake. The frescoes of the church are quite lovely and well-preserved, and there are delightful, plant-filled courtyards to walk through. You'll also find the famed icon of the Virgin Mary here. It's a good place to stretch your sea legs after a day on a boat.

Food

NINTRI CAFE

Anafonitria; lunch and dinner; from €7

This is a lovely little romantic spot on an unnamed road not far from Shipwreck Bay, with a terrace shaded by stone arches. The food is typical Greek taverna fare, served in copious portions by the friendly staff. It's a nice place to relax for a few hours, and it doubles as a café-bar.

Lefkada (Λευκάδα)

In Greek, *lefkes* means "white." It's ironic, because, with the exception of its rock strata along the island's ridges, Lefkada (pop. 23,000) is an explosion of seemingly every color *but* white. Like all the Ionian islands, Lefkada is incredibly green and fertile (at times, it feels more like a jungle than a Greek island), but its real draw is the technicolor-blue water on its west coast. As you descend down the coastline, with each turn of the road you'll get another glimpse of the Ionian sea that will have you struggling to think of the appropriate Crayola color to describe it: Robin's-egg blue? Cerulean? Aquamarine? It's a fun game.

If we're splitting hairs here, Lefkada isn't technically an island. It was originally a peninsula, but Corinthian colonizers cut through the

Highlights

Look for ★ to find recommended sights, activities, dining, and lodging.

★ **Rachi:** The best sunset view can be found at this shockingly affordable molecular gastronomy restaurant perched high up in the clouds, with spectacular views of Lefkada (page 413).

★ **Egremni Beach:** The most stunning beach in Lefkada is hard to reach, but it's worth it (page 414).

★ **Windsurfing:** Lefkada is renowned worldwide for its windy beaches. Try your hand at windsurfing at Vasilikis Beach, where colorful sails whip around the bay (page 417).

★ **Ta Lytrata:** This traditional mountain village of Eglouvi Village produces some of the best lentils in the world. Sample them at this authentic rural Greek restaurant (page 422).

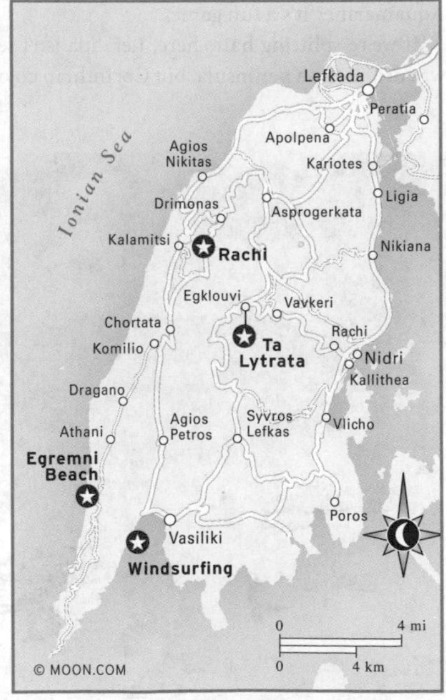

isthmus connecting Lefkada to the mainland in the 8th century BC, in order to create a passage to allow ships to sail through more quickly. These days there's an underwater tunnel, making Lefkada one of the few islands you can drive to; this also means it's become more popular with Greek tourists during the economic crisis (high-season ferry tickets can add up!). History and proximity make it a favorite island for Italians, and, somewhat more randomly, for Israeli tourists.

Lefkada has changed hands many times during its lifetime, and that's evident in the architecture, food, and even lilting speech of Lefkadians. Given its close proximity to the mainland, Lefkada has historically been an important strategic base, and thus a coveted one: In 1479, the Ottomans controlled the island, followed by the Venetians, who dubbed the island Santa Maura until they were overthrown by Napoleon in 1797. In 1810, the British had their turn until the island was reunited with Greece in 1864.

PLANNING YOUR TIME

Unless otherwise noted, businesses on Lefkada operate from **April** to **October.**

There's enough to do in Lefkada to satisfy everyone's tastes: extreme sports, languid walks on the beach, shopping, hiking, overeating...It's wise to spend **three to four days** on Lefkada, with at least one day devoted to exploring the island's **west coast,** and, if you're feeling adventurous, a morning spent **windsurfing** or **paragliding.** Spend an afternoon driving through the **mountainous interior,** and if you have the time, take a day trip to **Meganisi Island.**

I suggest basing yourself in the southeastern part of the island, where you'll find some of the island's nicest hotels (for every budget). You don't need to stay specifically in Nidri, though; there are plenty of nice options just outside the tourist bubble.

INFORMATION AND SERVICES

Banks and **ATMs** can be found in Lefkada Town, Vasilis, and Nidri. **Police** are headquartered in Lefkada Town (tel. 26450/22100), and have stations in the smaller towns. **Tourist police** can be reached at (tel. 26450/29379). The island's general **hospital** is located in Lefkada Town (tel. 26453/60244) and is equipped to handle serious injuries.

There is no official tourist agency in Lefkada, but **Kinissis Travel Agency** (Dimitroy Golemi, Lefkada Town; tel. 26450/25030; http://kinissis.gr) serves travelers' needs. Very practically situated, right on the harbor at the entrance of Lefkada Town, it is a one-stop shop for car/motorcycle rentals, reservations, and ferry/bus/airplane tickets.

GETTING THERE

Most visitors **fly** or **drive** into Lefkada. I recommend driving from Athens if there are spots on the mainland you want to see, or if you've found a cheap car rental in Athens.

Air

The closest airport is **Aktion Airport** (PVK) in Preveza, 20 km (12.5 mi) north of Lefkada Town. If you are flying between the Ionian Islands, use **Sky Express** (www.skyexpress.gr); flights from Athens are covered by **Olympic Air** (www.olympicair.com) and **EasyJet** (www.easyjet.com), as well as other budget airlines offering summer flights from around Europe. There is no airport shuttle between Lefkada and the airport, but **KTEL services** (tel. 26450/22364; www.ktellefkadas.gr) stops at the terminal entrance (30 minutes; €2.90). There are plenty of available **taxis** at the airport, a trip into Lefkada will cost €40.

Ferry

Ferries are not available from the mainland, but you can take the boat between Vasiliki, on

Previous: the unbelievably clear water of Egremni Beach; on the drive to Egremni you'll pass plenty of stalls selling honey; a local relaxes in the village of Eglouvi.

Lefkada's south coast, and Kefalonia during the high season. The two companies operating ferries are **West Ferry** (www.westferry.gr) and **Ionion Pelagos** (www.ionianpelagos.gr).

Bus

The bus service is an increasingly popular way to reach Lefkada, with the recently constructed **bus station** located 1 km (.6 mi) from the center of Lefkada Town. The bus serves **Athens** (5.5 hours; €38.50), **Patra** (3 hours; €17.60), **Thessaloniki** (8 hours; €38.50), and the nearby port of **Igoumenitsa** (2 hours; €13.30). Check the KTEL website for summer hours.

Car

It's pretty easy to drive from **Athens** to Lefkada. The 360-km (223-mi) journey takes just over four hours, cutting west across the Peloponnese before heading up north at Patras.

GETTING AROUND

Lefkada is 325 square km (125 square mi); given its size, there's a lot of geographical diversity. The north is flatter, while the center of the island is mountainous (the roads here are mostly good and paved, but quite twisty). The west coast is incredibly rugged, with white cliffs dropping dramatically into the sea—the roads here become more problematic. The eastern part of the island is more humid, with bogs and marshes.

Given the size of Lefkada, and the cost of taxis, it's useful and usually more cost-effective to rent a **car.** I don't recommend renting a scooter or motorcycle in Lefkada, as the roads are very high and twisty, and the island is pretty regularly rocked by earthquakes.

Bus

Lefkada is well-serviced by **KTEL** in the high season, with regular buses from Lefkada town to **Agios Nikitas** (25 minutes), **Nidri** (35 minutes), and **Vasiliki** (50 minutes). If you're trying to get to villages in more remote areas outside of these towns, you should plan to drive or take a taxi. Tickets cost €1.80-3.70. Note that schedules are reduced during Sundays and holidays.

Car

Rentals start around €40 per day, and there's no shortage of rental places in Lefkada Town, Nidri, Vasiliki, and the Aktion airport.

Taxi

Taxis are expensive and generally not worth it, unless you need to be transported to/from the airport. Try giving **Lefkas Taxi Service** a call (tel. 697 585 1038) if you need a lift.

Itinerary Ideas

For this itinerary, I recommend staying either in the mountainous interior of the island, or along the eastern coast. I would also recommend renting a car for these days.

DAY 1

1 The best way to experience Lefkada's fantastic western beaches is by boat. Book a trip leaving from **Nidri** that will take you to Porto Katsiki and Egremni. Lunch is included, but pack a bathing suit and sunscreen.

2 The view from the boat of **Porto Katsiki Beach**—backed by giant cliffs dotted with trees—is stupendous.

3 You can only reach the Technicolor-blue beach **Egremni Beach** by boat, making it a must-see on any tour. You'll jump off the boat and swim in clear waters.

Lefkada

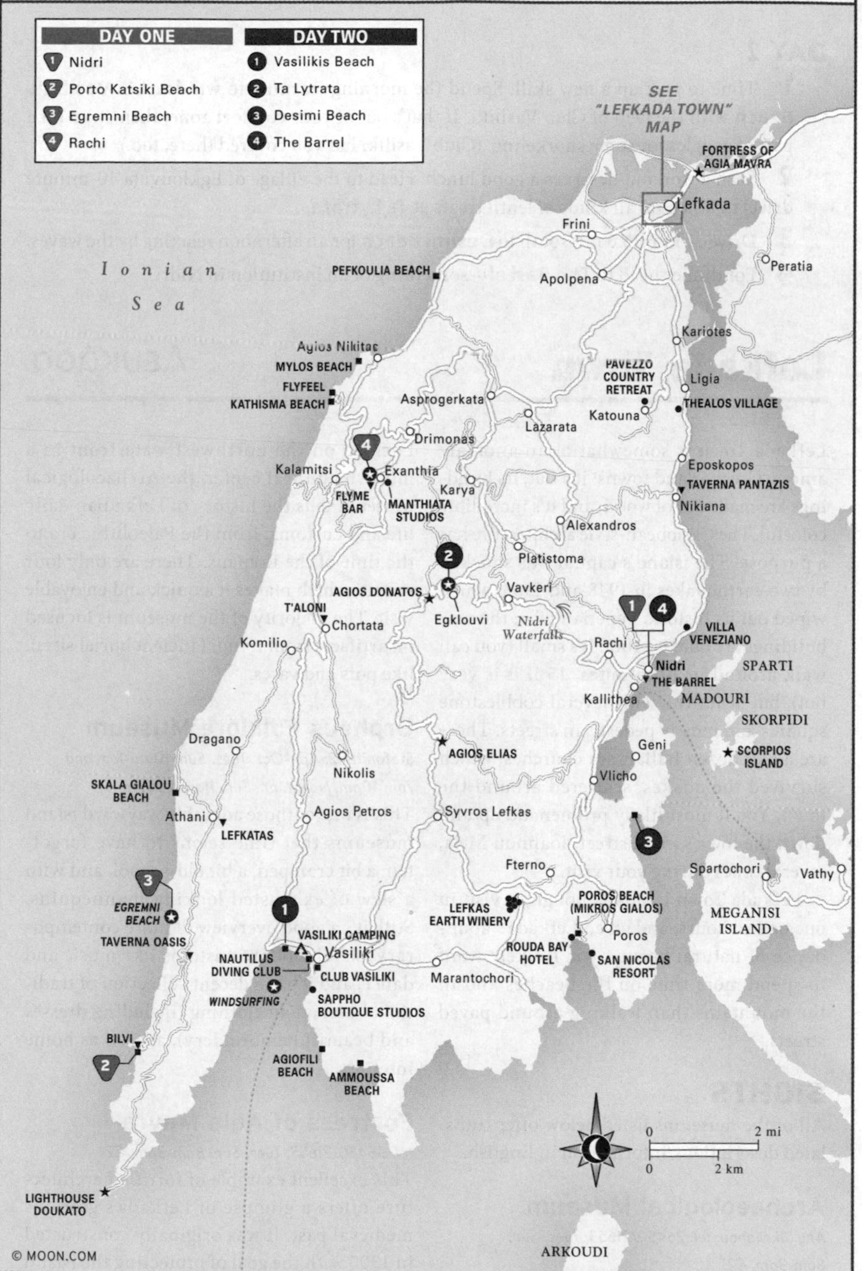
DAY ONE
1 Nidri
2 Porto Katsiki Beach
3 Egremni Beach
4 Rachi
DAY TWO
1 Vasilikis Beach
2 Ta Lytrata
3 Desimi Beach
4 The Barrel
SEE "LEFKADA TOWN" MAP
FORTRESS OF AGIA MAVRA
Lefkada
Frini
Peratia
Apolpena
Ionian Sea
PEFKOULIA BEACH
Kariotes
Agios Nikitas
MYLOS BEACH
FLYFEEL
KATHISMA BEACH
PAVEZZO COUNTRY RETREAT
Ligia
THEALOS VILLAGE
Asprogerkata
Katouna
Lazarata
Drimonas
Kalamitsi
Exanthia
FLYME BAR
MANTHIATA STUDIOS
Karya
Eposkopos
TAVERNA PANTAZIS
Nikiana
Alexandros
Platistoma
AGIOS DONATOS
T'ALONI
Chortata
Egklouvi
Vavkeri
Nidri Waterfalls
VILLA VENEZIANO
Rachi
Nidri
THE BARREL
SPARTI
Komilio
Kallithea
MADOURI
SKORPIDI
Dragano
AGIOS ELIAS
Geni
SCORPIOS ISLAND
Nikolis
Vlicho
SKALA GIALOU BEACH
Athani
LEFKATAS
Agios Petros
Syvros Lefkas
Fterno
Spartochori
Vathy
EGREMNI BEACH
TAVERNA OASIS
LEFKAS EARTH WINERY
POROS BEACH (MIKROS GIALOS)
MEGANISI ISLAND
Poros
VASILIKI CAMPING
NAUTILUS DIVING CLUB
Vasiliki
CLUB VASILIKI
WINDSURFING
ROUDA BAY HOTEL
SAN NICOLAS RESORT
Marantochori
SAPPHO BOUTIQUE STUDIOS
BILVI
AGIOFILI BEACH
AMMOUSSA BEACH
0 2 mi
0 2 km
LIGHTHOUSE DOUKATO
ARKOUDI
© MOON.COM

4 You'll be back in town around 6pm. For dinner, drive to **Rachi** in Exanthia (20 km/12 mi), where you'll watch the sunset while enjoying some thoughtful contemporary twists on classic Greek food.

DAY 2

1 Time to pick up a new skill: Spend the morning learning to windsurf in **Vasilikis Beach** with the help of Club Vasiliki. If that's out of your comfort zone, then strap on a pair of goggles for some snorkeling. (Club Vasiliki has you covered there, too.)

2 Such a workout deserves a good lunch. Head to the village of Egklouvi (a 40-minute drive) to fill up on all kinds of lentil treats at **Ta Lytrata.**

3 Drive 22 km (13.6 mi) south to **Desimi Beach** for an afternoon relaxing by the waves.

4 For dinner head to **The Barrel**—something of an institution in Nidri.

Lefkada Town Λευκάδα

Lefkada Town is somewhat of an anomaly among Greek island towns: it's flat, its buildings are made out of wood, and it's incredibly colorful. The Caribbean-style architecture has a purpose. The island's capital was shocked by two earthquakes in 1948 and 1953, which wiped out its historic Venetian vibe; the new buildings are quake-proof. It's small (you can walk around in 10 minutes, 15 if it is very hot), but beautiful, with several cobblestone squares and mostly pedestrian streets. There are a half dozen Italian-era churches, which survived the quakes, scattered around the town. You'll most likely promenade up and down the town's main street, Ioannou Mela, several times during your visit.

Lefkada Town is small enough to visit in one or two hours, and given Lefkada's abundance of natural beauty, you'll likely want to spend more time on the beaches and in the mountains than walking around paved streets.

SIGHTS

All of the museums listed below offer translated descriptions/information in English.

Archaeological Museum

Ang Sikelianou; tel. 26450/21653; Tues.-Sun. 8am-3pm; €2

Located on the northwest waterfront in a modern cultural center, the Archaeological Museum tells the history of Lefkadian daily life and customs, from the Paleolithic era to the time of the Romans. There are only four rooms, which makes it a quick and enjoyable visit. The majority of the museum is focused on artifacts from *timuli* (ancient burial sites), like pots and vases.

Orpheus Folklore Museum

Stefanitisi 2; Apr.-Oct. Tues.-Sun. 10am-1pm and 7pm-10pm, Nov.-Mar., Sun. 11am-1:30pm; €2

This is one of those adorably wayward island museums that time seems to have forgotten: a bit cramped, a bit old-school, and with a slew of exhausted looking mannequins. Still, it's a good overview of more contemporary island folklore customs like music and dance, and it has a decent collection of traditional Lefkadian clothing (including dresses and beautiful embroidery), as well as home interiors.

Fortress of Agia Mavra

tel. 26450/21653; Tues.-Sun. 8am-3pm; €2

This excellent example of fortified architecture offers a glimpse of Lefkada's glorious medieval past. It was originally constructed in 1300 with the goal of protecting the island

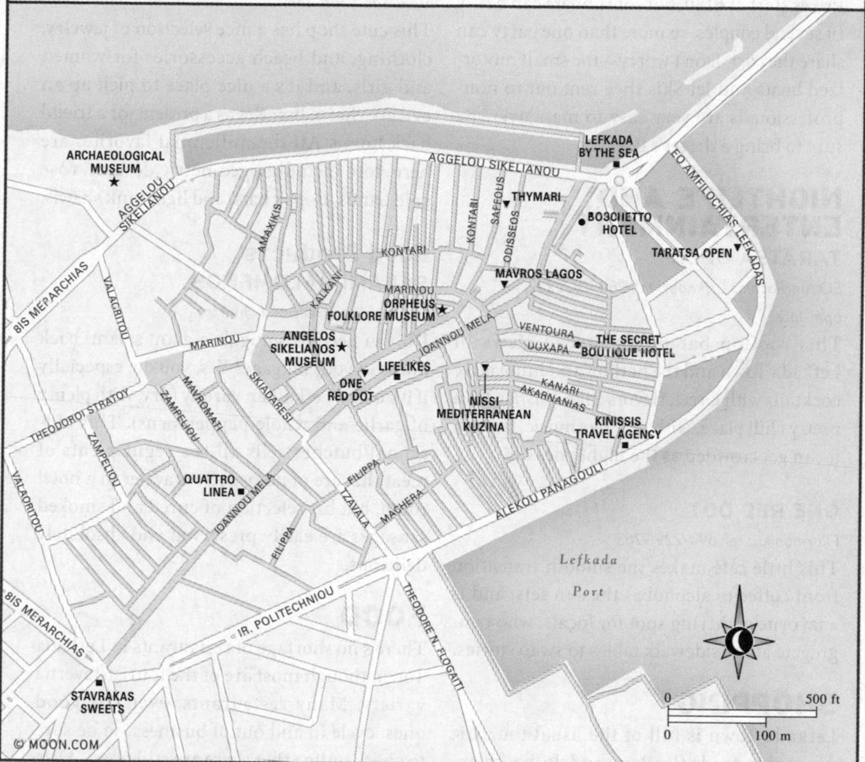

from frequent pirate invasions. The interior is now ruined, and parts of the fortress were destroyed by earthquakes, but it's still a nice place to stroll around, to soak up the history and look out at the beautiful views of the sea and port. It's located 2 km (1.25 mi) north of Lefkada Town, on the causeway connecting the island to the mainland.

Angelos Sikelianos Museum

Ang. Sikelianou and N. Svoronou Str.; tel. 26450/21635; http://odysseus.culture.gr; Tues.–Sun. 8am-3pm; €3, kids under 12 €2

Nobel Prize-nominated Angelos Sikelianos is one of Greece's most beloved poets. Sikelianos is famously difficult to translate, but his work, which focuses on the mysticism and beauty of Greece, is often compared to that of W. B. Yeats. This wonderful museum is located in Sikelianos's beautifully restored childhood home, and features an overview of the poet's life and work. The best exhibits include recordings of the poet's own voice, reciting his poetry. The museum is located just off Ioannou Mela.

RECREATION

Boat Rentals

LEFKADA BY THE SEA

Golemi and Machaira; tel. 694/472 1751; www.lefkadabythesea.com

Few things will make you feel as fabulous as renting a boat and cruising along the cerulean blue waters of the Ionian Sea. Choose from small motor boats or bigger sailboats, to be chartered on your own or with a captain. Prices start at €180, but some boats can easily fit several couples, so more than one party can share the cost. Don't worry—the small motorized boats and Jet Skis they rent out to nonprofessionals are very easy to maneuver! Be sure to bring a driver's license.

NIGHTLIFE AND ENTERTAINMENT

TARATSA OPEN

EO Amfilochias Lefkadas; tel. 26450/22232; 6pm-late

This rooftop bar offers breezy views of Lefkada Town and the harbor, and innovative cocktails with Greek flavors (like *mastic*). It's a pretty chill place, with nice live music, though it can get crowded as the night goes on.

ONE RED DOT

Filarmonikis; tel. 694/229 9763

This little café makes the smooth transition from coffee to alcohol as the sun sets, and is a favorite gathering spot for locals, who congregate at the sidewalk tables to swap stories.

SHOPPING

Lefkada Town is full of the usual touristic consumer goods (leather sandals, beach accessories, jauntily painted magnets made out of rocks, cheap jewelry), but there are a few places that stand out.

Clothing and Accessories

QUATTRO LINEA

Ioanna Mela 114; tel. 26450/22883; Mon.-Sat. 10am-10pm

Easily the most chic retailer in town, Quattro Linea offers the sort of dark, sexy, asymmetrical designs that are more suited to London or Berlin than a Greek island. They've got a selection of clothes from high-end designers like Vivienne Westwood, as well as contemporary Greek designers. Men and women's clothes are sold here, though there's much more choice for women.

LIFELIKES

Ioanna Mela 31; tel. 26450/25292; www.lifelikes.gr; Mon.-Sat. 10am-1am

This cute shop has a nice selection of jewelry, clothing, and beach accessories for women and girls, and it's a nice place to pick up an evil eye charm bracelet as a present for a friend back home. All the millennial favorites are here, too, including geometric designs, rose gold bands, floppy hats, and light pink shawls.

Food Products

SALAMI BALOMENOS

Filarmonikis Street and Quattro

Do you need to smuggle a giant salami back home in your luggage? Yes, you do, especially if it's of the Lefkadian variety (dry, with plenty of garlic and whole peppercorns). This old-school butcher sells all the regular cuts of meat that are of no use to a traveler in a hotel room, but his selection of cured and smoked sausages are easily preserved and absolutely delicious.

FOOD

There's no shortage of restaurants in Lefkada Town, though most are of the tourist-taverna variety. Many restaurants, even the good ones, cycle in and out of business, so be sure to check online that these are still open. Also, don't be alarmed to see cockroaches in restaurants and cafés, particularly in the bathrooms. I know it's startling, but the Ionian islands are full of them, especially in summertime (the hardcore ones can even fly). Seeing a cockroach in a restaurant isn't necessarily a sign of a lack of cleanliness.

Greek

MAVROS LAGOS

Pinelopis Street 4; tel. 698/696 0000

This beautiful wine bar, located in the terrace of the Aigli Hotel, has an astonishingly extensive list of Greek wines, and a tasty, if somewhat limited, selection of mezes. It's a great place for a tapas-style dinner.

NISSI MEDITERRANEAN KUZINA

Plateia Ethnikis Antistaseos; tel. 26454/00725; mains from €8

This Greek-Italian fusion restaurant is an excellent culinary example of Lefkada's Venetian influence—and a delicious one at that. Their specialties are seafood (prawns, octopus) and carbs (risotto, pasta), at shockingly affordable prices, and the service is great.

THYMARI

19 Pinelopis Street; tel. 26450/22266; www.thymari-lefkada.gr; from €16

Upscale taverna food with a creative twist is served inside a beautiful, traditional Lefkadian home in the heart of town. It's a bit of a "date night" restaurant, with the prices to match, but the food is delicious. FYI, most of the excellent-quality meat is imported from New Zealand or North America, which is uncommon in Greece (most of the meat is local).

Sweets

STAVRAKAS SWEETS

31 Ag. Mina Square; tel. 26450/22813; www.stavrakassweets.com

The only thing better than ice cream on a summer day might be semifreddo. It originated in Italy; is made of eggs, sugar, and cream; and has the consistency of frozen mousse. Stavrakas is the best place in town to try it, and they have a dozen flavors to choose from. Across the street is **Stavrakas Andreas** (22 Derpfeld St, Lefkada Town; www.stavrakassweets.gr), where the family owners sell traditional food products from Lefkada, like *ladopita* (sweet olive oil pie) and *soumadu* (a traditional drink made of almond extract that tastes like liquid marzipan). Preserved foods (jams, spoon sweets, nougats, etc.) can be easily wrapped up to bring back home.

ACCOMMODATIONS

There's no real reason to be based in Lefkada Town; you're much better off finding lodging in the west or southeastern parts of the island, where things are calmer and you're closer to nature and beaches. If you want to spend one day seeing the sights without driving anywhere afterward, or you want to be close to the airport for an early morning flight, it's worth spending the night.

BOSCHETTO HOTEL

Dorpfeld 1; tel. 26450/20244; www.boschettohotel.com; from €114, breakfast included

This medium-sized boutique hotel is one of the most attractive in Lefkada Town. It's located in a 100-year-old neoclassical-style building right on the harbor. Rooms are large and well-appointed (think wood floors, marble bathrooms, and adorable balconies looking out to the sea).

THE SECRET BOUTIQUE HOTEL

Ventoura 9; tel. 26450/21474; www.secretboutiquehotel.gr; €140, breakfast included

Tucked away into a little, cobbled side street of Lefkada Town, you'll find this cozy hotel. The five rooms, each designed with a specific concept, are all modern and spacious. The private garden is the perfect place to enjoy the delicious breakfast buffet. Amenities include bicycles that guests can use for free, Apivita products, and private airport transfers.

Agios Nikitas and the West Coast

The wild western coast of Lefkada boasts what may be some of the most beautiful landscapes of any Greek island. It's best to rent a car to drive south down the paved and (mostly) unbroken road from Agios Nikitas (12 km/7.5 mi southwest of Lefkada Town) to Porto Katsiki (a total of 40 km/25 mi), stopping along the way to buy honey from the local producers shacked up on the side of the road, and (carefully!) pulling over to marvel at the view of sheer white cliffs dropping down to that amazing blue. It will take you about an hour to drive down the length of the coast.

The best beaches on Lefkada, including Kathsima, Porto Katsiki, and Egremni, are located in the southwest. Most are accessible by road. A huge earthquake in 2015 devastated much of the west coast's best beaches, including Egremni and Porto Katsiki. Luckily, as of 2018 much of the area had been rebuilt. It's now possible to visit Porto Katsiki easily by road, although Egremni is still accessible only by boat from Nidri.

AGIOS NIKITAS
(Άγιος Νικήτας)

The beaches around Lefkada Town are not the cleanest or most beautiful the island has to offer. For swimming at the northern part of the island, head 12 km (7.5 mi) southwest of Lefkada Town to the quaint seaside village Agios Nikitas. This traditional settlement, snuggly nestled along the curved coastline, is considered one of the most enchanting villages in Lefkada. The small village boasts traditional architecture, stone pedestrian paths, and the beautiful **Saint Nikitas church**, with views out to the sea.

Beaches Near Agios Nikitas

MYLOS BEACH

A bit past Agios Nikitas is the stunning beach of Mylos, accessible via a 700-meter footpath leading south from the village. You can also hire a water taxi from the Agios Nikitas to take you to the beach (€6 one way). Boats depart from the harbor every 15-20 minutes and take just a few minutes. Note that the path becomes a little steep and difficult. It's worth it, though, as you'll arrive at a long sandy beach backed by cliffs and topped with pine trees and olive groves, with an unbroken expanse of that lovely blue in front of you. The water is calm and it's good for swimming. At time of this writing, Mylos Beach was one of the last unorganized beaches in Lefkada, although that's probably (sadly) changed.

PEFKOULIA BEACH

Located a five-minute drive south of Mylos is Pefkoulia Beach, which is pebbled and organized with lawn chairs and beach bars. The waves here can be quite big, so be careful. The beach is located right off the main road.

KATHISMA BEACH

This long sandy beach, backed by green mountains, is known on the island for the crystal quality of its water. This is an organized beach, with plenty of cafés, beach bars, umbrellas, etc. It's located 3.5 km (2.2 mi) south of Agios Nikitas (an 8-minute drive).

Paragliding

FLYFEEL

Kathisma, 3.4 km (2 mi) south of Agios Nikitas; tel. 697/418 7706; www.flyfeel.gr; €85 for flight and video

Are your dopamine levels feeling neglected? Why not jolt them awake with a quick paragliding jaunt? From March to November, weather permitting, the folks at FlyFeel will strap you to a tandem paraglider (or solo if you are experienced) and fly you over Lefkada's beautiful beaches and mountains. It's just like being a bird! FlyFeel is located in 3.4 km (2 mi) south of Agios Nikitas in the town of Kathisma; you'll meet there.

EXANTHIA (Εξανθία)

Located 12 km (7.5 mi) south of Agios Nikitas (on very winding roads that will take you 25 minutes to drive up), the small village of Exanthia is perched up in the mountains and has arresting views of the western coast of Lefkada.

Paragliding

PARAPENTE PARAMOTOR

tel. 694/455 5701; www.flyparapente.gr; from €120

This is a good option for paragliding, especially if you are feeling invincible after several cocktails at the FlyMe Bar (though they definitely won't let you fly if you're inebriated). Pick up some info on your way out of the bar/restaurant, and the next morning, decide if you're still feeling so courageous. The business doesn't have its own address; look for staff holding a Parapente Paramotor sign outside the FlyMe Bar. You can also make a reservation by phone.

Nightlife and Entertainment

FLYME BAR

tel. 26450/99231; www.flymelefkada.gr; 10am-2am

With the success of Rachi restaurant, the owners recently decided to open an adjacent bar. This has more of a lounge feel, with plenty of big cushions for draping your body just so as you watch the most beautiful sunset of your life. They have small snacks available, and in the summer, they often host DJs or live music events.

Food

★ RACHI

tel. 26450/99439; www.rachi.gr; from €10

I was not expecting to find a molecular gastronomy menu—with offerings like deconstructed salads and crispy fish skin served with foam—in the middle of the mountains, but Rachi is an extraordinary restaurant. The view is superb—you truly feel like you are perched in the clouds—and the gourmet food, with an emphasis on local ingredients with a modern twist, is more than affordable. This restaurant is a real treat, and the cocktails are good, too. During high season, call for reservations, especially if you want a seat on the terrace.

Accommodations

MANTHIATA STUDIOS

tel. 698/106 6885; from €150

English-speaking hosts Vicki and Dimos exude hospitality with their small collection of stone studios and apartments (most sleep two; the largest sleep up to five). Studios are small but clean and well-appointed, with absolutely fantastic views of the mountains.

CHORTATA (Χορτάτα)

This little village, 6 km (3.75 mi) south of Exanthia, runs along the main west coast road. It's a small, traditional settlement virtually untouched by tourists, who mostly drive through on their way to the more southern beaches. It has a good selection of tavernas and a couple of rooms to rent, as well as beautiful vistas visible from virtually anywhere in town.

Food and Accommodations

★ T'ALONI

Epar. Od.; tel. 26450/33240; Apr.-Oct. 8:30am-11pm; from €10

Okay ... the real reason to come to Chortata is to eat at T'Aloni, one of the best restaurants on the island. It's typical Greek taverna food, but they only use fresh, local products. In my years living in Greece, I've eaten a countless amount of feta, but T'Aloni's briny, crumbly version was the best I've ever had. They excel at meat dishes (if it's available, try the lamb), and the service is friendly without being intrusive. Grab a seat at the terrace, where there's an excellent view for sunset (bring a sweater, as it gets chilly at night). They also have a few rooms to rent upstairs, starting from €35.

ATHANI (Αθάνι)

The last populated village before Porto Katsiki, Athani (9 km/5.6 mi south of

Chortata) is a tiny hamlet with a fascinating history: The first settlers here were Italians; in the 15th century Athani became home to a small population of Sephardic Jews. During the 1950s and '60s, much of the village emigrated in search of work, and today only 200 inhabitants remain. It's got a bustling tourist infrastructure, and you should stop here to pick up any supplies from the minimarket. If you've forgotten cash, you'll need to stop at Vasiliki (15 southeast of Athani) before heading to the beaches further south. As you drive out of Athani towards the beaches you'll notice a slew of roadside vendors selling local honey for less than €10. They are all good!

Beaches

SKALA GIALOU BEACH

This vast beach features a long strip of white sand and gorgeous turquoise water. You can easily drive here off the main road, and there's a large parking that usually has spots. It's located 4 km (2.5 mi) south from Athani, and the road is partly unpaved but manageable. The beach is partly organized, with some umbrellas for rent and a canteen, but most of it is pristine. It's popular with campers, who park their vans in the lot, and with families, who take advantage of the shallow waters.

Food

LEFKATAS

tel. 26450/33149; www.lefkatas.gr; from €8

This is a true family taverna: The family's actual home was transformed into a restaurant serving standard taverna fare. The service is excellent (though a bit slow during peak hours), and the view of the mountains and the sea is superb.

TAVERNA OASIS

Athani; tel. 26450/33201; from €10

The real draw at this beachy taverna is the view, especially during sunset. Snag a table under the palm tree leaf veranda and enjoy rustic Greek classics. There is a decent selection of vegetarian options, though their specialty is fish.

★ EGREMNI BEACH (Εγρέμνη)

Egremni beach is the stuff of dreams. The white sand stretches out for 2.5 km (1.5 mi), hugged by impossibly high cliffs. The water is vibrant to the point of hurting your eyes. It's considered one of the most beautiful beaches in all of the Mediterranean, but with great beauty comes great difficulty: It's nearly impossible to access. Before the 2015 earthquake, you had to descend a steep, 720-step staircase, but that was destroyed during the quake, and parts of the cliff fell as well, making the beach inaccessible on foot or by car. You can only reach Egremni by boat, which makes it feel all the more *Mission Impossible.*

Boat Tours to Egremni

Boats leave regularly from Nidri; you can do a day trip (9am-6pm; €25) that includes several other stops, including to Porto Katsiki and Agiofili. Another option is to rent a private boat, for significantly more money and spend all day just in Egremni.

You'll notice several tour operators with boats docked at the Nidri harbor. Tickets can be bought directly from the boat staff the evening before you depart, or from travel agencies (hotels can also organize boat tours for you). The boats all do more or less the same tour, but you can try **Nikolaos Boat** (tel. 26450/92528), which is helmed by the gregarious Captain George. If you want a more private experience, take a chartered yacht with **Ionian Sail** (on the Quay in Vlicho, 5 km/3 mi south of Nidri; tel. +44 800 321 3800; www.sailionian.com). Private chartered yachts cost about €450 per day.

PORTO KATSIKI BEACH (Πόρτο Κατσίκι)

Katsiki means "goat" in Greek, and it sure feels like Porto Katsiki, which is similar in

1: A boat drops off passengers on Egremni Beach. **2:** The meat dishes at T'Aloni are cooked to perfection. **3:** The crumbly feta at T'Aloni is out-of-this-world delicious. **4:** the view of Porto Katsiki beach before you descend the stairs

1
2
3
4

landscape to Egremni, is better suited to the agile climbing skills of goats than humans. Though it was also partially ravaged in the earthquake, Porto Katsiki is now accessible again by car from the main coastal road that cuts through the island's south (from Athani, it's 10.7 km/6.5 mi south). There's a parking lot at the stairs of the beach, though it gets incredibly crowded and finding a spot can be a nightmare; your best bet is to arrive very early in the morning, even before 8am. The beach is organized, with a canteen and bar at the top. Standing at the top of the cliff and looking down at the water is unreal—the water is mesmerizing. Note that you do have to climb down 100 stairs to reach the beach itself.

Food

BILVI

tel. 697/330 9604; www.bilvi.gr

Once you've made it down to Porto Katsiki beach, the last thing you want to do is clamber up and down those 100 stairs to get drinks and snacks. Luckily, Bilvi, the only restaurant in the area, will come to you. You can order by phone—or from the waiters who jog down to the beach—from a menu of beverages and food, including sandwiches, pasta Bolognese, and moussaka (which begs the question, *who* eats bechamel-covered food at the beach?). Delivery is available on orders over €3.50.

LIGHTHOUSE DOUKATO

At the very tip of Lefkada, 15.5 km (9.5 mi) past Porto Katsiki beach, where the world seemingly ends, you'll find the Lefkada Lighthouse, precariously situated at the top of a cliff that suddenly drops down 75 meters (246 feet) below. Though it was built in 1861, like all good Greek things, the lighthouse has dramatic roots in mythology: According to legend, the lovesick could jump into these waters to cure a broken heart. The ancient poet Sappho leapt from this point on the cape after her lover Phaidon rejected her, and promptly died. During the Roman era, priests would select someone who had been rejected from society to perform *katapondismos* (the jump) as a sacrificial purification rite. For centuries after, heartbroken local youths imitated Sappho's jump, strangely believing it could fix their anguish. If you come here in July, you can see hang-gliders jumping (to safety). It's not possible to go inside, but you can hike (if you're athletic enough) somewhat close to it.

Vasiliki Βασιλική

Everything's relative, but compared to the west coast, the southern part of the island is more developed in terms of tourism, and this is most apparent in Vasiliki. This part of the island is popular with windsurfers, too, as Lefkada is considered to have some of the best windsurfing in Europe.

The seaside town of Vasiliki is a convenient ferry hub (boats arrive here from neighboring Kefalonia), and makes a decent base for exploring the island. It's got all you could want from a Greek island harbor town: nice scenery, bobbing boats, and plenty of restaurants, cafés, shops, and supermarkets. The main street is a bit depressing, in that commercialized way that many island towns have succumbed to, but the waterfront is nice for an evening stroll.

BEACHES

VASILIKIS BEACH

Vasilikis is one of the most popular beaches in Lefkada, as it is easily accessible from the main village. It's most popular with windsurfers, who take advantage of the bay's peculiar weather conditions. There's a lot of activity going on here, and it can get overwhelming, but the more social and extreme sport-loving among us will like this spot.

AGIOFILI BEACH

The unspoiled cove of Agiofili lies 3.2 km (just under 2 mi) south of the village of Vasiliki. This is an unorganized beach, so bring your own snacks and umbrellas. You can access the beach either via a 50-minute walk from the village of Vasiliki, or by taking a small water taxi from the port of Vasiliki. Taxi boats cost around €6 round-trip, with the first boats leaving around 10am and returning around 6:30pm. It's a small beach, so arrive early to snag a spot!

AMMOUSSA BEACH

Beautiful Ammoussa beach is perfect for families with small children (thanks to the shallow waters), and it's great for snorkeling (there's a whole world to explore living between the rocks). You can either buy a mask at the tourist shops in town or rent equipment from Club Vasiliki. The beach is pebbled and almost entirely taken up by sun beds (€3 for the day), and it's backed by a row of restaurants and cafés. It's located 11 km (6.75 mi) southeast of Vasiliki; it's best to drive there.

RECREATION

★ Windsurfing

Though Lefkada is known as a windsurfers' paradise, you don't need to be a pro to try your hand at it. Most of the diving clubs and rec centers offer beginner courses (though you might find yourself surrounded by children).

CLUB VASILIKI

tel. 26450/31588; www.clubvass.com

This family-run windsurfing shop and rental place is somewhat of an institution in Vasiliki. You can purchase all-inclusive windsurfing packages for beginners (with flights and accommodation, special offers from €750), as well as equipment rental, private lessons, and group classes. You can rent snorkel gear here, or go on a snorkeling day tour with lunch included (€50). Individual scuba dives with equipment start at €50, and courses start at €280.

Diving

NAUTILUS DIVING CLUB

tel. 693/618 1775; www.underwater.gr

Take advantage of Lefkada's crystal-clear waters with the help of Nautilus Diving Club. In addition to sea-kayak and snorkeling excursions, experienced divers can go on individual dives (€60), while others can take PADI open-water courses (€140). They have a specially designed program for kids called the Bubblemaker, which teaches young ones how to safely enjoy the "thrill of breathing underwater"!

FOOD

Vasiliki offers many dining options, but no restaurant stands out enough to warrant a recommendation. There are tavernas on the beachfront as well as along the street behind the beach.

ACCOMMODATIONS

VASILIKI CAMPING

tel. 26450/31308; https://campingvassilikibeach.com; from €6

For nature-lovers on a budget, Vasiliki Camping has you covered. You can park your camper or pitch your tent just 50 meters (164 feet) from Vasilikis Beach, and take advantage of amenities, including showers, toilets, washing machines, a minimarket, and restaurant/café. It's most popular with windsurfers, European tourists (who drive their campers from their native countries), and Greeks.

SAPPHO BOUTIQUE STUDIOS

Villa Agora Rd; tel. 694/888 4252; http://sapphoboutiquesuites.com; from €100 d

This cute, affordable cluster of modern studios is right next to its own semi-private beach, with a foliage-covered path (though if you're too blissed out to move, you can just take a dip in the hotel's infinity pool). Some studios feature individual plunge pools, while others have balconies that overlook the Ionian Sea. There's 24-hour concierge service offering everything from babysitting to private boat tours.

SAN NICOLAS RESORT

Epar.Od. Lefkas; tel. 26450/95050; www.sannicolas.gr; from €150 d

This (somewhat) newly built hotel is a modernist jumble of glass, infinity pools, lightly stained wooden beams, and chrome, all nestled in the green hills of Vasiliki. It's definitely a resort hotel, which means it's big, with luxuriously appointed rooms, plenty of optional upgrades, and lots of buffet dining options, but it's also a favorite among traveling couples and families. Note that there is a four-night minimum stay.

Nidri and East Lefkada

The eastern part of Lefkada is the most tourism-developed part of Lefkada, largely thanks to the busy resort town of Nidri. The farther south you go, the more the tourism dwindles, and though there are only a handful of beaches worth mentioning on this side of the island, there are nice waterfalls and hiking trails to discover.

Past Nidri, at the eastern tip of Lefkada, the coast sharply cuts in twice, revealing two lovely bays: Dhessimi and Rouda. Dhessimi is particularly dreamy, with grottos and white rocky promontories crowned with olive and pine trees. It's still a pretty quiet spot; that can be said less and less for Rouda, which is increasingly becoming a developed touristic area. To be honest, these are the only two beaches on the east side of Lefkada worth going out of your way for.

LIGIA (Λυγιά)

The small fishing port of Ligia is just a few kilometers south of Lefkada Town. It's a cute little fishing town that surrounds a small, tranquil bay. If you want touristic comforts and amenities without the resort-like feel of Nidri, it might make a good base.

Accommodations

THEALOS VILLAGE

tel. 26450/72035; www.thealosvillage.gr; €100 d

"Affordable luxury" is the rallying cry of this cluster of suites, villas, and studio apartments, although the interiors, while comfortable, are definitely Ikea-inspired. The rooms are built using traditional stone techniques, and the villas (some of which can fit up to 13 people!) come with private pools. This is a good choice for large groups and families.

KATOUNA (Κατούνα)

Three km (1.85 mi) west of Ligia, perched higher up in the mountains away from the coast, is the traditional settlement of Katouna. There's not a whole lot to see in the village, aside from a small church and a couple of architecturally pleasing buildings, but you'll be surrounded by lush mountains, and it's quite a relaxing place. You can also walk between the villages (30 minutes).

Accommodations

PAVEZZO COUNTRY RETREAT

tel. 26450/71782; www.pavezzo.gr; from €120

In the traditional Lefkadian dialect, *pavezzo* means "shelter," and this gorgeously restored hotel is exactly that. These cottages—made out of stone and decorated in a rustic chic style—are adorable mountain getaways. Some of them feature fireplaces or clawfoot bathtubs, and there's a wonderful restaurant onsite, serving traditional Greek food. There's a pool, of course, though your view takes in green mountains, not the sea.

NIKIANA (Νικιάνα)

Past Katouna, and back on the coast, you'll come across the small fishing village of Nikiana, 3.2 km (2 mi) south of Ligia. It's seen

Boating to Meganisi Island

There are four satellite islands that hang out right off the east coast of Lefkada—two are inaccessible, one is a semi-private island, and the largest, Meganisi, is easily accessible from Nidri. Nidri is also the launching point for boat trips to **Egremni Beach** on the island's west coast. Those same tour operators that serve Egremni have day trips that will take you around these satellite islands, and sail past Scorpios before stopping in Meganisi (from €55).

SCORPIOS ISLAND (Σκορπιός)

If you're approaching Lefkada by boat from Kefalonia, you'll notice a lush, beautiful island with just one house on it. Like all the best things in Greece, it belongs to the Onassis family. Scorpios island is famous as the place where Jackie Kennedy married Aristotle Onassis. It's possible to approach the island by boat (though it's not actually possible for us mere peasants to go *onto* the island), with regular boat tours leaving from Nidri.

MEGANISI ISLAND (Μεγανήσι)

The small, colorful island of Meganisi makes an excellent day trip from Nidri (€12-20); boat tours usually include swimming stops and a taverna lunch. There are three traditional villages, **Katomeri, Spartohori,** and **Vathy,** of which Vathy is the largest and the main harbor. Walking between the three of them is 10 km (6 mi), and takes two and a half hours. If you only have time for two, you can visit Vathy and walk 1 km (.6 mi) west to Katomeri.

Spartohori is a beautiful whitewashed, bougainvillea-laced traditional Greek island village, and well suited for a meandering walk. You can also visit the **Cave of Papanikolis** (located 10 km/6 mi south from Vathy), a lovely grotto that became a famous submarine hiding spot during World War II. If you want to spend the night, book a simply furnished room at **Hotel Meganisi** (tel. 26450/51240; www.hotelmeganisi.gr; €80).

some tourism growth in the past few years, but it remains a bit more peaceful of a harbor spot. The village surrounds a tiny harbor, and there's a string of restaurants, cafés, and rooms for rent on the waterfront.

Food

TAVERNA PANTAZIS

tel. 26450/71211; www.pantazistaverna.gr; fresh fish from €45/kilo

I firmly believe one should never miss an opportunity to eat lunch beachside, and this family-run taverna delivers. You'll find the usual list of Greek classics, but their specialty is seafood, which is freshly caught each day and grilled to order. They also have some bungalows for rent (€40).

Accommodations

★ VILLA VENEZIANO

Epar.Od. Lefkas, Vasilikis, Perigiali; tel. 2310/522422; www.villaveneziano.com; from €300 d

If you're going to splurge on one hotel during your time in Lefkada, make it the Villa Veneziano, where you can live like a member of the Onassis family for the night—literally! The villa was built in 2009 by the Russian shipbroker Sergei Kauzov in loving memory of his wife Christina Onassis. Five luxury suites are arranged around beautifully landscaped gardens and a pool (it's not uncommon for the whole villa to be rented out by one group). You'll find the luxury touches you would expect: four-poster beds, Bose sound system, walk-in showers, plus excellent service by the in-house manager, Giorgos, who goes out of his way to make guests feel at home.

NIDRI
(Νυδρί)

The island's touristic heartbeat thumps loudest in Nidri, where most package tourists end up, and that means lots of souvenir shops, cafés, and mediocre tavernas catering to out-of-towners. A lot of yachts end up stopping here, and the beach, which is located in the town, isn't half bad, with a decent array of water sports providers. However, it's not the most relaxing area, and I wouldn't recommend staying here, or even eating here, unless you've booked a package deal.

Nidri is the jumping off point for any touristic information you might want, though, and that includes booking boat tours to Lefkada's satellite islands. This is also the spot to hop in a boat headed for Egremni Beach, accessible only by boat.

Sights

NIDRI WATERFALLS

It's a lovely trek through the woods to this waterfall, but come early in summer—by the end of the season, if there hasn't been rain, the waterfall is dried up! You can drive up to the Nidri café (located right before the waterfalls), and from there it's an easy 15-minute hike to the waterfall, which also has a little pool that's deep enough to swim in. On a recent visit, I was disappointed to see how tourists treat the place: littering, carrying giant inflatable devices to use in the waterfall. It's best to come very early in the morning, with the sunrise, so you'll have the place to yourself; it gets crowded by mid-morning.

LEFKAS EARTH WINERY

tel. 26450/95200; www.lefkaditikigri.gr

Lefkada has some delicious wines, with the white vardea and vertzami grapes grown only on this island. The varieties are characterized by their crisp and bright taste. Lefkas Earth Winery offers free guided tours in English that last anywhere from 20 minutes to an hour, depending on the individual's oenological interest. You'll learn about traditional wine-making techniques in Lefkada, tour the vineyards, and sample a few bottles. You can also buy individual bottles or cases to ship back home. Lefkas Earth Winery is located on the 8th kilometer of the Nidri-Vasiliki road (13 km/8 mi south of Nidri).

Food

THE BARREL

tel. 26450/92906; from €8 euros; daily 11am-1am

This restaurant is something of an institution in Nidri, with oversized portions of everything from moussaka to good-quality steaks the size of a human face. Snag a table at the outdoor patio.

DESIMI BEACH
(Δεσιμι)

This relaxed beach on Desimi Bay isn't very large, but makes up for its size with excellent snorkeling and exploring possibilities. You can rent a motorboat or kayak from **Dessimi Boats** on the beach (https://dessimiboats.gr; from €15) to explore the grottos along the beach. Most visitors drive 6.2 km (4 mi) south from Nidri to get here (15-minute drive).

POROS
(Πόρος)

The seaside village of Poros sits around Rouda Bay.

Beaches

POROS BEACH (MIKROS GIALOS)

The village of Poros is home to Mikros Gialos beach (also called Poros Beach), an increasingly busy but still beautiful stretch of unspoiled beach. The beach is set on a fertile hillside, and the contrast of the green trees with the blue water is just fantastic.

Accommodations

ROUDA BAY HOTEL

Epar.Od. Porou; tel. 693/256 7502; www.roudabay.gr; from €70

What more could you want: rooms and food,

1: It's a short walk to the cascading Nidri Waterfall. **2:** Eglouvi makes some of the best lentils in the world.

1

2

right on the beach. This taverna/hotel offers six comfortable and modern studios and rooms in the center of town, with the sea just steps away, and breakfast included. The home-cooked food is quite good, and at €10 euros or less, this makes an excellent mid-range stay.

Egklouvi Εγκλουβη

The mountain village of Egklouvi, located right in the mountainous middle of the island, is one of the most delightful spots on the island. The village has preserved its traditional architecture, and the small cluster of stone houses and buildings is situated around a tree-shaded *platanos* (main square).

Egklouvi is renowned for its lentil production—so much so that chefs from around the world source their lentils from here, and locals refer to it as "black gold." If you think of lentils as the sad refuge of dieters, monks, and broke college students, just wait till you arrive in this village. There's something about the altitude and the high potassium levels in the soil that make Egklouvi particularly well-suited to producing lentils. If the village has had a bad production year, they won't sell you any lentils, but one way around that is to visit in August, when the village holds its annual **Lentil Festival,** featuring music, dancing, free-flowing wine, and bubbling cauldrons of lentils.

From Nidri, it's a beautiful 30-minute drive (15 km/10 mi) through the interior of the island. There are two route options; both are quite scenic but one road (through Rachi) involves more twisting turns. If you're coming from Lefkada Town, there's one road straight down the interior of the island (19 km/12 mi, 40 minutes).

SIGHTS

Agios Donatos and Agios Elias

There are two churches in town, Agios Donatos and Agios Elias, which are best known on the island for their stone and pebble exteriors and their panoramic views. Agios Donatos is located 2.4 km (1.5 mi) from the main square (a 6-minute drive, or 30-minute walk) and Agios Elias is 5.4 km away (3.25 mi, 13-minute drive).

FOOD

★ TA LYTRATA

tel. 26450/41261; Apr.-Oct. 11am-9pm; from €8.50

Right across from the main square is this delightful restaurant serving up delicious home-cooked foods. It's a really authentic rural Greek restaurant that mostly caters to locals, and the kind owner is happy to explain what's in the different dishes. They have a whole section of their menu devoted to lentils. Be sure to try the crunchy, vinegary lentil salad.

Crete (Κρήτη)

Greece's largest and most populous island is

also its jewel: Stunning Crete (pop. 633,000) is home to the oldest civilization in Europe. It's the birthplace of Zeus, and boasts the largest gorge in Europe. Crete is renowned for its beautiful, mountainous landscape, which gives way to turquoise beaches and moody villages steeped in tradition. Pastel-covered harbor towns dot the coast and lend Crete a modern flair; here you'll find some of the best nightlife in the country.

If you're a foodie, settle down in Crete, where "local" is not an ideological concept but a completely normal way of life. Crete is widely known across the country as having some of the best food, including local cheeses, *dakos* (dried bread), fried snails, lamb with wild greens,

Highlights

Look for ★ to find recommended sights, activities, dining, and lodging.

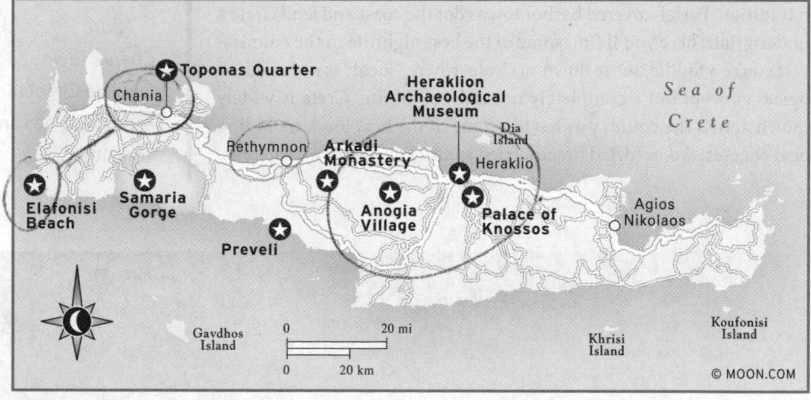

★ **Heraklion Archaeological Museum:** Most of Crete's BC discoveries are on display here—everything from gold headgear to ceramic vases (page 430).

★ **Palace of Knossos:** The most important of the Minoan palaces, Knossos is a lovingly restored ruin with beautifully painted frescoes (page 434).

★ **Arkadi Monastery:** This stunning monastery looks like a wedding cake (perks of Venetian baroque architecture) and is one of the most important monuments in the Cretan resistance against the Ottomans (page 444).

★ **Anogia Village:** Visit Anogia and get to know the locals, who are remarkably welcoming (page 446).

★ **Preveli:** This magical beach is located at the mouth of a gorge that spits out a river flanked by palm and date trees (page 448).

★ **Toponas Quarter:** The most beautiful town in Crete is worthy of at least a day's visit. Do like the locals and *volta* (stroll) down the Venetian harbor before exploring the narrow streets of Chania's Toponas Quarter (page 450).

★ **Samaria Gorge:** Hike through one of the longest gorges in Europe, passing through forest, rivers, and abandoned villages and monasteries, before ending at the Mediterranean sea (page 459).

★ **Elafonisi Beach:** This oblong-shaped peninsula, where shallow azure waters lap at pink sand beaches, looks like something out of a tropical fairy tale (page 462).

smoked pork, and special pies. You'll be urged to wash it all down with fire-y shots of raki.

Cretans are incredibly proud of their heritage, and they wear that pride on their sleeve—quite literally. It is one of the few places where you'll still see people dressed in traditional outfits (knee high leather boots, knotted scarves). You'll also hear the heritage in the music that pours out of homes, cafés, and restaurants, and you'll feel the Cretan spirit as you traverse the big island's stunning coast and mountainous interior.

PLANNING YOUR TIME

Thanks to its sizable population, Crete is a **year-long** island, and outside of resort-y areas, you'll find most places open throughout the year. Certainly from **April** to **October,** any touristic spots will be open. **July** and **August** can be cramped in Crete, as it's become one of the most popular tourist destinations for both foreigners and Greeks. It's best to visit in **autumn;** Crete is southernly enough that the water is still warm and the sun still strong, but the crowds will have thinned out.

Don't be overly ambitious with your time on Crete. Part of the joy of traveling around the big island is getting to know the people, slowing down to enjoy the scenery, and nursing some exquisite hangovers. If you want to see the whole island, I recommend that you allot at least **five days** to each of the four provinces: Lasithi, Heraklio, Rethymno, and Chania. It's technically possible to visit all of Crete in one week, but you will be exhausted from the long distances. If your time is limited, choose one region and stick to exploring it as much as possible. Head to **Lasithi** for an off-the-beaten path taste of Crete with few tourists; to **Heraklio,** the central region of Crete, to see the island's vibrant capital and its famed Knossos Palace; to **Rethymno** for mountain villages and a slice of traditional Cretan life; and to **Chania** for its stunning beaches and Venetian-inspired towns. Anywhere you go, there will be some constants: excellent food, the sound of Cretan music coming from the *lyra* floating in the air; impossibly beautiful landscapes; and lots of hospitable people who are proud to show you their island way of life.

If it's your first time on Crete, I recommend staying in either **Chania** or **Heraklio** (both have airports that you can directly fly into from Athens or other European cities, minimizing travel time). Most visitors will end up flying to Herakio.

INFORMATION AND SERVICES

In each of the four major towns (Chania, Rethymno, Heraklio, and Agios Nikolaos), and most smaller villages, you'll find plenty of **ATMs, police,** and **hospitals** (both private clinics and public). In Chania there's free **Wi-Fi** in most public spaces. The best and biggest hospitals are in Heraklio, where there's also the medical university. For major emergencies, you can go to the **University Hospital of Heraklion** (Stavrakia; tel. 2810/392 111; www.pagni.gr; 24 hours).

In Heraklio the main **post office** can be found on Plateai Daskalogianni (tel. 2810/289 994; www.elta.gr; Mon.-Fri. 9am-8:30pm, Sat. 9am-4pm). In Hania it's found on Peridou 10 (tel. 2821/091 500; Mon.-Fri. 7:30am-8:30pm). In Agios Nikolaos (28 Iktovriou 9; Mon.-Fri. 7:30am-2:30pm).

Crete's emergency number is **171.** In Heraklio, the **tourist police** is in the Halikarinassos suburb close to the airport (Dikeosynis 10; tel. 2810/283 190; 7am-10pm daily). In Chania (tel. 2821/025 931; 24 hours). In Agios Nikolaos (Erythrou Stavrou 47; tel. 2841/091 409).

Each region has its own tourist office:

- **Heraklio Tourist Info Point** (Nikiforou Foka square/Lions square; tel. 2813/409

Previous: the pink sand at the tropical Elafonisi Beach; the fortress on a blustery day in Heraklio; at Knossos, you'll find fantastic refurbished frescoes.

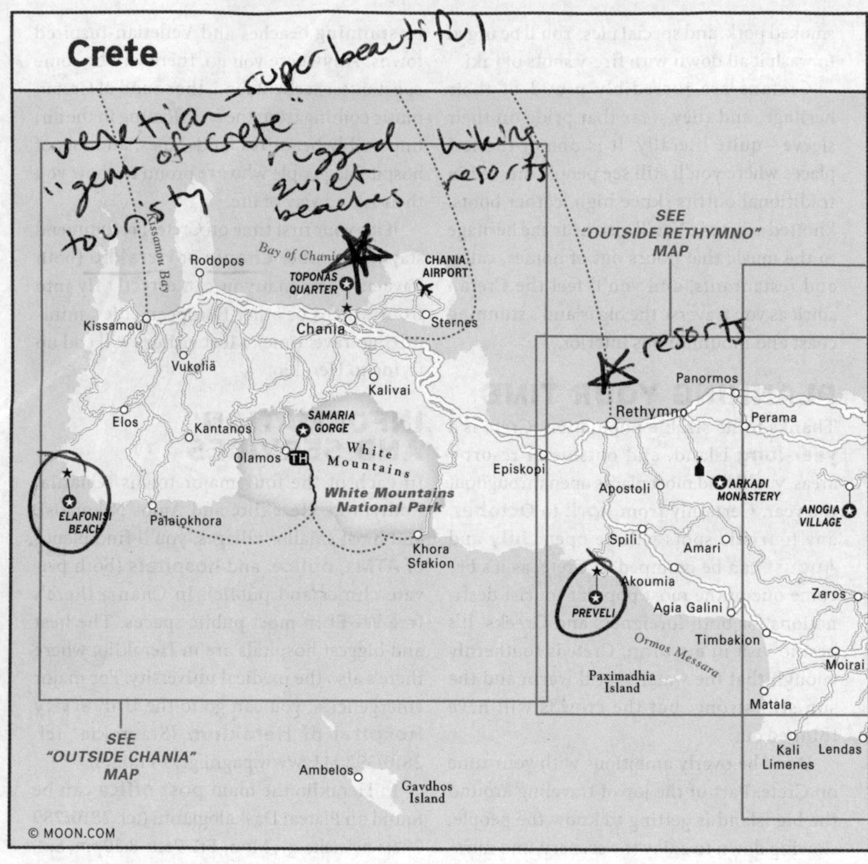

777; Mon.-Fri. 8:30am-2:30pm; www.heraklion.gr)

- **Rethymno Tourist Office** (Sofokli Venizelou; tel. 2831/029 148; www.rethymnon.gr; Mon.-Fri. 8am-2pm)
- **Chania Tourist Office** (Kydonias 29; tel. 2821/336 155; Mon.-Fri. 8am-2:30pm)
- **Lasithi Tourist Office** (Akti Kondourou 21; tel. 2841/022 357; www.agiosnikolaos.gr; Apr.-Nov. Mon.-Fri. 8am-10pm)

GETTING THERE

Unless you're traveling from Athens with your car, I recommend **flying** into Crete. **Ferries** from Athens can take up to 18 hours to reach Crete—not the best option if you get seasick easily. It's also not necessarily cheaper; food costs a fortune, and you'll probably want to lie horizontal for part of the way, so you'll end up springing for a cabin.

Air

Crete has several airports, the largest of which is the **Nikos Kazantzakis International Airport** (HER; tel. 2810/397 800; www.heraklion-airport.info) in Heraklio, which has international flights from across Europe. There are buses at the airport waiting to take passengers 5 km (3 mi) into town. Every few minutes **City Bus #10** leaves the airport, making stops at both bus terminals, the port, and Plateia Eleftheris (Maronisi Fountain). A **taxi** into the center of Heraklio costs €11.

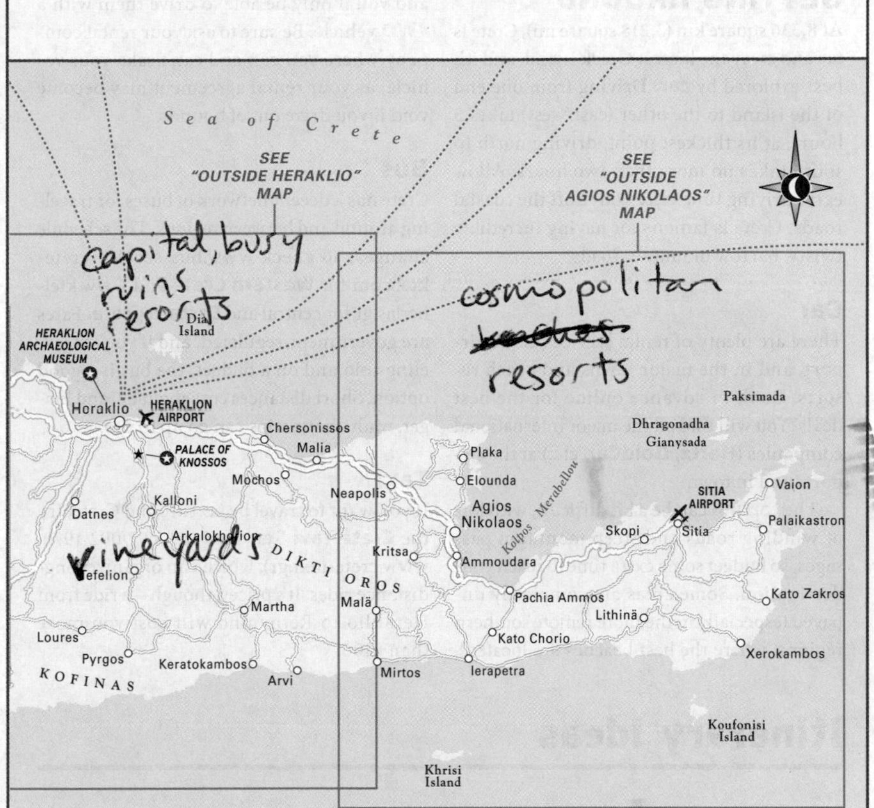

If you are leaving from Heraklio airport to a destination that is farther away than the city center, I recommend renting a **car** (you'll save more money than going in a long-distance taxi).

Chania International Airport Daskalogiannis (CHQ) has international and domestic flights throughout the year, and **Sitia Public Airport** (JSH) has domestic flights. From Chania, a **taxi** to the center costs €24, and the **bus**, which leaves regularly and takes 30 minutes, costs €2.50.

There are plenty of connecting flights between **Athens** and **Thessaloniki** to Crete. During the summer season, you'll find a good amount of direct flights between European cities and Crete, run by budget-airlines like **easyJet** (www.easyjet.com) and **Ryanair** (www.ryanair.com). If you're coming from another Greek island, you'll likely fly with the Crete-based **Sky Express** (www.skyexpress.gr). There are flights (with stops on the mainland) to/from Santorini, Mykonos, Lesvos, Corfu, Zakynthos, Ikara, Milos, Karpathos, and Naxos.

Ferry

There are daily ferry departures from **Piraeus** to Heraklio, Sitia, and Chania. In the summer months, there are several ferries a day. Ferries from Athens cost around €40 (though the prices can go up in the summer).

GETTING AROUND

At 8,336 square km (3,218 square mi), Crete is far and away the largest Greek island, and it's best explored by **car.** Driving from one end of the island to the other (east/west) takes 5 hours; at its thickest point, driving north to south takes no more than two hours. Allow extra driving time once you're off the coastal roads. Crete is famous for having incredibly twisty, narrow mountain roads.

Car

There are plenty of rental services at the airport, and in the major towns and beach resorts. Book in advance online for the best deals. You will find all the major international companies (**Hertz, GoldCar,** etc.) at the airports and in town.

The **terrain** can be a bit difficult, with lots of winding roads and steep mountain passages, so budget some extra time to reach your destination. Some areas are completely unpaved (especially in the more remote southern regions, where the best beaches are located), and you'll only be able to drive them with a **4WD** vehicle. Be sure to ask your rental company where you can and can't take your vehicle, as your rental agreement may become void if you drive out of bounds.

Bus

Crete has a decent network of buses for traveling around and between regions. The schedule changes, so check www.bus-service-crete-ktel.com for **Western Crete** and www.ktel-herlas.gr for central and **Eastern Crete.** Fares are government-regulated, and if you're traveling solo and on a budget, the bus is a good option. Short distances cost about €2, and longer, multi-hour trips can go up to €15.

Taxi

If you want to travel by taxi around Crete, try the **Crete Taxi Services** (tel. 697/002 1970; www.crete-taxi.gr), which can organize long-distance rides. It's pricey, though—a ride from Heraklio to Rethymno will cost you more than €100.

Itinerary Ideas

This quick two-day itinerary has you based in Chania, a recommended place to explore for first-time visitors. You won't need a car for the first day, but do rent one for day two.

DAY 1

1 Take time to walk around the **Toponas Quarter,** Chania's old Venetian quarter and the city's architectural jewel. A couple of streets worth seeking out are Angelou, Theofanous, and Moscho. On Theotokopoulou Street, you can also stop by the Etz Hayyim Synagogue.

2 Nearby the Toponas Quarter, you'll find **Thalassino Ageri.** Snag a table outside and have a lunch of grilled fish and beer.

3 Spend an hour brushing up on history at the **Chania Archaeological Museum,** taking a few extra minutes to marvel at the well-preserved Roman mosaics.

4 Have dinner at **Tamam,** a restaurant that used to hold public baths.

5 Stroll along the **Venetian Harbor** at sunset, stopping at **Sketi Glika** for a scoop of ice cream for a sweet note to end the evening.

6 When the sun dips down, head to **Fagotto Jazz Bar** for live music and cocktails.

Itinerary Ideas

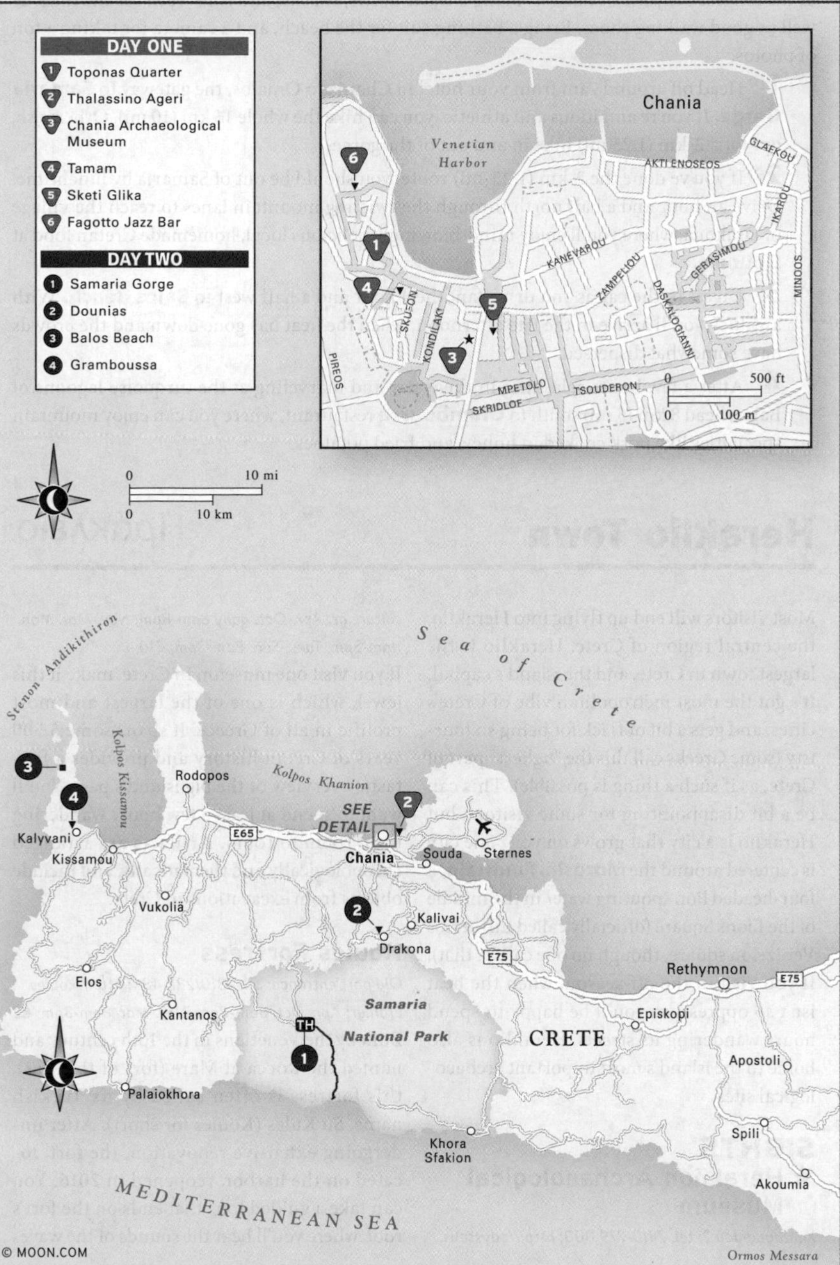
DAY ONE
1 Toponas Quarter
2 Thalassino Ageri
3 Chania Archaeological Museum
4 Tamam
5 Sketi Glika
6 Fagotto Jazz Bar
DAY TWO
1 Samaria Gorge
2 Dounias
3 Balos Beach
4 Gramboussa
Chania
Venetian Harbor
GLAFKOU
AKTI ENOSEOS
IKAROU
KANEVAROU
GERASIMOU
ZAMPELIOU
DASKALOGIANNI
MINOOS
SKUFON
KONDILAKI
PIREOS
MPETOLO
TSOUDERON
SKRIDLOF
0
500 ft
100 m
0
10 mi
10 km
Sea of Crete
Stenon Andikithiron
Kolpos Kissamou
Kolpos Khanion
Rodopos
SEE DETAIL
E65
Kalyvani
Kissamou
Chania
Souda
Sternes
Vukoliä
Kalivai
Drakona
E75
Rethymnon
Elos
Kantanos
Samaria National Park
TH
CRETE
Episkopi
Apostoli
Palaiokhora
Khora Sfakion
Spili
Akoumia
MEDITERRANEAN SEA
© MOON.COM
Ormos Messara

DAY 2

Today is your day to enjoy the beach and Crete's incredible landscape at Samaria Gorge, one of the longest canyons in Europe. Bring a water bottle, snacks, and sunscreen for the hike, as well as good walking shoes. Bring a bathing suit for the beach, and a camera for taking a ton of photos.

1 Head off around 7am from your hotel in Chania to Omalos, the gateway to **Samaria Gorge.** If you're ambitious and athletic, you can hike the whole 16 km (10 mi). Otherwise, opt for a 2-km (1.25 mi) hike in and out of the gorge.

2 If you've done the 2-km (1.25-mi) route, you should be out of Samaria by lunchtime. Drive an hour and a half north through the twisting mountain lanes to reach the village of Drakona, where you'll enjoy mind-blowingly delicious local, homemade Cretan food at **Dounias.**

3 Digest in the car as you drive (another) hour and a half west to **Balos Beach.** With any luck you'll arrive in the late afternoon, when the heat has gone down and the crowds have somewhat dispersed.

4 After a few hours splashing in the water and marveling at the turquoise lagoons of Balos, head 8 km (5 mi) south to **Gramboussa** restaurant, where you can enjoy mountain specialties like pork cooked in honey, and fried potatoes.

Heraklio Town Ηράκλειο

Most visitors will end up flying into Heraklio, the central region of Crete. Heraklio is the largest town in Crete, and the island's capital. It's got the most metropolitan vibe of Crete's cities, and gets a bit of flack for being so touristy (some Greeks call this the "ugliest" part of Crete, as if such a thing is possible). This can be a bit disappointing for some visitors, but Heraklio is a city that grows on you. The city is centered around the **Morosini Fountain,** a four-headed lion spouting water in the middle of the Lions Square (officially called Elftherios Venizelou square, though no one calls it that). If you visit in the off-season, when the heat isn't so oppressive, you'll be happy to spend hours wandering its streets. Heraklio is also home to the island's most important archaeological sites.

SIGHTS

★ Heraklion Archaeological Museum

Xanthoudidou 2; tel. 2810/279 000; http://odysseus.culture.gr; Apr.-Oct. daily 8am-8pm, Nov.-Mar. Mon. 11am-5pm, Tues.-Sun. 8am-3pm; €10

If you visit one museum in Crete, make it this jewel, which is one of the largest and most prolific in all of Greece. It spans some 5,500 years of Cretan history and provides a fantastic overview of the big island's past. You'll want to spend at least a few hours wandering from room to room. Artifacts are arranged chronologically and thematically, and include objects from excavations in Crete.

Koules Fortress

Old port entrance; tel. 2810/288 484; http://koules.efah.gr; Apr.-Oct. 8am-8pm, Nov.-Mar. 8am-3pm; €2

Built by the Venetians in the 16th century and named the Rocca al Mare (fort of the seas), this fortress is often called by its Turkish name, Su Kules (Koules for short). After undergoing extensive renovation, the fort, located on the harbor, reopened in 2016. You can take a guided tour that ends on the fort's roof, where you'll hear the sounds of the waves

Heraklio Town

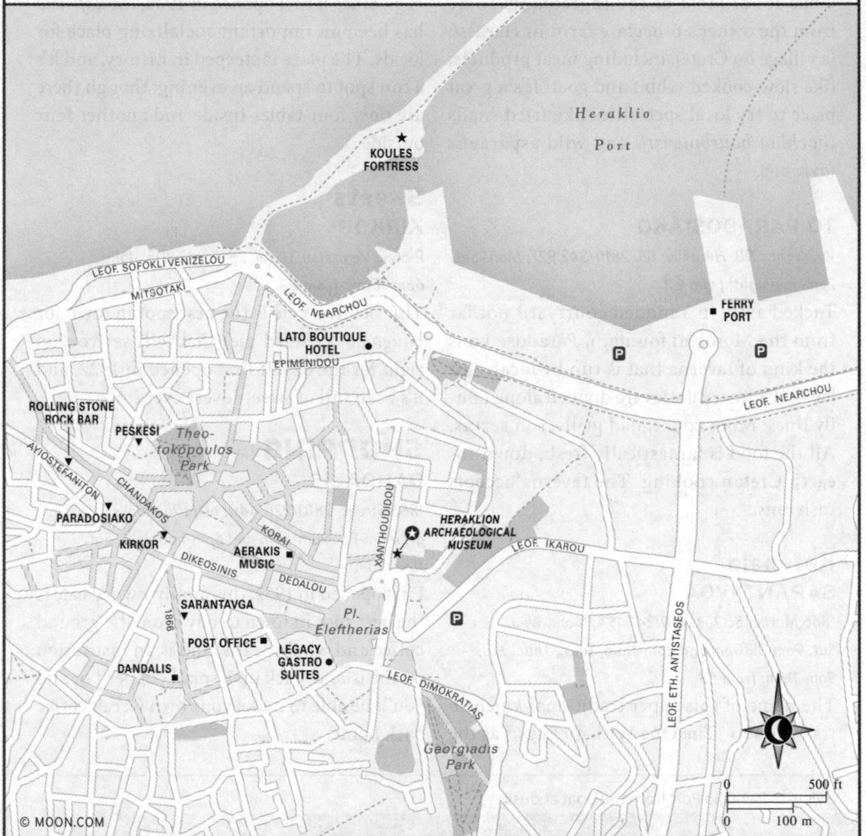

crashing against its old stone walls and take in a fantastic view of the city.

NIGHTLIFE

ROLLING STONE ROCK BAR

Ayiostefaniton 19; tel. 698/071 5658; daily 10pm-late

If you want a break from all that raki and meze, head to this rollicking music venue that showcases local rock acts and plenty of good, cheap drinks. The music, as the name suggests, is mostly rock, and the crowd is an intergenerational mix of tourists and locals.

SENSES CLUB

Papandreou 277, Amoudara; tel. 2810/824 509; summer daily 9pm-6am

With great cocktails, a nice lounge area, and local DJs spinning house and techno tunes till early in the wee morning, Senses Club is a quintessential summer beach club. It's located about 6.5 km (4 mi) west of Heraklio Town in the town of Amoudara.

FOOD

Greek and Cretan

PESKESI

Kaptean Haralampi 6-8; tel. 2810/288 887; www.peskesicrete.gr; daily 10am-2am; from €8

Beloved by both locals and tourists, Peskesi offers fantastic Cretan hospitality and delicious food. Most of the ingredients come from the owner's 6-hectare farm in Harasso (a village on Crete), including meat products, like slow-cooked rabbit and goat. It's a great place to try local specialties like fried snails (*hochlioi bourbouristi)* and wild asparagus (*avronie).*

TO PARADOSIAKO

Vourváhon 9B, Heraklio; tel. 2810/342 927; Mon.-Sat. 2pm-midnight; from €11

Tucked away in a hidden courtyard not far from the Morosini fountain, Paradosiako is the kind of taverna that is run by locals, for locals. Culinary duties are divided along family lines: Mom cooks, dad grills, son serves. All the food is fantastically fresh, down-to-earth Cretan cooking. The taverna accepts cash only.

Kafeneio

SARANTAVGA

1866 Market St. 16; 2810/341 494; Mon., Wed., Sat. 9am-3:30pm and 8pm-11pm, Tues., Thur., Fri., 9am-11pm; from €3

The name of this super traditional *kafeneio* translates to "The One With 40 Eggs," as the original owner was known around the neighborhood for his fanatic obsession with eating eggs. Since it first opened in 1924, the *kafeneio* has been an important socializing place for locals. The place is steeped in history, and it's a fun spot to spend an evening, though there are only four tables inside and another four outside.

Sweets

KIRKOR

Plateia Venizelou 31; tel. 2810/242 705; daily 6am-10pm; from €2

This beloved café is the best spot in town for *bougatsa* (custard pie) that will set you up right for the day. It first opened in 1922, and it's been full of sweet-lovers ever since.

SHOPPING

DANDALIS

1866 Street; 2810/220 440; http://dandalis.gr; Mon.-Fri. 9am-5pm and 8pm-midnight, Sat. 11pm-2am

First opened in 1952, this family-owned café is the best spot in town to buy aromatic ground coffee and whole beans, and is an institution on the island. Pick up a small copper pot and you'll be able to make your own Greek coffee back home.

a view of Heraklio Port from the boat at dusk

AERAKIS MUSIC

Korai Sq. 14; www.aerakis.net; Mon.-Fri. 9am-9pm, Sat. 9am-5pm

Something of an institution in Heraklio, Aerakis Music is the place to pick up Cretan music CDs and records (the shop even has its own record label). They also have some musical instruments and music books, and the knowledgeable shop owners can help you shift through their curated collection.

ACCOMMODATIONS

LATO BOUTIQUE HOTEL

Epimenidou 15; tel. 2810/228 103; www.lato.gr; from €120

This charming hotel located across from the Koules Fortress is a good option for those who want to stay in the city center at a moderate price. Perks include a small spa and a gourmet restaurant on-site. Staff is super friendly and helpful, and the decor is relaxed modern. The best part of the hotel is the rooftop, with amazing views of the fort and the sea beyond. Note that it is not handicapped-accessible. There are 71 rooms and 8 suites in the hotel.

LEGACY GASTRO SUITES

Pl. Eleftherias 43; tel. 2810/221 200; https://book.legacygastrosuites.com; from €212

All the rooms in this boutique hotel are spacious suites with sea views. With just 12 rooms, each decorated in a different theme, this is a fairly reasonably priced five-star hotel in the heart of the city. It's housed in a refurbished 1950s building, and gastronomy plays a central role: You can have Cretan meals, including breakfast, delivered to your room.

AMIRANDES GRECOTEL EXCLUSIVE RESORT

Kato Gouves; tel. 2897/041 103; www.amirandes.com; from €270

For next-level luxury, book a room at Amirandes, a stunning five-star resort is located 20 km (12.5 mi) east of Heraklio Town in the town of Kato Gouves. The only resort really worth staying at in the area, it's built around a lagoon, and it has its own Picasso collection and an Olympic size swimming pool. It is definitely a "see and be seen" type of hotel (bring your designer duds). Excellent service, exquisite food, and stunning views round out the amenities. You can find good deals in the off-season.

GETTING THERE AND AROUND

Air

Most visitors will fly into **Nikos Kazantzakis International Airport** (HER; tel. 2810/397 800; www.heraklion-airport.info), which is 5 km (3 mi) outside Heraklio Town. **City Bus #10** connects the airport with Herakio's two bus terminals, port, and and Plateia Eleftheris (Morosini Fountain). A **taxi** into the center of Heraklio costs €11.

Ferry

Ferries arrive daily in Heraklio from Piraeus. The **ferry terminal** is about a 20-minute walk northeast of Morosini Fountain.

Bus

Buses serving Heraklio, as well as central and Eastern Crete, are run by **KTEL Heraklion-Lasithi S.A.** (www.ktelherlas.gr). Bus Station A is located at the harbor.

Outside Heraklio Town

It's true that the area around Heraklio Town is awash in capitalistic resort towns; ignore those and head for the charming villages and wine country in the center of the region. The most important sight here is the Palace of Knossos. Towards the south, there are a couple of interesting beaches worth checking out, too.

The roads here are in relatively good condition, and for most of this trip, you'll be driving south along Highway 97. You can take three days to explore the region outside of Heraklio.

★ PALACE OF KNOSSOS

5 km (3 mi) South Heraklio, Knossos; tel. 2810/231 940; http://odysseus.culture.gr; Apr.-Oct. daily 8am-8pm, Nov.-Mar. 8am-5pm; €15

It's worth braving the crowds to see the fantastic Palace of Knossos, the most famous—and the busiest—of Crete's tourist attractions. This was the capital of Minoan Crete, and the sprawling sight gives you a glimpse into what life was like in Europe's oldest city.

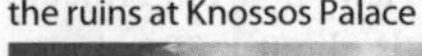

The area was settled around 7000 BC, and the first palace was constructed around 1700 BC. It was an epicenter of Mediterranean trading and immense wealth, which is seen in the storage rooms, palaces, tombs, and rock-cut caves. The most impressive sight is the Fresco Gallery, which houses restored replicas of the palace's most famous frescoes, including the Lady in Blue and the Bull Leaper.

Knossos is also the stuff of legends: It's here where the fabled tales of Minotaur, Labyrinth, and Ikaros unfolded, in the various tunnels and rooms of the palace. Your entry ticket will cover all of these sights. The whole site has been stunningly restored, including the colorful frescoes.

The entire palace covers a region of 22,000 square meters (5.4 acres). Serious history buffs could spend a whole day here, but for the rest of you, count two hours. There is a café selling snacks and refreshments at the entry to the palace, along with bathrooms. Note that there's almost no shade in Knossos, so be sure to pack a hat, or come very early in the morning or later in the evening. There are official guides waiting outside the gates who can take you on guided tours of the complex (in groups

the ruins at Knossos Palace

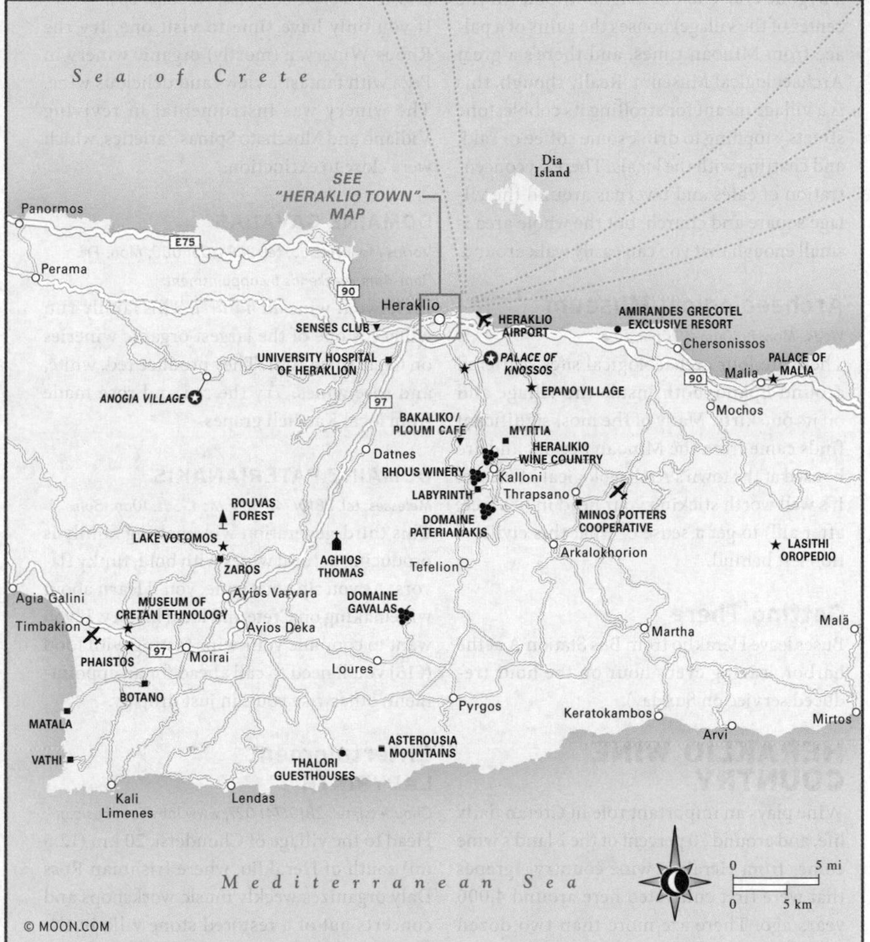

of up to eight people); these tours are worthwhile to get a more in-depth overview of the site and Minoan history (€10).

Getting There

There are public transportation options to Knossos: Take city bus 2 from the center (either from Bus Station A or from outside the Hotel Capsis Astoria). Buses leave every 15 minutes and cost €2.50 on the bus (or €1.70 if you purchase from a kiosk). If you're going by car, you're driving south on Highway 97, and the route is signposted to Knossos. Note that parking spots (free) fill up relatively quickly in the height of summer. Taxis cost no more than €12 from the port of Heraklio.

EPANO VILLAGE (Επάνω)

Epano (you might also see it written as Archanes), 5 km (3 mi) from Knossos (signposted), was awarded the European Award for Village Restoration, and for good reason: This charming hamlet feels like stepping into a bygone era. The old neighborhood (in the center of the village) houses the ruins of a palace from Minoan times, and there's a great Archaeological Museum. Really though, this is a village meant for strolling its cobblestone streets, stopping to drink some coffee or raki, and chatting with the locals. There's a concentration of cafés and tavernas around the village square and church, but the whole area is small enough that you can easily walk around.

Archaeological Museum

Weds.-Mon. 8:30am-2:30pm, free

There are four archaeological sites scattered around Epano, both inside the village and on its outskirts. Many of the most significant finds came from the Minoan period, and are housed at the town's Archaeological Museum. It's well worth sticking your head in (it's free, after all!) to get a sense of what this civilization left behind.

Getting There

Buses leave Heraklio from Bus Station A at the harbor, leaving every hour on the hour (reduced service on Sunday).

HERAKLIO WINE COUNTRY

Wine plays an important role in Cretan daily life, and around 70 percent of the island's wine comes from Heraklio wine country—grapes that were first cultivated here around 4,000 years ago. There are more than two dozen wineries scattered around the area (which is headquartered in Peza, 18 km/11 mi south of Heraklio Town). If you're lucky enough to have a designated driver in your group, it's a pleasure to meander around the fertile valleys and stop at different wineries. In the summer season, it's best to call ahead to make a reservation, as they can get quite crowded with tourists. Tastings from €2.

Wineries

RHOUS WINERY

Peza; tel. 2810/742 083; Mon.-Fri. 10am-6pm

If you only have time to visit one, try the Rhous Winery, a (mostly) organic winery in Peza with fantastic views and delicious wine. The winery was instrumental in reviving Vidiano and Moschato Spinas varieties, which were close to extinction.

DOMAINE GAVALAS

Vorias Monofatsiou; tel. 2894/051 060; Mon.-Fri. 8am-4pm, weekends by appointment

Prefer your wine *au naturel?* This family-run winery is one of the largest organic wineries on Crete since 2001. They produce red, white, and rosé wines. Try the red and rosé made from local Katsifeli grapes.

DOMAINE PATERIANAKIS

Melesses; tel. 2810/742 083; Mon.-Sat. 10am-5pm

This third-generation winemaking family is producing natural wines with bold, funky flavors. As you sip your wine, you'll learn about winemaking on Crete and local history. If you want to combine your wine tasting with food (€16) you'll need to call ahead for an appointment; otherwise you can just drop by.

Entertainment

LABYRINTH

Choudetsi; tel. 2810/741 027; www.labyrinthmusic.gr

Head to the village of Choudetsi, 20 km (12.5 mi) south of Heraklio, where Irishman Ross Daly organizes weekly music workshops and concerts out of a restored stone villa in the countryside. The music is traditional Cretan, and it's a fantastic way to get an intimate look into the culture.

Food

Wander through the flower-filled, cobblestone streets of Archanes (16 km/10-mi south of Heraklio Town), a well-preserved, traditional Cretan village with plenty of good restaurants.

PLOUMI CAFÉ

Archanes; tel. 693/453 3882; Wed.-Sun. noon-midnight

This lovely cooperative café is the best place in Archanes to people-watch, throw back fiery shots of raki, and nibble at some mezes. The cooperative was started by five friends, three of whom are musicians. Most nights, there's impromptu live music and singing.

BAKALIKO

Eleftherios Venizelos Square 13, Arhanes village; tel. 2810/751 117; www.bakalikocrete.com; daily 10am-10pm; from €5

For many foreigners, a visit to Crete turns into a lifetime on the big island. This happened to Agnes and Susanna, two Hungarian women who fell in love with Crete and have since opened Bakaliko, a restaurant/store/cooking class operation that has a fantastic selection of delights from across the island. They also have a good cellar and can arrange wine tastings.

THRAPSANO (Θραψανό)

Thrapsano is famous for its pottery, in particular, its *pitharia,* or large-scale jugs that have been used as storage containers since the times of the Minoans. There are pottery workshops around the village that you can pop into to see workers throw pots on the wheel, and to pick up some pots for yourself. The name Thrapsano comes from *thravo* (to break) and *psino* (to bake)—likely a play on all the pots that get broken when fired in the kiln.

Thrapsano is located 30 km (18.5 mi) southeast of Heraklio town (40 minutes), in the interior of the island.

Shopping

MINOS POTTERS COOPERATIVE

Thrapsano; tel. 2891/041 598; www.minos-ceramics.gr/en; Mon.-Sat. 8am-3:30pm

To watch the ceramicists in action, head to Minos Potters Cooperative, where you can watch them throw pots and vessels on the wheel. Everything is made by hand before being fired in a wood-burning kiln. They have plenty of goods for sale, too, from cups and plates to pitchers.

AGHIOS THOMAS (Άγιος Θωμάς)

For a macabre interlude to your sunny vacation, make a pit stop at Aghios Thomas, 36 km (22 mi) south of Heraklio Town, a village known for being the site of the "Hole of Hades"—the gateway into the underworld. The world won't swallow you up here, but you can visit the cave churches that were originally built in Roman times. From the village square, follow the stone pathway up to the churches; there are 49 churches in total (free). It's quite an impressive feat of architecture, and if you have any interest in Greek mythology, it can feel quite trippy to stand in front of the hole to the underworld.

It's pretty much a direct shot south from Heraklio to Aghios Thomas, and the road is straight most of the way. The drive will take you half an hour.

PHAISTOS AND VICINITY

This Bronze Age settlement was one of the most important places for the Minoans. There is a fantastic archaeological site to visit and it's nowhere near as crowded as Knossos.

Sights

PHAISTOS (Φαιστός)

Heraklio, Phaistos Road; tel. 2892/042 315; http://odysseus.culture.gr; Apr.-Oct. daily 8am-8pm, Nov.-Mar. 8am-3pm; €8

Located on the southern edge of Heraklio county (70 km/43.5 mi; 45 minutes southwest of Heraklio), this Minoan archaeological ruin is famed for being the site of discovery of the mysterious "Phaistos Disc." The 4,000-year-old disc, stamped in Minoan hieroglyphics, had scientists scratching their heads since it was first discovered in 1908. In 2014, they deduced it was a prayer to a Minoan fertility goddess. You can see the disc in the Heraklion Archaeological Museum. The site is sprawled

Nikos Kazantzakis: A Cultural Icon

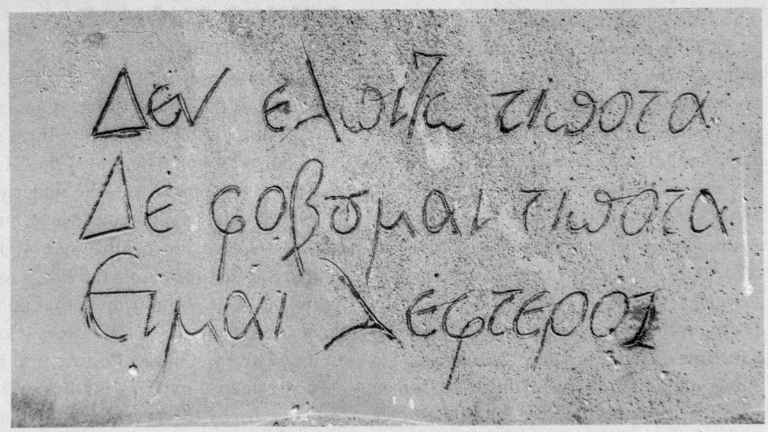

The inscription on Nikos Kazantzakis's grave reads: "I hope for nothing. I fear nothing. I am free."

If there's only one name to associate with Crete, it's Nikos Kazantzakis: The literary behemoth who penned *Zorba the Greek* and *Freedom or Death* is the modern cultural icon of the island. During his prolific career, Kazantzakis (1883-1957) was nominated for the Nobel Prize in Literature nine times. He was as much a philosopher as he was a writer. Born during the Ottoman occupation, and raised during the Greek Independence War and two World Wars, Kazantzakis wrote about liberty, freedom, human suffering, and spirituality.

His ancestral village, **Myrtias** (17.2 km south of Heraklio), makes a worthy pilgrimage to pay homage to the great writer. The Nikos Kazantzakis Museum on the village's main square will tell you more about his life and work; anything else you wish to know can be gleaned from the friendly locals, who are all very proud to share a birth place with Kazantzakis.

out across a hill and offers fantastic views of the green valleys laid out below.

Though there's no direct bus from Heraklio to Phaistos, you can take the bus to Moires (leaves hourly from Heraklio; 1 hour 50 minutes; €8) and then take a taxi to Phaistos (7.7 km/4.75 mi, no more than €10 one way).

MUSEUM OF CRETAN ETHNOLOGY

Voroi Prigiotissis; tel. 2892/091 110; www.cretanethnologymuseum.gr; Apr.-Oct. 11am-5pm; €3

In the charming town of Voroi (signposted on the Mires-Tymbaki Road) is a small museum devoted to showcasing the rural life of Cretans into the 20th century. Exhibits are labeled in English (a rarity for a rural island museum) and divided into different ethnological sections, including customs and traditions, social organization, food, handicrafts, and transportation. It's worth visiting if you're in the area.

Beaches

MATALA (Μάταλα)

The most famous of Heraklio's beaches, thanks to the hordes of hippies that lived in the caves for a while in the 1960s, Matala (11.6 km/7 mi southwest of Phaistos) is the ancient port of Phaistos. Fishing was the main activity until the hippies arrived, and now it's a well-established tourist beach with loads of people coming to check out the ruins and the naturally occurring caves that are located on the north side of the beach. It's worth a visit, especially if you can go in the early morning to beat the crowds.

VATHI (Βαθύ)

Travel 22 km (13.5) south of Matala and you'll come to Vathi, one of the beaches that requires a bit of exertion to reach. Though it's geographically close, the drive will take one hour, (no) thanks to the roads. It's no surprise that this beach used to be a pirate hangout. These days there are no pirates, just a couple of wild olive trees, the cool waters of the Libyan Sea, and a small taverna. Because visitors need to travel such a long dirt path to reach the beach (about a 30-minute walk from Odigitria Monastery), it's usually quiet.

Shopping

BOTANO

Kouses; tel. 2892/042 295; https://botano.gr; daily 10am-7pm

About 15 km (10 mi) northeast of Matala, you'll find the village of Kouses, with this cute shop that stocks all you'll need to feel like a true Cretan: spices, oils (essential and extra virgin), soaps, and herbs that can be brewed into healing teas. There's a small café as well, and you can relax on the patio and sip your drink while looking out at the beautiful view of the Messara Plain.

PALACE OF MALIA

tel. 2897/031 597; daily 8:30am-3pm; €6;

The third-largest of the Minoan palaces, thought to have been constructed around 1650 BC, the Palace of Malia (3 km/1.85 mi east of Malia) doesn't get as many visitors as its sister palaces. It was built around arable land and was important in cereal production (there are eight grain silos). The area is somewhat unique in that a good amount of its structures are still standing tall at two meters. Most of the place is also well-shaded from the strong sun.

The Palace is located 41 km (25 mi) east of Heraklio, on the easy coastal highway (it'll take you 35 minutes). There are regular buses from Heraklio's Bus Station A to Malia (buses stop 250 meters/820 feet from the site).

Rethymno Town Ρέθυμνο

The third-largest city in Crete, Rethymno is something of a laid-back version of Chania. It was ruled by the Venetians for some 400 years, and during that time, it became one of the most important cities in Crete. A slice of the Renaissance was brought to Rethymno, and one of the most beloved meeting points in the city, the Rimondi Fountain, was built by the Venetians. In 1646, Rethymno was taken over by the Ottomans, who left their mark on the city: Churches were turned into mosques, wooden lattice work appeared over doors and windows, and the city took on a decidedly eastern flair. You'll want to spend at least a day just wandering through the colorful streets of Rethymno and taking in the relaxed air of the city.

SIGHTS

Rimondi Fountain

This historic fountain serves as a meeting point for Rethymnians. It was built in 1629 and features three Corinthian columns, three water basins, and three lions' heads, which still spout water to this day.

Venetian Fortress

Apr.-Oct. 8am-8pm, Nov.-Mar. 10am-5pm; €4

Dominating the Rethymnon harbor is the imposing Venetian Fortress, which succumbed to the Ottomans in 1646. In the centuries that followed, people lived in and around the fort, creating a city that was destroyed by the Germans during World War II. Today the ruins still stand, and the views

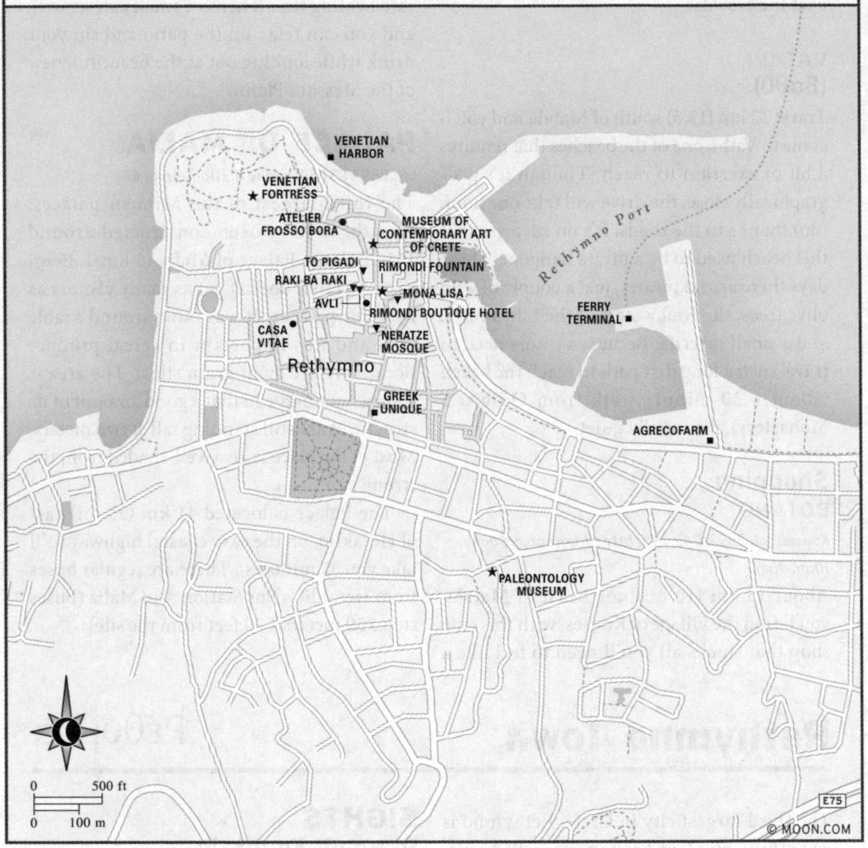

up here are incredible. You can walk around the ramparts and wander into the twin buildings of the Bastion of Agios Nikolaos, which hosts art exhibits. The **Sultan Bin Ibrahim Mosque,** located in the complex of the fortress, adds another layer of history (and hosts occasional summer concerts); it's worth poking your head in there if only to marvel at the huge dome.

Your ticket covers entry into all the buildings. Wear shoes with a good sole, as the rocks are incredibly slippery and it's somewhat of an uphill climb. Also, avoid coming here in the middle of the day, as there's almost no shade.

After the fortress, you can continue your walk along the colorful harbor with its bobbing fishing boats, and head to the Egyptian-built **lighthouse** from the 19th century, which you can admire from the outside.

Museum of Contemporary Art of Crete

tel. 2831/052 530; www.cca.gr; Tues.-Fri. 9am-2pm and 7pm-9pm, Sat.-Sun. 10am-3pm; €3, Thurs. free

For a welcome change of pace from all the ancient history, head to this charming museum that first opened in 1992. The permanent collection is heavily weighted toward local artist Lefteris Kanakakis, but plenty of other Greek artists working since the 1950s are represented. Kanakis's original work focused on still life and portraiture, but his style evolved to become a critique of Greece's political system at the time. Check the website for temporary exhibits.

Paleontology Museum

tel. 2831/023 803; May.-Oct. daily 9am-3pm, Nov.-Apr. Tues., Thurs., Sat. 9am-3pm; €4

The best part of this odd museum is certainly the building. It's housed in the 17th-century Temple of Mastaba (also known as the Veli Pasha Mosque), which has the city's oldest minaret. The gardens of the mosque are beautiful in the spring. (By August, they can get quite dry and brown.) The museum's permanent collection includes fossils from 10,000-year-old mammals and Cretan elephant bones. In the wintertime, the museum seems to close at random times, so take the official opening hours with a grain of salt.

NIGHTLIFE AND ENTERTAINMENT

Bars

CAVO

13 Akrotiriou; tel. 2831/036 700; https://cavorethymno.gr; daily 1pm-11pm

A quintessential (fancy) summer island bar with fantastic sunset views. Cavo operates as an all-day café-bar, but it really comes alive when the sun slips behind the sea and there's a cocktail in your hand. You'll want to dress up ever so slightly to fit in.

Concerts

NERATZE MOSQUE

tel. 2831/341 301

Like everything else in Rethymno, the Neratze Mosque has a past: It was originally the main church of the Augustinian monastery. The Ottomans converted it into a mosque in 1657, eventually adding a 27-meter (88-foot) tall minaret. Under its three domes, there are fantastic atmospheric concerts. If you're in town when there's a performance, don't miss it! It no longer functions as a mosque. Instead, it's a conservatoire with concerts and lessons. Visit www.rethymno.guide for concerts.

FOOD

Greek and Cretan

RAKI BA RAKI

Arbatzoglou 17; tel. 2831/058 250; daily 10am-midnight; from €3

With its cute and colorful design, Raki Ba Raki looks more like the inside of a country grocery store than a restaurant. It's the perfect place for a quick meze dinner. You can't go wrong with any of the appetizers (all the ingredients are sourced from local farmers around Greece), but the fried snails and warm feta with caramelized figs are especially delicious.

AVLI

Xanthoudhidou 22; tel. 2831/058 250; www.avli.gr; daily 11am-midnight

For a more elegant and romantic dinner, head to Avli, located inside of an atmospheric Venetian villa. The food is upscale Cretan (carob bread bruschetta, beef liver with wild greens). There's a wine cellar on the premises, and it's worth deferring to the waiters to choose a suitable Greek wine to accompany your meal.

TO PIGADI

Xanthoudidou 31, Old Town; tel. 2831/027 522; www.pigadi-crete.com; Mar.-Nov. lunch and dinner

Located in the garden of a 16th-century Venetian building, To Pigadi ("The Well") is a fantastic upscale taverna with plenty of good vegetarian options. The decor is a bit old-world, with plenty of dark furnishings and antiques, but the food is decidedly modern Greek. Call to book a table outside.

Sweets

MONA LISA

36 Konstantinou Paleologou; tel. 2831/023 082; daily lunch and dinner; from €3

Have you ever had ice cream made from sheep's milk? If not, make a beeline for Mona Lisa, a beloved local sweets shop that's been

1

2

3

going strong for nearly 70 years. If ice cream isn't your thing, then try their famous *galaktoboureko* (custard pie) and wash it down with a Greek coffee.

SHOPPING

GREEK UNIQUE

3 Vosporou; tel. 2831/402 829; Mon.-Fri. 10am-3:30pm and 5:30pm-10:30pm, Sat. 10am-8pm, Sun. 10am-4pm

This cute concept gift shop sells modern souvenirs; all of them have been designed and made in Greece. From the notebooks to the ceramic mugs, everything is made with an extra touch of elegance, and the kind owner will hand-wrap your purchases for free.

AGRECOFARM

33-35 Sofokli Venizelou; tel. 2831/072 129; www.agreco.gr; Mon.-Sat. 10am-10pm

Located on the coastal road a few minutes outside of Rethymno Town, AgrecoFarm is an organic farm with a restaurant and shop. They sell traditional food products like raki, olive oil, herbs, and beauty products made from their farm. The packaging is absolutely fantastic—bright, bold, and playful—and places these keepsakes a notch above anything you'd find in town.

ACCOMMODATIONS

Under €150

ATELIER FROSSO BORA

Chimaras 25; tel. 2831/024 440; www.frosso-bora.com; from €45

You'll want to book well in advance to snag one of the charming four rooms run by local artist (and hotel namesake) Frosso Bora. Located in the heart of the old town, rooms are clean and include kitchenettes. This is an excellent budget option, and if you can get a room with a bougainvillea-covered balcony, you'll be all the happier. Frossa also runs ceramics workshops in her downstairs studios for those wanting to add an artistic tilt to their vacation.

CASA VITAE

Neophytou Patelarou 3; tel. 2831/035 058; www.casa-vitae.gr; from €100

With just three villas located inside a renovated Venetian house from the 16th century, Casa Vitae exudes privacy. The decor is all exposed stone and light wood, with calming taupe and nude color schemes that are a bit more Cycladic than Cretan. The bathrooms—under vaulted stone—are particularly exquisite. A homemade breakfast is served in the courtyard, and you're walking distance from all the city sights and beaches.

€150-300

★ RIMONDI BOUTIQUE HOTEL

Xanthoudidou 10; tel. 2831/051 289; www.hotelsrimondi.com; from €150

This beautiful luxury boutique hotel brings to mind a Moroccan *riad,* thanks to its columns and courtyard pool. The hotel is housed in the Rimondi Palazzo, which dates to Venetian times; subsequent additions were made by the Ottomans. The air is rich with history, and the rooms (20 rooms and 13 suites) with stone-vaulted ceilings, make you feel like royalty. There's a wonderful spa and restaurant on-site as well.

Over €300

GRECOTEL CRETA PALACE

Missiria; tel. 2831/055 181; www.cretapalace.com; from €390

On the outskirts of Rethymno, you'll find several big-budget resorts. Grecotel Creta Palace is the best of them all, with more than 200 rooms set around a pristine white sand beach. Choose from double rooms up to 160 square meters (525 square feet) and villas with private pools. There's a spa, communal pool, beach area, and plenty of activities for kids, including an open-air cinema. Prices are cut in half in the off-season.

1: characteristic wooden doors of Rethymno **2:** Is this the most fabulous door in Rethymno? Answer: yes. **3:** the ruins of the Venetian Fortress

GETTING THERE

Rethymno Town is located west of Heraklio Town, and **KTEL Heraklion-Lasithi S.A. buses** (www.ktelherlas.gr) run between the two towns. A **taxi** from Heraklio to Rethymno will cost more than €100. **KTEL Chania-Rethimnon buses** (www.bus-service-crete-ktel.com) run from Chania to Rethymno.

Outside Rethymno Town

The area outside of Rethymno Town is rich with history; here you'll find archaeological ruins from ancient cities, restored Venetian villas, and traditional pottery as it's been made for centuries. There are mountains to explore (on foot or by car), and locals to meet and drink raki with. The air feels more mystical here, maybe due to all the monasteries and ancient cities that pepper the interior landscape. The pace of life is much slower in the villages around Rethymno; factor that in as you're planning your itinerary. I would allow at least three days in the region, though because the mountain roads can be tiring to drive, you might want to spread out your time over four or five days.

VILLA CLODIO

Chromonastiri village; tel. 2831/075 135; Tues.-Fri. 10am-3pm, Sun. 10am-2pm; €3

This stunning Venetian mansion now houses Chromonastiri Military Museum, but the interior of the house, which was built in the 16th century for the aristocratic Clodio family, is much more interesting than the weapons on display. Particularly noteworthy are the hammam (built by a pasha who used to live in the house during Ottoman times) and the inner courtyard with wells and cisterns.

Villa Clodio is located in Chromonastiri Village, 10 km (6 mi) south of Rethymno Town. It's a 20-minute drive on the Akademis Vivi.

MAROULAS VILLAGE (Μαρούλας)

Game of Thrones fans will feel right at home in Maroulas. No, this village was never a set for the dragon slayers, but you'll be forgiven for thinking otherwise. Seemingly stuck in the Middle Ages, this village is something of an oddity (with very few tourists). Maroulas is a jumble of stone Venetian and Ottoman architecture. Most impressive are the two stone towers that still stand in the center of the village. The towers were used as communication centers, through smoke and fire, with the fortress in Rethymno, and you can still see the so-called "murder holes" where soldiers would pour boiling oil and tar on their enemies' heads.

Maroulas is 10 km (6 mi) southeast of Rethymno Town. It's a 20-minute drive on the Platanon-Moni Arkadiou highway.

ARKADI TO MARGARITES

The southeast interior of Rethymno is full of some fantastic sights that have historical and cultural significance in Crete. You can visit all three sites below in one day, provided you leave early enough in the morning by car. From Rethymno, it takes half an hour (20 km/12.5 mi) to reach the Arkadi Monastery. A further 11 km (6.75 mi, 18 minutes driving) over mountain roads will have you in Eleutherna; you can continue 4 more km (2.5 mi) to Margarites.

★ Arkadi Monastery

tel. 2831/083 135; www.arkadimonastery.gr; Apr.-Oct. daily, 9am-7pm, Nov.-Mar. daily 9am-4pm; €3

The last and bloodiest of the fights for Cretans' independence from Ottoman rule occurred in 1866 and culminated in Cretan

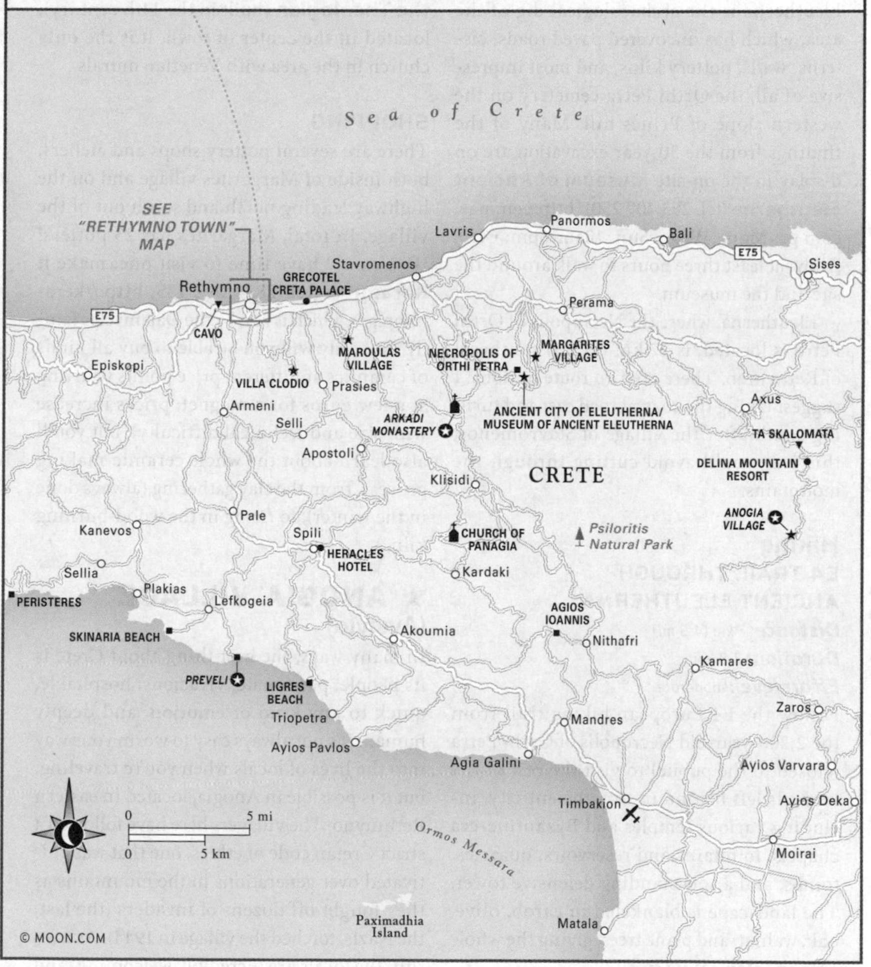

independence three years later. The Arkadi Monastery (you might also see it written as Moni Arkaidou) is the site where Cretans like to say their liberation began. As such, it's the best-known monastery on the island. During the uprising, Cretan rebel soldiers blew up the monastery (which was moonlighting as a munitions storehouse) and themselves so as not to surrender to the Ottomans. There's an entire building complex to explore, and aside from the history, it's a real work of art. The monastery, with its three-belled tower and wedding cake–like façade, are beautiful.

The area around the monastery is serviced by the bus (40 minutes, three daily from Rethymno, twice daily on weekends; €3). You'll have 90 minutes to explore the area. By car, it's 20 km (12.5 mi, 30 minutes) southeast from Rethymno.

Ancient City of Eleutherna

The ancient city of Eleutherna is believed

to have been inhabited since 3000 BC. Now spread across the Prines and Nisi hills in Eleutherna is the archaeological dig of the area, which has uncovered paved roads, cisterns, walls, pottery kilns, and most impressive of all, the Orthi Petra cemetery on the western slope of Prines hill. Many of the findings from the 30-year excavation are on display in the on-site **Museum of Ancient Eleutherna** (tel. 283 409 2501; http://en.mae.com.gr; Mon., Weds.-Sun. 10am-6pm; €4;). Allow at least three hours to walk around the site and the museum.

Eleutherna, where the Necropolis of Orthi Petra is located, is 27 km (17 mi) southeast of Rethymno. There are two route options. I suggest taking the coastal road east and turning south after the village of Stavromenos; this way you'll avoid cutting through the mountains.

Hiking

E4 TRAIL THROUGH ANCIENT ELEUTHERNA

Distance: *7 km (4.3 mi)*
Duration: *2-3 hours*
Effort level: *moderate*

Follow the E4 European hiking trail from the 2,200-year-old Necropolis of Orthi Petra (closed to the public) to visit the rest of the marvels left behind in this ancient city, including various temples and Byzantine-era chapels, fountains and reservoirs, quarries, tombs, and a sole standing defensive tower. The landscape is blanketed in carob, olive, oak, walnut, and plane trees, giving the whole area an intoxicating smell.

Margarites Village (Μαργαρίτης)

Margarites, one of the most beautiful villages in central Rethymno, has had its share of bad luck: It was sacked several times by the Ottomans and the Venetians, but somehow, its beauty survived. Today, the village is known as one of the four largest pottery centers in Crete. Take a few hours to walk around the Venetian streets. You'll notice plenty of *pitharia*, or large ceramic vessels decorating buildings. Stop by the **Chapel of Aï Yiannis the Theologian** (built in the 14th century); located in the center of town, it is the only church in the area with Venetian murals.

SHOPPING

There are several pottery shops and ateliers, both inside of Margarites village and on the highway leading north and south out of the village. In total, Margarites has 23 potters! If you only have time to visit one, make it **Keramion** (tel. 2834/092 135; http://keramion.gr), which is run by the Dalamvelas family. Not only will you be able to buy all kinds of ceramics at different price points (starting at a few euros for a magnet; prices increase with size and technical difficulty), but you'll also learn about the whole ceramic-making process, from the clay gathering (always done in the winter), to firing in the wood-burning kiln.

★ ANOGIA VILLAGE (Ανωγια)

In many ways, the best thing about Crete is its people: passionate, vivacious, hospitable, quick to any kind of emotion, and deeply human. It's not always easy to worm your way into the lives of locals when you're traveling, but it is possible in Anogia, located in eastern Rethmyno. The villagers here have followed a strict Cretan code of ethics, one that was cultivated over generations in the mountains as they fought off dozens of invaders (the last, the Nazis, torched the village in 1944). As a result, the locals are incredibly welcoming, and they appreciate the finer things in life—wine, music, good conversation. This is a village for sitting and drinking at the local *kafeneio*. Also worth a visit is the church of **Aghios Ioannis,** built in the 14th century.

From Rethymno, the 56-km (35-mi) drive takes a bit over an hour. You'll drive east along the coast before turning south onto the Peramatos Panormou highway. From Heraklio, the 37-km (23-mi) drive takes just under an hour, as most of the drive is through mountainous roads with lots of twists and turns.

Food

TA SKALOMATA

31 August 1944 St; tel. 2834/031 316; 9am-midnight; from €5

This lovely family-run taverna has been doling out hearty Cretan platters for the past four decades or so. The views from its perch, at the upper edge of the village, are stupendous. The food is fresh and local, with copious amounts of homemade bread and wine. Here you'll find kindly owners, excellent grilled meat, and good vegetarian options.

TO KAFENEION TOU SKOULA

tel. 2834/031 396

Hidden between two mulberry trees in the village's main square, this *kafeneion* is something of a time capsule. Out in front sit straight-backed elderly men dressed in traditional Cretan outfits; the pride in their culture radiates off them as they sip their coffee and smoke hand-rolled cigarettes. Oh, the stories they could tell you. Inside, the *kafeneion* walls are covered in photographs memorializing the Skoulas' family's participation in Nazi resistance during World War II.

Accommodations

DELINA MOUNTAIN RESORT

tel. 2834/031 701; www.delina.gr; from €115

Set over a sprawling 11 hectares (27 acres), which includes a lake and an old stone theater, Delina Mountain Resort is a good combination of plush luxury and Cretan hospitality. Each of the 13 clean and spacious rooms comes with a fireplace, veranda, and jacuzzi. There's a spa and restaurant on-site.

SPILI TO PSILORITIS NATURAL PARK

The lovely village of Spili (Σπήλι) is a great example of a traditional Cretan village. It's incredibly picturesque, with traditional stone homes, beautiful fountains, and twisting cobblestone streets shaded by trees. The Rethimou-Agiou Galinas highway connects Rethymno with Spili in 35 minutes (26 km/16 mi). Note that the whole interior of Rethymno is very mountainous, so allow extra driving time. From Spili to Amari (where the Church of Panagia is located) the 20-km (12.5-mi) drive takes 30 minutes. To get to the Psiloritis National Park, give yourself 2 hours (80 km/50 mi). It's easier to base day trips to these places out of Rethymno, as the highway roads are easier to drive.

Sights

CHURCH OF PANAGIA

Meronas Village In Amari

One of the more impressive churches in the area, the Church of Panagia ("Holy Mother of God") was built in the 13th century, and the rest of the lovely Meronas village was built around the church. The building was financed by the Byzantine family Kallergis, who commissioned some of the top artists from Constantinople (Istanbul) to paint murals, which survive today. The faded frescoes are painted in the classic Byzantine style, and depict scenes from the Bible. Keep your eyes peeled for the impressive *Tree of Jesse* mural, which covers the whole western wall of the church.

PSILORITIS NATURAL PARK

Psiloritis Natural Park, Anogia Center for Environmental Education; tel. 2834/031 662; free

Covering nearly 1,200 square km (463 square mi), Psiloritis National Park is split between the municipalities of Heraklio and Rethymno. Psiloritis Natural Park is a beautiful and wondrous place: You'll come across caves, gorges, plains, thick forests, and babbling brooks. Most interesting are the *mitata* (slate stone huts built by shepherds) that are strewn about the park and were used by shepherds and farmers for centuries. Some are still in use today. There are seven villages that serve as base points for entry into the park: Anogia, Garazo, Margarites, Fourfouras, Zaros, Gregeri, and Krousonas (all accessible from either Rethymno or Heraklio, and all the roads are paved, though slow to drive thanks to the curves).

You will find the *mitata* all over the park, but if you only have time for one hike, drive to the Nida Plateau (located in the park, parking available, 68 km/42 mi) southeast of Rethymno). You'll see signs (first white flags, then red paint sprayed on rocks) leading you up to the **Ideon Cave** on Mt. Plistorits, where, according to ancient myth, Rhea gave birth to a baby Zeus. Allow at least five hours to ascend and descend back to the plateau.

Accommodations

HERACLES HOTEL

Spili; tel. 2832/022 111; www.heracles-hotel.eu; from €40

For a budget option with a big heart, rent a room from Heracles, the kind and charming owner (and the namesake) of this hotel (he speaks fluent English). There are five clean and sparsely furnished rooms, each with a balcony. A homemade breakfast can be added for an additional €5. The location is a bit isolated, which is good for those searching for something off the tourist path at an affordable price. However, plan on staying here only if you have a car.

SOUTH COAST BEACHES

Rethymno has 55 km (34 mi) worth of shoreline, with more than 30 beaches. You can't really go wrong at any of them, but as a general rule of thumb, head south and away from Rethymno Town.

From Rethymno Town, it's a straight shot south to Preveli. The 35-km (22 mi) drive is mostly along the highway, and you can get to the southern part of the region in 50 minutes. There are also four daily buses leaving from Rethymno. Tickets cost €4.50, and you'll have to change part-way through the journey at Plakias. The last bus back to Rethymno leaves at 6:30pm, and the buses stop near the stairs to the beach, next to the monastery.

★ Preveli (Πρέβελη)

Located at the mouth of a gorge that spits out a river flanked by palm and date trees before flowing into the salty Libyan Sea, Preveli Beach is a magical, unmissable spot. You can jump from natural pools and then run to the sandy beach to dip into the sea, or get lost in the date trees—it's fantastic. Come very early in the morning, or late in the afternoon when the forest is filled with the sound of chirping swallows. The beach is partly organized; you

an aerial view of stunning Preveli Beach

can rent pedal boats and canoes at the mouth of the river (around €7 for 30 minutes), and lawn chairs under umbrellas can be rented for €3 per person. (It's one umbrella shared between two people with two chairs).

For food, walk 10 minutes along the signposted path to the next-door beach of Ammoudi, where there are two tavernas.

The beautiful ochre-colored monastery of **Moni Preveli** (free) (2.8 km/1.7 mi from the beach) stands in a prominent position overlooking the Libyan Sea. It dates back to 1594, but its greatest significance is connected to the resistance movement during World War II, when the monks (along with the local villagers) provided supplies, lookouts, and safe haven to the Allied forces. A memorial to peace and remembrance was erected on the 60th anniversary of the war. There's also a small museum inside the monastery, with a collection of icons, vessels, and garments.

Ligres Beach (Λιγκρες)

This long sandy beach is surprisingly quiet even in the peak season. At the southern end of the beach there's a small waterfall and a nice taverna where you can enjoy a drink and some meze as you watch the sun go down. The beach is located 15.6 km (9.5 mi) east of Preveli, but the drive will take 45 minutes, thanks to the twisting coastal road.

Skinaria Beach (Σκινάρια)

Skinaria Beach is a fantastic white sand, teal blue beach that is partly organized, but it's not very well known, even by locals. It's a fantastic place for snorkeling, as the rocky seabed has become a home for all sorts of fish, morays, and octopus. There's a small kiosk selling refreshments and snacks that manages the umbrellas (free with a purchase). Located 7 km (4.25 mi) west of Previli.

Peristeres (Περιστερές)

Grab a spot in the shade under the carob trees at Greek Prime Minister Alexis Tsipras's favorite beach (or so it is rumored). The beach is separated into two coves, both of which are quiet throughout the summer. There are no organized lawn chairs or beach bars—just a couple of tavernas. It's favored by nudists and free campers. Located 27 km (17 mi) west of Skinaria (a 47-minute drive; again, the road is quite twisty).

Chania Town Χανιά

TOP EXPERIENCE

Good luck getting out of Chania. Not only will the winding, colorful streets have you walking in charmed circles, but also this is far and away the most beautiful city on Crete—one of the most stunning in all of Greece, and some even say the most gorgeous on the whole Mediterranean. Even if you don't get lost, you'll find it hard to leave, ever.

Nestled around a turquoise blue harbor, Chania is a relic of the people who passed through here: Venetians (it's often called "the Venice of the East"), Andalusian Arabs, Ottoman Turks, Genoese, and Egyptians, just to name the more recent ones. Modern Chania has a university, and a big student population ensures plenty of activity year-round. Note that during the summer months, it can become incredibly crowded with tourists.

You'll want to spend at least two days in Chania itself. To explore the whole region, allow at least five to six days (though you could easily spend two weeks here without scratching the surface). Pick a few must-see destinations, like Balos Beach and Samaria Gorge, and build your itinerary around them. Don't try to cram too much into each day: Driving

Chania Town

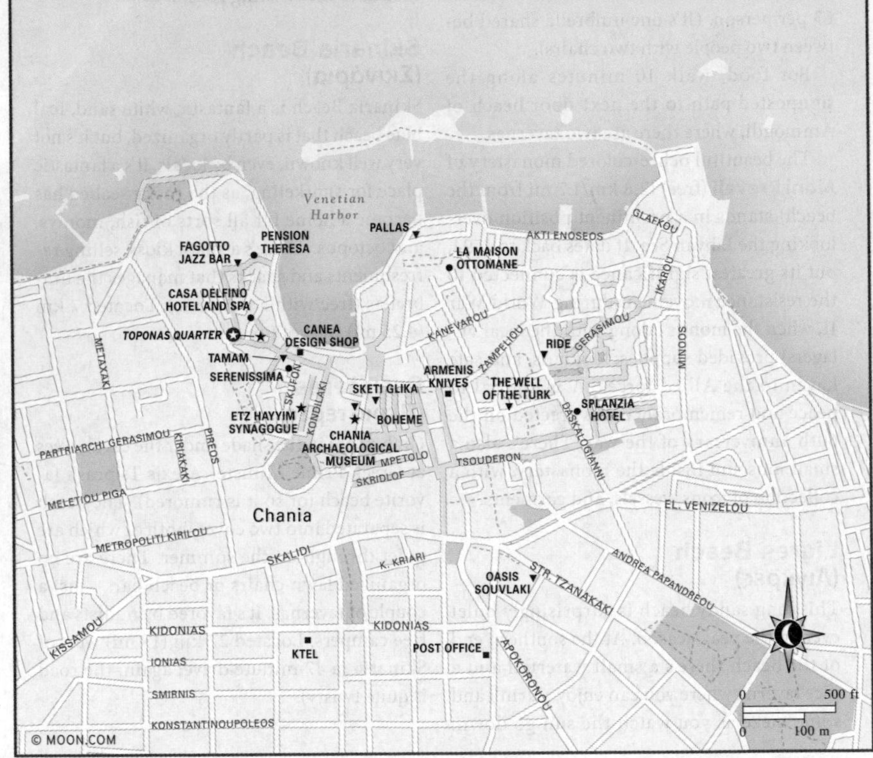

distances are long, and the roads, which are incredibly twisty, can easily exhaust you.

SIGHTS

★ Toponas Quarter

Chania's old Venetian Quarter—better known as Toponas—is an architectural jewel. It's a joy to wander around the streets, each corner revealing an even more beautiful facade or doorway. A couple of streets worth checking out include **Angelou, Theofanous,** and **Moscho;** on **Theotokopoulou Street,** you'll find remnants of Venetian fortifications.

Chania Archaeological Museum

Halidon 28; tel. 2821/090 344; http://chaniamuseum.culture.gr; Tues.-Sun. 8am-3pm; €4

Located inside of a 16th-century Venetian Church (which has moonlighted as a mosque, a movie theater, and an ammunitions dump later in its life), the Chania Archaeological Museum displays a delightful collection of goods from neolithic to Roman times. There's a charming courtyard with a Venetian fountain in the church's interior. Standout exhibits include the meticulously assembled Roman mosaics.

Etz Hayyim Synagogue

Parados Kondylaki; tel. 2821/086 286; www.etz-hayyim-hania.org; Mon.-Thurs. 10am-6pm, Fri. 10am-3pm; free

Crete was once home to a sizable Romaniote Jewish population, but 2,300 years of Jewish life was pretty much wiped out when the Nazis landed on Crete's shores. Originally built in the 15th century, the synagogue is the only remaining one on the island. It reopened in 1999 after being badly damaged during the war. A small congregation still comes for prayers, and the synagogue is open to the public. There's a small memorial to the Jews murdered during the war and tombs of buried rabbis.

Venetian Harbor

The most dominant site in Chania is undoubtedly its harbor. Originally built by Venetian occupiers in the 16th century, it was later refurbished in the 19th century by the Egyptians. The harbor is flanked by a lighthouse on one end, and the Mosque of Kioutsouk Hasan (free) on the other; in between are plenty of shops, cafés, tavernas, and bars. Come here around dusk, for an evening *volta* (walk) when the sun has bathed everything in a golden light.

NIGHTLIFE

Chania has some of the more chic nightlife in Crete. The harbor comes alive at night, as people dressed in their nicest outfits stroll up and down. You'll find bars and lively tavernas scattered throughout the city.

Bars

RIDE

52 Daskulogianni; tel. 2821/058 585

This very cool café-bar does both roasted coffee and craft beer equally well. In addition to the usual Greek beers, they brew their own IPA. As the name suggests, this is also a cycle shop; you can stop by to rent a bike (from €10) for a tour around the city, or to repair yours.

BOHEME

Chalidon 26; tel. 2821/095 955; daily 10am-3am; www.boheme-chania.gr

Every spot in Chania has a history, including the newly opened Boheme. The plane tree in the courtyard is over 400 years old, and the bar itself is located in the old cells of the Franciscan monks. It's as much a restaurant (the food is great) as it is a bar, and they have plenty of specialty cocktails.

Live Music

FAGOTTO JAZZ BAR

Aggelou 16; tel. 2821/071 877; daily 9am-3am

Tucked away in a 15th-century Venetian house, Fagotto is one of the oldest jazz bars in the city, and it's certainly one of the most atmospheric places to spend an evening, sipping cocktails and listening to live music. Check their Facebook page for musical guests.

FOOD

In general, there's good food in Chania, though the restaurants along the harbor, and those with aggressive barkers out front of the restaurants waiting to pounce on tourists, are less delicious than the rest. Don't be afraid to deviate from this list of recommended restaurants, as long as you follow this tips: If a restaurant is full (and there are some Greeks in there), and if you can smell the food cooking, it's probably going to be a nice meal.

Greek and Cretan

TO MAGAZAKI

Akti Papanikoli 14; tel. 2821/099 177; breakfast, lunch, and dinner; from €5

A no-frills, no-pretense local taverna on the western edge of town, To Magazaki is a favorite with locals and the tourists who manage to venture far enough from the Venetian belly of Chania. Weather permitting, a local fisherman is employed to catch the restaurant's fresh fish of the day; other standouts on the menu include roasted chicken and baked feta.

THALASSINO AGERI

Vivilaki 35; tel. 694/793 9146; www.thalasino-ageri.gr/en; daily 7pm-midnight; from €7

Located in the old section of Chania known as Tabakeria (where leather tanners used to work), Thalassino Ageri is a fantastic fish taverna. You'll munch on grilled octopus and fresh salads on white cloth-covered tables overlooking the Mediterranean. Book a table outside around sunset for the best experience.

OASIS SOUVLAKI

Voloudaki 2-4; daily, lunch and dinner; from €2

For the best sandwich in town, head to Oasis Souvlaki, where expertly grilled cubes of pork and lamb are stuffed inside roasted pitas and finished with yogurt sauce and parsley. Unlike other joints, this one doesn't stuff the sandwich with french fries; the focus is on the meat.

TAMAM RESTAURANT

Zampeliou 51; tel. 2821/096 080; www.tamamrestaurant.com; daily noon-1am; from €10

The building of Tamam, constructed in the 14th century, used to host public baths, or *hammam,* as it's known in Turkish and Arabic. When the owners of the restaurant were pondering a name, they were inspired by the location's history. The name Tamam is a nod to both *hammam* and *temem,* the Egyptian word for "all good." The food is made with Cretan products, and you'll find traditional dishes like octopus cooked in wine, grilled lamb chops, and homemade savory pies. They also have an excellent wine list of exclusively Greek wines.

International and Fusion

THE WELL OF THE TURK

1-3 Kallinikou; tel. 2821/054 547; https://welloftheturk.gr; daily 6-11:30pm; from €10

Featuring a literal well, the Well of the Turk is a fun taverna with an exotic mix of food. It's located in the old Turkish quarter, Splantzia, and the flavors are more Turkish and Middle Eastern than they are Greek. You'll find dishes like falafel, raisin-studded couscous, and mint tea.

PALLAS

Akti Tombazi 15; tel. 282 104 5688; www.pallaschania.gr/en; daily 8am-4pm; from €8

Located in a beautiful 19th-century building, Pallas offers stylish Mediterranean cuisine, plus an extensive sushi menu. Try the sautéed scallops with pork belly and sweet potatoes, or the pork marinated in ginger and kimchi. The café/restaurant has something of an upscale bohemian vibe, and is beloved by both locals and tourists. Call ahead to snag a table on the terrace, which juts out into the harbor.

Sweets

SKETI GLIKA

18 Isodion; tel. 2821/302 801; daily 9am-11:30pm; from €2

Located conveniently close to the Venetian Harbor (you'll need some fuel after all that strolling!) is this old-school sweets shop that's a beloved institution in Chania. They have traditional desserts like baklava, but most of their creations look more like something out of a Parisian patisserie.

SHOPPING

CANEA DESIGN SHOP

45 Zampelou; tel. 2821/098 639; www.caneagiftshop.com

For one-stop souvenir shopping with none of the tacky tourist trappings, head to Canea Design Shop. Owner Konstantinos Konstantinidis is a born and bred Cretan, and after spending several years abroad, he decided to come home to open a store showcasing local Greek talent and designs, including everything from textiles to jewelry to ceramics.

ARMENIS KNIVES (Αρμενης Μαχαιροποιειο)

14 Sikifa; tel. 694/621 8264

With any luck, you'll spot a Cretan man in traditional garb on your trip. Tucked away in the folds of his pants, tied snugly at his hip, will

1: people strolling along Chania's port **2:** the lighthouse of Chania **3:** detail of a door in Chania's backstreets **4:** olives for sale in Chania

PORTO DEL COLOMBO
1
2
3
4
ΤΣΑΚΙΣΤΕΣ

be a short knife. If you want your own, head to Armenis, where silversmiths make knives emblazoned with *mantinades* (short poems, like a Greek haiku).

ACCOMMODATIONS

Under €150

PENSION THERESA

Angelou 8; www.pensiontheresa.gr; tel. 2821/092 798; from €50

The cheapest decent hotel in town, the small Pension Theresa, features rooms that may be tiny (unless you splurge for a "big room"), but pack a punch when it comes to ambience. There are lovely antique furnishings in each room, and there's a communal kitchen upstairs on the rooftop. Mercifully, air conditioning is included in the low price.

SPLANZIA HOTEL

Daskalogianni 20; tel. 2821/045 313; www.splanzia.com; from €135

A good affordable option in the heart of the city, and located in an 18th-century Venetian mansion, Splanzia is an eight-room, family-run hotel. Service is exceptional, though the room designs, with green lights and walls full of oval-shaped mirrors, won't be to everyone's tastes. There's a communal terrace on the roof with a hammock, and a fantastic breakfast (included in the price, and if you're hiking Samaria early in the morning, they'll pack you a breakfast picnic) served in the shady courtyard.

€150-300

AMMOS HOTEL

5 km (3 mi) west of Chania; tel. 2821/033 003; www.ammoshotel.com; from €165

This is the best beach resort (well, mini resort) next to Chania, with only 33 rooms located across a sprawling complex of Cycladic-style buildings. Inside, the colors are bright and cheerful and outfitted with huge marble bathrooms. Other perks: you're only seconds from the beach (or the outdoor pool), and it's worth splurging on the copious breakfast buffet. The hotel is located a 15-minute drive from Chania.

CASA DELFINO HOTEL AND SPA

Theofanous 9; tel. 2821/087 400; www.casadelfino.com; from €175

With 22 rooms in a refurbished 17th-century manor, Casa Delfino is one of Chania's nicest hotels, tucked away on a quiet street from the harbor. There's a fantastic rooftop bar and a restaurant with breakfast, plus a spa, and the service is top-notch. Try to get a room with a balcony.

LA MAISON OTTOMANE

Parodos Kanevarou 32; tel. 2821/008 796; www.lamaisonottomane.com; from €180

This truly luxurious five-star, boutique hotel is heavy on the history and the charm. There are only three rooms in the hotel, and each is named after an important person or city in Ottoman Turkey. The decor is fit for a pasha, with plenty of antique furniture, Egyptian cotton, and oil paintings, and there's a lovely courtyard where you can have breakfast.

SERENISSIMA

Skoufon 4; tel. 2821/086 386; www.serenissima.gr; from €200

Located in a beautifully renovated Venetian manor from the 16th century, this lovely, medium-sized boutique hotel is big on design and ambiance. All the rooms come outfitted with cult favorite Coco-Mat mattresses and a pillow menu, and are done up in taupes and nude tones. Rooms face the courtyard or out onto the harbor. Breakfast is included.

ERIA RESORT ACCESSIBLE HOLIDAYS FOR DISABLED TRAVELERS

Maleme (16 km/10 mi from Chania); tel. 2821/062 790; www.eria-resort.gr; from €220

There are many places in Crete that can be difficult for disabled travelers to reach—not so at Eria Resort, which was designed with complete accessibility in mind. There are 11 rooms and two suites, all of which are spacious and feature accessible bathrooms. There's a swimming pool with a sloped ramp (and waterproof chairs). In addition, there are motorized scooters and other specialized equipment for rent.

GETTING THERE AND AROUND

Chania International Airport Daskalogiannis (CHQ) is located on the peninsula east of town. A **taxi** to the center costs €24, and the **bus,** which leaves regularly and takes 30 minutes, costs €2.50. **Ferries** arrive daily from Piraeus. Buses serving Chania and Western Crete are run by **KTEL Chania-Rethimnon** (www.bus-service-crete-ktel.com).

Outside Chania Town

The region of Chania might be the most beautiful section of Greece; these may sound like bold words, but this little corner of the world is home to some outstanding scenery: gorges that cut through the mountains before emptying into the sea; tropical beachscapes with secret coves and lagoons, and pink sand; stone villages and rock-hewn churches nestled in the green mountains. You can't really go wrong driving any direction out of Chania town.

You'll also be hard pressed to find a bad meal in the Chania region. In general, any roadside taverna (the farther off the beaten path the better) should be a safe bet, and even the beachside tavernas in the more resort-y areas have good food choices. Always ask if the seafood is fresh; it should be, given that you're on an island, but some places might try and trick sun-dazed tourists. If you're driving in the mountains, I urge you to stop along anywhere you see a bunch of Greek people, or even just a few wizened Cretans sitting in the shade and knocking back raki; that means something magical is probably happening in the kitchen.

AVLAKI GORGE

On an island full of gorges, Avlaki stands out for its religious connections; the name literally translates to "the saint's way." A half-hour walk (follow the signs) from where you park your car, you can access the **Aghia Triada (Holy Trinity) Tzagarolon Monastery,** which was built in the 17th century by a Cretan-Venetian family. You'll also find the **cave of Panagia Akroudiotissas,** the **chapel of the Virgin Mary** and the **sanctuary of Artemis,** and the **monastery of Saint John the Hermit.** The churches and chapels are built into and around the gorge, and it makes for a beautiful hike.

Avlaki Gorge is 16 km northeast (10 mi) of Chania, near to the sea. To get here, follow the signs to the Chania International Airport, and then continue north for another 7 km (4.25 mi).

Hiking the Gorge

Only one section of the gorge is accessible to hike. Leave your car at Gouvernetou Monastery (marked on Google maps as Moni Kirias ton Aggelon Agiou Ioannou Erimitou Gouvernetou, Chania, Hellas—phew!) and follow the clearly marked path that features a lot of stairs and ends at the Katholiko monastery. The whole walk will take you around 3 hours round-trip, because it's quite steep. Be sure to take a flashlight (better if it's the kind that's strapped to your head), as the walk goes through unlit caves. Bring water and snacks.

GRAMVOUSA PENINSULA

The Gramvousa peninsula is located in the northwest corner of Crete, a little arm sticking out and waving hello to the rest of the

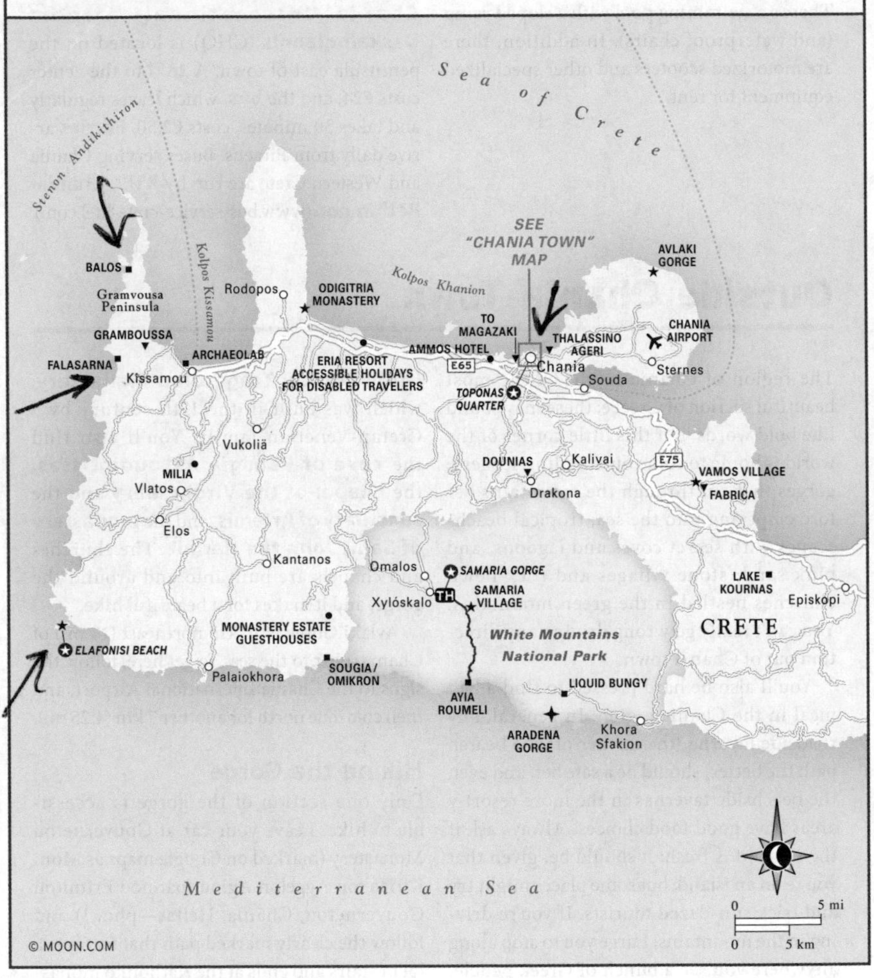

Mediterranean. From Chania, it's located 53 km (33 mi) west (1 hour 20 minutes driving).

Beaches

FALASARNA (Φαλάσαρνα)

The tropical-looking Falasarna beach, with its powder-white sand and azure waters, is 59 km (36.5 mi) west of Chania. Falasarna is actually five consecutive beaches; the middle two are the most popular, and thus, the most busy, though given the size, it never feels crowded. The whole area around the beach is a protected nature reserve, and in the middle of the beach, you'll find tavernas and snack bars. Some parts of the beach are organized with umbrellas and chairs. Note that because the beach is west facing, it can be quite windy—good for windsurfers, but a bit annoying for the rest of us.

BALOS
(Μπάλος)

Perhaps the best known of Chania's beaches, Balos is something of a natural wonder, with shallow waters and crisscrossing strips of powdery white sand crowned with wild grass. It gets very, very busy in July and August, and boats from Kissamos arrive in the afternoon, somewhat ruining the vibe; come in the morning to avoid them. It's located 52 km (32 mi) west of Chania (1 hour 20 minutes) and 20 km (12.5 mi) north of Falasarna (though note that the drive will take an hour, as the roads are full of switchbacks).

Recreation

ARCHAEOLAB

Kasteli village; tel. 693/930 5668; €20

Crete has been inhabited by people for thousands of years, which makes it a fitting site for this unique workshop. Designed by archaeologist Koula Borboudaki, Archaeolab is a unique workshop that simulates the highs and lows of an archaeological dig. They have classes for all ages and specialties, and your dig will use real tools and archaeological techniques. You'll also grill souvlaki on an ancient souvlaki grill! And, yes, you'll definitely unearth something in your dig!

Food

★ GRAMBOUSSA

Kalyvani; tel. 2822/022 707; http://gramvousarestaurant.com; daily 11:45am-midnight; from €8

Named for the peninsula it lies on, Gramboussa is a traditional Cretan restaurant with a beautiful, verdant garden. Special dishes are cooked over a wood-burning stove—such as pork with vine leaves and honey, and fried potatoes with sheep's butte—giving it an edge over the rest. In the summer, it's best to book a reservation, and be sure to take your time! Portions are copious and you'll want to order everything on the menu.

VLAOS
(Βλάτος)

Vlatos is located 56 km (35 mi) southwest of Chania (1 hour 20 minutes). Located up in the mountains, it's a great spot to base yourself if you want to be secluded in nature. The coast isn't far, but the roads down to the western beaches are incredibly narrow and twisty, and it'll take you an hour to go from the village to the coast.

Accommodations

★ MILIA

Vlatos; tel. 694/575 3743; www.milia.gr; €145

For ecotourism at its finest, head to the fantastic Milia, where stone houses (originally built in the 15th century!) are hidden in the green foliage of the mountains. Milia means "back to basics," and that's what you'll get here, with a definite luxurious twist. All the rooms are solar-powered, and the water comes from a natural source; outside your window you'll be greeted by chirping birds making their homes in chestnut trees. Additionally, there's a fantastic restaurant on-site that offers cooking classes, and there are art exhibits year-round. It's off the beaten path, but it makes for a fantastic respite from all the crowds in Chania. You will need a car if you're planning on staying here, but it's worth it.

VAMOS VILLAGE
(Βάμος)

Vamos village was first an experiment: In 1994, a group of friends decided to turn their ancestral village into a veritable agritourism destination. The gamble paid off, and today Vamos is a must-visit for anyone interested in sustainable tourism, or to get a taste of Cretan life. Though it seems like it has a sort of faux-authentic vibe, Vamos is actually a great place to learn about Cretan culture and historical preservation. It's even popular with Greeks, which means you know it's worth your time.

You can stay in wood and stone houses (from 80 euros), take cooking classes (€60) or guided botanical walks (€35), or harvest and

1
2

gather wild herbs and olives. Organize different activities through Vamos Village's friendly tourist office, or just show up in the village and walk around (though I recommend organizing an activity). Even the most ornery children will have a good time here, leaving mom and dad to fire back shots of raki in peace.

The village is located 28 km (17.25 mi) southeast of Chania (40 minutes), and for more information, there is a tourist office (tel. 282 502 2190; www.vamosvillage.gr).

Festivals

Vamos Village's old olive press, built in the 19th century and fittingly renamed **Fabrica,** is the site of concerts and performances all summer long. Check www.vamosvillage.gr for a complete list of local festivals. Some of the best include the August 15th *panigiri,* the Jazz in July festival, and the celebration of the summer solstice on June 23.

Food

STERNA TOU BLOUMOSIFIS

tel. 2825/083 220; from €8

This village taverna has been around since 1905, when the building was first used as a café. They serve up classic Cretan fare, and all the meat dishes are cooked in a traditional stone oven. Try the cuttlefish with fennel, or the rooster cooked in wine sauce. All the ingredients are local, including the wine, and everything is cooked using extra virgin olive oil. In the summer, dine al fresco under the *platanos* trees; in the winter, cozy up inside next to the fireplace. They occasionally have live Greek music in the evenings.

LAKE KOURNAS

As the only natural lake in Crete, Kournas is something of a destination spot for the Chania region. The water looks more like the sea—it's turquoise and clear water, nothing like the muddy lake water you might be imagining—and it's backed by beautiful hills that are covered with wildflowers in the spring. You can rent pedal boats (from €10) from one of the operators on the shore, and swim in its placid waters.

Lake Kournas is located 45 km (28 mi) east of Chania (50 minutes), and just 16.5 km (10 mi, 25 minutes) from Vamos.

DRAKONA (Δρακόνα)

The little mountain village of Drakona is worth a visit for the delicious food at Dounias taverna. The village also has a small Byzantine church (built in the 9th century) at the entrance of the village. There's a brown sign indicating the church. It's a tiny one-room structure that warrants a visit before dinner. Drakona is located 22 km (13.5 mi) south of Chania (38 minutes).

Food

★ DOUNIAS

Drakona; tel. 2821/065 083; daily 11am-6pm; from €7

For next-level slow cooking, come to Dounias, a taverna beloved by locals and far enough off the beaten trail that most tourists don't venture there. Everything is cooked over an open fire, and all the ingredients are sourced locally—most are grown at the owner's farm, and herbs are harvested from the nearby White Mountains. Call ahead, as there are only a few tables. It's a 20-km (12.5-mi, 40-minute) drive from Chania; it makes a good return dinner after hiking in the Samaria Gorge.

★ SAMARIA GORGE

Omalos; tel. 2821/045 570; www.samaria.gr; May-mid-Oct. 6am-4pm; €5

The stunning, 16-km (10-mi) long Samaria Gorge is one of the longest canyons in Europe, and a definite bucket-list item for any athletic visitor to Crete. Sheets of rock zoom up into the blue sky, and bubbling brooks cut through the rocky terrain. The gorge is partly forested, and it's home to dozens of endemic plants and wildflowers that the Cretan goats like to

1: the stunning Balos lagoon 2: passage through Samaria Gorge

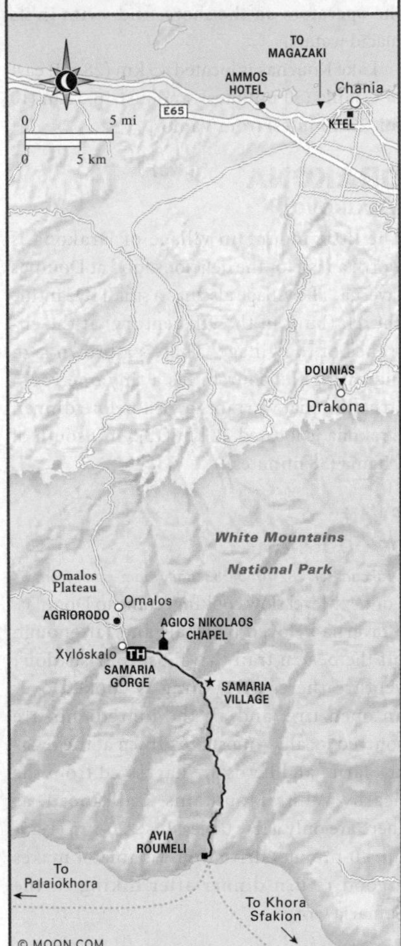

nibble. The gorge ends at the sea, and you'll be able to go for a dip after your hike.

The gorge forms the whole region known as **White Mountains National Park** (the only national park in Crete). Hiking is the best way to experience the gorge; you can't drive through it.

Chania is 40 km (25 mi) away (1.5 hours driving). There are morning buses from Chania to Omalos (www.e-ktel.com; one hour; €7.50).

Hiking the Gorge

Distance: *16 km (10 mi) one-way*

Duration: *4-8 hours*

Effort level: *moderate*

This hike takes you through the gorge itself. You'll start the hike in the village of **Xylóskalo** just south of Omalos, following a steep, stony path before catching a glimpse of the **Agios Nikolaos** chapel. Say a quick prayer (you may need it for the next dozen kilometers), and continue through the abandoned village of Samaria, a geological feature known as the **Sideroportes (Iron Gates)** at the 11-km (6.8-mi) marker, and the final stretch to **Ayia Rouméli** (the exit of the gorge), where the turquoise Mediterranean laps at the beach. You can stop here to have a beer and dip your feet in the cool water. In Ayia Roumeli, **Anendyk** (www.anendyk.gr) ferries wait to take hikers to Sougia or Hora Sfakion (€8.50). From there, you can take a public bus (2 hours) or taxi (€75) back to Chania.

It's best to start the hike in the early morning, as the park rangers don't let anyone hike more than 2 km (1.25 mi) after 2pm, and you'll need to be out of the gorge by sunset (camping overnight is strictly forbidden). Bring a water bottle (you can fill up at taps along the way), wet wipes (for the bathrooms along the trail, which may or may not have paper), snacks, sunscreen, and good walking shoes. Most people choose to go on an organized hiking tour (you'll see operators around Chania advertising). Tours cost around €20 and include transportation to and from the gorge to your hotel, but it's also feasible to hike on your own.

Accommodations

AGRIORODO

Omalos; tel. 2821/067 237; from €60

If you want to get an early start on the Samaria Gorge, spend the night here first. The seven modern stone cottages (two of them are larger maisonettes) make a reliable base to get a good night's sleep before your long hike. The cottages can sleep up to five and are outfitted with kitchens and fireplaces. It's a 15-minute walk to the start of the trail.

OMALOS PLATEAU

If you're looking for total solitude, head to the Omalos Plateau, where your cell phone won't work and the only signs of life are a few sheep and their herders. During the Ottoman occupation, the Omalos plateau served as a shelter and meeting point for both locals and rebels. In Xiloskalo (signposted) you'll find a kiosk and forest ranger; it's a good starting point for several hikes of varying length and difficulty. Located 56 km south of Chania, it also makes a good stopover if you're coming to the Samaria gorge.

ARADENA GORGE

At 138 meters (453 feet), this is the deepest gorge in Crete, making it ideal for bungy jumping.

Bungy Jumping

LIQUID BUNGY

Aradena Gorge; tel. 693/761 5191; www.bungy.gr; June-Sept. Sat.-Sun. noon-5pm; €40 euros

Channel your inner Icarus—hopefully with better results—and jump into the abyss with Liquid Bungy, the (very) safe operator with the second-largest bungy jump in Europe. Located on the bridge of Aradena (originally built by one of the richest families in Greece, the Vardinogiannis), it's a 138-meter (453-foot) plunge. Participants must be over 14 years, and weigh between 40-140kg.

Hiking

Those who prefer to keep their feet firmly planted on the ground (I'm with you) can walk sections of the 15-km (9.25-mi) long gorge. The most common hiking trail starts from the abandoned village of Aradena and ends up at the Marmara beach. The trail is 5.5 km (3.5 mi) long and takes about 2.5 hours to complete (moderate, bring water and snacks and a bathing suit for a dip at the end).

Aradena is reached from the road to Chora Sfakion (72 km/45 mi south of Chania, 1.5 hours) through the village of Anopolis (signposted) and then to Aradena.

SOUGIA (Σούγια)

One of the last places in Crete that can all itself a hippie hangout, Sougia village is the most relaxed of the resort towns. There's not a whole lot to do here, which is the point: It has the longest beach in southwest Crete, and the village is built around the kilometer-long strip of sand. There are a few seafood tavernas and cafés in the town, but the best part of this village is the low-key vibe. The locals are incredibly chill, and most of the tourists who visit here have been coming since the 1970s; it still retains something of a bohemian vibe. It's easy to strike up a conversation with a stranger and make friends in Sougia.

From Chania, there are two driving options to get to Sougia: the shorter road, at 60 km (37 mi), cuts through the interior of the island and takes an hour and a half, thanks to the stomach-churning twisting roads. The second road will have you first driving west along the coast before cutting south (72 km/45 mi, an hour and 40 minutes). It's 10 minutes longer but the roads are straighter.

Beaches

Sougia has a long gray pebble beach with deep waters. There are a couple of taverns and bars at one end of the beach. It's not the most beautiful, but the vibe is chill and it's not overcrowded. The beach is mostly pebbles; nudism is common on the eastern side of the beach, which locals call "Matala."

Food

OMIKRON

Sougia Beach Rd; tel. 2823/051 492; daily 8am-late; from €7

If you're tired of grilled fish and Greek salad, head to this modern European eatery on the beach. The food is more western and eclectic, featuring *flammenukuchen,* pizza, crepes, and steak. Portions are big, and the staff is exceedingly friendly.

Accommodations

MONASTERY ESTATE GUESTHOUSES

Sougia; tel. 694/224 3232; www.monasteryestate.com; from €70

Forged out of stone and wood, and with a nod to the Cycladic style of interior design, Monastery Estate is a relaxing, nature-filled holiday spot. It's located 4.5 km (2.75 mi) from Sougia beach, and is tucked away in nature to give you a true sense of relaxation. Rooms are bright and spacious and come with kitchens. Breakfast is a tasty affair (included), and the friendly owners will point you in the direction of the best hiking trails and beaches. They have a luxurious sister hotel in Chania.

★ ELAFONISI BEACH (Ελαφονήσι)

For pink sand (yes, pink—the unique color of the sand comes from the crushed seashells) and crystal-clear turquoise waters, head to the magical, Caribbean-esque lagoon of Elafonisi. It's in between an island and a peninsula—a fantastically strange, oblong bit of geography, and you'll have to cross over some water on foot to reach the beach—and the area is full of tiny sand islets. The water at the breaking point of the lagoon isn't more than 1 meter (about 1 yard) deep, and it's great for small kids. The eastern part of the lagoon is quite organized, and you can rent beach umbrellas and buy cold drinks; on the west end of the peninsula, there are a couple of coves that are preferred by nudists. If you want to get away from the crowds, just keep walking west until you find a cove that's empty.

Elafonisi is about a two-hour drive (73 km/45 mi) from Chania, through beautiful mountain ridges, but note that the road is quite narrow and very twisty. If you go in the high season, you will find a crush of people that will detract from the ambience. It's better to go during the shoulder season, or, if you're there in July/August, in the very early morning. There are regular buses from Chania (€11).

Agios Nikolaos and Lasithi

Lasithi (Λασίθι), the easternmost region of Crete, is often overlooked by visitors who flock to the island's center and western shores. All the better for the intrepid traveler who ventures here: You'll find a corner of the world full of sandy beaches that are blessedly quiet, dense forests, charming archaeological ruins, and sweet villages. You can go way off the beaten path here.

A tour of the whole region covers about 250 km (155 mi) from Agios Nikolaos around the perimeter of the region, and will take five hours to drive. You should plan on staying at least four days here to see all the sights.

AGIOS NIKOLAOS (Άγιος Νικόλαος)

The capital of Lasithi, Agios Nikolaos, is the smallest of the four Cretan cities. It's built around the Mirabello Bay, and was constructed on the ancient site of Kamara, where followers worshipped Eileithyia, the goddess of midwifery and childbirth. The town has something of a resort feel to it, and the streets are wide and framed with trees—a far cry from the twisting labyrinth of Heraklio or Chania.

The town congregates around the cute Voulismeni Lake, which is connected by a thin passage to the sea. (You know summer has started in Lasithi when the cliff divers arrive from around the world, putting their daredevil antics on full display.) It's also worth seeing the open-air **Horn of Amalthea,** a larger-than-life sculpture of the horn that was used to feed Zeus a never-ending supply of milk and honey, and the charming

Agios Nikolaos and Lasithi

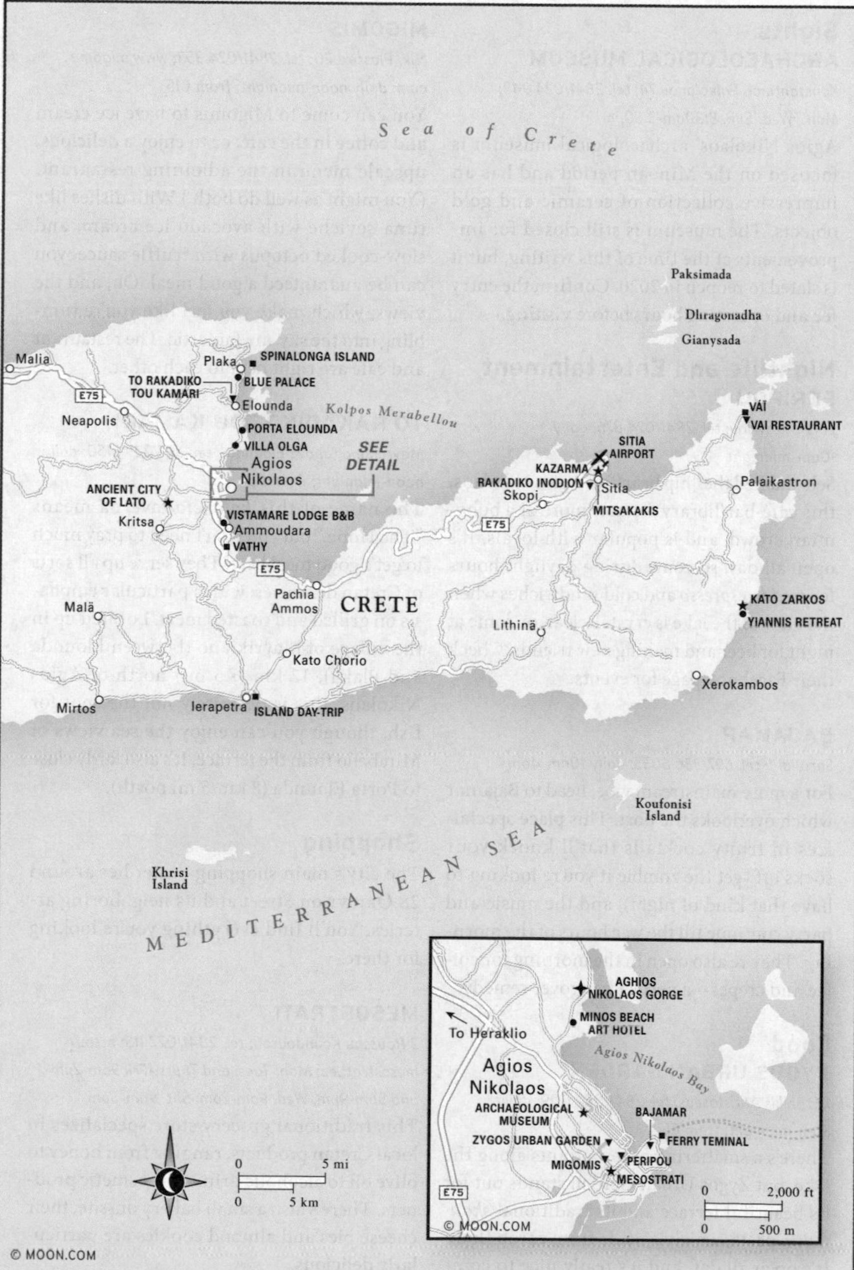
Sea of Crete
Paksimada
Dhragonadha
Gianysada
Malia
Plaka
SPINALONGA ISLAND
BLUE PALACE
TO RAKADIKO TOU KAMARI
E75
Elounda
Neapolis
Kolpos Merabellou
PORTA ELOUNDA
VILLA OLGA
Agios Nikolaos
SEE DETAIL
ANCIENT CITY OF LATO
Kritsa
VISTAMARE LODGE B&B
Ammoudara
VATHY
Pachia Ammos
CRETE
Malä
Kato Chorio
Mirtos
Ierapetra
ISLAND DAY-TRIP
VÁI
VAI RESTAURANT
SITIA AIRPORT
KAZARMA
RAKADIKO INODION
Sitia
Skopi
MITSAKAKIS
Palaikastron
KATO ZARKOS
YIANNIS RETREAT
Lithinä
Xerokambos
Koufonisi Island
Khrisi Island
MEDITERRANEAN SEA
0 5 mi
0 5 km
© MOON.COM
AGHIOS NIKOLAOS GORGE
MINOS BEACH ART HOTEL
To Heraklio
Agios Nikolaos Bay
Agios Nikolaos
ARCHAEOLOGICAL MUSEUM
BAJAMAR
ZYGOS URBAN GARDEN
FERRY TEMINAL
PERIPOU
MIGOMIS
MESOSTRATI
E75
0 2,000 ft
0 500 m
© MOON.COM

Kitroplatia (Citrus Square), which is located on the harbor at the Kitroplateia beach.

Sights

ARCHAEOLOGICAL MUSEUM

Konstantinou Paleologou 74; tel. 2841/024 943; Mon., Wed.-Sun. 8:30am-3:30pm

Agios Nikolaos' archaeological museum is focused on the Minoan period and has an impressive collection of ceramic and gold objects. The museum is still closed for improvements at the time of this writing, but it is slated to reopen in 2020. Confirm the entry fee and operating hours before visiting.

Nightlife and Entertainment

PERIPOU

28is Oktovriou; tel. 2841/024 876; daily 10am-midnight

Self-dubbed the "hip heart" of Agios Nikolaos, this café-bar/library attracts more of a bohemian crowd, and is popular with locals. It's open all day, so come during daylight hours for *freddo espresso* and cold sandwiches when the view of the lake is crystal-clear, or come at night for beer and making new friends. Check their Facebook page for events.

BAJAMAR

Sarolidi 1; tel. 697/336 6035; daily 10am-4am

For a more mainstream vibe, head to Bajamar which overlooks the port. This place specializes in fruity cocktails that'll knock your socks off (get the zombie if you're looking to have that kind of night), and the music and party continue till the wee hours of the morning. They're also open in the morning for coffee and crepes—a perfect hangover remedy.

Food

ZYGOS URBAN GARDEN

1 Ethnikis Antistaseos; tel. 2841/082 009; daily 8am-midnight; from €5

There's a smattering of restaurants along the lake, but Zygos Urban Garden stands out for its beautiful terrace and its traditional *skoufichta* pasta, which is made from carob flour. It's open all day, and it's really nice to come here for a coffee and breakfast in the morning, too.

MIGOMIS

Nik. Plastira 20; tel. 2841/024 353; www.migomis.com; daily noon-midnight; from €15

You can come to Migomis to have ice cream and coffee in the café, or to enjoy a delicious, upscale menu in the adjoining restaurant. (You might as well do both.) With dishes like tuna ceviche with avocado ice cream, and slow-cooked octopus with truffle sauce, you can be guaranteed a good meal. Oh, and the views, which make you feel like you're tumbling into the sky, are fantastic. The restaurant and café are right next to each other.

TO RAKADIKO TOU KAMARI

Mavrikiano (above Elounda); tel. 697/229 5150; daily noon-midnight; from €5

The name of this *kafeneio*/taverna means "The Hope," but you won't need to pray much to get a good meal here. They serve up all sorts of Cretan delicacies, with a particular emphasis on grilled and roasted meat. Located up in the village of Mavrikiano (between Elounda and Plaka), 12 km (7.5 mi) north of Agios Nikolaos, this is definitely not the spot for fish, though you can enjoy the sea views of Mirabello from the terrace. It's also fairly close to Porta Elounda (8 km/5 mi north).

Shopping

The city's main shopping center lies around 28 Oktovriou Street and its neighboring arteries. You'll find everything you're looking for there.

MESOSTRATI

2 Roussou Koundourou; tel. 2841/027 115; http://mesostrati.eu; Mon.-Tues. and Thurs.-Fri. 9am-2pm and 5pm-9pm, Wed. 9am-2pm, Sat. 9am-5pm

This traditional grocery store specializes in local Cretan products, ranging from honey to olive oil to alcoholic drinks to cosmetic products. There's also a small bakery on-site; their cheese pies and almond cookies are particularly delicious.

Accommodations Near Agios Nikolaos

There's not much point to staying in Agios Nikolaos proper. The best hotels (both budget and luxury) are located a few kilometers north or south of the city.

VILLA OLGA

Anapafseos 18 Ellinika; 2841/025 913; www.villa-olga.gr; from €40

If you prefer more independence on vacation, make a beeline to the charming studios of Villa Olga, run by local Michalis (English speaking). Decor is traditional with a bohemian flair, and the apartments—which include kitchenettes and sleep up to six—are ideal for families. All suites come with terraces that have views of the bay of Mirabello. Located 6 km (3.75 mi) north of Agios Nikolaos (12-minute drive).

VISTAMARE LODGE B&B

Amoudara; tel. 2841/028 886; www.vistamareapartments.com; from €100

Choose from airy and colorful studios or self-catering apartments at this beachfront lodge, which is situated around an olive grove and features a pool. Breakfast, somewhat annoyingly for a bed-and-breakfast, is an additional €7, but it's homemade. It's a good option for families. Located 5.6 km (3.5 mi) south of Agios Nikolaos (12-minute drive).

MINOS BEACH ART HOTEL

Akti Ilia Sotirchou; tel. 2841/022 345; www.minosbeach.com/el; from €290

For something close to town, head to Minos Beach Art Hotel, where, as the name suggests, there's a focus on the beach (it's a waterfront hotel) and art (there's an abundance of original works around the resort). There are four restaurants, three bars, a spa and fitness center, and everything is done up in a minimalist style. Located 1.7 km (1 mi) north of Agios Nikolaos (6-minute drive).

★ PORTA ELOUNDA

Elounda; tel. 2841 068 000; www.portoelounda.com; from €320

With its own private beach, a golf club, and top-notch wellness facilities, there's not a lot more you could want from a resort. Rooms have a bit of a business feel to them, but the addition of prints by famed Greek artist Alekos Fassianos adds a soft, artistic touch. Rooms face out onto the beach, and there's a fantastic breakfast. For dinner, head to the nearby To Rakadiko Tou Kamari restaurant (8 km/5 mi

the port city of Agios Nikolaos

north). Located 8.2 km (just over 5 mi) north of Agios Nikolaos (15-minute drive).

BLUE PALACE

tel. 2841/065 500; https://luxuryconcierge-greece.com.gr/portfolio_page/blue-palace-agios-nikolaos-crete; from €400

The fantastic five-star Blue Palace resort is 15 km (9 mi, 26-minute drive) north of Agios Nikolaos. With the steep price tag comes an endless supply of infinity pools, gauzy white fabrics, a top-notch spa, several restaurants, and an isolated beachfront with views of Spinalonga island. There are several restaurants to choose from, and it's so luxurious, you'll feel like you've melted into your four-poster bed.

ANCIENT CITY OF LATO

Lato; tel. 2841/022 462; Tues.-Sun. 8am-3pm; €2

Nestled into between two hills, Lato is famous as the birthplace of Nearchos, Alexander the Great's admiral. Given the city's importance in maritime and trade since it was founded in the 7th century BC, it's little surprise it would produce an admiral for one of the world's greatest armies. You can walk around the formerly glorious Dorian city, wandering through the Agora with its market stalls, stoa, and council house. Lato is located 10 km (6 mi) west of Agios Nikolaos (15-minute drive) on easy roads.

LASITHI OROPEDIO

Lasithi Oropedio (Lasithi Plateau) is one of the stranger faces of Crete: It's actually a series of villages built in a circle around a wide plain. The villages include Avrakontes, Aghios Georgios, Psyhro, Lagou, Tzermiado and a couple others. The villages are similar, with traditional buildings, old people hanging out in front of cafes, and shops selling local products. The villages seem stuck in time, as do the houses and windmills that dot the landscape. It's located 43 km (27 mi) southwest of Agios Nikolaos. I recommend putting aside 2-3 hours to drive between the villages—or walk if you're feeling fit—occasionally stopping to admire the view and walk around.

The most famous site in the area is Dikteon Cave (daily 8am-8pm; €6 entry, €2.50 car park), where, according to myth, Rhea came to give birth to Zeus. It's become much more of a tourist attraction in recent years, which is reflected in the price. In addition to the entry fee, there are donkeys waiting by the car park to take tourists up the steep hill (€10 one way). I recommend walking up the hill if you are able to. In the summer months, try to come early in the morning, when the cave is coolest and the crowds are thinnest.

It's worth stopping by the village of Agios Giorgous to see the Cretan Folklore Museum (daily 10am-6pm; €2) and, located just across the street, the Elftherios Venizelos Museum (daily 10am-6pm; €2 euros), which houses a collection of personal belongings of one of Greece's most important politicians.

Food

VILAETI

Agios Konstantinos; tel. 697/724 8456; daily 2pm-midnight; from €10

This traditional guesthouse also runs a restaurant, whipping up delicious Cretan meals. Their specialty is meat (we're nowhere near the sea, after all) that's roasted in the wood-burning oven. Try the asado-style lamb, called *antikristo*. This spot is popular with locals.

SITIA
(Σίτια)

The little seaside town of Sitia is a beautiful jumble of white cube houses on a green hill, arranged around a fishing harbor with boats bobbing in the bay. The jewel of Sitia is the Kazarma, the old Venetian fortress that presides over the town and has arresting views of the sea. It's much more laid-back than Agios Nikolaos (it's located 70 km/43 mi east of the city), as it hasn't been picked up by the tourist crowds (yet).

Sights

KAZARMA

Sitia; tel. 284 302 7140; Nov.-Mar. Tues.-Sun.8:30am-3pm, Apr.-Oct. Tues.-Sun. 8:30am-7:30pm; free

Easily the most beautiful site in Sitia, Kazarma is an old Venetian fort that is surprisingly well-preserved. It was built by the Venetians in the 13th century as a guards barrack (named Casa di Arma, which on Cretan tongues, got twisted into Kazarma). Later, the Ottomans fashioned it into a fortress. It's got a great view of the harbor and the town, and in the summer, there are concerts.

Food

RAKADIKO INODION

El Venizelou 157, Sitia; tel. 2843/026 166; daily noon-midnight; from €8

You'll find a bevy of restaurants lining the harbor of Sitia. The family-run Rakadiko Inodion is a cut above the rest, thanks to ingredients from their own farm (plus homemade raki and olive oil!) and beautiful interior decor. Go for the Cretan specialties, including the cheese pies and snails, plus anything that's been roasted to juicy perfection in their wood oven.

MITSAKAKIS

Karamanli 6, Sitia; tel. 2843/022 377; daily 8am-12pm; from €4

Head to the best sweets shop in Sitia for thick Greek coffee and any of their fabulous homemade desserts. I particularly like the *loukoumades* (fried dough), which you can have covered in honey or Nutella. They have a nice patio with a view of the sea, too.

Getting There

There are seven daily buses from **Sitia's bus station** (Sitia-Paleokastro-Vai Road; tel. 284 302 2272;) to Agios Nikolaos (1 hour 45 minutes; €8.30) and six buses to Heraklio (3 hours; €16).

VÁÏ BEACH

(Βαϊ)

Váï is the most popular beach in Lasithi, though until the 1980s it was something of a hippie hangout. The area around the beach is protected, as all the trees are Cretan date palms, a unique species endemic to the island. The beach is organized, with umbrellas and food/drink.

If you want the same look of Váï but with none of the organized resort vibe, head for nearby **Erimoupolis Beach,** for equally stunning sand and water. Windsurfers can head 1.5 km (1 mi) away to the blustering **Kouremeno Beach** to rent equipment and take classes (from €40) from the beachfront **Gone Surfing Crete** (Kouremenos-Plakopoules Area, Palekastro; tel. 694 142 7787; www.gonesurfing.gr).

Food

VÁÏ RESTAURANT

Vai beach; tel. 2843/061 129; www.vai-restaurant.gr; daily noon-7pm; from €8

Specializing in "creative" Cretan cuisine, Váï has been certified by the Agro Nutritional Cooperation of the Region of Crete and awarded their Cretan Cuisine quality label—you know you're getting the good stuff here. All of the products are local, and the raki and wine come from the nearby Toplou Monastery. It's located right on the beach, with a huge terrace sticking out, where you can enjoy freshly grilled fish and chopped salads with a sea breeze ruffling your hair. It's located 23 km (14.25 mi) east of Sitia, but it's worth the 30-minute drive.

Getting There

Váï is located a long 90 km (56 mi) from Agios Nikolaos; it's worth a visit only if you're staying in Sitia (24 km/15 mi). There are hourly buses to Vai from Agios Nikolaos (1 hour 50 minutes; €10 one way).

KATO ZARKOS

tel. 2843/026 897; http://odysseus.culture.gr; daily 8am-8pm; €3

Given its remote location, there's a good chance you'll have these stunning ruins of Kato Zarkos all to yourself. The area was built up around 1900 BC during the Minoan period, and though all the artifacts are now on display at the archaeological museum in Heraklio, it's still worth it to walk through the stunted walls and archways of this formerly glorious port city. This is the edge of Crete, and there's a certain lightness in the air here. You really feel like you've reached the end of the world (or at least, the Mediterannean). Kato Zakros is also located around a beautiful bay, and you can swim in the blue waters after you explore the site.

Nearby is the desolate and hauntingly beautiful **Valley of the Dead**—so called because the ancient Minoans used to bury their dead here. It's a natural gorge that forms the last section of the E4 European Trail, and is accessible at the entrance of Kato Zakros. It's a beautiful place to hike through, and it's nowhere near as crowded as the Samaria gorge. The whole trail is 5.5 km (3.5 mi, bring water and food) and ends at the beach.

Accommodations

★ YIANNIS RETREAT

Kato Zarkos; tel. 2843/025 726; from €60

The smell will hit you first at this friendly hotel—nestled in the Kato Zarkos valley, the area is full of wildflowers and herbs. It's a complex of five renovated stone houses set around a fantastically lush garden with, thankfully, hammocks for lazily passing your days. Each little house has a kitchenette equipped with basic pantry items, including fresh olive oil, and patios or terraces that look onto the garden. This is an astonishingly good value.

Getting There

It's a hike out to Kato Zarkos: 110 km (68 mi) from Agios Nikolaos (2.5 hours driving) or 44 km (27 mi, 1 hour) from Sitia. Note that the phone reception out here is quite spotty, so be sure to load your maps beforehand (or use paper).

SPINALONGA ISLAND

Before Spinalonga was popularized in Victoria Hislop's 2005 bestselling novel, the island served as a protective buffer for coastal Dorian cities; a refuge for Christian refugees and so-called "fugitive rebels"; an Ottoman port city; and finally, a leper colony from 1903-1957. Today it's got pending UNESCO World Heritage approval and a bevy of tourists who visit each summer. It's easiest to come by one of the boats that depart regularly (daily 9am-6pm) from Agios Nikolaos (€16), Plaka (€8), and Elounda (€10); all prices round-trip. The boats take about half an hour from Agios Nikolaos, and a full tour with lunch will cost you €25 (entry fee excluded). Try **Nostos Cruises** (30 Rousou Koundourou; tel. 2841/022 819; www.nostoscruises.com). Note that the tourist buses only run in the summer; if you're in the region in winter and desperately want to go to Spinalonga, you can ask the fisherman along the harbor in Plaka if they can take you.

There is an €8 entry fee to the archaeological site on the island. Once you arrive on the island, you'll walk through the 20-meter-long tunnel dubbed Dante's Gate that lepers had to walk through—presumably to their own version of hell on earth. There's a looping trail that'll take you through the island's desolate sites, ending in the cemetery.

Background

The Landscape

GEOGRAPHY

Greece is located in southwest Europe. The island of Gavdos, off the coast of Crete, is the southernmost point of the continent. To the east lies Turkey, which shares a land border with Greece, and to the west sits Italy, separated by the Ionian Sea. To its north, Greece shares a land border with Albania, North Macedonia, and Bulgaria. The total country measures 131,957 sq km (50,949sq mi).

Around 80 percent of Greece's topography is mountainous, and the country has 16,000 km (9,942 mi) of coastline, making it one of

the longest in the world. Scattered throughout the Aegean and Ionian Seas are 6,000 Greek islands, 227 of which are inhabited. Their climate ranges from lush and fertile in the west, to rocky and dry in the south.

ISLAND GROUPINGS

There are six major island groupings in Greece; this book has listings for five of them. To the west are the **Ionian** Islands, which are known for their Italian-influenced cuisine and dialect, vivid greenery, and mild climate. Across the mainland are the **Sporades** Islands, which are quieter and more laid-back. Above the Sporades Islands are the **North Aegean** Islands, which are split between proximity to northern mainland Greece and Turkey.

The **Cyclades** are located in the middle of the Aegean and feature the most islands—and some of the most famous, including Mykonos and Santorini. These islands are known for their dry climate and beaches. To the east are the **Dodecanese,** much closer to mainland Turkey than to Greece. These islands have a rugged beauty and a strong Ottoman influence.

CLIMATE

Greece is generally blessed with a Mediterranean climate, though the country also has a significant number of microclimates. Despite the country's relatively small size, there's a sizable variance in climate: Crete, the Cycladic, and Dodecanese islands have drier, hotter weather. The north of Greece sees more snowfall and cooler weather; around Thessaloniki, the humidity in the summer is through the roof. Generally speaking, the weather is warm from April to October. In the south, winter means heavy rainfall and mild temperatures; it snows in the north. There has been an increasing number of thunderstorms across Greece in the past years, which can impact travel. You'll also want to watch out for the *meltemi,* the high-frequency winds that peak in July and August across the Cycladic and Dodecanese.

ENVIRONMENTAL ISSUES

Years of government corruption, prioritizing the interests of international conglomerates and companies; the increased urbanization and development of land for agricultural use; and the lack of a comprehensive education system around the environment have all contributed to a rather depressing state of affairs in Greece. The country's major environmental issues include water and air pollution, degradation of coastal zones, overfishing, deforestation, and littering. During the economic crisis, the air quality worsened considerably as Greeks, unable to pay for the rising cost of heating, began burning painted and treated wood, and occasionally their trash, to keep warm. In the past few years, Greece has had two major economic catastrophes: a massive oil spill in the Saronic Gulf, and a devastating wildfire in Rafina (near Athens) that killed 100 people. Travelers should try to minimize their use of plastic, make sure never to leave burning cigarettes or fire embers around, and clean up after themselves.

Recycling and Garbage Collection

Plastic is a plague on Greece, and a startling amount ends up in the sea. Part of the problem is a lack of education around recycling (though private organizations led by young Greeks have started to do some excellent campaign work), and part of it is a lack of will. Greece's recycling rate is 17 percent—well below the EU threshold of 39 percent. You may notice some big blue dumpsters beside roads (though in some cases you may have to walk for a long time to find them). These are designated for recyclable materials, but 40 percent of that recyclable waste ends up in

Previous: Palm trees frame Preveli Beach.

Island Groupings

TIRANA
MACEDONIA
BULGARIA
ALBANIA
Seres
Xanthi
Thessaloniki
Katerini
Kerkira
GREECE
Aegean Sea
IONIAN ISLANDS
SPORADES
NORTH AEGEAN
Mitilini
TURKEY
Agrinio
Chalkida
Izmir
ATHENS
Adriatic Sea
CYCLADES
DODECANESE
Rodos
Mediterranean Sea
Heraklio
CRETE
0 50 mi
0 50 km
© MOON.COM

landfills. Tourism contributes to the problem as well: Tourists often leave their trash behind on the beach, where it gets swept into the sea. Make sure to collect all your trash, and bring refillable bottles, especially for filling up with iced coffee.

Most summers there's at least one strike by Greek garbage collectors. In 2018, the island of Corfu was so overrun with garbage that riot police had to be deployed to control protests against the use of an illegal landfill.

Plants and Animals

TREES

Greece was once entirely blanketed in forests, but much has been razed to make way for housing, urban expansion, animal grazing, and other activities. Athens is rather noticeably void of trees; flying over the city, you'll look down on what looks like a white block. The north of Greece has more forests, but even those are threatened, as oil companies and gold mines begin to set up large-scale operations around Chalkidiki and Epirus. On the islands, you'll still find plenty of trees, particularly olive trees, Cyprus plane, hop hornbeam, fir trees, poplars, oak trees, and cypress trees. There are plenty of beaches on the islands that are backed by fir trees; their piney scent mixed with saltwater is a very strong summer memory for most Greeks.

WILDFLOWERS AND HERBS

One of the greatest things about Greece is walking through an island in the summer, the air heavy with the smell of oregano, wild thyme, and mountain tea. With more than 6,000 species of flora, 1,600 of which are endemic, Greece accounts for half of the flora in the European Union. Aristotle was the first to try to describe all of Greece's flora and fauna; while his work was lost over time, the physician Dioscorides was able to publish "De Materia Medica" in the 1st century AD, describing more than 600 types of plants and their medical properties. Different wildflowers can be found across Greece, depending on the season. Wildflowers also feature prominently in Greek mythology, like the pink colchicum that Medusa uses to poison her own children.

MAMMALS

On the islands, you're more likely to see a well-fed stray cat, or perhaps a goat, than any other kind of exotic animal. In urban places, or where there's a sizable human population, you might see a hare, rabbit, fox, or weasel. The largest Greek mammal is the brown bear, which lives in the Pindos mountain range, though the bears are hanging on by a thread—there are only 200 of them left. They mix with the gray wolf, a protected animal that lives in Pindos and the Didia Forest Reserve area. Like the bears, there are only 200 surviving in the wild. Farmers, attempting to protect their stock, are often accused of killing the wolves. If you go to Skyros, you'll see the fantastic, tiny Skyrian horses. They're forever immortalized on the Parthenon's frieze, and in Skyros, only 70 percent of their original population remains.

SEALIFE

The Mediterranean Sea used to be teeming with sea life. Today, thanks to commercial fishing, offshore oil drilling, increased boat traffic, and climate change, numbers are declining. The most remarkable marine animals include monk seals, sperm whales, the common dolphin, loggerhead turtles, and basking sharks (totally harmless). Even ten years ago, it was common to see dolphins, but on all my ferry trips and beach jaunts, I only once saw a pod of dolphins swimming behind our small ferry to Lefkada. It's truly a fantastic site, and I hope you'll be able to see it, though it's becoming increasingly less common. There's also plenty of smaller fish in the sea, including cod, mullet, sardines, anchovies, and eels. Depending on where you're snorkeling, you'll see at least one!

Greece has two marine parks: one in Zakytnthos (National Marine Park of Zakynthos), where it serves as a refuge for loggerhead turtles; and one in Alonnisos (National Marine Park of Alonnisos), where monk seals and dolphins can live in relative peace.

BIRDS

Sitting between three continents—Africa, Asia, and Europe—Greece is a migratory point for birds and is something of a bird-watcher's paradise. Four hundred fifty different bird species have been recorded across the country, and one of the best places for birdwatching is in Lesvos, where some 279 recorded species stop annually. Sixty percent of the world's population of the rare Eleonora's falcon can be found on the islands, including Piperi in the Sporades, Tilos, and Karpathos. Everyone's favorite pink bird, the flamingo, can be found on Lemnos island. For more information on birdlife and bird-watching, visit www.birdingingreece.gr or www.ornithologiki.gr.

REPTILES AND AMPHIBIANS

Greece has a pretty diverse collection of reptiles and amphibians, including turtles, lizards, snakes, frogs, newts, and salamanders. If you're hiking in the spring or summer, you might encounter a snake; most are harmless, but there are viper and coral snakes whose bite can be extremely dangerous. In Samothrace, thanks to the abundance of rivers and streams, you'll see plenty of frogs and other little reptiles.

History

ANCIENT CIVILIZATION

The earliest known civilization in Greece was the Cycladic civilization, based in the Cyclades islands (3000-1100 BC). They were small fishing and farming communities that are particularly well remembered for their art. Picasso is said to have been inspired by the pared down, sophisticated statuettes carved from Parian marble (most are on display at the Cycladic Museum of Art in Athens). Around the same time, Crete was inhabited by Europe's first advanced civilization, the Minoans. The Minoans were so named after the mythical ruler of Crete, King Minos, and their civilization was inspired by both Mesopotamia and ancient Egypt. Minoans are best known for the construction of the architecturally complex Knossos palace; the advent of the Bronze Age helped them also build fantastically advanced boats, giving them maritime prowess (this is also how they came in contact with the Cycladic people). By establishing trade routes across Europe, Asia, and North Africa, the Minoans spread their economic prosperity.

It's still unclear exactly what led to the decline of the Minoans. One of the more popular theories is that the disastrous volcanic eruption on Santorini in 1500 BC created a strong enough tsunami and cloud of ash that it irreversibly weakened the civilization on Crete. As the Minoans were declining on the big island, the Mycenaean civilization (1600-1100BC) was rising on the mainland. Characterized by authoritarian rule and goldsmithing, the Mycenaeans were no match for the Dorians, an ancient Hellenic people who set up camp around the Peloponnese area in the 8th century. The Dorians would control many of the Greek islands in addition to the mainland, and the 400-year period of Dorian rule is often referred to as Greece's "dark age." However, the Dorians did give the local population polytheism—the precursor to the Greek gods we know of today—as well as iron smithing and more sophisticated forms of pottery.

EARLY HISTORY

The ancient Greece that the average reader is probably most familiar with, at least in passing form, is the Classic period, which was preceded by the Archaic Age (800-650 BC). By this time, the Dorians had divided Greece into a collection of independent city-states that saw the rise of Athens and Corinth. As land and wealth were redistributed, art and culture began to flourish in earnest, and important developments in architecture, literature and poetry, sculpture, theater, and philosophy began to take shape. Around this time the *Iliad* and the *Odyssey* were written, the Olympic games were founded, and the Greek alphabet was developed.

This renaissance came to a head during the 6th-4th century BC, and the rapid growth of Athens, stunted only by the Persian Wars. The leader Pericles was fundamental in shifting the center of power from Delos to Athens, and to funding massive construction projects, including the Parthenon. Growth, however, put the Athenians directly in the line of fire with Sparta, a neighboring city-state and warrior society. Sparta is most famous for its rigorous state-sponsored military training, which indoctrinated all healthy boys at the age of 7. Every Spartan male from the age of 20 till 60 stayed on active soldier duty. Sparta managed to defeat Athens during the Peloponnese War, which was destructive enough that historians point to it as the decline of Greece's Golden Age. Athens eventually surrendered and found itself under Roman rule.

At the same time, Alexander the Great (334-323 BC) was expanding his empire eastward, all the way to Central Asia. Alexander the Great, born in the ancient Greek kingdom of Macedon (now an area split between Greece and North Macedonia, and a hotly contested geopolitical topic), is one of history's most impressive military leaders. Before the age of 30, he created the ancient world's largest empire, from Greece to northwest India. Tutored by Aristotle and undefeated in battle, he remains an important icon in Greece.

Also around the same time, the Romans had expanded west into southern Greece. The Romans, however, revered Classical Greek art and learning, and this was a time of relative peace and stability. The so-called Pax Romana lasted until 250 AD.

BYZANTINE EMPIRE

The collapse of the Pax Romana was brought on by the Gothic invasion of Greece in 250 AD. The Roman Emperor Constantine I, who had converted to Christianity, shrewdly moved his center of power in an effort to bring peace from Rome to Byzantium, later renamed Constantinople. As Rome declined, this new eastern capital grew as a wealthy and strong Christian state that spread across Greece and the Balkans, despite constant opposition from the Venetians, Arabs, Persians, Slavs, Normans, Franks, and various other ethnic groups that lived in the area. During this time, some Greek islands fell, like Crete to the Arabs and Rhodes to the Persians, though most remained Byzantium. The Byzantines are also responsible for the decline of Athens' classical philosophy, which was outlawed by Emperor Justinian in 529 in favor of Christian theology. The Byzantine Empire left a lasting legacy in Greece. The Orthodox religion is still the most powerful religion in the country, and much of the country's architecture is Byzantine-influenced. But the ill-fated Crusades in 1204, in which Constantinople was sacked by the Frankish soldiers, would mark the ultimate demise of the Byzantines. To the west, the Venetians were rapidly encroaching on the Ionian islands and the western flank of the mainland.

OTTOMAN EMPIRE

May 29, 1453 marked the beginning of Ottoman rule over Greece for the next 400 years. The yoke of occupation is still indelible in many Greeks' collective memory, and Greeks often refer to this time period as *sklavia* (slavery). In reality, the Ottoman Empire was one of the least oppressive occupying forces. In exchange for agreeing to submit to Muslim rule and paying taxes, Greeks (both Christian and Jewish) were left in charge of their own religious and civil affairs, and were free to practice their religion. At the same time, there was much intermingling between different religions and cultures, including culinary, linguistic, and creative exchanges. During this time, the Greek Church grew in strength and wealth, as Greeks preferred to hand over their lands to the Church than to the Turks (to this day, the Church is the single-largest landowner in Greece). The Ottomans, for their part, preferred to deal with the administrative efficiency of a centralized Church.

The Ottomans peaked under the rule of Sultan Suleiman the Magnificent, followed by Selim the Sot, whose biggest claim was capturing Cyprus in 1570. Aside from the capture of Crete in 1669 following a 25-year war (the Cretans are renowned for their fearsomeness and strength in battle), the succeeding sultans in the later 16th and 17th centuries were largely ineffective. By the 18th century, as elsewhere in the region, pockets of Turkish officials and affluent Greeks took advantage of the Ottoman decentralized ruling approach to create pockets of self-government, as well as Greeks who began to work earnestly for independence.

INDEPENDENCE AND THE MODERN GREEK NATION

The seeds for independence began to be sown in the early 19th century, particularly in the Greek diaspora, further aided by the romantic notion of a Christian nation fighting "barbaric" Muslims that many Western European countries held about the Christian Greek nation under Ottoman Muslim rule. In 1814 the independence party Filiki Eteria (Friendly Society) was formed, and their message of a free nation burned like wildfire around the country, leading to the breakout of the War of Independence on March 25, 1821. Fighting broke out nearly simultaneously across much of Ottoman-controlled Greece and the islands. The death and destruction were equally horrific on both sides. Notably, 12,000 Turks were killed in Tripoli, and massive deaths of Greeks occurred in Chios. The Greeks scored enough victories and gained enough ground to announce their independence on January 13, 1922, but the situation escalated into civil wars in 1824 and 1825. Only with the help of the Russian, British, and French naval and military interference did the Sultan officially accept Greece's independence. After the Treaty of Adrianople, independence was officially recognized in 1830.

Despite finding itself free of the Ottomans, Greece was firmly in the hands of Britain, France, and Russia, who declared Greece a monarchy, following a rather disastrous few years wherein the first elected president of the republic, Ioannis Kapodistrias, was assassinated. Prince Otto, a 17-year-old Bavarian, was given the throne in January 1833; the inexperienced non-Greek would rule over Peloponnese, Sterea, Ellada, the Cyclades, and the Sporades rather ineffectively. He was thrown out by popular revolt in 1862, but was replaced by another European king, this time the Danish George I. His ascension is best remembered as the time Britain returned the Ionian islands to Greece, as well as a time when borders were extended, roads were built and modernized, and land reform began in the south.

A central tenet to the modern Greek state was Greece's foreign policy, known as the *Megali Idhea* (Great Idea), which would reunite the Greek ethnic populations outside the Greek borders and reclaim the old Byzantine territories. As revolts broke out, Thessaly and Epirus ceded to Greece, but despite fierce fighting, the Ottomans retained control of Crete. The big island was only officially united with Greece in 1913. Ironically, Greece's most important modern statesman, Eleftherios Venizelos, was elected the country's prime minister in 1910. An avid proponent of the *Megali Idhea,* Venizelos organized alliances to fight the Balkan Wars (1912-13), which successfully drove the Ottomans out of almost all of northern Greece and the Balkans. With the success of the wars, the borders of Greece extended to the northeast Aegean islands, northern Thessaly, central Epirus, and sections of Macedonia.

Victory got the best of Venizelos, as he launched a campaign in 1919 to invade Smyrna (modern-day Izmir), which had a predominantly Greek population. This cataclysmic failure would launch what is known in Greece as the *Katastrofi* (Catastrophe). By 1922, Turks had razed much of the city, massacring a significant portion of the Greeks and Armenians in Smyrna. For the Turks, led by Ataturk at that time, this marked a successful end to their own War of Independence. In 1923, the Treaty of Lausanne established the borders of Turkey as we know them today, and created the framework for an unprecedented population exchange based on religion; many view this as a state-sanctioned mass ethnic cleansing. About 1.3 million Christian refugees were resettled from Turkey in Greece (at a time when the population was 5 million), while Turkey brought in nearly 400,000 Muslims who had been living in Greece. This put incredible strain on the Greek and Turkish states.

WORLD WAR II

This explosive time was also marked by a series of coups (and counter-coups), which saw the monarchy abolished in 1924 and a republic restored (though the monarchy would be reinstated a few years later, in 1935). King George II brought in the right-wing General Ioannis Metaxas as prime minister. In typical right-wing fashion, Metaxas imposed press censorship, created a secret police force, suppressed any dissidents, and bolstered a fascist-tinged youth movement.

As World War II broke out across Europe, Greece faced an immediate threat from Italy, its westerly neighbor, which still controlled the Dodecanese. Despite his political learnings, Metaxas remains forever imprinted in the Greek memory for his famous 'OXI (No!) to Mussolini's ultimatum on October 28, 1940. An incensed Italy invaded, but the Greeks managed to kick them out and take control of northern Epirus. Victory was short-lived, however, as Hitler invaded Greece on April 6, 1941, quickly taking control of the whole country. During this time, the Jewish population of Greece was almost entirely wiped out. Eighty percent of industry was destroyed, 90 percent of transportation, too, and more than 11 percent of the total population was murdered or starved to death. At the same time, resistance movements mushroomed, divided along royalist and communist factions that would sadly sow the seeds for the devastating civil war to come. The Nazis began to retreat in October 1944, but the local fighting continued.

CIVIL WAR AND DICTATORSHIP

Following World War II, as the Allied powers divided up Europe, the newly formed Yugoslavia was given to the Soviets as a communist bloc, while Greece—still romanticized by the West—was kept as a right-wing, Western country. Winston Churchill specifically ignored advice about the left-wing resistance groups and made sure that only the right-wing groups received British funding and machinery. A three-year civil war ensued, wreaking even more havoc on an already fragile, shell-shocked country. Indeed, more people died during the civil war than in World War II, and by the time the fighting finished, a quarter of a million people were left homeless. The loss of life and livelihood led to a massive exodus, with nearly a million Greeks abandoning entire villages (and entire islands) to seek a better life across the oceans, in the US, Canada, and Australia. In total, 12 percent of Greece's 1940 population was killed, and the country's infrastructure was decimated.

As reconstruction began, the US began to exert overt control over Greece, enlisting the country in the Korean War and in NATO. It was also the Americans who influenced the elections, ensuring that the US-backed Greek Rally party would win the elections in 1952. The right wing dominated the political sphere, and overt leftist activity was banned. Many dissidents were killed, imprisoned, or sent into exile. After the death of General Papagos, who won the first post-civil war election, Constantine Karamanlis took over party leadership. Under his rule, there was a moment of peace, stability, and economic growth, but he resigned over issues in Cyprus and the presence of US nuclear bases in Greece.

Greece's Shipping History

The moment I realized just how prevalent Greeks were around the world was a few years ago in Honduras, when I sat down to interview a middle-aged sailor in San Pedro Sula and he started speaking to me in fluent Greek. Shipping is probably the oldest occupation by Greeks, and it's been an important part of the country's economy since ancient times. Thanks to its strategic location on the Mediterranean, with access routes to Asia, Africa, and Europe through the Balkans, and a bevy of islands to use as stopping and refueling points, Greek ports are some of the most coveted in the world. Greek sailors are some of the best in the world as well, and up to the 1980s, it was not unusual for foreign sailors to be trained on Greek boats, picking up some of the language along the way. Shipping is still the country's most important economic activity, accounting for 7.5 percent of total GDP and employing some 4 percent of the country's workforce. Most of the country's shipping activity is ruled by a handful of families with familiar names such as Onassis and Niarchos.

After Karamanlis resigned, new elections in 1964 brought the Center Union Party led by George Papandreou to power. It was the first non-right government in Greece since 1935, and Papandreou took many symbolic steps to heal Greece from the civil war, including allowing exiles to return and releasing political prisoners.

Tensions continued to grow over Cyprus and American intervention in Greece, alarming the right-wing and foreign powers. A few weeks before planned elections in May 1967, a group of colonels staged a coup and implemented a military junta that lasted for seven years. Led by chief colonel Papadopoulos, it was a dark time for Greece, with censorship, martial law, banned political parties and trade unions, imprisonment, torture and exile (including to the islands) of thousands of dissidents, and secret police to enforce it all. One of the turning points against the junta was on November 17, 1973, when tanks were sent in to the Athens Polytechnic university against a student protest. At least 20 students were murdered by the junta, and hundreds more were injured. A year later, the junta attempted a disastrous plan to unite Cyprus, provoking a Turkish invasion. Both events led to the collapse of the junta, which ushered in a new era under the New Democracy (ND) party and its leader Konstantinos Karamanlis.

CONTEMPORARY TIMES

The 1980s and 1990s were marked by general stability, though economic growth was pendulous. In 1981 Greece became the tenth country to join the EU, though it was the organization's least rich and smallest member. Still, this step opened up the Greek economy and encouraged growth, at least in the beginning. That same year the socialist party PASOK, led by Andreas Papandreou, came to power and would remain so for the next two decades (except for an interlude from 1990-95; Greek politics have essentially oscillated between PASOK and ND). PASOK's time was marked by long-overdue social reforms on women's rights and wage increases. But the late 1980s to mid-1990s were a time of economic lag. Inflation hit 25 percent and the national debt rose alarmingly high. In an echo of what would come some decades later, Papandreou was forced to take a huge loan from the European Community, with substantial austerity measures attached. The breakdown of Yugoslavia and the creation of new countries and wars along Greece's northern borders added to the difficulties of the PASOK government. It also brought a huge influx of immigrants to Greece, particularly Albanians.

By the late 1990s, growth had stabilized, and the country entered the eurozone in 2001 with a particularly self-confident swagger.

The Economic Crisis

Greece entered the new millenium in full swing, joining the EU in 2001, hosting the Olympics in 2004, and giving the impression of an affluent, healthy country with a functioning economy. That came to a screeching halt in 2008, when Greece experienced an unprecedented economic collapse that persisted for nearly a decade. A year later, then Prime Minister George Papandreou admitted that Greece had purposefully misreported its budget-deficit figures when entering the European Union after the country's fudged numbers were revealed in the now infamous LaGarde list. Political corruption (Greece is the second most corrupt country in the EU according to Transparency International) and mismanagement have long been major issues in Greece, and are partly to blame for the crisis—so are Western European countries like Germany, which gained a cool €2.9 billion from the crisis. Rating agencies were quick to downgrade the government's debt, and as interest rates soared, the economy badly contracted.

Greece's hand was forced, and it turned to the International Monetary Fund and the EU for salvation that came at a steep price: three bailout programs that cost $346 billion (€312 billion), with strict austerity measures attached. As a direct result of troika austerity measures, severe budget cuts slashed public sector funds, including money for hospitals, schools, and employee wages. The biggest impact was felt by average Greeks. Economic depression was followed by a period of stagnation. It's difficult to overstate just how difficult the economic crisis was for most Greeks: Greece has the highest unemployment in the eurozone; the rate stands at 18.6 percent, and it's as high as 40 percent for youth. The country continues to suffer from a "brain drain," as well, as educated Greeks seek employment opportunities in other E.U. countries. In 2016, 34,000 people aged 20-29 left; few have returned.

After eight torturous years Greece exited its bailout program, and on August 20, 2018, the country returned to borrowing on financial markets, prompting governments, press, and international organizations around the world to declare that Greece's economic crisis was over. Last year, the country's economy grew by 2 percent for the first time in a decade, and growth is projected at 2.2 percent for 2019. That said, real problems persist on the streets: thousands of Greeks remain unemployed or underemployed, many cannot afford homes, the birth rate continues to decline, and the public sector has yet to fully recover.

Some islands have fared slightly better, thanks to a healthy surplus of tourism. Mykonos, Santorini, and Crete, for example, have all continued to do well, and the crisis has had a less dramatic impact on those islands. All that said, though you might hear people talking about the crisis or the high taxes, it won't have an impact on your travel experience.

The Olympics were held in Athens in 2004, as were the Euro football championships. There were widespread investment projects, and the early aughts were marked by spending and a generally positive outlook. However, it would come crashing down rather quickly, when it became apparent just how much Greece (as other European countries) had fudged their figures to meet the Euro's strict criteria. The corruption that had long plagued Greek politics came to a head, when it was revealed by Papandreou that the country had a national debt of €262 billion and a deficit that was four times the euro limit. New Democracy briefly came to power in summer 2012 and accepted the terms of the EU bailouts in exchange for incredibly harsh austerity measures. Those measures, of course, fell most squarely on the heads of working and middle-class Greeks, who still suffer today. The left-wing government Syriza, which campaigned on a platform of "OXI !" (No!) against the EU, won in 2014 and again in 2016. The party leader Alexis Tsipras did not, however, say "OXI!" to Brussels, and accepted even more EU bailout terms. Disillusionment with Syriza has grown in Greece, and New Democracy has retaken power.

People and Culture

DEMOGRAPHY AND DIVERSITY

There are more than 11 million people living in Greece. As of spring 2019, there were 75,000 asylum seekers living in Greece, primarily from the Middle East, North and sub-Saharan Africa, and Central Asia. The north of Greece is a particularly ethnically diverse place, with Romani, Pomaks, Vlachs, Slavophones, Arvanites, and Turks sharing the region. Following the fall of the Ottoman Empire and the Treaty of Lausanne, Greece and Turkey agreed to a population exchange of two million. Christians living in Turkey were moved to Greece, and Muslims living in Greece moved to Turkey. Most of those who were relocated had no physical connection to their new home, and the traumatic experience has had an indelible impact on the Greek psyche. Still today, if you ask a Greek with family origins in Turkey where they are from, they will tell you from "Constantinople" (never Istanbul!), Izmir, or another Turkish city. The same goes for people with origins in the islands; they might live in Athens, but they are Cretan, or Corfiat, or Samothrakian first!

Throughout the 20th century, due to war and economic desperation, millions of Greeks moved abroad, primarily to the United States, Canada, and Australia. In some cases, entire villages were depopulated by immigration, though the remittances Greeks send back contribute greatly to the local economy, particularly in Karpathos. Greece also has a significant problem with birth rates—they've dropped 10 percent in the past few years. Coupled with an aging population, this makes for a worrisome demographic trend.

RELIGION

Orthodox Christianity

The primary religion in Greece is Orthodox Christianity, and the Church's presence is strongly felt: There are countless churches across Greece, and the Orthodox cross is a symbol strongly associated with the country. Holidays are celebrated on the Orthodox calendar, most Greeks carry an Orthodox name, priests roam the streets in full garb, and up to 90 percent of the population identifies as Orthodox. Orthodox Christianity has seeped into the everyday culture also. You'll see evil eyes dangling from car windows, people crossing themselves whenever they pass a church, and people softly spitting after complimenting you (to ward off the evil eye).

Islam

After so many centuries of Ottoman rule, there is an undeniable imprint of Islam across Greece, particularly in the northern part of the country. To this day, minarets still point skyward, and Arabic calligraphy can be found in Ottoman ruins. The Muslim minority in Greece is the only official minority group recognized by the Greek government. During the Treaty of Lausanne, around 86,000 Muslims living in Greek Thrace (northeast) were exempted from the population exchange. They still live in Greece today, and Muslims account for more than 1 percent of the total population in Greece. Aside from a historic population of Muslims, many of the refugees and asylum seekers coming to Greece in the past years are also Muslim. A mosque was finally scheduled to open in Athens during summer 2019.

Judaism

Jews have lived in Greece since the 4th century BC. In fact, one of the oldest Jewish ethnic groups in existence are Greek Jews, or Romaniote. Greece also had a significant number of Sephardic Jews in Thessaloniki. During the Ottoman Empire, Greece became a haven for Jews fleeing from the Spanish Inquisition, and at one point, Jews

Greek Mythology

Daily life in ancient Greece was structured around the worship of twelve central gods and goddesses, the integral figures in *mythos* (mythology), as well as an endless number of nymphs, mythical creatures, and others who were to be pleased or avoided. At that time Greeks believed their dues would come in this life, and the relationship between deities and mortals was based on gift-giving. The gods lived on Mount Olympus, though they could also walk among the plebeians, usually wreaking havoc. Zeus ruled Olympus, and his siblings Poseidon, Hera, Demeter, and Hestia were given other realms to control, along with his children Athena, Apollo, Artemis, Ares, Aphrodite, Hephaestus, Hermes, and Dionysus.

One of the most fascinating things about the gods is just how human they seem. All those human characteristics that seem beyond the gods—bitterness, jealousy, shallowness—feature prominently in Greek mythology, and indeed are the driving forces for a lot of the tensions and tantrums between the gods. ("Who is the nicest Greek god" is one of the top Greek mythology–related questions on Google. The answer: none). We can find a lot of ourselves in the myths around the gods; indeed, Sigmund Freud built a lasting reputation after concluding that the story of Oedipus and his mother was an expression of our psycho-sexual development as a child. Of course, immortality and impunity are what separates the humans from the gods.

Though worshipping the Greek gods may seem like a thing relegated to the past, there is a small community of modern Greeks who continue the Hellenistic practice of their ancestors. Only recognized as an official religion in 2018 after decades of discrimination in Christian Greece, the Supreme Council of Ethnikoi Hellenes has about 2,000 worshipers, with a temple in an old office building in downtown Athens. They regularly gather to pray in ancient Greek, dress in robes, and perform ceremonies.

There are hundreds of Greek gods, ruled by the twelve Olympians and Hades of the Underworld. In addition, you'll come across a countless amount of nymphs, half-gods, smaller gods, and more. Here is a couple worth knowing:

- **Zeus:** King of the Gods and ruler of Mount Olympus. In Athens, check out the Temple of Olympian Zeus.
- **Hera:** Queen of the Gods and wife of Zeus.
- **Poseidon:** God of the sea. The Temple of Poseidon is located in Sounio, an hour's drive from Athens.
- **Demeter:** Goddess of harvest and agriculture. In Naxos, you'll find the Sanctuary of Demeter.
- **Athena:** Goddess of wisdom and warfare. The Temple to Athena is located in the Acropolis.
- **Apollo:** God of light and sun, philosophy, music, and healing. In Naxos you'll find the arresting Temple of Apollo.
- **Aphorodite:** Goddess of love, fertility and beauty. In Milos you'll find a replica of the Venus de Milo.
- **Dionysus:** The youngest god, in charge of wine, festivity, and madness. In Ikaria, you'll find homages to him everywhere.

represented 68 percent of the total population in Thessaloniki. Jews made innumerable cultural, social, and economic contributions across Greece. During World War II, Nazi Germany occupied Greece, and a tragic number of Jews were murdered or sent to concentration camps. Greeks went to heroic lengths to save their Jewish neighbors from the Gestapo: In Volos, 74 percent of the Jewish population was saved, and in Zakynthos, the entire Jewish population was saved. After the war, a large portion of the remaining Jewish community moved to Israel; today there are 8,000 Jews left across Greece.

LANGUAGE

Greek is the local language throughout the country. English is widely spoken, and you will have no problems communicating in any of the major islands or towns. Most road signs are written in both Greek and Latin script, and many restaurants have menus in English. If you go off the beaten path to remote villages or far-flung islands, you'll likely encounter older Greeks who can only speak their native tongue. Though Greek can sound positively mind-boggling to the untrained ear, you likely already know more than you think—many English words are derived from Greek.

Learning a few words goes a long way: *Yassas!* ("hello"); *Efgharisto!* ("thank you"). So does a familiarity with Greek body language: two kisses to greet someone, an upward tick of the head with a click of the tongue to mean no, and a hand on the heart to express gratitude.

Greeks also have an endless stream of blessings and phrases that correlate to specific life events. *Xronia pola* ("many years") is used for birthdays and holidays. *Na tou sas zisi* ("to you to live") is said to parents for their children to live a healthy life. Greeks also have an impressive arsenal of creative curses, damning everything from the Virgin Mary to your automobile, which are entirely acceptable to use, even in Parliament.

LITERATURE

Greeks are rather prolific readers. Even during the economic crisis, the number of books (particularly poetry books) being bought actually increased. And it's no surprise; this country has produced some of the Western world's most important authors. From Herodotus (arguably the Western world's first journalist), to the prose of Homer, to the philosophical musings of Plato, to the historical overviews succinctly (if rather depressingly) written down by Thucydides, ancient Greece's contribution to literature is undeniable. A lot of modern Greek literature has been influenced by nationalism and struggles for independence, as well as deeply Greek feelings around love, honor, and family. One of the most important Greek writers to know is Nikos Kazantzakis.

Greeks also have an affinity for poetry, and have a dynamic culture around poetry. Poets are elevated in society as national heroes, like Kostis Palamas, C.P. Cavafy, and Yiannis Ritsos. One of the modern masterpieces is the Cretan resistance poem *Erotokritos;* the country's national anthem (the longest in the world) is actually a poem by Dionysios Solomos set to a musical score. George Seferis and Odysseus Elytis have both won Nobel prizes for their poetry.

VISUAL ARTS

Greece has a wonderfully rich history of visual arts, though outside of the country, only its ancient artwork—particularly sculpture—is known. Many ancient Greek sculptures feature nude, beautifully proportioned young men: The ancient Greeks did not make a distinction between art and science, but rather thought of them holistically. The result is a stunning number of pieces that stir both our soul and mind. Women were occasionally sculpted, usually to signify fertility or productivity.

Under Ottoman rule, Greece did not experience the artistic Renaissance that swept Western Europe, aside from islands like Crete or Corfu, which were under Venetian rule and did assimilate some of the major artistic transformations underway across the continent. Modern Greek art began to develop in earnest around the 19th century with Romanticism. There were limited resources for native Greek artists at the time, so most went to Munich or Paris, eventually returning to Greece with an interest in portraits and landscape. Many painters also dedicated themselves to depicting the everyday realities of Greek life, and to documenting historical moments.

The second half of the 20th century was one of the most dynamic periods for Greek art, as artists began experimenting with light and challenging notions of shape and dimension. Important figures include Constantine Andreou, recipient of the French Légion

Greek Instrument Guide

- **Baglamas:** An important *rembetika* instrument, it's a long-necked bowl-lute that is small enough to hide in a jacket (thanks to the dictatorship's ban on *rembetika* music).
- **Bouzouki:** Brought over by Greek immigrants from Turkey, the bouzouki is a pear-shaped string instrument that's often found in *rembetika* music.
- **Laouto:** a long-necked lute that has the back of an oud, which is a staple sound in Greek music, often played with the violin, lyra, and *tsampouna.*
- **Lyra:** This pear-shaped instrument with metal strings is played upright and parallel to the musician's body. It's one of the oldest island instruments.
- **Tsampouna:** The island bagpipe made of goatskin can be played alone, in a duet with another tsampouna, or with the lyra or laouto.
- **Toumbaki:** One side of this two-headed drum is struck with bone or wood drumsticks, and the whole affair is hung from the musician's body.

d'honneur; Takis, an internationally acclaimed Kinetic sculptor; Jannis Kounellis, one of the most important figures in the Arte Povera movement; and Alekos Fassianos, whose J. Dubuffet-inspired figures have effectively become symbolic of the spirit of modern Greek people.

MUSIC AND DANCE

Spend enough time in Greece, and it's likely that the patrons at whatever restaurant or bar or even street-side party you happen to stumble across will eventually break out into song and dance. Rhythm—from both music and choreography—is absolutely central to Greek life, and has been for centuries. Probably the quickest way to make friends in Greece is to bring along an instrument to any sort of social event. There's a huge diversity of music across the mainland and the islands, and customs, songs, and dance vary between islands (and even between villages).

Folk music, generally taught by ear, can be roughly divided into the *nisiotika* of the islands, and the *dimotika* of the mainlands. *Nisiotika* is more upbeat and lighter music, but the lyrics between both genres focus on universal themes of humanity: desire, love, war, freedom, the hardships of rural or seafaring life. Generally speaking, there is a strong influence from Byzantine and Ottoman music and instruments. The exception is the Ionian islands, which were occupied by the Venetians; their music is more confined to Western musical tradition. Another important musical tradition in Greece is *rembetika,* or the Greek blues, which emerged in the mid-19th century from Greece's underground and is very much tied to the artistry and struggles of the lower class and recently arrived refugees from Turkey. The music was so abhorrent to the upper echelons of society that it was actually outlawed during the Metaxas dictatorship. More recently, there has been an intellectual renaissance, and renewed, mainstream interest in and around *rembetika.* For example, the opening credits to Pulp Fiction include surf guitarist Dick Dale's rendition of the popular *rembetika* song "Misirlou."

Like music, dancing varies across the country. There are slower and more serious dances like the *tsamikos* found in the mountains, the dramatic and athletic *pentozali* in Crete, and the more bouncy and light dances of the Cycladic islands. In group dances, the steps range from a simple one-two to a more complicated rhythmic movement. In general, dancing doesn't rely on gyration of hips, but a more up-down move. If dancing's not

Panigiri

During the summer months, islands host *panigiri*, or traditional festivals that celebrate the island's main saint. Villagers gather together, bolstered by good food, alcohol, and music, to celebrate all day and night. Religious in principle, *panigiri* are usually nothing of the sort in practice. Karpathos and Ikaria have some of the most impressive *panigiri*, which are open to the public. If you go, keep an open mind and prepare to dance; it's likely that someone will grab your hand and force you into a circle. Don't worry about perfecting the steps; just do your best to follow along. You'll be lauded for trying.

PANIGYRIA ON IKARIA

Some of Greece's wildest *panigyria* occur on this island, taking place in summer on **June 24, June 29, July 1, July 17, July 27, August 6, August 15-20,** and **September 17.** The most raucous *panigyria* take place in the village of Raches, including the town's biggest, the Metamorfosi tou Sotiros (Transfiguration of the Savior) on August 6.

PANIGYRIA ON KARPATHOS

The can't-miss village of Olympos hosts its most important *panigiri* on **August 29.** Meanwhile, the village of Vroukounda hosts its own **August 28-30.** The latter is totally unique in Greece, hosted in a cave till the party moves on to the beach. Bring a sleeping bag and camp out with the locals.

There's also a big *panigiri* in the village of Menetes every **August 15.**

OTHER ISLANDS

Ikaria and Karpathos may have the wildest *panigyria,* but all the other islands have their own celebrations as well. Every church or village that you come across that bears a saint's name, and most of them will have a celebration on the Feast Day of that particular saint. August 15 is a particularly important day in Greece (second only to Easter and Christmas) as it is the day of the Dormition of the Virgin Mary.

- **Naxos:** August 15; village of Filoti
- **Kalymnos:** August 15; Panagia Kyra Psili Monastery
- **Lesvos:** August 15; Petra's Panagia Glykofilousa
- **Corfu:** August 15; town of Kassiopi
- **Crete:** August 15; Vamos Village
- **Zakynthos:** August 24; Zakynthos Town's Church of St Dionysios
- **Santorini:** October 20; village of Finikia

your thing but you still want to join in, you can bend on one knee and clap your hands to the beat.

FESTIVALS AND EVENTS

Greece's calendar is governed by the Greek Orthodox religion. Throughout the year, there are dozens of festivals to celebrate the holy days. The biggest celebration takes place on **August 15** (Feast of the Assumption). Athens is a ghost town as city dwellers leave in droves for the islands. **Orthodox Easter** is another important holiday (the date, which changes yearly, has nothing to do with the non-Orthodox Easter date), and is celebrated with local flair. In Corfu, residents drop giant red pots from balconies.

Essentials

Getting There

If you're coming from the US, you'll most likely fly into Athens and then either take a connecting flight to the islands (especially those that are far away, like Crete or Rhodes) or spend a couple of days exploring Athens before heading to Piraeus port. I personally love the ferries, and I think it's an experience you should try at least once in Greece. If you're coming from the UK, you'll have many more options to fly directly to the islands. This is a good choice if you're short on time or visiting one larger island, like Crete.

AIR

Airports

In addition to smaller island airports, Greece has four main international airports:

- **Eleftherios Venizelos International Airport** (ATH; tel. 210/353 0000; www.aia.gr), located 27 km (16.75 mi) east of Athens
- In Thessaloniki, **Macedonia International Airport** (SKG; tel. 231/098 5000; www.thessalonikiairport.com), 17 km (10.5 mi) southeast of the city
- In Crete, **Nikos Kazantzakis International Airport** (HER; tel. 281/039 7800; www.heraklion-airport.gr) is 5 km (3 mi) east of Heraklio
- **Diagoras Airport** (RHO; tel. 224/10 8 8700; www.rhodes-airport.org) in Rhodes

Airports on the following islands have international flights:

- Santorini (JTR)
- Mykonos (JMT)
- Rhodes (RHO)
- Lesvos (MJT)
- Lefkada (PVK)
- Corfu (CFU)
- Zakynthos (ZTH)
- The Cretan cities of Heraklio (HER) and Chania (CHQ)

Airports on the following islands have only domestic flights:

- Milos (MLO)
- Naxos (JNX)
- Karpathos (AOK)
- The Cretan city of Sitia (JSH)
- Kalymnos (JKL)
- Ikaria (JIK)
- Skyros (SKU)

There are no airports on Folegandros or Anafi. Santorini is the nearest airport to both of these islands. Samothrace and Alonnisos are also without airports and are best accessed via ferry from the mainland.

Airlines

FLYING FROM THE US

Emirates (www.emirates.com) has a direct flight between Athens and Newark. These tend to be the most expensive but best-quality flights, and you get a two-bag allowance. In summer, **Delta Airlines** (www.delta.com) runs two daily nonstop flights from New York to Athens. **American Airlines** (www.aa.com) runs direct summer flights from Philadelphia to Athens. There are currently no direct flights from the West Coast to Athens. There are no direct flights from any state in the US to any of the Greek islands—you will need to transfer either in a European hub or in Athens.

FLYING FROM EUROPE

Aegean Airlines (tel. 801/112 0000; www.aegeanair.com) is Greece's national carrier and has been consistently voted one of the top airlines in Europe. Its subsidiary is **Olympic Air** (tel. 801/801 0101; www.olympicair.com); both have regular flights around Europe.

Easyjet (tel. 210/967 0000; www.easyjet.com) offers very cheap tickets between European hubs and Athens and Thessaloniki as well as some of the islands, including Corfu, Crete, Mykonos, Santorini, Zakynthos, and Lesvos, as does **Ryanair** (www.ryanair.com), though you'll be choosing money over comfort and the bag allowance is miniscule.

FLYING FROM AUSTRALIA AND NEW ZEALAND

Budget airline **Scoot Airways** (www.flyscoot.com) currently has the cheapest travel between Australia and Greece. **Air China** (www.airchina.com) currently has the cheapest travel between New Zealand

Previous: Cruise ship near Mykonos.

Getting to the Islands: By Ferry or Plane?

Although flying can be quicker and cheaper, travel between the Greek islands is best experienced slowly, and by boat, as it has been for thousands of years. Approaching the island of Santorini in late afternoon, just as the setting sun glitters on the Aegean Sea, is as magical an experience as it sounds.

That being said, if you are traveling on a budget, be sure to compare to the prices between planes and ferries; sometimes the plane tickets can be significantly cheaper than the boat. Flying to some islands cuts down significantly on time as well. The ferry from Piraeus to Lesvos takes 16 hours, but a flight takes less than one. If you are only visiting one island, far from the coast, it's worth it to fly; if you are covering a cluster of islands or visiting those just a few hours from Athens, the boat is your best option.

and Greece. **Qatar Airways** (www.qatarairways.com), which has fantastic economy-class options and some of the best business seats in the world, runs flights from New Zealand and Australia to Greece with a stop in Doha. **Singapore Airlines** (www.singaporeair.com) offers flights from Australia and New Zealand to Greece with a stopover in Singapore.

FLYING FROM SOUTH AFRICA

EgyptAir (www.egyptair.com) runs flights from Johannesburg to Athens with a stop in Cairo. **Qatar Airways** (www.qatarairways.com) offers flights from South African cities to Athens with a stop in Doha. **Air France** (www.airfrance.com) flies from Cape Town to Athens with a stop in Paris.

FERRY AND CRUISE SHIP

International Routes

There are ferries run by multiple companies, including **ANEK Lines** (www.anek.gr), **Blue Star** (www.bluestarferries.com), **Grimaldi Lines** (www.grimaldi-lines.gr), **Hellenic Seaways** (www.hellenicseaways.gr), **Superfast Ferries** (www.superfast.com), and **Minoan Lines** (www.minoan.gr), from Italy to Igoumenitsa in western Greece (also occasionally stopping in Corfu or Zakynthos). There are also ferries run by multiple companies, including **Sea Dreams** and **Phoenix Marine,** from the Turkish coast to several Dodecanese islands, including Rhodes and Lesvos.

From Mainland Greece to the Islands

A comprehensive network of ferries connects Greece's mainland ports (Piraeus, Rafina, Lavoro, Igoumenitsa, Kymi, Volos, Agios Konstatntinos, Alexandroupoli, and Kyllini) to the major inhabited islands. Overnight ferries leave regularly to the most far-flung islands, like Karpathos and Lesvos, while high-speed ferries are a good option for medium-distance islands like Mykonos. Pricing depends on the ferry's speed, and the season (there are deep discounts during the winter months).

PORTS

Piraeus (the main access point for most of the islands in this book), **Rafina,** and **Lavrion** are all fairly easy to access from Athens. However, these ports don't serve the following islands. Here's how to get to each one from a mainland port:

- **Samothrace:** Head to **Alexandroupoli,** an hour-and-a-half flight from Athens.
- **Alonnisos:** Head to **Volos** and **Agios Konstantinos,** a 3-hour drive from Athens.
- **Skyros:** Head to Kymi in Evia, a 3.5-hour bus ride from Athens.

- **Corfu:** Head to **Igoumenitsa,** 470 km (292 mi, 7 hours) northwest of Athens.
- **Zakynthos:** Head to **Kyllini** or **Igoumenitsa,** a respective 287 km (178 mi, 3 hours) and 470 km (292 mi, 7 hours) northwest of Athens. Buses are available from the Athens' main bus terminal to the ports.

Lefkada has no mainland ferry access. However, you can access it easily by plane, bus, or car. (It's connected to the mainland via underwater tunnel.)

BUYING FERRY TICKETS

There is no official government-run website for Greek ferries, but there are several private websites where you can buy tickets. The sites **www.ferries.gr** and **www.ferryhopper.com** are good options. If you are planning multiple trips to different islands, though, I suggest going through a tour operator who can help you book your tickets. **Priority Travel & Tourism** (Sofokelous stoa inside the alley; tel. 210/331 4476; www.prioritytravel.gr) in Athens is one good option. You can also buy tickets directly at the port, though I suggest that you do this only on return trips from more relaxed islands. (Navigating the ticketing at Santorini or even Piraeus is not for the faint-hearted.)

On overnight trips, you can book a private cabin or first-class seats. Cabins are worth it on long trips to Crete or Lesvos; first-class seats usually mean you're sitting on airplane-style seats next to a window. Slow ferries are longer, as the name implies, and cheaper. These are also the only ferries big enough to hold vehicles, and they're preferred by Greeks who bring their personal car on vacation. Note that car rental companies will not let you bring your rental car on ferries.

RIDING THE FERRY

Fast ferries usually have assigned seating; slow ferries only have assigned seating if you purchase air seats (instead of general seating). Boats are usually comfortable and hilariously decorated like the inside of a 1980s hotel. Fast ferries have snack bars, and the overnight boats have full restaurants. My Greek husband has a special place in his heart for "boat Bolognese," a spaghetti dish that I guess speaks to the childhood memories of many Greeks! In general, though, food is overpriced and not that good (it's also not included in the price of your ticket). I always pack plenty of snacks and water. Plus, it's fun to share snacks with your fellow passengers.

On slow ferries, my biggest tip is to park yourself on a comfortable couch; these are the prime spots on the boat and are especially coveted on overnight ferries where people haven't sprung for a cabin. For quicker trips, I like to take a seat on the deck and watch the world go by.

You likely won't get seasick on the big, slow boats, but if you are prone to seasickness, it's best to pack some medication. Sometimes the air-conditioning can be on full blast; I like to bring a big cozy scarf or even a blanket up on deck with me.

TRAIN

Greece is part of the **Eurail** network (www.eurail.com) and the **Inter-Rail Pass** system (www.interrail.com), as well as the **Rail Plus Balkan Flexipass** (www.raileurope.com). Train lovers can ostensibly take the train from London all the way to Athens in two days, with stops in Paris, Vienna, Budapest, the Balkans, and Athens.

Greek railway organization **Oranismos Sidirodromon Ellados** (14511; www.trainose.gr) runs multiple daily trains from Athens to Thessaloniki and vice versa (half rate at night). From Thessaloniki there are trains to Belgrade (via Skopje) and Sofia, with a weekly onward train to and from Budapest.

Getting Around

Aside from really tiny, walkable islands like Alonnisos or Anafi, it's best to rent your own scooter, ATV, or car for at least part of your trip. While islands do have a pretty reliable bus service that will take you to the most touristic destinations, you'll be tied to a schedule and unable to visit more unique sites. Note that hitchhiking is a pretty common practice on the smaller islands.

Villages and cities on the islands are all walkable. Most of the islands have a town called Hora—this is just the Greek word for village—that can range from a few streets to a larger town.

CAR

Road Rules

The **minimum driving age** in Greece is 18, though most places won't rent to you unless you're 21, and bigger cars will only be rented to those above the age of 23.

EU drivers can drive in Greece with their country's **driver's license.** American drivers will need an international driving license.

Seatbelts are required in the front seat. Children under 12 years old are not allowed to sit in the front seat (though this rule is regularly, and brazenly flouted across the islands).

As of 2019, **smoking** in your car nabs you an eye-watering €1,500 fine.

The **blood alcohol limit** is 0.04 percent. At 0.05 percent you'll be fined €150; anything over 0.08 percent is considered a criminal offense. Honestly, dude, just call a taxi.

On highways the **speed limit** is 120 km/hour (75 mi/hour); 90 km/hour (56 mi/hour) on country roads; 50 km/hour (31 mi/hour) in the city. There are an increasing amount of CCTV in Greece, especially on the highway. If you drive 20 percent over the speed limit, you'll be fined €60; over 40 percent costs €150. You have two months to pay the fine.

Driving on the Islands

Island roads are notoriously difficult to drive. Most of the Greek islands are mountainous, and the roads are two-lane, 1960s-style roads without lights or guard rails. There are still plenty of places that have dirt or unpaved roads, and if you want to visit remote beaches, you'll need to rent a car with 4WD.

Most island rental companies have an excess of manual cars; for automatic transmission, make sure to book ahead of time.

The biggest hazards of the islands are other drivers—your fellow tourists, who creep along slowly and confused—and the Greeks, who plow forward at breakneck speed and double park cars illegally. My best tips are to drive defensively, don't use your phone while driving, and have someone with you to navigate.

Parking

Ah, parking in Greece: an exercise in patience. Forget it in places like Mykonos or Santorini; you will lose your mind trying to find a spot in the Hora in the height of summer. It's easier to find parking in smaller villages and on beaches. In most places, parking is free (and it's always free on Sundays), but you should have some cash on hand for city parking.

SCOOTER

The biggest benefits of a scooter are 1) you'll live that romantic dream you have of riding a scooter in Greece while clutching a handsome man/woman with the wind in your hair, and 2) it's easier to find parking. That being said, if you don't know how to drive a scooter or ATV, a Greek island shouldn't be your first time. Rental companies don't check your experience level, but you don't want to suddenly find yourself trying to drive a scooter up switchbacks, surrounded by a dozen honking cars.

BUS

The Greek bus network is comprehensive and operated by **KTEL** (www.ktelbus.com), which manages the long-distance buses as well as island buses. Bus fares are fixed by the government and it remains one of the cheapest ways to travel (approximately €5 per 100 km/62 mi). Buy tickets ahead of time in the station.

TAXI

Taxis are available on every island, and there's a particularly heart-warming amount of women taxi drivers on the islands. You don't need to tip drivers, but I usually round up to the nearest euro. It's best to carry small bills.

Visas and Officialdom

PASSPORTS AND VISAS

Greece is a member-state of the European Union (EU), and normal EU travel rules and restrictions apply. Your passport should have at least six months validity and one blank page for a stamp. Currency restrictions for entering and exiting the country are capped at €10,000.

United States and Canada

American and Canadian passport holders can stay in Greece up to three months without a visa. If you want to spend more than three months in Greece within a six-month period, apply for a visa from your country of residence's Greek embassy or consulate.

European Union/Schengen

Greece is part of the Schengen Zone, and EU passport holders do not need visas. You can also enter Greece with your European I.D. card.

Australia and New Zealand

Australians and New Zealand passport holders can stay in Greece up to three months without a visa. If you want to spend more than three months in Greece within a six-month period, apply for a visa from your country of residence's Greek embassy or consulate.

South Africa

South African passport holders need a Schengen visa to enter Greece. Visas can be obtained through the embassy or consulates in Johannesburg, Cape Town, or Durban. Plan at least two to three months ahead for visa application.

EMBASSIES AND CONSULATES

- **US Embassy** (91 Vasilissis Sofias, Ilissia, Athens; tel. 210/721 2951; www.athens.usembassy.gov) with a branch in Thessaloniki (Tsimiski 43 7th floor; www.gr.usembassy.gov)
- **Canadian Embassy** (Ethnikis Antistaseos 48, Halandri, Athens; tel. 210/727 3400; www.greece.gc.ca)
- **UK Embassy** (Ploutarchou 1, Athens; tel. 210/727 2600; www.ukingreece.fco.gov.uk) with a branch in Thessaloniki (Tsimiski 43; tel. 231/027 8006; www.britishconsulate.net/Thessaloniki)
- **Australian Embassy** (5 Hatziyianni Mexi Street, Athens; tel. 210/870 4000; https://greece.embassy.gov.au)
- **Consulate General of New Zealand** (Leof. Kifisias 76, Athens; tel. 210/692 4136; www.mfat.govt.nz/en/countries-and-regions/europe/italy/new-zealand-embassy/new-zealand-consulate-general-athens-greece)
- **South African Embassy** (Leof. Kifisias 60, Marousi, Athens; tel. 210/617 8020; www.dirco.gov.za/foreign/sa_abroad/sag.htm)

Accommodations, Food, and Nightlife

ACCOMMODATIONS

With nearly 10,000 hotels across mainland Greece and the islands, you can find whatever you're looking for at any price point. Greek accommodations are regulated by the tourist police, and are subject to strict price controls. Prices generally double to the maximum legal price during the summer months; in the off-season costs drop dramatically. Prices include VAT and tax, but note that a mandatory charge of 20 percent is added for an extra bed (usually ignored if it's for a young child).

Hotels and pensions are divided into A, B, C, D, and E categories. A, B, and C have private bathrooms, while D and E have shared bathrooms. Nearly all of the hotels listed in this guide are in the A, B, and C categories. Some pensions and hostels are D and E categories; shared bathrooms have been indicated.

A popular option for budget travelers are ***domatia*** ("rooms"), which are bare-bones accommodations that cost €30-80 a night. On the islands, a lot of tavernas also have some rooms for rent, and in the summer *domatia* owners will come to the port hawking their rooms. **Camping** is another good option, and there are 350 campgrounds across the country, usually open between April and October. For a comprehensive list of campgrounds, check the **Panhellenic Camping Association** (tel. 210/362 1560; www.greece-camping.gr).

Airbnb and **apartment rentals** are increasingly common on the islands, though they're not always cheaper than hotels. I suggest renting a larger apartment or house if you are with a big group of friends and family, or are planning on staying a longer amount of time in one place. Although you'll notice some hostility toward Airbnb in Athens (rents have been hiked up for the local population because of it, and there have been some protests around the issue), this is less the case on the islands.

Bellhops expect a €2-3 **tip.**

FOOD

There's a good reason the Mediterranean diet has reached such worldwide popularity. With a focus on fresh and local products, Greek food is both delicious and healthy. Aside from some more conceptual restaurants in Athens and Mykonos, Greek food is staunchly traditional and based in grains, vegetables, olive oil, meat, and fish. The Aegean and Dodecanese islands were dominated by the Ottoman Empire for centuries, and you'll notice cross-culinary traditions between Turkey and Greece; Italy's influence on the Ionian islands is strongly felt in Zakynthos and Corfu.

Cooking preparations are deceptively simple: Meats are roasted, stews slowly bubble away, octopus is dried in the sun, but Greek cuisine mainly stands out for its incredible quality. The country has over 1,600 endemic plants—that's more than 50 percent of the total European Union—that are used to flavor dishes. Fertile soil tinged with salty seawater gives island-grown produce an amazing taste, and the animals that graze on the island grass have a unique flavor. The seas are rich with fish and crustaceans, grilled to perfection and served with freshly squeezed lemon. Each island has its own specialty, like hand-rolled pasta from Karpathos or tomato fritters from Santorini. All this said, you can still eat badly in Greece, especially if you go to the tourist trap restaurants or chain bakeries. A good tip is to always look for restaurants that don't have moussaka (they only put it on there for tourists) or book-sized, plastic menus that are written in various languages.

A server will bring you your check at the end of the meal, usually with a free shot of alcohol and/or dessert (this is particularly true in Crete and on some of the smaller, less touristic islands). You can also flag down your waiter for the check, or make the universal hand scribble gesture. You can sit for a longer time at the table once you're finished, talking and drinking your raki, as long as there isn't a huge line of people waiting.

Restaurant Types

I can't tell you the number of times I've seen tourists patiently waiting for someone to seat them at an *estiatoria* or *tsipuradika.* Unless it's a fancier restaurant with a very obvious *maitre d'*, you seat yourself in Greece. At the below places, a server comes to take your order; you usually only order from the counter if it's a souvlaki joint or fast-food restaurant.

- ***Esiatoria:*** Meaning "restaurant," *esiatoria* have cooked, prepared foods waiting to be served, plus meats and fish grilled *tis oras,* (to order, or literally "on the hour").
- ***Psistaria:*** These are grill houses that are usually found in less populated areas.
- **Taverna:** A taverna is very similar to an *esiatoria,* the difference being that tavernas usually have smaller tables covered in paper tablecloths. My favorite thing is that each island usually has its own type of tablecloth with a map of the island and some important Greek phrases written in English and Greek, so you can learn something while you wait for your food.
- ***Psarotavernas:*** This literally means "fish taverna," and it's just that: a taverna specializing in fish. These are most commonly found along the beach.
- ***Tsipuradikas:*** The closest equivalent to a tapas bar (though most Greeks might take offense to that!), these are places where a bottle of *tsipuro* comes with small plates of meze (snacks) that are meant to partially sop up the alcohol. It's a quintessentially Greek environment, and you should try to go to one at least once. There's usually live music. A similar style of restaurant also serves raki with the same music/meze concept.

Meals and Meal Times

Lunch is usually the biggest meal of the day, and it's best enjoyed in a local taverna over several hours. Dinner is a smaller version of lunch (though still copious), while the local joke is that a Greek breakfast is coffee and cigarettes. Keep the coffee but ditch the cigarette for local pies made with flaky phyllo dough and stuffed with a variety of fillings. Different islands or places on the mainland have their own special flavors. In Folegandros, for example, the local specialty is watermelon pie. Vegans should try *hortopita,* which is wild greens in phyllo dough without butter or cheese.

Lunch is eaten around 1pm or 2pm, while dinner is between 8pm and 10pm. Meals can stretch on for a long time, and if you are invited to someone's house, you shouldn't show up empty handed. The quintessential Greek host gift is a bouquet of flowers and some sweets.

Dietary Restrictions

A growing number of restaurants offer gluten-free options. Greece largely adheres to a Mediterranean diet, so there are naturally plenty of options for vegetarians and pescatarians. Once a year, religious Greeks fast before Easter and stick to a vegan diet (plus seafood) that's called *nistisimo.* Vegans can always ask for *nistisimo* foods in a restaurant or bakery, and they'll be given foods cooked without butter, cream, cheese, or meat. Most ice cream parlors have sorbet options as well, and a lot of Greek desserts, like halva, are naturally vegan.

Tipping

Waiters and bartenders make a living wage and don't rely on tips. Service charges are usually included in the price; however, it is customary to leave a few coins.

Greek Cuisine

Greece is the only country I know of where people can talk about food for hours—I mean that literally. I'll often overhear my husband or close friends on the telephone recounting in exquisite detail the merits of one recipe for stuffed vegetables over another, or the precise taste of a Cretan tomato.

Greek cuisine focuses on simple, fresh ingredients, and slow-cooked foods preserved with olive oil. Common ingredients include olives, dairy (from goat, sheep, and cow's milk), whole grains, seasonal vegetables and fruit, fresh herbs and wild greens, fish, and meat (including goat, lamb, and beef). Many dishes are inspired by Ottoman times, and you'll notice plenty of similarities with Turkish food, particularly in the Dodecanese and North Aegean islands. The Ionian islands are more influenced by Italy. Though you'll be tempted to taste many creative twists on food, don't forget that the national dish of Greece is bean soup, and therein lies a perfect truth: the simplest food is often the best.

MEZE AND SALADS

Most restaurants offer a selection of meze to start your meal; if you go to a *tsipuradiko* or *ouzeri*, you'll be served meze along with your drinks. Below is a sampling of traditional meze and salads to start your meal. It is also common to eat cheese at the start of the meal in Greece.

- ***Tzatziki:*** This dip made of strained yogurt, cucumber, and salt is usually served alongside fried vegetables or patties. (It's rare to order tzatziki alone to eat on bread; only tourists do this!)
- ***Fava:*** Pureed fava beans are often served with caramelized onions. Santorini is famous for having the best fava beans.
- ***Dakos:*** Dried barley rusks are served with raw vegetables and olive oil.
- ***Saganaki:*** This fried cheese is often served with a savory marmalade.
- ***Horiatiki Salad:*** Also known as Greek salad, this is a simple combination of peppers, cucumbers, onions, tomatoes, olive oil, and olives (no lettuce!), served with a slice of feta cheese.

SEAFOOD

- ***Kalamari:*** This is squid, either fried or grilled; you'll sometimes find it stuffed.
- ***Baccalaro:*** Salty cod is usually served with potatoes and a pungent garlic sauce.

BAKED DISHES

- ***Yemista:*** In this dish, seasonal vegetables are stuffed with a mixture of rice and meat, sometimes served with *avgolemono* (an egg-and-lemon sauce that's similar to hollandaise).

NIGHTLIFE

Drinking is a normal and encouraged part of Greek culture. It's rude to decline a glass, so be prepared to drink whatever is offered to you, and to lift your glass and say, *"Yammas!"* (cheers). Most drinks are derived from grapes: ouzo, *tsipouro* (a distilled liquor made from grapes), and wine are some of the islands' preferred beverages. While Greeks do drink a lot, it's usually accompanied by mezes (small snacks) that absorb the alcohol and keep the drunken debauchery at bay.

Although each island's town has bars, restaurants, and live music venues, nightlife does vary greatly between the islands. Mykonos is legendary for its beach bars and discos filled with celebrities and models, though you'll have to dress the part and shell out the cash to gain access. Everyone is beautiful in Crete and seems to dress the part too, while in

- ***Moussaka:*** This is a layered vegetable dish with meat, eggplant, potatoes, tomato, and bechamel sauce.
- ***Pastitsio:*** Like Greek lasagna: This baked pasta dish is made of ground beef, long hollow noodles, bechamel sauce, and cheese.
- ***Gigandes:*** "Giant" beans are baked in a tomato sauce with herbs.
- ***Spanakorizo:*** A great vegetarian option, this is a mixture of rice, spinach, herbs, and lemon.

MEAT

You'll find plenty of baked and grilled options for meat, including:

- ***Souvlaki:*** These grilled skewers of meat are usually made with pork, though you'll also find chicken, beef, or lamb versions.
- ***Soutzoukakia:*** Spicy meatballs are served in tomato sauce.
- ***Giovetsi:*** In this dish, lamb is cooked in a clay pot.
- ***Gyros:*** Usually pork (but sometimes beef or chicken, or a combination) meat is cooked on a rotating spit that is sliced and eaten in sandwiches with pita bread and vegetables.

SWEETS

Greeks love their sweets, and you'll see plenty of pastry shops and bakeries dotting the islands. Fruit is often served at the end of meals, or strained yogurt with walnuts and honey, but there will always be other dessert options, too.

- ***Baklava:*** This dessert is made of phyllo pastry swimming in honey and nuts (pistachio is considered the best).
- ***Loukoumades:*** Fried donuts are served with powdered sugar, honey, or Nutella.
- ***Galaktoboureko:*** This custard pie is made with phyllo, and is often drizzled with an orange or lemon sauce.
- ***Halva:*** There are two types of halva in Greece: the dense confection made of tahini and sugar or honey and flavored with chocolate, vanilla, nuts or dried fruit; and the cake halva, made of semolina flour. If it's being offered at a restaurant for dessert, it's probably the latter.

more laid-back islands like Alonnisos and Samothrace, you can get away with more beachy outfits. Corfu, which has a large university, caters more to students, and blockbuster islands like Lefkada, Zakynthos, and Rhodes are full of British stag and hen parties. In general, Greeks clean up when going out, and you'll want to at least change out of your bathing suit and brush the sand off your feet to go out.

Bars start picking up around 11pm. The legal closing time for Greek bars and restaurants is 3am, though this isn't always followed and places generally stay open until the last customer leaves. Any situation can turn into a party in Greece, though, so go with the flow to have the best time.

Conduct and Customs

Though it's impossible to sum up this dynamic culture, this quintessential Greek phrase gives good insight into the local psyche: *pan metro ariston* ("everything with a measure").

GREETINGS

Greeks customarily kiss twice on the cheek (between all sexes), though if they are meeting you for the first time, a handshake is more normal. There are also specific greetings depending on the holiday, the day of the month, or someone's birthday or name day.

SMOKING

Greece ranks 12th in the world for smokers, and smoking is a firmly entrenched part of the culture. In September 2010 Greece passed a law banning smoking in public places. This law is so regularly flouted that even the country's minister of health appeared in a televised conference smoking a cigarette. Most bars, music venues, and restaurants still allow smoking (aside from wine bars and fancier restaurants), which can be really difficult for nonsmokers. As of 2019, the newly elected (or rather, re-elected) New Democracy party promised to crack down on smoking indoors. If you want to avoid smoking in the summer, you should probably head indoors—everyone will be sitting outside and smoking.

DRUGS

Greek law does not distinguish between drug possession or acquisition for personal use vs. commercial use. It is illegal to carry any drugs for personal use, even marijuana, and if you're caught with a small amount, you could get sent to jail for up to five years. That said, cannabis is widely consumed in Greece, and in certain neighborhoods in Athens or on beaches it's not uncommon to catch a whiff of weed. On party islands like Mykonos or Rhodes, as well as Athens, drugs like Ecstasy, MDMA, and cocaine are prevalent. Since the crisis, there's been a tragic increase in the number of heroin and *sisha* (a hardcore drug made from gasoline and shampoo) users; in central Athens, you might find people shooting up directly in the street.

DRESS

There is no particular dress code (although Greeks generally err on the side of fancy) in daily life. You can enter village churches or roadside churches wearing anything you like, though if you are going to a bigger church with more people, it's a sign of respect for men and women to cover their shoulders and knees. At larger churches, women are required to cover their knees and shoulders, and are provided with scarves if they aren't "modest" enough.

BUSINESS HOURS

Between 3pm and 5pm each day you will find most shops and cafés closed in towns and villages across the island. The relentless heat reaches its peak during these hours, and it's considered rude even to call someone or make noise in your house at this time. That being said, most island economies depend on the tourist season, and shops and restaurants may be open all day, and late into the night. Almost all shops and supermarkets are closed on Sundays. Opening hours for different business are as follows:

- **Banks:** Mon.-Thurs. 8:30am-2:30pm, Fri. 8am-2pm, closed weekends and holidays
- **Post Offices:** Mon.-Fri. 7:30am-2pm in rural places plus Sat. in urban areas
- **Shops:** Mon., Wed., Sat., 8am-3pm; Tues., Thurs., Fri. 8am-2:30pm and 5pm-8pm or all day

Health and Safety

While Greece is generally a safe country, it's a good idea to be up to date on your vaccines and to bring plenty of sunscreen and mosquito repellent. The Greek islands lend themselves to excess, and perhaps the most dangerous thing is the allure of hedonism. Overeating, over drinking, and spending too much time in the sun are common culprits for headaches, hangovers, stomach aches, and sun burns. A few other health and safety tips:

In high tourist areas, like Mykonos or Santorini, be aware of **pickpockets.** Don't carry more money than you need for the day, and keep your phone and wallet off the table when you eat outdoors. Keep your bag close to you, with the zipper facing inwards, and don't stop if someone bumps into you or asks you to sign a strange petition. Pickpockets usually work in teams, and one will try to distract you while the other goes for your bag.

Most beaches have no lifeguards, so keep an eye on your children. (In general, the seas around the islands are calm and clear, without jellyfish, but it's best to be cautious.)

Greece does have a high rate of **motor accidents** (the little churches that dot the roadsides are memorials to victims). If you are renting a car or motorcycle, drive defensively and be aware of drunk drivers, particularly at night. Always wear a helmet if you're on a motorcycle.

It is safe to drink the **tap water** on the mainland, though in most of the islands, including Mykonos and Santorini, you should stick to bottled water.

EMERGENCY NUMBERS

- **Emergency:** 112
- **Ambulance:** 166
- **Fire Department:** 199
- **Police:** 100
- **Anti-drug Police:** 109
- **Coast Guard:** 108
- **Tourist Police:** 171

PHARMACIES

Pharmacies are a dime a dozen in Greece, and are marked with a flashing green cross. Note that they close on Wednesday afternoons and Sunday. You can buy skincare products, shampoo, female hygiene products, over-the-counter pills, diabetes-approved snacks, sunscreen, etc. Medicine for heartburn and constipation can be bought at any pharmacy. I particularly like the local Greek brands of Frezyderm, Korres, and Apivita.

Practical Advice

MONEY

Currency

Greece is part of the eurozone and uses the euro, though some would like to return to the *drachma* (Greece's old currency). It's a good idea to carry small denominations of cash on you, and I wouldn't go out with more than €200 at a time, in case of loss or theft.

Currency Exchange

You can change your money at the airport, at currency exchange shops in town, or at banks. The fees are pretty standard, and you won't find a lot of variance between places. One tip: When you charge your credit card, you'll be asked if you want the purchase to go through in euros or dollars. Always choose the *opposite* of whatever is highlighted on the machine (for example, if the highlighted option is Euros, choose dollars)—you'll save a few cents that way.

ATMs

Note that while the country's financial crisis has had a less severe impact on the islands than the mainland, you may have some difficulties taking out money. Some of the more remote islands only have a few ATMs, or none at all. It's a good idea to stock up on cash, especially smaller bills, when you can.

Credit and Debit Cards

Credit cards and debit cards are widely accepted, but in some of the more off-the-beaten path locations, you might only be able to pay with cash. **MasterCard** and **Visa** are two widely accepted and used credit cards. Some places do not accept American Express. Make sure you inform your bank ahead of time that you are traveling to Greece; if not, most banks' antifraud mechanisms will be triggered and they will automatically block your card when you try to spend money abroad.

Sales Tax

Greece has a rather eye-watering 24 percent sales tax as part of austerity measures. Tax is bundled into the price you see, so you don't need to calculate it separately. Some fancier shops have a tax return for tourists, and they usually advertise this outside the shop.

COMMUNICATIONS

The country code for Greece is +30.

Cell Phones

I recommend purchasing a SIM card upon arrival. It's cheap and really useful to have a bit of 4G at your fingertips. If you're traveling around Europe, it's better to buy an **Orange** SIM (https://orange.simoptions.com; €49.99 for 10GB and 2 hours calling in 30 European countries including Greece) that works around the EU.

If you're only staying in Greece, you can try **Vodafone, Wind,** or **Cosmote.** You can either purchase directly in the shop (there's at least one provider on each island, and plenty in Athens and at the airport) or from vendors on the street. You'll notice plenty of young people hawking Vodafone SIMs on Ermou street in Athens, this is legal and normal. I use Vodafone (www.vodafone.gr; 2.5 GB data cost €10 is valid for 1 month and gets you 1,500 minutes calling times).

Wi-Fi

Most restaurants, bars, and cafés have Wi-Fi. It's either written directly on the menu or you can ask the waiter. There's currently no city-wide free Internet in Athens.

Traveler Advice

ACCESS FOR TRAVELERS WITH DISABILITIES

Unfortunately, Greece as a whole is not a very architecturally friendly place to travel if you are in a wheelchair. Athens is particularly difficult to navigate: The sidewalks are tiny, and cars often block the curbs, though most hotels and apartment buildings do have elevators, and public transportation is wheelchair-friendly. Poor urban planning and a string of budget cuts means this is unlikely to improve in the future. More developed islands like Crete or Mykonos have slightly more up-to-date infrastructure, but they can be quite crowded in the summer months.

If you are traveling in a wheelchair, I recommend calling your hotel ahead of time to let them know you'll need a wheelchair-accessible room. If you want to relax as much as possible, consider organizing a trip through **Christianakis Travel** (tel. 210/322 1483 and

Going to the Beach

I truly believe that a Greek beach in the summertime, as the sun is setting over the Aegean, is paradise. That said, there are a few rules—or at least, useful things to know—about paradise.

ORGANIZED AND UNORGANIZED BEACHES

In this book you'll come across references to "unorganized" and "organized" beaches. **Organized** beaches refer to those that have gone the capitalistic route: You'll find lawn chairs, umbrellas, beach bars, etc. Greek law stipulates that businesses must place chairs and umbrellas 5 meters (16 feet) from the sea; in practice, this rarely happens. Organized beaches sometimes have facilities like showers and bathrooms, as well as water sports. Prices on organized beaches can vary wildly—you'll find umbrellas for rent for a couple of euros in smaller islands, while the biggest beach bars in Mykonos sell a day on a chair for upwards of €200. **Unorganized** beaches are those that are still wild—you'll have to bring your own supplies here.

NUDITY

Nudity is also technically illegal in Greece, but is widely practiced by both locals and tourists. This book has attempted to specify when beaches are nudist. If you find yourself on an unorganized beach alone, you can take your clothes off. If you find yourself surrounded by clothed families, you may offend a lot of people by stripping down to your birthday suit. A good rule of thumb is to pay attention to the crowd and follow along. Women can go topless anywhere.

210/322 1484; www.christianakis.gr), the country's only tour operating company specializing in tours for those with physical disabilities. They can organize special trips for you around Athens and Mykonos.

TRAVELING WITH CHILDREN

Greeks *love* children. This is both good (children are accepted everywhere, even bars; your kids will likely get free snacks) and a little invasive (cheeks might be pinched without asking, unsolicited advice might be given). Be warned that in the center of Athens it's difficult to navigate with a stroller, and there are very few playgrounds for kids. On the islands, especially the less touristic ones, children run wild in that kind of free-spirit, magical childhood sort of way.

WOMEN TRAVELING ALONE

Generally speaking, Greece is a pretty safe place, and aside from verbal harassment (which has greatly reduced in recent years), there isn't a ton of risk from locals. In beach resorts on party islands, however, you're at risk of sexual assault by other travelers. Please never accept a drink that you haven't seen poured, and don't accept a ride from a stranger alone late at night. In Athens, like any big city, you'll want to exercise caution at night. Note that it is illegal to own or use pepper spray in the country, but you can carry a rape whistle.

SENIOR TRAVELERS

With a warm climate and laid-back lifestyle, the Greek islands have long been a preferred choice for senior travelers. Islands like Crete and Ikaria are particularly beloved by seniors, but in general, there's little age differentiation in Greece. Tavernas, bars, and cafés, are full of people of all ages. Indeed, social inclusion well into old age (actually, until death!) is a strong contributing factor to Greeks' overall health and happiness.

LGBTQ+ TRAVELERS

Greece is mostly a safe destination for LGBTQ travelers, particularly on Mykonos, Folegandros, Anafi, Samothrace, and Lesvos.

Athens as a whole, particularly in the center and around Exarchia, is also safe. However, there have been some instances of violence or discrimination amongst LGBTQ people, like during the 2018 Gay Pride Parade in Thessaloniki, when right-wing assailants attacked some of the Pride participants. More recently, a well-known figure and activist in the gay community, Zak Kostopoulos, was beaten to death during the day in Omonia, though it's still unclear if this was over his sexual identity. Greece remains an Orthodox Catholic country, and the church has a strong stance against homosexuality. This bleeds into the everyday, and especially among the older generation, there can be a frustratingly backward way of thinking and talking about homosexuality. Though it's unlikely you will be physically assaulted, you might receive some stares or hear slurs muttered at you.

There's a strong LGBTQ community in Athens, including organizations dedicated to gay refugees, such as **Athens Housing Collective** (www.safeplaceinternational.org) and the intersectional **Athens Queer Collective** (https://athensqueercollective.org).

TRAVELERS OF COLOR

There have been racist attacks, led by right-wing and fascist groups, against immigrants from the Middle East and Africa, across Greece for the past several years. While Greeks are on the whole open-minded and the culture is rapidly changing with immigration, there is prejudice and racism. The Golden Dawn, a Nazi party responsible for many attacks against immigrants, held seats in Parliament for several years. As of 2019, they had no government representation, but their ideology still lingers. In 2017, an American college student was beaten to death on an island; his family has insisted it's because he was black. More subtle forms of racism exist: overt staring is the most common in the least touristy islands. You may also experience people asking about your family origins or to touch your hair (or rather, not asking), or assuming that you can't pay for something.

I've heard both good and bad things about traveling in Greece from black travelers. Several people have told me they've had pleasant experiences, while others have had some humiliating encounters. For a black woman's first-hand account of traveling in Greece, check out this travel blogger on the **Travel Noire** site (https://travelnoire.com/black-woman-travel-greece).

Resources

Glossary

Αα
(alpha)
Αεροδρομιο (aye-air-o-dhromio): airport
Αεροπλάνο (aye-air-o-plano): airplane
Αφίξεις (ah-fee-ksees): arrivals
Αυτοκινητόδρομος (af-to-kee-nee-to-dro-mos): highway
Αναχωρήσεις (ah-na-cho-ree-ses): departures
Άνοιξε (ane-ksi): open
Ανταλλαγή (an-ta-la-yee): exchange
Αμμος (ah-mos): sand
Αργός (ahr-gos): slow
Αντηλιακό (antiliakio): sunscreen
Ακριβός (a-kree-vos): expensive
Αυτοκίνητο (afto-kee-nee-to): car
Αστυνομία (as-tee-no-mee-A): police
Αγαλμα (A-gal-ma): statue

Ββ
(beta)
Βιβλιοπωλείο (vivliopoleio): bookstore
Βούτυρο (voo-tee-ro): butter
Βόλτα (vol-ta): walk, ride
Βουνό (vou-NO): mountain

Γγ
(gamma)
Γάλα (gha-la): milk
Γιατρός (ya-tros): doctor
Γλυκα (glee-ka): dessert, sweets
Γρήγορα (gree-go-ra): fast
Γυαλιά ηλίου (ya-lia iliou): sunglasses
Γέφυρα (yEF-ee-ra): bridge
Γειτονιά (ye-to-nee-A): neighborhood

Δδ
(delta)
Διαβατήριο (dee-ah-va-teerio): passport
Δρόμος (droh-mos): street
Δωμάτιο (doh-MA-tee-oh): room

Εε
(epsilon)
Εισιτήριο (ee-see-tee-ree-o): ticket
Εκκλησία (ek-lee-see-ah): church
Είσοδος (ee-so-dhos): entrance
Εξοδος (eks-o-dhos): exit
Ελεύθερος (el-ef-ther-os): free
Επείγον (eh-pee-yon): emergency
Ευχαριστώ (ef-ghar-is-TO): thank you

Ζζ
(zêta)
Ζαχαροπλαστείο (za-ha-ro-plasti-kee-a): pastry shop
Ζεστό (zes-TOE): hot

Ηη
(êta)
Ήλιος (EE-lee-yos): sun
Ηλιοθεραπεία (EE-lee-o-therapia): sunbathing, literally sun therapy

Θθ
(theta)
Θάλασσα (tha-la-sa): sea
Θέατρο (theatro): theater

Ιι
(iota)

Ιδέα (e-dhe-a): idea
Ιστορία (e-sto-ria): history, story

Κκ
(kappa)

Καλός (kah-los): good
Καρπός (karpos): fruit
Κάρτα (KA-rta): card
Κακό (kah-ko): bad
Κλειστό (klee-sto): closed
Κρύο (kree-oh): cold
Κλιματισμό (klee-mah-tis-mo): air-conditioned
Κρασί (kra-see): wine
Κρεβάτι (kreh-va-tee): bed
Κτίριο (kt-EE-ree-o): building
Κίνδυνος (Keen-dee-nos): danger
Κρέας (kray-as): meat
Κράτηση (krA-tee-see): reservation

Λλ
(lambda)

Λεωφορείο (lee-oh-fo-ree-oh): bus
Λογαριασμός (loh-gor-yas-mos): bill
Λαϊκή (lie-ee-kee): market
Λιμάνι (lee-mahn-i): port
Λεωφόρος (le-o-for-os): avenue

Μμ
(mu)

Μαλάκα (malaka): asshole (an insult, a loving term, the most commonly used word in Greek)
Μαγιό (may-o): bathing suit
Μπαρ (bar): bar
Μουσείο (moo-seh-oh): museum
Μνημείο (mni-me-YO): monument

Νν
(nu)

Νοσοκομείο (noh-so-ko-mee-oh): hospital
Νόμισμα (NO-mis-ma): coin

Ξξ
(xi)

Ξενοδοχειο (xen-o-do-chio): hotel

Οο
(omikron)

Οδηγός (oh-dee-yos): driver

Ππ
(pi)

Παραλία (pah-ra-lee-ya): beach
Πάρκο (parko): park
Πρεσβεία (presvia): embassy
Πόλη (PO-lee): city
Πολλά (po-LA): many, a lot
Πέτρα (petra): stone, rock
Πρόβλημα (prov-lee-mah): problem
Πλατεία (plah-tee-a): square
Πετσέτα (pet-set-ah): towel
Ποτάμι (po-TA-mi): river
Περίπτερο (per-IP-ter-o): newsstand
Προξενείο (prox-en-e-O): consulate

Ρρ
(rho)

Παιδί (pae-dhi): child
Παιδιά (pae-dhia): children
Πάγος (pa-ghos): ice
Παγωτό (pa-gho-to): ice cream
Πωπω (po-po): "Wow"—this is my favorite Greek expression, and you'll hear it used in excitement, disgust, confusion, and more. For extra emphasis, draw out both the "po"s.

Σσ ς
(sigma)

Σουπερμάρκετ (soo-per market): supermarket
Σερβιτόρος (serviTORos): waiter
Συναγωγή (sin-a-yo-yee): synagogue
Σπίτι (spee-tee): house
Σόδα (soda): soda
Σκάφος (skafos): boat
Σινεμά (see-nema): movie theater, cinema
Συναυλία (see-nav-lia): concert
Σταθμός (stath-MOS): station

Ττ
(tau)
Τρένο (treno): train
Τουαλέτα (twa-leta): bathroom
Τράπεζα (TRA-eza): bank
Τζαμί (ja-mee): mosque
Τσιγάρο (tsee-garo): cigarette
Τιμή (tee-ME): price

Υυ
(upsilon)
Υγεία (ee-yee-ah): health

Φφ
(phi)
Φούρνος (foor-nos): bakery
Φτηνός (ftee-nos): cheap

Χχ
(chi)
Χρόνος (chrO-nos): time
Χρονοδιάγραμμα (chrono-diA-gramma): timetable

Ψψ
(psi)
Ψάρι (psari): fish

Ωω
(omega)
Ωπα (OH-pa): Oops!
Ωρα (OH-ra): hour

Greek Phrasebook

Greeks speak excellent English, especially among the youth and in any touristic place, though it's always nice to know a few phrases in the local language. Most tourists, put off by the alphabet and complicated grammar, make no attempt to learn any Greek, so even just learning to say *efgharisto* ("thank you") will make people very happy. After all, Greek is one of the oldest known European languages, with an oral tradition of 4,000 years and a written tradition of 3,000, and learning a few words and phrases will show that you respect that history.

It's true that Greek isn't the easiest language to learn, but I will give you a few tips that will make you instantly feel more confident. First, much of English is derived from ancient Greek, and you already know a lot of words. *Hypno*, for example, means sleep in Greek; think of the English word "hypnosis." The word "hygeine" comes from the Greek word *ygina* for "health." See where I'm going? Greek pronunciation is also more straightforward than it appears. There's only one accent per word, so you only inflect once. Finally, if you've spent any time on a college campus in the US, you've already got a passing familiarity with the Greek alphabet.

PRONUNCIATION

Alphabet

There are 24 letters in the Greek alphabet. Beginners are often confused by some letters that look like English letters but are pronounced differently. Those include the "B" (pronounced "V"), the "P" (pronounced "R"), and the lowercase "v" (pronounced "n"). You'll notice that Ηη, Ιι, and Υυ are all pronounced the same; the distinction is only really clear to nonspeakers when a word is written. Combinations of letters create different sounds as well: ΜΠ μπ (b) as in "bee" and ΝΤ ντ (d) as in "do" are the most important combinations to know.

Αα a as in *father*
Ββ v as in *vet*
Γγ gh / y as in *yield*
Δδ dh as in *this*
Εε e as in *pet*
Ζζ z as in *zone*
Ηη i as in *meet*
Θθ th as in *theme*
Ιι i as in *feet*
Κκ k as in *kip*
Λλ l as in *line*

Μμ m as in *map*
Νν n as in *no*
Ξξ x as in *fox*
Οο o as in *hot*
Ππ p as in *pill*
Ρρ r as in *roll* (slightly trilled like in Spanish)
Σσ ς s as in *straw*
Ττ t as in *top*
Υυ i as in *meet*
Φφ f as in *free*
Χχ kh as in *Bach* (There is no equivalent sound in English.)
Ψψ ps as in *lapse*
Ωω o as in *hot*

Essential Phrases

Hello Γεια σας. (YAH sahss). Literally means "to your health"
Hi Γεια σου. (YAH soo)
Good morning Καλημέρα (kali MERa)
Good evening Καλό απόγευμα (kali apoyevMA)
Good night Καληνυχτα (kali NICHta)
Good-bye Αντίο. (AHN-dee-oh)
Nice to meet you Χάρηκα (HA-reeka)
Thank you [very much] Ευχαριστώ [πολύ]. (ef-hah-rees-TOH [po-LEE])
You're welcome Παρακαλώ. (Pah-rah-kah-LOH)
Please Παρακαλώ ((pah-rah-kah-LOH)
Do you speak English? Μιλάτε αγγλικά; (mee-LAH-teh ang-glee-KAH?)
I don't understand Δεν καταλαβαίνω. (dhen kah-tah-lah-VEH-no)
I love you Σ'αγαπώ (sa-gha-POH)
Leave me alone Αφήστε με ήσυχο (male)/ ήσυχη (female). (a-FIS-te me EE-si-kho / EE-si-khee)
Yes Ναι (neh)
No Όχι. (OH-hee)

Transportation

Where is...? Που είναι...; (poo EE-ne)
How far/long is...? Πόση ώρα/μακριά; : (Posi ora/makria)
Is there a bus to...? Υπάρχει λεωφορείο για (Ee-par-hee le-oh-fo-ree-oh ya)
Where does this bus go to? Πού πηγαίνει αυτό το λεωφορείο (Poo pee-yeh-ne afto to le-oh-fo-ree-oh?)
Where do I get off? Πού βγαίνω; (Poo vga-no)
What time does the bus leave? Τι ώρα φεύγει το λεωφορείο (Tee ora fev-yee to le-oh-fo-ree-oh?)
What time does the bus arrive? Τι ώρα φτάνει το λεωφορείο (Tee ora fta-nee to le-oh-fo-ree-oh?)
Where is the nearest subway station? Πού είναι το κοντινότερο μετρό (Poo ee-ne to kon-tee-no-tero metro?)
Where can I buy a ticket? Από πού μπορώ να αγοράσω ένα εισιτήριο (A-po poo bo-roh na agorazo ena ee-see-tee-ree-oh)
One ticket... Ένα εισιτήρι (ena ee-see-tee-ree-oh)

Food

A table for one/two... Ένα τραπέζι για ένα άτομο/δύο άτομα, παρακαλώ (Ena trapezi ya ena atoma/dhio atoma, parakalo)
Do you have a menu in English? Έχετε ένα μενού στην αγγλική (eh-ye-te ena meh-noo steen an-glee-kah?)
What is the dish of the day? οιο είναι το πιάτο της ημέρας; (Pio einai to piato tis e-meras?)
We're ready to order. Είμαστε έτοιμοι (E-maste eh-tee-moh)
I'm a vegetarian. Είμαι χορτοφάγος (E-mae chortofayos)
May I have... Μπορώ να έχω (Boro na e-xho)
The check please? Το λογαριασμό, παρακαλώ. (To logoryasmo parakalo)
beer μπύρα (beer-ah)
bread ψωμι (pso-ME)
breakfast πρωινό (pro-yee-no)
cash μετρητά (me-tree-ta)
check Το λογαριασμό (To logoryasmo)
cheese τυρί (tee-REE)
coffee καφές (kafes)
dinner δείπνο (dh-eep-no)
fish ψάρι (ps-AH-ree)
glass ποτήρι (po-tee-ree)
hors d'oeuvre ορεκτικό (oh-rek-ti-ko)

ice πάγος (pa-yos)
ice cream παγωτό (pa-yo-to)
lunch μεσημεριανό (me-see-mer-ee-a-NO)
meat κρέας (kray-AS)
restaurant εστιατόριο (es-tee-ah-to-ree-oh)
sandwich σάντουιτς (sandh-weech)
waiter σερβιτόρος (se-rvee-TOE-ros)
water νερό (ne-ROH)
wine κρασί (kra-SEE)

Shopping

money χρήματα (KHRI-ma-ta)
shop μαγαζί (ma-ga-ZEE)
What time do you close? Τι ώρα κλείνετε? (Tee ora KLEE-steh?)
How much is it? Πόσο κάνει (Poso kan-ee)
What is the local specialty? Ποια είναι η τοπική ειδικότητα (Pya eina i topiki eidiKOtita?)

Health

drugstore φαρμακείο (far-ma-kEE-oh)
pain πόνος (POH-nos)
fever πυρετός (pee-reh-TOS)
headache πονοκέφαλο (pono-KES-ta-lo)
stomachache μστομαχόπονος (sto-ma-to-XHO-ponos
toothache πονόδοντος (po-NO-dhon-tos)
burn έγκαυμα (En-kav-mah)
cramp κράμπα (kr-AH-mpa)
nausea ναυτία (naf-TEE-ah)
vomiting εμετό (eh-me-TOE)
medicine φάρμακο (fArm-ako)
antibiotic αντιβιοτικό (anti-vio-ti-ko)
aspirin ασπιρίνη (aspirini)
I need a doctor. Χρειάζομαι γιατρό. (hree-AH-zoh-meh yiah-TROH)
I need a hospital. Χρειάζομαι νοσοκομείο (hree-AH-zoh-meh no-so-ko-mEE-oh)
I have a pain here... Έχω πόνο εδώ (e-xho PO-no eh-do)
I have been stung/bitten. Έχω κτυπηθεί (e-xho kt-y-pee-thee)
I am pregnant. Είμαι έγγυος (Ee-may en-gee-yos)
I am allergic... Είμαι αλλεργικός (E-may ah-ler-yee-kos)
My blood type is...positive/negative. Ο τύπος μου είναι θετικός / αρνητικός (O tee-pos mou einai the-ti-kos / ar-nee-tee-kos)

Numbers

0 μηδέν (miden)
1 ένας (enas)
2 δύο (dio)
3 τρία (tria)
4 τέσσερα (tessera)
5 πέντε (pede)
6 έξι (eksi)
7 πτά (efta)
8 οκτώ (okto)
9 εννέα (ena)
10 δέκα (dheka)
11 έντεκα (endheka)
12 δώδεκα (dhodheka)
13 δεκατρείς (dhekatris)
14 δεκατέσσερα (dhekatessera)
15 δεκαπέντε (dhekapente)
16 δεκαέξι (dhekaeksi)
17 δεκαεπτά (dhekaepta)
18 δεκαοκτώ (dhekaochto)
19 δεκαεννέα (dhekaenyah)
20 είκοσι (eksi)
21 είκοσι ένα (eksi enyah)
30 τριάντα (trianta)
40 σαράντα (saranta)
50 πενήντα (penanta)
60 εξήντα (eksenta)
70 εβδομήντα (evdomanta)
80 ογδόντα (ogdonta)
90 ενενήντα (eneninta)
100 εκατό (ekato)
200 διακόσια (diakosia)
500 πεντακόσια (pendhakosia)
1,000 χίλια (hee-lia)
10,000 δέκα χιλιάδες (deka hee-lee-ades)
100,000 εκατό χιλιάδες (ekato hee-lee-ades)
1,000,000 εκατομμύριο (ekato mee yee ro)

Time

What time is it? Τι ώρα είναι; (Ti ora einai?)
It's two o'clock. Γίναι δύο ή ώρα (Ei-nai dhio e ora)
midday μεσημέρι (mesi-merry)

midnight μεσάνυχτα (mesa-nee-hta
morning πρωί (pro-ee)
afternoon/evening απόγευμα (ah-poy-ev-ma)
night Νύχτα (neeh-ta)
yesterday εχθές (ech-thes)
today σήμερα (see-me-rah)
tomorrow αύριο (av-ree-oh)

Days and Months

week εβδομάδα (ev-dho-MA-dah)
month μήνας (MEE-nas)
Monday Δευτέρα (dhef-TER-ah)
Tuesday Τρίτη (TREE-tee)
Wednesday Τετάρτη (te-TAR-tee)
Thursday Πέμπτη (PE-mpti)
Friday Παρασκευή (para-ske-VEE)
Saturday Σάββατο (SAH-vah-to)
Sunday Κυριακή (kee-yee-ra-KEY)
January Ιανουάριος (yan-you-AH-ree-os)
February Φεβρουάριος (fev-rou-AH-ree-os)
March Μάρτιος (MAR-tee-os)
April Απρίλιο (apr-EE-leo)
May Μάιος (MAI-os)
June Ιούνιος (YOU-nee-os)
July Ιούλιος (YOU-lee-os)
August Αύγουστος (AV-goo-stos)
September Σεπτέμβριος (sep-TEM-vree-os)
October Οκτωβρίου (och-tom-VREE-ou)
November Νοέμβριος (nov-EM-vree-os)
December Δεκέμβριος (dhek-EM-vree-os)

Verbs

Verbs are shown below in the present tense, first person, which is also how their conjugation begins.

to have έχω (e-xho)
to be είναι (ee-nai)
to go πάω (pow)
to come έρθω (ER-tho)
to want θέλω (the-LO)
to eat τρώω (tro-o)
to drink πίνω (pee-no)
to buy γοράζω (ah-go-ra-zo)
to read διαβάζω (dhia-va-zo)
to write γράφω (ghrap-so)
to stop σταματώ (sta-ma-TOE)
to stay μένω (mEH-no)
to leave φύγω (fee-YO)
to look κοιτάζω (kee-TA-zo)
to give δίνω (dh-EE-no)

Suggested Reading and Films

BOOKS

Travelogues

Bakken, Christopher. *Honey, Olives, Octopus: Adventures at the Greek Table.* This book is part cookbook, part travelogue. Bakken delves into one of Europe's most misunderstood food cultures with all the zeal and gusto you'd expect of such a *bonhomme.*

Durrell, Gerald. *My Family and Other Animals.* This beloved account of one eccentric family's relocation from damp and gray England to sunny Corfu in the 1950s was also made into a popular television series.

Miller, Henry. *The Colossus of Maroussi.* When Henry Miller traveled to Greece in 1939 to see his friend Lawrence Durell, we were all blessed with the publication of this fantastic travelogue. Miller considered it one of his greatest works.

Fiction

Eugenidis, Jeffrey. *Middlesex.* Greek grandparents feature heavily in this blockbuster novel, which traces a family's roots from modern America to a tiny rural Greek village.

Highsmith, Patricia. *The Two Faces of January.* This fantastically horrifying novel set in Crete involves a scammer, a conman, and a hotel in Athens. I won't spoil the rest.

Hislop, Victoria. *The Island.* You'll find this paperback sold everywhere. It's a heart-warming story about a daughter who digs into her secretive Greek mother's past.

Homer, *The Odyssey.* Maybe this summer vacation is the time to finally cross this epic poem off of your must-read list?

Kazantazakis, Nikos. *Freedom or Death.* You must read something by Kazantzakis if you go to Crete, and this book, which showcases the strength and resilience of the Cretans (and sums up their overall mentality in a succinct title) during the end of the Ottoman era, is my favorite.

Miller, Madeline. *Circe.* This is a feminist retelling of the story of one of Greek mythology's most misunderstood nymphs, Circe, who was exiled to a Mediterranean island. It's transcendently good.

Nikolaidou, Sophia. *The Scapegoat.* Inspired by the real-life story of CBS journalist George Polk, this murder mystery ties together politics, journalism, and modern history into one intriguing read.

History and Politics

Clogg, Richard. *A Concise History of Greece.* This is one of the best and most digestible books about Greece's history, from ancient times to the present.

Jones, Reece. *Violent Borders: Refugees and the Right to Move.* The refugee crisis into Europe has claimed more than 40,000 lives. In this thought-provoking and empathetic book, Jones explores the political and economic role of borders—a must read for anyone with a heart.

Mazower, Mark. *Salonica, City of Ghosts: Christians, Muslims and Jews, 1430-1950.* Mazower is one of the pre-eminent historians on Greece and the Balkan countries and has published many books, but this one, which highlights the ethnically rich tapestry of Thessaloniki, is critical for understanding the cultural and economic contributions of minorities in Greece's history.

Varoufakis, Yanis. *Adults in the Room.* Varoufakis, the infamous Syriza finance minister during the peak troika years of the economic crisis, is a love-him-or-hate-him figure in Greece (and in Brussels). But this first-hand look into the worst years of the country's economic crisis is illuminating and entertaining, if not vastly depressing.

Art and Architecture

Beard, Mary and Henderson, Jon. *Classical Art: From Greece to Rome.* A comprehensive critique of Greek art through Roman eyes, this book is by two professors of the classics at Cambridge University.

Turner, Victoria and Jenkins, Ian. *The Greek Body.* The human body is at the forefront of ancient Greek art and architecture, the epitome of youth, sensuality, and beauty. This comprehensive book explores the use and politics of the body in art.

FILMS

Dogtooth (2009) Yiorgos Lanthimos. Lanthimos is considered to have ushered in the third wave of Greek cinema, and this fantastically strange family drama was the director's first Academy Award-nominated film. It takes the archetype of the controlling Greek family to an absurd, nightmarish level.

Mia Treli Treli Oikogeneia (1965) Dimos Dimopoulos. In this very funny 1960s comedy, a quirky family's eccentricities threaten to be too much for their daughter's new husband.

Stella (1955) Michael Cacoyannis. Starring the inimitable Melina Merkouri, this beloved classic is a Greek retelling of *Carmen*. Merkouri oozes wit, charm, and a strong sense of self as she navigates the world of love and commitment on her own terms.

Suntan (2016) Argyris Papadimitropoulos. An unremarkable, middle-aged doctor on the island of Antiparos becomes deeply infatuated with—you guessed it—a super hot, super young woman, eventually losing all sense of self-respect and self-control.

Online Resources and Apps

TRAVEL AND TIPS

www.visitgreece.gr
This is the official website of the Greek Tourism Organization (GTO).

www.discovergreece.com
On this site you'll find a good guide to the islands, including info on events and itinerary ideas.

www.xe.com
Calculate what a buck is worth and know exactly how much you're spending. The site's sister app is ideal for the financially conscious and allows travelers to track expenditures on the go.

TRANSPORTATION

www.skyscanner.net, www.kayak.com, www.hipmunk.com
These flight aggregators help find the cheapest fares. Hipmunk is one of the latest and has paid a little more attention to design and practical features like timelines and maps that simplify planning. They also offer hotel and car-rental services.

www.rome2rio.com
Here you'll find door-to-door transportation details with distances, departures times, and prices for planes, trains, buses, and ferries. There's also a carbon emissions estimate for the ecologically inclined.

www.seatguru.com
Learn your legroom options and read unbiased advice on where to sit on a flight. The database includes all major airlines, along with diagrams, photos, and descriptions of Airbus and Boeing interiors.

www.jetlagrooster.com
Avoid jet lag by creating a personalized sleep plan for a smooth transition between time zones. Just log on 3-4 days before departure and follow their recommended bedtimes.

www.trainose.gr
This official train company website provides timetables and ticket purchasing options.

www.e-ktel.com
Greece's official bus company website has timetables and ticket purchasing options.

www.ferriesingreece.com
This is a useful website for finding ferry itineraries across the islands and for booking tickets.

ACCOMMODATIONS

www.airbnb.com, www.slh.com, www.tablethotels.com, www.mrandmrssmith.com
Search for bed-and-breakfasts, apartments, or boutique hotels. These sites include realistic visuals and advice from previous guests. Airbnb is hugely popular across Greece.

APPS

Taxibeat: There isn't Uber in Greece, but there is TaxiBeat, which is one of the more reliable ways of finding a taxi in Athens.

ToposText: You'll enjoy having a great app that geolocates archaeological sites and matches them with ancient texts.

Duolingo: This popular language-learning platform offers an option to learn Greek in just 5 minutes a day.

BLOGS

www.greecetravel.com

Run by Matt Barrett, an expat who is married to a Greek woman, this is probably one of the most widely used and popular guides online.

https://mygreecetravelblog.com

This blog is a particularly good resource for travelers to Mykonos.

Index

A

B

C

D

E

F

G

H

IJ

K

L

M

P

R

S

UV

W

XYZ

List of Maps

Photo Credits

All interior photos © Nikolaos Symeonidis except; title page photo © Lefteris Papaulakis | Dreamstime.com; page 2 © Sven Hansche | Dreamstime.com; page 3 © Smallredgirl | Dreamstime.com; page 6 (top left) © Darikya Maksimova | Dreamstime.com; (top right) © Vasilis Ververidis | Dreamstime.com; (bottom) © Patryk Kosmider | Dreamstime.com; page 7 (top) © Jekaterina Voronina | Dreamstime.com; (bottom left) © Beriliu | Dreamstime.com; (bottom right) © Mila Atkovska | Dreamstime.com; page 8 (top) © Totophotos | Dreamstime.com; page 9 (top) © Xiaoma | Dreamstime.com; (bottom left) © Georgios Tsichlis | Dreamstime.com; (bottom right) © Shivashakti555 | Dreamstime.com; page 10 © Jaumescar | Dreamstime.com; page 13 (top) © Andrei Stancu | Dreamstime.com; (bottom) © Freesurf69 | Dreamstime.com; page 14 © Carafoto | Dreamstime.com; page 15 © Costas1962 | Dreamstime.com; page 16 (top) © Orcun Koral Işeri | Dreamstime.com; (middle) © Vkarafill | Dreamstime.com; (bottom) © Milan Gonda | Dreamstime.com; page 17 (top) © Aleh Varanishcha | Dreamstime.com; (bottom) © Milan Gonda | Dreamstime.com; page 18 (bottom) © Ktree | Dreamstime.com; page 19 (bottom) © Charis Anagnostopoulos | Dreamstime.com; page 30 (bottom) © Salparadis | Dreamstime.com; page 32 (bottom) © Dbdella | Dreamstime.com; page 35 © Ivan Bastien | Dreamstime.com; page 36 (top left) © Photostella | Dreamstime.com; (top right) © William Perry | Dreamstime.com; page 49 © Pavlos Tsokounoglou; page 51 (top left) © Emmanouil Pavlis | Dreamstime.com; (top right) © Ollirg | Dreamstime.com; (bottom) © Saiko3p | Dreamstime.com; (top right) © Milan Gonda | Dreamstime.com; page 59 © Lornet | Dreamstime.com; page 61 © Milan Gonda | Dreamstime.com; (bottom) © Saloni1986 | Dreamstime.com; page 73 © Kurylo54 | Dreamstime.com; page 85 © Desislava Vasileva | Dreamstime.com; (top right) © Andrei Stancu | Dreamstime.com; page 97 (top) © Ionut David | Dreamstime.com; (bottom) © Gianluca Rosselli | Dreamstime.com; page 101 (top left) © Justin Black | Dreamstime.com; (bottom) © Michal Bednarek | Dreamstime.com; page 113 © Jekaterina Voronina | Dreamstime.com; page 114 (top left) © Alexander Shalamov | Dreamstime.com; (top right) © MDFotori | Dreamstime.com; page 122 © Sven Hansche | Dreamstime.com; page 123 © Asteri77 | Dreamstime.com; page 127 © Pulpitis | Dreamstime.com; page 133 © Jaumescar | Dreamstime.com; page 134 © Jekaterina Voroniva | Dreamstime.com; page 145 © Serban Enache | Dreamstime.com; page 146 © Sarah Souli; page 150 © Paraskevas Karvouniaris; page 151 (top left) © Paraskevas Karvouniaris; (top right) © Freesurf69 | Dreamstime.com; page 157 (top) © Zoipap | Dreamstime.com; (bottom) © Georgios Tsichlis | Dreamstime.com; page 161 (top left) © Paraskevas Karvouniaris; (top right) © Paraskevas Karvouniaris; (bottom) © Paraskevas Karvouniaris; page 165 (top) © Paraskevas Karvouniaris; (bottom) © Paraskevas Karvouniaris; page 170 © Mila Atkovska | Dreamstime.com; page 177 © Milan Gonda | Dreamstime.com; page 182 © Paolo Giovanni Trovo | Dreamstime.com; page 185 (top left) © Sarah Souli; (bottom) © Paolo Giovanni Trovo | Dreamstime.com; page 193 © Milan Gonda | Dreamstime.com; page 204 © Freesurf69 | Dreamstime.com; page 215 © Hector Christiaen | Dreamstime.com; page 219 (top left) © Thevirex | Dreamstime.com; (bottom) © Freesurf69 | Dreamstime.com; page 222 © Freesurf69 | Dreamstime.com; page 223 (top left) © Kellydt | Dreamstime.com; (top right) © Allouphoto | Dreamstime.com; page 231 (top left) © Kutt Niinepuu | Dreamstime.com; (top right) © Kutt Niinepuu | Dreamstime.com; (bottom) © Wieslaw Jarek | Dreamstime.com; page 233 (top) © Tommason | Dreamstime.com; (bottom) © Saiko3p | Dreamstime.com; page 238 © Lubos Kovalik | Dreamstime.com; page 241 © Ciolca | Dreamstime.com; page 244 © Milan Gonda | Dreamstime.com; page 245 (top left) © Imagin.gr Photography | Dreamstime.com; (top right) © Milan Gonda | Dreamstime.com; page 252 © Sakis Pilatos | Dreamstime.com; page 257 (top) © Marbenzu | Dreamstime.com; (bottom) © Jedynakanna | Dreamstime.com; page 261 © Eremia425 | Dreamstime.com; page 262 (top left) © Fritz Hiersche | Dreamstime.com; (top right) © Fritz Hiersche | Dreamstime.com; page 267 © Eleni Seitanidou | Dreamstime.com; page 268 © Fritz Hiersche | Dreamstime.com; page 272 © Diamantis Seitanidis | Dreamstime.com; page 274 © Neagoemartin2000 | Dreamstime.com; page 285 (top) © Milan Gonda | Dreamstime.com; (bottom) © Salparadis | Dreamstime.com; page 297 © Josef Bosak | Dreamstime.com; page 298 (top left) © Rudmer Zwerver | Dreamstime.com; page 309 (top left) © Motto555 | Dreamstime.com; (top right) © Julie Mayfeng | Dreamstime.com; (bottom) © Kokixx | Dreamstime.com; page 311 © Julie Mayfeng | Dreamstime.com; page 315 (top) © Martin Hatch | Dreamstime.com; (bottom) © Rexwholster | Dreamstime.com; page 320 © Roy Pedersen | Dreamstime.com; page 322 (top right) © Jana Kleteckova | Dreamstime.com; page 330 (top left) © Milan Gonda | Dreamstime.com; page 358 © Allouphoto | Dreamstime.com; page 359 (top right)

© Valentini Amasiadi | Dreamstime.com; page 362 © Donka Zheleva | Dreamstime.com; page 368 (top left) © Valentini Amasiadi | Dreamstime.com; page 372 © Fotokon | Dreamstime.com; page 377 (top left) © Patrick Angerave | Dreamstime.com; (top right) © Antonis Karvelas | Dreamstime.com; (bottom) © Lornet | Dreamstime.com; page 403 © Lucianbolca | Dreamstime.com; page 415 (top) © Grigor Ivanov | Dreamstime.com; page 421 (top) © Maksym Topchii | Dreamstime.com; page 423 © Milafedotova | Dreamstime.com; page 424 (top left) © Panagiotis Karpanagiotis | Dreamstime.com; (top right) © Bernard Foltin | Dreamstime.com; page 432 © Petros Papakonstantionou | Dreamstime.com; page 435 © Vladimir Timofeev | Dreamstime.com; page 438 © Charalambos Andronos | Dreamstime.com; page 442 (top left) © Freesurf69 | Dreamstime.com; (top right) © Amlw71 | Dreamstime.com; (bottom) © Njarvis5 | Dreamstime.com; page 448 © Georgios Tsichlis | Dreamstime.com; page 452 (top left) © Tupungato | Dreamstime.com; (top right) © Mirc3a | Dreamstime.com; (bottom left) © Milangonda | Dreamstime.com; (bottom right) © Simon Edwards | Dreamstime.com; page 458 (top) © Georgios Tsichlis | Dreamstime.com; (bottom) © Aleh Varanishcha | Dreamstime.com; page 465 © Vladamir Skylarov | Dreamstime.com; page 469 © Jarino47 | Dreamstime.com; page 484 © Saiko3p | Dreamstime.com

MOON
CAMINO DE SANTIAGO
SACRED SITES, HISTORIC VILLAGES, LOCAL FOOD & WINE
BEEBE BAHRAMI

MOON
AMALFI COAST
LAURA THAYER

MOON
BARCELONA & MADRID
JESSICA JONES

MOON
CROATIA & SLOVENIA

MOON
EDINBURGH, GLASGOW & THE ISLE OF SKYE

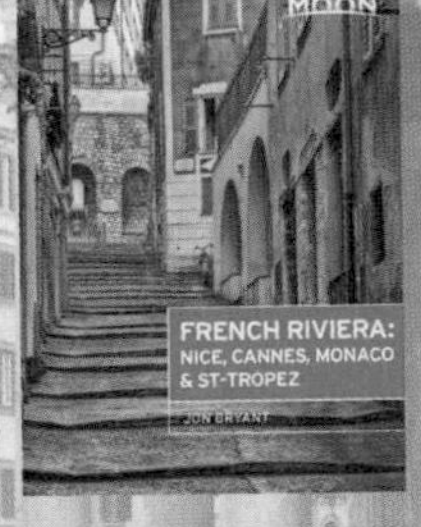
MOON
FRENCH RIVIERA: NICE, CANNES, MONACO & ST-TROPEZ

MOON
ICELAND

MOON
IRELAND
CAMILLE DeANGELIS

MOON
NORMANDY & BRITTANY

MOON
NORWAY

MOON
PORTUGAL

MOON
PRAGUE, VIENNA & BUDAPEST

MOON
PROVENCE

MOON
ROME, FLORENCE & VENICE

Trips to Remember

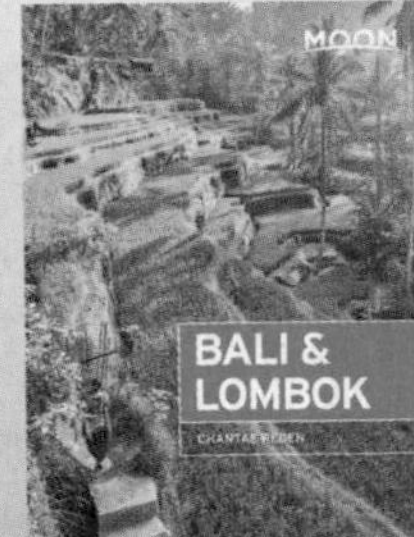

Epic Adventure

MAP SYMBOLS

- Expressway
- Primary Road
- Secondary Road
- Unpaved Road
- Trail
- Ferry
- Railroad
- Pedestrian Walkway
- Stairs
- City/Town
- State Capital
- National Capital
- Highlight
- Point of Interest
- Accommodation
- Restaurant/Bar
- Other Location
- Information Center
- Parking Area
- Church
- Winery/Vineyard
- Trailhead
- Train Station
- Airport
- Airfield
- Park
- Golf Course
- Unique Feature
- Waterfall
- Camping
- Mountain
- Ski Area
- Glacier

CONVERSION TABLES

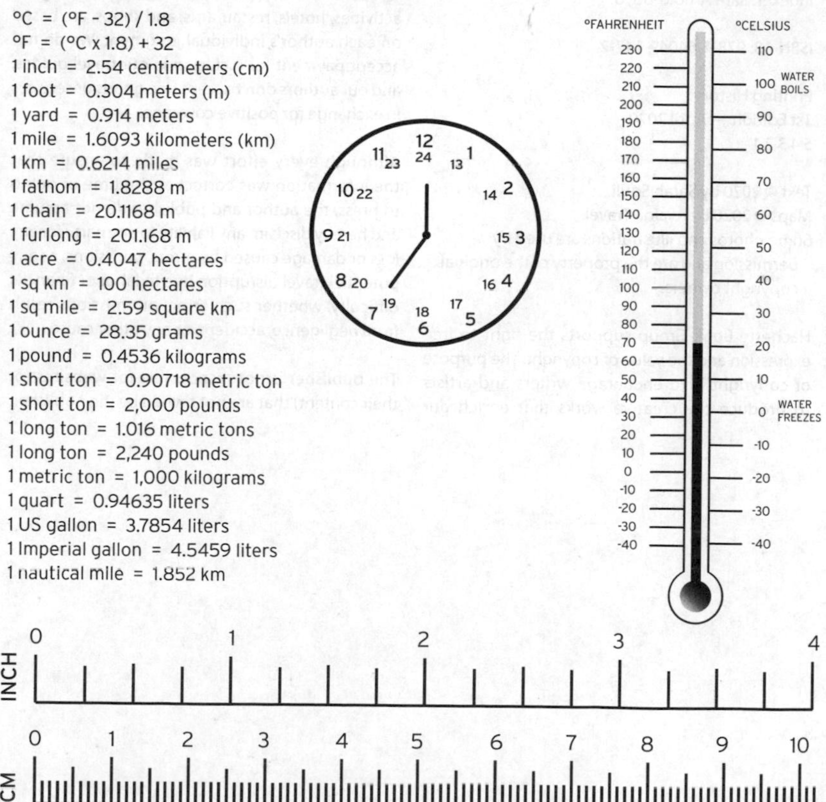

°C = (°F - 32) / 1.8
°F = (°C x 1.8) + 32
1 inch = 2.54 centimeters (cm)
1 foot = 0.304 meters (m)
1 yard = 0.914 meters
1 mile = 1.6093 kilometers (km)
1 km = 0.6214 miles
1 fathom = 1.8288 m
1 chain = 20.1168 m
1 furlong = 201.168 m
1 acre = 0.4047 hectares
1 sq km = 100 hectares
1 sq mile = 2.59 square km
1 ounce = 28.35 grams
1 pound = 0.4536 kilograms
1 short ton = 0.90718 metric ton
1 short ton = 2,000 pounds
1 long ton = 1.016 metric tons
1 long ton = 2,240 pounds
1 metric ton = 1,000 kilograms
1 quart = 0.94635 liters
1 US gallon = 3.7854 liters
1 Imperial gallon = 4.5459 liters
1 nautical mile = 1.852 km

MOON GREEK ISLANDS & ATHENS
Avalon Travel
Hachette Book Group
1700 Fourth Street
Berkeley, CA 94710, USA
www.moon.com

Editor: Nikki Ioakimedes
Managing Editor: Hannah Brezack
Copy Editor: Barbara Schultz
Graphics Coordinator and Production Designer: Suzanne Albertson
Cover Design: Faceout Studio, Charles Brock
Interior Design: Domini Dragoone
Moon Logo: Tim McGrath
Map Editor: Kat Bennett
Cartographers: Moon Street Cartography (CO), Kat Kalamaras, Karin Dahl, John Culp
Proofreader: Lina Carmona
Indexer: Sam Arnold-Boyd

ISBN-13: 978-1-64049-147-2

Printing History
1st Edition — April 2020
5 4 3 2 1

Front cover photo: Little Venice by Tuul / Alamy Stock Photo
Back cover photo: Samothrace © Vkarafill | Dreamstime.com

Printed in China by RR Donnelley

Avalon Travel is a division of Hachette Book Group, Inc. Moon and the Moon logo are trademarks of Hachette Book Group, Inc. All other marks and logos depicted are the property of the original owners.